AF606004

Accumulating Culture

Accumulating Culture

The Collections of Emperor Huizong

PATRICIA BUCKLEY EBREY

A China Program Book

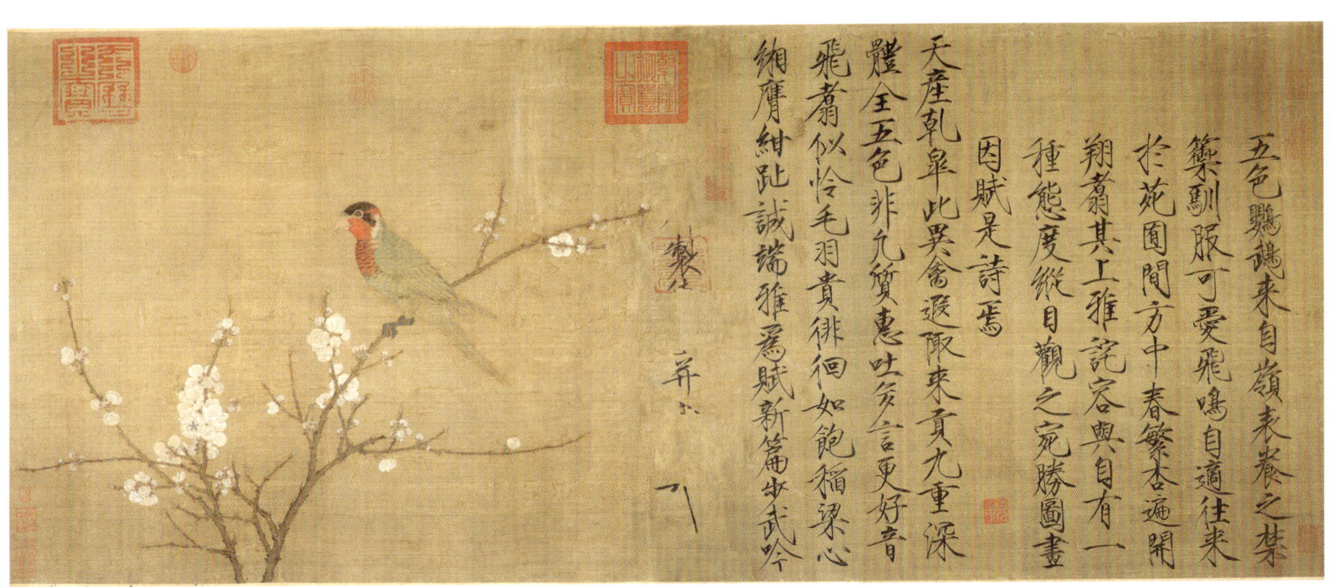

University of Washington Press *Seattle & London*

For Tom

This book was supported in part by the China Studies Program, a division of the Henry M. Jackson School of International Studies at the University of Washington.

Designed by Veronica Seyd
Printed in Canada
15 14 13 12 11 10 09 08 10 9 8 7 6 5 4 3 2 1

University of Washington Press
P.O. Box 50096, Seattle, WA 98145, U.S.A.
www.washington.edu/uwpress

Library of Congress Cataloging-in-Publication Data

Ebrey, Patricia Buckley, 1947–
Accumulating culture : the collections of Emperor Huizong / Patricia Buckley Ebrey.
p. cm.
"A China Program book."
Includes bibliographical references and index.
ISBN 978-0-295-98778-1 (cloth : alk. paper)
1. Song Huizong, Emperor of China, 1082-1135—Art collections. 2. Art—Collectors and collecting—China. 3. China—Kings and rulers—Art collections. I. Title.
N5285.C52S664 2008
709.51'07451—dc22 2008003999

The paper used in this publication meets the minimum requirements of American National Standard for Information Sciences—Permanence of Paper for Printed Library Materials, ANSI Z39.48–1984.

Jacket photo: Attibuted to Huizong, *Copy of Zhang Xuan's Lady Guoguo on an Outing*, ink and color on silk handscroll. Collection of the Liaoning Provincial Museum.

Title page: Huizong, *Five-Colored Parakeet*, ink and color on silk handscroll. Photograph © Museum of Fine Arts, Boston.

Contents

Illustrations

FIGURES

Tables

Preface

I FIRST BECAME INTRIGUED BY HUIZONG (1082–1135, R. 1100–1125) a decade ago. As a Song historian, I knew the dramatic appeal of his story. In his fifty-three years, he went from brother of the reigning emperor, anticipating a life of cultured leisure, to ruler of the largest and richest country in the world, able to pursue his deep interests in art and Daoism, to humiliated captive, transported to the far north by those who had invaded his country and captured his capital. What attracted me to Huizong, however, was the prospect that analyzing his reign would allow a deeper understanding of the visual and material dimensions of Chinese rulership. I began by pursuing many strands of Huizong's rule, but eventually decided to focus on the magnificent collections of art and antiquities that he assembled.

It may seem odd that a book on collecting is being written by a social and cultural historian rather than an art historian. When I have had my own doubts about venturing into this territory, I have reminded myself that in the Song period our modern concept of art did not exist. What both the court and the educated class collected were cultural relics, material objects that were traces of the past and gave one access to the minds of great men of former times. These objects were not just aesthetically pleasing decoration but were comparable to books and documents. Ancient bronze vessels were viewed as authentic relics of the rituals of the ancient kings, solid evidence that could be used to correct misunderstandings of the classics. Calligraphy and paintings were physically much like manuscript books. All three were rolls of paper or silk on which ink had been applied by brush. Paintings and calligraphies were also like books in that they revealed the thoughts and feelings of great men of bygone ages. Concentrating these culturally highly valued objects in the palace was a political act with all sorts of ramifications worth exploring.

I have tried to write this book in such a way that students of both history and art history can learn from it. This means that some of what I discuss will seem familiar to historians (such as discussions of the New Policies) and some familiar to art historians (such as traditions of art criticism). I have included this background material in order to make the book more accessible to less expert audiences. I realize that I am covering a huge range of material that experts often deal with in much smaller chunks. Art historians regularly write specialized studies of small fractions of what I touch on here—mirrors, not antiquities in general; landscape painting of a single century, not all paintings up to the early twelfth century; one calligrapher, not all schools, styles, and scripts. I have relied on art historians' close studies in the hope of avoiding making the worst mistakes, but undoubtedly I have sometimes stretched myself too thin. My goal in taking such a broad view is to see dimensions that do not come into focus at a micro level. In the broadest terms, I look at art and politics together. But just as crucial is the intermediate level, where I look at collecting books and collecting calligraphy together, or collecting contemporary paintings and old masters together.

In working on this project, I have accumulated debts of many kinds. I am above all grateful to the John Simon Guggenheim Foundation, the Chiang Ching-Kuo Foundation, and the University of Washington's Royalty Research Fund for funding the time off from teaching that made possible the research and writing of this book. Funds from the UW China Studies Program and the UW history department enabled me to employ three graduate research assistants at various stages of research and manuscript preparation. Sumei Yi, Jeong Won Hyun, and Hsiao-wen Cheng cheerfully and capably took on chores of all sorts, from fetching books from the library to preparing the glossary and checking citations. The China Program also funded the trips to libraries and museums that have made it possible for me to see many of the works discussed here.

Opportunities to present my research to other scholars at seminars and symposia not only helped me formulate my ideas but also sustained my commitment to this project. Particularly valuable have been occasions I have had to engage art historians, beginning with the "Symposium on Visual Dimensions of Chinese Culture" at the Institute for Advanced Study in 1999, the symposium "Daoism and Art" at Chicago in 2000, the workshop and conference "Huizong and the Culture of the Northern Song" in Seattle and Providence in 2001, the "Conference on Court Art" at the Palace Museum, Beijing, in 2003, the "Conference on Chinese Art: Concepts and Contexts" at Bonn in 2003, the Association for Asian Studies meeting panel "Emperors as Collectors" in 2004, the "Conference on Antiquarianism in East Asian Art and Visual Culture" at Chicago in 2006, and the "Conference on Founding Paradigms: The Art and Culture of the Northern Sung Dynasty" at the National Palace Museum in 2007. When I reached the point where I needed readers for my manuscript, Amy McNair, Richard Barnhart, Maggie Bickford, Charles

Hartman, Lothar von Falkenhausen, and R. Kent Guy were generous with their time and knowledge. I am particularly indebted to Maggie, who was with me at the Institute for Advanced Studies in 1998–99 when I began working on Huizong in earnest, and who joined with me in organizing the two Huizong meetings and in editing the resulting book, and was always available to listen to my ideas when I needed a sounding board. I have also had the pleasure of being able to share chapters as I wrote them with a small reading group in Seattle. I could not have had a better incentive to keep writing than knowing that smart and demanding readers like Shih-shan Susan Huang, Kyoko Tokuno, and Hsueh-man Shen were waiting for me to complete the next chapter so that we could discuss it together (and go out for dinner afterwards). I have also benefited from the thoughtful comments of two anonymous readers for the University of Washington Press and my editor there, Lorri Hagman. As often happens, readers have pushed me in different and often contradictory directions, wanting me to make Huizong more central or less, to recapitulate more or less often, and so on. Since I thus have not been able to adopt all advice, none of my readers should be held responsible for remaining flaws.

I have dedicated this book to my husband Tom, in honor of our fortieth wedding anniversary. Tom has not only supported my forays into Chinese history and culture for all these years but is also largely responsible for introducing me to the world of Chinese art collecting.

A Note on Dates, Measurements, and Other Conventions

THE CHINESE LUNAR YEAR, IN SONG TIMES AS TODAY, DOES NOT correspond exactly to the Western solar year. It begins weeks later, the exact difference varying from year to year. In this book, unless otherwise noted, dates are Chinese dates, with the Chinese year converted to the Western year with which it overlapped most. Thus, the first day of the eighth month of the fourth year of the Zhenghe reign period is given as "1114/8/1" or spelled out as "the first of the eighth month of 1114." Chinese dates are adequate for most purposes, and their use makes reference to Chinese sources much simpler. However, it should be recognized that events that took place in the twelfth month of the Chinese year would generally have fallen in the next year of the Western calendar (which sometimes leads to discrepancies in the dates given for people or events in English-language works). Another difference between the Chinese dating system and the current western calendar is the use of intercalary months inserted every few years to keep the lunar calendar from diverging too far from the solar year. Thus 1114/i6/3 would mean the third day of the intercalary month that fell between the sixth and seventh months in the year 1114.

The Chinese system for describing ages is also different from the Western one. A person is said to be one *sui* during his first year of life, two *sui* during his second year, and so on. On average these ages make the person seem to be 1.5 years older than the use of Western years would. (That is, someone born in the middle of the year, on the first of the sixth month, would become two *sui* at the next new year, when he had been alive six months.) Accurate conversion is possible only when one knows the person's day of birth, and for most purposes such precision is not necessary. Therefore, most ages in this book are *sui* ages. An exception is made for children, as the difference is much greater there. For instance, since Huizong was born in the tenth month of 1082, when his father died in the third month of 1085, he was two years and five months old, but four *sui*.

Chinese units of measurement generally cannot be converted with any precision for periods as early as the Song. Moreover, often more than one ruler or scale was in use. Here, for convenience, *cun* 寸 is translated as inch, *chi* 尺 as foot, *jin* 斤 as pound, *liang* 兩 as ounce, and *sheng* 升 as pint; all of these measurements should be seen as approximate, based on references in Song texts. By contrast, when metric measurements are given, they are based on modern measurements.

To Romanize Chinese words, I have used the pinyin system consistently, even when quoting from someone who wrote in English using another system. The only exception is that I have not changed authors' names or book or article titles. Since many books and articles by authors with Chinese or Japanese names are now written in English, as an aid to those who do not read Chinese or Japanese, I have signaled that the cited work is in English by using initials. Thus, an article by James Liu in English is cited as "J. Liu" but one in Chinese is cited as "Liu Zijian."

To keep the text as uncluttered as possible, I have avoided inserting romanizations after translated titles and terms, and instead have supplied characters in the glossary-index. Thus, anyone wishing to know the Chinese characters for Grand Celebration Hall or Han Gan's *Night Shining White* can look for them in the glossary-index. (One exception to this is the translation for names of government offices. Neither romanizations nor characters are given if they conform to the usage in Charles Hucker, *A Dictionary of Official Titles in Imperial China,* [Stanford: Stanford University Press, 1985]). When an individual's dates are important to the discussion, they are included in the text; in all other cases they are given only in the glossary-index.

Chronology

CHINA PROPER	NORTHERN REGIMES
Xia dynasty, ca. 1800–1600 BCE	
Shang dynasty, ca. 1600–1045 BCE	
Zhou dynasty, 1045–256 BCE	
Qin dynasty 221–206 BCE	
Han dynasty, 202 BCE–220 CE	
Former (Western) Han, 202 BCE–8 CE	
Wang Mang's Xin dynasty, 8–23	
Later (Eastern) Han, 25–220	
Three Kingdoms, 220–265	
(Western) Jin dynasty, 265–316	
(Eastern) Jin dynasty, 317–420	
Northern and Southern Dynasties, 420–589	
Sui dynasty, 581–618	
Tang dynasty, 618–907	
Five Dynasties and Ten Kingdoms, 907–960	Liao dynasty (Khitans), 907–1125
Later Zhou, 951–960	
Southern Tang, 937–935	
Song dynasty, 960–1276	
Northern Song dynasty, 960–1127	
Taizu, r. 960–976	
Taizong, r. 976–997	
Zhenzong, r. 997–1022; Empress Liu (wife), 969–1033	
Renzong, r. 1022–1063	
Yingzong, r. 1063–1067; Empress Gao (wife), d. 1093	

Shenzong, r. 1067–1085; Empress Xiang (wife), d. 1101
Xining period, 1068–1077
Yuanfeng period, 1078–1085
Zhezong, r. 1085–1100
Yuanyou period, 1086–1093
Shaosheng period, 1094–1097
Yuanfu period, 1098–1100
Huizong, r. 1100–1125
Jianguo jingzhong period, 1101
Chongning period, 1102–1106
Daguan period, 1107–1110
Zhenghe period, 1111–1117
Zhonghe period, 1118
Xuanhe period, 1119–1125
Qinzong, r. 1125–1127
Jingkang period, 1126–1127
Southern Song dynasty, 1127–1276
Gaozong, r. 1127–1162
six more emperors

Jin dynasty (Jurchens), 1115–1234
Zhangzong, r. 1189–1208

Yuan dynasty, 1215–1368
Wenzong (Tugh Temür, r. 1328–1329, 1330–1332)
Ming dynasty, 1368–1644
Taizu, r. 1368–1398
Qing dynasty, 1644–1912
Kangxi reign period, 1662–1722
Qianlong reign period, 1736–1795

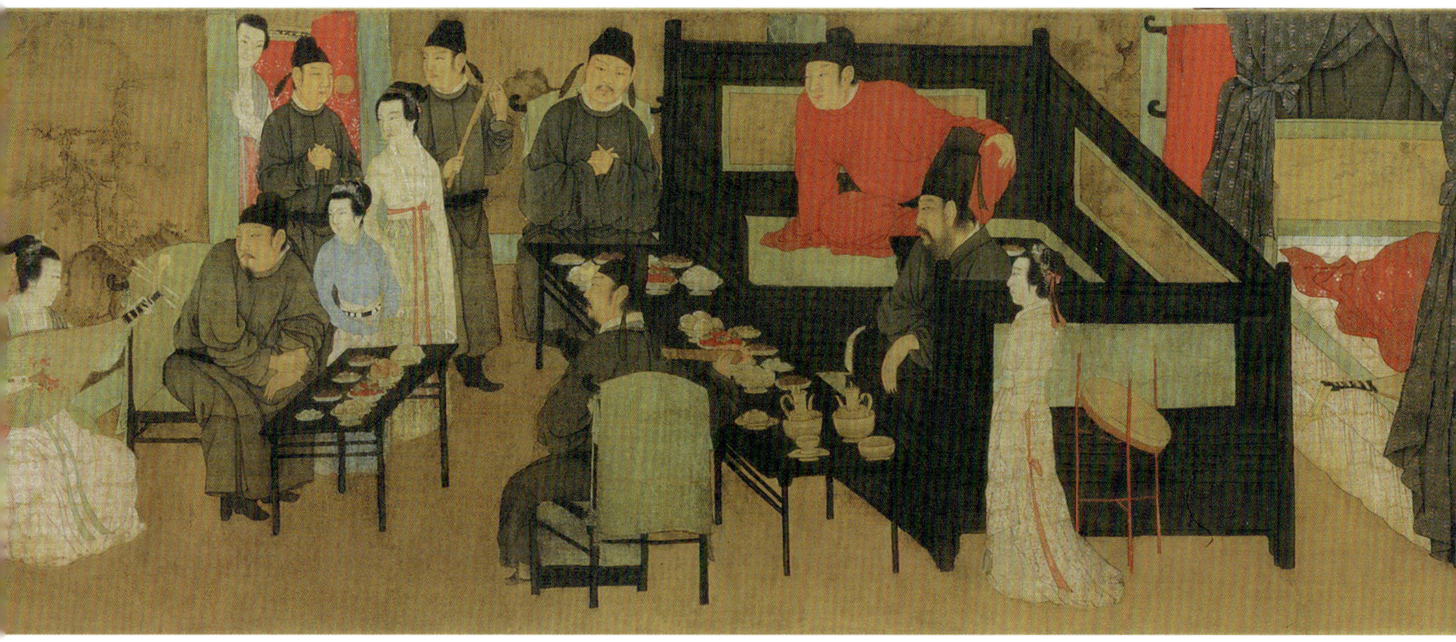

Plate 1
Attributed to Gu Hongzhong (tenth century), *The Night Revels of Han Xizai* (detail). Handscroll, ink and color on silk, 28.7 × 335.5 cm. Palace Museum, Beijing. There were many ways to make life more elegant in Song times. The wealthy official whose social gathering is depicted here is shown surrounded by fine wooden furniture (some decorated with landscape paintings), attended by women wearing colorful silk dresses and entertained by musicians. He serves his guests a wide array of wine and food on fine ceramic dishes.

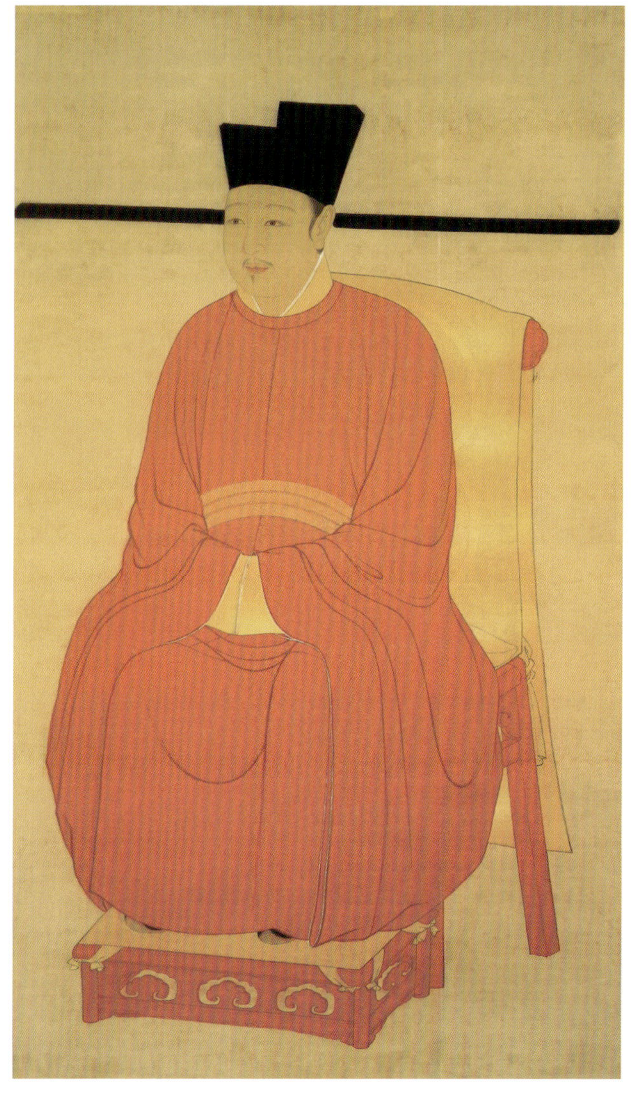

Plate 2
Portrait of Huizong. Hanging scroll, ink and color on silk, 188.2 × 106.7 cm. National Palace Museum, Taiwan, Republic of China.

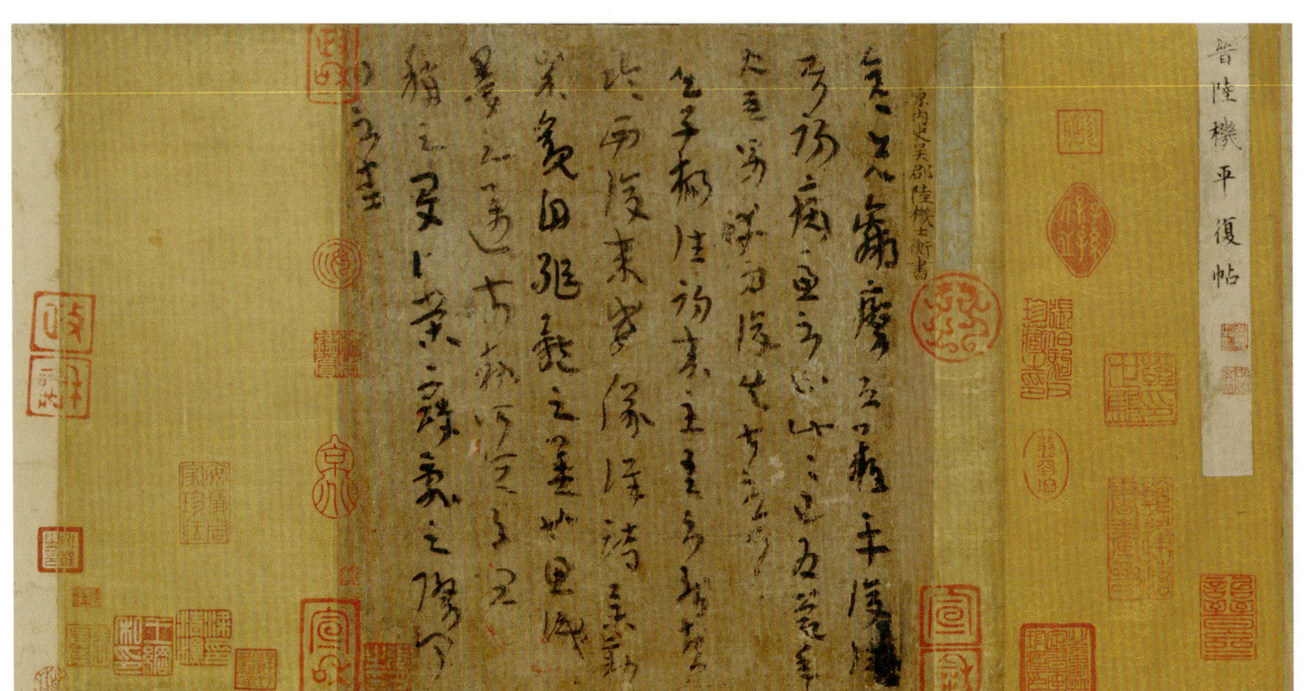

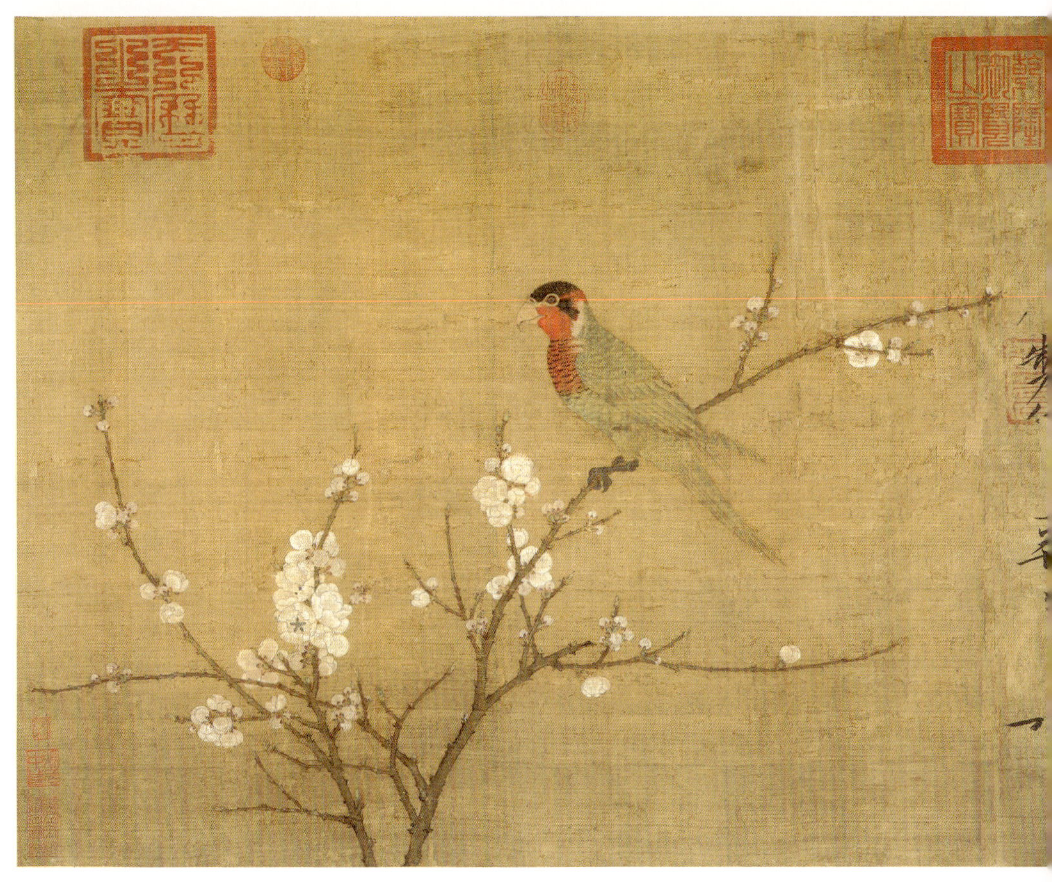

Plate 3

Lu Ji (261–303), *Pingfu tie.* Handscroll, ink on paper, 23.8 × 20.5 cm. Palace Museum, Beijing. This short letter, consoling a friend on his serious illness, is the oldest extant work once in Huizong's collection. Huizong's title strip, in barely legible gold ink, is to the right of the work itself. Below it is Huizong's round double dragon seal. Like other works with the "Xuanhe mounting set" of seals, at the bottom right of the work is a double seal reading "Xuanhe," at the top left is an oblong seal reading "Zhenghe," and bottom left an oblong seal reading "Xuanhe." At the center of the next seam is a double seal reading "Zhenghe" (Zhenghe and Xuanhe are the names of two of Huizong's reign periods). The other seals visible in the picture belong to later collectors. The three in the middle of the left seam are those of the collector An Qi (1683–1742).

Plate 4

Huizong, *Five-Colored Parakeet.* Handscroll, ink and color on silk, 53.3 × 125 cm. Photograph © 2008 Museum of Fine Arts, Boston. Marie Antoinette Evans Fund, 33.364. This work combines Huizong's poetry, calligraphy, and painting. The poem describes the delightful bird from the far south. The calligraphy is in Huizong's distinctive Slender Gold style. The painting represents the colorful bird in profile on the branch of a flowering tree.

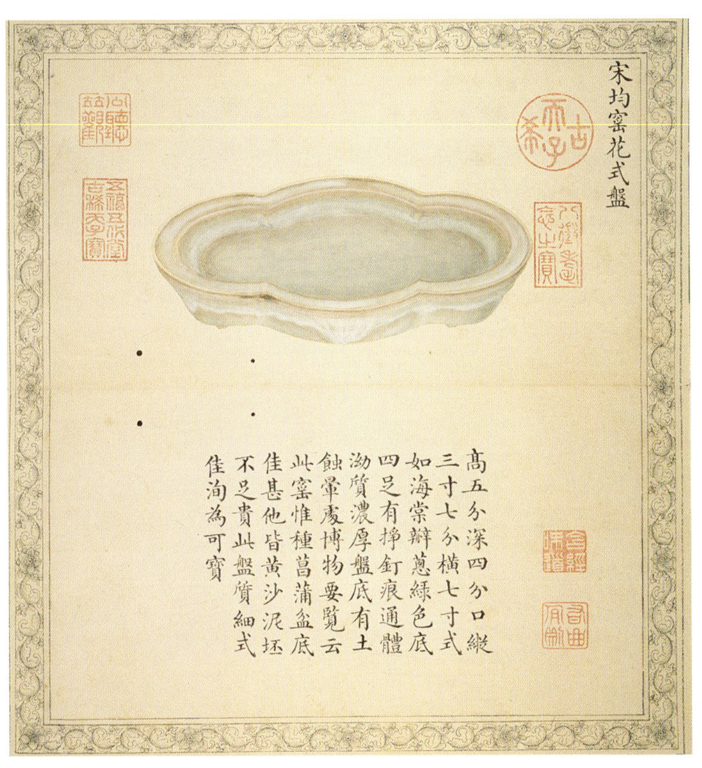

PLATE 5
Page from Qianlong's catalogue of his ceramics, *Taoci puce*. National Palace Museum, Taiwan, Republic of China. The Jun ware bowl of the Jin or Yuan period depicted on it still survives in the National Palace Museum. The description below the image gives dimensions and discusses the shape and glaze. The illustrations of the porcelains were hand painted in color.

PLATE 6
Viewing Books at Grand Clarity. Handscroll, ink and color on silk, 33.1 × 60 cm (detail). National Palace Museum, Taiwan, Republic of China. This picture, one of the *Four Events during the Jingde [Reign Period]*, depicts Zhenzong's 1007 visit to the building in the inner palace that held newly copied duplicates of books. In the painting, some officials are inside, viewing opened books, while others outside wait their turn to enter.

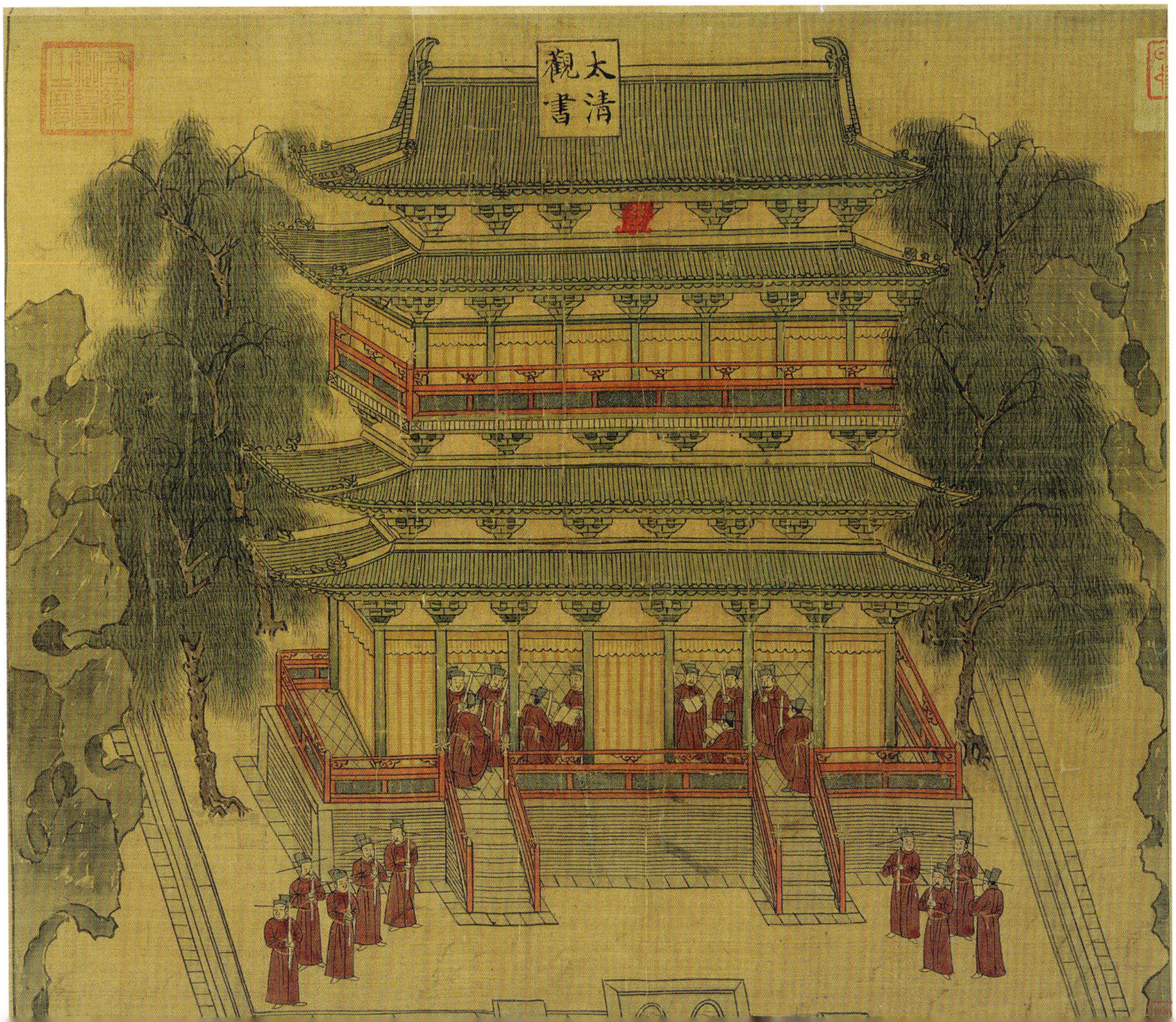

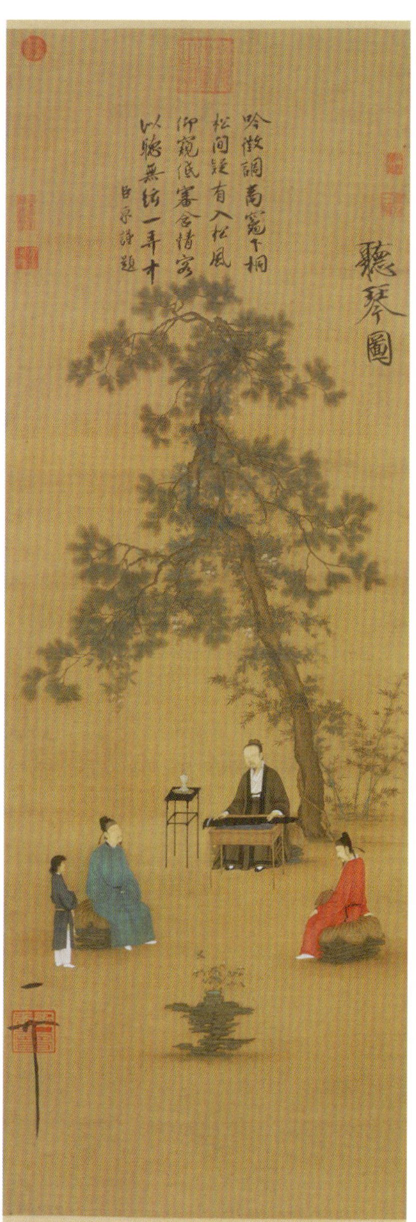

PLATE 7
Attributed to Huizong, *Listening to the Zither*. Hanging scroll, ink and color on silk, 147.2 × 51.3 cm. Palace Museum, Beijing. Both Cai Jing and Huizong inscribed this painting. Huizong gave it the title *Listening to the Zither*. In the lower left are his seal and mark interpreted to mean "The first person under Heaven." Cai Jing inscribed the poem at the top that alludes to the music and the pine tree. The painting itself was probably done by a court artist and depicts the sort of cultivated cultural interaction that Huizong and Cai Jing engaged in.

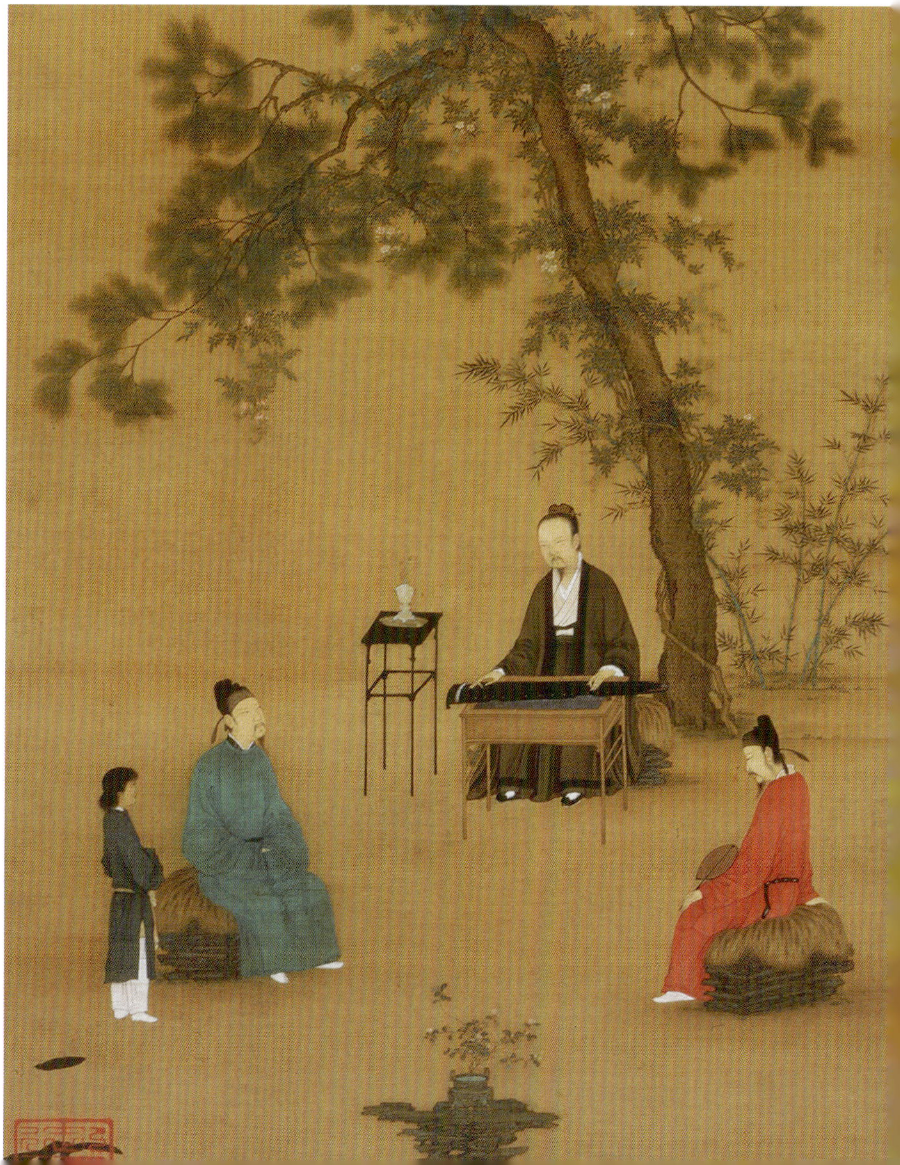

PLATE 8
Detail of *Listening to the Zither*, (plate 7).

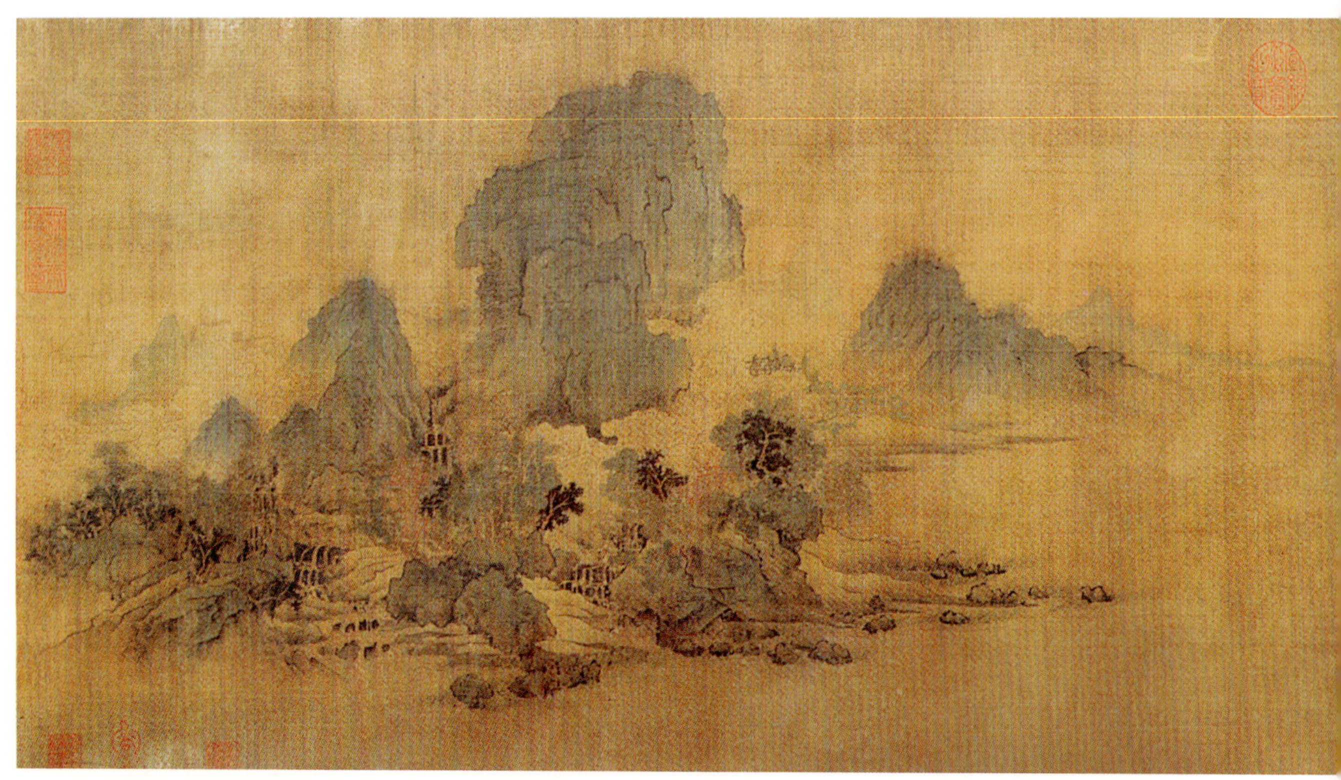

PLATE 9
Wang Shen (ca. 1048–1103), *Rivers and Mountains in Mist.* Handscroll, ink and color on silk, 45.2 × 166 cm. Shanghai Museum.

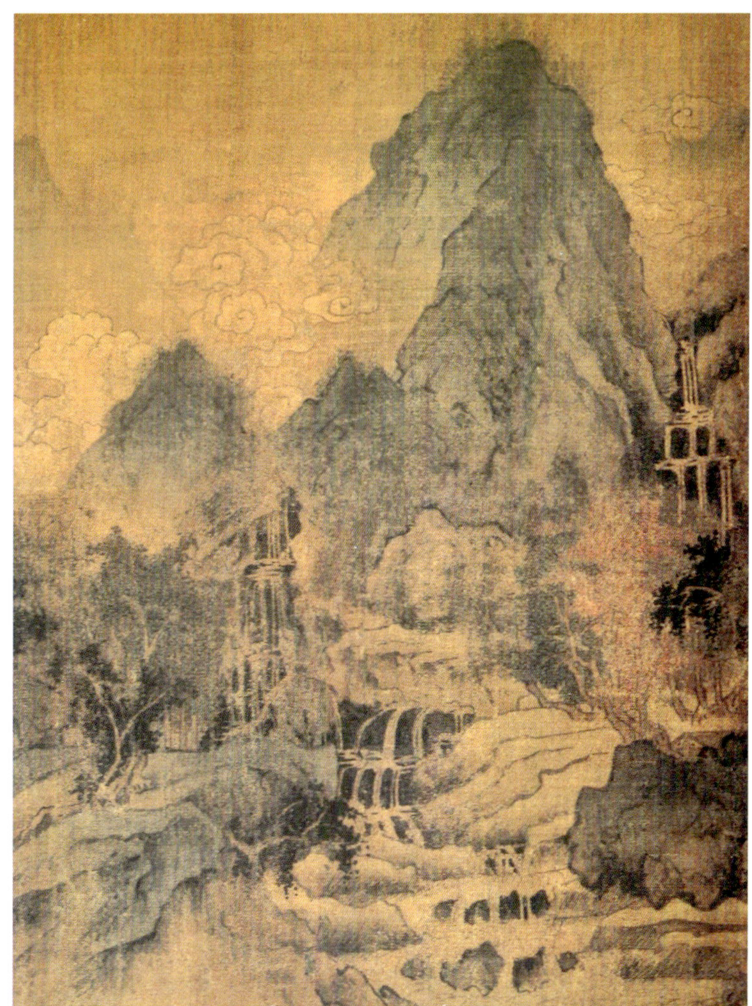

Plate 10
Detail of *Rivers and Mountains in Mist* (plate 9).

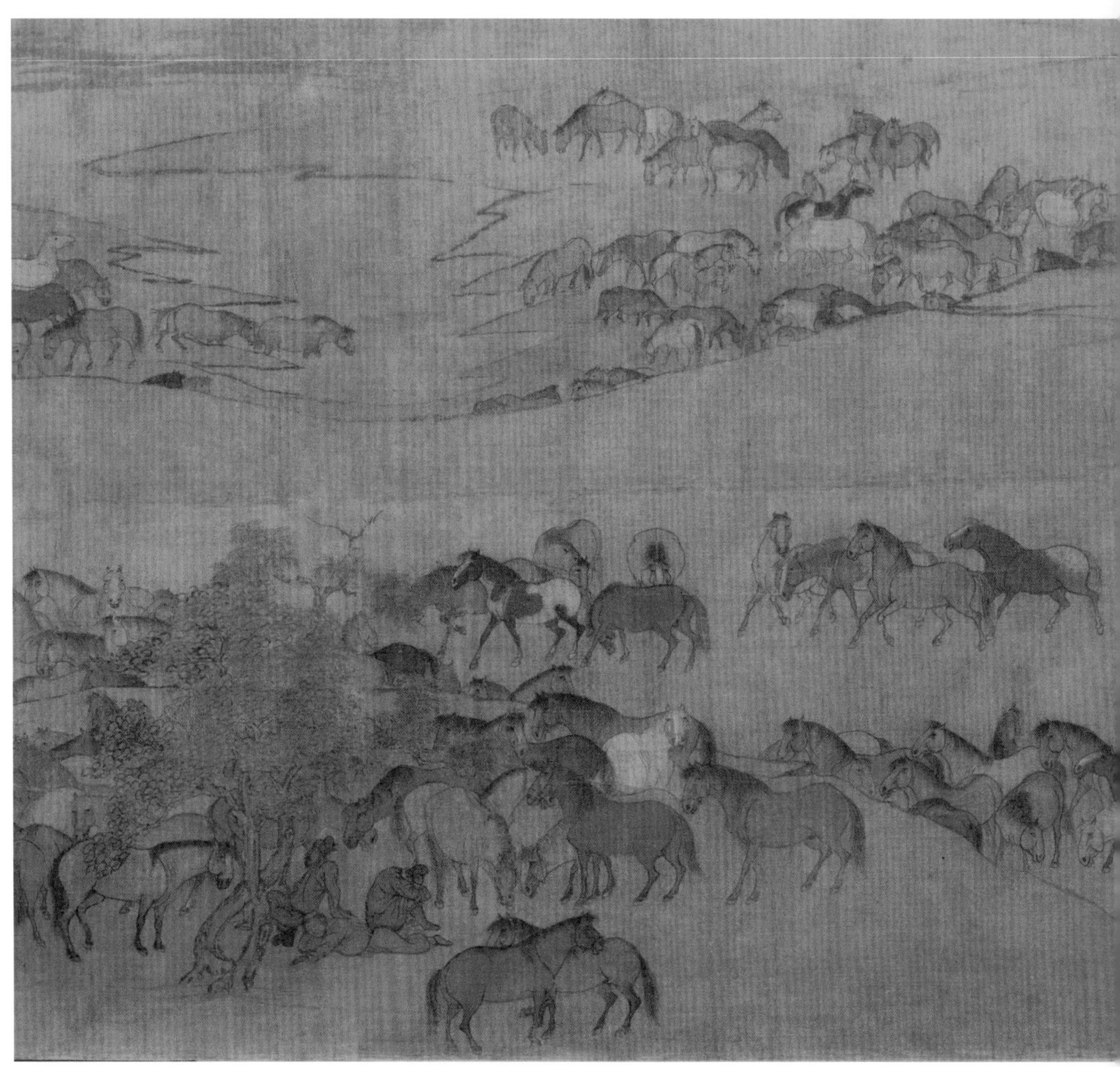

PLATE 11
Li Gonglin (ca. 1041–1106), *Copy of Wei Yan's Pasturing Horses* (detail). Handscroll, ink and color on silk, 46.2 × 429 cm. Palace Museum, Beijing. In Li's inscription, he says he did this painting on imperial order.

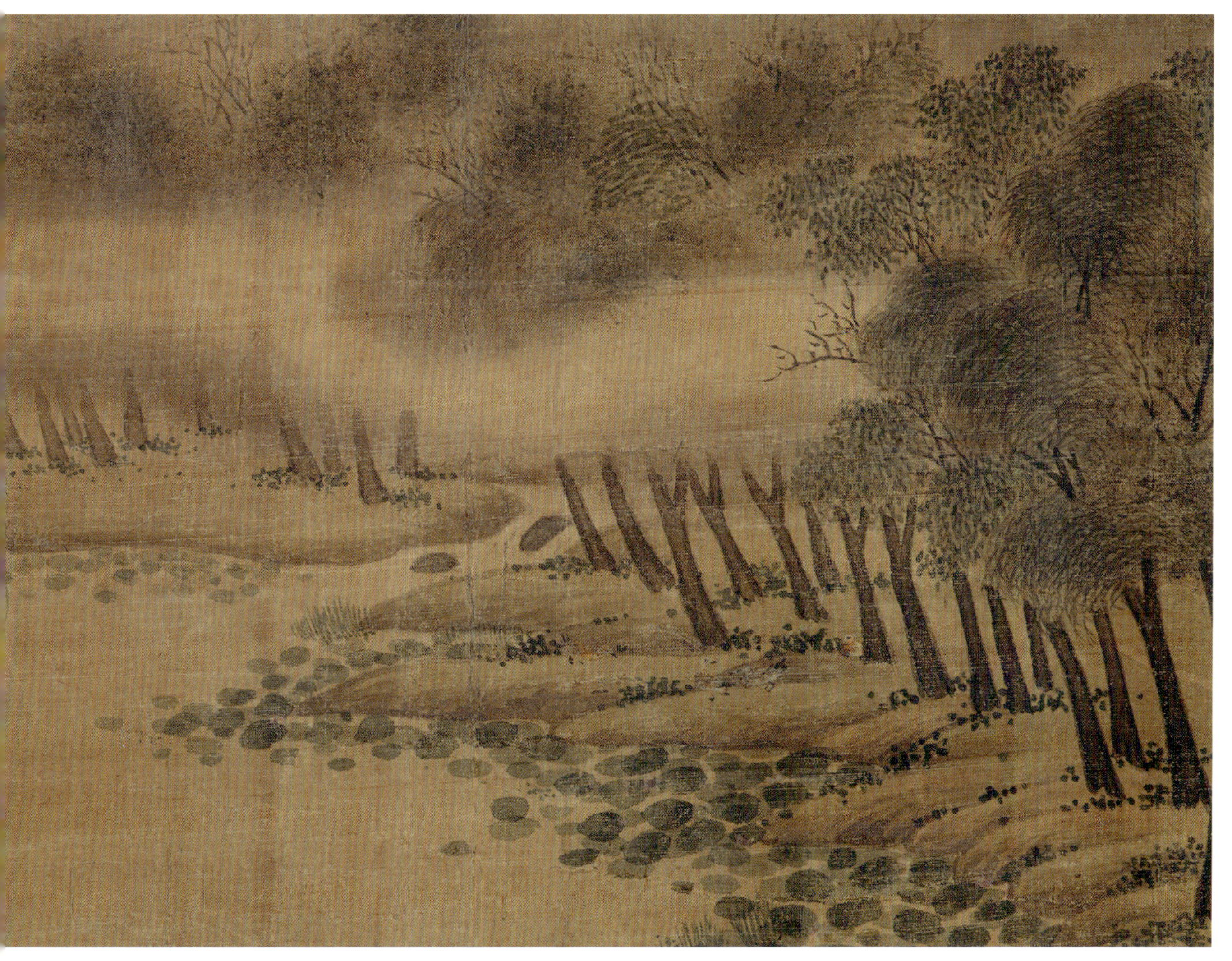

PLATE 12

Zhao Lingrang (ca. 1070–ca. 1100), *Summer Mist along the Lake Shore* (detail). Handscroll, ink and color on silk, 19.1 × 161.3 cm. Photograph © 2008 Museum of Fine Arts, Boston. Keith McLeod Fund, 57.724. Zhao signed this painting, dated it to 1100, and put two seals on it. For the entire painting, see figure 8.9, p. 302.

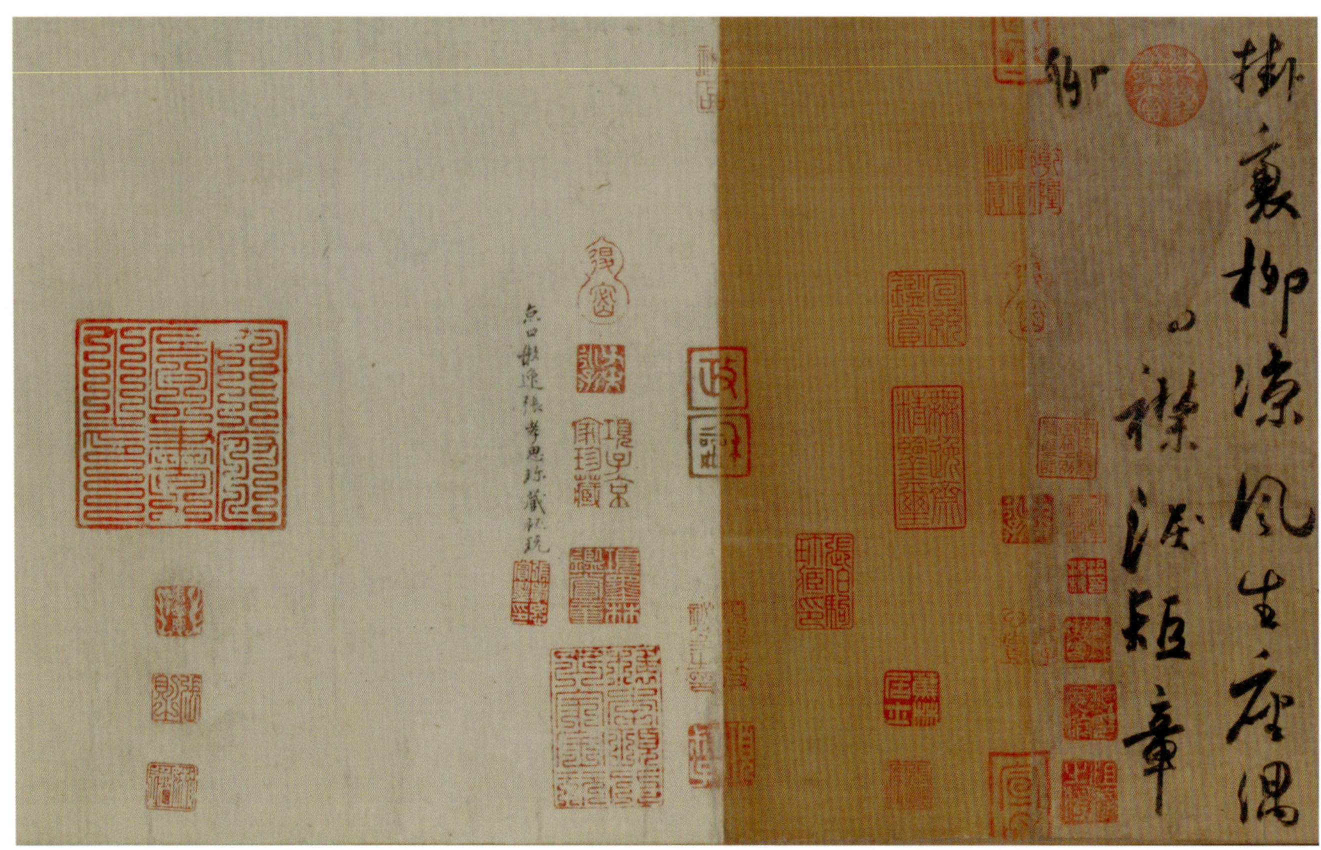

PLATE 13

Du Mu (803–852), *Poem Dedicated to Zhang Haohao* (two details). Handscroll, ink on paper, 28.1 × 161 cm. Palace Museum, Beijing.

The beginning and end of this scroll show Huizong's use of the seven seals in the Xuanhe mounting set.

唐杜牧之張好好詩 蕉林秘玩 神品上上

張好好詩 并序

牧大和三年佐故吏部沈公江西幕好好年十三始以善歌舞來樂籍中後一歲公鎮宣城復置好好於宣城籍中後二年沈著作述師以雙鬟納之又二歲余於洛陽東城重覩好好感舊傷懷

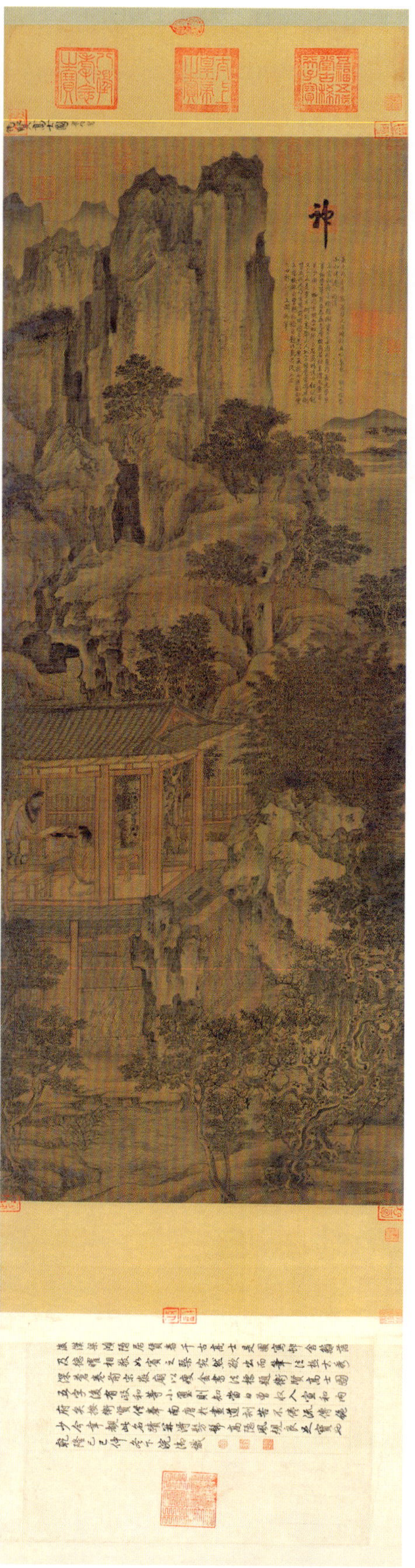

Plate 14
Wei Xian (fl. 937–975), *Lofty Scholar.* Hanging scroll, ink and color on silk, 134.5 × 52.5 cm. Palace Museum, Beijing. This scroll shows all of the seals in the Xuanhe mounting set, from the gourd-shaped "imperial writing" seal at the top seam, to the large square Inner Palace seal in the middle of the white sheet of paper attached to the end of the work. For a detail of this work, see plate 29.

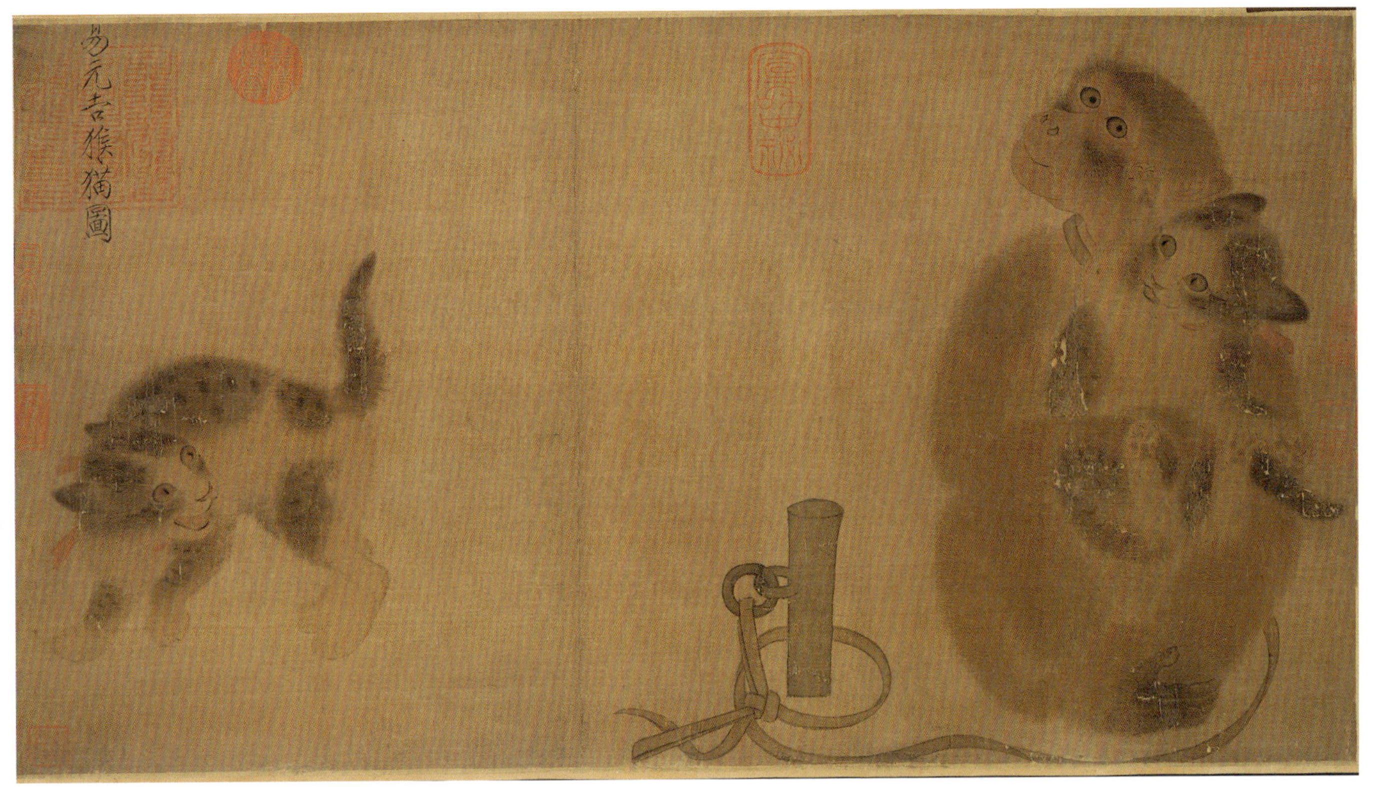

PLATE 15

Yi Yuanji (eleventh century), *Monkey and Cat.* Handscroll, ink and color on silk, 31.9 × 57.2 cm. National Palace Museum, Taiwan, Republic of China. The seal near the center of the top is the Secret Treasure of Harmony Revealed Hall seal. In the upper left Huizong inscribed "Yi Yuanji's *Monkey and Cat.*" On top or underneath it is the large square seal reading "Seal of the Inner Palace Paintings and Calligraphies."

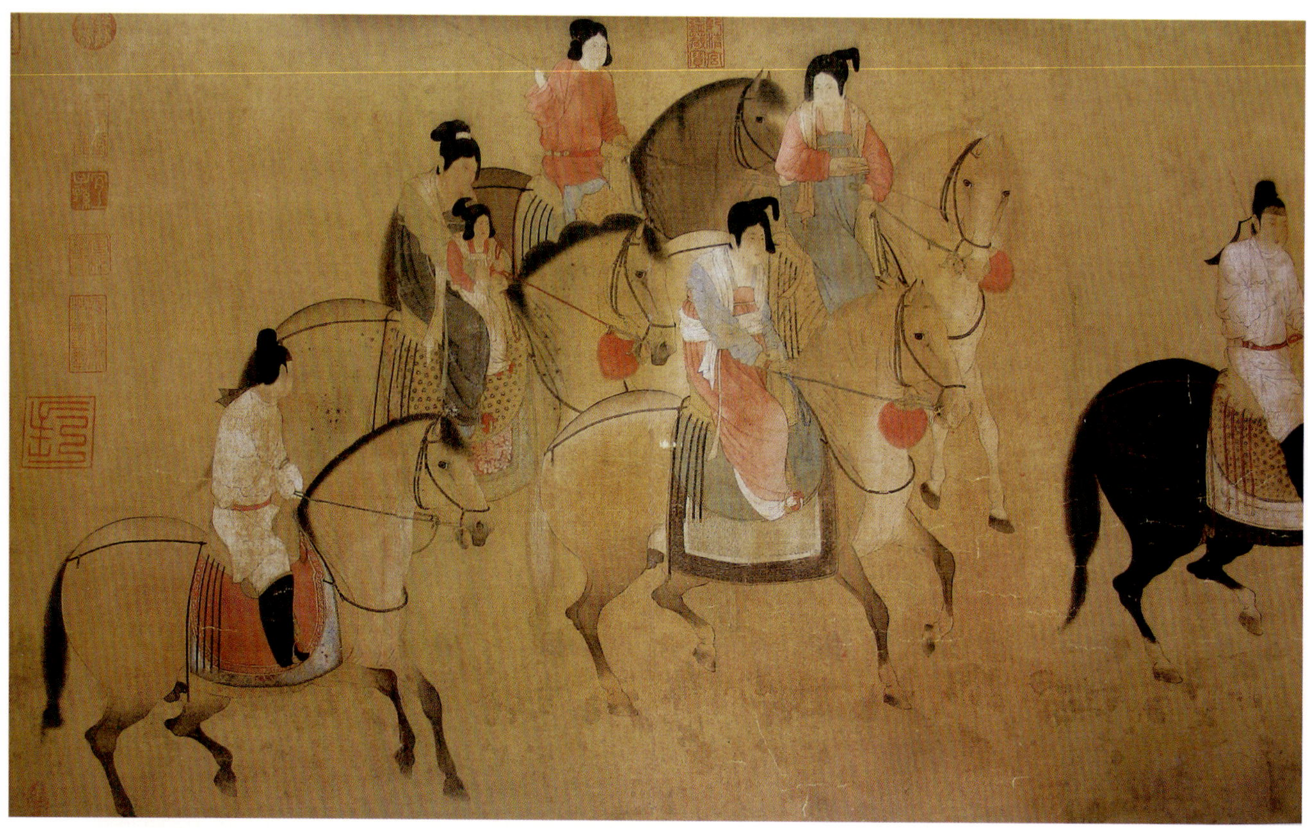

Plate 16

Attributed to Huizong, *Copy of Zhang Xuan's Lady Guoguo on an Outing* (detail). Handscroll, ink and color on silk, 51.8 × 140 cm. Liaoning Provincial Museum. Zhang Xuan's original painting illustrated a scene depicted in a poem by Du Fu (712–770) titled "Beauties on an Outing" about the sisters of Yang Guifei, the beloved consort of the Tang emperor Xuanzong. The figures in male dress may be palace ladies wearing men's clothes as a fashion statement, or they may be eunuchs. Huizong or the court painter working at his direction preserved the plump faces of the Yang sisters from the Tang original, but seems to have been even more concerned to capture the details of the elaborately decorated saddles.

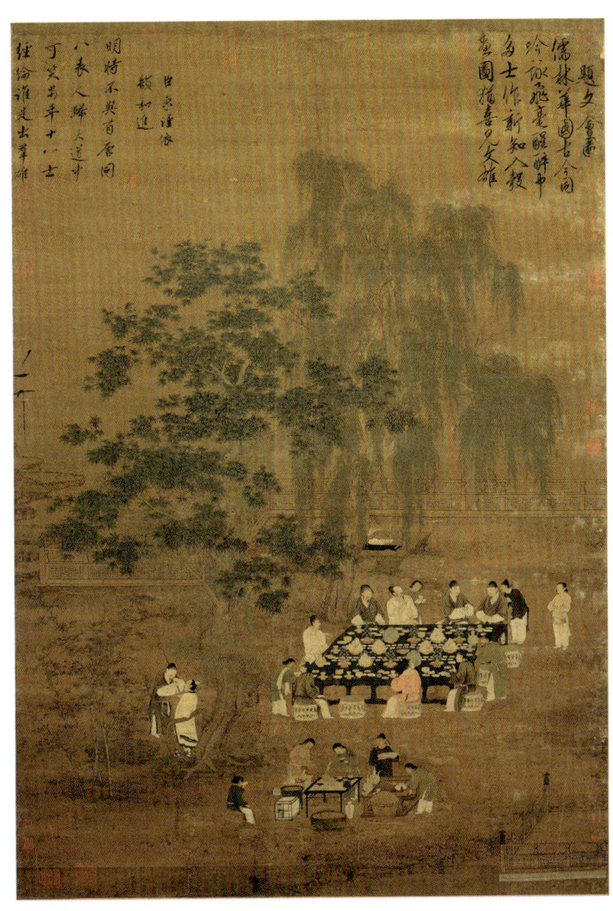

PLATE 17
Attributed to Huizong, *Literary Gathering.* Hanging scroll, ink and color on silk, 184.4 × 123.9 cm. National Palace Museum, Taiwan, Republic of China. Huizong's poetic inscription is in the upper right, Cai Jing's poem using matching rhymes in the upper left.

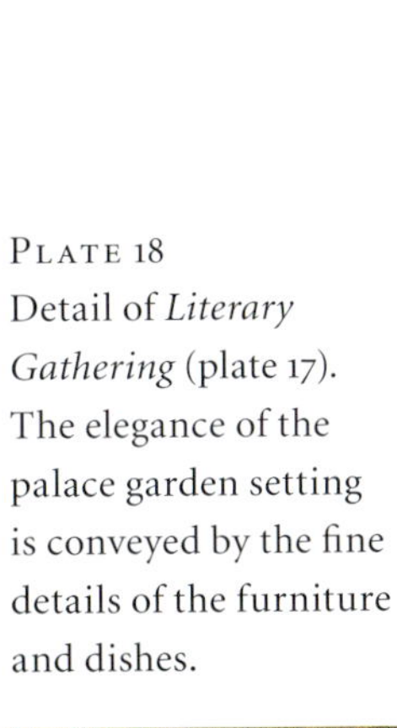

PLATE 18
Detail of *Literary Gathering* (plate 17). The elegance of the palace garden setting is conveyed by the fine details of the furniture and dishes.

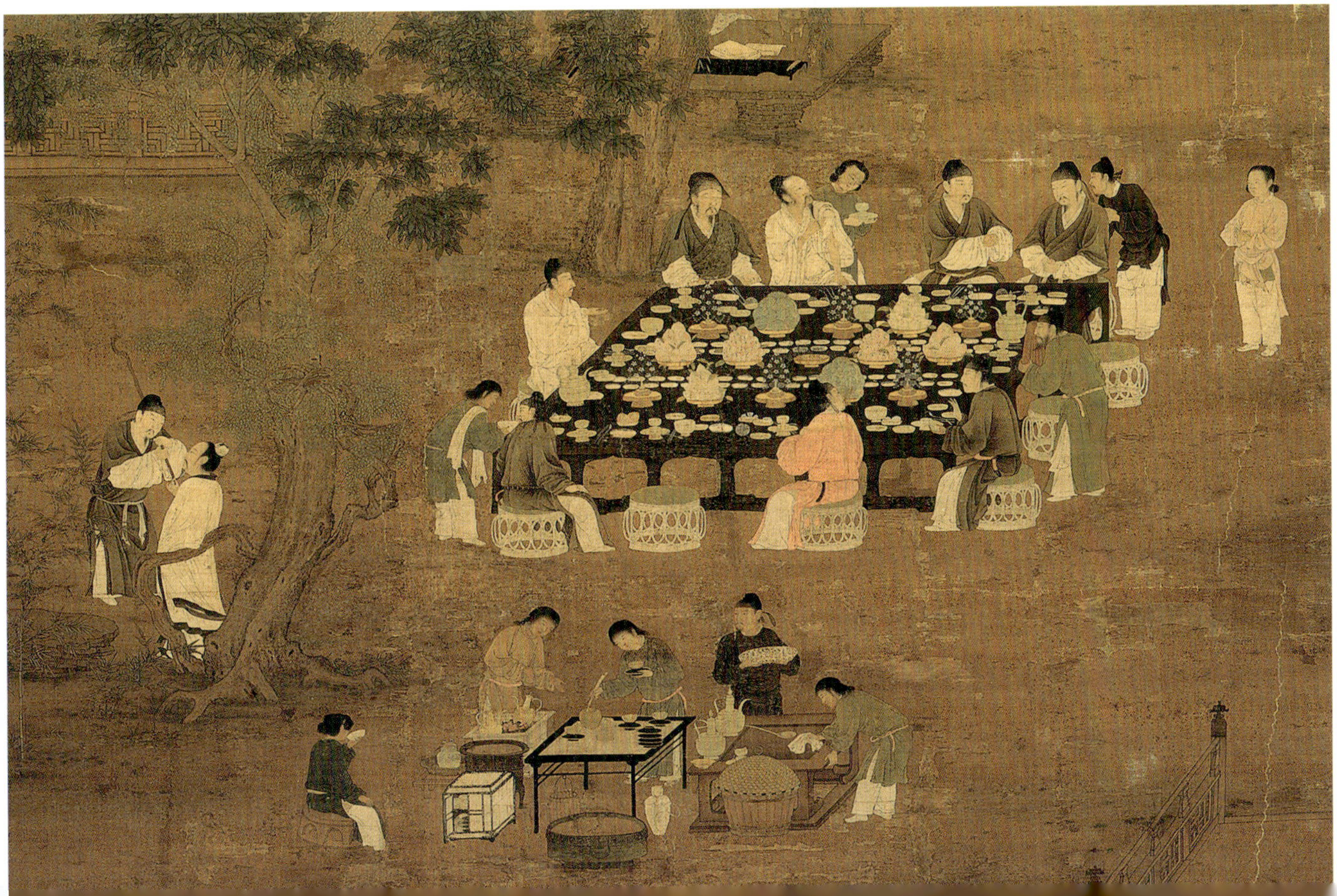

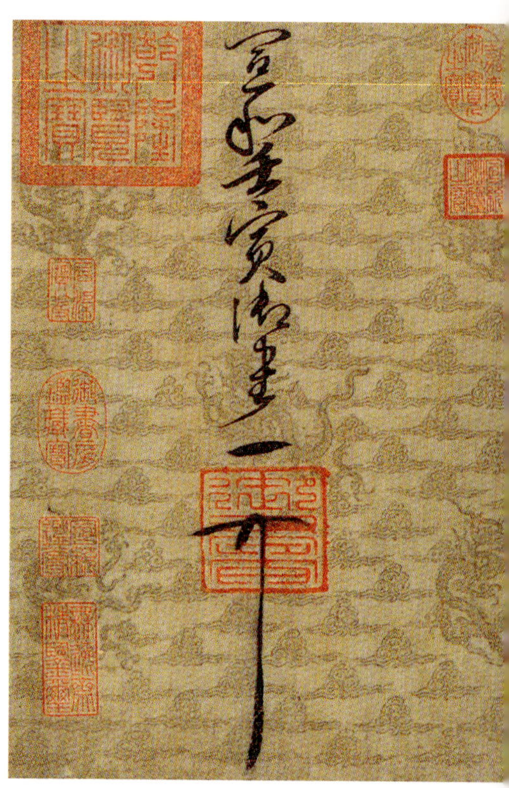

Plate 19

Huizong, *Thousand Character Essay in Cursive Script* (detail). Handscroll, ink on decorated paper, 31.5 × 1172 cm. Liaoning Provincial Museum.

Huizong's calligraphy on this piece is remarkably free and fluid, in sharp contrast to his Slender Gold regular script calligraphy.

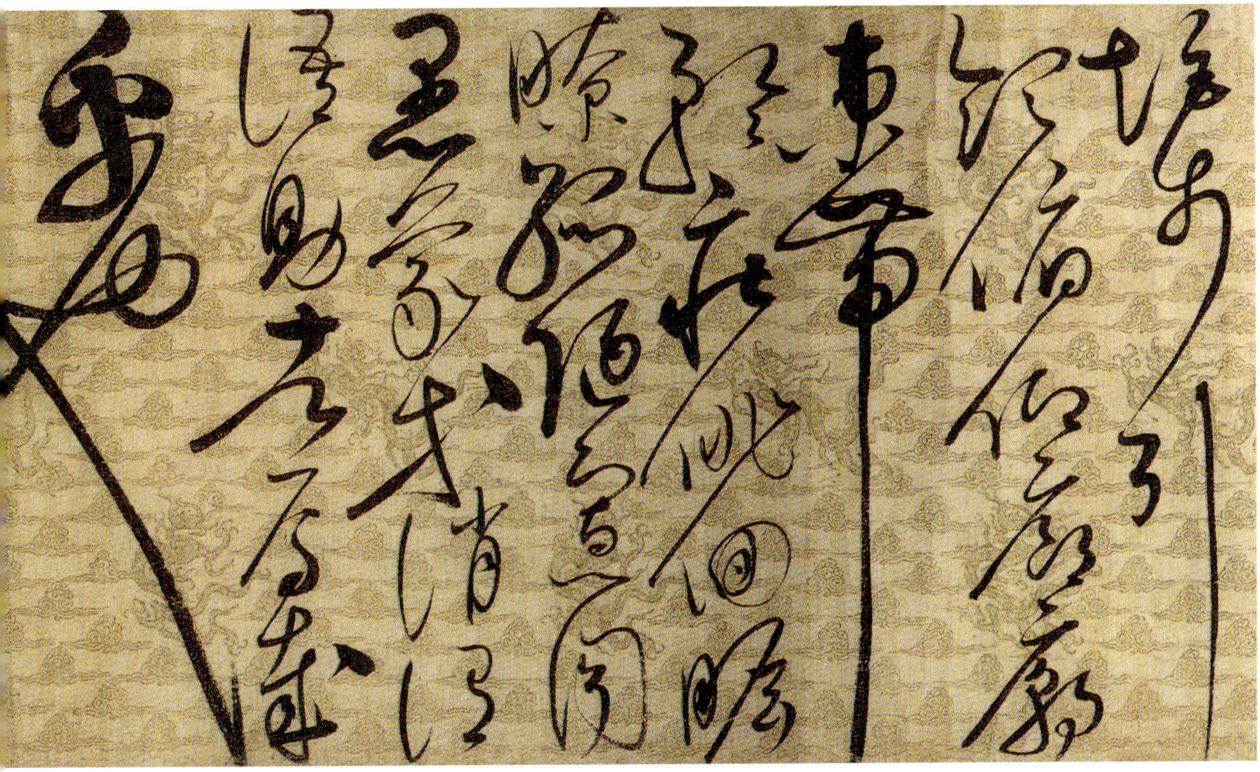

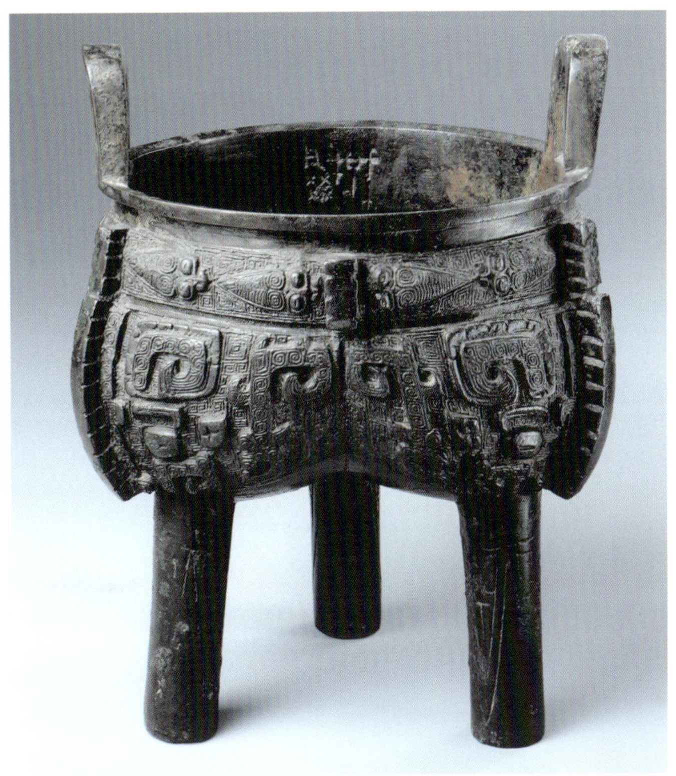

Plate 20
Fugui cauldron. Height 22.5 cm, weight 3.0 kg. National Palace Museum, Taiwan, Republic of China.

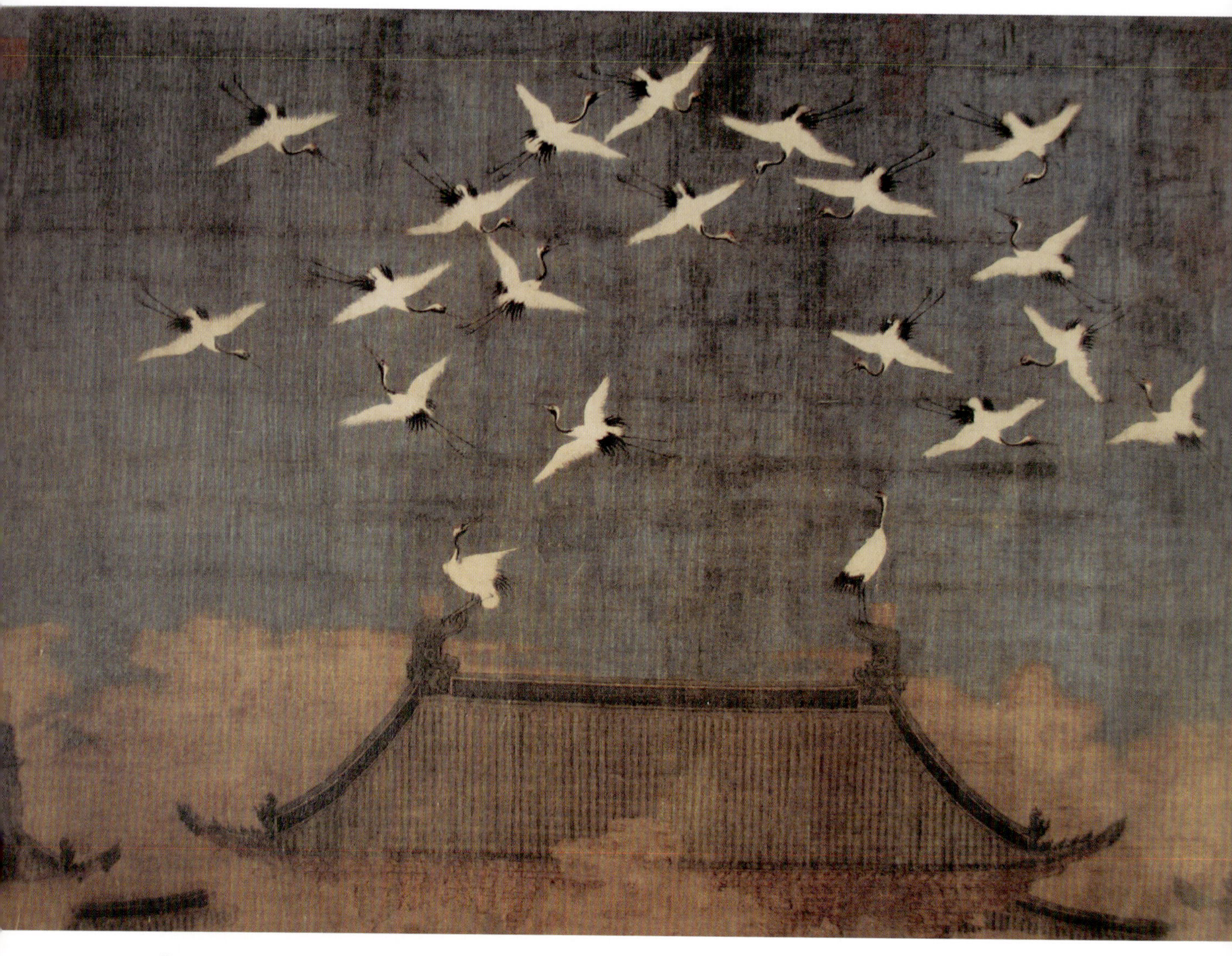

PLATE 21

Attributed to Huizong, *Auspicious Cranes* (detail). Handscroll, ink and color on silk, 51 × 138.2 cm. Liaoning Provincial Museum. Huizong's inscription on this painting says that it was done to record an occasion in 1113 when cranes appeared at the gate to the palace complex.

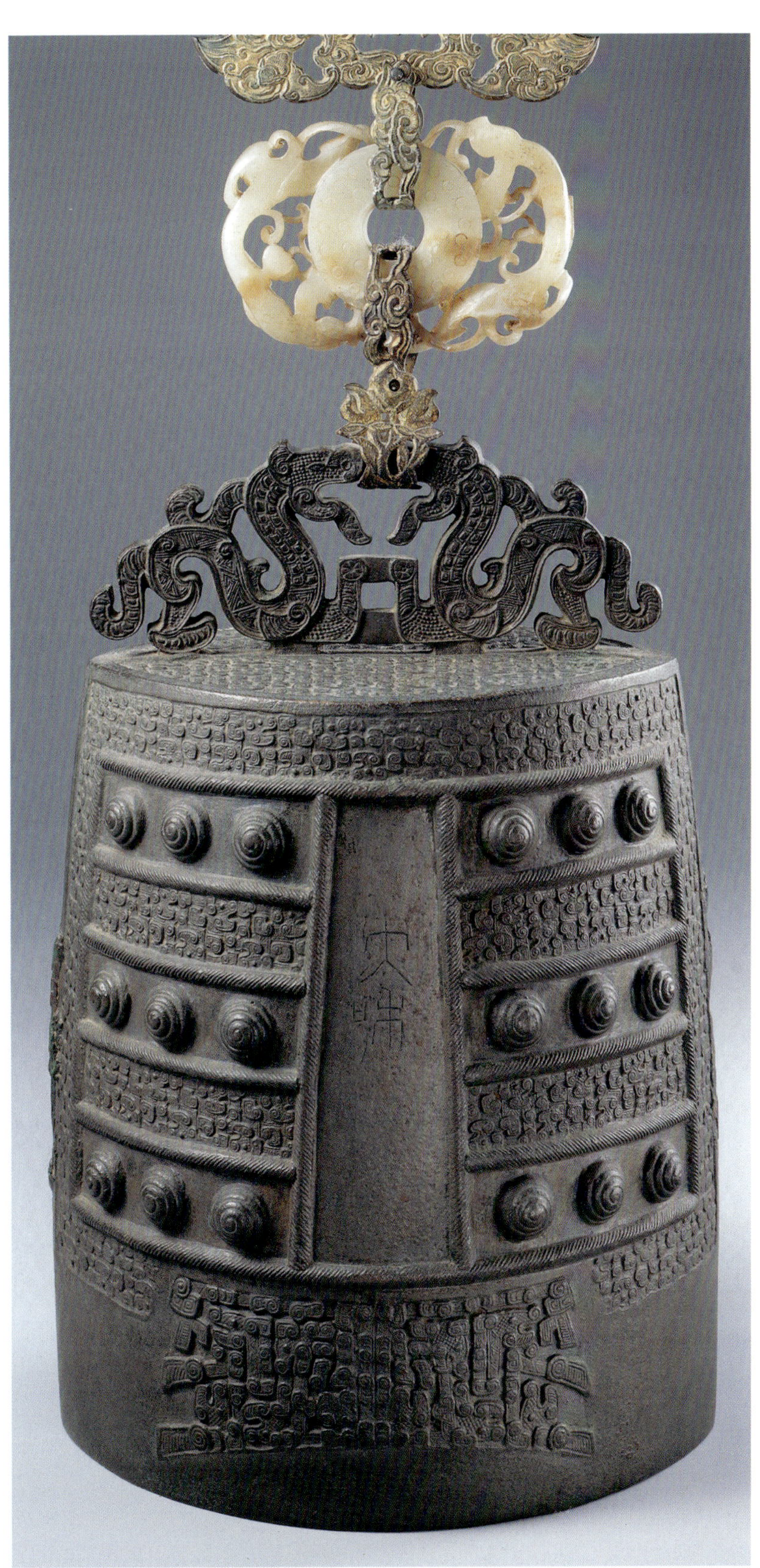

PLATE 22
Dasheng bell. Height 28.2 cm, weight 6.5 kg. National Palace Museum, Taiwan, Republic of China.

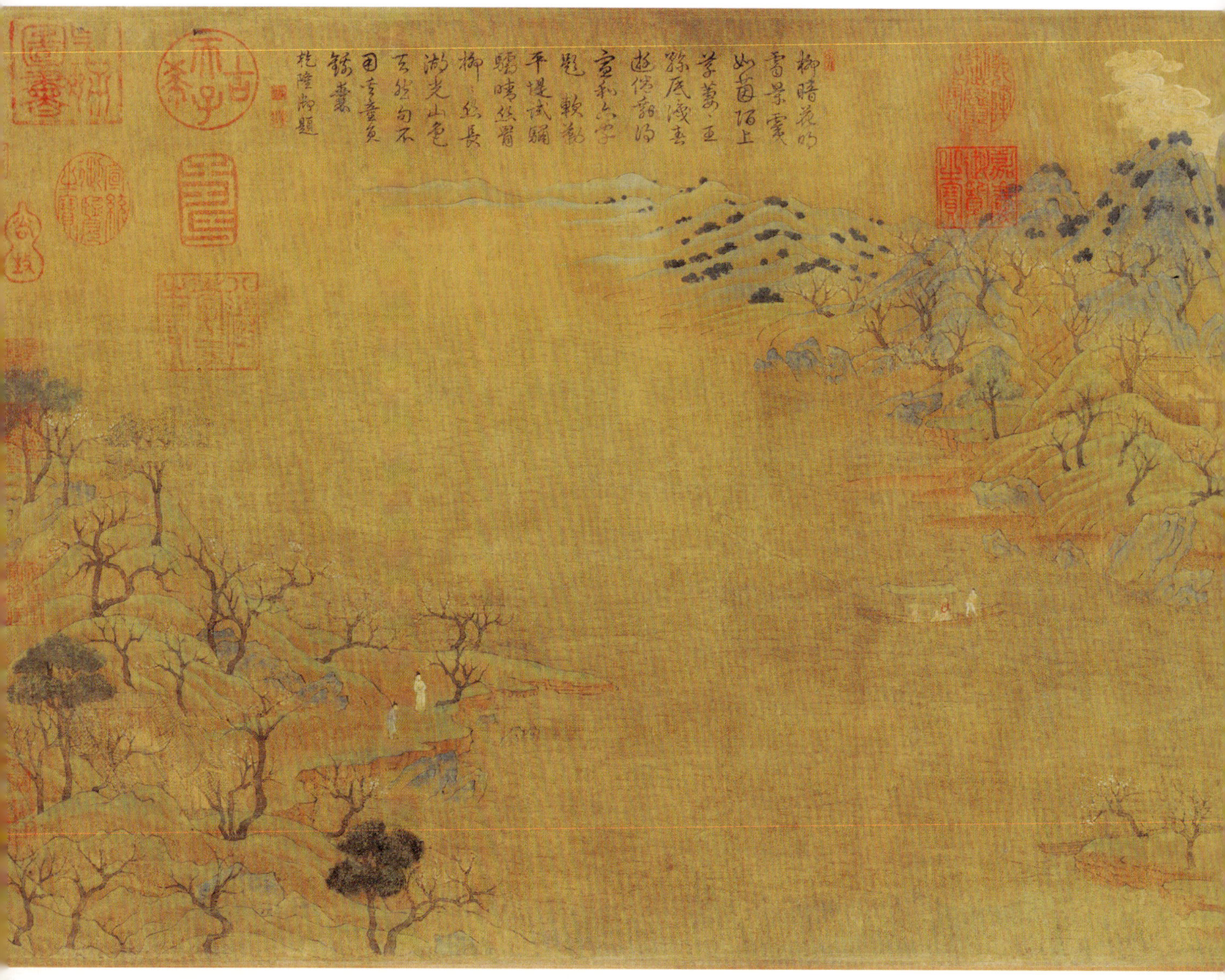

PLATE 23
Attributed to Zhan Ziqian (fl. 570s–580s), *Spring Outing.* Handscroll, ink and color on silk, 43 × 80.5 cm. Palace Museum, Beijing. This relatively short handscroll depicts a landscape that extends many miles. Near the center of the picture is a boat being sculled, carrying three women across the water. We know it is spring because of the trees with white and pink blossoms.

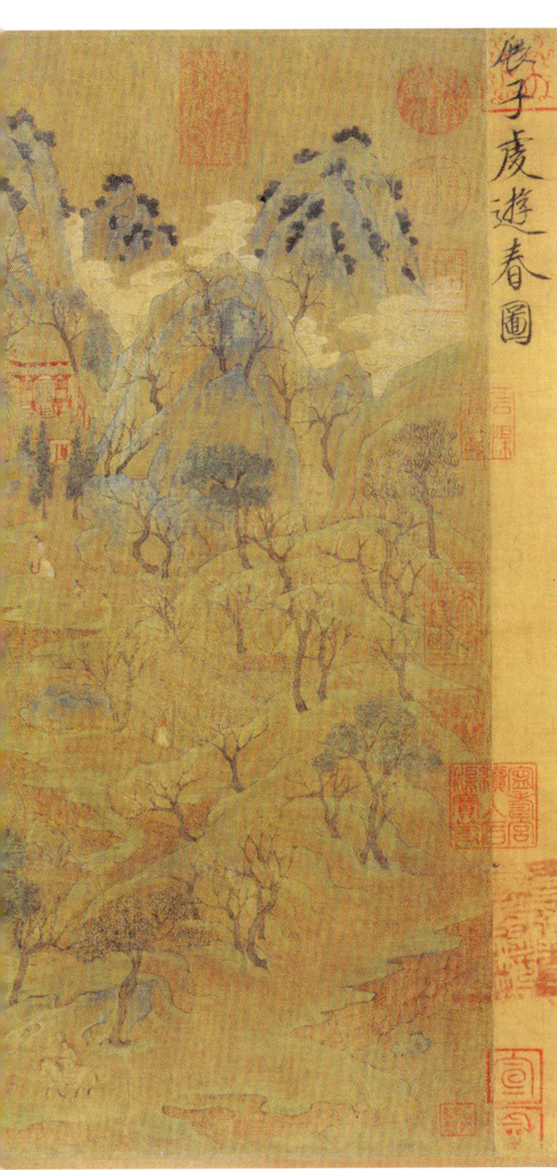

PLATE 24
Detail of *Spring Outing* (plate 23).

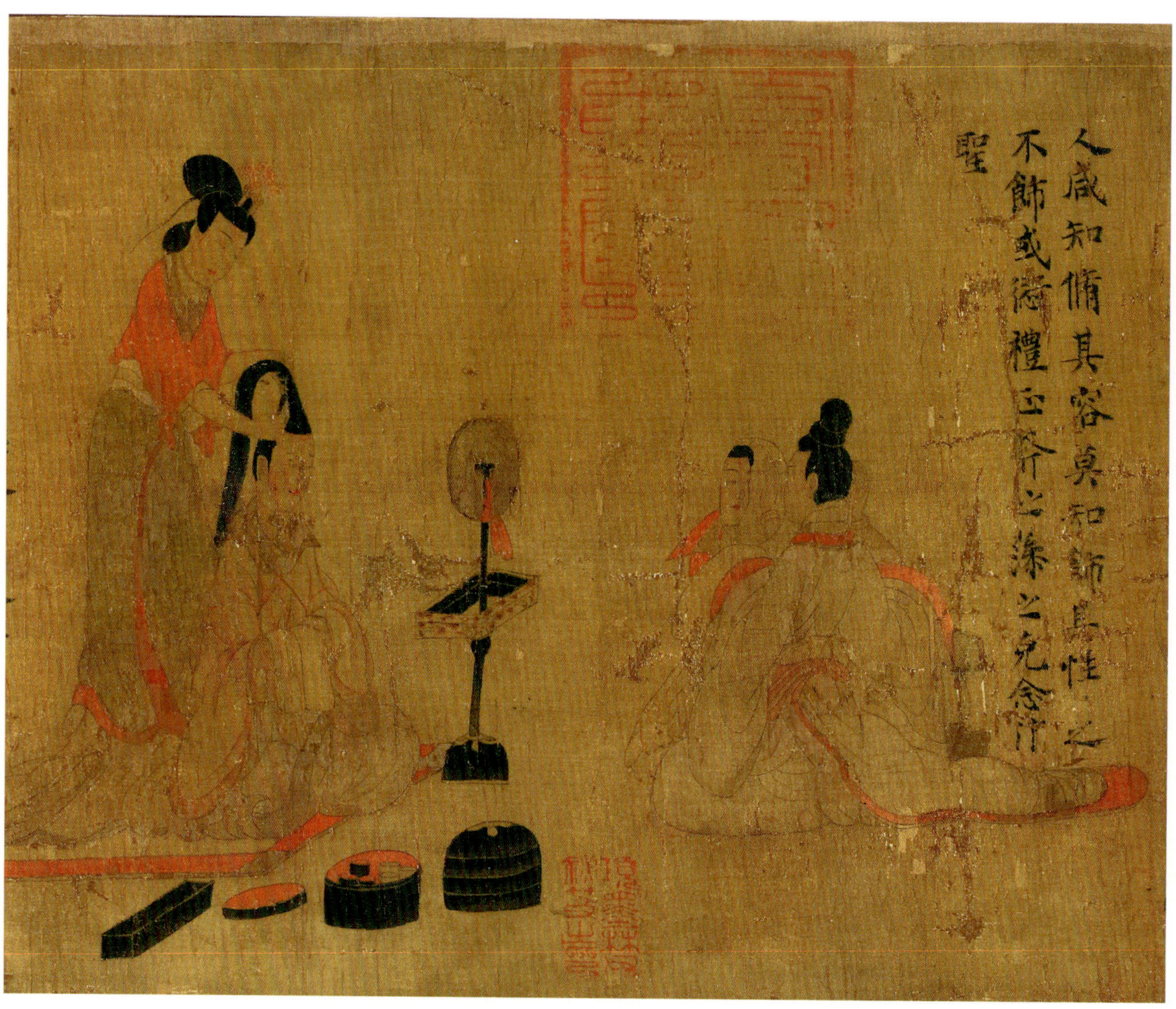

PLATE 25

Attributed to Gu Kaizhi (ca. 345–ca. 406), *Admonitions of the Instructress* (detail). Handscroll, ink and color on silk, 24.8 × 348.2 cm. © The Trustees of the British Museum. All rights reserved. The scene shown here illustrates the statement, "People know how to adorn their faces, but not how to polish their character." Yet rather than depict the action encouraged, the painter shows two women doing what was ostensibly being discouraged.

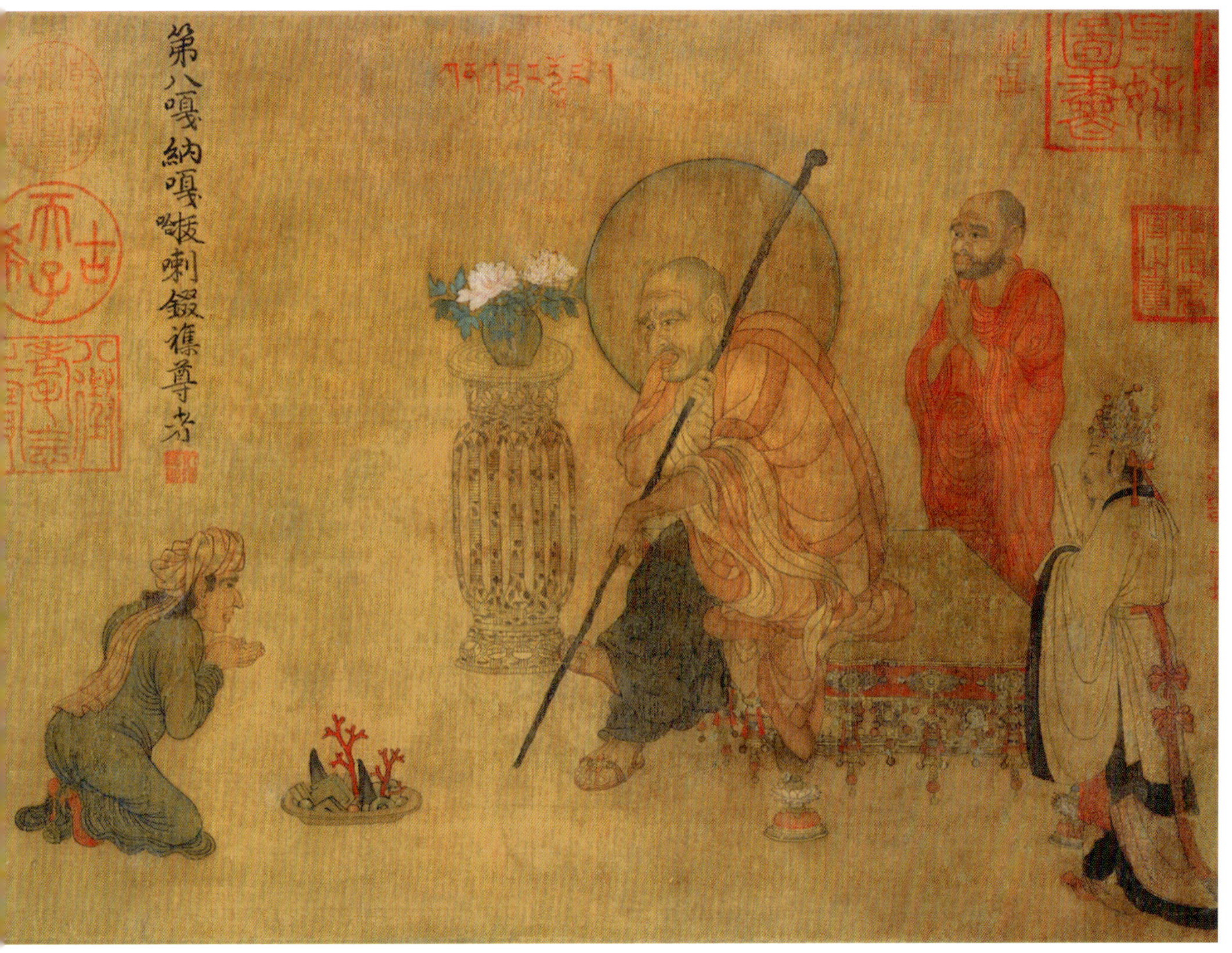

PLATE 26

Attributed to Lu Lengqie (fl. 750s–760s), *Six Arhats* (detail). Handscroll with four scenes, ink and color on silk, each scene 30 × 53 cm. Palace Museum, Beijing.

In each scene of this work, the arhats are accompanied by attendants or worshippers, whose smaller size emphasizes the centrality of the arhats.

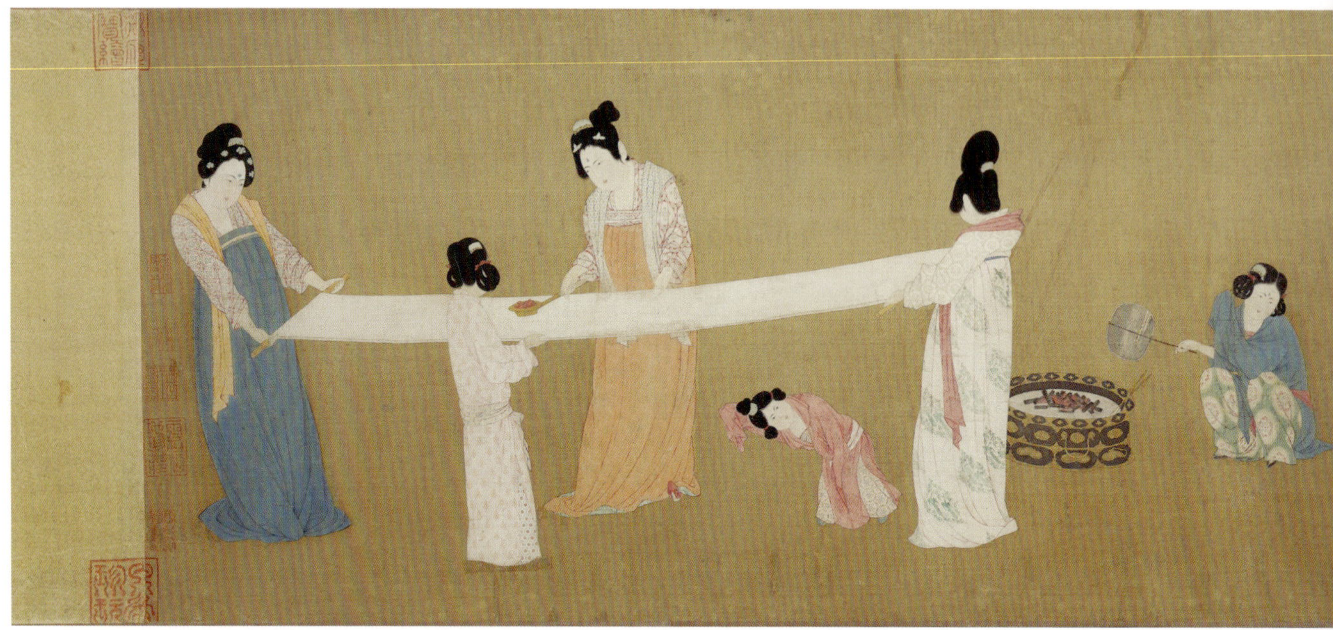

PLATE 27

Attributed to Huizong, *Copy of Zhang Xuan's Court Ladies Preparing Newly Woven Silk*. Handscroll, ink and color on silk, 37 × 147 cm. Photograph © 2008 Museum of Fine Arts, Boston. Special Chinese and Japanese Fund, 12.886. Done at Huizong's court, this finely detailed painting shows three groups of palace women, first a group of four beating the silk, then two sewing, then three women and three girls involved with final processing: Two women stretch a bolt of silk, which a third irons with a pan of burning coals. One girl helps with the silk, another fans the coals, and an even younger one, too small to help, runs under the stretched silk.

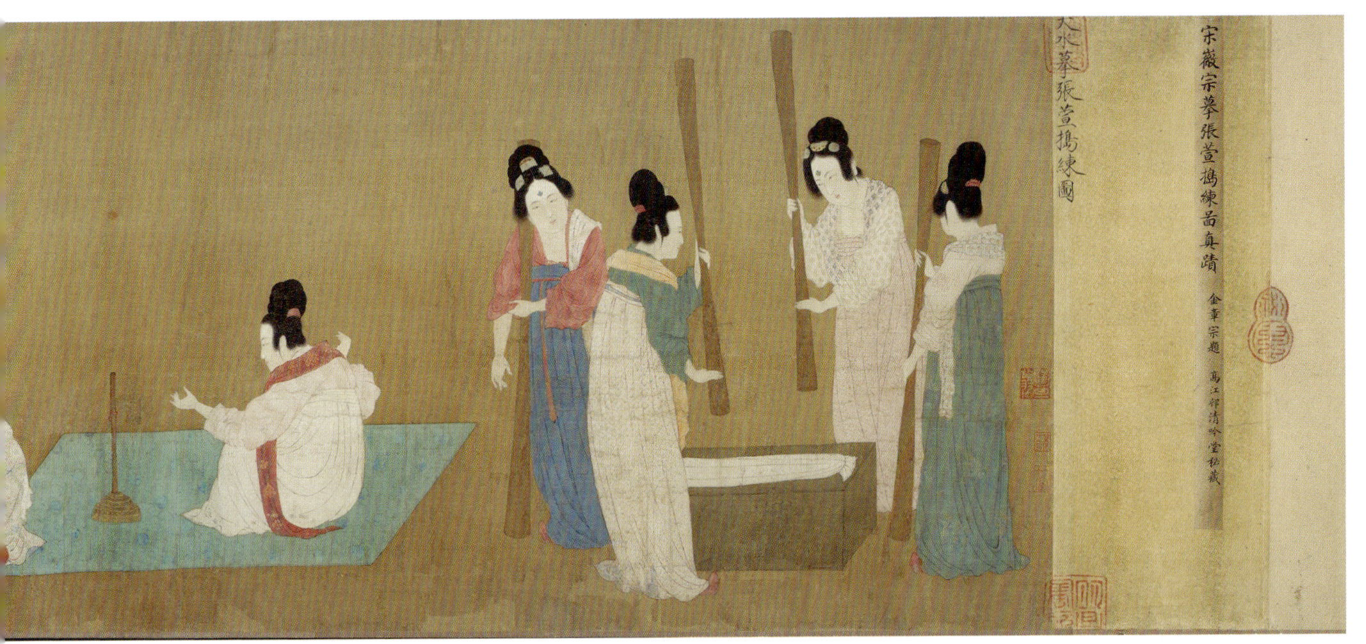

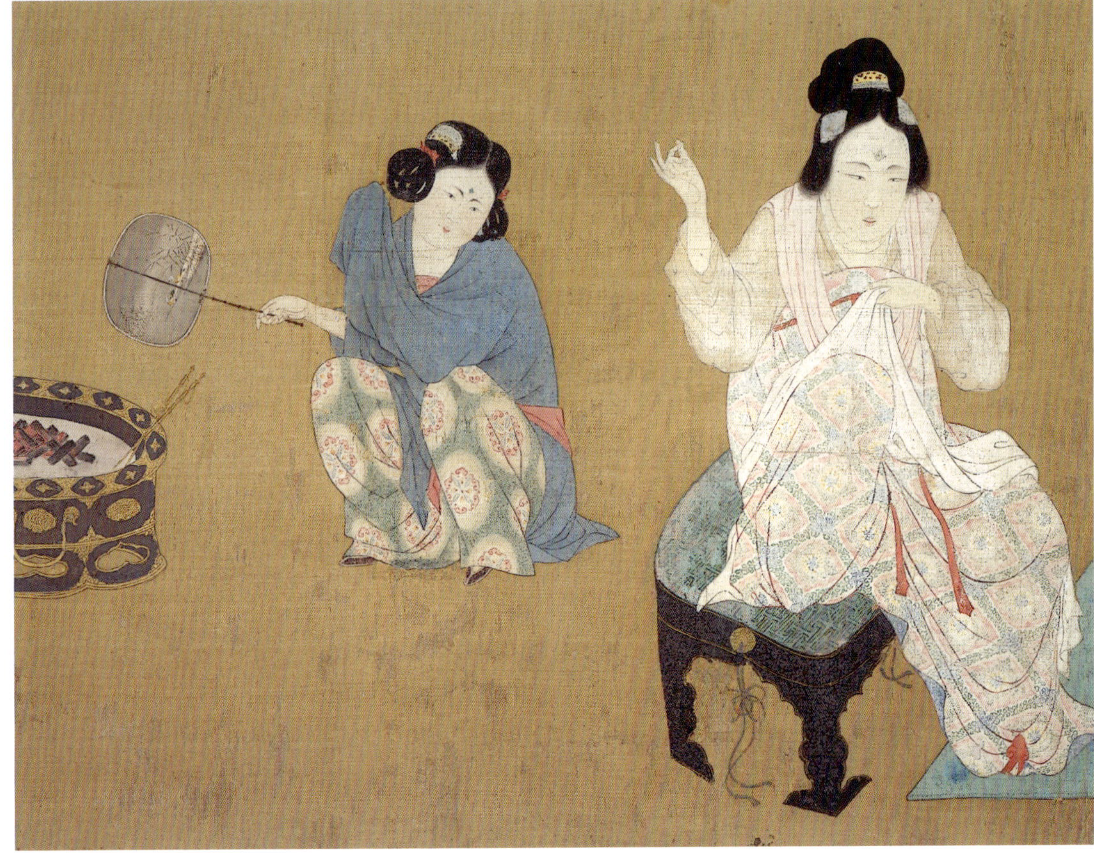

PLATE 28
Detail of *Copy of Zhang Xuan's Court Ladies Preparing Newly Woven Silk* (plate 27).

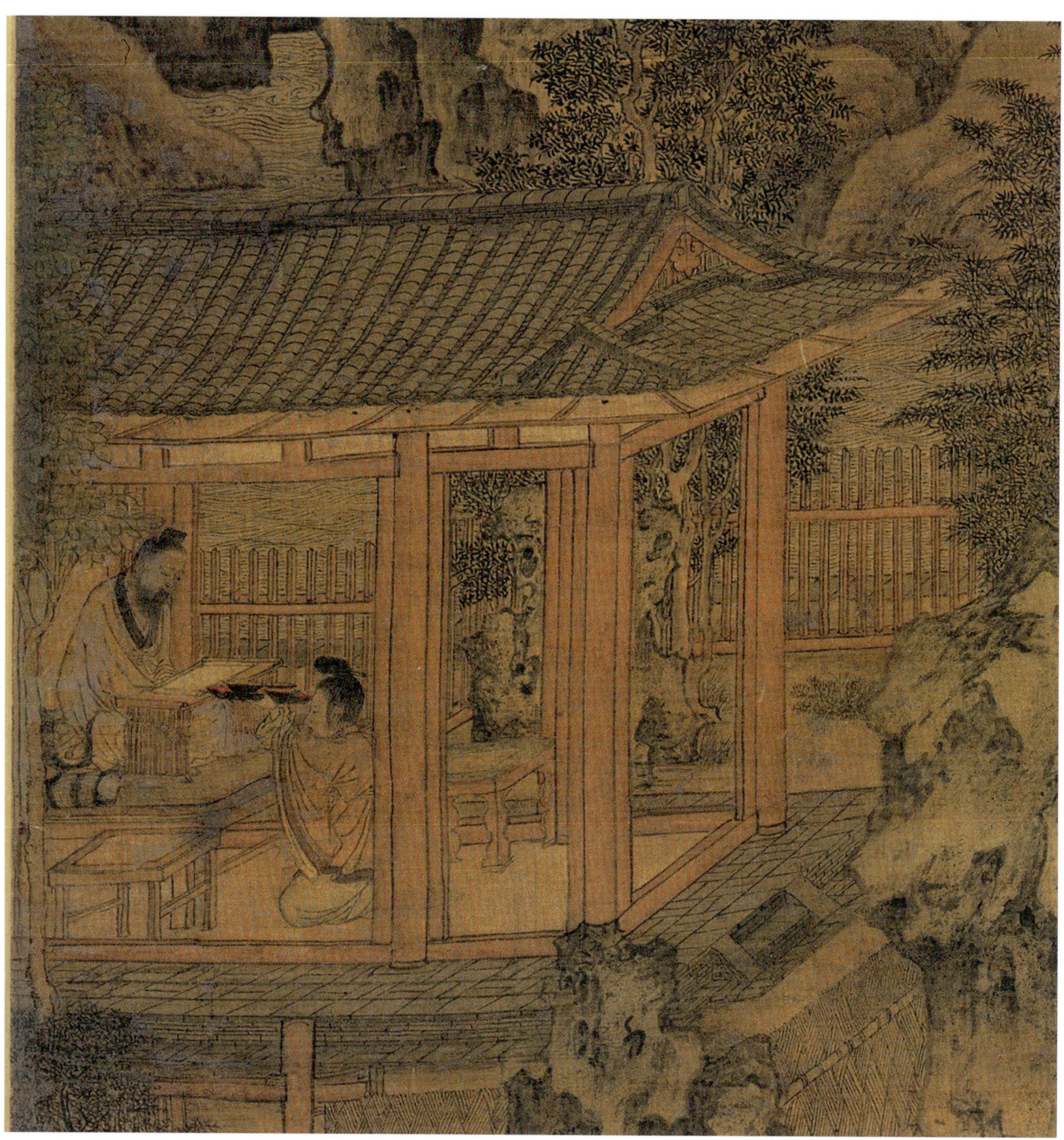

PLATE 29
Detail of *Lofty Scholar* (plate 14). This detail shows Liang Hong's wife raising a tray to eyebrow level when presenting it to her husband, busy with his scholarly work.

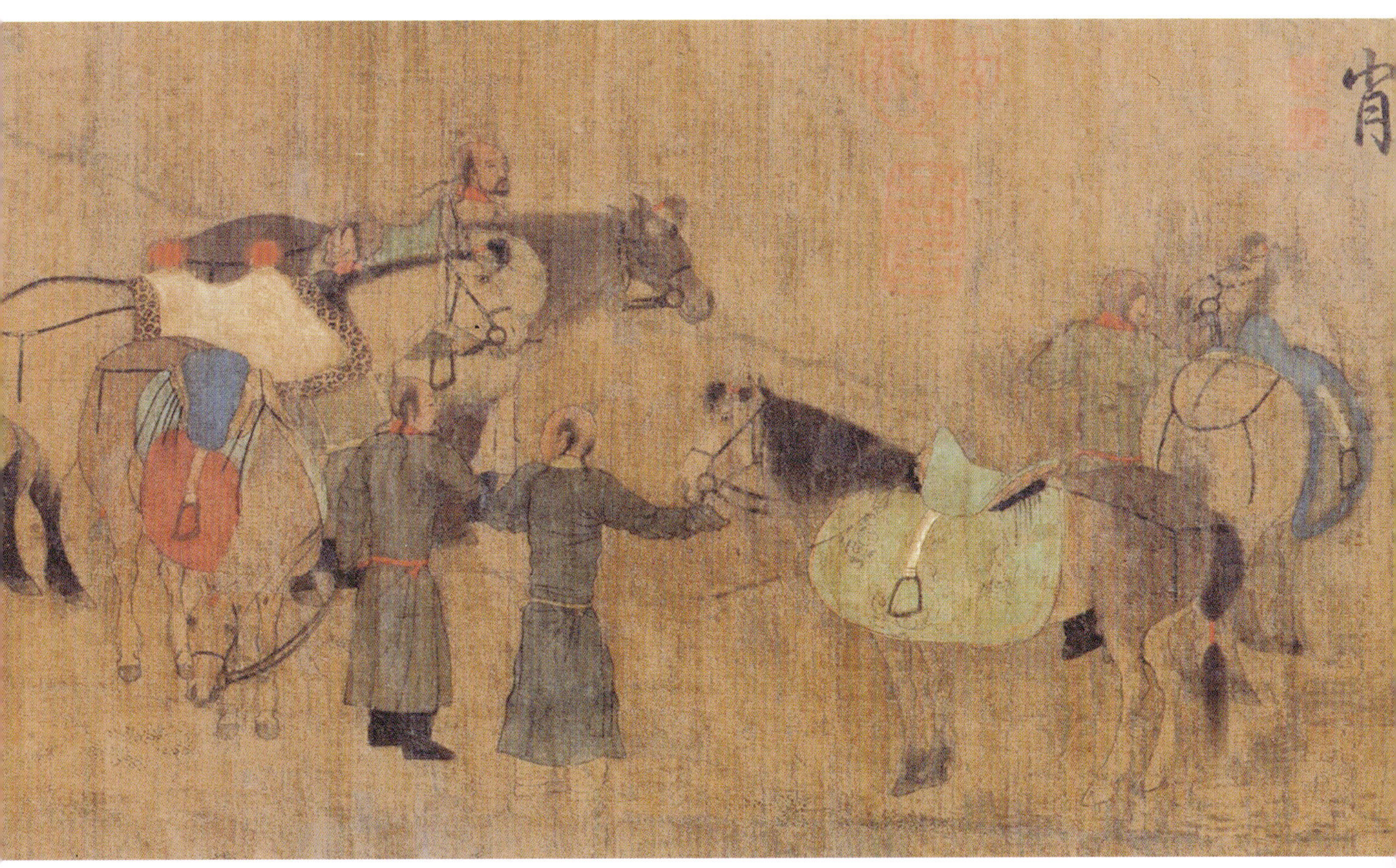

Plate 30
Attributed to Hu Gui (tenth century), *Drinking Party* (detail). Handscroll, ink and color on silk, 33 × 256 cm. Palace Museum, Beijing. The hairstyles of the men depicted here show that they are Khitans.

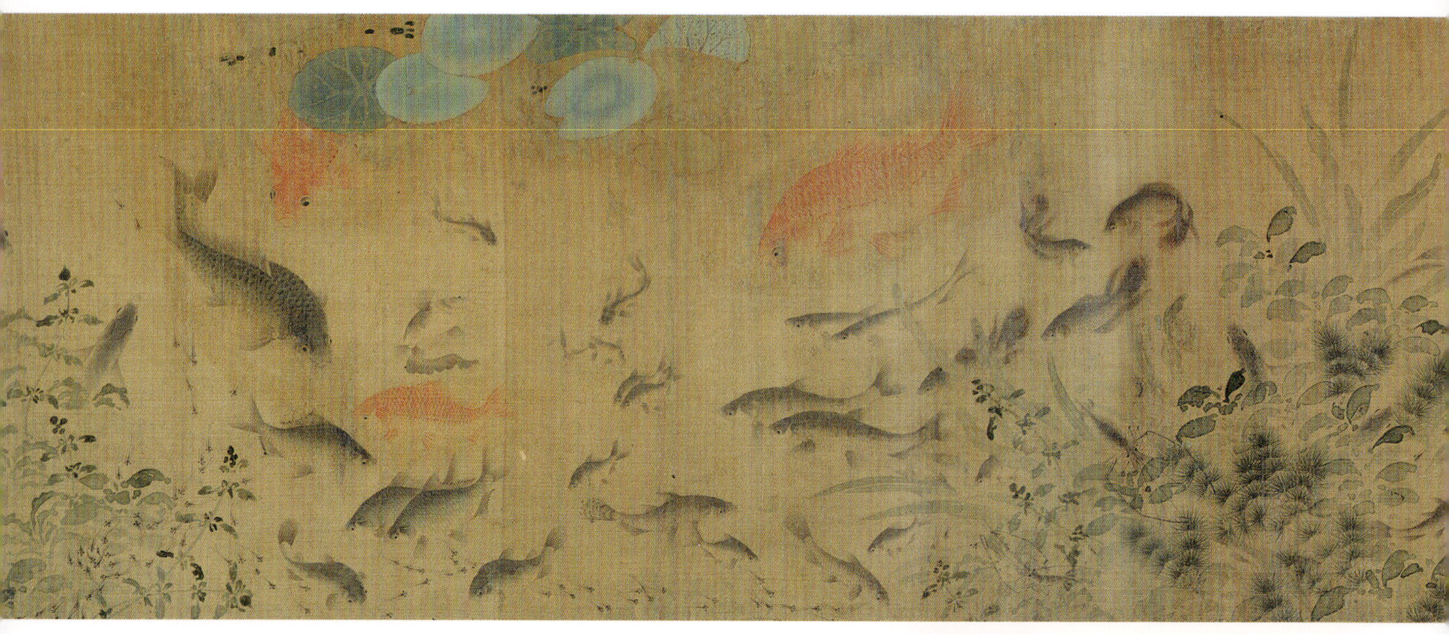

Plate 31
Liu Cai (fl. 1070s–1080s), *Fish Swimming amid Falling Flowers* (detail). Handscroll, ink and color on silk, 26.4 × 252.2 cm. Saint Louis Art Museum. William K. Bixby Trust for Asian Art.

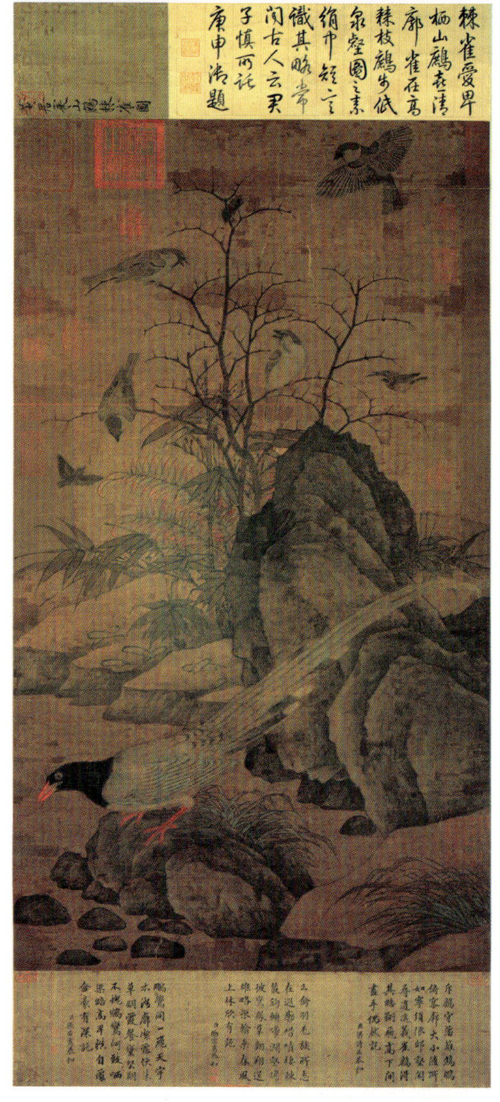

Plate 32
Huang Jucai (933–993+), *Partridges by a Thorny Bush.* Hanging scroll, ink and color on silk, 976 × 53.6 cm. National Palace Museum, Taiwan, Republic of China. The feathers of the birds are depicted with great attention to detail, and the feet of the long-tailed bird are done with red dots to catch the knobby texture of the skin.

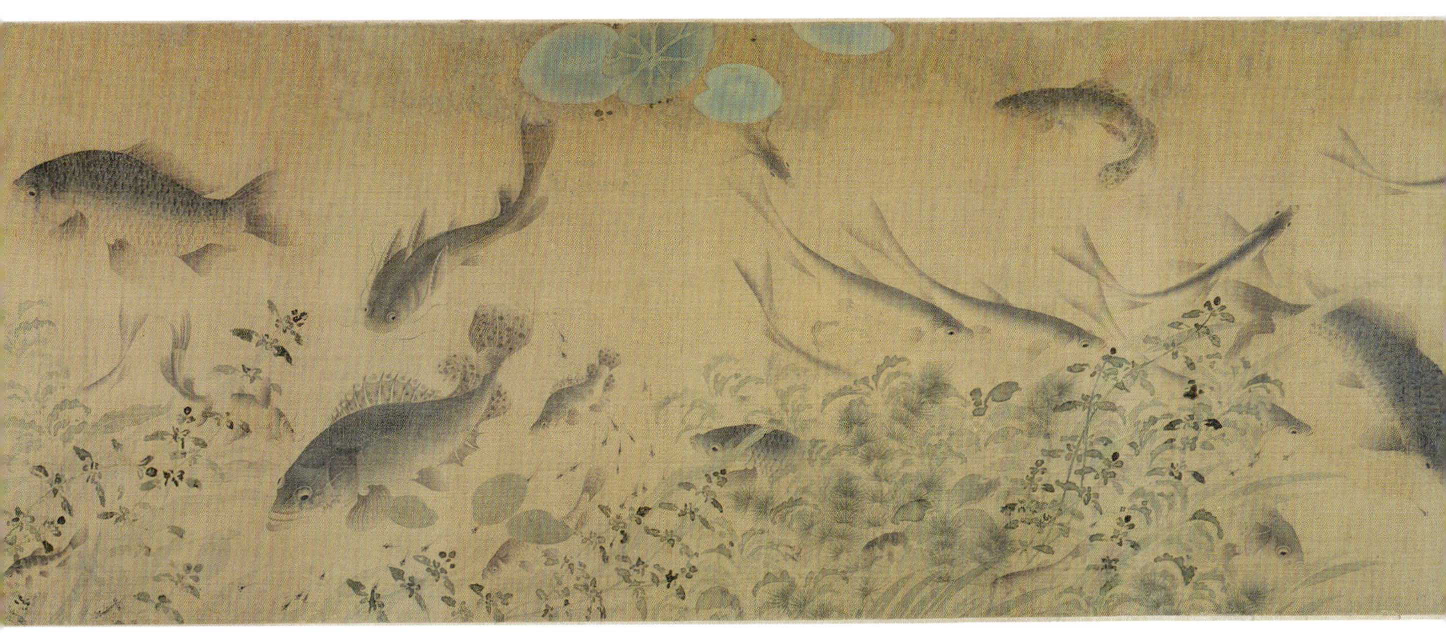

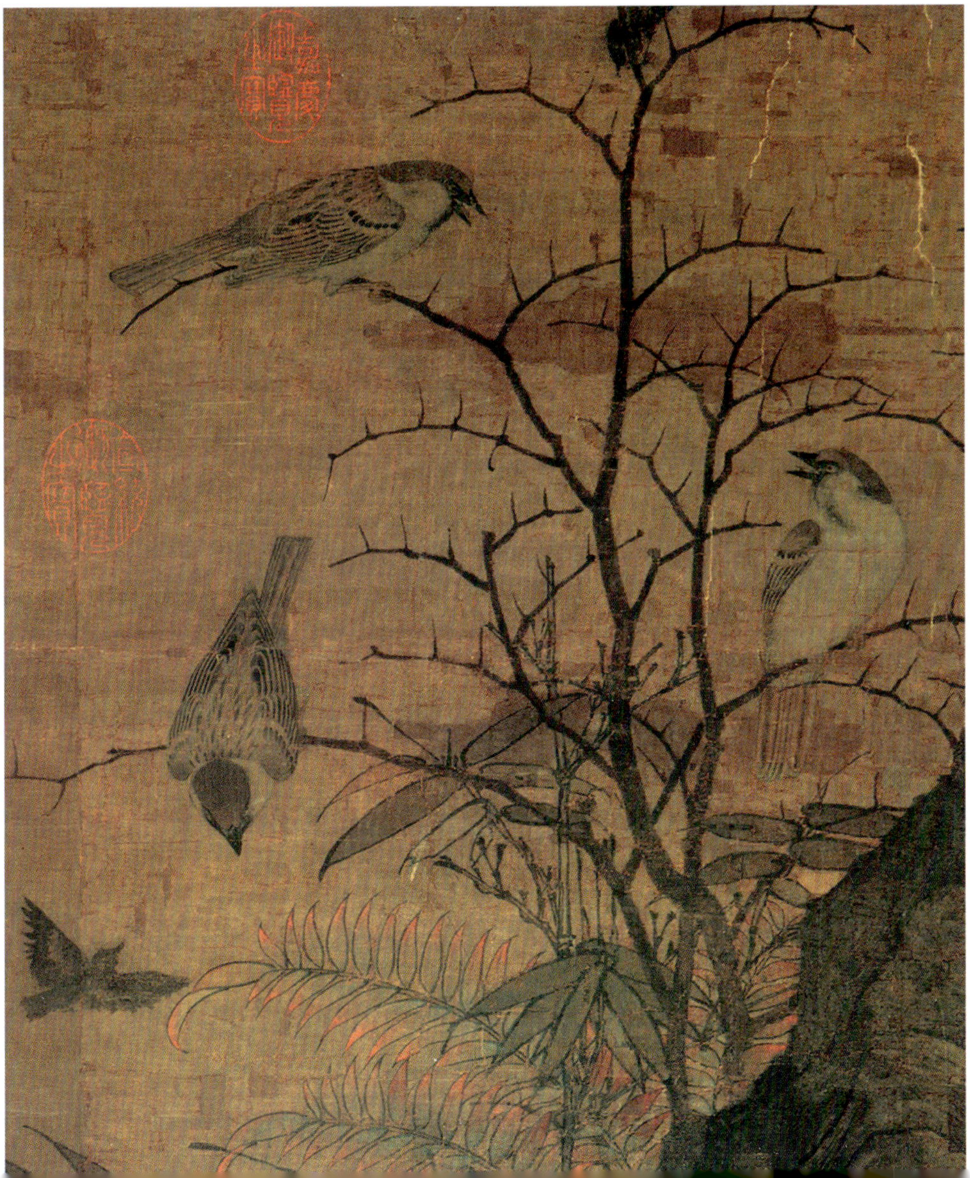

PLATE 33
Detail of *Partridges by a Thorny Bush* (plate 32).

Plate 34
Attributed to Yan Liben (c. 600–c. 674), *Taizong in the Sedan Chair* (detail). Handscroll, ink and color on silk, 38.5 × 129.6 cm. Palace Museum, Beijing.

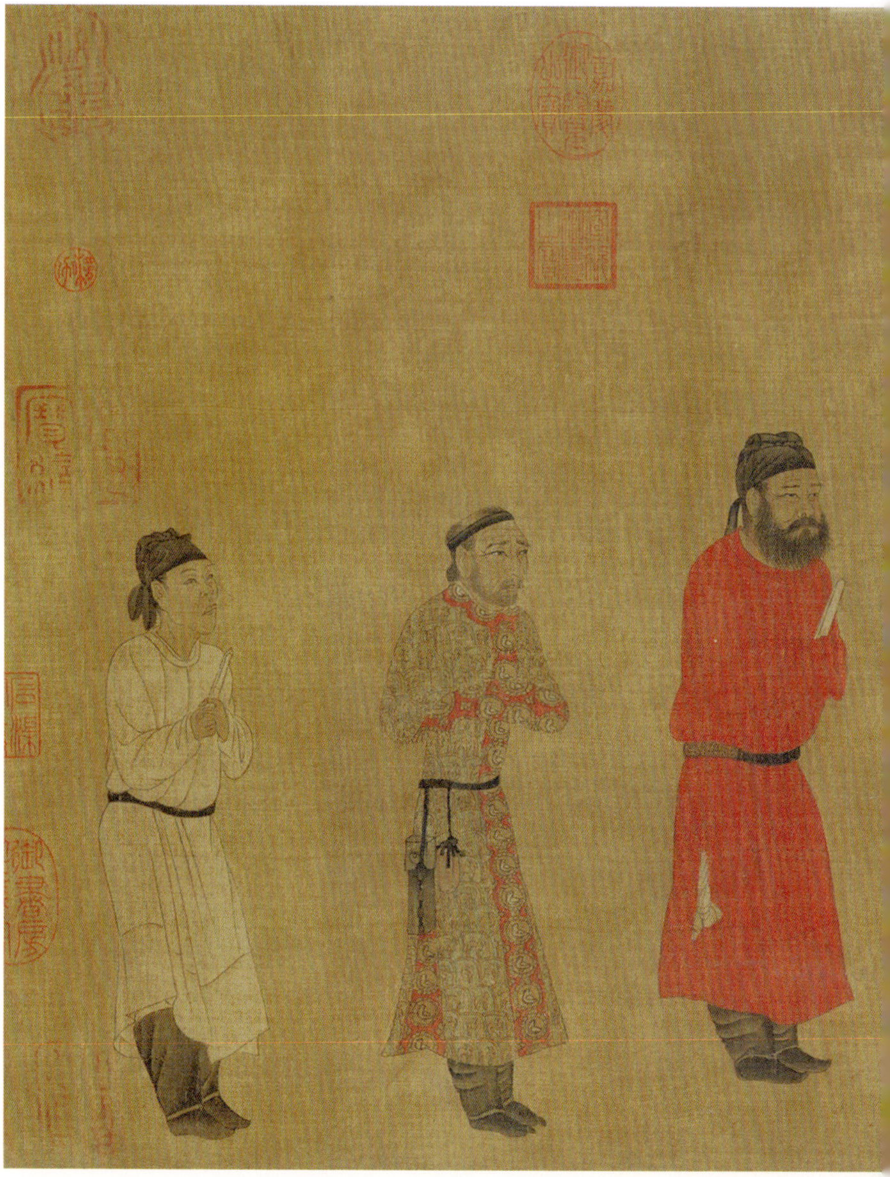

Plate 35
Attributed to Han Huang (723–787), *Five Oxen*. Handscroll, ink and color on hemp paper, 20.8 × 139.8 cm. Palace Museum, Beijing.

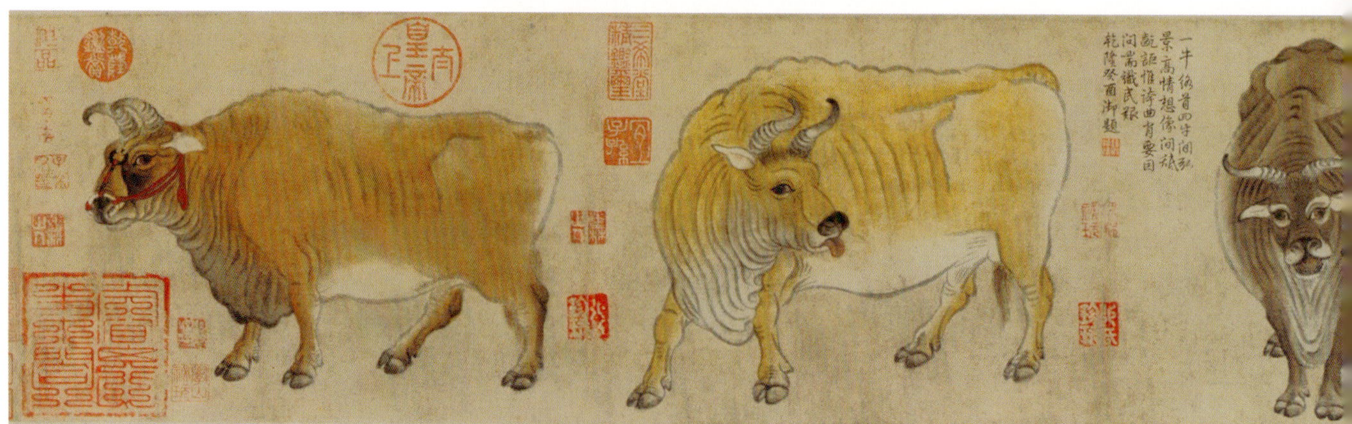

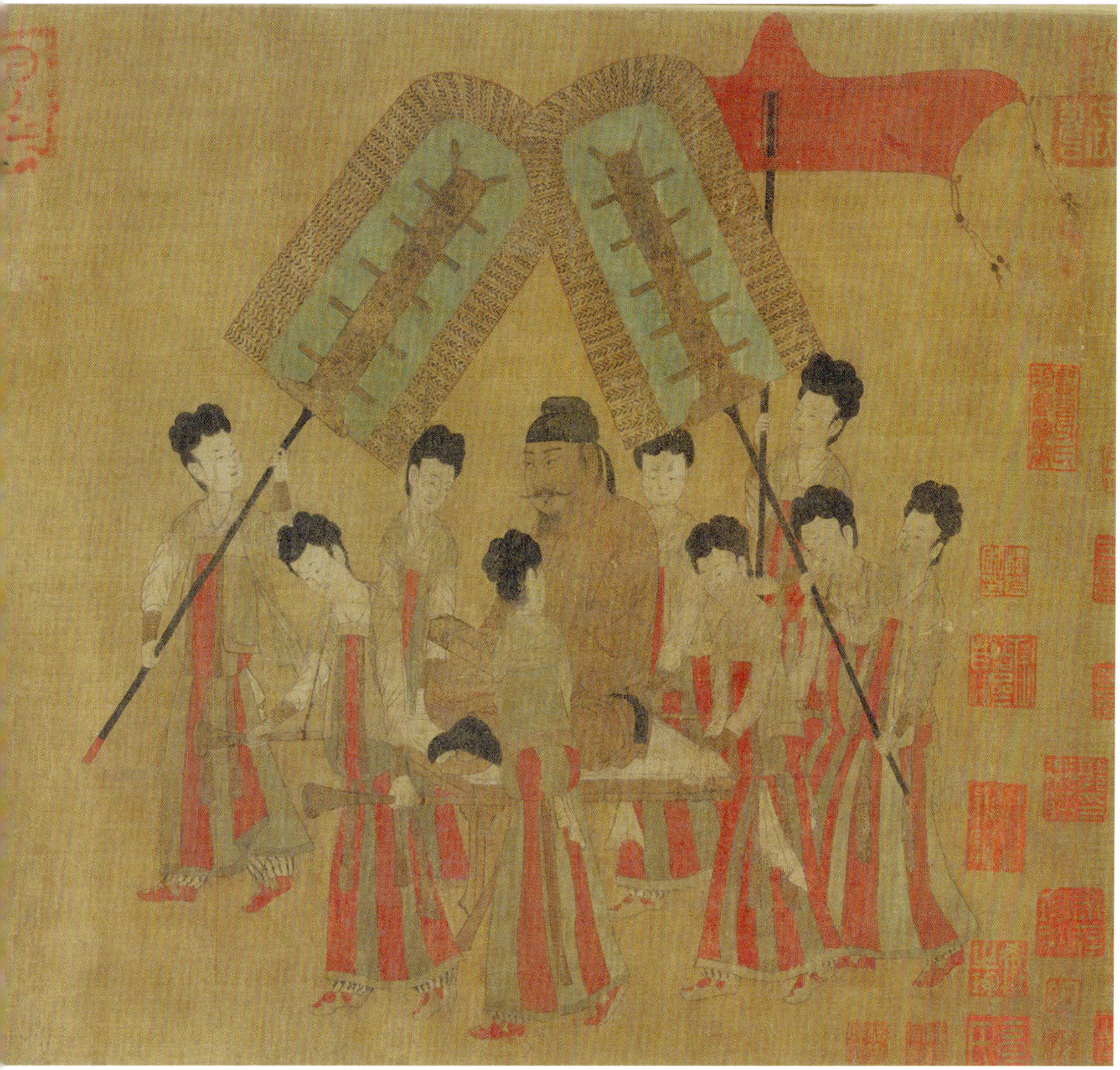

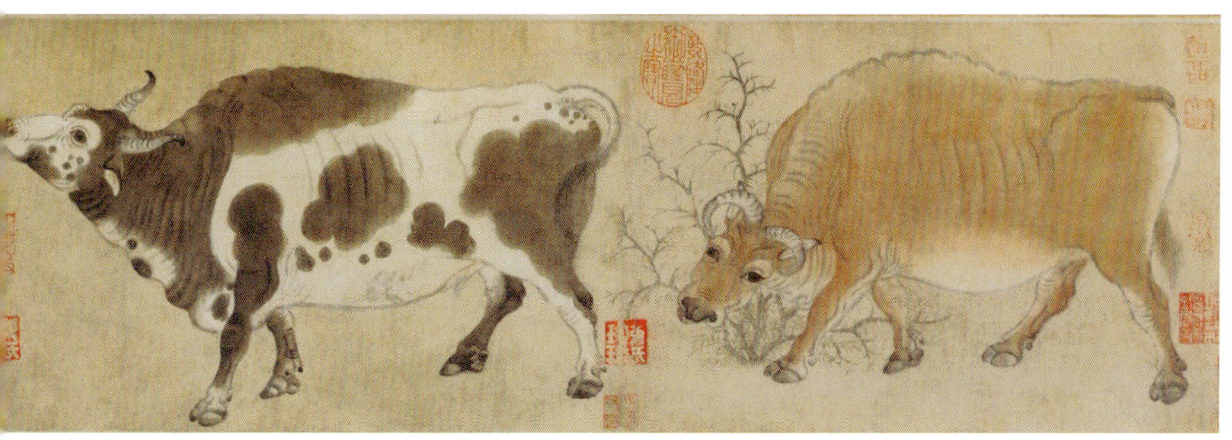

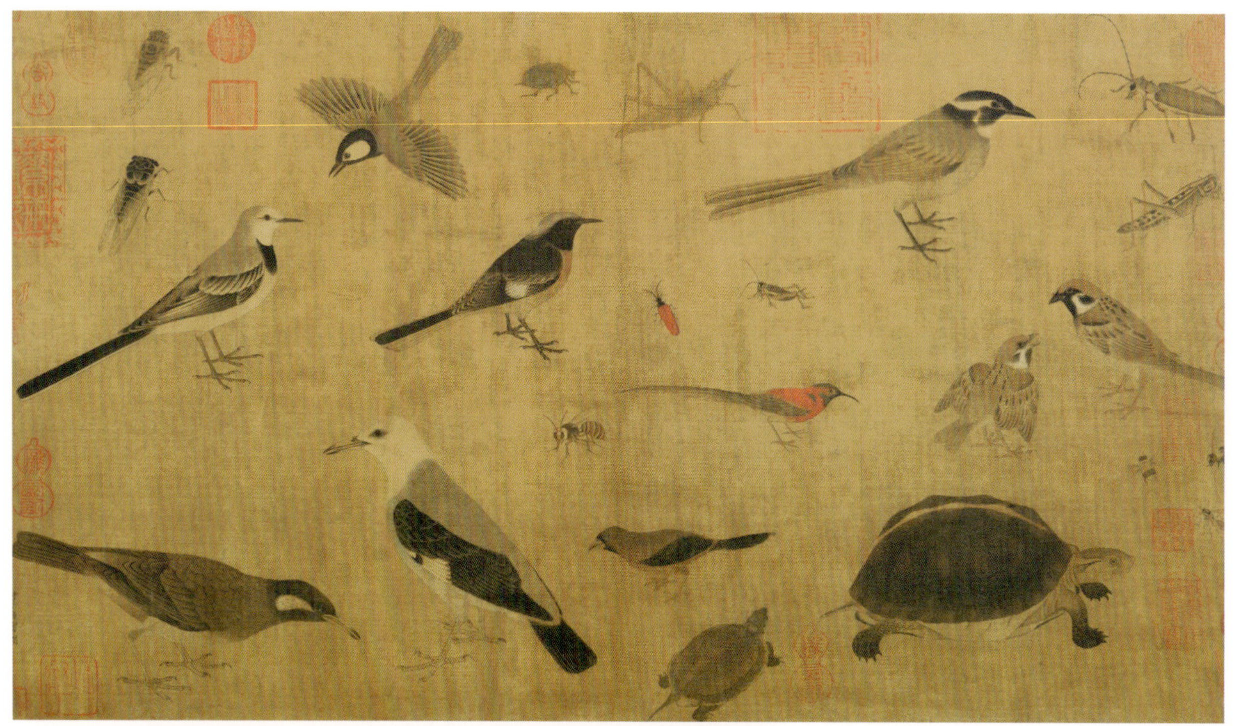

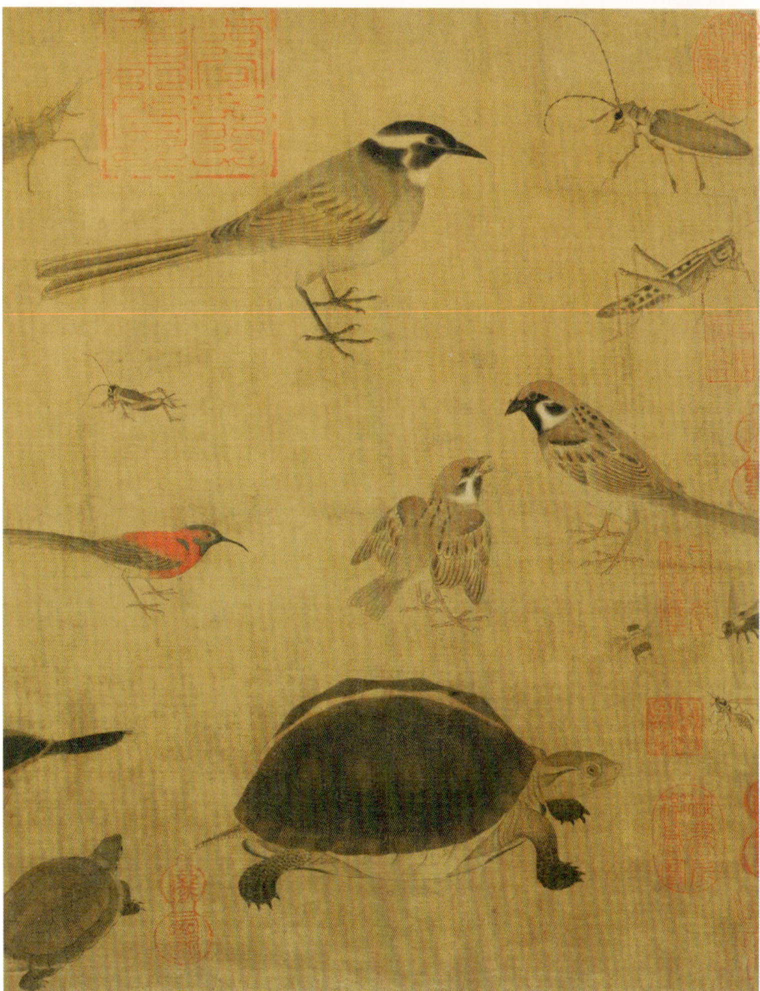

Plate 36
Huang Quan (903–968), *Studies from Nature*. Handscroll, ink and color on silk, 41.5 × 70 cm. Palace Museum, Beijing.

Plate 37
Detail of *Studies from Nature* (plate 36).

Accumulating Culture

Introduction

WHY INVESTIGATE COLLECTING? THE SIMPLE ANSWER IS THAT COLlecting is a key cultural activity. It is fundamental to the ways knowledge is created, transmitted, and contested. Throughout history, the gathering of books into government, church, or school libraries has drawn together scholars and students and thus facilitated intellectual inquiry. Arraying large numbers of examples—whether of books, ancient pottery, or dinosaur bones—allows people to gain insights not possible from a few scattered pieces. Collecting objects for their aesthetic appeal leads to discussion of what makes one object better than another and also to recording the names of masters. It thus fosters art history and art criticism. Collecting art objects also affects their supply. Collectors preserve the objects they collect, in that things that might well have been discarded after their initial use are carefully repaired and protected. However, the development of art markets can lead to such high prices that only the wealthy can acquire fine examples. These high prices in turn stimulate the circulation of copies and forgeries.

Comparative Perspectives

Although collecting is a widespread phenomenon, found in many kinds of societies, the social, cultural, and political dynamics of collecting vary widely, depending very much on what is collected, who does the collecting, and the political and social context in which the collectors act. Consider, for example, the contrast between the Western classical world and China. In Greece and later in Rome, Greek sculptures were collected by the elite to adorn their homes and gardens. The demand for statues meant that they would be removed from temples, transported long distances, and repaired if they were damaged. A critical literature on the art of sculpture appeared, along with histories of the greatest masters. In Roman times, a secondary market for copies of Greek sculpture developed, with the copies treated like art objects, even if ones not equal in value to the originals.[1] China also developed a sculptural tradition with the spread of Buddhism in the second to sixth centuries. During that era, Chinese sculptors embellished Buddhist temples all over the country with images of buddhas, arhats, and bodhisattvas. Those statues were not collected as art, however, until Westerners in the nineteenth century saw them as comparable to Western religious sculpture. By then, early Buddhist sculpture was scarce because Buddhist temples treated statues much the way they did candlesticks or altar tables, replacing them when they were worn or broken.

During the centuries when Buddhist sculpture first flourished in China, especially the Eastern Jin (317–420) and Southern Dynasties (420–589), members of the Chinese elite did collect, but not sculpture. The educated class had long collected books, and in these centuries developed a passion for calligraphy. Both private collectors and rulers prized casual correspondence for its aesthetic qualities and would pay large sums of money for short notes written by the handful of men considered to be the greatest masters. People made freehand or tracing copies of calligraphy that they admired, and these copies also came to be collected, sometimes as copies, sometimes mistaken for originals. In the early Tang period (618–907), Emperor Taizong developed a consuming desire for works by the "god of calligraphy" Wang Xizhi (309– ca. 365). Taizong drew on the resources of the throne to acquire every example of Wang's calligraphy that he could locate, more than 2,000 pieces altogether.[2]

Books and calligraphy retained their hold on Chinese collectors into modern times, but gradually other objects attracted collectors as well. Already in the Southern Dynasties scroll paintings were collected, and by the late Tang dynasty critics described the "irresistible craving" painting collectors feel.[3] During Song times (960–1276) scholars began collecting rubbings of old inscriptions as well as ancient bronzes and jades. In later eras, collectors developed interests in old ceramics, lacquerware, coins, and other objects.

A particularly important period in the expansion of collecting was the Northern Song dynasty (960–1127). The Song dynasty today is thought of above all as a time of economic growth and prosperity. The population approximately doubled in the three centuries from 800 to 1100, from about 50 million to about 100 million. In the same period the supply of money increased at least eightfold and paper money came into widespread use—signs of the expansion of the commercial economy. Trade fueled the growth of cities—none more than Kaifeng, the capital during the Northern Song period (see fig. 1). The better-off in this society lived in considerable comfort; they dressed in lustrous silks, ate from finely glazed ceramic dishes, and furnished their homes with elegant tables, couches, chairs, and even screens decorated with paintings (see plate 1 and fig. 2). The scholar-official class grew rapidly, no doubt reflecting the expansion of educational opportunities, the impact of printing on the availability of books, and the flowering of the civil-service examination system. During this period, collecting books, calligraphies, antiquities, and paintings reached new levels of popularity. Many highly educated scholars viewed collecting as an elevated pastime.

Of the many Northern Song collectors, the one who stands out most is the dynasty's eighth emperor, Huizong (see plate 2).[4] Rulers are a special category of collector, in China as elsewhere. A ruler who lets his subjects know of his love of old master paintings or ancient coins will most likely find it easy to acquire fine examples, not only because his resources are sufficiently ample to reward agents who find things for him but also because those who might benefit from the monarch's favor will welcome the chance to please him with appropriate gifts. Jonathan Brown, in a study of European collector-kings, argues that a ruler's entry into the art market removes many objects from general circulation and pushes up prices for other collectors, just at the time that demand for those objects increases because of the ruler's influence on taste. When Philip IV of Spain (r. 1621–1665) avidly collected Flemish and Italian paintings, not only did he acquire hundreds of them, making it more difficult for others to obtain them, but the Spanish nobility also came to feel that they too ought to have paintings by such men as Titian and Rubens, in part in order to make presents to the king.[5] Very similar sorts of dynamics operated in China.

During Huizong's twenty-six year reign (1100/1 to 1125/12), he assembled the most impressive collections that anyone had put together to that date. Moreover, no earlier collection, either court or private, is known in as much detail as Huizong's, because book-length catalogues of his paintings, calligraphies, and antiquities all survive, listing more than eight thousand objects (see fig. 3). Although the catalogues did not circulate during his reign (and two of them were not printed until the early fourteenth century), they offer excellent evidence of what Huizong collected and how he wished his collections to be understood.

What did Huizong collect? The oldest of the surviving scrolls in Huizong's collection can serve as an example of the sorts of things he treasured as well as how he handled them (plate 3). When Huizong acquired this short letter by Lu Ji (261–303), it was already about 800 years old. Because it was written in an early form of the cursive script and because the paper is worn, scholars have not been able to decipher eleven of its eighty-five characters.[6] Huizong had the letter remounted as a handscroll, wrote out a title for it that is still attached to it, and added several seals. The catalogue of Huizong's calligraphy collection, the *Xuanhe Calligraphy Catalogue* (Xuanhe shupu), lists this piece as one of two works by Lu Ji in Huizong's collection, referring to it by the same term commonly used for it today, *Pingfu tie*, based on a phrase in the first line.[7]

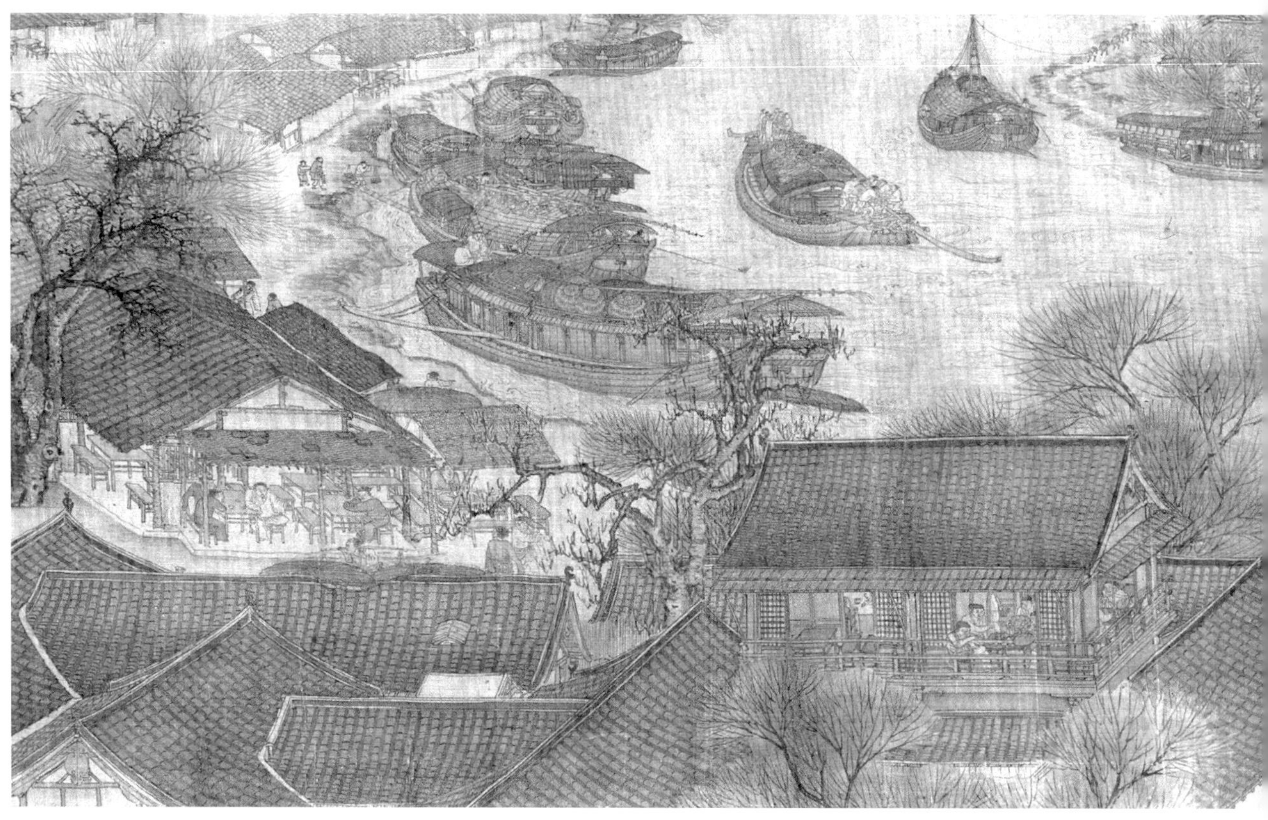

Fig. 1
Attributed to Zhang Zeduan (Song), *Along the River at the Clear and Bright Festival* (detail). Handscroll, ink and color on silk, 24.8 × 528.7 cm. Palace Museum, Beijing. The vitality of Northern Song cities is captured in this famous handscroll, which depicts river boats carrying cargo, inns, restaurants, peddlers, craftsmen, and much more.

One can describe what Huizong did in acquiring this letter as "accumulating culture," but only if it is recognized that the English word "culture" is being used as a loose translation of the Chinese word *wen*. The core meaning of *wen* is "text" or "writing," making it narrower in its connotations than the English word "culture." When Confucius referred to "this culture of ours" (*siwen*; *Analects* 9.5), he was referring to the culture of those who knew and respected the ancient texts and the values expressed in them. *Wen* was also the culture of those who governed through ritual and tradition rather than force, expressed in the common distinction between *wen* and *wu* (military force). Some Song emperors took an interest in other facets of culture in the more extended sense common in English, such as music, drama, architecture, sculpture, textiles, ceramics, and so on. The court employed low-status craftsmen and entertainers to furnish luxury goods, decoration, and entertainment. But these forms of culture were viewed as providing pleasure, not advancing learning or morality. In the Confucian tradition, love of everything that could be classed as luxury carried overtones of self-indulgence and moral weakness and stood at a far remove from the love of literature and antiquity. Gathering and

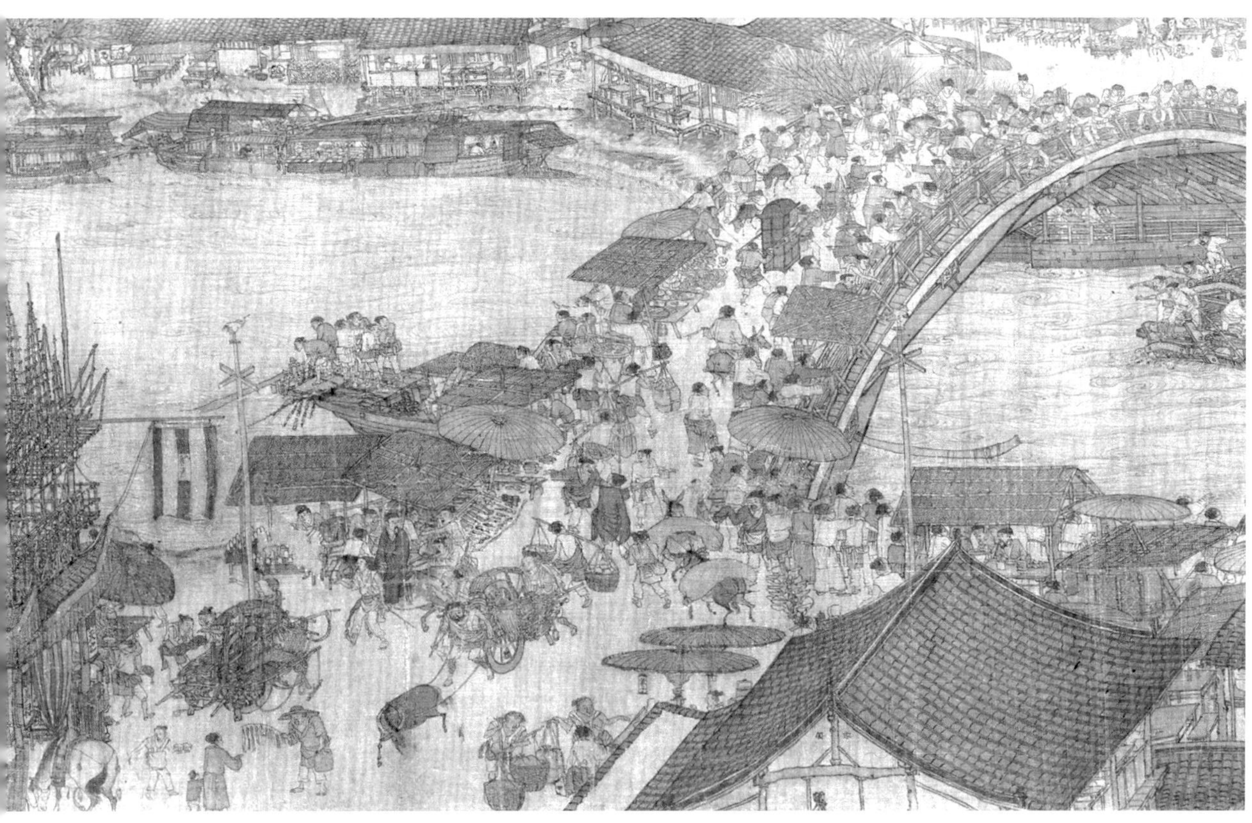

preserving books and book-like objects, by contrast, was a prime way to honor culture and men of culture.

Both in China and in Europe, rulers who collected on an immense scale were relatively rare. Jonathan Brown identified a few European collector-kings as "megacollectors" because they sought quantity as much as quality. "Great collections were also meant to be huge, as a sign of the acquisitive power of the collector. The number of works owned by Philip [II, of Spain] set a new standard and entitled him to be called the first megacollector, a term which can be applied to those who amassed 1500 or more paintings. (While seemingly arbitrary, this quantity represents approximately the largest total that individual collectors of the sixteenth and seventeenth century acquired.)"[8] Huizong, whose catalogue lists 6,397 paintings, surely also merits the epithet of "megacollector."

By far the best-documented megacollector in Chinese history is the eighteenth-century Qing (Manchu) emperor Gaozong (r. 1735–1796), commonly known by his reign name as the Qianlong emperor or even just Qianlong. Like Huizong, Qianlong assembled a broad spectrum of objects—like Huizong, books, calligraphy, paint-

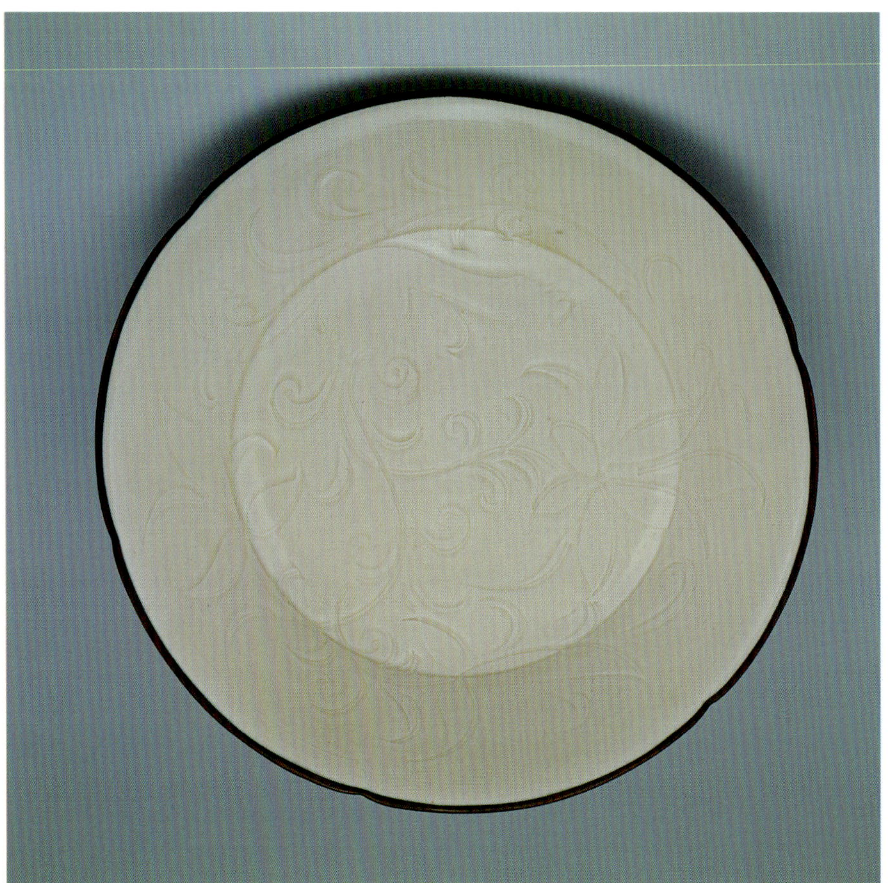

Fig. 2
White-glazed dish with incised flower design. Ding ware porcelain, 4.5 × 20.3 cm. National Palace Museum, Taiwan, Republic of China. The clean lines, muted colors, and spare decoration of Song ceramics reflect an appreciation of the elegance of simplicity.

ings, and antiquities—but in Qianlong's case also ceramics, lacquerware, coins, and foreign objects such as clocks. Harold Kahn links Qianlong's activities as a collector to his activities as a patron and to his taste for the monumental and grandiose. To Kahn, "Monumentalism was essentially a political aesthetic," designed to inspire and awe, part of the universal claims of the monarchy.[9] Qianlong's collections manifested hegemonic sovereignty and dynastic grandeur.

Fig. 3
Entry in Huizong's antiquities catalogue, *Antiquities Illustrated*, titled "Shang Tureen Inscribed Siding." Each object in the antiquities collection is given at least two pages in *Antiquities Illustrated*. The first page gives the name of the vessel and a detailed drawing of it. In this case the drawing takes up two pages, but this occurs only in the Yuan and 1528 editions. If there is an inscription on the vessel, next comes a rubbing of the

Huizong as Emperor, Artist, and Collector

In popular Chinese memory, Huizong is known as the Artist-Emperor. Like a handful of earlier rulers, he is viewed as having been talented enough to have made a name for himself as an artist if he had not become emperor. He painted in several genres, ranging from landscape to bird-and-flower to bamboo.[10] A good example is the *Five-Colored Parakeet* in the Boston Museum of Fine Arts (plate 4), a work in

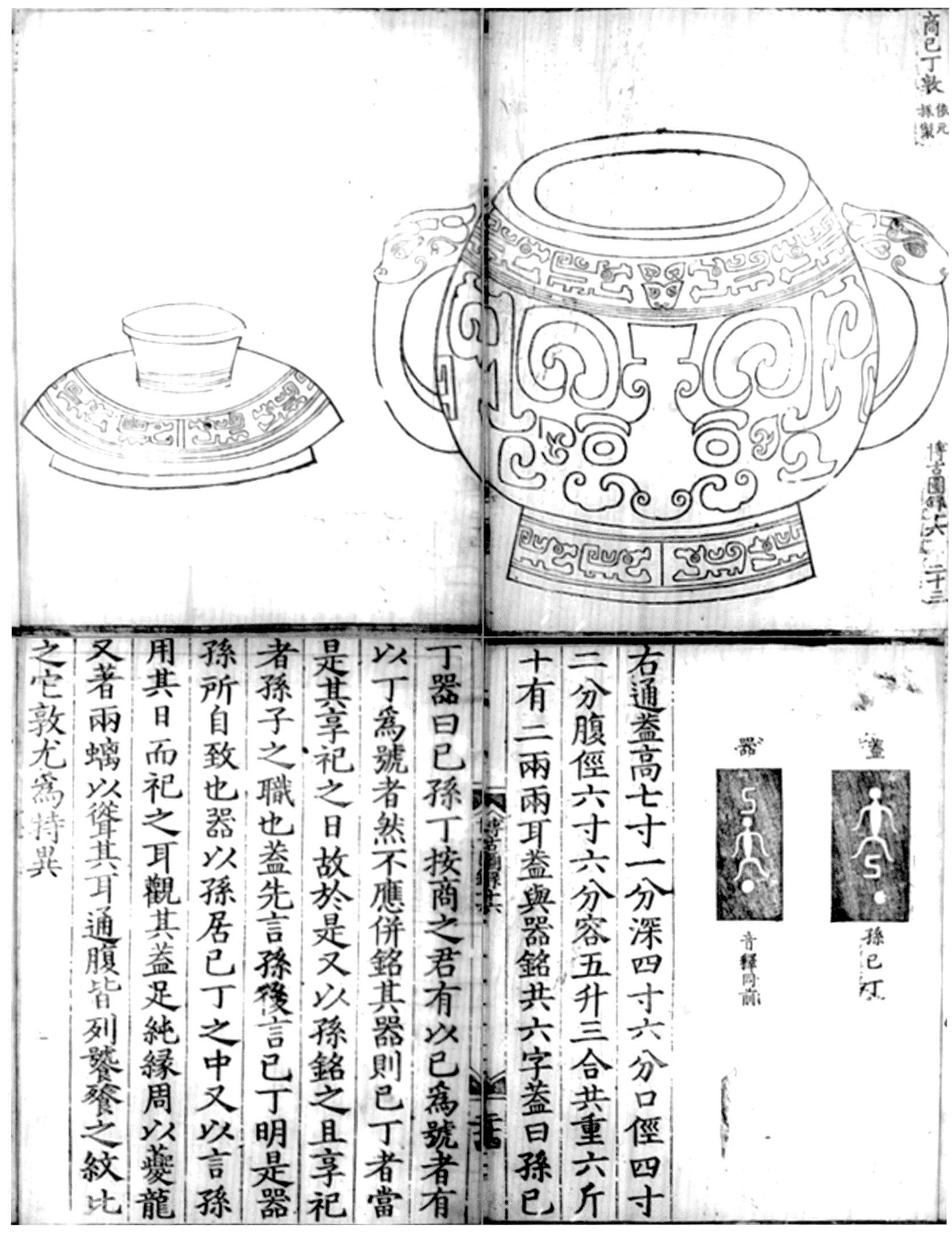
商己丁敦 依元樣製

博古圖錄 十六 二十三

蓋 孫己丁

器 音釋同前

右通蓋高七寸一分深四寸六分口徑四寸
二分腹徑六寸六分容五升三合共重六斤
十有二兩兩耳蓋與器銘共六字蓋曰孫己
丁器曰己孫丁按商之君有以己爲號者有
以丁爲號者然不應併銘其器則己丁者當
是其享祀之日故於是又以孫銘之且享祀
者孫子之職也蓋先言孫後言己丁明是器
孫所自致也器以孫居己丁之中又以言孫
用其日而祀之耳觀其蓋足純緣周以夔龍
又著兩螭以聳其耳通腹皆列饕餮之紋比
之它敦尤爲特異

博古圖錄 十六

inscription and under it a reading of it in modern transcription. There follows a discussion of the object, beginning with precise measurements. In the case of the tureen shown here, we are told that it is 7.1 (Chinese) inches tall, 4.6 inches deep (that is, excluding the bottom foot); that its opening is 4.2 inches; that at its widest it is 6.6 inches; that it holds 5.3 pints; that it weighs 6 pounds, 12 ounces; that it has two handles and a cover; and that it has an inscription on both its cover and body. The discussion of the vessel concentrates on the unusual features of the decor and the inscriptions, which vary in the order of the characters. BGT 1528 ed. 16.23a–24b.

which he presents himself as a painter, a poet, and a calligrapher.[11] The painting shows a bird in profile, perched on the twig of a flowering tree, against a blank background of unpainted silk. Huizong's skill as a painter is evident in the meticulous way he conveyed the distinguishing features of the bird. The sharp edge of the beak was drawn with a precise, thin line; the texture of the feathers was conveyed by layers of semi-transparent red, yellow, and green wash. The poetry is part of the lengthy text Huizong inscribed on this painting. In the prose prefatory remarks, Huizong records that the delightful, docile, brilliantly colored bird had come from the far south and looked very attractive sitting on the branch of an apricot tree in full bloom. Huizong then shows his skill as a poet through an eight-line poem on the same subject. The third part of the artistry of this work is the calligraphy, written in Huizong's highly distinctive regular script calligraphy called Slender Gold.[12] This style is characterized by thin, angular lines with sharply chiseled corners. Horizontal strokes end with pronounced stops; that is, they reveal rather than hide the fact that the brush is brought back in the reverse direction. Another distinctive feature of this style is the long and curling upward hooks at the end of strokes. By writing in this unprecedented way, Huizong was presenting himself as an innovative artist who had developed his own style, a style that displayed his discipline and flair.

Huizong not only practiced the arts of poetry, calligraphy, and painting himself; he also involved himself in the work of court painters. Early in his reign he established a school for court painters with a three-year curriculum. Painting students were selected by examination and divided into two groups of thirty students each. One group concentrated on painting, probably in preparation for traditional court painting jobs such as painting murals on palace and temple walls. The other group was given a concurrent literary education and was expected to be able to produce poetic paintings. The examinations for the latter group required them to be able to develop the ideas in a poetic couplet by painting a scene that used the subtle indirection and allusion customary in poetry.[13]

Huizong's success as an artist and patron of artists was not coupled with comparable political success. It was Huizong's misfortune that on his watch China was invaded by the Jurchens, who after a siege of the capital took Huizong and much of his court captive in 1127. Subsequently the Jurchens were able to hold on to north China for about a century (the Jin dynasty, 1115–1234) before themselves falling to the Mongols. Men who had disapproved of Huizong's political policies got the last word after his reign ended in debacle. Resettled in the South, where the Song state retreated (the Southern Song, 1127–1276), Huizong's critics were the ones to write the voluminous histories of this period.

The sorts of history they wrote took for granted that the decisions made by emperors and their ministers determine the fates of dynasties. In this traditional historiography, Huizong is treated as ultimately responsible for everything that went wrong during his reign, and historians see their task as that of identifying his mistakes. Some point to poor judgment in trusting unworthy men who encouraged him to waste money on palaces and gardens or deluded him with talk of Daoist heavens and military glories.[14] Some historians give Huizong's failed leadership a romantic gloss. To them, it is because Huizong loved the beautiful so intensely that he had no head for the tough side of governing. The dozen or more historical novels about Huizong and his period help sustain this romantic vision.[15]

Modern historians do not need to treat history-writing as a search for examples to use to admonish the emperor. Here no effort will be made to assess whether Huizong's enthusiasm for collecting had deleterious effects on his ability to govern. Every effort will, however, be made to place Huizong's actions in context, to view them as responses to his circumstances and not just as expressions of his character. When approached that way, Huizong does not seem frivolous or muddle-headed, but instead seems an ambitious man who wished to strengthen the ancient roots of the monarchy and make his court the cultural center of the realm.

Imperial Collecting in China

Royal collecting began in China long before Huizong. From classical times on, rulers collected both sacred and secular objects, ranging from sacrificial vessels, documents, and maps to treasures such as gold, silver, pearls, and jade, not to mention dogs, horses, and rare birds and animals. In the Zhou period (1045–256 BCE), when one state destroyed another, the victors would take such treasures as trophies, so that the collections of the most successful states could grow rapidly. By the Warring States era (481–221 BCE), men of wealth sought many of the same objects, sometimes vying with rulers in the splendor of their possessions. Confucian scholars in Han times (206 BCE– 220 CE) scorned those who collected jewels and animals as decadent but esteemed those who collected books. During the Southern Dynasties, this more scholarly side of collecting was stretched to include works that we today class as art, notably calligraphy and painting scrolls by known artists.

From the start, rulers were among the most avid collectors. Unfortunately, concentrating large numbers of books and works of art in one place made them vulnerable to political and other catastrophes. In the sixth century, Emperor Wu of Liang is said to have amassed a collection of more than 140,000 scrolls (presumably the bulk of them books). Most of them were destroyed either during the uprising of

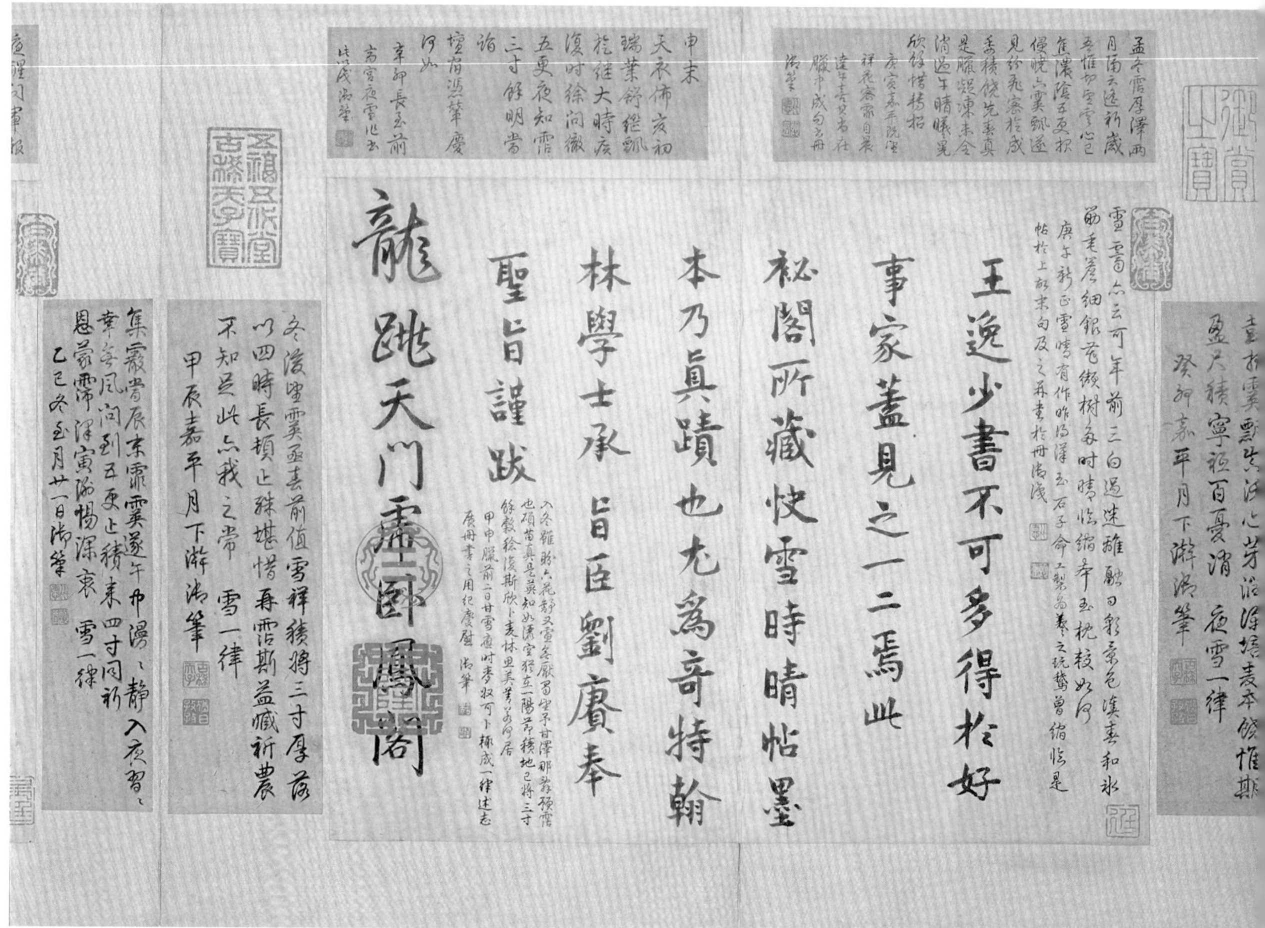

Hou Jing in 540 or the burning of the palace in 554. Much of the huge Sui (581–618) collection perished when Emperor Yang took his treasures with him on a boat journey to Yangzhou and the boat carrying them capsized. Large parts of the Tang imperial collection were lost with the capture of Luoyang by the rebel An Lushan in 756, and much of the remainder disappeared six years later when a Tibetan raid on the capital resulted in the burning of the palace library.[16]

The best-studied imperial collection is that of the eighteenth-century emperor, Qianlong. A large majority of the thousands of objects that he collected survive today, primarily in the palace museums of Beijing and Taipei. There is an extremely rich textual record as well, ranging from the catalogues he commissioned to the inscriptions he wrote on objects, the notes of the officials working on his collections, and the original memorials and edicts found in the archives (see plate 5 and fig. 4).[17]

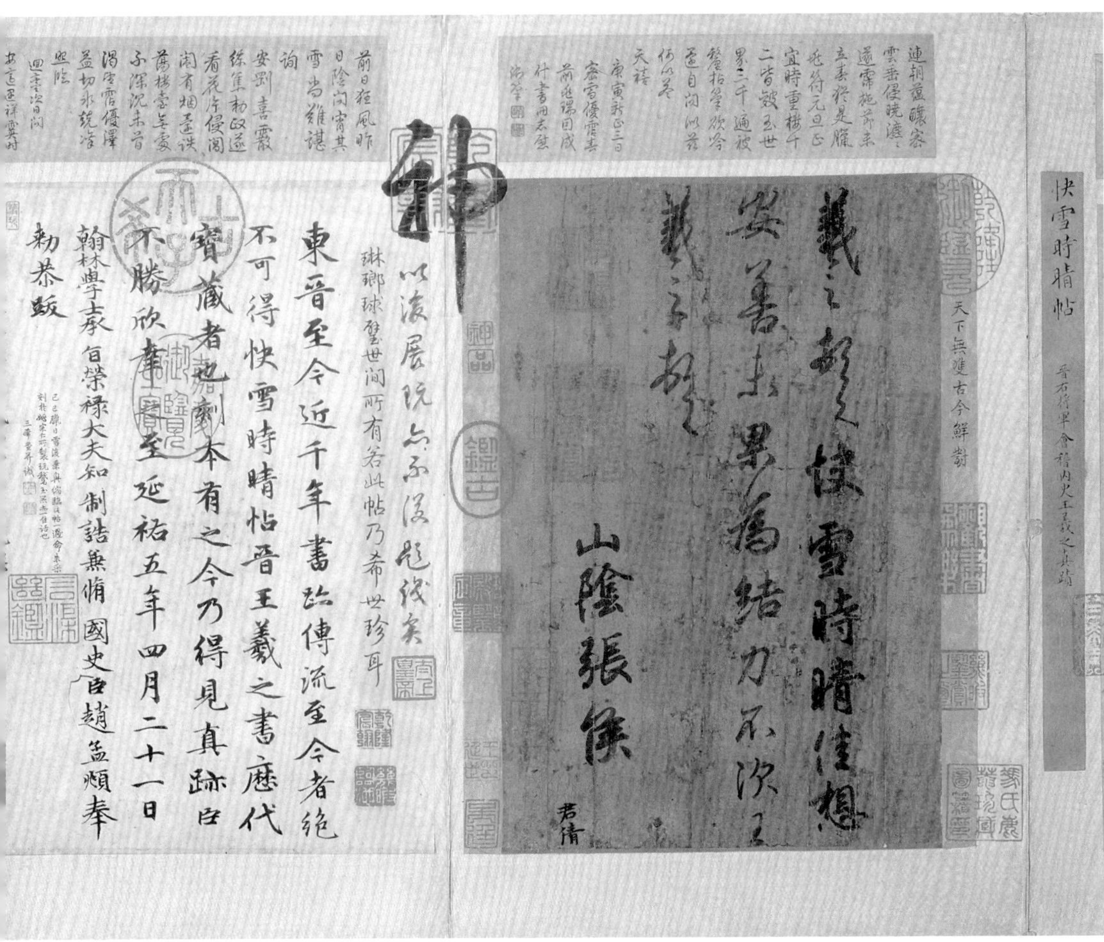

FIG. 4
Wang Xizhi (309–ca. 365), *Kuaixue shiqing tie.* Handscroll, ink on paper, 23 × 14.8 cm. National Palace Museum, Taiwan, Republic of China. This calligraphy scroll was one of Qianlong's favorite art works. Over the years he added numerous inscriptions and colophons, and even a painting. No trace is left of Huizong's possession of this piece (it was in his catalogue, but later passed to his son Gaozong, who regularly had his father's seals removed). Rather, Qianlong's presence dominates the surviving piece. Between 1746 and 1792 the emperor viewed it thirty-two times, each time writing something on it. He also made a painting of Wang Xizhi watching geese and a copy of a landscape by the Yuan painter Ni Zan, both of which he added to the scroll.

This wealth of material has encouraged scholars to study Qianlong's collecting from many perspectives. R. Kent Guy and Patricia Berger have examined the politics of Qianlong's collecting projects. Guy, focusing on Qianlong's book collecting, cataloguing, and copying project, shows that for the emperor, this project demonstrated "his right to be leader of the literate community of the most civilized empire in history." At the same time, the several hundred officials who worked on this project were able to turn an imperial initiative to their own ends, thus "to accomplish scholarly goals beyond their own resources."[18] Patricia Berger links Qianlong's collection of Buddhist art to the multi-ethnic nature of the Qing empire and especially the Tibetan and Mongol components. How Qianlong acquired objects has also been studied. Qianlong referred both to buying objects and also to receiving them as gifts. Harold Kahn sees a competition between private collectors and the throne for the "scarce resources of the art market" that he thinks "might help explain the remarkable drive by the court under Qianlong to collect art quantitatively as well as qualitatively." Private parties were at a serious disadvantage: "The emperor's claim to the lion's share of the market was primary and assured."[19]

Many observers have been struck by Qianlong's penchant for writing on paintings, calligraphies, and even ceramics and jades in his collection (see figs. 4 and 5). Jan Stuart writes, "Time and again, he permanently altered great masterpieces by embellishing them with his writing, but he never acted with maliciousness or out of stupidity. Rather, he studied art and treasured it, and with the self-confidence of a Universal King turned his art patronage into an expression of his role as China's moral exemplar." As Gerald Holzwarth puts it, Qianlong's inscriptions "were a mark of distinction for the work and a visible sign of his rightful role as Emperor." Kohara Hironobu is somewhat less generous in his assessment of these many inscriptions, pointing to ways Qianlong's discernment as a painting connoisseur was limited by his reliance on the textual material connected to a work—the seals, signatures, inscriptions, and colophons.[20]

These studies of Qianlong's collecting offer insights into cultural and political dimensions of imperial collecting in China and suggest ways to think about Huizong's collecting. But it is important not to assume that Huizong and Qianlong collected for the same reasons or in the same ways. Qianlong was well aware of Huizong's collecting activities and in his catalogues often evoked Huizong's precedents, but the political situation of Qianlong's reign was very different from that of Huizong. Their tastes were also not at all alike—Huizong had none of Qianlong's love of ostentation. Still, comparisons of Huizong and Qianlong as collectors are interesting and will be explored further in the last chapter.

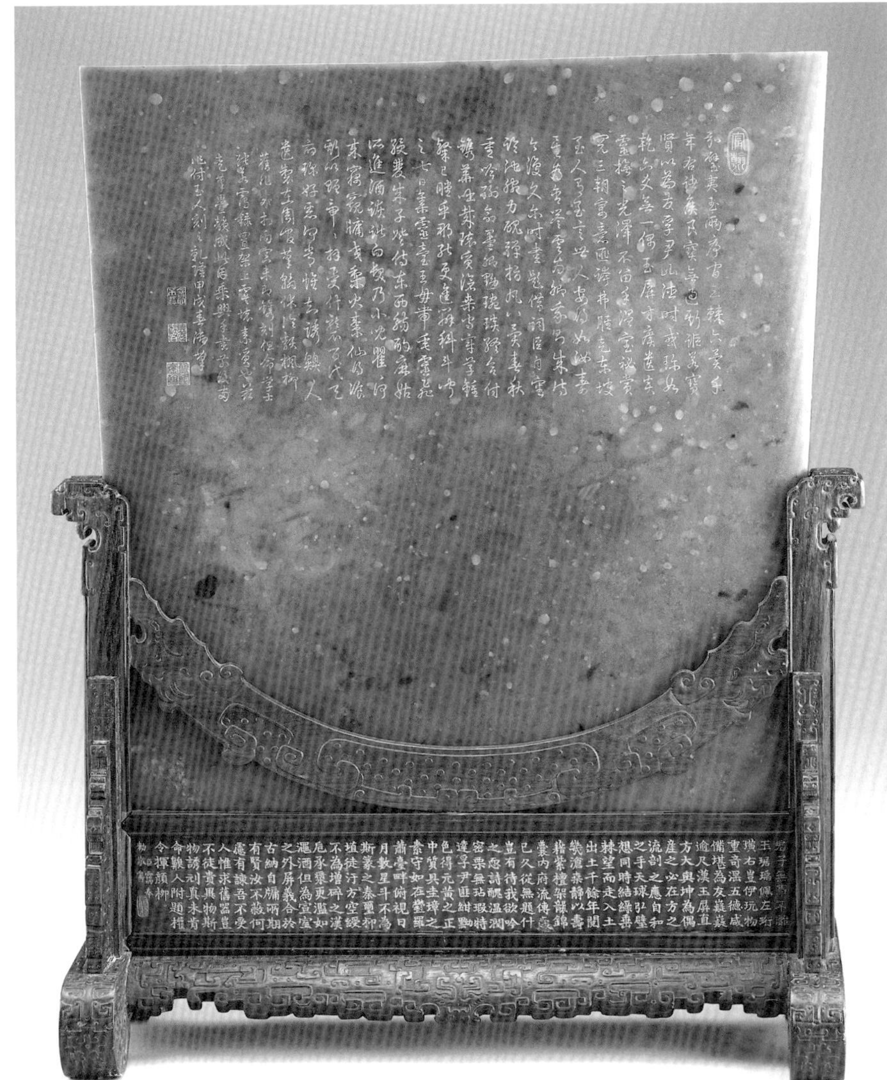

Fig. 5
Inscribed Neolithic jade tablet. 37.4 × 35.8 cm (.8 cm thick). National Palace Museum, Taiwan, Republic of China. The mottled red jade itself dates to about 2600–2000 BCE. The inscription is of poems written by the Qianlong emperor in 1746 (the emperor wrote more poems in 1754, which are inscribed on the other side). The wooden stand has poems written by officials to match the emperor's.

Theorizing Imperial Collecting

Scholars who have written about royal collecting in China have generally seen it as a dimension of rulership, a part of statecraft. Some stress its antiquity and its sacred character; even more view it as one of the many steps rulers take to claim and maintain their legitimacy, their right to rule.

The art historian Lothar Ledderose is generally credited with developing the idea that the origins of royal collecting in China should be traced back to the sacred side of ancient kingship. In an influential article, he argues that Chinese imperial art collections began as palace collections of numinous treasures, such as the Nine Cauldrons and the charts and registers secured from conquered rivals, "tangible proof that their owner had received the mandate of Heaven." The substitution of art objects for magical objects occurred gradually in the fourth century, Ledderose argues, when handwritten pieces by famous calligraphers entered the palace collection as works of art. By the sixth century, scrolls of painting and calligraphy were considered the most precious part of the royal collections and, like the earlier treasures, acted to guarantee and manifest Heaven's favor.[21]

Other scholars have picked up on these ideas and regularly treat imperial collecting as above all an act intended to increase the legitimacy of the emperor and his dynasty. These ideas raise as many questions as they answer. Almost anything a ruler does that lacks the obvious utility of maintaining an army or collecting taxes can be said to help boost his image as a rightful king. How does accumulating cultural treasures compare to hosting banquets, bestowing largesse, building magnificent palaces, performing sacred rituals, or any of the other activities regularly said to enhance a monarch's legitimacy? Some of these activities virtually all rulers perform, and to fail to perform them undeniably weakens the ruler's legitimacy. But many rulers had little or no interest in art or antiquities. Is collecting pursued more vigorously when the dynasty's legitimacy is most in question? Or is personal preference the only reason some rulers devote substantial resources to this activity and others ignore it? Does the intensity of private collecting in the period make much of a difference? Do collections add to a ruler's or dynasty's prestige no matter how the objects in them were acquired? Do the cultural and political processes work the same way in different periods? For instance, can we assume that Huizong and Qianlong had similar reasons for producing catalogues?

In the European case, scholars have connected royal collecting to the perceived need for royal magnificence. Especially from the Renaissance on, interstate competition in Europe led rulers to compete with each other in the magnificence of their courts, and building collections was one way to awe rivals.[22] The same logic does not seem to have applied in China. During periods when a single ruler reigned over all or most of China, it would not have occurred to him or his advisors that a rival ruler could preside over a more magnificent court. (It is true that in Northern Song times China had to treat its northern neighbor, the Khitan state of Liao, as a diplomatic equal. But Song never considered Liao a cultural rival.) As the Chinese understood it, China's neighbors sought Chinese goods and adopted Chinese practices and institutions because they too saw the superiority of the culture of the Central Kingdom. Moreover, Chinese rulers did not use their collections to awe audiences in any blatant way, since they were largely kept boxed up and out of sight, not displayed on palace walls as in Europe. One could even go further and question whether magnificence was a universal goal of rulers. In medieval Japan, where there were two potential political and cultural centers—the imperial court and the shogunate—competition did not center on magnificence. The shogun Yoshimasa (r. 1443–1473) had enormous influence on Japanese aesthetic standards by avoiding grandeur and promoting an aesthetic of unadorned austerity. His collection of Chinese ink paintings was central to his promotion of this aesthetic.[23]

Even if neither the need for legitimacy nor the desire for magnificence seems adequate to explain which Chinese emperors built up impressive collections, that does not mean collecting was outside the realm of politics. In the Song case, at least, collecting linked the throne to other social groups that also collected, most importantly the scholar-official class. (This class is also referred to in English as the "educated class" or the "literati"—all terms used interchangeably in this book—and in Chinese as the *shi* or *shidafu*.) In my view, the politics of imperial collecting in China, from at least the Southern Dynasties on, was deeply intertwined in the complex relationship between the throne and this class. Modern historians of the Song period have done important work on the emperor-elite relationship from the perspective of civil-service recruitment and factionalism.[24] But they have yet to probe in depth the more cultural and symbolic side of this relationship in the way that scholars of the Ming (1368–1644) and Qing (1644–1911) periods have done.[25] In Song times, collecting and writing about books, art, and antiquities became an arena in which the educated elite and the throne subtly competed for cultural leadership. Examining imperial collecting in Song times thus has the potential to enlarge our understanding of Song emperorship.

Such an examination can also further understanding of the social and political dimensions of the Chinese art world. In the scholarship on Chinese art history, the literati and the court are both well-established topics. The last two generations of Song art historians have done much to add to our understanding of literati painting, calligraphy, and art criticism by placing it in the context of literati political and cultural life.[26] The court often figures in their discussions, but usually as a foil against which the literati defined themselves.[27] This book instead gives the court center place and views the world of art from its perspective in order to treat the social and political complexities of the court as an actor in the world of art with the same attention previous scholars have given the literati.

Another way to go beyond previous studies of Chinese imperial collecting is to take account of the fact that collections carry messages. As the scholar of collecting

Susan Pearce has argued, collections that aim at some level of completeness can be seen as microcosms of a larger whole and thus convey truths about this whole.[28] Well-chosen and well-documented collections of many kinds of objects (not just of art but also of natural history or other sorts of curiosities) gain meaning by their connection to some larger truth—whether the structure of the cosmos or the limit of human creativity—a truth more effectively communicated through arrayed material objects than through words. Beginning well before Song times, the imperial book collection was taken to represent the sum of human knowledge. As will be seen in later chapters, the objects Huizong collected and documented in his catalogues carried messages about antiquity, human creativity, Huizong's court, and Huizong's own vision and acumen.

Interpretations of royal collecting in terms of its sacred origins, its political functions, or the messages it communicates are not mutually exclusive. Any Chinese ruler acted with a mind to the past: He could not launch an initiative without regard to what had been done by his predecessors, since his contemporaries would interpret his actions with the past in mind. Yet departures from precedent, especially costly ones, were unlikely to be sustained unless they were thought to provide some political benefit to those pursuing them. Moreover, it is certainly possible for an act such as collecting to communicate messages about fundamental truths or current political realities while also adding to the court's political legitimacy or placing pressure on political rivals. This book aims to do justice to the many different facets of imperial collecting during Huizong's reign.

Emperor-Literati Relations and Imperial Collecting

In imperial China the relationship between rulers and the educated elite had many built-in sources of tension. Men imbued with the Confucian values of loyalty to the ruler, responsibility for the welfare of the common people, and personal integrity made good officials, but they were not always easy to manage. Many stubbornly insisted that it was their duty to point out to the emperor the errors of his ways. Emperors got tired of listening to Confucian critics charge them with failing to choose the most upright men as their councilors or with giving in to the Confucian sins of indulgence and extravagance; scholars felt frustrated when rulers ignored their advice or did not appreciate the depth of their sincerity. The powers of the educated elite were considerable, as they could make it difficult for a ruler to act in disapproved ways—at least when they were largely in agreement. Many rulers felt that their officials tried to hem them in, surrounding them with ritual and convention. Yet the ruler retained ultimate authority; his officials served at his pleasure;

they could advise him but not dictate to him. Frustrated officials took solace in their ability to shape "public" opinion and eventual historical judgment.

These relatively constant patterns of emperor-literati relationships played out in different ways in different periods of Chinese history. In some eras, rulers were relatively weak; in some, military men held much more power than Confucian scholars. The Northern Song period was one in which the imperial institution was strengthened, yet the educated elite became more solidly entrenched than ever before. As we will see in chapter 1, to bring the armies and their commanders under control, the early Song rulers turned to men trained in the literary traditions. In this favorable environment, the educated class grew rapidly and gained a stronger hold over government office. By the middle of the eleventh century, court ministers were usually men of high culture, accomplished not only in politics and scholarship but also in poetry, calligraphy, and sometimes even the connoisseurship of art. Ouyang Xiu, a leading political figure of this period, was not only a respected poet and historian, but also a collector of rubbings of ancient inscriptions and the author of the first catalogue of a rubbing collection.[29]

This happy situation did not last long. When Shenzong took the throne in 1067, he made Wang Anshi his grand councilor, and together they initiated a comprehensive overhaul of the Song government that aroused enormous resistance from key segments of the scholar-official class. When the chief critics were reassigned out of the capital or dismissed from the government, they felt that the implicit contract between them and the throne had been violated. After Shenzong died in 1085, his policies were reversed. Once those who had been ousted were brought back to power, they quickly retaliated against those who had targeted them. As the court repeatedly shifted course over the next couple of decades, cycles of recrimination and retaliation steadily worsened. By Huizong's day, the sense of common cause between the emperors and their literati officials had worn thin on both sides. Huizong undertook a major expansion of the educated class by providing more financial support to aspiring literati at government schools, but also became increasingly fascinated by Daoist masters and Daoist revelations and even instituted a Daoist examination system. The evolving strains in relations between the educated elite and the throne during the reform era are sketched in chapter 2.

Northern Song literati were passionate not only about politics but also about art. The eleventh century was an exciting period in art history. Landscape painting reached unprecedented creative heights and came to be considered the highest form of painting. Educated men took to collecting calligraphy, paintings, and antiquities as never before. They also took new interest in painting themselves, giving impetus to the tradition of literati painting. Lively discussion of standards of artistic merit was coupled with advances in connoisseurial practice as collectors tried to distinguish original works from copies and forgeries. These developments in the world of literati art lovers are the subject of chapter 3.

Because so many advances were made in connoisseurship, by the end of the eleventh century the Northern Song imperial collections needed to be upgraded, a responsibility Huizong was more than happy to undertake. The decisions Huizong made concerning what to collect were shaped by both his own personal interests and the government agencies given curatorial charge over the collections. Huizong's personal involvement in the collections is the subject of chapter 4. As discussed there, he built new halls to house his collections, arranged occasions to display his favorite objects to select groups of officials, and at times even made copies of paintings in the collection. The institutional side of the management of his collections is taken up in chapter 5. The staff of the Palace Library served as curators of Huizong's collections. They were highly learned men, knowledgeable about the evolution of scripts and well-read in historical and religious texts. They strove to classify each object correctly and to maintain records of its condition and location.

There were other rulers before Huizong who collected on a large scale, but none who came close to him in documenting his possessions through catalogues. None of Huizong's three extant catalogues is a simple inventory of all objects in the palace; rather, all three are select lists of objects that passed a screening process. The catalogues divide works into meaningful categories, put these in hierarchical order, and provide lengthy discussions of the categories as well as capsule accounts of each artist. In this way, the catalogues offer an intellectual framework for fitting individual items into larger wholes and explaining the relations among items.

Drawing on these catalogues, chapters 6, 7, and 8 each look at a single field of collecting and its distinctive political meanings and connoisseurial challenges. In the case of antiquities, court collecting was fundamentally different from private collecting because of the emperor's ritual roles. Rulers were expected to perform the rituals specified in the classics, and knowledge of ancient vessels helped them do so in more authentic ways. As discussed in chapter 6, Huizong decided that the bells and ritual vessels he collected should be used as models to cast new instruments and vessels. In the case of calligraphies and paintings, discussed in chapters 7 and 8, the curators had to attribute works to specific artists and select artists and objects for inclusion in the catalogues. This gave them opportunities to promote artists that others had neglected, demote some artists or genres that they deemed overrated, and shift the focus from one subspecialty to another. Even if Huizong started his collecting with the aim to update the collections so that they could regain the prestige they had had early in the dynasty, eventually he embraced the more ambitious goal of using his collections to influence critical opinion and strengthen the position of the court in the cultural life of the time.

The collections Huizong assembled had a short life. Chapter 9 relates the story of the dispersal of Huizong's collections with the fall of Kaifeng to the Jurchens in 1127. This unplanned outcome inverted the image of emperorship that Huizong had taken such efforts to project. In the end, Huizong became not the architect of a glorious centering of cultural power but the hapless witness to its fragmentation.

CHAPTER 1

Early Song Precedents

During the years of disorder, records were lost and scattered, and the teachings of the Duke of Zhou and Confucius were nearly abandoned. Since I took the throne, books have been collected from all over either by copying or purchasing them, so that now there are tens of thousands of chapters. One can find the principles of order and disorder in them.

—Taizong to his officials on a visit to the Imperial Repository in 992

ALTHOUGH THE FIRST STEPS IN CREATING THE SONG IMPERIAL COLlections were accomplished by force—by seizing the collections of defeated states—the larger project of gathering into the palace the works of China's scholars and artists was viewed by the Song court as a way for the dynasty to demonstrate its commitment to culture (*wen*). The early emperors restored the Palace Library and other hallowed institutions and presented themselves as patrons of the educated class. They welcomed men of learning into their governments and sponsored literary projects of many kinds. In addition, they exemplified the cultured man themselves, through their personal performance of such literati activities as reading, composing poetry, practicing calligraphy, and promoting the education of their relatives. They also gathered together culturally valued objects—primarily documents, books, calligraphies, and paintings. Collecting these objects was seen as a way to "honor Confucian scholars" (*chong ru*).

The First Four Emperors as Patrons of Culture

The overriding need of the initial decades of the Song dynasty was to rein in the military. During the last century and a half of the Tang dynasty (618–907), military governors controlling province-size territories had been able to act independently of the court, resulting in both political decentralization and the ascendance of the

THE FIRST FOUR SONG EMPERORS

1. Taizu (927–976), dynasty's founder, r. 960–976
2. Taizong (939–997), Taizu's younger brother, r. 976–997
3. Zhenzong (968–1022), Taizong's second surviving son, r. 997–1022
4. Renzong (1010–1063), Zhenzong's only surviving son, r. 1022–1063

military. Men of letters seeking government careers frequently had little choice but to seek the patronage of military men. After the fall of the Tang, the dominance of the military increased. In the north, whoever controlled the Emperor's Army and the Palace Corps (the successors of the Tang central armies) was paramount. A series of these generals declared themselves founders of new dynasties—"the Five Dynasties"— but none of these "dynasties" lasted more than sixteen years. Meanwhile south China was fragmented into province-size states, each with its own ruler and army.

The Song dynasty was founded by Taizu (r. 960–976), a general in the service of the Later Zhou dynasty (951–960, the last of the Five Dynasties). In 960, when a child succeeded to the Zhou throne, Taizu seized the throne himself with the support (some sources say the instigation) of his troops. Throughout his reign, Taizu remained above all a military commander, leading the armies that gradually subdued the rival states. In 966 Sichuan in the west was incorporated, but through the 960s most of the south was at least semi-independent. In 975–976, the state of Southern Tang with its capital at Nanjing was conquered, after which the other southern states submitted voluntarily. When Taizu died in 976, only two important rivals remained.[1]

Taizu's government was staffed largely by military men who had served the Northern Zhou. Nevertheless, Taizu is given credit by historians for shifting the balance from *wu* to *wen*. He did this by circumscribing the power of his generals and placing men without military credentials in important posts. Taizu also presided over the restoration of key cultural agencies, such as the Directorate of Education and the Palace Library.[2] During Tang times, the Palace Library had offered prestigious employment to highly educated men, served as the center for the collection of books, documents, and related materials, and carried out many compilation projects.[3] To declare that his dynasty was different from its immediate predecessor, and that the period of division was over, in 973–974 Taizu had a team of scholars at the Library compile the history of the Five Dynasties.[4]

Taizu was not a man of culture himself. He was certainly literate, and sometimes wrote edicts out by hand, but he made no claims to having skill as a poet or calligrapher. Moreover, Taizu never came to place a high value on literary education per se. Even in 975, after fifteen years on the throne, he was so exasperated by the lack of military proficiency of the 270 candidates for the civil-service examination sent from Puzhou that he threatened to draft them into the army.[5]

Taizu was succeeded by his younger brother Taizong (r. 976–997) even though he had adult sons. The official explanation for this anomalous succession was that in 961 their mother, on her deathbed, had made Taizu promise to pass the throne to his brothers. From that time on, however, many people suspected that Taizong had taken matters into his own hands.[6] Be that as it may, Taizong proved an effective ruler who went much further than his elder brother in showing honor to educated men. He employed them in large numbers, regularly acted like a man of culture himself, and encouraged his sons and nephews to cultivate the arts of the literati.

Taizong particularly deserves credit for recognizing the potential of the civil-service examination system to find for him suitable men of letters. In the first examination he supervised, that of 977, he passed more men than Taizu had during his entire reign. John Chaffee sees the Song dynasty, through its reliance on the exam system, as "attempting to create a meritocratic elite beholden to the emperor and large enough so that its own most powerful members would not threaten the dynasty." Peter Bol sees favoring men with literary education as expedient for Taizong because such men "were willing subordinates, without independent power, who depended on a superior authority for their political position, and who brought to their duties a commitment to the civil culture invaluable to the institutionalization of central authority."[7]

It was also Taizong who incorporated into the government southern officials with literary rather than military accomplishments. Among those Taizong favored was Xu Xuan, who had strongly defended the importance of literary values in government while serving Li Yu, the last ruler of the Southern Tang. Under Taizong he was assigned literary tasks, such as re-editing the Han period dictionary, *Shuowen jiezi*. Larger literary projects employed even more southern literary officials.[8] Taizong had long had an interest in medicine, and in 978 ordered the compilation of a medical manual, which eventually included 16,834 prescriptions classified into 1,670 categories and a preface by Taizong. In 981 he commissioned a collection of medical texts, which, when submitted five years later, came to 1,000 chapters. In 988 Taizong ordered the editing and printing of the Five Classics and their commentaries.[9] Other large-scale literary projects included a 200–chapter national geography (*Taiping huanyu ji*), a 500–chapter collection of stories and anecdotes (*Taiping guangji*), and a 1,000–chapter collection of literary pieces (*Wenyuan yinghua*). These huge encyclopedic compilations have been described as "museums of thought in which things of the past are exhibited for the interested connoisseur."[10]

Taizong set the example of how an emperor could honor men of learning by acting like one himself. In 977, when the encyclopedic *Taiping yulan* was completed, Taizong undertook to read it at a rate of three chapters a day. When an official advised that such a pace would be exhausting, Taizong is said to have responded:

> By nature I love to read. Opening a book benefits me; it doesn't weary me. Every time I come across cases of the rise or decline of former dynasties, I learn a lot, even

if I cannot remember all of the new things I find. This book has a thousand chapters, and I wish to read through it in a year. I now realize that a scholar who loves learning would not find it difficult to read ten thousand chapters. With reading, if you do not enjoy the act of reading, you will not absorb what you read. Yesterday, after I read from *si* to *shen* [9 A.M. to 5 P.M.], cranes appeared on the staircases of the hall, and they left when I stopped.[11]

Taizong also presented himself as a writer. Wang Yinglin (1223–1296) records many instances when Taizong wrote poems for officials, including the banquets for new examination graduates. Taizong also responded to poems by his officials by writing matching ones, and offered his own poems for them to match. For instance, in 979 he gave his close associates some new tea and a poem on tea for them to match. By 990, Taizong's collected works had 41 chapters, and after his death it grew larger as pieces which had been scattered were gathered together.[12]

Taizong became a major patron of the Palace Library. When he visited it in 977, he was so dismayed at its physical condition that he personally designed new quarters for it. He made trips to observe the progress of construction, which one of his trusted eunuchs supervised. When the new quarters were completed in 978, he gave the complex a new name: Hall for Exalting Culture. A gate was placed on the west side of the complex to make imperial visits easier (see fig. 1.1). Six storehouses were filled with 80,000 books. A decade later, in 988, Taizong ordered a new building added to hold Exalting Culture's books along with his own old paintings and calligraphies, and named it the Imperial Repository.[13]

Taizong said that he enjoyed practicing calligraphy and trying to master the different scripts. At the same time, he was clearly aware that using the brush in this way created objects that made excellent gifts. In 992 he gave each of his grand councilors a scroll with his calligraphy of the *Thousand Character Essay* in cursive script, and the next year another one in *bafen* (a version of clerical script). Two years later he gave them each twenty scrolls done in flying white with large characters several feet in size.[14] When the councilors came to thank him, Taizong told them,

> Flying white is based on the small cursive script and is different from clerical script. Given my duties to the realm, how do I have time for brush and ink? It is just that in my heart I love [calligraphy] and cannot lightly set it aside. As the years and months have gone by, I have mastered its techniques. But it is difficult to grasp the characters of the small cursive script. The brush configuration of my flying white is rarely skillful, but by practicing this script, I keep it from dying out.[15]

Soon Taizong was agreeing to have his calligraphy inscribed on stone. In 992, at a banquet at the newly built Imperial Repository, Taizong wrote a piece to celebrate the occasion, which the grand councilor Li Fang asked permission to have carved on stone at the base of the Repository. Another official supported the request by pointing out that the Tang Palace Library had had paintings of cranes by Xue Ji, of phoenixes by Lang Yuling, and cursive script calligraphy by He Zhizhang, the three works referred to at the time as the "three excellences." The official also cited the fact that in the Tang dynasty, Yan Zhenqing had asked Emperor Suzong to do the title for a commemorative stele at the Buddhist Releasing Life ponds, and that more recently Su Yijian had gotten the emperor to do a title in flying white for the Hanlin Academy. Taizong consented and sent a eunuch to deliver his calligraphy of the two characters "Imperial Repository." After repeated requests, Taizong also wrote out in his own hand his essay in praise of the Repository so that it could be carved into stone.[16]

After a subsequent visit to the Imperial Repository, Taizong sent to the Palace Library his transcription of the *Thousand Character Essay* in cursive script. The director of the library promptly asked permission to have it carved on the reverse of the stele erected with his encomium, to which he responded that the transcription had been written out for practice, not to be preserved for the ages; for that purpose, he would instead copy out the *Classic of Filial Piety*.[17]

Once his calligraphy was being carved on stone, Taizong realized the possibilities for reaching a larger audience through duplication. In 995, he had several hundred copies made of his transcription of stories from the histories and classics in cursive script. The copies were made by first engraving his text on stone, then making rubbings of it. The copies were then sent to Buddhist and Daoist temples as well as to local worthies in the Southeast who had contributed books to the Palace Library.[18] Although no copies of this work in cursive script survive, the National Palace Museum in Taipei has one of similar date and content in running script (fig. 1.2). As Ho Chuan-hsing has observed, in this piece Taizong wrote in the style of the most famous of earlier calligraphers, Wang Xizhi, thus emulating the Tang emperor Taizong, whose esteem for Wang was boundless.[19]

Taizong also considered himself a connoisseur of paintings, and took credit for writing a continuation of a Tang treatise that evaluated painters. According to Liu Daochun (fl. 1050s), "Taizong, who had been given great capabilities by Heaven and who devoted himself to all of the arts, made an examination of those painters who came after the Tang. He compiled the names of another one hundred and twenty artists, along with critical remarks, and called the work *Opinions on Painters of Renown*."[20] This book unfortunately has not survived.

Besides acting as a man of culture himself, Taizong took steps to see that his sons, nephews, and their descendants (in other words, the imperial clan) received literary

FIG. 1.1
Plan of the Kaifeng Palace during the final years of Huizong's reign. Generally speaking, the halls toward the front were used by officials and the halls to the rear were the personal quarters of the emperor, the palace ladies, and the court eunuchs. Grand Celebration Hall is in the center, near the front. The Palace Library had been to the right of it, but was replaced by the Hall of Enlightenment after 1116. Harmony Revealed Hall is left rear. The halls for objects connected to Taizong and Zhenzong, Dragon Diagram and Heavenly Emblems Pavilions, are in the front left. After SLGJ Houji 6.6a–b.

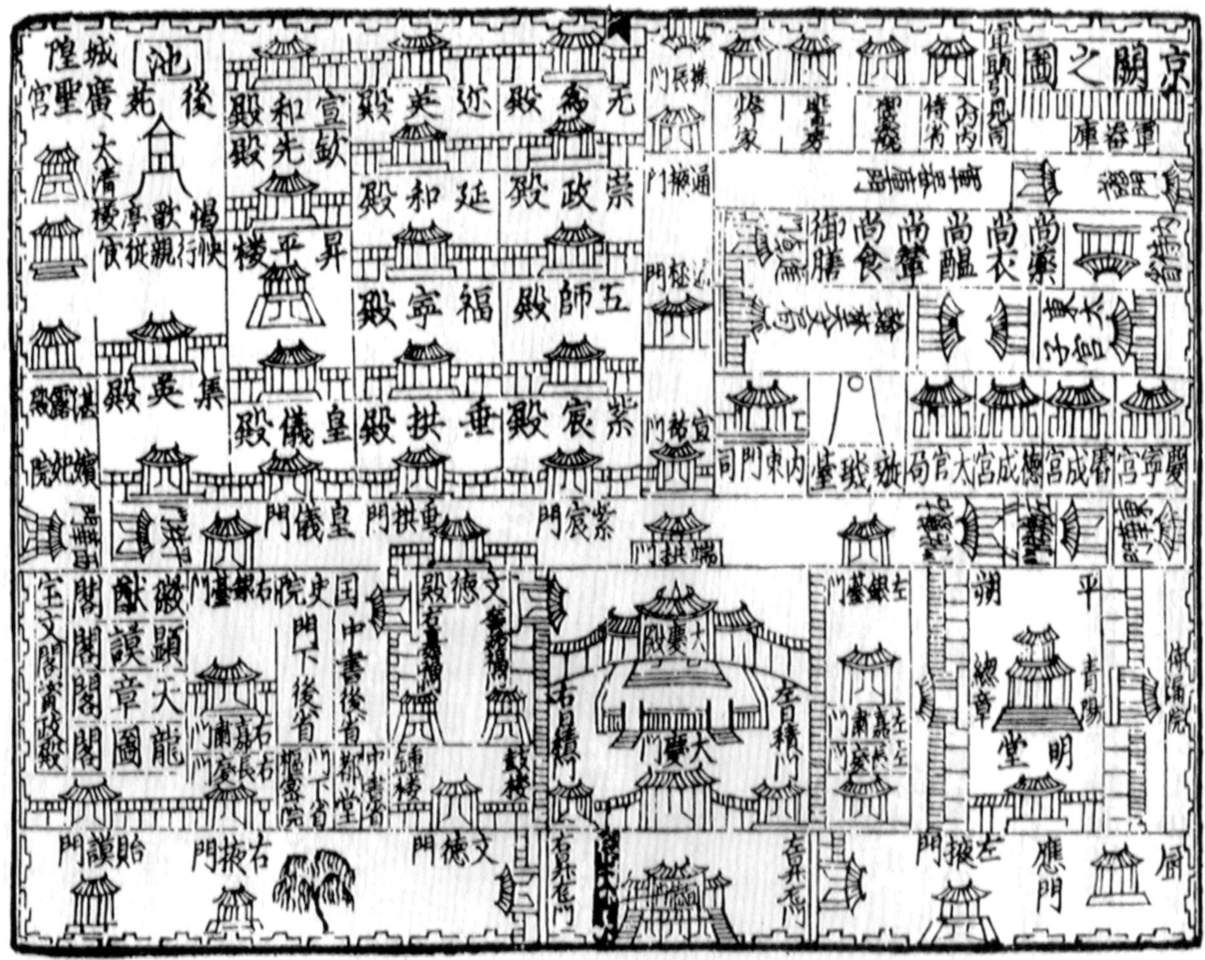

educations. In 983 he appointed teachers for the princely establishments to give them moral as well as literary educations. One of Taizong's sons, Zhao Yuanjie, showed talent in poetry and calligraphy and built up a 20,000–chapter book collection.[21]

Taizong's son and successor, Zhenzong (r. 997–1022), who was thirty when he came to the throne, continued most of Taizong's cultural initiatives. Like his father, he favored officials with literary talent, such as Ding Wei, who was not only widely read and a prolific poet, but also knowledgeable in matters of painting and music.[22] Zhenzong continued the policy of drawing more southern scholars into the government through the examination system. To reduce favoritism, he made it difficult for examiners to recognize who wrote an examination paper by first ordering that their names be covered and then, in 1015, that the entire examination paper be recopied.[23]

When the project of editing and printing the Five Classics and commentaries was completed in 1005, Zhenzong visited the Directorate of Education where the work was done to inspect the books and woodblocks. He asked about the work, including how many woodblocks had been used (about 100,000), and approved an expansion of the academy's book-storage facilities.[24]

Zhenzong was not as devoted to the practice of calligraphy as his father, but he liked to write. He regularly wrote poems with new examination graduates and close associates at banquets and similar occasions. Zhenzong also wrote prolifically in prose genres, resulting in a 300–chapter collected works with nearly 100 chapters devoted to verse of one sort or another. Some of his essays were printed, others were carved on stone and placed at temples or government schools. After Zhenzong became deeply interested in Daoism, he wrote many commemorative essays and inscriptions on Daoist matters.[25]

Zhenzong similarly followed his father's example in encouraging imperial clansmen (his first cousins and their descendants) to become men of culture. He expected them to be able to write poetry at clan gatherings and gave them personal advice and instruction. In 1012 he told his councilors, "I continually urge the imperial clansmen to read books, write poetry, do calligraphy, and practice archery. If I hear that any of them attain some degree of proficiency, I go to his home to observe." At times, he invited clansmen and officials to join him in honoring princes who excelled in these arts. Occasionally he gave clansmen gifts with strong literary associations, such as his own calligraphy or poetry.[26]

Zhenzong added to the repertoire of ways emperors could honor *wen* by building a hall to celebrate his father's cultural accomplishments. This hall, called Dragon Diagram Pavilion (Longtu ge), held cultural objects connected to Taizong, such as documents produced during his reign, his own writings, and anything in his own hand, as well as objects submitted to the court during his reign because they carried auspicious meanings. In the upper floor of the main hall at Dragon Diagram Pavilion were 5,115 scrolls or albums of Taizong's works, as well as several dozen of his personally inscribed silk fans, together with other objects associated with him. Besides the main hall, there were six subordinate halls, each of which held a category of books, with one holding the paintings and calligraphy.[27] Zhenzong celebrated Taizong's literary and artistic accomplishments in other ways as well. In 1012 he approved distributing copies of Taizong's collected works to several government libraries and literary organs, including the Palace Library. He also granted permission to the Directorate of Education to set up a special pavilion to house Taizong's collected works.[28]

Zhenzong's only son, Renzong (r. 1022–1063), came to the throne as a child of thirteen *sui*. Zhenzong's widow, Empress Dowager Liu, served as regent until her

FIG. 1.2
Rubbing of Taizong's calligraphy, dated 994 (detail). 27.3 × 31.2 cm. National Palace Museum, Taiwan, Republic of China. Taizong had his own transcription of passages from the classics reproduced as rubbings, probably in order to give them out as gifts. Like many Tang emperors, this Song emperor emulated the style of the great calligrapher Wang Xizhi.

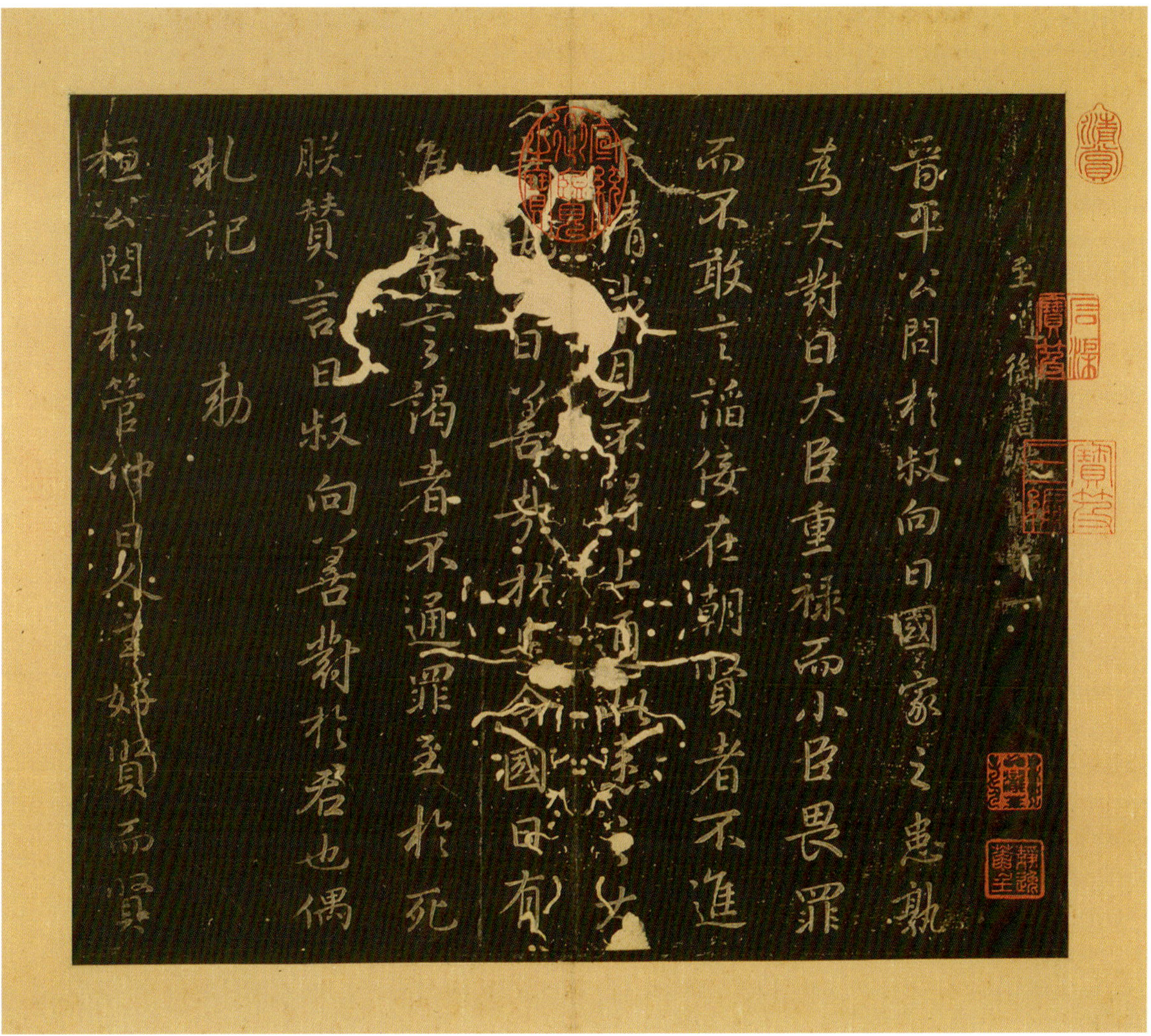

death in 1033. Renzong became perhaps the strongest patron of Confucian education among Song emperors. In 1034 he introduced the practice of having Confucian scholars and officials lecture the emperor on passages from the classics or histories. Renzong also oversaw an expansion of government schools. In the 1030s, he encouraged governments at the county and prefectural levels to set aside land to endow government schools to assure them reliable income. Higher education in the capital was also expanded. In 1042, because more and more candidates had to be turned away from the Directorate of Education's school for the sons of officials, a new school that admitted students without regard to their father's status was established, the National Academy. The new Academy appointed well-respected scholars as professors, including Sun Fu, appointed when the university was opened, and Hu Yuan, appointed in 1052. By 1058 the Academy had 600 students.[29]

Renzong further strengthened the *wen* side of government by nurturing the offices of criticism. The old office of the Censorate and the new Bureau of Policy Criticism became under Renzong major organs through which literati could challenge and ultimately alter government policies and personnel. Even low-ranking "speaking" officials were able to get grand councilors to resign by submitting memorials detailing their failings. Men like Fan Zhongyan, Han Qi, Ouyang Xiu, Fu Bi, Cai Xiang, and Zhang Fangping gained reputations for integrity by criticizing those in power while serving in the Bureau of Policy Criticism during Renzong's reign.[30]

Like his grandfather Taizong, Renzong claimed to enjoy practicing calligraphy. In 1039, when his officials thanked him for the calligraphy scrolls he had given them, he modestly turned away their praise by saying, "When I have moments free from government business, with nothing to distract me, this is what I most enjoy."[31] Even more than Taizong and Zhenzong, Renzong let his calligraphy be seen on the name plaques for halls. In 1045 he wrote out the plaques for nearly a dozen temple halls in several parts of the country. He also often wrote the titles for the funerary stelae of his highest officials.[32] Renzong's interest in calligraphy also extended to ancient scripts. He once gave his highest officials rubbings of the inscriptions on eleven ancient bronzes held by the palace. Most could not decipher the ancient scripts.[33]

As a man of the brush, Renzong was more a calligrapher than a writer, and as a writer he preferred prose to poetry. Although he at least occasionally gave poems to favored officials, after more than forty years on the throne, only 4 chapters of his 100–chapter collected works were devoted to poetry.[34]

The imperial clan grew rapidly during Renzong's long reign, and he continued the practice of offering incentives to clansmen to become educated in the literary traditions. The biography of one clansman mentions that Renzong would not only entertain clansmen with poetry-writing competitions but would also commend those who did well, sometimes with edicts of encouragement, other times with gifts of gold or silk. Renzong also organized examinations for imperial clansmen. Even though these did not bring government appointments like the regular civil-service examinations, they brought honor and encouraged clansmen to pursue the sorts of education that more and more of the educated class were pursuing in the hopes of passing the civil-service examinations.[35]

Where Renzong was innovative was in dabbling in painting. Guo Ruoxu, writing not long after Renzong's death, was lavish in his praise:

> His Imperial Majesty Renzong was endowed by Heaven with a store of keen understanding. His sagely artistry had an inspired originality; when in the flush of enthusiasm he wielded his brush, he far outstripped common men. I have heard that when the imperial aunt Lady Xianmu of Qi was beginning to lose her sight, the emperor personally painted the Bodhisattva Nagarjuna, which was then traced by a painter-in-attendance and printed by woodblock for distribution. The goodness and filial piety of his sagely heart defy this unworthy subject's attempts at praise.[36]

By the end of Renzong's reign, when the Song dynasty was a century old, the emperor's role as patron of scholarly culture was fully institutionalized. It was taken for granted that the government should be in the hands of men with literary educations. Officials who had access to the emperor were expected to be men who had achieved reputations for their literary abilities, usually by placing high in the civil-service examinations. There were disagreements on the importance of being able to write good poetry and on how to discern moral character, but not on the idea that men trained in the classics made better officials than men trained in the arts of war. Emperors themselves were expected to be able to entertain their clansmen and high officials in ways that demonstrated their cultural facility. Even if court officials may have sometimes polished (or even drafted) an emperor's poems, the emperor had to have enough command of the art of poetry to respond properly to his subjects' contributions. In addition, it was best if he was skillful enough with the brush that gifts of his calligraphy were presentable.

During the first century of the Song, as in Tang times, emperors' gestures of support for literary culture and Confucian learning were not seen as being in conflict with concurrent support for Buddhism and Daoism. Taizu was personally attracted to Buddhism and sent a delegation of 157 monks to the Western Regions "in search of the Dharma." In 971 he ordered a printing of the Buddhist canon, using 130,000 printing blocks. In 980 Taizong set up the Institute for the Translation of Scriptures to translate the newly acquired scriptures. He also built or rebuilt many Buddhist temples, especially in Kaifeng.[37] Zhenzong, by contrast, lavished more support on Daoism. Probably modeling himself on the Tang dynasty's claim of descent from Laozi, he claimed that dreams revealed that the Song royal family was descended from an incarnation of the Yellow Emperor. He was soon building huge Daoist temples in the capital and ordering every prefecture in the country to erect a Heavenly Felicity Daoist temple. Many painters were given employment covering the walls of these temples with Daoist imagery. It is true that Confucian scholars wrote many memorials urging emperors to curtail their patronage of Buddhism and Daoism, but by Renzong's time, such patronage was well-established.

Renzong believed that imperial patronage of religions should be maintained on the grounds that it was part of the established traditions of the former emperors.[38]

The Palace Collections

Like the other ways Song emperors showed their respect for Confucian culture, imperial collecting began early in the dynasty, following precedents set in earlier dynasties. From the beginning, all sorts of document-like objects were collected together: books, documents, calligraphy, paintings, and occasionally ritual vessels. Officials reminded the emperors of the glorious history of the Palace Library going back to the Han dynasty and encouraged efforts to enhance its collections.[39]

A key to appreciating the distinctive features of Chinese royal collecting is to recognize the close connection in the Chinese case between collecting books and collecting calligraphy and painting. The acquisition of these products of the brush was viewed as different from the acquisition of gold, jewels, and other objects valued primarily in monetary terms. Perhaps because of the condemnation heaped on the short-lived Qin dynasty (221–206 BCE), which had decreed the destruction of much of the written record, the efforts of subsequent dynasties to collect together, preserve, and catalogue books was always presented as a positive, pro-culture measure. The sorts of paintings and calligraphies that became objects of collection shared a material similarity with manuscript books. Although printed books most commonly had pages (and this format was gaining popularity for hand-copied books as well), older manuscripts were often still in the form of rolls of paper or silk.[40] It was thus easy to think about collecting paintings and calligraphies as an extension of collecting books and to view the larger enterprise as a way to promote learning.

FIG. 1.3
Li Yu (937–978), inscription on a painting by Zhao Gan (detail). Handscroll, ink and color on silk, 25.9 × 376 cm. National Palace Museum Taiwan, Republic of China. Along the opening edge of this painting, Li Yu wrote the title, *Along the River at First Snow*, and said the work was by a painter of his Painting Academy, Zhao Gan. This painting probably entered the Song palace collection with Li Yu's defeat by Song in 976.

ACQUIRING OBJECTS BY CONFISCATION

Taizu deserves some credit for starting the Song palace collections because he seized the treasures and documents of the courts he defeated and sent them back to his capital at Kaifeng, much as he did their court artists, palace ladies, and other spoils of war.[41] In 963, when the small state of Jingnan in the middle Yangzi region was annexed, Taizu ordered that its libraries be confiscated and transferred to Kaifeng. In 966 when the much larger state of Shu was defeated, Taizu instructed Sun Fengji to seize the state's ritual paraphernalia, diagrams/pictures (*tu*), books/calligraphies (*shu*), and seals. When Sun returned to Kaifeng, Taizu had the ritual paraphernalia destroyed, but sent the remaining booty to the History Institute (one of the units of the Palace Library).[42]

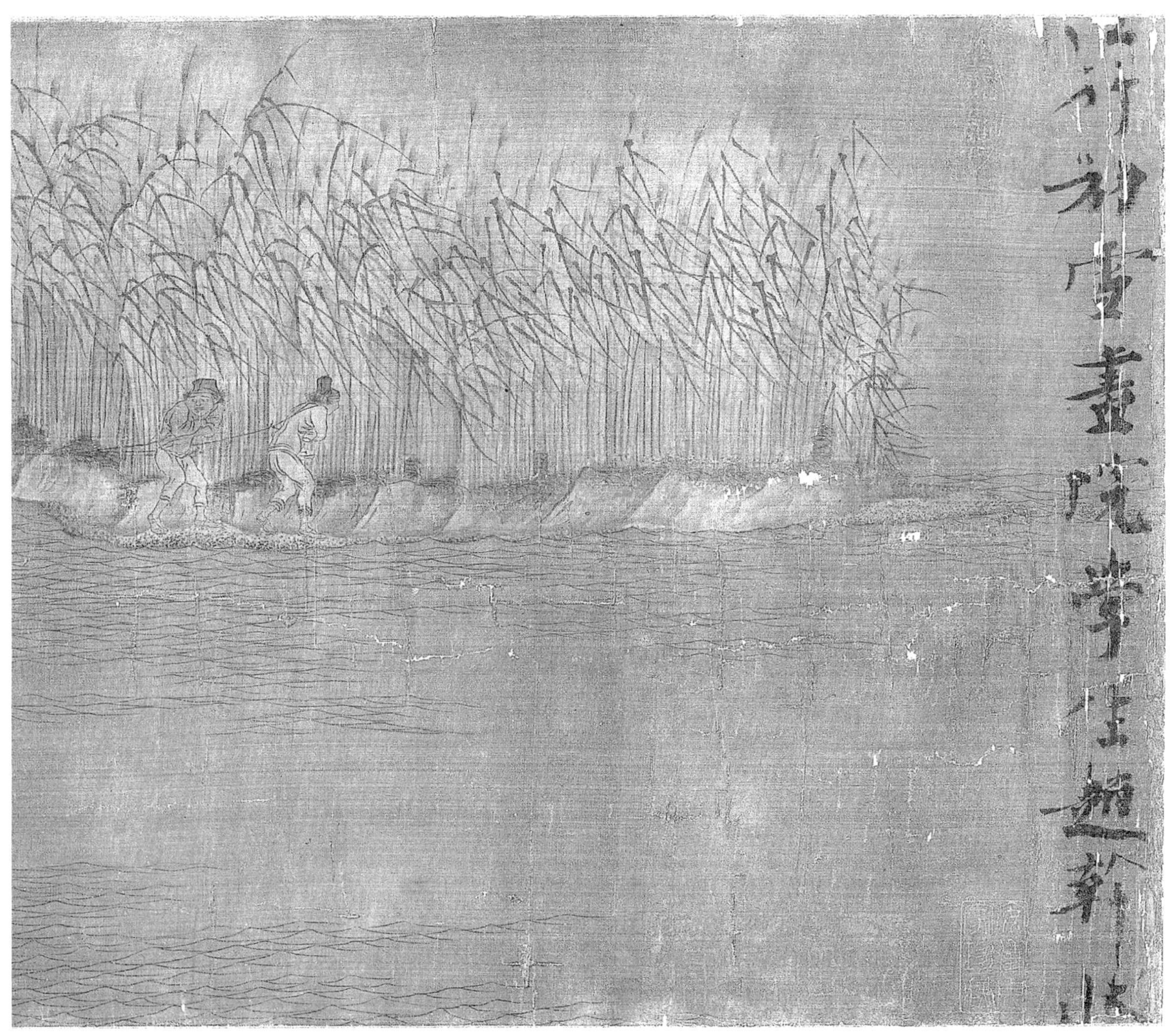

Similarly, in 976, after the defeat of the Southern Tang court, Lü Guixiang was sent to inventory its palace library. Li Yu, the last ruler of the Southern Tang, had devoted much time and attention to his collections, which certainly contained many treasures. He nurtured several talented court painters and sometimes inscribed their paintings (see fig. 1.3).[43] Although Li Yu told a palace lady to destroy his collection rather than let it fall into the hands of the Song, the Song agent was able to send back to Kaifeng more than 20,000 chapters' worth of books, which were sent to the History Institute. Duplicates, though, the court gave to favored officials. The book-loving grand councilor Wang Pu ended up with more than 10,000 chapters of books, as well as "many famous paintings and calligraphies."[44]

Once all of the rival states were subjugated, confiscations became rare events. Occasionally officials found guilty of corruption or other charges had their property seized, which could include substantial collections of books and artworks. Soon after Zhenzong died, his widow Empress Dowager Liu saw to the downfall of Ding Wei and the confiscation of his property, which included a large collection of painting and calligraphy, including a reported ninety scrolls by the landscape master Li Cheng.[45]

ORGANIZING SEARCHES

In addition to emptying out the palaces of defeated rivals, Taizu and his successors tried many different tactics to secure works held in private hands. Just six years after the dynasty was founded, the government announced that it would buy books missing from the palace collections. To tempt major collectors to submit large numbers of works, the prospect of official appointment was dangled before them. Some 1,228 chapters of books were acquired in this way. After Taizong took the throne, he made many similar announcements. In 977 he ordered prefects to search for pictures and calligraphies that were "traces of the brush of former worthies." One official submitted a piece of calligraphy in cursive script by the early master Zhang Zhi, along with three paintings of horses by the famed Tang painter Han Gan. Other officials submitted calligraphy by the Tang emperor Xuanzong, a portrait of the Tang official Zhang Jiuling along with his nine-chapter collected works, and a book of rubbings by twenty-eight masters including the Two Wangs, Wang Xizhi and his son Wang Xianzhi. As paintings and calligraphies arrived at the palace, they were examined, authenticated, and shown to the emperor, then stored in the Palace Library.[46]

All throughout Taizong's reign, with generous rewards as an incentive, calligraphies, paintings, and books were regularly sent to the capital. In 981, Taizong asked officials to search specifically for calligraphy by the third-century calligrapher Zhong You. In response, one official turned in seven scrolls of calligraphy by Zhong You, Wang Xizhi, and Tang Xuanzong. Objects submitted by other officials included eight scrolls by Zhong You and Wang Xizhi, a painted portrait of Wang Xizhi, and his inkstone. In 985 an official submitted thirty pieces of calligraphy by the early Tang calligraphy masters Chu Suiliang, Ouyang Xun, and Yu Shinan.[47]

In 984 officials at the Palace Library organized searches for specific titles the Palace Library lacked, using the eighth-century catalogue of the Tang palace library as a checklist to compile a list of missing books and chapters. Those able to supply

300 or more missing chapters were promised a government post; those contributing fewer would receive financial compensation. Some donors were additionally given rubbings of Taizong's own calligraphy. Those unwilling to part with their books permanently were asked to lend them so that they could be copied. Zhenzong announced similar policies in 1001. He made the rewards as simple and clear as possible: 1000 cash for each chapter of a book the Library lacked, and official appointment for those who submitted 300 or more chapters.[48]

Occasionally it happened that collectors approached the throne directly. In 994 a family was rewarded with 100,000 cash for turning in over a hundred chapters of historical documents relating to the late Tang and Five Dynasties periods.[49] A collector named Sun Sihao who had connections to the palace (his daughter was one of Taizong's consorts) twice made gifts of paintings to Taizong. Once a painting done for him of the ancient King Wu attracted so much praise that Sun Sihao "would not dare be selfish, so he presented the painting to the Son of Heaven."[50] Another man named Wang Yizheng, whose father had built up a substantial collection of paintings and calligraphies, presented fifteen to the court. Taizong selected eight to keep and returned the rest.[51] By returning half the paintings offered, Taizong showed that his desire to build up the palace collections was not so extreme that he wanted everything for himself.

COMMISSIONING AGENTS

Besides the general calls for individuals to submit books and for prefects and other officials to keep their eyes open for objects the Palace Library needed, Taizong also sent emissaries to conduct searches. In 993, wanting to increase the palace's holdings, Taizong sent a court painter to purchase paintings from throughout the realm, giving him one hundred bolts of silk to pay for them. Another source reports that two court painters who had formerly served at the Shu court in Sichuan, Gao Wenjin and Huang Jucai, were given commissions of this sort.[52]

The south was known to have books and art works unavailable in the north, so Taizong sent scouts south. On one such trip in 995, the palace eunuch Pei Yu found more than sixty missing chapters of old books, forty-five "famous" paintings, nine old zithers (*qin*), and eight pieces of calligraphy by famous calligraphers, including Wang Xizhi and Huaisu. The emperor also gave a similar commission to Su Yijian, an official whose experience with painting was as a collector rather than as an artist. According to Guo Ruoxu, Taizong remembered that Su was familiar with the Nanjing region, which had been the capital not only during the Southern Dynasties but also under the Li family of the Southern Tang, so he sent Su there to seek out calligraphies and paintings by famous masters. Su secured more than a thousand scrolls, and Taizong rewarded him with a hundred of them. On another occasion Taizong gave him several dozen more. In fact, once when he noticed that Su kept looking at a painted screen, Taizong gave him the screen.[53] Thus one of the many uses of the palace collection of paintings was a ready supply of rewards for art-loving subjects.

VIEWING OBJECTS

Taizong and Zhenzong found many occasions to view objects from the palace collections with their officials, thus using the collections to strengthen their cultural links to their officials. After the Imperial Repository was built in 992, Taizong visited several times. On a visit of 992/9, Taizong viewed a display of books set out there. He remarked to his attending officials, "During the years of disorder, records were lost and scattered, and the teachings of the Duke of Zhou and Confucius were nearly abandoned. Since I took the throne, books have been collected from all over, either by copying or purchasing them, so that now there are tens of thousands of chapters. One can find the principles of order and disorder in them." Taizong then summoned his top officials, invited them to sit, and had them served three rounds of wine. Next he invited the officials of the Library to join, letting them sit as well. After he returned to his quarters, he sent a eunuch to tell the leading military figures to read books in the Imperial Repository, reportedly because "the emperor wanted them to know the splendor of literary and Confucian culture."[54]

Zhenzong especially liked to meet with his officials at the hall dedicated to his father, Dragon Diagram Pavilion, where they would view together the tangible cultural remains of his predecessor along with the fruits of his own cultural and political initiatives.[55] In the winter of 1002, he had his officials first view the recently printed Five Classics downstairs, then ascend to see Taizong's writings. With the catalogue of Taizong's calligraphy in his hand, Zhenzong said to them, "The late emperor put effort into his writing and calligraphy. I try to preserve every scrap, not letting a single piece be discarded. As for the screens and fans that he wrote on, if they suffer any damage, I have them remounted." This occasion also involved poetry writing. Zhenzong composed a seven-character poem, to which the officials responded, and Yang Yi, on imperial command, wrote a poem to commemorate the event. Three years later, during a visit to Dragon Diagram Pavilion, Zhenzong assured the officials present that he appreciated their work, telling them, "When at leisure from court business, I gather together pictures and calligraphy/books to amuse myself."[56]

On occasions like this, Zhenzong simultaneously displayed his appreciation for culture and his filial piety. In 1007 Zhenzong invited his leading officials to Grand

Clarity Edifice to see both the calligraphy and writings of Taizong and the collection of books housed there. The occasion was turned into a banquet, with Zhenzong writing poems for his officials to match.[57] The event was commemorated in a painting, *Four Events during the Jingde [Reign-Period]*, a later version of which survives in the National Palace Museum, Taipei. The last scene, titled *Viewing Books at Grand Clarity* (see plate 6), depicts Zhenzong's 1007 visit to the hall in the inner palace that held newly copied duplicates of books.[58]

THE SIZE OF THE COLLECTIONS

The palace collections of books grew relatively rapidly. At the beginning of the Song dynasty, one source reports, the Palace Library had only 12,000 chapters of books, but gained another 13,000 with the confiscations of the royal library of Shu, and another 20,000 from that of Jiangnan. By 978, after the initial attempts to gather more books and the building of new quarters for the Library, the six storehouses had 80,000 chapters of books, counting duplicates.[59]

A large number of these books must have been duplicates, as later figures which exclude duplicates are significantly smaller. A tally of the collections in 1005 showed nearly 29,000 chapters of books and a little under 1,000 works of art, broken down as follows:

Classics	3,341 chapters
Histories	7,258 chapters
Philosophers	8,489 chapters
Collected Works	7,108 chapters
Technical treatises, manuals	2,561 chapters
Paintings	701 scrolls or booklets
Calligraphies	266 scrolls[60]

Both to aid preservation and to expand access, extra copies were made of both books and calligraphies held by the Palace Library. Copies of calligraphies were made first. As the palace calligraphy collection grew, Taizong put his own calligraphy tutor, Wang Zhu, in charge of developing it. To provide better models for calligraphy practice, Taizong had Wang select the best pieces of calligraphy from the collection to be reproduced. Over half the pieces he selected were by the Two Wangs, and most of the rest by other calligraphers of the Southern Dynasties. Copies of the resulting book, known as the *Chunhua Model Letters*, were given to officials.[61]

In 999 Zhenzong initiated a copying project to make two extra copies of each book in the Imperial Repository, one to be placed in Grand Clarity Edifice in the more residential rear part of the vast palace complex, the other in Dragon Diagram Pavilion.[62] Five years later, when the project was complete, Zhenzong told his officials:

> Beginning when I lived in the prince's quarters and continuing after I took the throne, I have tried to buy missing books to complete the collection. Whenever we borrow a volume from a book collector, we always record it so that once the copying is done, it can be promptly returned undamaged. As a consequence, unusual books and unknown documents are no longer hidden away. In cases where the classics and histories now in the palace and academy had not been printed, we have had blocks carved for printing. Some said that the *Record of the Three Kingdoms* [Sanguo zhi] was a book about the rivalry among treacherous warlords and so should not be printed, but I thought that one can learn from and take warnings from both good and bad rulers and subjects. After all, Confucius' *Spring and Autumn [Annals]* also deals with a period of contending states.[63]

Unfortunately, in 1015 a palace fire destroyed the Imperial Repository, where the originals of the books were kept. Because two copies had already been made of most books, with each stored in a different building, the lost books could be replaced, but not without another major book-copying and collating project. Collecting books that were in private hands was renewed, leading to the acquisition of 18,754 chapters and to nineteen men gaining official status by donating books. A new building also had to be built to house the restored collection.[64]

Although later copying projects were not as massive, books seem to have continually been lost, so that supplementary copies had to be made. From 1059 to 1061, clerks copied some 6,496 chapters on yellow paper treated to repel insects, and 2,954 chapters on regular paper.[65]

By Renzong's reign, the palace book collection was complete enough to merit cataloguing. A distinguished group of scholars, including Ouyang Xiu, spent seven years on the project, completing it in 1041. The resulting *Chongwen Catalogue* (or *Catalogue of Exalting Culture [Hall];* Chongwen zongmu) was sixty chapters long. It had entries for 3,445 books, which contained a total of 30,669 chapters.[66] The full version of this work has not survived, but the books it listed are known from an abridged version, published a century later, and some of the introductions to sections and entries on titles have been recovered from other works. Books were divided into forty-five categories, largely following the divisions into classics, histories, philosophers, and literary collections of earlier book catalogues, but adding seven chapters on Daoist and five chapters on Buddhist books. Each category began with a general introduction, thirty of which Ouyang Xiu drafted.[67] Within each category, books were listed chronologically. Each had its title, number of chapters, and author listed, followed by a brief assessment. Below is an example:

> *The Record of Great Clarity [Reign Period]* (Taiqing ji), in 10 chapters, was written by Wang Shaozhi of the Liang dynasty. It begins with the first year of Great Clarity [547] and ends with the sixth year. Earlier when Hou Jing destroyed [the Liang capital] Jianye, Wang Shaozhi fled west to Jiangling. Gentlemen there frequently asked him what had happened within the walls [during the siege]. Rather than describe the events to people one by one, Shaozhi wrote down his account, which he showed to those who asked. Emperor Yuan heard about it and got a copy to read. He said, "Previously Wang Shaozhi wrote a *Record of Splendid Peace [Reign Period]* about the disorder at the end of the Jin dynasty. [His current manuscript] should be called the *Record of Great Clarity [Reign Period]*." Shaozhi used his idea for the title. But in his discussions he apologizes for this and rarely uses the emperor's ideas. The narrative is full of mistakes, so this is not an accurate account.[68]

One benefit of compiling the catalogue was that it could be used as a checklist of the Library's collection. Within twenty years, so many books had been lost that a new call was issued for people to submit books missing from the Palace Library.[69] The new incentive structure was more generous in its financial rewards, but raised the bar for gaining office through book donation to 500 chapters.[70]

❧ ❧ ❧

At the early Song court, collecting was deeply entangled with other ways emperors showed their devotion to culture. Among the most treasured objects were books and calligraphy that former emperors had written or read. The Palace Library was not merely a place to house the cultural objects collected but also a place where literary projects could be initiated and distinguished scholars given employment. Visits to the Palace Library offered emperors opportunities to show that they were men of culture by composing poems or leaving samples of their calligraphy, which could then be carved onto stone for all visitors to see.

Imperial patronage of men of culture was different from other sorts of imperial patronage. The English term "patronage" is used to refer to a wide range of relationships. When the court hired or gave commissions to painters, builders, merchants, and the like, the patronage relationship may well have defined the social and political positions of those being patronized. Court patronage of the educated class was much more diffuse and multi-stranded; demonstration of appreciation of their literary and cultural activities coexisted with more direct patronage, such as appointing them to office or providing schools for them to prepare for the examinations. In other words, support for the arts and letters colored the relationship between the throne and the educated class, but did not define it—too much else was going on.

Collecting differed in interesting ways from other ways emperors showed themselves as patrons of the educated class. Offering talented men jobs in the government was of direct economic benefit to the men. Although the government offered financial incentives to those who turned over their books and art treasures to the court, the bargain may not have been financially advantageous for the owners, and at times they may have felt coerced. Ambitious local officials who discovered that a local collector had a calligraphy that the emperor would be delighted to receive may have given the collector little choice about "offering" it to the throne. There was a way out in the case of books; if collectors wanted to keep them, they could lend them while a copy was made. But in the case of paintings and calligraphies, copies were valued less highly than originals.

Another difference between collecting and other ways emperors could testify to their appreciation of culture was in its cumulative effects. Zhenzong had to demonstrate his own appreciation of poetry composed at his parties; he could not rest satisfied that his father had done enough in that regard. But he did not need to collect books already collected by his father—so long as they were not destroyed by fire, at any rate. Thus, the dynasty's standing as the guardian of culturally valued objects rose over time as more objects were added to the collections.

A third difference is that the collections did not have as public a character as the displays of the emperors' calligraphy or the many book projects that they sponsored. Officials favored with appointments in the Palace Library got to see objects held there; sometimes other officials got to see them as well, but most of the time the objects were concealed from view. The main way to make the collections more visible was not to invite people to view them but to produce a catalogue of them. This was done for the first time in 1041, but only for books.

Song emperors may have shown their respect for scholars and scholarly activities, but scholars didn't necessarily respond with enthusiasm. Many gestures could be interpreted more than one way. Taizong's readiness to have his calligraphy reproduced and distributed could be seen as megalomania or a crude attempt to promote his own style rather than an expression of his love of calligraphy. Buying up books and art works for the palace collection could be seen as strengthening the center at the expense of distant regions. Moreover, politics inevitably intruded. Thus, honors bestowed on one group of scholars might displease another. Scholar-officials displeased with an emperor's foreign policy, support for Daoism, or choice of grand councilors were not always easy to win over through gifts of calligraphy. These sorts of tensions do not seem to have been especially acute during the first century of Song rule, but during the subsequent reform era, initiated by Shenzong, strains in emperor-literati relationships become more pronounced, placing in question many of the ways emperors showed honor to the culture of the educated class.

CHAPTER 2

Strains in Emperor-Literati Relations during the Reform Era

Formerly, during the Yuanyou period [of Zhezong's minority, 1086–1093], powerful officials monopolized the government and led evil factions to slander the good government and excellent institutions of the former worthies and make reckless charges against them. During the Shaosheng period [1094–1097] when Zhezong personally took charge of the government, he clearly saw this group's deceptions and banished them in full accord with the law. When I took over, the slate was wiped clean and the [banned officials] were all taken back and brought to court. And yet they conspired to restore [the Yuanyou system]. Stubbornly they took ruining [the New Policies] to be payback and hostility to be their job as they uttered slander after slander. They would not stop until they had totally replaced the institutions of [Shenzong's] Xining and Yuanfeng eras by those of the Yuanyou period.

—Huizong's edict of 1102/5/23

SONG SOURCES PORTRAY EMPERORS AS MAGNANIMOUSLY GRANTING favors to the educated among their subjects. In reality, of course, the relationship between Song emperors and the educated class was not one-way; the educated elite, especially those holding office, could exert pressure on emperors by prolonged resistance to appointments and policies. In other words, although Song China was in theory an autocracy, with the emperor empowered to choose his officials freely and issue new laws at will, Song emperors were often frustrated by their inability to get their officials to comply with their wishes. This was especially true during the reform period (the reigns of Shenzong, 1067–1085, Zhezong, 1085–1100, and Huizong, 1100–1125).

Neither Shenzong nor Zhezong expended much effort on presenting themselves as men of culture. They did not draw attention to their love of reading or practicing calligraphy, nor did they devote as much time to poetry parties or other culture-centered entertaining of their high officials as Taizong, Zhenzong, and Renzong had done. Neither one of them initiated major book projects or an expansion of the Palace Library. Thus, the bitter factional disputes of their reigns became the dominating element in their relationship with educated men. Huizong's collecting initiatives should be seen as part of his campaign to recast emperor-literati relations, to return to the political climate of the first century of Song rule, when emperors, by embracing their role as patrons, were viewed as fundamentally on the side of the literati.

The political side of the emperor-literati relationship was worked out in two principal arenas, which can loosely be termed the "audience hall" and "literati opinion circles." The small group of officials who met regularly with the emperor—members of the Council of State, censors and policy criticism officials, and the top officials of major bureaus and agencies, who can be thought of as the "audience hall"—had the most direct say on the issues referred to the emperor. Chief among these were personnel issues, such as whom to appoint or promote, or whom to dismiss or demote. The emperor had to give explicit authorization for major initiatives, ranging from military campaigns to changes in tax-collection procedures. Decisions made in the audience hall were high-stakes decisions, upon which men's careers and fortunes depended; they could result in major expenditures and affect the economic fate of different regions of the country and sectors of the economy. It is not surprising that many educated men were intensely interested in what went on in the audience hall and who had influence there.

Literati opinion circles were much less concrete entities referred to at court as "outside discussion" (*waiyi*), "the common opinion" (*zhonglun*), "public discussion" (*yuyi*), "the literati" (*shiren*), "scholar-officials" (*shidafu*), and the like. These terms referred vaguely to what was discussed among educated men outside the audience hall. Officials serving in censorial and policy criticism posts were charged with bringing outside opinion to the ruler's attention and thus played a major role in articulating "the common opinion." In theory, when policy criticism and censorial officials fulfilled their duties well, no single group of officials could monopolize access to the emperor. From the point of view of those who felt like outsiders (most of whom were nevertheless officials of some sort), imperial deference to "public opinion" was part of the implicit contract between the ruler and his officials (or even the educated class as a whole): they would serve loyally, but he would listen to their concerns and ideas.[1]

When first on the throne, Huizong tried to change the political culture of factional strife. He brought leading men from both the reform and the anti-reform camps to court and attempted to get them to moderate their language and work together. When these steps failed to work, he sided with the reformers and appointed Cai Jing as his grand councilor. With Cai Jing's advice and encouragement, Huizong took three simultaneous steps to try to alter the ruler-literati relationship. He initiated a huge expansion of the government school system, establishing direct relations between the government and the wider educated class at the county and prefectural level. He issued three successive lists of men he did not want in his government (and did not want others to admire). And he began addressing the literati more directly by issuing large numbers of edicts in his own hand and having replicas of key edicts placed where literati in and out of office could see them. All three of these efforts had a similar goal: to gain support for his administration among potential office-holders and the wider educated class.

At the same time that Huizong promoted Confucian education, he also took a gradually deepening interest in Daoism. He was intrigued by the ideas and special powers of Daoist masters, sponsored several Daoist book projects, and built a series of Daoist temples. From 1119 to 1120 he even went so far as to make Buddhist temples and clergy adopt Daoist names and costumes. These measures certainly were not part of any campaign to win allies in the literati class, and generally made that task more difficult as scholar-officials came to resent the privileges granted to Daoist clergy.

Although the outlines of these events are well-documented, historians are much better informed about the thoughts of the most vocal of the anti-reformers than about the ideas of the thousands of men who served in Huizong's government—even his half-dozen highest officials. This is because when the histories were compiled during the Southern Song period, Huizong's leading officials were viewed as so evil that their words should not be preserved. Not only do Cai Jing's collected works not survive but even his biography in the *Song History* quotes very little of his writings, even his memorials.[2] By contrast, indictments of Cai Jing have been preserved in large quantity. To understand the situation as it appeared to Huizong, not to men two or three generations later, these biases in the sources must be taken into account.

The Reform Movement and the Reaction It Evoked

Shenzong had large ambitions when he took the throne at age twenty-one. He wanted to solve the problem of inadequate government revenues so that he could afford to launch military campaigns to push Song's northern neighbors out of territory he believed was properly Chinese. The high officials he had inherited from his father discouraged his ambitions. Fu Bi urged him to not even mention war for twenty years. His chief censor, Sima Guang, urged him to concentrate on rectifying his own heart and to leave to his officials the bothersome details of government. He also objected to Shenzong disrupting the normal process of government by sending palace eunuchs to investigate provincial officials. Shenzong became more and more irritated with the limitations the senior officials tried to place on him. Then an official warned him that the grand councilor, Han Qi, had monopolized power in the Council of State for so long that the position of emperor had been weakened. Han Qi soon retired, and Shenzong began bringing in new men who could help him pursue a more activist course.[3]

The man Shenzong eventually turned to was Wang Anshi (1021–1086), an experienced, intelligent, and hardworking official with original ideas (see fig. 2.1). Some years earlier, in 1058, Wang Anshi had submitted a long memorial with detailed criticisms of many government institutions—especially the civil-service examinations, which he believed selected self-serving and unimaginative men rather than problem solvers.[4] At his first audience with Wang Anshi in 1068/4, Shenzong asked him how his predecessors had managed to keep things going if the government was in as bad shape as he argued. In the memorial he wrote in response, Wang Anshi painted a dire picture: Because the peasantry was overburdened by labor service, the army full of unfit soldiers, the bureaucracy staffed by obstructionist time-servers, and the emperors surrounded by women and eunuchs, the government was not prepared for a major natural disaster or a barbarian invasion, either of which could happen at any time. Shenzong soon announced that Wang was the one to help him achieve his goals, and by early 1069 he had put Wang on the Council of State. Wang cautioned Shenzong that the mediocrities and evil men in the government would do everything they could to keep them from accomplishing their goals, and that they would therefore have to begin by removing those who would stand in their way. The only way to maintain imperial authority, he argued, was to subdue the cacophony of conflicting opinions.[5]

Over the course of the next three to four years, Wang Anshi proposed and Shenzong approved a long series of measures that came to be called the New Policies. Many of these policies were designed to solve the government's financial shortfalls. To increase revenues, state monopolies on tea, salt, and wine were expanded. Land was resurveyed to make land taxes more equitable. Farmers were offered low-cost loans and a tax in place of compulsory labor service. The cost of defense was reduced by forming a militia. To speed up the introduction of these reforms, Wang Anshi set up a Finance Planning Commission to bypass the existing bureaucracy.[6]

Another problem Wang Anshi tackled was the civil-service recruitment system, a subject that had been widely discussed by reformers since Fan Zhongyan in the 1030s and 1040s. Like earlier reformers, Wang saw the goal as finding and nurturing men of ability. He wanted the government to play a larger role in education and wanted the examinations to select men based more on their understanding of policy issues than on their ability to write poetry. Like the Confucian teacher Cheng

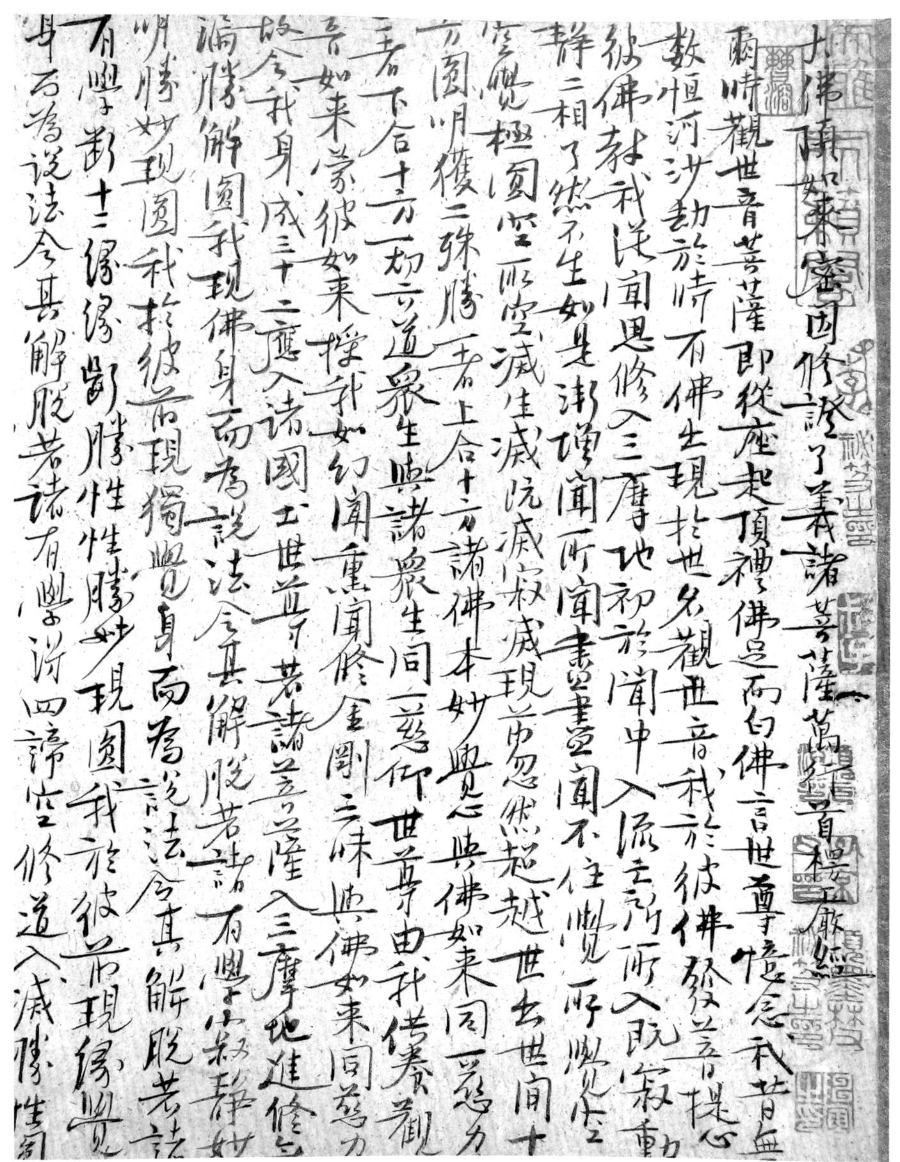

FIG. 2.1
Wang Anshi (1021–1086), *Précis of the Lengyan Sutra* (detail). Handscroll, ink on paper, 29.9 × 119 cm. Shanghai Museum. Even Wang Anshi's political opponents recognized that he was an accomplished poet and a man of learning. His calligraphic style, seen here, was also quite distinctive. This piece was written in 1085, during his retirement, when he had time to pursue his interests in Buddhism.

Hao, he thought that ideally the examination system should be replaced by a network of local schools. He believed that if everyone were taught the way of the ancient kings found in the classics, it would be possible to achieve agreement on basic values; deviant ideas then would no longer find adherents.[7]

Wang Anshi turned to *The Rites of Zhou,* one of the Confucian classics, to justify many of these measures. Past reformers had turned to this book many times, for it described a perfectly designed government said to have operated in the early Zhou period.[8] As James Liu notes, Wang was attracted to *The Rites of Zhou* because of its utopian nature. "It extols the ancient Zhou period by showing the active leadership of the state in setting up a number of political, economic, and social systems which regulated these respective phases of the people's life. It was this highly idealized picture of a perfect order that furnished inspiration and theoretical justification to those who endeavored to discard the existing systems in favor of new ones." In other words, *The Rites of Zhou* validates an assertive government that uses regulation to achieve a moral society.[9]

The New Policies' expansion of state schools directly aided scholars but was also intended to mold them in ways that served state needs. Wang had the poetry component of the civil-service examination dropped. He commissioned new commentaries on the classics, which became required reading for candidates hoping to do well on the examinations. In 1080 the campus of the National Academy was expanded to eighty buildings and reorganized into three grades or "halls." The lowest or outer hall was expanded to accommodate 2,000 students, the inner or intermediate hall, 300, and the upper hall, 100. Monthly and annual tests were instituted to promote students from one level to the next, and, in theory, students at the highest level could test directly into office.[10]

The New Policies evoked an outpouring of criticism and resistance almost from the start. Some critics charged that it was disrespectful to former emperors to change their policies. In 1069 the censor Lü Hui wrote a vituperative ten-point memorial accusing Wang Anshi of arrogance, nepotism, and forming a faction. When Wang Anshi offered to resign, Shenzong had Lü Hui demoted instead. Han Qi charged that the Green Sprouts Loan policy would end up being too attractive to the poorest farmers, who would take loans they could not repay, which in turn would mean that better-off farmers would likely end up having to cover the arrears. When Shenzong was not swayed, Han Qi retired, as did many other senior officials.[11]

From the perspective of Wang Anshi and Shenzong, opposition to the New Policies was tantamount to obstruction, and challenged the emperor's authority. To implement their program, they needed officials who supported it, not ones dead set against it. Officials deemed obstructive were usually assigned offices outside the capital, but when the court wanted to be harsher, it could send them far away. To many in the educated class, however, these steps were fundamentally illegitimate, since the "speaking" officials were as much a part of the body politic as the emperor and had an obligation to warn the ruler when bad policies or appointments were proposed.

The men who came to function as leaders of the opposition played a crucial role in this political drama. Several traits enabled particular men to function as spokesmen for "common opinion." It helped greatly if they wrote well, so that their

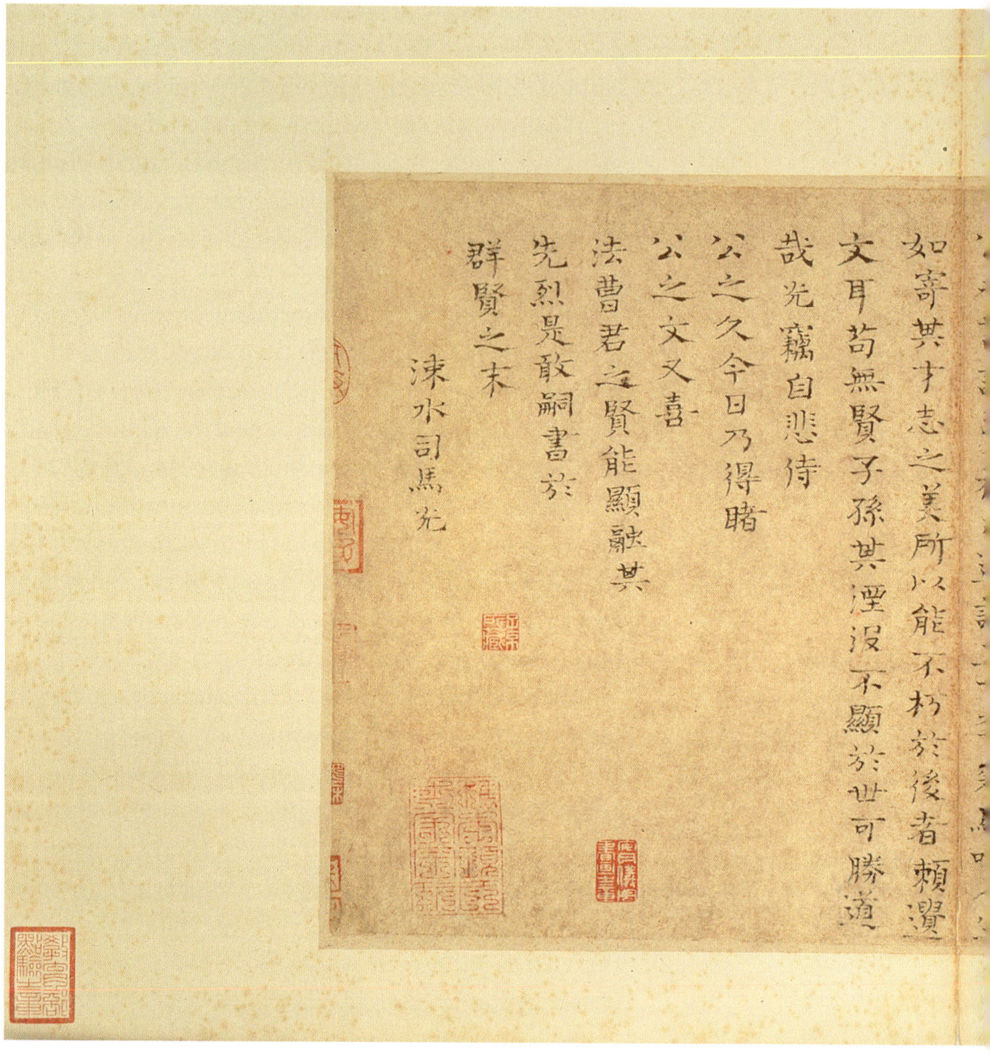
如寄其才志之美所以能不朽於後者賴選
文耳苟無賢子孫其湮沒不顯於世可勝道
哉光竊自悲侍
公之久今日乃得睹
公之文又喜
法曹君之賢能顯融其
先烈是敢嗣書於
群賢之末
涑水司馬光

memorials were worth passing around. Officials were also much admired for speaking up to power, for seeming to jeopardize their own careers to inform the emperor of serious shortcomings in his closest advisors or their chosen policies. Connections also helped, whether based on kinship, friendship, or teacher-student or superior-subordinate relationships. These traits help explain how Sima Guang and Su Shi became leaders of the opposition. They were at different stages of their careers, but were alike in evoking imperial ire that lasted beyond their lifetimes.

Sima Guang (1019–1086) came from a north China family that had long produced officials.[12] He passed the examinations at nineteen and began a steady rise through

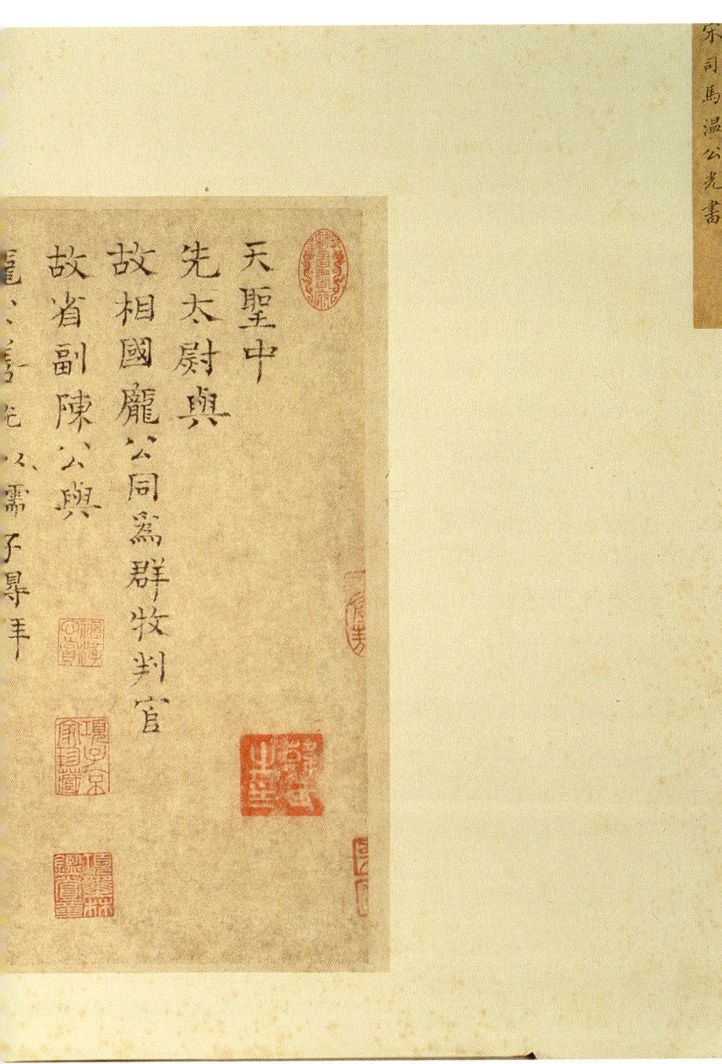

FIG. 2.2
Sima Guang (1019–1086), colophon, dated 1079. Album leaf, ink on paper, 30.3 × 48.6 cm. National Palace Museum, Taiwan, Republic of China. This colophon was written for a piece of calligraphy done fifty years earlier by the grandfather of a friend. Sima Guang was not known for his calligraphy, but his self-discipline and respect for established norms can be seen in his precise and careful writing.

the ranks of office, helped by friends of his father. He wrote excellent prose, but was not much of a poet. By his late thirties, he was in the capital, serving in the top post in the Bureau of Policy Criticism. He played a key role in several crises; he helped urge Emperor Renzong to adopt a son as a potential heir and then, after that heir succeeded as Yingzong, he helped him rule on his own without the interference of Renzong's widow. Still, Sima Guang was not someone who always took the emperor's side; he strongly protested when Yingzong wanted to elevate the honors for his natural father.[13] Sima Guang's memorials to the throne on this issue circulated widely among his contemporaries, adding to his reputation (see fig. 2.2).

By the time Shenzong came to the throne in 1067, Sima Guang, then in his late forties, was one of the senior statesmen. After Shenzong chose Wang Anshi as his grand councilor, Sima Guang brought up objections to each of Wang's proposals. He argued, for instance, that training peasants in the use of weapons would give rise to banditry.[14] When Shenzong politely dismissed most of his critiques, Sima Guang warned him that he was listening only to those who agreed with him, which was dangerous for an emperor whose experience outside the palace was limited. After his repeated protests failed to dampen Shenzong's enthusiasm for the reforms, Sima Guang insisted on leaving court. Shenzong continued to treat him respectfully, however, and gave him a sinecure that allowed him to move to Luoyang and devote his time to writing the *Comprehensive Mirror for Aid in Government,* the most ambitious history attempted in over a thousand years. In this era, Luoyang became a center for the opposition, home not only to Sima Guang but to several of the most eminent retired officials (including Fu Bi and Wen Yanbo), as well as the influential Confucian thinkers Cheng Yi, Cheng Hao, and Shao Yong. These men regularly visited one another, which undoubtedly helped them retain their conviction that their stance was right. They also corresponded with like-minded men around the country.[15]

Seventeen years younger than Sima Guang, Su Shi (1036–1101) grew up in Sichuan in western China.[16] He was ranked second when he passed the *jinshi* exams in 1056, then in 1061 he passed the much more exceptional decree exam for "direct speech and full admonition," for which he had to submit fifty essays. His score on that exam was the highest ever given in the dynasty, making him an instant celebrity. Still a junior official when Shenzong began introducing the New Policies, he was appointed to a post in the censorate, where he wrote critiques of each new policy in turn.[17] He quickly attracted the support of Sima Guang and the anger of Wang Anshi. In 1071 Su Shi requested reassignment out of the capital. For the remainder of Shenzong's reign, he served in provincial posts, mostly in the south. He was thus not a part of the Luoyang opposition circles, but he had such a high reputation as a writer that his ideas quickly reached a national audience.

Su Shi thrived during the years he served in the provinces, and wrote many of his most famous works then. He often wrote in a satirical vein, poking fun at those in power. For instance, to celebrate the first bath of his month-old son, he wrote:

> All I want is a son who is doltish and dumb.
> No setbacks or hardships will obstruct his path to the highest court posts.[18]

Su Shi went further than his contemporaries in using poetry to vent his frustrations, and his friends tried to curb his jibes. Huang Tingjian wrote in a letter to a nephew,

"Su Shi's writing is the most marvelous in all the world. His only shortcoming is that he likes to rebuke people. In that you must not follow him."[19]

In 1076 Wang Anshi retired, and Shenzong took over personal management of the reform program. This change troubled one censor, who in 1077 charged that officials on the Council of State, by letting the emperor make all of the decisions, were failing in their duty to govern.[20] One can easily imagine that Shenzong saw the situation differently.

In the late 1070s Su Shi was arrested and thrown in prison on the grounds that his poems slandered the emperor and his appointed officials. Su later claimed that he had thought of committing suicide by starving himself, but changed his mind after Shenzong sent a special envoy to make sure he was not mistreated.[21] After he had been interrogated for about five weeks, Su Shi agreed to "tell all" and explain the indirect criticisms in his poems. He had written this poem in 1073:

> An old man of seventy, sickle at his waist,
> Feels guilty the spring bamboo and bracken are sweet.
> It's not that the music of Shao has made him lose his sense of taste,
> It's just that he's eaten his food for three months without salt.

In his confession Su Shi explained the poem as follows:

> This says that the people in the mountains are impoverished and have nothing to eat. Although old, this man must still pick himself bamboo shoots and bracken to satisfy his hunger. The salt laws of the time were too severe and strict. People in poor and remote places had no salt to eat. This had been the situation for several months, as when the sage of old lost his appetite when hearing the music of Shao (cf. *Analects* 7.13). How can the mountain people enjoy eating bland food? By this I criticized the severity of the salt laws.[22]

The prosecutors, in making their case, were particularly concerned that Su Shi's poems had been printed and, as a consequence, circulated widely. They complained that whenever a famine or flood occurred, people expected to learn that Su Shi had written a poem blaming the New Policies for the disaster.[23]

When Su Shi's case was presented to Shenzong, he threw out some of the more strained interpretations, insisting that not every poem was a covert political protest. Shenzong did not approve the prosecutors' request for the death penalty, but he did banish Su Shi to an unimportant city on the Yangzi River (Huangzhou) and forbade him to speak out on government matters. In addition, the friends of Su Shi who had received his poems or helped him get them printed faced penalties. Three were also banished, and twenty-five, including Sima Guang, were fined.[24] Su Shi's reputation as the consummate literatus was if anything enhanced by his persecution. Not only his poetry and prose but also his calligraphy and paintings were highly admired (see fig. 2.3).

The Yuanyou Period Under Empress Dowager Gao

Shenzong died of illness in his thirties and was succeeded by his eldest son, then only ten *sui*, known as Zhezong. For the next eight years, known as the Yuanyou reign period (1086–1093), Zhezong was under the domination of his grandmother, Empress Dowager Gao, who served as regent. Gao had never approved the New Policies, and once she was in charge of the government, she promptly brought back to court the most famous of the opponents, Sima Guang. He was by then in his midsixties and ailing, but he wanted so much to dismantle the reform program that he accepted the post of grand councilor. Soon the reformers in top offices were replaced with conservatives. One of the most strident of the new speaking officials was Su Shi's brother Su Che, who called the reformer Cai Que obsequious, incompetent, and wicked. The conservatives quickly saw to it that the reformers were treated even worse than they had been during Shenzong's reign. In 1089 Cai Que was banished to Lingnan because a poem he wrote could be read as covert slander of Empress Dowager Gao. This was the first time in seventy years that an official had been banished to the "deadly" regions of the far south; some of the conservatives realized that they were setting a dangerous precedent.[25]

Su Shi, by then forty-eight, returned to the capital in 1085 and was given an important court post. He immediately disagreed with Sima Guang on a key matter, the commutation of labor service to a monetary assessment, which he believed was a good policy worth retaining. The personnel of the Censorate, now all followers of Sima Guang, quickly attacked Su Shi. Su came to think that little had improved in how the government operated since the speaking officials were no more independent than before.[26]

When Sima Guang died in 1086/9, his reputation was enormous. Both the empress dowager and the boy emperor went to his home to express their grief by his coffin. Su Shi, in the epitaph he wrote for Sima Guang, reported that a commoner had printed copies of a portrait of Sima Guang that people all over the country had purchased in order to make offerings to his image. Tens of thousands of people traveled to the capital to take part in the funeral, and more than a hundred followed his funeral procession all the way to his home, more than a hundred miles away.[27]

Su Shi's relationships with other conservatives deteriorated after Sima Guang's

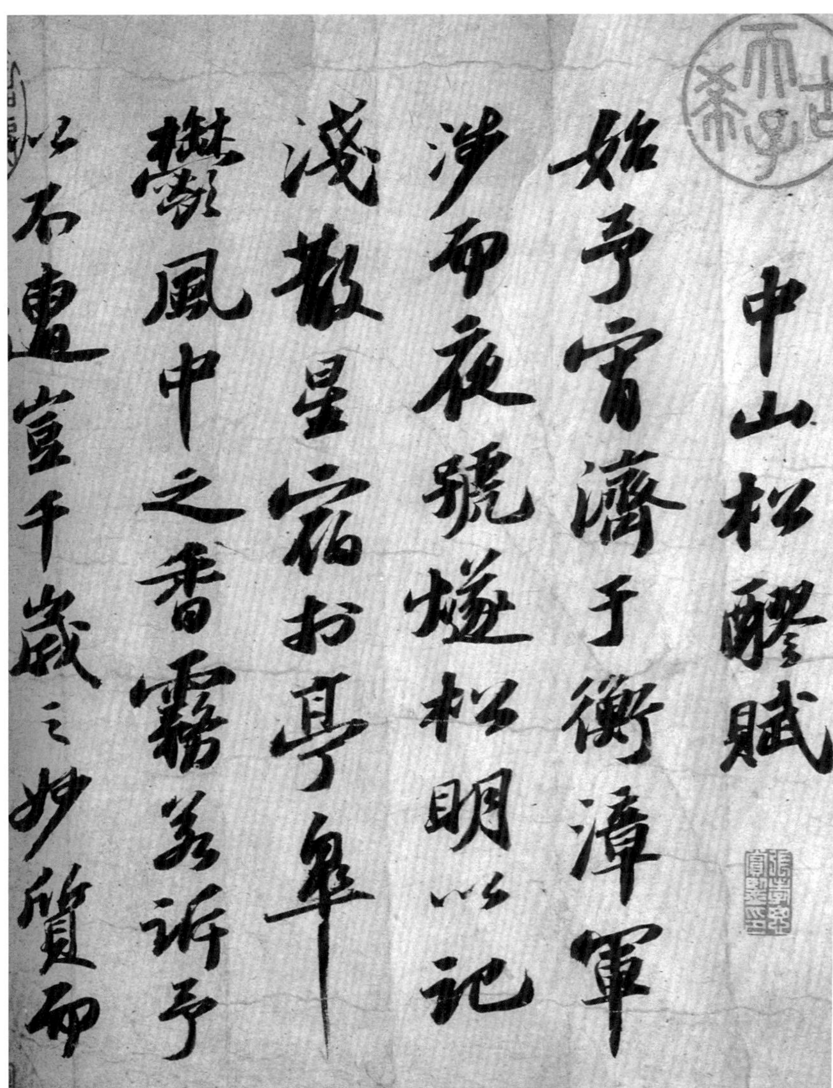

Fig. 2.3
Su Shi (1036–1101), *Pine Trees and Dregs of Wine at Central Mountain* (detail). Handscroll, ink on paper, 28.3 × 306.3 cm. Jilin Provincial Museum. Su Shi was considered an excellent calligrapher, with a bold, fluid hand. Especially appreciated are works like this one that he both composed and wrote out. After Shen Peng 1986:26.

death, and by 1088 he asked to be assigned outside the capital to get away from the censors who seemed to have it in for him. When he returned to the capital in 1091, a follower of Cheng Yi serving in the censorate accused him of malfeasance. Soon he left the capital to take up another prefectural appointment. His return to court in 1093 was similarly unsuccessful. These banishments did not hurt his reputation, however. While serving as prefect of Hangzhou, Su Shi wrote dozens of memorials requesting famine relief, which helped form the image of Su as a compassionate conservative who worked hard to alleviate the people's suffering.

Zhezong's Personal Rule

Empress Dowager Gao died late in 1093, making it possible for Zhezong to rule on his own. He deeply resented his grandmother's domination and returned to the policies of his father. Wang Anshi was no longer living, but Zhezong brought back men who had been purged in the Yuanyou period, such as Zhang Dun and Cai Bian. Sima Guang was posthumously demoted and castigated for deceiving the empress dowager, monopolizing power, and being intolerant of disagreement. Although Zhezong did not approve a request to open Sima Guang's tomb and smash his coffin, he did approve destroying the stele inscribed with Su Shi's epitaph. A few years later someone suggested that the woodblocks of the *Comprehensive Mirror* be destroyed, but because Shenzong had written the preface for it, the blocks were spared. It was decided that the historical records of Shenzong's reign would have to be rewritten, since the conservatives had portrayed Wang Anshi and other reformers very negatively. Wang Anshi's scholarship came back into favor and his etymologies were again printed by the Directorate of Education.[28]

Campaigns against the "Yuanyou faction" recurred several times during Zhezong's personal rule. In 1095 memorials submitted during the period 1085 to 1094 were scrutinized to compile a list of those who had been most critical of the New Policies. Two years later, a group of leading conservatives accused of having plotted with Empress Dowager Gao to depose Zhezong were banished to Lingnan. Moreover, an official blacklist was issued naming thirty-seven men to be deprived of official status. Many of those on this list were deceased, but their demotions had an impact on their descendants, who lost the benefit of their ranks, such as entering office through the protection privilege.[29]

With the reformers back in power, Su Shi's banishment was made more punitive. First he was banished to a remote prefecture in Guangzhou and forbidden to speak out on government matters. Then, in 1097, when he was over sixty, he was sent to the most distant place of all, Hainan Island, where his health deteriorated.[30]

A particularly illuminating source on court infighting in this period is the administrative diary of Zeng Bu (1035–1107). The part that survives, covering the period from the third month of 1099 to the seventh month of 1100, attempts to record all important conversations Zeng Bu had with the emperor and at least some of the more important ones he had with other councilors outside the imperial presence. In 1099 Zeng Bu was one of four officials on the Council of State (the others were Zhang Dun, Cai Bian, and Xu Jiang). All four had very strong credentials in the reform movement. Zeng Bu and Zhang Dun, in their late fifties to early sixties, had both passed the *jinshi* exams before Wang Anshi came to power and had moved into court offices during the New Policies period. Cai Bian was more than a decade younger, but had the distinction of personally studying under Wang Anshi and marrying his daughter.[31]

Although to those excluded from Zhezong's court, those serving there seemed a coherent faction, those on the inside were aware of all sorts of friction. No two of the four on the Council of State seem to have consistently sided together. For instance, on 1099/7/28, Zeng Bu and Zhang Dun got into an argument; Zhang Dun complained that Zeng Bu had called him mentally defective, and Zeng Bu countered that Zhang Dun had said he talked like a woman nattering away in the courtyard. Threats to resign if one of the others was retained were not uncommon. Interestingly, even the brothers Cai Bian and Cai Jing were portrayed as frequently at odds with each other. In 1099/10, Zhezong discussed with Zeng Bu the friction between Cai Bian and Cai Jing. He had noticed that Cai Bian would not praise people close to Cai Jing, and that Cai Jing did not like people close to Cai Bian. Zeng Bu speculated that their wives probably did not get along, which Zhezong agreed was a common problem.[32]

Huizong's Initial Attempts to Manage Literati Opinion

Huizong succeeded to the throne in the first month of 1100 after Zhezong died without a son. Shenzong's widow Empress Dowager Xiang had been the one to select Huizong, and for the next half year she was consulted on major court decisions.[33] Even though quite young (nineteen *sui,* but only seventeen years and three months in full-year counting), Huizong would not have been totally ignorant of how the government actually worked or of the problem of factional politics. Just a few months earlier he had lost two of his tutors because they had given money to the conservative Zou Hao when he was banished from the capital.[34] Still, Huizong had much to learn, as Zeng Bu makes clear in his diary. Zeng Bu did not hide the fact that whenever he got the chance to speak to Huizong alone, he tried to undermine Huizong's confidence in his fellow councilors. Dealing with such men every day, Huizong had to learn how to evaluate their often conflicting advice and come up with ways to keep them under control.

Huizong started with a strong bias toward bringing back those who had been purged during his brother's reign and mentioned particular men. He thought it inappropriate that some of them had been banished to deadly places merely for what they had said. One of the first to return was Han Zhongyan, who had served in high posts during Empress Gao's regency. Cai Bian was worried by the prospect of the return of men whom he had helped send away, but Zeng Bu tried to reassure him that he could at least count on the emperor not to bring back Su Shi or Su Che, apparently already detecting Huizong's antipathy toward them.[35]

In this period Huizong enjoyed being told that his actions were well received. Zeng Bu pointed to the fact that someone had printed the edict appointing Han Zhongyan and seven others as evidence of literati opinion. Huizong asked in amazement, "Was it really printed?"[36] On 1100/2/13, when Zeng Bu again spoke of the need to fill vacancies in the speaking offices, Huizong on his own brought up Zou Hao and remarked on the injustice of his having been banished to a deadly place. On 2/26 a long list of prominent men were called back from banishment, including Su Che, Cheng Yi, Huang Tingjian, Zhang Lei, and Zou Hao.[37]

Usually Zeng Bu saw Huizong in the company of the other members of the Council of State, but he had opportunities to remain after they left to talk to Huizong privately. Moreover, because Zhang Dun was put in charge of Zhezong's burial, Zhang was away for extended periods, giving Zeng Bu opportunities to try to convince Huizong that neither Zhang Dun nor Cai Bian could be trusted. On 2/21, for instance, Zeng Bu remarked that Zhezong was intelligent but had been overly influenced by Zhang Dun's opinions, and that Zhang Dun, motivated by the desire for revenge, often went too far in demoting people.[38]

After three months on the throne, Huizong still thought he had the power to do many things by fiat. When he made the assumption that he could get rid of Zhang Dun by issuing a rescript, Zeng Bu corrected him. The matter was not so simple. He would first have to appoint new censors who would make accusations against Cai Bian, which would prompt Cai Bian to resign. Only after Cai Bian was out of the way would it be possible to get Zhang Dun himself to resign. Huizong, we are told, was impressed with Zeng Bu's grasp of political tactics.[39]

Zeng Bu had occasions to explain to Huizong that "outside opinion" was often faulty. One occasion concerned reassigning Cai Jing out of the capital, which had required the cooperation of Zhang Dun and Cai Bian. As it turned out, however, Empress Dowager Xiang liked Cai Jing and insisted on keeping him in the capital. When people outside the court learned that Cai Jing would stay in the capital after all, they assumed Zhang Dun had used his influence to keep him there. As Zeng Bu explained to Huizong, this was evidence that outsiders do not understand what happens at court, since in reality Zhang Dun detested Cai Jing. Moreover, the other members of the Council of State did not obediently do whatever Zhang Dun told them.[40]

When it was in his interest, however, Zeng Bu urged Huizong to listen to common opinion. For instance, when Cai Bian urged Huizong not to appoint the conservative Chen Guan on the grounds that he was too close to Zeng Bu, Zeng Bu countered that his own view was the common one, and that this was a case of "When the superior man calls the inferior man evil, the inferior man calls the superior man evil." In other words, in this case, he argued that the ruler should value the "common opinion of the world" over "one person's private view."[41]

Memorials were one way Huizong could judge "common opinion" for himself. On 4/13 Huizong told Zeng Bu that he had already received more than 100 memorials attacking Zhang Dun, and the next day he said he had 200 to 300 attacking Zhang Dun and Cai Bian.[42] Everyone, it seemed, wanted to influence the course Huizong would take. Many of the memorials submitted to him were ad hominem attacks on particular men, often based on a mishmash of rumors. To give an example, in the ninth month of 1100, the policy criticism official Chen Guan, a favorite of the conservatives, wrote a long memorial indicting Cai Jing. The main accusation was that he had formed friendships with relatives of Huizong's legal mother, the Empress Dowager Xiang. The main evidence was that Cai Jing had written a funerary inscription for a relative named Xiang Zai in which Xiang said "My whole life I have made friends with *shidafu*, and among them, no one has been closer to me than Recipient of Edicts Cai." Chen also quoted an elegy Cai had written for another Xiang, in which he wrote, "He had good words at the end of the Yuanfeng era," which Chen interpreted to mean that he must have slandered Empress Dowager Gao, the heroine of the conservative faction. Why it would be a crime to be on friendly terms with a man in the eminent family from which Empress Xiang came is never made clear. Chen wrote as though Empress Dowager Xiang was running the government, when in fact while she had participated the grand councilors had always called on Huizong first, and she had very rarely objected to Huizong's decisions. Moreover, she had withdrawn totally from participation in court decisions two months earlier. Chen also accused Cai Jing of conspiring with Cai Bian. Huizong, who knew that Cai Jing and Cai Bian frequently tried to undermine each other, must have found this memorial rather hysterical.[43]

By the sixth month of 1100, Huizong had effectively curbed the followers of Zhang Dun and Cai Bian, by both assigning them outside of the capital and bringing in many of those they had ousted just a few years earlier. But the tone of many of the new appointees disappointed Huizong. On 6/8 he told the councilors, "Most of the censorial and policy criticism officials you have recently recommended lost their posts during the Shaosheng period [i.e., when Zhenzong began ruling on his own, 1094–1097]. I am concerned that they harbor resentment. Their statements are often too extreme. You councilors ought to tell them not to go too far in their comments." Zeng Bu advised Huizong that this was not possible because the councilors and the speaking officials did not meet together, an answer Huizong refused to accept. Zeng Bu then pointed out that speaking officials did not like being warned, and suggested that Huizong cope by taking their tendency to exaggerate into account when assessing their charges.[44]

The next day Huizong told Zeng Bu that Han Zhongyan was reasonably balanced, but that Li Qingchen was extremely biased. To him, "everything done under Empress Gao was right." He also objected to Huang Lü on the same grounds. The following day Huizong came up with a way to make his disapproval of vituperative language known: he would dismiss the censor Xing Shu for it. Just as important, he wanted the edict dismissing Xing Shu to be clear on the reason for his dismissal. Zeng Bu's brother Zeng Zhao was given the task of drafting it, and Huizong met with him in person to be sure he understood his assignment. This step did not yield much in the way of moderation, however. Just a few days later, on 6/16, Gong Guai's impeachment of Cai Jing made Huizong fume.[45]

In 1100/10, with Zhang Dun finally removed from power, Zeng Bu was promoted to junior grand councilor. Through much of 1101, Huizong maintained a balance between the two opposed factions, with both Han Zhongyan and Zeng Bu serving the full year. Zeng Bu consistently spoke to Huizong of the need to work around factional hostilities, to make use of the best ideas from both sides and employ men with connections to each side, so long as they were not unrelentingly hostile or incapable of compromise. As reasonable as this sounds, Zeng does not seem to have been able to attract many officials to his position, and ad hominem attacks on him remained a constant irritant to Huizong.

Eventually, Huizong gave up hope of getting the two sides to work together. Realizing he had to choose, he opted for the reformers. On 1101/5/16, posthumous demotions were issued for high officials of the Yuanyou period, including Sima Guang and Wen Yanbo, as well as ones still living, such as Su Shi (who, however, would die two months later).[46]

What accounts for Huizong's change of heart? Zeng Bu gave his interpretation in a letter to his brother Zeng Zhao. In an earlier letter, Zhao had voiced his concerns that "good and upright scholars" had been leaving the court, while most of those taking their places had served under Zhang Dun and Cai Bian. Zhao warned Bu that since he had previously worked so hard against Zhang Dun and Cai Bian, he should not expect their followers to be willing to work with him now. Thus, if they returned to power, it would be a disaster for the entire Zeng family.[47] Zeng Bu wrote in reply:

> Ever since Huizong took the throne he has been acutely aware of the evils of the past, so he took in the men who had been banished in the Yuanyou period [when Empress Gao was regent] and sent away those who had acted vindictively in the Shaosheng

> period [when Zhezong ruled on his own]. His aim was to destroy factional thinking and eliminate evidence of differences, in order to unite the scholar stratum. And yet the Yuanyou partisans remained as one-sided as ever. Those who presented their views to the emperor all praised the Yuanyou period and denigrated the Xining and Yuanfeng eras [of Shenzong], just as was done in the Yuanyou period, disregarding the contrary direction of the previous reign and taking no account of the ruler's correct direction. Because of their own private ambitions, they want to force the emperor to cast aside Xining and follow Yuanyou. This has angered and depressed Huizong, and he increasingly resents the Yuanyou faction, who in turn put the blame on me. They conspire together and devise all sorts of strategies in their desire to oust me. This has upset the emperor even more.[48]

On 1101/8/23 Chen Guan submitted a memorial indicting Zeng Bu. When Huizong reacted negatively to it, Han Zhongyan and the others present urged that Chen Guan be banished to a prefectural post. Huizong then proposed a heavier punishment, but the officials tried to dissuade him, arguing, "What Guan said was definitely not appropriate, but if he is punished for it, he will become famous as a result. It would be better for Zeng Bu to bear it."[49] In other words, the emperor could inadvertently help his critics by making martyrs of them.

Cai Jing and the Attempt to Find New Allies

Having made the decision to side with the reformers, Huizong put Cai Jing on the Council of State and dismissed Zeng Bu. Huizong came to put great trust in Cai Jing, and also admired him as a calligrapher. On several occasions Huizong and Cai Jing collaborated on calligraphy and painting (see plates 7 and 8, and figs. 2.4, 2.5, and 2.6).[50]

During Cai Jing's first and second terms on the Council of State (1102–6 and 1107–9), Huizong experimented with several ways to gain the cooperation of the scholar-official class. He became a generous patron of education, the defining characteristic of the class. He made lists of the men they should not take as their models, the men he did not want in his government (or, if already deceased, not honored by his government). And he addressed educated men directly through edicts he claimed came from his own brush.

On 1102/5/10, after Cai Jing was back in the capital but before he had joined the Council of State, a memorial was submitted asking Huizong to expel from court all the petty men who had opposed reform. It argued that the leaders of the Yuanyou period had "committed crimes against Shenzong," and that when they had been allowed back into the government after Huizong first took the throne, they had

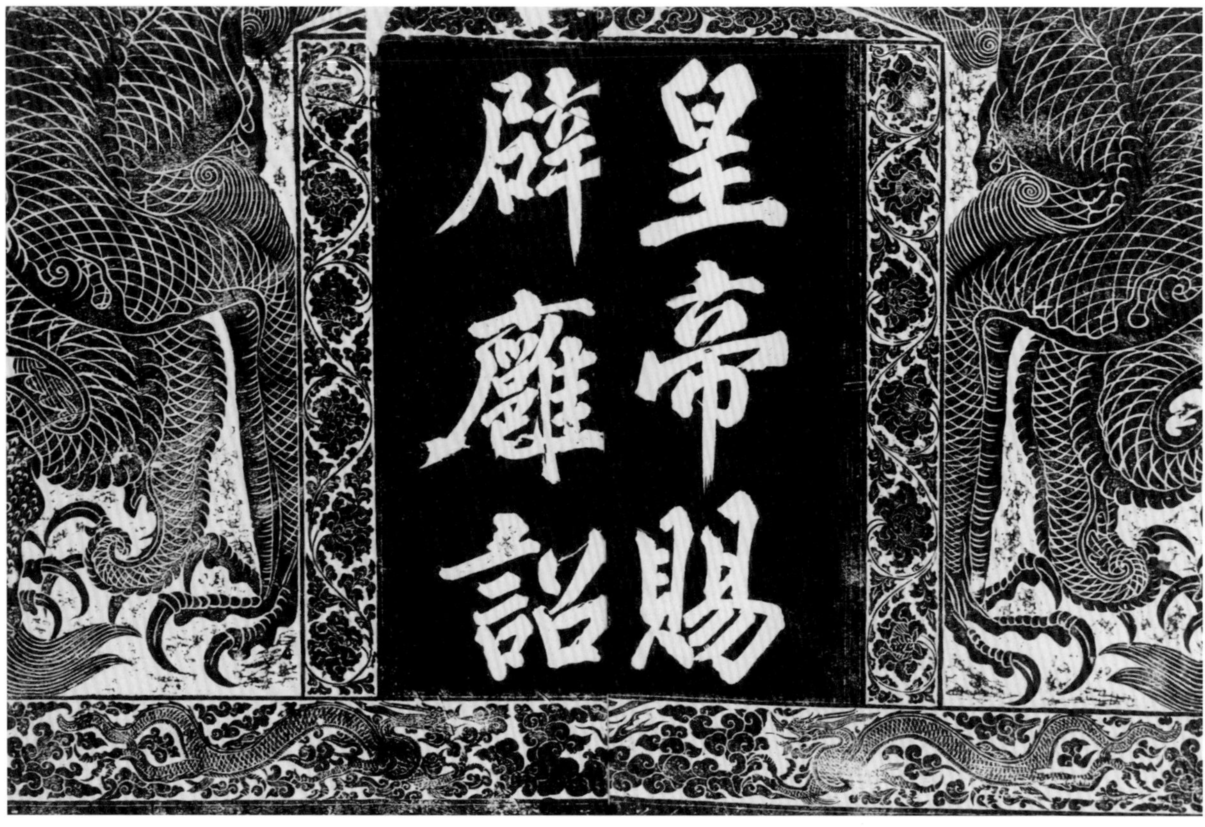

FIG. 2.4
Cai Jing (1047–1126), title for the Biyong stele. The stele itself, in Huizong's calligraphy, discusses the Three Halls educational system begun by Shenzong on the model of ancient precedents. Cai Jing's title reads "An Edict Bestowed by the Emperor on the Biyong Academy." From the rubbing held by the National Library of China.

spent their time indicting the true reformers. The memorial also claimed that only by removing these men could Huizong achieve Shenzong's great enterprise.[51] Soon other memorials followed, some listing specific men who needed to be ousted for their perfidy. Ten days later, on 1102/5/20, Huizong demoted more than fifty leading members of the conservative faction (including many already deceased, such as Sima Guang and Su Shi), and ruled that those still alive could no longer be given assignments in the capital. The next day charges were brought against the remonstrators who during the past two years had asked that these men's honors be restored. Two days after that (5/23), Huizong issued an edict that drew a contrast between his generosity to the conservatives, whom he had given good posts, and their refusal to cooperate. "Those in censorial and policy criticism posts continually vilified the reformers and could not be restrained, making it necessary to remove the most extreme of them." On 1102/i6/20 Huizong wrote out in his own hand an edict explaining Zou Hao's demotion, claiming that a memorial of his had maliciously attacked Zhezong.[52]

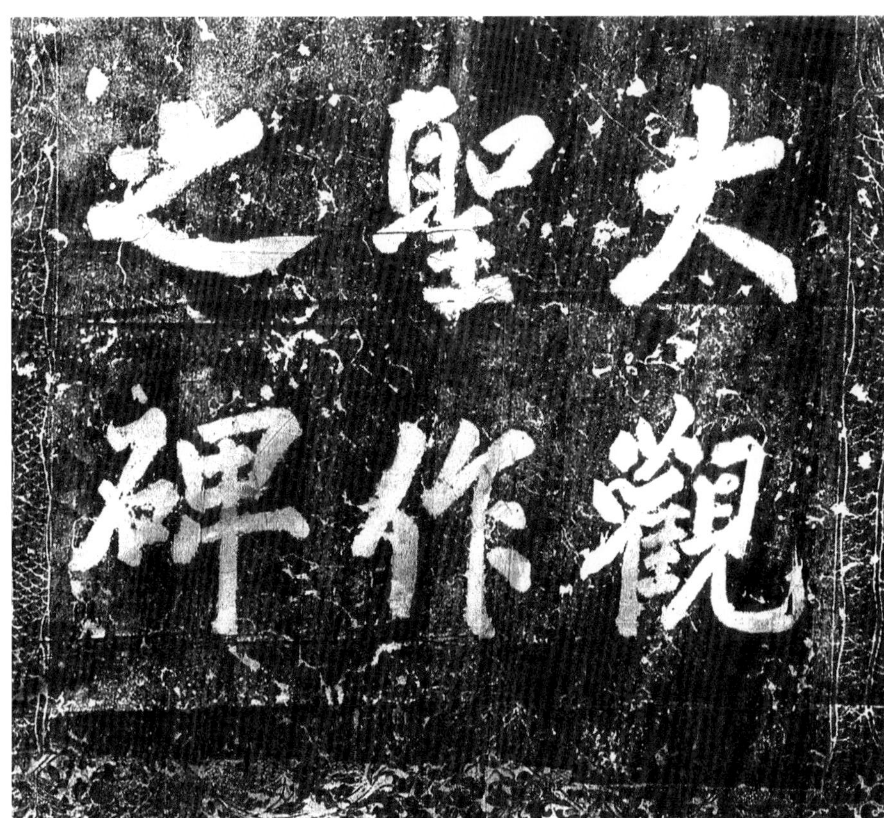

FIG. 2.5
Cai Jing's title for the Eight Virtues stele. The title reads "The Stele Done by the Sage in the Daguan Period." After Onoe et al. 1954–68 15:217.

About three months later (1102/8/22), Cai Jing proposed revamping the government school system, implementing ideas Wang Anshi had earlier articulated. He began by stating that education was a major priority and that schools needed to be set up throughout the country to nurture scholars. Cai Jing's plan involved increasing the number of teachers, students, and schools, as well as the size of lands set aside to cover school expenses. Not only prefectures but also counties should have schools, including primary schools for elementary education. Each school would have three grades, and tests would be used to promote students from one grade to the next within and between schools. Students who reached the National Academy could test directly into office. To support these expanded schools, local governments were instructed to draw on income from the "ever-normal" granaries and land that fell to their jurisdiction because there was no heir to inherit it.[53]

Two months later (1102/10/27), Huizong approved Cai Jing's proposal to expand the National Academy. To handle the increase in students being promoted into it from prefectural schools, the spaces in the upper and inner halls would be doubled

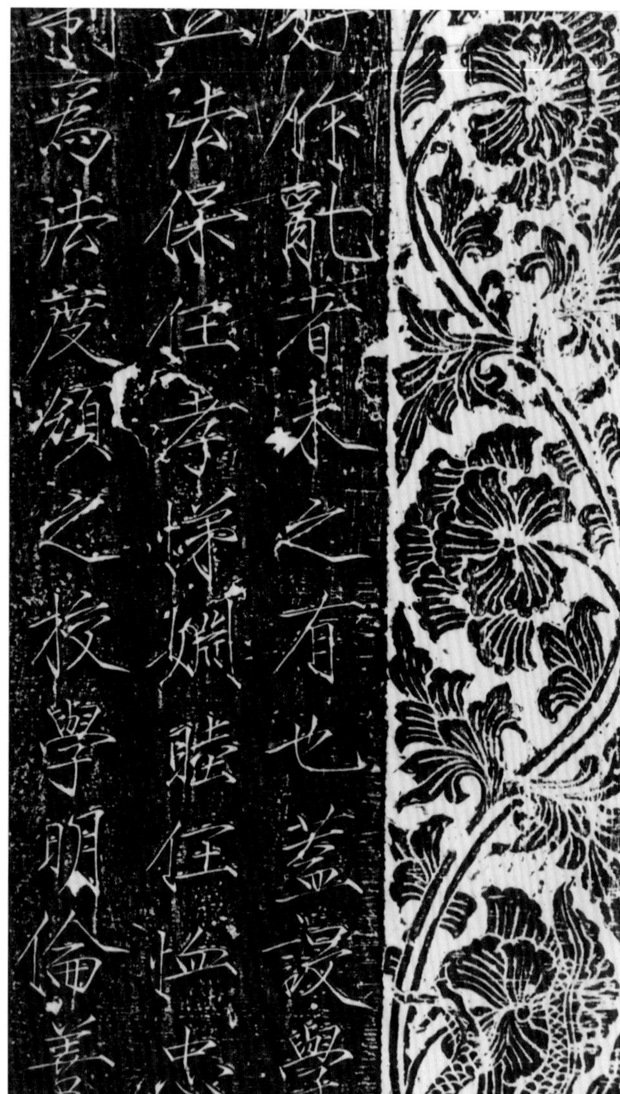

Fig. 2.6
Huizong, calligraphy for the Eight Virtues stele. Notice also the fine floral design on the border. From rubbing in the National Library of China.

and a new campus built for a new lower school outside the southern walls of the city. The architect Li Jie was given charge of constructing the new campus's four lecture halls and one hundred residence halls housing thirty students each.[54]

At the same time that Cai Jing was putting forward these education proposals, he was systematically identifying opponents, using the same method employed during Zhezong's reign—the analysis of memorials.[55] In the ninth month of 1102, a list of 117 men deemed unfit for service in the capital was issued, mostly men who had served in prominent posts during the Yuanyou period, many of whom were no longer living. In the next month, 1102/10, specific demotions were issued. The forty-one men considered to be "very unorthodox" were sent to small, remote places, and the thirty-eight in the next to worst category were sent to remote places. In the twelfth month local officials were ordered to keep those banished to their jurisdictions under supervision. The ban and the schools were explicitly linked in an edict of 1102/12/27 that insisted that students be taught only the works of the sages and worthies, and threatened the expulsion of any student at government schools who violated that rule by studying "Yuanyou learning."[56]

During 1103 and 1104 many details on the administration of both the school system and the purge were issued. For schools, the newly issued rules ranged from land allocations to testing, selection ratios, numbers of teachers, and avoidance of heterodox thought. On 1104/1/9 Huizong approved a proposal to increase the stipends for students at the government schools. On 1104/1/17 the number of students given stipends at the county schools was increased: large counties could have fifty, medium-sized ones, forty, and small ones, thirty.[57]

The ban on the Yuanyou partisans was repeatedly clarified and elaborated. On 1103/3/6 the sons and younger brothers of the banned Yuanyou and Yuanfu partisans were prohibited from entering the capital. On 1103/4/9 an order was issued to destroy the woodblocks used to print Su Shi's collected works. A few weeks later this order was expanded to include eleven other authors (including Su Shi's father and brother).[58] On 1103/5/7 a list was issued of thirteen officials who had recently served Huizong, including Chen Guan and Zou Hao, who were now given the heavy penalty of being stripped of official rank and placed under administrative supervision in distant prefectures. On 1103/9/25 a revised list of those banned was issued, bringing the total down from 117 to 98 men, nearly half of them deceased.[59]

Eight months later the final list of men to be excluded from office was issued. The edict of 1104/6/3 listed 309 former officials as "the treacherous faction of the Yuanyou period" and divided them into six tiers. The first tier included civil officials who had once served on the Council of State. It began with Sima Guang and Wen Yanbo, both long dead, and ended with several who had served in Huizong's own Council of State, such as Zeng Bu. The second tier consisted of men who had formerly served in high court posts. It began with a long list of deceased officials, beginning with Su Shi and ending with officials who had recently served under Huizong. The third tier was composed of "other officials," beginning with men known to be friendly with Su Shi, including Qin Guan, Huang Tingjian, Chao Buzhi, and Zhang Lei, and many who can no longer be identified. Fourth came a group of men with military ranks, including two imperial clansmen. Fifth was a list of twenty-nine eunuchs, most of whom are not recorded elsewhere but who had probably served Empress Dowager Gao. The sixth and final tier consisted of two men who were identified as "disloyal ministers who once served as grand councilors," Wang Gui (who served under Shenzong) and Zhang Dun.[60] A copy of this list was written out by Huizong, then carved into a stone placed on the east wall of Cultured Virtue Hall. Soon replicas of it were ordered erected in all prefectures. A pamphlet listing those banned was also printed.[61]

Cai Jing, in the preamble he wrote for the version of this stele distributed to the prefectures, asserted that the emperor had a duty to distinguish the good from the evil and that he had done this by scrutinizing the memorials of a very large number of officials, only 309 of whom were deemed unacceptable for further appointment. The copies of the stele would help to publicize the emperor's filial and fraternal desire to continue the legacy of his father and elder brother.[62]

Copying the list of banned officials in his own hand identified Huizong closely with the blacklist. Huizong made similar efforts to identify himself closely with the expansion of the school system. Once construction of the new lower academy (the Biyong Academy) was complete in the eleventh month of 1104, Huizong paid a visit. The high official Xue Ang reported that while there, Huizong paid his respects to the image of Confucius in the Great Completion Hall and summoned the two directors of study, whom he told, "I have unrolled some of my own favorite writings to give to the school," and asked that everyone be allowed to view them. Also on this occasion, Huizong asked the director of studies, Wu Yin, to lecture on the *Book of Changes*. According to Wu's biographer, who saw this as the high point of Wu's career, Huizong complimented Wu on the profundity of his scholarship, made him a gift of a purple robe chased in gold, and promoted him one rank, with the result that Wu's reputation soared among the large number of scholars who had collected in the capital at the time.[63]

After this visit Huizong conferred on the new academy a hand-drafted edict extolling the virtues of the new school system and declaring that from then on, promotion from the schools would replace the open civil-service examinations. This edict was carved on a stele erected at the academy. Cai Jing did the calligraphy for its title, "An Edict Bestowed by the Emperor on the Biyong Academy" (fig. 2.4). Cai also proposed that copies of the stele be made and distributed to all the prefectural schools so that they could erect copies of it.[64] The timing of Cai Jing's suggestion, in late 1104, only a few months after the order to duplicate the stele listing the banned partisans, suggests that the new stele was intended to counter any sense that the new emperor was an enemy of literati, education, or Confucian principles.

Less than a year later, one of the directors of study at the lower academy asked that Huizong's visit be further commemorated through a written record of the event. The record, composed by Xue Ang, summed up Huizong's accomplishment in extending the Three Halls system to the entire country in this way: "At present, there is the worry that scholars might not study, but not the worry that they have no place to study. There is the worry of people lacking talent, but not the worry of them having no way to develop their talent."[65] This record was soon carved below Huizong's original edict.

By the time this record was written in 1105, Huizong had come to consider the blacklist a mistake. In his first year as emperor, members of his Council of State had advised him not to punish Chen Guan for his wild accusations against Zeng Bu because harsh treatment would just make Chen famous. This lesson did not seep in deeply enough, because Huizong did not anticipate the full reaction to his lists. Because so many of the listed men (such as Sima Guang and Su Shi) were highly admired, even those not well-known gained fame by association.

Thus, less than a year after the final blacklist was issued, Huizong began reducing the penalties associated with it. On 1105/5/11 the restrictions on fathers, sons, and brothers of those banned were removed. Two months later, Huizong issued an edict in his own hand allowing those who had been banished for writing memorials to return home. Six weeks after that, on 1105/9/5, those whose offenses were too serious to be allowed to return home were moved to closer regions. Before the end of the year, on 1105/12/24, Huizong issued an edict saying that the punishment for the Yuanyou and Yuanfu partisans was already sufficient, and that they could be restored to the ranks of those eligible for office. Moreover, he mentioned that he had already ordered the inscribed stone at court destroyed, and that any prefectures that had set up a copy should destroy it. At the same time, he once again reiterated his demand that officials stop submitting accusations of factionalism, and asked the Censorate to report anyone who disobeyed.[66]

A few days later, on the last day of 1105, in an imperial brush edict, Huizong reported frustration with getting officials to carry out his reduction of penalties on those formerly blacklisted. A similar edict had to be issued two weeks later on 1106/1/12. Within a few days the Three Departments began issuing new ranks and appointments for those earlier banned, and soon the Ministry of Justice was ordered to destroy the blacklist pamphlets as well as the woodblocks used to print them.[67]

As Huizong backpedaled on the use of a blacklist, he put more effort into his school initiatives. In 1107 a way of recruiting students outstanding for their virtue was introduced. Based on the system described in *The Rites of Zhou,* this "Eight Virtues, Eight Offenses" school promotion system was intended to allow the rapid promotion of students nominated as excelling in eight specified virtues.[68] Students recommended by their villages or county or prefectural schools for two or more of the virtues would attend those schools for a year, after which they could be directly admitted to the upper hall of the National Academy without taking an exam. After they had been investigated there, they could be given degrees and official rank. The other side of bringing morality into the school system was the Eight Offenses, the crimes or improprieties that would warrant expulsion from the schools.[69]

An edict on this system that Huizong issued in the ninth month of 1107 was soon inscribed on stones erected at government schools around the country, most of them again in his handwriting (figs. 2.5 and 2.6). Early the next year Huizong issued an edict in his own hand that brought up the problem of the schools becoming a haven for the banned partisans:

> In antiquity, first teachers were appointed, then study commenced. Recently someone submitted a memorial that reported that partisans have attracted large numbers of students whom they teach heterodox ideas. What they study is not correct; it violates reason and harms morality. How could such study make possible the unification of moral virtue and the standardization of customs? Besides the scholars who are appropriately in the schools, from now on anyone who teaches youth in villages, towns, and cities should report to the county or prefecture and explain the principles he teaches and tests. Those whose statements are not in violation of moral principles will be permitted to continue. This does not apply to people on the list of banned partisans. Anyone who violates this will be held to have violated an imperial injunction.[70]

Among the other hand-drafted edicts concerning government schools that Huizong issued in 1108 was one on the name to be given the libraries at prefectural schools. Since Wang Anshi had disapproved of the histories as reading matter for aspiring scholars, Huizong did not want "Histories" in the name of the libraries:

> I have recently heard that prefectural schools with buildings for storing books generally call them "Classics and Histories" [halls]. At present we are honoring the Eight Virtues as the way to lead scholars. We honor the Six Classics and downgrade the writings of the miscellaneous schools. How are the histories even worth discussing! Since the schools already have the buildings, let them be renamed "Searching for Antiquity."[71]

Notice that although the histories are downgraded, antiquity is not. The histories, from the *Spring and Autumn Annals* to the dynastic histories, had been read by conservatives such as Sima Guang as justifying retaining as much as possible of what had been inherited from the past. Wang Anshi and his followers held up antiquity as a much better model of the ideal to strive towards.

In 1112/5, after an absence of three years, Cai Jing returned as grand councilor. Soon many new regulations were issued concerning the schools, ranging from exemptions from the grain tax to handling of surpluses, problems with discipline of students and recruitment of teachers, and men who had entered officialdom through the privilege extended to them as sons or grandsons of high-ranking officials who nevertheless wanted to study at the schools.[72] On 1114/8/9 Huizong increased the quotas of students at government schools. He summed up the progress that had been made: "For twelve years, schools have served to improve the cultivation of men; we have appointed teachers, constructed school buildings, and supplied food in order to instruct the scholars of the realm. Every day the Way is better illuminated; every day scholars become more numerous. We are getting close to antiquity."[73] In 1118, Huizong again had an edict on education in his own hand inscribed on stones erected at government schools around the country.[74]

Why did Huizong write out himself so many of the edicts that dealt either with schools or with the men to be excluded from his government? Earlier Song emperors, most notably Shenzong, had sometimes issued edicts in their own hand, but none to the extent that Huizong did. Taking the time and making the effort to compose and write out an edict certainly demonstrated that he considered a matter serious. Beyond that, however, it linked the decision to Huizong personally. These were not issues Huizong had let his top officials handle by themselves, but ones he cared about deeply. Moreover, by having duplicates of his hand-drafted edicts distributed to county and prefectural schools, where they would be engraved on stone slabs set out for all to see, he was making his presence felt throughout the country. In Chinese understanding, calligraphy is a trace of the heart-and-mind and reveals the true person. Huizong and his advisors undoubtedly hoped that the local literati who read the inscribed stones would be moved by Huizong's sincere concern for their education. Subjects rarely saw the emperor either in person or in portraits. The emperor's calligraphy could, however, function like a portrait to make the imperial presence felt at a distance.

Promoting Daoism

Huizong did not single-mindedly court Confucian scholars. His strong faith in Daoism led him to concurrently support Daoist projects that many Confucian scholars considered a waste of money.

From early in his reign, Huizong was attracted to both learned Daoist masters and *fangshi*, men capable of tapping into mysterious powers to work wonders.[75] In 1104, he put into practice some of the proposals of the seer, wonder worker, and musical theorist Wei Hanjin (see chapter 6). He also was in correspondence with Liu Hunkang (1035–1108), twenty-fifth patriarch of the Shangqing lineage at Maoshan, who had already been favored at court under Shenzong and Zhezong.[76] After Liu returned to Maoshan in 1103, Huizong wrote several dozen letters to him, preserved in the history of Maoshan.[77] Huizong repeatedly urged Liu to come to the capital. Huizong inquired about methods for curing illness, the names to be given newly constructed temples, and how to deal with misfortunes like the continuous rains that were harming farmers. He repeatedly asked for detailed analyses of disasters and anomalies. Huizong made reference to his own religious practices, such as the use of talismans. The two discussed the construction of buildings Huizong was providing at Maoshan. Liu Hunkang encouraged Huizong to support Daoism in its competition with Buddhism, and they carried on a correspondence concerning the problem of Buddhist temples incorporating shrines to Daoist deities. Cai Tao, a son of Cai Jing, thought it was Liu Hunkang's slanders of the Buddhists that turned Huizong away from Buddhism.[78]

In 1106 Huizong sent several items for Liu's new temple. These included a plaque with the title of the temple in his own calligraphy, an essay written by Cai Bian, plus ten fans with Huizong's own painting and calligraphy on them, which Huizong told Liu to use to summon a breeze on a hot day.[79] Cai Bian's essay mentions that Huizong sent as gifts for the new temple several chapters of Daoist scripture that he had written out himself, plus a painting of Laozi that he had painted himself. The next year, when Huizong was sending another group of presents, he included two paintings he had done of two of the most important Daoist deities, the Venerable Celestial of the Primal Beginning (Yuanshi tianzun) and the Supreme Lord Lao (Taishang daojun). Huizong wrote that if these were put together with the painting of Laozi he had done the year before, they would make a complete set of the Three Pure Ones (San qing). In another letter Huizong also mentioned the completion of an image of the Third Mao Lord (San Mao jun).[80]

Daoist texts also attracted Huizong's patronage. In 1108 he ordered that liturgies for the Rite of the Golden Register be collected in order to send sets to each county and prefecture with a Daoist temple.[81] According to Michel Strickmann, "The purpose of the Rite of the Golden Register ever since its inception in the fifth century had been to guarantee the welfare of the imperial house. Thus the distribution of a newly codified redaction of the Golden Register Rites was intended to ensure that a vast chorus of supplication of the interests of the Song would rise from every corner of the empire."[82] In 1113 Huizong issued a general call for the collection of Daoist texts, ordering prefects and circuit intendants to conduct wide searches, and for priests, laymen, gentlemen, and commoners all to submit their Daoist books. In addition, in the third month of 1114, he ordered every circuit to send ten Daoists to the capital, where they were to receive advanced training. Some of the learned Daoists who arrived in the capital were brought into the project of editing a new Daoist canon. This editorial project did not just look for the best editions of old classics but incorporated the key texts of relatively recent teachings, such as the Celestial Heart, Thunder Rites, and Divine Empyrean schools. In 1116 the manuscript of the texts prepared in the capital was sent to Fuzhou to be carved on blocks. This was the first complete printing of the Daoist canon.[83]

As work on the canon was completed, other editorial jobs were found for the assembled Daoists, including a *History of the Dao* and an *Institutes of the Dao*. The *History* was to cover the period through the Five Dynasties, with chronicles of the rulers who had attained transcendence, twelve monographs on Daoist subjects, and biographies of male and female immortals. The *Institutes* would cover the Song period.[84]

Huizong's intensified interest in Daoism was attributed by Cai Tao to a dream:

> Early in the Zhenghe period the emperor was ill. After a hundred days he was on the mend, then one night he had a dream that someone summoned him. In the dream it was like the time when he lived in his princely mansion and attended Zhezong's court. In response to the summons he entered a Daoist temple where two Daoist masters acted as ushers. They arrived at an altar where the exalted one told Huizong: "It is your destiny to promote my religion." Huizong bowed twice and accepted the command. As he left, the two ushers led him away. When he woke up he made a record of the dream and sent it to Cai Jing, who at the time was living in Hangzhou.[85]

It was Huizong's text-oriented projects that led him to meet Lin Lingsu, the Daoist master who he came to feel had the greatest powers.[86] Lin came to the capital in 1113 or 1114, probably in response to Huizong's call for unusual texts and adepts. Originally from Wenzhou (Zhejiang), Lin was a master of Thunder Rites and an exponent of a new sect of Daoism, Divine Empyrean Daoism, which he had learned from a Daoist master in Sichuan. The Divine Empyrean, they proclaimed, was a celestial region far superior to those that governed the other Daoist orders. In Isabelle Robinet's words, "The style of this movement was essentially liturgical. A complete cycle of recitations ensures the salvation of humankind, equivalent to a Return to the Origin. It breaks the circle of life and earth and permits rebirth in the Taiping heaven. An important place is reserved for the cosmic and apotropaic power of thunder and lightning, which the master must interiorize in order to make use of its power."[87]

What makes Lin Lingsu notorious in Chinese historiography is his revelation in 1116 or 1117 that Huizong was an incarnation of the elder son of the Jade Emperor, named the Great Sovereign of Long Life.[88] Huizong was so pleased with learning this from Lin that he had the palatial Supreme Purity Precious Treasure Temple built for him. He also ordered Divine Empyrean temples established in every prefecture to house images of the Great Sovereign of Long Life and his brother the Sovereign of Qinghua. Existing Daoist temples could be converted for this purpose, but in places without any Daoist temples, Buddhist ones could be converted instead, and there is evidence that Buddhist temples were in fact taken over by Daoists in this period. The construction or conversion of these temples must have created a lot of work for painters and sculptors, as one observer noted that they typically had twenty-two immortals depicted on their eastern and western walls, in addition to images of the main deities at their altars.[89]

In 1117/2 Lin Lingsu announced that the Sovereign of Qinghua had descended to earth. Huizong assembled huge numbers of Daoist priests at Precious Treasure Temple to hear Lin tell of this great event. From then on Huizong made frequent trips to this temple and would always distribute large quantities of cash. Wanting his subjects to know of the strength of his commitment to Daoism, in 1117/4 Huizong issued an edict stating that he believed he had been given the mission of saving China from the foreign religion (i.e., Buddhism) and returning it to the correct way. Two years later, in 1119/8, Huizong composed and wrote in his own hand a record of the Divine Empyrean Jade Clarity Longevity temples that was carved on a stele. Paper copies were distributed throughout the realm, so that stone copies could be erected at Divine Empyrean temples everywhere.[90]

Huizong did not confine his Daoist compositions to commemorative pieces. Like Emperor Xuanzong in the Tang dynasty, he wrote a commentary on the *Laozi*.[91] Huizong's commentary was engraved in stone at the Divine Empyrean temple in the ninth month of 1118 and printed in 1123. Scholars were encouraged to read and comment on it.[92]

In 1118 Huizong decided to incorporate Daoism into the government school system. Students of Daoism could attend the county and prefectural schools, where they would study two major classics, the *Laozi* and the *Inner Classic of the Yellow Emperor*, and two minor classics, the *Zhuangzi* and the *Liezi*. They were also to familiarize themselves with classics of the Confucian tradition, with the *Book of Changes* listed as the major classic and the *Mencius* as the minor classic. Students in the standard Confucian curriculum would for their part add to their studies a major and a minor Daoist classic. Students who did well in the Daoist curriculum could be appointed to Daoist offices.[93] In 1118, in an edict on Daoist schools, Huizong asserted the common origins and purposes of Confucianism and Daoism. As he saw it, until the Han period, the Dao had not been differentiated, but since then it had split: "I am bringing the teachings of the Yellow Emperor, Laozi, Yao, Shun, the Duke of Zhou, and Confucius to proceed in harmony from now on."[94]

After promoting the Divine Empyrean teachings for a couple of years, Huizong began placing curbs on Buddhist establishments. In 1118 the Daoist Bureau reviewed over 6,000 volumes of Buddhist texts to discover ones that slandered Daoists or Confucians. Nine volumes were singled out to be destroyed, though a copy of each was to be kept for evidence. Lin Lingsu wrote a treatise detailing the slanders in them, which was printed and circulated. Anti-Buddhist measures went a step further in 1119/1, when Buddhist temples and monasteries were forbidden to increase their land or buildings. Then the foreignness of Buddhism was to be erased through a process of renaming. Buddhist monks were renamed "scholars of virtue" (*deshi*, to correspond to Daoist priests who were called *daoshi*). They were to wear Daoist-style robes, use their original surnames, and salute with raised fists, not joined palms—in other words, they were to make themselves visually indistinguishable from Daoist clergy. Buddhas, bodhisattvas, and arhats were given new names—Śakyamuni, for instance, was to be called the Golden Immortal of Great Enlightenment. Temples could retain the old statues of these newly renamed deities, but had to clothe them in the robes and caps of Daoist divinities.[95]

Not surprisingly, Huizong's support of Lin Lingsu and Divine Empyrean Daoism provoked resistance and protest. Huizong's eldest son, the heir apparent, a young man in his mid teens, was the boldest, calling Lin a fraud who used tricks like paper cranes to create the illusions that dazzled Huizong. Cai Jing went along with most of Huizong's projects, dutifully offering praise whenever called for, but he too began complaining. Supporters of Buddhism circulated texts ridiculing the Divine Empyrean. By late 1119 Lin Lingsu had become a political liability and was sent back to Wenzhou. The following year most of the restrictions on Buddhism were removed.[96]

Literati Reception

How did men in the educated class respond to the various strategies Huizong adopted to try to refashion relations with them? This question is not easy to answer. The vast majority of the thousands of men who served in office during Huizong's reign have left no trace in the written record. "Outside opinion" or "literati opinion" did not have as clear leaders in Huizong's reign as it had during Shenzong's. Men on the banned lists gained fame just from being listed, but it is difficult to identify a core group who both supported each other and developed the intellectual and political rationale for opposing current policy, in the way that the group around Sima Guang had during the first phase of the reform period. Moreover, as it became apparent that Huizong was unlikely to change his mind about the New Policies agenda or about Cai Jing, it made little sense for officials to continue bringing up objections to them.

As one would expect, the educated elite responded differently to the educational expansion than to the ban on partisans. Certainly young men were happy enough with the expansion of educational opportunities that they entered the schools in large numbers—up to 200,000 at a time, and presumably several times that number over the course of the nearly two decades that the full school system was in operation. In other words, there was never a lack of men ready and eager to enter the schools and to try to make their way into office by doing well at them. The close association of the school system with the New Policies does not seem to have led to a boycott of them, not even by opponents of the reform program. Reformers sometimes charged that opponents of the reform were using the schools to spread their ideas; they never charged them with staying away from the schools or ostracizing those who entered them.

Many officials, especially ones with scholarly leanings, spent a good part of their careers in school offices. Ge Shengzhong (1072–1144) can serve as an example. Three years after passing the *jinshi* examinations in 1097, he took two further exams (the examination for examiners and the "abundant talent" exam), getting the highest score both times. The next year he was appointed as preceptor at the Yan prefectural school, where, we are told, he did such a good job that his school became the best in its circuit. Then, according to his biographer, "In 1103 the Three Halls system was extended throughout the country. The court, considering the National Academy to be the central place in this system, would consider only men of the highest caliber to staff it. They appointed Ge as instructor." Ge was thus there during Huizong's visit of 1104, and the congratulatory composition he wrote was judged the best of the thousands submitted. After a period of mourning, Ge returned to take a court scholarly post, and was soon assigned the task of writing a report on the entire government school system. In 1114 he was appointed director of studies, the second highest post in the Directorate of Education, in which capacity, his biographer reported, he gained an excellent reputation as a teacher and administrator. In 1115 he was appointed one of the instructors of the heir apparent, in 1116 was made chancellor of the Directorate of Education, and in 1117 was made rector of the lower school of the National Academy.[97]

The report Ge wrote on the school system came to twenty-five volumes and gave detailed statistics on all of the government schools. Although this report does not survive, Ge summarizes some of the key findings in the memorial he submitted with it. He pointed to the remarkable generosity of the system, which went far beyond anything the Han or Tang dynasties had done. Indeed, nothing on its scale had been attempted since high antiquity. The two most significant figures he gave were the size of land set aside to support the schools, which was 105,990 *qing* (each *qing* is 100 *mu*, or about sixteen acres), and the number of students, including students in the elementary schools, which was 167,622. He also gave statistics on the amount of money expended, the grain distributed, and the room-space devoted to schools.[98]

The schools were not perfect, of course. Many memorials pointed to problems in the administration of the schools, such as inattentive teachers, and students who cheated on exams, but they invariably praised the larger goals of the system and its impact on education. Stelae erected at local schools opened in this period often credited Huizong. For instance, an inscription dated 1103 erected by local officials in Hebei is titled "In Praise of the Sagely Virtue of Promoting Education of the Chongning Period" and began, "The year after the emperor ascended the throne. . . ," explicitly tracing the initiation of their new school to Huizong. Another inscription from the same year erected by officials in Henan began with a reference to Huizong's decision to return to the policies of Shenzong's time, as did one from Hubei. Yet another from that year, erected in Shaanxi for a county school, explicitly cited the edict of the year before ordering schools established in counties, and included the sentence, "Our lord is treating the scholars (*shi*) of the realm generously. The scholars of the realm ought to give thought to how to assist him."[99] During the period 1109–1112, when Cai Jing was out of office, some criticism was voiced of relying entirely on the school system to recruit officials. The examination system should be retained as a temporary expedient for those unable to secure places in the schools, such critics advised.[100]

Two generations later, the leading thinker Zhu Xi said that the school system had largely succeeded in its goal of gaining the favor of scholars. In a discussion with a disciple, he mentioned that after Cai Jing expanded the school system, "current discussion" had come to favor him more and more. He would visit the schools and eat with the students, where he would be praised for the attention he had devoted to the school system.[101] A contemporary of Zhu Xi's, the grand councilor and man of letters Zhao Ruyu, similarly had good things to say about the extension of the Three Halls system throughout the country under Huizong. He thought it approximated the ancient ideal of selecting men on the basis of their reputations in their local communities. Its main drawback was requiring students to study Wang Anshi's commentaries and skip the *Spring and Autumn Annals*. Moreover, because the open civil-service examinations were cancelled, those aspiring to office had no alternatives to the school curriculum.[102]

Literati reaction to Huizong's promotion of Daoism was relatively muted. The elements that most directly impinged on Confucian literati were those that altered the school curriculum and offered government posts to Daoist clergy. Some students voluntarily switched from the Confucian to the Daoist curriculum in the hope of improving their chances for office. Others saw these policies as disturbing, but did not voice their objections. As Shin-yi Chao shows, many local officials were perfunctory at best in establishing Divine Empyrean temples in their jurisdictions, but they did not put up a united front or protect each other when Huizong ordered circuit intendants to report resisters. On the other hand, Edward Davis, who believes that Huizong's goal of uniting the Dao of the Daoists and the Dao of the Confucians was widely shared, presents a much more positive account of the reaction of the elite to Huizong's pro-Daoist projects. In his view, "The major effect of Huizong's religious policy was, I believe, to create the atmosphere in which classical and Daoist ritual could be performed enthusiastically."[103] A generation or two after Huizong, Hong Mai, not by any means hostile to religion, expressed the suspicion that Lin Lingsu's séances were staged like a play with actors.[104]

What about literati reaction to Huizong's blacklist and its rapid reversal? Although many high officials had asked Huizong to distinguish clearly between upright men and men too untrustworthy to be employed in high office, few seem to have approved when he actually took the recommended step and made his judgments fully explicit. Huizong must have heard some grumbling, or he would not have so quickly issued directives canceling or lessening the penalties. Moreover, he probably realized that resentment continued to linger long after most penalties were removed. After the Jurchen invasion, when Huizong's reign was on the point of collapse, Huizong issued an edict of self-indictment. It was written by one of his top officials, but Huizong read it through and approved it, presumably believing that the accusations were ones that his critics would want to hear him make. Two passages refer in general terms to the blacklists:

> I inherited a flourishing dynasty but the avenues for criticism were blocked so that on a day-to-day basis I heard only sycophants. Favorites gained power and the greedy could do as they pleased. Scholars of wisdom and ability were caught in the proscriptions. . . .
>
> I am aware that in the past, in response to disturbances in the heavens, I have often issued edicts requesting the expression of honest opinion to improve the government. However, such calls were not in effect for long before powerful ministers made use of them to levy accusations against those who spoke up. Thus my calls for advice were not trusted and the spirit of the literati was frustrated.[105]

From the early Southern Song on, having been blacklisted was treated as a badge of honor, something to be mentioned in one's epitaph. Some epitaph writers even went to lengths to explain why someone had not been listed. Zhu Xi's *Words and Actions of Famous Song Officials* (Song mingchen yanxing lu) gave prominent biographies to Zou Hao and Chen Guan, featuring them as courageous critics of the evils of their day.[106] The rapid reversal of the ban, by contrast, was barely mentioned in these sorts of texts, since it did not serve in the same way to celebrate literati courage and willingness to stand up to power.

ꕥ ꕥ ꕥ

The educated class that Huizong had to deal with was in many ways more powerful than the one Taizong had successfully courted more than a century earlier. The growth in education and participation in the civil service examinations in the intervening decades meant that by the early twelfth century there were many more educated men than there had been in the mid- to late tenth century. Printing had grown enormously in this period, and gave the educated class more cultural independence. Huizong's efforts to forbid the printing of works by Su Shi and his circle probably did more to popularize them than to keep people from reading them. Huizong could not keep the educated class from choosing its own heroes.

From the perspective of the emperor, the relatively pro-literati policies of the early Song seem to have fostered in officials a sense of entitlement. Many officials denied the ruler the right to dismiss officials for resisting or obstructing his policies. They regularly cited the common opinion of the literati as a way to try to limit the emperor's choices, even while the vituperative language they directed at each other gave the lie to any notion that the literati had a common opinion. The degeneration of political culture during the reform era was widely lamented, but even as determined a grand councilor as Zeng Bu was unable to get politically committed men to treat their opponents with courtesy.

Educated men who found the political culture of this era distasteful could choose to opt out. As will be seen in the next chapter, some men stayed clear of politics, devoting themselves to the less political dimensions of literati life, such as collecting books or art works. Some, perhaps, were too absorbed in such pursuits to have the time or energy for politics. Others may have turned to apolitical activities because they found politics unpleasant. Huizong, as emperor, could not opt out of politics. He could, however, do his best to revive the image of the emperor as a patron of culture, as one who not only excels as a man of culture himself, but also gathers together the finest products of culture.

CHAPTER 3

Collecting As a Scholarly Passion during the Northern Song Period

Wang Xizhi's *Diagram of the Battle Formation of the Brush* is preceded by a self-portrait done on paper as thin and stiff as gold leaf, which makes a rustling sound. Zhao Song acquired it from a Daoist. Zhang Dun borrowed it from him and has not returned it. Wang Xizhi's *Family Genealogy* belongs to the Wang family of Shanyin county. Wang Xizhi's *Appreciation of the Portrait of Dongfang Shuo* has some damaged areas that were repaired by Ouyang Xun. It used to be owned by the academician Ding Feng, then passed to the imperial clansman Zhao Lingzhi. Liu Jing acquired it from him by trading a portrait of Emperor Wu of Liang [r. 502–549] done by Zhang Sengyou.

—Mi Fu, in his *Chronicles of Calligraphy*

DURING THE FIRST SIX DECADES OF THE SONG DYNASTY, THE COURT was the dominant force in the collection of books, calligraphies, and paintings. Once the palace collections had been built up to a respectable size, however, the court largely withdrew from the active pursuit of art and books still in private hands. From 1020 until the beginning of Huizong's reign, members of the educated class (including imperial kinsmen) took the lead as collectors. Growing prosperity, the impact of printing on scholarship, and the withdrawal of the court as a competitor probably all contributed to the lively interest literati took in acquiring objects associated in one way or another with the written tradition—books, above all, but also calligraphies, paintings, and objects from the remote past that could be treated as documents, a category that included ancient bronze vessels and rubbings of inscriptions found on such vessels or on stone monuments. During the Reform administrations of Shenzong and Zhezong, when political passions were at their height, there were men who felt even more passionately about the acquisition, study, and care of cultural relics.[1]

The objects that scholarly collectors sought were commonly classed into such categories as books, documents, calligraphies, paintings, and antiquities, but the divisions between these categories were not rigid. There were many objects that could be fit into more than one category, and many collectors who sought more than one type of object. Rubbings of inscriptions, for instance, were saved both as historical documents and as specimens of calligraphy. Scholars treasured antiquities, especially ancient bronzes, in large part because the inscriptions on them provided clues to early stages of the writing system and could be read as historical documents. Paintings in handscroll format often had text inserted between the pictures, blurring the distinction between an illustrated book and a painting with lengthy captions.

Historians of libraries, archaeology, painting, and calligraphy have long used material about Northern Song collectors to document the development of their fields.[2] Some have used lists of objects in collections as evidence of the types of objects available in a particular time and place. Collectors' opinions of what was most worth collecting have been used to analyze the development of critical standards and connoisseurial practices. The emergence of markets to meet the demands of collectors has also attracted attention. Modern scholars have not, however, looked together at all the different things that Song scholars collected. As this chapter shows, many aspects of scholarly collecting were broadly shared across fields of collecting.

From the perspective of social and cultural history, scholarly collecting was among the ways status was gained and maintained in the educated class.[3] Collecting demonstrated both wealth and cultivation; it entailed asserting and contesting claims of cultural leadership. By putting together impressive collections, even those who did not distinguish themselves as writers or government officials could claim a respected place for themselves as men of culture. In addition, collections were a form of property that could be handed down to heirs without any of the crass associations of money or businesses. Moreover, passing down traditions of learning to descendants was made easier when one could also pass to them the physical tools of their trade in the form of collections of books and related objects.

Was there also a political dimension to collecting? Avid collectors were as likely to be found among reformers as conservatives.[4] Some collectors probably eschewed taking stands that would have made it difficult to visit the owners of objects they dearly wished to see. Others probably simply found themselves more drawn to the search for objects of lasting cultural value than to the volatile world of government service. Perhaps the accelerating political animosities helped stimulate interests viewed as apolitical.

Five Collectors

Five men notable in one way or another for their collections can serve to illustrate the range and style of Song scholar-collectors. They are Song Shou, Ouyang Xiu, Wang Shen, Li Gonglin, and Zhao Mingcheng.

One of the leading officials of the 1030s, Song Shou (991–1040) acquired his love of books in his childhood from his mother's father, the high-ranking official Yang Huizhi. Having no sons, Yang gave his daughter an excellent education, and later her son Shou continued the Yang family's sacrifices. Yang Huizhi also passed to Shou his collection of books. Song Shou's parents helped expand the collection by arranging for him to marry the daughter of another book collector, Bi Shi'an. Bi's books in time also passed to Shou. Carrying on the tradition of his father-in-law, Shou became an obsessive collator, checking each word in a newly copied book three or four times in the attempt to eliminate copying errors. Song Shou's contemporaries thought that his access to so many books and the long hours he spent copying and collating them had added greatly to his store of knowledge and improved his calligraphy.[5]

Song Shou succeeded in instilling the collector's passion in his son, Song Minqiu (1019–1079). When Minqiu was at home, he would collate books with his sons and nephews, and they would make extra copies that could be lent to others without risking the integrity of their collection (in other words, archival copies were distinguished from reading copies). Minqiu reportedly had read nearly all of the 30,000 books in his family's collection and had such a remarkable memory that he could recall everything in them. People of the time, we are told, would turn to him when they came across an obscure allusion. It was even claimed that scholars would take lodgings near the Song house to make it easier for them to borrow the family's books.[6]

Song Shou's younger contemporary Ouyang Xiu (1007–1072) also came from an official family. He had an equally eminent career in government service and was one of the two or three leading men of letters of his day, renowned for his poetry, essays, and historical writing.[7] He also was a collector of both books and rubbings.

There is no evidence that the Ouyang family had been collectors before Ouyang Xiu's time, so some of his interest in books may date from his years of service in the Palace Library, where he was involved in the compilation of the *Chongwen Catalogue*. He also developed an interest in rubbings of inscriptions, which no one before him seems to have collected on a large scale. In the course of his career, as he crisscrossed the country, he searched for local stelae to rub. Soon friends who knew of his interest sent him rubbings from places he had not visited himself. When Ouyang Xiu's collection of rubbings reached a thousand items, he gathered together his notes on them, calling the work *Record of Collected Antiquities* (Jigu lu).[8] In his erudite annotations, he traced the historical circumstances of an inscription or identified the people mentioned in it. Often he showed complex feelings about learning of people not recorded in the histories:

> To the right is Liu Xi's *Stele for the Students' Graveyard*, from within the borders of Gucheng county in Xiang prefecture. When I was prefect of Qiande, I once passed through Gucheng on official business. I saw several unkempt graves in a grassy area. To the side was a toppled ancient stele, half buried in the ground. I asked the villagers whose graves these were, but no one could tell me, and the text of the stele was damaged. I had to leave before I could decipher it. Several years later, when I was in Hebei and began to collect and record ancient texts, I recalled the stele I had previously seen in Gucheng and wondered if it could have been a Han dynasty stele. I tried for several years to get a copy of it before I finally succeeded. According to the *Illustrated Records of Xiang Prefecture*, Students' Graveyard lies in the northeast of the county. The *Annotated Classic of Rivers* records that Liu Xi (style, Deyi) of Jinan in [Three Kingdoms] Wei was a widely knowledgeable scholar who loved antiquity. He set up a stele to record the names of more than a hundred students who died before finishing their studies and who were buried there. He gave it the name "Students' Graveyard." Even though today the stele is damaged and incomplete, the names of Xi and some students can still be made out. Most likely what I saw was the Students' Graveyard, and the stele was a Wei period stele, and Xi the magistrate of Gucheng.
>
> Written on the tenth day of the first year of Zhiping [1064].[9]

Ouyang Xiu's comments sometimes are confined to historical issues, but often also deal with calligraphic style and its links to the writer's moral character. He wrote of a rubbing of a work by Yan Zhenqing, "This man's loyalty and integrity were rooted in his nature, hence his brushstrokes are resolute, forceful, and distinctive, not following the paths of earlier masters. Marvelous and majestic in its own way, his calligraphy resembles his conduct."[10]

Rubbings were not the only cultural relics Ouyang Xiu enjoyed owning. In his later years, when he was over sixty, he described himself as gaining enormous pleasure from his zither, his chessboard, and his large collections of books and of rubbings. "When I am enjoying myself with my five possessions, Mt. Tai could loom up in front of me and I would not notice it, thunderclaps could shatter pillars beside me and I would not flinch."[11] Ouyang Xiu also used positive language to describe what other people got from their possessions. For an old painting of an ox owned by a Mr. Yang Zimei and inscribed by Ouyang Xiu's friend, the prominent poet Mei Yaochen, he wrote:

> I see that Mr. Yang truly loves the extraordinary,
> Now he possesses both the painting and the poem.
> Such pleasures are sufficient, bringing their own kind of wealth,
> What need has he of gold and jade, fame or property?
> He will look at the painting in the mornings and read the poem in the evenings.
> Mr. Yang shall thus no longer know hunger.[12]

In the preface that he wrote for his collection of rubbings, Ouyang Xiu admitted that collecting could be a dubious activity, pointing to the lengths people went to acquire such rare things as ivory, rhinoceros horns, jade, pearls, and gold. But collecting rubbings was different. He saw himself as performing a public service by saving from obliteration marvelous examples of calligraphic art and records of the past.[13]

Song Shou and Ouyang Xiu gained prominence during the reign of Renzong in the early and mid-eleventh century. Collecting seems if anything to have become more popular in subsequent decades, during the reigns of Shenzong and his son Zhezong.

Wang Shen (ca. 1048–ca. 1103) came from a different sort of family than Song Shou or Ouyang Xiu. His family had gained prominence as military men who were generously rewarded by the Song founding emperor. As a young man, Wang Shen had been selected to marry one of Yingzong's daughters (thus making him a brother-in-law of Shenzong). Wang did not pursue a military career himself, but rather devoted himself to collecting paintings and calligraphies, as well as practicing both arts.[14]

Wang Shen was one of the most prominent collectors in Kaifeng in the 1180s and 1190s and is mentioned as a collector by several contemporaries, including Guo Ruoxu, Mi Fu, and Su Shi. Guo mentioned that Wang had a painting of onions by Ding Qian that had formerly been in the collection of Li Yu, the last ruler of the Southern Tang. Mi Fu recorded that every time he went to Kaifeng, Wang Shen would invite him to his home to view calligraphy together and allow him to copy any pieces that interested him.[15] Among the works owned by Wang Shen that Mi Fu mentioned are a set of six Huang Quan paintings of peonies in wind and Han Gan's painting of a horse, *Night Shining White*, that was inscribed "Possession of the Family of Director of the Chancellery Wang" (see fig. 3.1). Mi Fu spoke highly of many items in Wang Shen's collection, but also made disparaging comments about Wang's

FIG. 3.1
Han Gan (fl. 713–756), *Night Shining White*. Handscroll, ink on paper, 30.8 × 34 cm. Image © The Metropolitan Museum of Art, New York. Purchase, The Dillon Fund Gift, 1977.78. Most of the inscriptions visible on this painting were put on it after Wang Shen owned it, with the exception of the title written out by Li Yu, in the upper right of the painting proper.

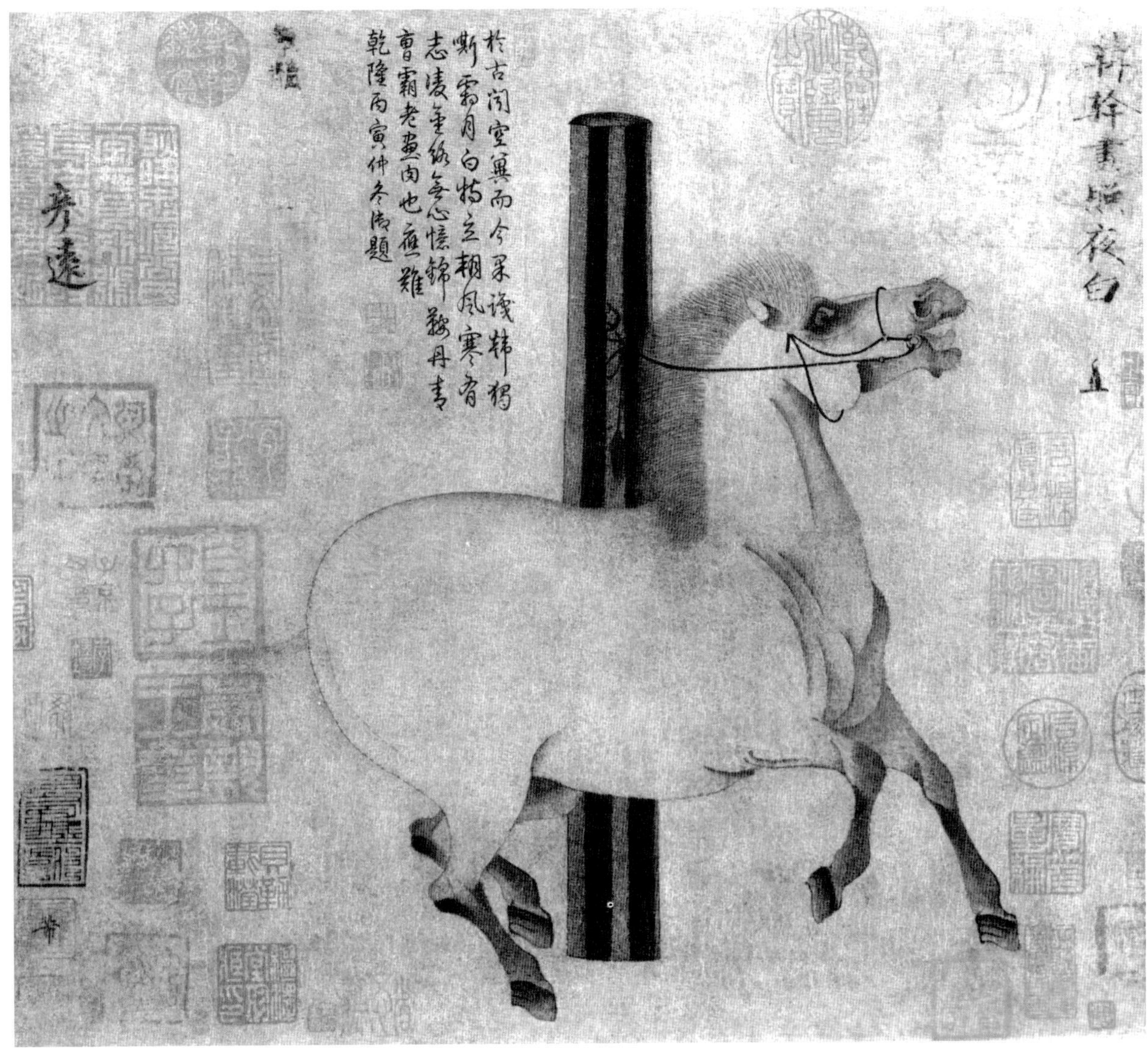

connoisseurship, implying that he often failed to detect fakes. He also noted that Wang himself was not above altering works to make them seem something other than what they were. Mi looked down on collectors who could be fooled by fakes, but did not necessarily hold the perpetrators in contempt, and some sources say he perpetrated frauds himself.[16]

Mi Fu recorded trades that Wang Shen made with a half-dozen other collectors, including another imperial son-in-law, Li Wei, and Wang Gong, a close friend of

Su Shi. Mi Fu recorded nearly a dozen trades he himself made with Wang Shen. Paintings and calligraphies were traded interchangeably, and sometimes other items were included as well, such as, in one case, a one-year-old tree, but never the crude medium of cash.[17]

The art critic Han Zhuo (fl. 1100–1121) portrayed Wang Shen as an exceptionally discerning connoisseur of paintings. After citing examples from history of men who were excellent judges of jades or horses, he went on to explain the particular challenges of judging paintings. Paintings seem different upon repeated examination, and it is easy to be misled by others' praise. Marvelous paintings need to have truth as well as spirit, harmony as well as verisimilitude. Han Zhuo then discussed Wang Shen's skill in assessing paintings:

> I fortunately received his favor and each time there was a viewing of paintings, he would summon me to look at them together with him; he would discuss the subtleties of the paintings and talk about their fame and authenticity. One day it happened that at the Cishu Hall a Li Cheng was hanging on the east wall and a Fan Kuan on the west. Wang first looked at the Li Cheng and said: "Li Cheng's painting method was that of moist ink and fine brushwork; he depicts mists that lightly move, scenery of a thousand *li* that seems to be right before one's eyes; he possesses a fresh spirit which one can almost grasp." Next he looked at Fan Kuan's painting and said: "It is just as if the densely packed mountain ranges were truly lined up before one's eyes; the spirit is strong and unfettered, and its brushwork is extremely vigorous. As for the effects of these two paintings—truly, one is like a civil [thing] and the other like a military [thing]." It seems to me that the appropriateness of his words truly can be called criticism that penetrates to the very marrow.[18]

FIG. 3.2
Wang Shen (ca. 1048–ca. 1103), colophon for Sun Guoting's *Thousand Character Essay* (detail). Liaoning Provincial Museum. In the colophon, Wang Shen discusses his reaction to the calligraphy, defends Sun as a calligrapher against Dou Ji, who had disparaged him, and mentioned viewing the work with Su Shi. After Liaoningsheng bowuguan 1998:69.

Wang Shen did not just collect paintings and calligraphies; he also produced them. A few examples of his calligraphy survive, some as colophons attached to works once in his collection (see fig. 3.2).[19] Two very impressive landscape handscrolls by Wang Shen survive (see plates 9 and 10). On the basis of these scrolls, Richard Barnhart has characterized Wang Shen as a highly creative landscape painter who "created a landscape of exile, in which the alienated artist finds his place amid a landscape that had been until now an imperial realm, shaped by the imperial gaze and power."[20] Wang Shen's practice of painting was undoubtedly enriched by his access to old paintings in his collection. In turn, his skill in painting should have helped him as a collector to recognize an artist's individual hand.

Wang Shen was not the only major collector with imperial kinship connections. The imperial son-in-law Li Wei was at least as major a collector. Several imperial

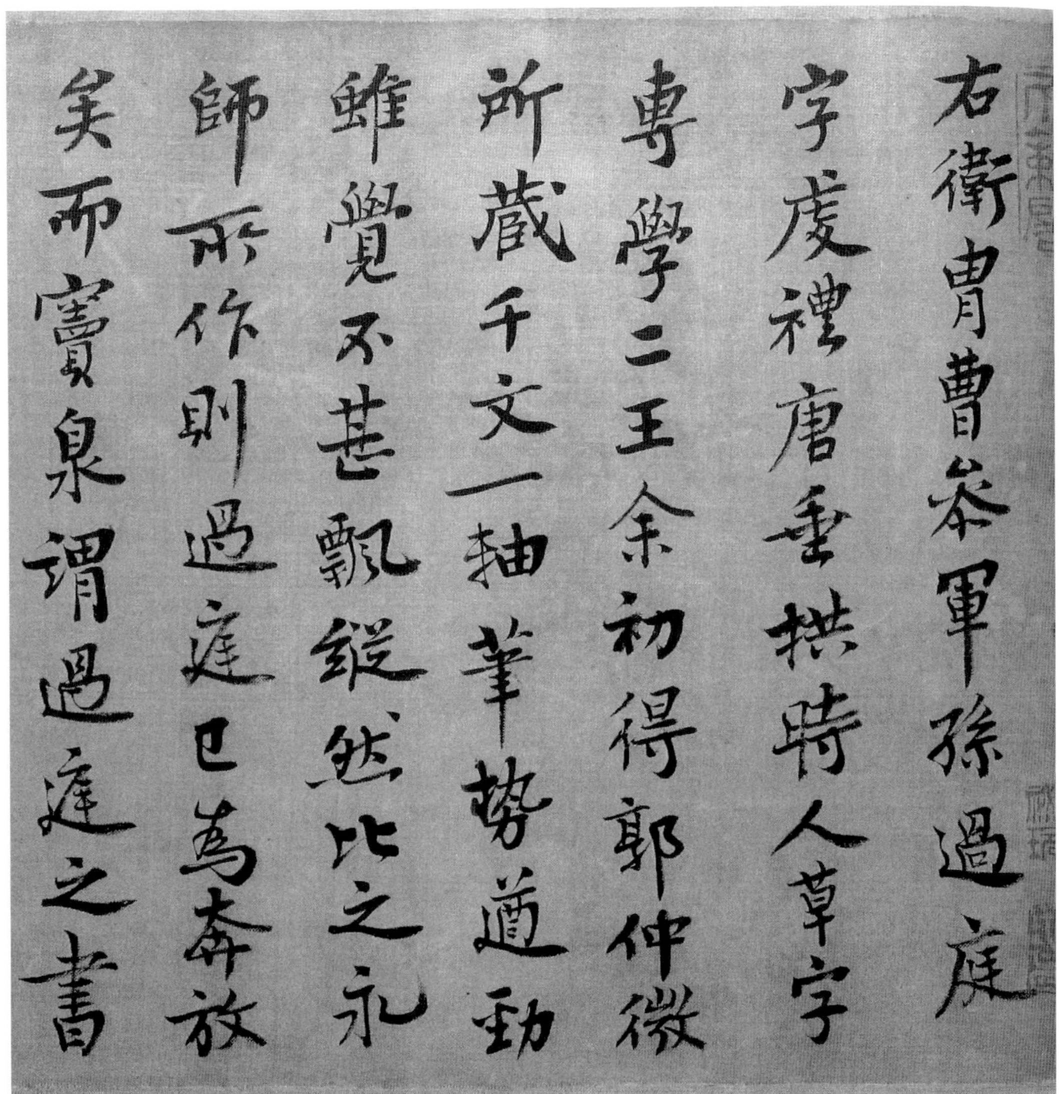

clansmen also were significant collectors. Zhao Zhonghu seems to have been especially prominent as a collector of antiquities.[21] Zhao Lingrang, known today primarily as a painter, was also a collector of paintings and calligraphies mentioned several times in Mi Fu's writings. He owned, for instance, a three-line calligraphy by the Sui monk Zhiyong, three pieces of calligraphy by the Tang artist Ouyang Xun, a calligraphy by Lu Jianzhi, a Wu Daozi painting that Mi Fu considered genuine, as well as a fine Tang copy of five horses and another of a black ox, both attributed to major Tang painters.[22]

Wang Shen's contemporary and acquaintance Li Gonglin (ca. 1041–1106) was also both an artist and a collector. Like Song Shou, Li was not the first in his family to collect, as his father had already put together a large collection of paintings and calligraphies. Compared to Song Shou and Ouyang Xiu, Li had an undistinguished civil-service career, which gave him more time to both paint and collect. Li collected more broadly than any of the collectors mentioned so far, acquiring not only books, calligraphies, and paintings, but also inkstones, rocks, ancient money, ancient bronze vessels, and ancient jades.[23]

Li pursued antiquities with a passion. He searched widely for ancient vessels, would pay top price to get them, and had rooms filled with them in his house in Kaifeng. Much as Ouyang Xiu produced a catalogue of his rubbings, Li compiled a five-chapter *Investigations of Antiquities Illustrated* (Kaogu tu) to record his bronzes and jades. Although this catalogue does not survive, it was probably the basis for the entries on the fifty-five bronzes and sixteen jades of Li's included in Lü Dalin's *Kaogu tu* of 1092 (see fig. 3.3). These objects were acquired from many places—some when Li was serving outside the capital, others near his home in Anhui, and others in the capital. Li justified collecting ancient vessels on the grounds that it deepened one's knowledge of the ancients. "The sages made vessels and adorned them with forms to record the Way and to pass down admonitions," he wrote. "They lodged in the use of vessels subtleties that otherwise could not have been transmitted and passed these on to later men."[24]

Li Gonglin's stature as a painter was if anything higher than Wang Shen's, as he was more prolific and excelled not only in landscapes but also in paintings of people, horses, and religious subjects. Robert Harrist has called him "the most versatile and accomplished of all Northern Song scholar-artists."[25] Li Gonglin's painting was tied to his collecting through his practice of copying. Li would make copies of paintings, much as Mi Fu did of calligraphy. One copy he made of a Tang painting in the palace collection has survived. He inscribed on it in seal script, "the subject Li Gonglin, on imperial command, copied Wei Yan's *Pasturing Horses*" (see plate 11).[26] By such extensive and painstaking copying, Li perfected technical mastery of the brush.

The fifth collector to be discussed here, Zhao Mingcheng (1081–1129), was a generation younger than Wang Shen and Li Gonglin. He was from a well-established official family, his father a high official in the reform administration.[27] We would not know much about Zhao as a collector were it not for the postface his widow, the famous poet Li Qingzhao, wrote for the thirty-chapter catalogue of his rubbings that she published after his death. She described collecting as a source of joy that the two of them shared from the early years of their marriage, when Zhao was a student at the National Academy. Every fifteen days, when he got a day off from his

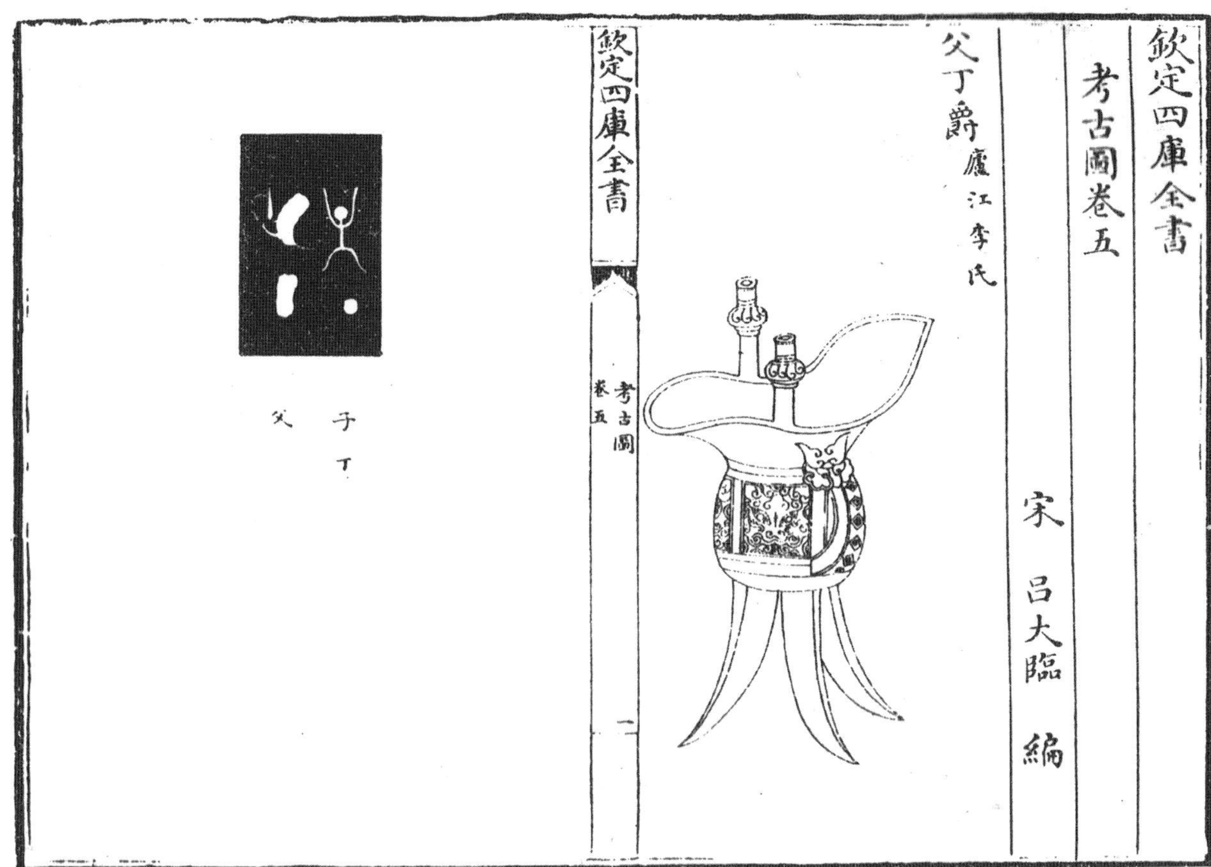
欽定四庫全書
考古圖卷五
宋 呂大臨 編
父丁爵 廬江李氏
欽定四庫全書
考古圖 卷五
一
子丁
父

Fig. 3.3
Page from *Investigations of Antiquities Illustrated*, showing ancient bronze collected by Li Gonglin and the rubbing of the inscription on it. KGT 5.1a–b.

studies, he would stop at the Xiangguo Temple market on his way home and buy both fruit and rubbings of ancient inscriptions. In the evening, by candlelight, they would eat the fruit and discuss the rubbings. Zhao also gradually built up his book collection by making copies. He had relatives with appointments in the Palace Library, which gave him access to its vast collections. "He would work hard at copying such things, drawing ever more pleasure from the activity, until he was unable to stop himself."[28] Nearly as eclectic in his interests as Li Gonglin, Zhao wanted to own all sorts of other objects besides books and rubbings. According to Li Qingzhao,

> Later, if he happened to see a work of painting or calligraphy by some person of ancient or modern times, or unusual vessels of the Three Dynasties of high antiquity, he would still pawn our clothes to buy them. I recall that in the Chongning Reign [1102–1106] a man came with a painting of peonies by Xu Xi and asked two hundred

> thousand cash for it. In those days two hundred thousand cash was a hard sum to raise, even for children of the nobility. We kept [the painting] with us a few days, and having thought of no plan by which we could purchase it, we returned it. For several days afterward husband and wife faced one another in deep depression.[29]

Zhao took an interest in the physical qualities of the objects he collected and would remount or repair those needing attention. He and his wife also liked to discuss each piece: "When he got hold of a piece of calligraphy, a painting, a goblet, or a cauldron, we would go over it at our leisure, pointing out faults and flaws, setting for our nightly limit the time it took one candle to burn down." Sometimes the couple would make a game of their displays of erudition. For instance, they would challenge each other to identify not only the source of a passage but also the exact page on which it could be found. Li wrote that their collections were "what took our fancy and what occupied our minds, what drew our eyes and what our spirits inclined to; and our joy was greater than the pleasure others had in dancing girls, dogs, and horses." In time Zhao's collections grew so large that he had a set of huge bookcases built to hold the books, and kept a ledger to keep track of any books taken out or needing repair.[30] The surviving catalogue of rubbings lists two thousand pieces.

Justifications for Scholarly Collections

On the whole, although authors were quick to note the obsessiveness of collectors—even of themselves as collectors—they framed scholarly collecting positively. Collecting could lead to exhausting the family fortune, but it was usually treated not as a decadent indulgence, like a passion for dogs or horses, but as a sign of refined tastes and noble passions.

The most basic collection for a scholar was a collection of books—practically a necessity for a scholar in an age before public libraries. Book collectors were generally given the benefit of the doubt about their motivations. Books aided a person's moral development because they gave him or her access to the thoughts, emotions, and moral character of people of the past. If one memorized a book—the approved way to gain mastery over the classics and other important books—one would have access to it at all times and would not need a reference copy. Still, since ancient times, those who loved books strove to accumulate them. Much of the time they had earned their right to own their books by producing them themselves through their own labor of copying, freeing them of the taint of extravagant spending.

Su Shi saw many advantages in books as objects to collect:

> Precious objects such as ivory, rhinoceros horn, pearls, and jade are pleasing to the ears and eyes, but have no utility. Gold, stone, grass, wood, silk, hemp, the five grains, and the six materials, are all useful but get used up. There is only one thing that is pleasing to the senses, useful, inexhaustible, with something for both the worthy and the unworthy according to their abilities, to the benevolent and the wise according to their nature. No matter what your talents or station, if you seek from it, you gain. That thing is books![31]

Collecting other sorts of scholarly objects was often justified in similar terms. Liu Chang stressed the importance of ancient bronzes to the study of ancient scripts. Ouyang Xiu justified his collection of rubbings on the grounds that he was preserving documents that otherwise might disappear. He was aware that even though people thought of inscriptions on stone as permanent, in reality they deteriorated over time, proved by the fact that even some Tang inscriptions could no longer be deciphered. Lü Dalin, in the preface to his *Investigations of Antiquities Illustrated,* argued forcefully that ancient vessels should not be treated as toys. Rather scholars should look at them, recite their inscriptions, and copy their forms—all in order to gain a better understanding of the ancients, fill in gaps in the histories and classics, and correct errors of earlier scholars. Li Gonglin saw the justification for collections of antiquities in their links to men of the past, even if their names were no longer known or recognized. He made a point of refuting any suspicion that he sought objects for their beauty: "How could these merely be for dazzling beauty that provides amusement or a toy to delight the eye!"[32] It was instead the meanings inherent in the objects that made them worthy of assiduous study.

If the justification for collecting inscriptions and vessels often involved treating them like historical documents, the justification for collecting calligraphy often involved likening it to poetry and other forms of literature through which people expressed their thoughts and emotions. Examining a person's calligraphy was thought to bring one close to the person, because the calligraphy was a trace not just of his thoughts but also of his bodily movements. By imagining the movement of his brush in each character, one placed oneself, in a sense, behind the brush of the writer. Part of this desire to see the moral worth of the writer in his calligraphy was a distrust of anything that seemed merely beautiful. As Ronald Egan notes, "From a Confucian standpoint, any intricate and beautiful style of expression was open to suspicion as something that is potentially beguiling or deceitful—an attitude that may be traced back to Confucius' caution about 'clever words and comely faces' (*Analects* 1/3)."[33]

There were secondary justifications that could also be evoked for collections.

The great collector saw value where others did not recognize it; he in a sense earned the right to possess a great work by seeing its true worth. Another argument often implied was that collectors should not be blamed for extravagant spending because they made economies elsewhere. Li Qingzhao emphasized that she and her husband lived frugally in order to save money to purchase objects for their collections. Mi Fu, it should be noted, does not seem to have felt any need to justify his collecting. To him, the inherent value of the works made their collection an obvious good.[34]

Must-Have Names

The value placed on the ability of books, calligraphies, paintings, and ancient objects to link one to the men of the past led to a strong desire for works that could be directly connected to particular people. In the case of inscribed bronzes, collectors and connoisseurs scoured the classics for references that might link their objects to known individuals. For instance, Li Gonglin wrote about a bronze vessel: "The *Zuozhuan* mentions that the Marquis of Jin gave Zichan of Zheng two square cauldrons from the state of Ju. This one was found in Xinzheng, so is probably that Zheng cauldron."[35]

In the case of painting and calligraphy, the desire to link objects to known men converged with a desire to have objects by the most famous artists, a tendency criticized since the late Tang period when Zhang Yanyuan wrote, "Any collection must have famous scrolls by Gu, Lu, Zhang, and Wu before it can be said to 'have paintings.' It is like saying of a book collection that it must have the Nine Classics and Three Histories."[36] In the late eleventh century Shen Gua lambasted this insistence on famous names: "Of those who collect calligraphy and painting, the majority rely on names alone. Everyone who sees a work reputed to be from the brush of Zhong You, Wang Xizhi, Gu Kaizhi, or Lu Tanwei will compete to acquire it. This is known as 'appreciating by ear.'"[37] As a consequence, a scrap by a famous calligrapher would be more highly sought than a long, elegant, polished work in perfect condition but with no name attached (a situation critics often attempted to remedy by attributing unsigned works to known masters).

Must-have names were established through the circulation of texts that discussed and ranked calligraphers and painters. Chinese authors had been writing such books since the Six Dynasties, and the ideas they expressed influenced collectors' decisions. Northern Song authors who continued this tradition include Liu Daochun and Guo Ruoxu on painting, Zhu Changwen on calligraphy, and Mi Fu on both.

Acquiring Objects by Reproduction

Most of the cultural objects scholars collected could be reproduced in some fashion. Since early times, all one needed to obtain a book was paper, ink, time to copy, and a borrowed book. In handcopying books, the goal was to get every word right; it did not matter if the pages had fewer columns or the characters were written in a different calligraphic style so long as no words were left out or added. During the Northern Song period, despite the spread of printing, collectors still often transcribed books by hand. A good place to do this was the Palace Library, as we saw in the case of Zhao Mingcheng. Su Song served for nine years in palace literary organs and each day would copy 2000 words of a book in the Palace Library, building up his personal library to at least twenty or thirty thousand chapters, a majority of them copied from the Library.[38]

Much as book collectors made copies of books in their friends' libraries, those who loved calligraphy would make copies of pieces owned by their friends and acquaintances. In the case of calligraphy, of course, it was essential to reproduce the physical appearance of a work and to capture as much as possible the movement of the brush. This was most commonly done freehand, as making freehand copies was how people mastered styles and script types. When done well, freehand copies were appreciated as both reflections of the original and evidence of the skill and artistry of the copyist.

When very exact copies were desired, pieces of calligraphy could be traced and meticulously filled in. Mi Fu reported that Wang Shen provided housing for the son of a mounter who made tracing copies for him.[39] When multiple copies of a work were desired, a tracing copy could be transferred to a stone or wooden surface for engraving, from which rubbings could later be made. For calligraphies, there was thus a hierarchy of distance from the artist's hand—from original work to close tracing copy to freehand copy to rubbings of incised copies—and connoisseurs carefully distinguished between these types of copies. For books, by contrast, one rarely knew the genealogy from original manuscript to current copy; if the copyist's errors had been minimized by careful collation, a recent copy was better than a tattered old one.

Besides rubbings created to reproduce calligraphy originally on paper or silk, rubbings were regularly made of inscriptions on stone and metal. One could put together a collection of rubbings of inscriptions, like those assembled by Ouyang Xiu and Zhao Mingcheng, for a fraction of the cost of original autograph calligraphies. These rubbings were of particular significance to those interested in early history, because paper and silk did not survive in any quantity from the Han period or earlier. Moreover, a scholar did not need introductions to major collectors to view rubbings. He could, like Ouyang Xiu, make detours on his travels to make his own rubbings, ask friends to do them for him, or, like Zhao Mingcheng, buy them ready-made in urban markets.

Copies played a lesser role in painting collections, in part because fewer painting copies were made, and in part because copies were seen as much lesser reflections of the original than were copies of books or calligraphy. Still, copying paintings was an established practice, something painters did to improve their facility with the brush. Moreover, because paintings suffered deterioration over time, some men preferred having copies of paintings to having nothing to represent important works by early masters. Li Gonglin was not trying to deceive when he made copies; he would inscribe the painting as a copy. Painters could also imitate the style of an established artist without having a specific model in front of them, producing works that are better thought of as imitations than as copies. Whether or not the works were originally made to deceive, copies and imitations circulated in abundance and were a perennial problem for collectors. Mi Fu claimed to have seen only two genuine Li Chengs but 300 forged ones.[40]

Acquiring Objects by Purchase, Trade, or Gift

The most straightforward way to acquire an object one would not or could not reproduce was to purchase it for money. Since Han times, at least, it had been possible to purchase books, giving the better-off a significant advantage as book collectors. By Tang times, the most impressive book collections contained more than ten thousand chapters or scrolls (*juan*). With the wide availability of printed books in Song times, it became easier for scholars to obtain copies of basic texts such as the classics or histories, and the sizes of collections began to reach 30,000 or more chapters. Book shops were not rare in the Song capital. Even those who had to struggle to make ends meet sometimes still found ways to buy books. Sima Guang told of a Huang Xi who had hardly enough clothes to cover his body and lived on handouts from friends but would spend anything he got on books. The grand councilor Lü Dafang reportedly regularly spent half of his salary on books.[41]

The market for new paintings was also well developed. In the capital, paintings were hung in many places to attract buyers, including pawnshops, wineshops, and restaurants. One of the best-known markets was at the Xiangguo Temple, where Zhao Mingcheng stopped twice a month to look for rubbings when he was a student. Even Mi Fu sometimes acquired things there.[42]

Old paintings and calligraphies could also be purchased. Li Qingzhao mentioned 200,000 cash as the asking price for the Xu Xi painting of peonies. Even though Mi Fu once insisted that "one should not discuss the price of calligraphy and paintings," he frequently mentioned how much was paid for particular items. For instance, he reported that an imperial clansman paid 700,000 cash for a painting by the Tang artist Yan Liben. Another acquaintance bought 500 scrolls for a bulk price of 500,000 cash without examining them, doing quite well when it turned out that one of the scrolls, Lu Hong's painting of his thatched hut, could be sold for 100,000 cash. Mi Fu was disappointed not to get a copy made by Chu Suiliang of one of Wang Xizhi's masterpieces, even though he offered 50,000 cash. He was especially galled that Shen Gua later managed to get the piece for only 20,000 cash. Of course, paintings and calligraphies did not always fetch high prices. Mi Fu wrote that he acquired many pieces while living in Suzhou because families needing cash during a famine made use of old women brokers to dispose of their art works.[43]

When making heavy outlays for paintings and calligraphies, collectors naturally wanted to be sure that they were getting an original work, not a forgery or copy. Mi Fu mentioned that one good painting could be worth more than a hundred bad ones, meaning that those who purchased a painting later deemed a forgery had made a very bad investment. When judging the authenticity of a piece of calligraphy, Mi Fu made note of many features: he inspected the paper and silk closely and he identified the collectors' seals in order to trace the ownership of items. But forgeries were often difficult to detect. Shen Gua told a story of a Mr. Li, who, on visiting a high official, encountered a copy of a piece of calligraphy he owned. The copy had been presented to the official as the original by a man who had borrowed it from Mr. Li.[44]

Even rubbings could be other than they seemed, something Ouyang Xiu frequently discussed in his *Record of Collected Antiquities*. With inscriptions, the most common problem was that collectors mistook a re-cut stone for an original. Men who appreciated ancient monuments might recut a stele that had deteriorated so badly that it was barely legible. Even if recutting was done for the best of motives, dealers or collectors might knowingly or unknowingly represent a rubbing of a recut stone as a rubbing of the original.[45]

One way to escape the danger of forgeries was to acquire works directly from the artist. When one's friends, relatives, and acquaintances were known for their calligraphy, one could save the pieces of paper they had written on, including casual letters, poems written socially, government documents, and the like. It was of course a high compliment to learn that something you had written in haste had been preserved for its beauty. Men might also make gifts of works intended as calligraphies, much as they would write poems to give to friends. The same was true of paintings. Scholar-painters often made paintings for occasions that traditionally had called for poems, such as farewell parties. Many contemporary scholars had acquired paintings by Li Gonglin and Wang Shen in such ways.[46]

Treating Treasured Objects with Due Respect

Li Qingzhao mentioned that she and her husband carefully inspected the condition of books, scrolls, and ancient vessels that they had acquired, and made repairs as needed. Mi Fu wrote quite extensively about how he cared for objects in his collection and about the advice he gave Wang Shen. For instance, he regularly cleaned his paintings and calligraphies by placing a wet piece of paper on the surface, letting the water soak through, and pressing gently so that dirt and grease on the surface were absorbed by the top sheet, a process that could be repeated if necessary. Mi stressed that to avoid cracking, paintings and calligraphy should be backed with paper rather than silk, something he once demonstrated to Wang Shen:

> Calligraphy and painting on paper backed with silk will suffer damage as the days and months pass and the ink seeps into the silk. Wang Shen used to back his calligraphies with silk and did not believe me, but after a while he saw that the ink of his Huan Wen calligraphy had become blurry and the pattern of the silk showed through on the paper, which annoyed him. So he put a piece of paper from She on it and from then on did not use silk to back his works.

Mi Fu also reported that he convinced Wang Shen to avoid unnecessarily removing the backing of his paintings and calligraphies and to switch to small seals with thin lines so as not to cover up too much of a work with his seals.[47]

Besides taking good physical care of objects, respectful collectors studied them. Serious book collectors, including Song Shou, Song Minqiu, and Zhao Mingcheng, closely compared their books to the same titles owned by other collectors, eager to identify every discrepancy. This devotion to collation was widely shared among Song book lovers. One collector's son described his father's obsessive interest in the integrity of books:

> Whenever my late father obtained a book, he would make a copy of it in cursive script on scrap paper. Then he would seek a different edition of the work to compare it to. After all errors had been eliminated, he would make a good copy of it. He would always use paper from Puqi county in E prefecture for the pages, aiming to make each fascicle hit the mean in speed and thickness. Each would have no more than thirty to forty pages because thicker fascicles come apart too easily. Only this copy could be read by family members or lent to others. He would write out another copy, a particularly fine one with a silk cover, which he called the archival copy. No one could read it without a proper reason. Not all of his books had archival copies, only some 5000 or so. He once agreed to pass books on to Song Cidao [Minqiu]. They exchanged their

> catalogues, and when they found a title that the other lacked, they made a copy to send to the other, which is how their collections got so large.[48]

Scholars also enjoyed doing historical research concerning the objects in their collections. Highly learned collectors could explicate the allusions in a piece of calligraphy and the occasion upon which it was made. They could identify the story behind a narrative painting by using such details as the type of clothing worn by the figures. Similarly, they could identify the iconography of religious paintings. Erudition was especially valued for the study of antiquities, as ancient scripts were difficult to decipher and collectors often were not even sure of the name of a particular object. Notes by Ouyang Xiu, Li Gonglin, and Zhao Mingcheng on their antiquities are full of discussions of passages from the classics and the histories that they saw as related in one way or another to their objects.

We can compare Ouyang Xiu's and Zhao Mingcheng's notes on the Stone Drums, objects that would eventually find their way into Huizong's collection.[49] Ouyang Xiu wrote:

> To the right is the text of the Stone Drums. The Stone Drums of Qiyang were not known from early times till the Tang period, when people first praised them. Wei Yingwu[50] considered them the drums of King Wen of Zhou, inscribed during the reign of King Xuan.[51] Han Tuizhi [Han Yu, 768–824] considered them the drums of King Xuan. They are currently in the Confucian Temple in Fengxiang [Shaanxi province]. The drums belonged to a set of ten. Previously they had been scattered throughout the countryside, but Zheng Yuqing[52] put them in the temple, with one missing. In 1052 Xiang Chuanshi[53] found the missing one among the common people, thus completing the set.
>
> The legible parts of the inscriptions come to 465 characters, with more than half illegible. Of all the texts I have gathered and recorded, these are the earliest. Still, there are three or four reasons to be suspicious of them. Nowadays, there are quite a few stelae surviving from the time of the Han emperors Huan [r. 146–167] and Ling [r. 167–189], which is not quite a thousand years ago. Still eight or nine out of ten which had been written in large characters and deeply inscribed are too worn to read. According to the Grand Historian's chronological charts, 1,914 years have passed from the time of King Xuan, when common dating began, until this present year of 1063. The characters on the drums are fine and the carving is shallow. Logically, how could they have remained legible? This is the first doubtful point.
>
> The characters are ancient and yet are systematic; the language matches the elegant hymns [in the *Book of Songs*]. Even though there are no other examples of authentic writings from the Three Dynasties except for the *Book of Songs* and *Book of Documents*,

learned and curious scholars since the Han dynasty have said nothing about the Drums. This is the second suspicious point.

The Sui imperial house collected books on the grandest scale, and the treatise [on bibliography in the *Sui History*] lists the carved stones of the First Qin emperor and foreign Brahmanic texts.[54] Yet it does not list the Stone Drums. Since it valued ancient over modern texts, there is no reason for it to have left them out. This is the third suspicious point.

Accounts of far-off marvels are common in narratives of earlier times; they are full of fabrications and hard to believe. How much more so when the records have not recorded anything! I do not know on what basis Wei [Yingwu] and Han [Yu] could know that these were the drums of Kings Wen or Xuan. During Sui and Tang times ancient and modern writings were in a so-so state. It is unlikely that they had sources that we do not have access to today. Still, Han Yu loved antiquity and was not wild in his views. I thus for the time being accept his opinions. And with regard to the calligraphy, no one but Shi Zhou[55] could have done it.[56]

In this passage, Ouyang Xiu demonstrates his capacity for skepticism. He is inclined to doubt that any carved stone can remain legible for more than a thousand years and is particularly suspicious of something so large failing to attract notice until Tang times.

Zhao Mingcheng responded to Ouyang Xiu's arguments, making the assumption that his readers were familiar with them.

The traditional attribution is that King Xuan had [the Drums] carved and Shi Zhou did the calligraphy. Ouyang Xiu had doubts about them because Han stelae of the time of Emperors Huan and Ling, which is less than a thousand years ago, in eight or nine cases out of ten are too worn to read even when they have been written in large characters and deeply incised, so logically there is no reason for the Drums to have survived given that more than 1900 years have passed since the time of King Xuan and the characters are fine and the inscription shallow.

When I examine stelae and inscriptions from the Qin and earlier, such as these Drums, the *Cursing Chu* text, and the Qin inscriptions in seal script at Mt. Tai,[57] they are all on coarse-grained stones, like the sort we use nowadays for mortars and pestles. Because the nature of the stone is strong and unyielding, it is difficult to chip and, moreover, has no other uses. As a consequence, these [stones] have been able to survive until today. The stones used for stelae and markers since the Han period, although fine, are easily split and broken, and, moreover, frequently are taken by people to make bases for pillars and the like. It seems that people of ancient times had foresight, and there is a logic to these things. How much more so is this true given that the characters are written in a marvelously ancient way, beyond the ability of people after the Zhou period. Even Ouyang Xiu admitted that no one but Shi Zhou could have written them, which is a true observation.[58]

Collectors without the time or erudition to research all of their own pieces might ask the opinion of learned scholars who enjoyed such puzzles. Dong You (fl. 1100–1130) was such an expert, and in his collected notices he mentions dozens of examples of men who showed him items that were intriguing in one way or another. Sometimes he came to the conclusion that an object was forged or otherwise not what it seemed to be.[59] More often, he identified an object that seemed puzzling. For instance, Li Jie, mentioned in the last chapter as the architect of the new campus of the National Academy, had wide-ranging interests in collecting and once showed Dong You a bronze in the shape of an ox. Li Jie thought that it must be a "sacrificial animal beaker" (*xizun*), even though it did not look like the illustration of one in the *Illustrations of the Three Ritual Classics*. Dong confirmed his hunch, supporting it by reviewing references to the term "sacrificial animal beaker" in the classics and commentaries, and discussing two other examples that had come to light in recent times.[60]

Providing Access to Other Scholars

As the cases presented above show, scholarly collectors commonly let other scholars read, copy, or borrow their books, rubbings, calligraphies, and paintings. It was in order to use the Song family's books that scholars looked for houses near theirs. Lü Dalin was not only able to visit collectors of ancient bronzes but also to make drawings of the vessels and take rubbings of their inscriptions for his *Investigations of Antiquities Illustrated*. Li Gonglin was able to make copies of paintings in other people's collections. Mi Fu visited dozens of collectors of painting and calligraphy. He mentioned nearly a hundred collectors and some 330 pieces of calligraphy that he saw. Those he visited included well-known literati, high officials, imperial clansmen, imperial affinal relatives, and many people who can no longer be identified but apparently had enough means to collect.[61]

After their collections outgrew their houses, collectors sometimes built separate buildings to house them. Sima Guang, who had more than 10,000 chapters of books, built a Hall for Reading Books to house them in his Garden of Solitary Pleasure. The Daoist master Chen Jingyuan had separate halls built for his Daoist, Confucian, and medical books, which made it easier for visitors to go directly to the books that interested them. Although collections of paintings and calligraphy rarely occupied as much space as books, some collectors ended up needing to build new space for them as well. In 1072 Sun Jue built a hall for the rubbings and stelae he had collected as prefect of Wuxing. The hall was erected at the prefectural yamen, a site that would make it accessible to local literati. In 1077, Wang Shen had a building built for his paintings.[62]

Owners of paintings and calligraphies generally did not give visitors free run of the room where they were stored, but rather viewed pieces with their guests. During the Northern Song, painting and calligraphy viewings became occasions to ask those present to record their reactions, often in poems. These inscriptions and colophons often survive in writers' collected works even when the painting or calligraphy itself has been lost, and tell us not only about the works but also about the ways they were interpreted, used, and circulated.[63] This was also the period when it became common for collectors to put their seals on paintings. The seals Mi Fu put on the best works in his collections carried such messages as "authenticated," "of the divine class," "For Mr. Mi's private amusement," or simply "Mi Fu."[64]

Why were people so generous in allowing others access to the works they had accumulated? Some may have felt that ownership obligated them. In the age before libraries, museums, and photography, learning required such access. In the case of books, beginners needed works to copy or compare; in the case of calligraphy, paintings, and antiquities, they needed to view and discuss originals in order to learn to recognize authentic works of high quality. In other words, collecting was an intrinsically social activity, and those who enjoyed collecting must often have found the social interaction it engendered part of its attraction.

Another way to offer access to one's treasures was to issue a catalogue of them. Such a book allowed even those who could not visit in person to learn from one's collection. Ouyang Xiu, Li Gonglin, and Zhao Mingcheng all prepared catalogues of their antiquities or rubbings. Many book collectors also compiled catalogues.[65] For instance, Li Shu, who had a special interest in books on divination, mathematics, music, philology, and scripts, in 1049 compiled a ten-chapter catalogue of his family's books. The books were classified into fifty-seven categories, and an addendum listed other works in the family's collection, such as paintings, calligraphies, and Daoist books.[66]

A particularly interesting advance in cataloguing in Northern Song times was the addition of illustrations. During Renzong's reign the palace had illustrations prepared of its small collection of ancient bronzes. The first private illustrated catalogue, produced in 1063 by Liu Chang, was titled *Illustrations of Ancient Vessels of the Pre-Qin Era* and contained pictures of eleven vessels, along with the inscriptions on them. Both Li Gonglin's and Lü Dalin's catalogues of antiquities were illustrated. Lü's survives, and illustrates objects owned by several dozen collectors (see fig. 3.3). This catalogue is particularly notable for recording the names of the owners of objects and identifying where the objects had been found.[67]

Reservations about Collecting

Some Northern Song collectors were unabashedly acquisitive; Mi Fu is probably the best example, as his two *Chronicles* reveal his glee when a masterpiece came his way. Still Mi Fu knew it was best to be able to let go of things. He wrote, "Nowadays, people collect something and keep it their whole life, which is really silly. It is human nature to grow bored with things one has looked at for a long time. If one trades it for something new and amusing in a timely manner, both sides will get something they want."[68]

A few scholars, however, had ambivalent feelings about collecting. Ronald Egan has shown that Ouyang Xiu had misgivings even about collecting something as book-like as rubbings. In his view, Ouyang Xiu's frequent reference to the historiographical value of inscriptions is defensive, based on his unease with aesthetic attraction to what were, ultimately, material things.[69] As Stephen Owen has shown, Li Qingzhao related not only the joys she and her husband felt in their early years of acquiring cultural treasures but also the burden that the objects eventually became. Moving the collection proved enormously difficult, especially since it had to be done quickly to flee an invading army. She declared that greed for such things was at bottom no different from greed for money.[70]

The scholar most voluble on the dangers of collecting was Su Shi. In the account he wrote of a man who had donated his collection of nine thousand books to a Buddhist temple, Su Shi expressed reservations about the value of accumulating books. In the passage cited earlier, he began by noting that books, in theory at least, are the best of all objects, useful, pleasing, and inexhaustible. Su Shi then cited evidence that in the Zhou period books were hard to obtain. That led him to observe, "Not many of those born in that age got to read the Six Classics, making study difficult for them. And yet later scholars have never equaled their mastery of ritual and music or deep comprehension of morality." One problem was that as books became more widely available, scholars became less inclined to read them:

> Ever since the Qin and Han periods, authors have multiplied. Both paper and the writing script have become progressively more convenient. With the steady increase in books, every scholar owns some. And yet scholars have become shallower. Why is that? I once met an old Confucian scholar who said that when he was young he had trouble locating copies of the *Shiji* and *Hanshu*, so after he got hold of them, he copied them

all out by hand, and recited them day and night, fearful that he might miss something. In recent years, merchants print the works of philosophers and other authors, issuing ten thousand pages a day. The relationship between scholars and books changes when books are numerous and easy to get. It ought to be that modern scholars' writing and scholarship should be twice as good as that of the ancients, but more recent students and exam candidates have bundles of books that they do not read; as they travel about they offer opinions on things, but without any basis.

Su Shi went on to say that his friend was different, that he mulled over the words in his books, and moreover made them available to others. Su concluded by saying he had agreed to write this essay to let future visitors to the collection know "the difficulty that former scholars had in acquiring books and the pity that nowadays scholars do not read books even when they own them."[71]

Su Shi had just as strong feelings about collecting paintings and calligraphies. In 1077, when he was serving as a prefect out of the capital, he took the occasion of a request to write a commemorative essay for Wang Shen's new painting hall to chide Wang. Drawing on Buddhist ideas about attachment and ways to avoid it, Su began his essay by noting that the noble man may let his mind pay visit to material things, but should not let it stay there. If his mind just visits, then he can get pleasure from the most trifling things, and even the most alluring will not become an affliction for him. But if he lets his mind become preoccupied with them, he will not get pleasure from even the most enchanting. Su then mentioned some men in history whose love of their paintings and calligraphies caused them to lose all sense of proportion. Next he related his own experience:

As a young man I too was obsessively fond of calligraphy and painting. I worried constantly that my family might lose what works we owned, and I was also distressed that other people would not give us what they owned. Later, I laughed at myself, thinking that I made little of wealth and position but made much of calligraphy, and that I took death lightly but gave importance to painting. Were not my priorities upside down, and had I not lost my innate sense of things? After this, I overcame my obsession. When I saw a work I liked, although occasionally I would acquire it, if someone subsequently took it away from me I would not begrudge its loss. It was like the clouds passing before my eyes or bird songs pleasing my ears: naturally, I appreciated whatever I happened to encounter, but once they were gone I did not give them another thought. Thereafter, these two things, calligraphy and painting, became a constant source of joy for me but never an affliction.

Su ended the essay by telling Wang Shen that he worried that Wang "might suffer from the same obsessive fondness I had in my own youth."[72]

Huang Tingjian also had qualms about Wang Shen's collecting, part of his unease based on Wang's willingness to pay high prices for works. As Egan sees it, "In the view of Su and Huang, there is something unseemly about this willingness to spend extravagantly to amass large collections. They see it as taking the place of true discernment and connoisseurship. Money and connoisseurship are juxtaposed with each other as if they are incompatible."[73]

Scholars had collected books, paintings, and calligraphies before the Song period, but the social, cultural, and economic climate of the eleventh century made possible a major expansion in collecting as a cultivated pursuit of the educated class. By the eve of Huizong's reign, the collecting of books and related cultural relics had made many advances. The spread of printing had raised the stakes in the collation of books, as the edition that appeared in print would gain authoritative status. The connoisseurial challenges of distinguishing original calligraphy from tracing or freehand copies or imitations led collectors like Mi Fu to scrutinize tangible papers and seals and the intangible spirit and resonance of the works they inspected. Connoisseurs of paintings had begun to record their reactions to viewing art works, often in the form of poems written on the painting or an attached sheet of paper.

The most dramatic advance in collecting was the emergence of antiquities as a field of collecting. Men like Li Gonglin and Zhao Mingcheng collected ancient bronzes and jades, rubbings of inscriptions on such antiquities, and rubbings of stone inscriptions, mostly of Han to Tang date. The publication of catalogues that shared information about the objects collected helped spread interest in early scripts and antiquities in general. Catalogues that included illustrations of antiquities were especially influential, as they allowed scholars who did not live in the capital or other major cities to compare objects that they encountered to ones owned by major collectors. Printing rubbings of inscriptions on these vessels in addition allowed scholars who did not have access to the vessels themselves to join in the effort to decipher the texts and trace the evolution of early script forms. When Taizong and Zhenzong built up the palace collections in the late tenth and early eleventh centuries, these sorts of collections and associated scholarly activities were not yet common.

In the mid- to late-eleventh century, collecting books, art, and antiquities intersected with politics, but was not fundamentally political in nature. During Renzong's reign, Song Shou and Ouyang Xiu were major political figures and also major collectors, but most of the leading political figures during the reform era were minor collectors if they collected at all. Wang Anshi was a man of culture, a distinguished poet who wrote commentaries on the Confucian classics and learned inquiries into etymology, but he was not a collector. He undoubtedly had some books and perhaps had saved some friends' letters as calligraphy, but there is no sign that he pursued old masterpieces or even inexpensive rubbings. Much the same could be said of many of the other men active in politics during this period, both reformers and conservatives.

Some of those who were most active as collectors probably avoided politics because of their kinship ties to the throne. Imperial clansmen were not allowed to hold office and were discouraged from involvement in politics. Probably the imperial sons-in-law Li Wei and Wang Shen felt similar pressures. Other major collectors, notably Li Gonglin and Mi Fu, maintained reasonably good relationships with both reformers and conservatives. Although both considered Su Shi a friend, they also socialized and traded favors with Su's political opponents. Li Gonglin was on friendly terms with Wang Anshi, and even painted a picture of him riding on a donkey with a servant boy carrying his controversial study of etymology. Mi Fu was friends with Zhang Dun and Cai Jing, and turned to Cai Jing for help.[74] Zhao Mingcheng came from a family that supported the reform administration. Su Shi was of course politically engaged, but his place in this chapter has been more as a critic of collecting than as a collector. These collectors did not expect their collecting to be interpreted as a political statement. During Shenzong's and Zhezong's reigns, the court was not competing with private collectors for objects, so avid pursuit by individuals was neither following the lead of the court nor competing with it. Su Shi's qualms about collecting did not derive from the perception that reformers were more dominant in collecting than conservatives (though they may have drawn on his sense that the rich had too great an advantage).

Collecting did not align one with either the reformers or the conservatives—any more than writing poetry did—but it did help solidify one's position in the educated class. Collections were assets in many senses. First, they were social assets. If you had a collection, people would seek you out; you would be in demand. In addition, you would share in some of the honor accorded the objects you collected, in no small part because you had recognized their merits. This would be all the more true if you went further and enhanced their worth by doing research on them or making an annotated catalogue of them. Although observers noticed the obsessions of collectors, they were tolerant of them, seeing in them something akin to Confucius losing his interest in food after hearing the music of Shao.

Second, collections were financial assets. Objects in them could be traded or sold, sometimes at great profit. Most collectors, however, hoped that the bulk of their collection (preferably improved over time through appropriate trading up) would go to their descendants. The collection would, in a sense, add to their family's net worth, but in a way that would encourage sons and grandsons toward the scholarly life.

Third, collections were literary assets in that they gave rise to occasions for writing. Not only were the objects collected connected to texts in a variety of ways, but interaction with these objects frequently became occasions for writing about objects and people's relations to objects. There is a large literature surviving from the Song connected to collecting, ranging from poems scholars wrote about each others' paintings and calligraphy (meant to be shared with the owner and often written on the work itself or an attached colophon) to notes one made for one's own reference (probably recorded after leaving the owner's home and not meant to be shown to him) to catalogues of collections and works of criticism based on viewing many collections. Collections were literary assets both to those who themselves aspired to write and to those whose aspirations lay rather in being mentioned in others' writings. Collecting, as practiced among Song scholars, was not an activity for those who preferred tangible objects to immaterial words but rather one in which words and things were in constant interplay.

Fourth, collections were artistic assets, of value to men such as Wang Shen, Mi Fu, Zhao Lingrang, and Li Gonglin who aspired to artistic creation. Examining and copying old works would improve their technique and bring them into contact with the sorts of people who could acquire their works and spread word of their talent. Moreover, their standing as collectors would counter any suspicion that they painted for a living.

The apolitical way collecting was treated by the educated elite in Kaifeng at the end of the eleventh century may have been part of its attraction to Huizong. As an emperor, of course, his situation was different from even the most wealthy and high-ranking of the collectors of the capital. He could not pay visits to subjects to view their treasures. Nor could he bargain or make trades to acquire objects. Yet there was much in the contemporary culture of collecting that he could adopt.

CHAPTER 4

Huizong As a Collector

Once Huizong issued an order that the antiquities in the collection be displayed on the two side chambers of Promoting Governance Hall and had the officials summoned to view them. At that time Huizong was attentive to government matters, concentrated and serene. He would secretly peek through the cracks in the inner doors to hear his officials discuss the objects with each other. He could recognize each one and enjoyed listening to their displays of broad knowledge; he savored the flavor of their discussions and appreciated their eminence, all without the officials knowing he was there.

—Cai Tao

BECAUSE OF HUIZONG'S REPUTATION AS A MAN MORE INTERESTED in the arts than in statecraft, Huizong's personal involvement with his collections has largely been assumed. There are, after all, still surviving a dozen or so title slips written in Huizong's hand on paintings and calligraphies that also bear his seals.[1] On the other hand, Maggie Bickford has recently cast doubt on whether Huizong actually painted the works that bear his seals and signatures.[2] If court artists could be called on to paint the works Huizong claimed as his own, surely court calligraphers could be assigned the task of writing title slips for the thousands of scrolls in his collection. Therefore, it is useful to lay out in some detail the ways in which Huizong was personally involved with the collections assembled at his court.

By far the most important witness to this facet of Huizong's rulership is Cai Tao, a man who was as well placed as anyone to know what went on in Huizong's palace. Cai Tao was the youngest son of Huizong's long-term grand councilor, Cai Jing, and about fifteen years younger than Huizong himself.[3] His oldest brother, Cai You, was twenty years his senior and served throughout Huizong's reign. Another older brother, Cai Tiao, married Huizong's fifth daughter in 1118, tying the two families by marriage. Even before that, however, Huizong treated Cai Jing's sons with exceptional informality. Beginning in the early Zhenghe period (1111–1117), Cai Tao reported, Huizong copied the precedent of the Tang emperor Dezong (r. 779–805), who had addressed the eminent statesman Lu Zhi informally as "Lu Nine." Huizong thus began calling Cai You "Cai Six" and extended the practice to the other Cai brothers as well, calling Cai Tao "Cai Thirteen."[4]

Cai Tao was probably in and out of the palace as a teenager, but does not seem to have played much of a political role until he was in his midtwenties, near the end of Huizong's reign. By 1123 he held the high post of edict attendant of the Huiyou Hall (rank 4b). That year he was dismissed from the government on the grounds that he wrote a book on poetry that gave prominent places to Su Shi and Huang Tingjian, two of those whose writings had been banned by Huizong. Late the next year, Cai Jing was brought back as grand councilor for his fourth term. Because at age seventy-eight he was nearly blind, he had Cai Tao assist him. Cai Tao, we are told, would read aloud to his father, write for him, and substitute for him at audiences. At the time Tao was honored by being granted the status of "equal to a presented scholar" (*jinshi chushen*). Not surprisingly, other officials complained about the power he exercised, chief among those being his own brother, Cai You, who for some time had not gotten along with their father. Cai You is even said to have repeatedly asked Huizong to have Cai Tao executed. Although Huizong would not go that far, after only four months Cai Tao was demoted and Cai Jing once more retired.[5]

After the Jin invasion and Huizong's abdication, Cai Jing died on his way to exile, Cai You and his brother Cai Shu were executed by Huizong's successor (his eldest son, Qinzong), and Cai Tiao, as a son-in-law, followed Huizong into captivity. Cai Tao, although exiled to a remote area in Guangxi, survived for a couple of decades, giving him time to write not only his six-chapter *Collected Talks from My Little World* (Tiewei shan congtan) but also a widely cited history.[6]

In *Collected Talks* Cai Tao showed a broad familiarity with features of palace life during Huizong's reign. His topics range widely, from court etiquette to key personalities. He reported at length on Daoist masters prominent at court. He also provided revealing discussions of Huizong's interests in tea, inkstones, chess, and court artists. He even discussed relatively private matters, such as Huizong's relations with his sons. Cai Tao was, of course, not an unbiased witness. Many have pointed out that he showed his father in a more favorable light than the standard histories did.[7] Moreover, we need to keep in mind that he was writing after the events and after the destruction of Huizong's world. The incidents and personalities that he chose to write about undoubtedly would have been different if the Jurchen had never attacked and Huizong had reigned peacefully into old age. Like many of his contemporaries, in looking back to Huizong's reign, Cai Tao frequently returned to events and practices that seemed to him to foretell the fate that befell Huizong and his court.

Involvement with Painting and Calligraphy as a Prince

According to Cai Tao, Huizong's interests in painting and calligraphy were already well developed before he took the throne:

> In our dynasty princes have usually been fond of wealth and rank; Huizong alone while a prince loved the unusual. He devoted himself exclusively to practicing painting and calligraphy, collecting books and pictures, and mastering archery and riding. In the Shaosheng [1094–1097] and Yuanfu [1098–1100] periods, when he was just sixteen or seventeen, his sagely reputation had already spread, and those who knew him already suspected he would succeed to the throne. Early on, he was friendly with Wang Shen and the imperial clansman Zhao Danian [Lingrang], both of whom were good at writing prose and poetry and were marvelous painters. Zhao Danian was also good at Huang Tingjian [style calligraphy]. Therefore Huizong did Tingjian style calligraphy, and later formed his own style on that basis. From time to time he would also amuse himself with painting with Wu Yuanyu, who served in his princely mansion.[8]

This passage provides direct evidence that Huizong as a prince got to know two of the most prominent art collectors of the day, both of whom were relatives: his father's sister's husband, Wang Shen, and the imperial clansman Zhao Lingrang. Wang Shen was one of the five collectors discussed in the last chapter, and he was as well an accomplished painter and calligrapher (see fig. 3.2 and plates 9 and 10). Zhao Lingrang had similar interests, and, like Wang Shen, both collected art work and painted landscapes (see plate 12). The two men were a generation older than Huizong, and seem to have offered the fatherless young prince examples of how to fashion a life as an accomplished aristocrat. Following their lead, while still in his teens Huizong studied both painting and calligraphy. However, the painter Huizong studied with, Wu Yuanyu, was not a master of landscape but of bird-and-flower painting.[9]

In the passage above, Cai Tao makes only passing reference to Huizong's interest in collecting. Elsewhere Cai Tao records a specific occasion when Huizong became involved with Wang Shen's collecting:

> Wang Shen's family for a long time had possessed two sheets of a painting of mallows by Xu Bijian.[10] Wang Shen was always sighing that he was missing half of it and regretted that it was not complete. Huizong quietly searched for [the missing part] and one

> day succeeded in securing it. He then asked to borrow the other half from Wang Shen, and Wang Shen obeyed, thinking Huizong loved [the painting] and wanted its marvels for himself. Huizong had a mounter join the two as one scroll, and invited Wang Shen to look at it. He then made a present of it to Wang Shen.[11]

This anecdote implies that Wang Shen felt that he might have to make a gift of the painting to the young prince, whose rank in the imperial hierarchy was considerably higher than his own. We are thus surprised when we discover instead that the youthful Huizong was helping Wang Shen add to his already impressive collection.

As a prince, Huizong also collected the work of living artists, or at least the calligraphy of Cai Jing, then a mid-rank court official well-known for his calligraphy. In the item that reports this, Cai Tao first traced the evolution of his father's calligraphic style as he practiced the styles of different masters, ending with a study of the style of the Two Wangs. By then he had created his own style, "which the entire world honored." Cai Tao then records how Huizong as a prince acquired some of Cai Jing's calligraphy:

> When my father was working at the northern gate, he had two retainers who attended him with exceptional deference. Each carried a round white fan to fan him while he was working in summer time. Out of generosity, my father wrote a poem by Du Fu on each of their fans. A few days later, the two retainers appeared in high spirits, parading their new clothes. They said that a royal prince had purchased their fans for the handsome price of 200,000 cash. That prince was the present retired emperor [that is, Huizong]. Later, when my father was entertained by the emperor in Harmony Preserved Hall, the latter mentioned this incident to him, adding, "The two fans are now kept with the inner palace collections."[12]

Huizong, thus, not only saw Cai Jing's calligraphy as worth acquiring, but continued to treasure it for more than two decades.

Building Up the Palace Collections

Once on the throne, Cai Tao reports, Huizong set to gathering more objects for the palace collections:

> Once Huizong took the throne, he put his mind to searching the realm for calligraphies and paintings. In the Chongning period [1102–1106], he began by appointing Song Zifang [Qiaonian] to manage the imperial painting and calligraphy [school].[13] After Song's dismissal, Mi Fu was appointed.

The works the emperor accumulated, from first to last, numbered in the thousands; it really was a splendid accomplishment of a glorious dynasty. In 1123 I got to see the catalogue. There were more than 3,800 tracing copies of works by the Two Wangs done by men of the Tang, and more than 800 works by Yan Zhenqing. Pieces of calligraphy by such [Tang] masters as Ouyang Xun, Yu Shinan, Chu Suiliang, and Xue Ji, as well as ones by famous officials such as Li Bo and Bo Juyi, were uncountable. The admittedly countable items by men of the Western and Eastern Jin included many exceptional works such as the Two Wangs' *Poqiang*[14] and *Goddess of the Luo River.*[15] Furthermore, the palace collection of old paintings had some that dated way back. The earliest was Cao Buxing's *The Original Maiden Transmitting the Military Tallies to the Yellow Emperor. . . .*[16]

Today we will never look on these [masterpieces] again, which makes people feel short of breath. It seems that once Huizong's love of these objects was manifested from the Zhenghe period [1111–1117] on, people presented them as bribes to gain favors, which became a failing of the age. Allowing this to happen was a serious mistake.[17]

This passage brings up many aspects of Huizong's collecting that can be substantiated from other sources, such as Huizong's early interest in the court collections, how he acquired objects, his use of expert consultants, and the huge size of the collection. Other evidence that he took an interest in the collections from early in his reign can be found in the memorial submitted by a censor in his first year on the throne. The censor reported that he had heard that Huizong had asked to have some paintings brought from the Palace Library into the inner palace. The censor advised him to look at the classics, not at pictures.[18]

There is also corroborating evidence on the ways Huizong acquired works of art. According to one account the eunuch Tong Guan was sent south to search for art works soon after Huizong took the throne. Other eunuchs were sent to Luoyang late in his reign, ready to spend generously to obtain old paintings.[19] Deng Chun, writing in 1167, recorded a case in which an official recognized that a painting he saw should be in the palace collection:

Among the most precious works kept in the Council Chamber of Harmony Revealed Hall was a set of paintings by Zhan Ziqian called *The Four Conveyances.* The emperor loved and enjoyed each of them. Sometimes he could not tear himself away from them all day. Regretfully, there were only three [of the original four] pictures; the *Transport by Water* picture was missing from the series. One day an official went to Luoyang and happened to hear that one of Luoyang's old families had it. Immediately, he asked Luoyang's chief magistrate if he could see it. When he saw it, he said, startled: "This really is the Council Chamber's missing painting." Forthwith, it was presented to the emperor. As the saying goes: "When Heaven gives birth to a divine sage, all things will finally come to him."[20]

Elsewhere in the *Collected Talks,* Cai Tao gives other examples of how objects entered the palace. For instance, he reports that in the Zhenghe period, Huizong had a temple plaque brought to the palace because a Tang calligrapher had written a poem on it. This particular plaque was famous because Mi Fu had once tried to steal it from the temple which owned it.[21] In other places Cai Tao mentions how ancient artifacts were turned over to the palace:

> When Huizong took the throne he made manifest his love for antiquity and his desire to match [the ancient sage kings Yao and Shun of] Tang and Yu, and therefore [collecting antiquities] boomed. In the early Daguan period [1107–1110], he compiled the *Illustrations of the Antiquities in Harmony Revealed Hall*, styled on Li Gonglin's *Investigations of Antiquities Illustrated*. There were already more than five hundred ritual vessels, large and small, in his collection. Once the world realized what he loved, when anyone obtained a vessel, he would price it at several hundred thousand cash; later some even exceeded a million cash. As a consequence, soon practically all the tombs in the realm had been excavated. [Enthusiasm for antiquities] reached its high point in the Zhenghe period [1111–1117], when the ritual vessel storerooms contained over six thousand vessels. From them one can understand ancient writings on ritual, and can discard many of the interpretations of earlier Confucian scholars. First Duan prefecture submitted the bells of Duke Cheng of Song, which led to the creation of the Dasheng music.[22] Afterward other instruments were found. The rituals and music of our dynasty were thus made much closer to antiquity than any earlier dynasty's. . . .
>
> At the time what Huizong valued were the vessels of Xia, Shang, and Zhou; in the case of Qin and Han pieces, only exceptional ones were collected. From the Xuanhe period on [1119–1125], everything was kept and recorded, till the number reached more than 10,000. Famous objects, such as the Stone Drums of King Xuan from Qiyang and the painted portrait of Western Shu's Wen Weng in the ritual hall, were all brought to the palace, no matter whether large or small, from far or near.[23]

(One of the Stone Drums, which are still extant, is shown in fig. 4.1.)

In this account Cai Tao observed that Huizong's interest in antiquities led to a rise in the prices people could get for them and thus indirectly provided an incentive for grave robbing. His contemporary Ye Mengde also described these phenomena:

> In the Xuanhe period [1119–1125], the palace esteemed ancient vessels. Not daring to keep them hidden, scholar-official families offered all of their antiquities from Xia,

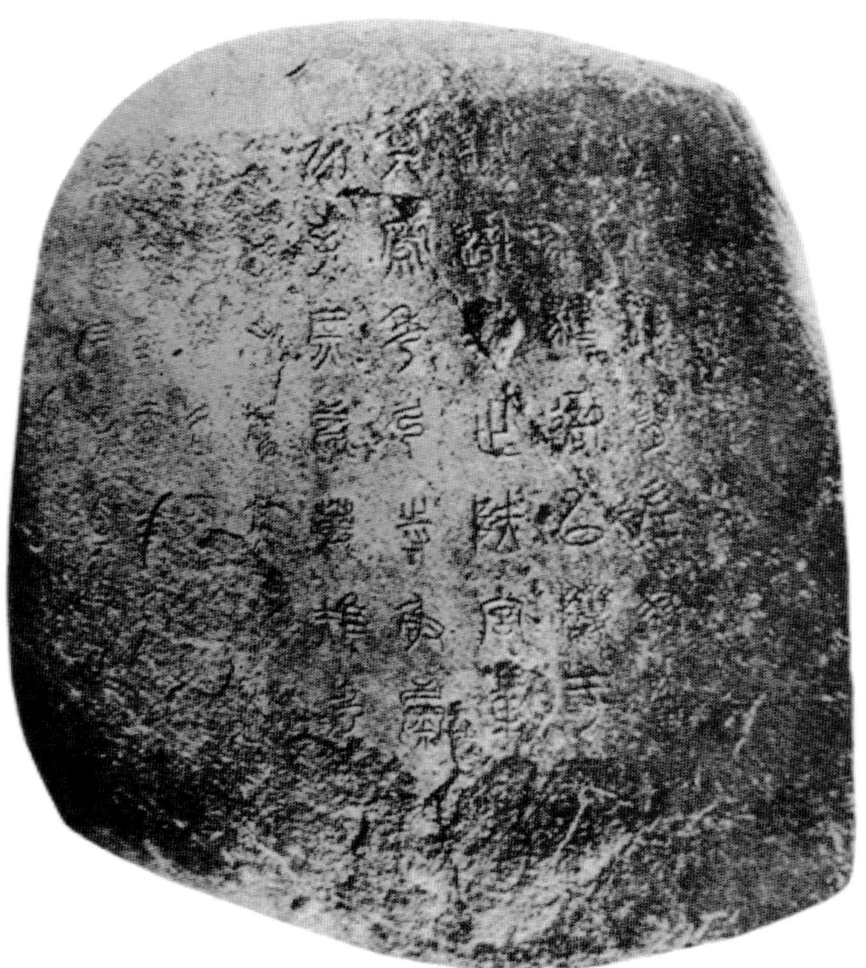

Fig. 4.1
The seventh of the ten Stone Drums. Height 56.5 cm, weight over 300 kg. Palace Museum, Beijing. These drums were transported from Shaanxi province to Kaifeng and installed in Huizong's palace. The text inscribed on this one is a poem concerning a hunting party led by the Duke of Qin.

Shang, Zhou, Qin, and Han to the throne. Those who loved these things then competed to find more, worried more about not getting a piece than its price, which could reach several million cash. In pursuit of profit people competed to scrape the hills and marshes and dig up graves, stopping at nothing. In innumerable cases objects hidden for several thousand years were suddenly exposed. Wu Jue was magistrate of Gushi in Guangzhou, which had been the state of Shenbo and an old fief of Chu. From time to time unusual objects appeared there, but because of the remote location, no one knew it. Wu ordered commoners found guilty of crimes to pay restitution in ancient vessels. When he finished his term he had fifty to sixty vessels. When I met him in the capital he took them out and showed them to me. Several dozen of them were of the Xia, Shang, and Zhou periods. Later my cousin succeeded him as magistrate and after learning what Wu had done made a little use of the practice himself, getting a dozen-odd vessels. From this it can be inferred that many vessels have still not been made public.[24]

Ye's account reminds us that the statements of Cai Tao and others that refer hyperbolically to "all" valued objects entering Huizong's collections should not be taken literally. Not only did grave robbers fail to discover all graves but most private collectors such as Wu Jue held on to the bulk of their possessions. Only about 30 percent of the privately owned bronzes listed in Lü Dalin's 1092 catalogue are listed in Huizong's catalogue.[25] Only four of nine bronzes listed as owned by the imperial clansman Zhao Zhonghu in another catalogue also appear in Huizong's collection, even though the two men were on close terms.[26] As seen in chapter 3, Zhao Mingcheng's widow Li Qingzhao still had their huge collection at the end of Huizong's reign, when she had to cope with moving it in advance of the invading Jurchens. In all likelihood, Huizong's collection of ancient vessels never actually reached the ten thousand objects Cai Tao claimed.[27]

Neither Ye nor Cai made clear exactly how antiquities ended up in the palace. Did palace agents buy objects from those who found them? Or did those who dug them up sell them to ambitious men who wanted to please Huizong by presenting them to him? Did local governments claim them and then submit them to the court? Probably objects reached Huizong in all of these ways, and in others as well. Zhao Mingcheng reported cases of ancient bronzes discovered by farmers that the prefectural government sent to the court in 1118 and 1123. Hong Mai recorded a story of two fiscal officials in Shaanxi who had the grave of a Shang official excavated and sent Huizong the large bronze pan they found in it. Huizong dismissed the officials and sent the pan back, rebuking them for digging up the grave of a past worthy.[28] In another case Cai Tao described how an object changed hands repeatedly before being presented to the throne. This object, called the Primal Tablet (Xuan gui), had once belonged to the early Song high official and art collector Ding Wei, but subsequently it had been sold. Later an official named Wang Minwen had purchased it for a substantial price. When the palace eunuch Tan Zhen was supervising defense in Hedong, he saw it and was amazed by it. Tan acquired it from Wang, then presented it to Huizong in 1112.[29] This jade object is described as twelve inches long, black on the edges, and red in the center. The top was tapered and the bottom square. On two sides twelve mountains were engraved with very fine workmanship. There were also cloud and thunder patterns at the top, and a hole in the middle, large enough for a finger to pass through.

Certainly people did offer objects to Huizong. In 1107 a man on the list of banned officials, Liu Fengshi, submitted an ancient vessel that he had inherited from his

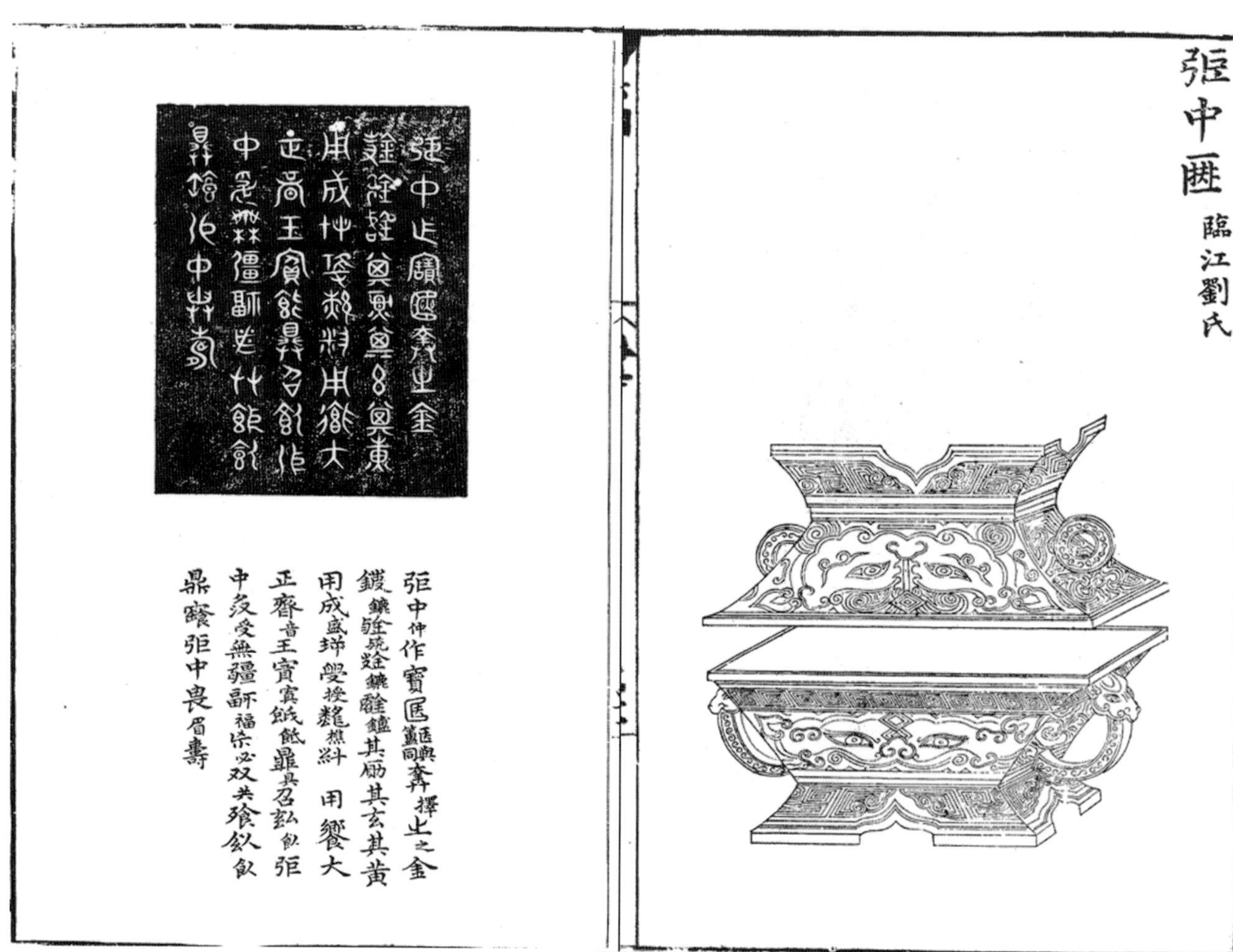

Fig. 4.2
Investigations of Antiquities Illustrated entry for a vessel that Liu Fengshi later submitted to Huizong's court. This vessel, interpreted as a tureen, was part of a set of four with identical fifty-one-character inscriptions found in Lantian, each 7.5 by 9.5 inches. The transcription under the rubbing gives both exact and equivalent readings of the characters. KGT 1752 ed. 3.41a–b.

father, the famous collector Liu Chang (fig. 4.2).[30] Mi Fu, according to his funerary biography, after being appointed professor offered Huizong choice works of calligraphy and painting from his collection, and Huizong rewarded him generously with money. The rewards naturally encouraged others to submit their possessions.[31] Mi Fu's son Mi Youren in 1137 reported that his father's four genuine pieces of Wang Xizhi calligraphy had been presented to the throne in the Daguan period (1107–1110), probably after Mi Fu's death in 1107.[32] Wang Shen probably also gave paintings and calligraphy from his collection. He, for instance, was the owner of Sun Guoting's *On Calligraphy* (fig. 7.1) as well as two pieces of Yan Zhenqing's calligraphy, all three of which eventually entered Huizong's collection. Those who gave treasured objects to the palace undoubtedly expected some return. Ye Mengde reported that Li Gonglin's eighty-chapter illustrated version of the *Flower Garland Sutra* was so highly valued by Huizong's court that one could get a good office for submitting even one or two sheets from it.[33]

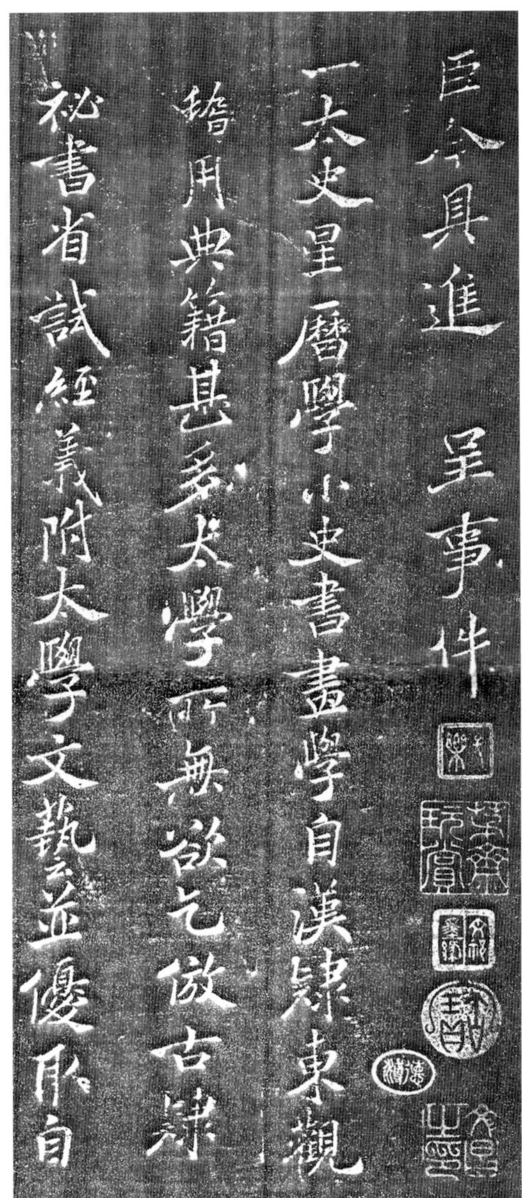

Fig. 4.3
Mi Fu (1051–1107), *Presentation of Duties* (rubbing, detail). In this memorial, datable to 1105, Mi Fu advocated upgrading the training of court artists. He also urged Huizong to try to improve the accuracy of the copies made at court of works in the palace collection. After CYTMT 3.1.

Cai Tao, in the passage cited above, also mentioned Mi Fu's appointment to Huizong's court. Perhaps on Cai Jing's or Wang Shen's recommendation, Mi Fu was first appointed to the Court of Imperial Sacrifices, then in 1105 was made professor of calligraphy and painting (see fig. 4.3).[34] From surviving anecdotes it is clear that Huizong and Mi Fu met several times, giving them the opportunity to discuss calligraphy and calligraphers. Zhang Bangji, in a text dated 1144, wrote:

> Mi Fu, when he was professor of calligraphy, was summoned for an audience with Huizong. Huizong asked him about a number of writers of the present dynasty who had achieved reputations as calligraphers. Mi Fu then characterized each of them, saying, "Cai Jing lacks brush. Cai Bian has brush but lacks untrammeled spirit. Cai Xiang labored his characters. Shen Liao arranged his characters. Huang Tingjian sketches his characters. Su Shi drew his characters." Huizong then asked Mi Fu about his own calligraphy. He answered, "I brush my characters."[35]

The professors at the painting and calligraphy schools were not the only ones Huizong could consult concerning objects in his collection. He routinely directed queries to the staff of the Palace Library, the topic of the next chapter. On other occasions, he turned to leading officials he respected for their scholarship, most notably Cai Jing. Cai Tao tells us, for instance, that after the receipt of the Primal Tablet, Huizong entrusted it to Cai Jing, saying, "Some say this is an ancient primal tablet. Investigate it for me."[36] Because Cai Jing had so many other responsibilities, he passed it on to his wife's nephew, Xu Ruogu, and Xu and Cai Tao found an appropriate passage in the *Record of Ritual* to argue that it was the ancient defense tablet (*zhen gui*, see fig. 4.4). Cai Jing and several other officials formally presented their analysis of the object and its implications at a court audience. They traced the origins of jade tablets back to the sage kings and interpreted the decoration of this tablet as symbols of Heaven and Earth. Since Huizong was enacting the policies of Yao, Shun, and Yu, they declared, Heaven had sent him this treasure. The next year Huizong announced that he would from that time on hold this jade tablet when he performed the winter sacrifices to Heaven.[37]

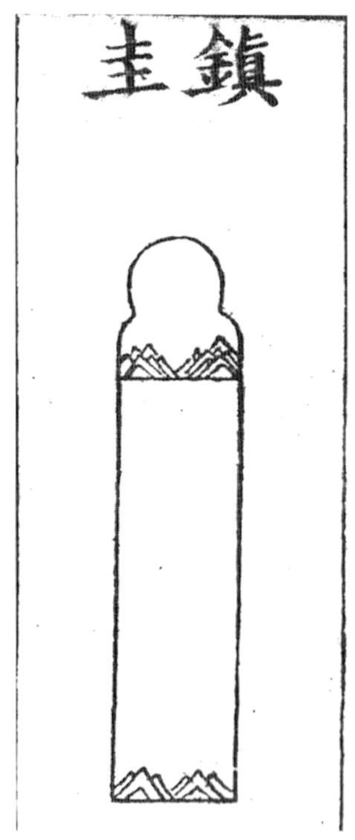

FIG. 4.4
Picture of a "defense tablet" in *Illustrations of the Three Ritual Classics*. After SLT 10.2a. In the *Rites of Zhou*, the king holds the one-foot-two-inch "defense tablet" to bring stability to his realm.

Housing the Collections

Huizong's collections grew so large that by 1113 he needed to construct special buildings to house them. Cai Tao briefly mentioned the buildings where he stored the objects from his collections that he valued most highly:

> Behind Harmony Revealed Hall, Huizong built Harmony Preserved Hall, which had pavilions on the left and right with names like Searching for Antiquity, the Broad Manifestations of Antiquity, and Honoring Antiquity. They were used as storehouses for the ancient jades and seals, bronze ritual vessels, calligraphies, and paintings.[38]

On the completion of these buildings, Huizong wrote (or took credit for writing) an account of them, in which he listed the different buildings and mentioned that they totaled seventy-five room-units in size. He remarked on the austere aesthetic adopted for the buildings and the fine workmanship of the construction. In keeping with his distaste for garish colors, the posts and beams were not painted. Nor were there colorful murals on the walls, which instead had monochrome paintings of wintry bamboo forests with birds. Concerning the chambers for the collections, Huizong wrote:

> The left side is filled with state papers and the classics and histories, which allow one to draw on antiquity in composing decrees and regulations. On the right are stored vessels of the Xia, Shang, and Zhou dynasties: cauldrons, libation cups, stands, raised dishes, tureens, pans, beakers, and tall jars. From observing the images on these vessels one can make vessels that reach the spirits during offerings at the altars and temples.
>
> On the eastern aisle are arranged the ancient and modern calligraphy and paintings, which have been classified according to quality. They allow one to amuse oneself and give free rein to thought. On the western aisle are [such scholar's objects as] zithers, brushes, and inkstones. With these one can flourish the brush and scatter ink, thus releasing sorrows and expressing emotions.[39]

Cai Jing provided a less lyrical description of these rooms as he saw them on a visit in 1119:

> Both the west and the east side rooms had laid out in them precious crafts, ancient bronzes, and jade objects. The studio on the left had the name, Marvelous Existence. In it were displayed Confucian works, histories, and calligraphy. The studio on the right had the name, The Way Revealed, and in it were the Daoist books of the golden casket and jade book box, along with the various secret Heavenly texts of the Divine Empyrean sect. The emperor proceeded forward to the Studio of Searching for Antiquity, which had the Stone Drums of King Xuan, then went to the series of other studios named Pursuing Antiquity, Honoring Antiquity, Examining Antiquity, Creating Antiquity, Transmitting Antiquity, the Broad Manifestations of Antiquity, and the Inner Secrets of Antiquity. In these were kept the writings of earlier emperors, various kinds of bronze vessels of the Xia, Shang, and Zhou dynasties, as well as paintings and calligraphies of the Han, Jin, Sui, and Tang dynasties, many of which I had never seen before.[40]

The second place Huizong's art and antiquities were kept was the Palace Library, which also came to need new quarters. After Huizong visited the Library in 1115, he issued an edict describing its buildings as cramped and dilapidated. The roofs leaked, and the walls looked as if they were bursting at the seams because too much was stuffed into them.[41] Soon the Library's site was designated for the construction of the new Hall of Enlightenment and a new larger Library was built south of the palace complex. The new complex included many office buildings and storerooms for books and was considered the most splendid of the government office complexes in the capital. On an official's request, Huizong himself wrote out the title plaques for the buildings.[42] Huizong's visit to these new quarters in 1122 is discussed later in this chapter.

Putting his Personal Imprint on the Paintings and Calligraphies in his Collections

Surviving paintings and calligraphies that were once in Huizong's collections are today recognized by the seals or inscriptions that he placed on them. Cai Tao made no mention of Huizong inscribing or impressing his seals on the paintings and calligraphies in his collection, but we have another witness with even greater access to Huizong's palace than Tao: Huizong's ninth son, who later reigned as Gaozong. In a discussion of the imperial calligraphy collection, Gaozong wrote:

> During our dynasty, ever since [the initial] Jianlong reign period and the pacification of the illegitimate [rival courts], famous pieces of calligraphy have all found their way to the palace collections. During the reign of my predecessor [Huizong], there was another search for objects, with rewards of official rank or wealth [for those who submitted them], and messengers sent to make inquiries. Thus nearly everything was located. The emperor assigned officials like Cai Jing, Liang Shicheng, and Huang Mian to classify the objects according to whether they were originals or copies, on paper or silk. Before storing them in the inner palace, they were mounted as scrolls or albums using [such fine materials as] black pheasant wood, brocade, white jade, and coral. The practice was to use Daguan, Zhenghe, and Xuanhe seals on them. Among the seals was one that used the calligraphic style of the Qin dynasty imperial seals. Later, each work would be stamped with the seal reading "neifu" [inner palace] and the emperor would write its title slip and ranking. Works that are not mounted this way are not from the most treasured collection. Those a grade below them were stored outside the inner palace at the Palace Library.[43]

Gaozong makes several important points in this passage. He reports that officials helped in the basic classification of works, with special attention to distinguishing copies from originals. Of the three men Gaozong mentions by name, two are well known for their close association with Huizong, but the third, Huang Mian, is of interest because he played the same role in Gaozong's court and could have been

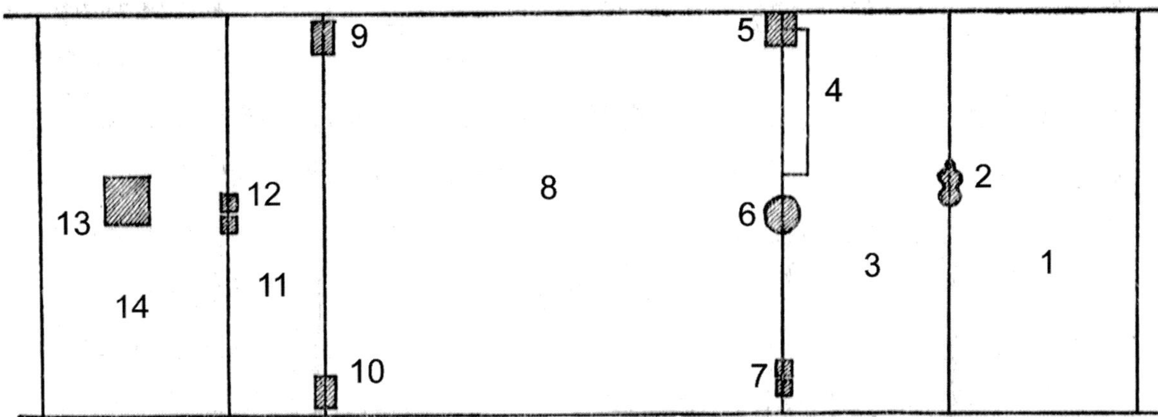

Fig. 4.5
Diagram of the position of seals in the Xuanhe program for a painting or calligraphy handscroll. The numbers identify the various parts. 1. Buff-colored outer mounting silk. 2. Gourd-shaped seal reading "imperial writing." 3. Buff-colored inner mounting silk. 4. Title with name of the artist and title of the work in Huizong's writing (for calligraphy on a separate piece of paper glued to the silk). 5. Square double dragon seal (on paintings). 6. Round double dragon seal (on calligraphies). 7. Linked Xuan and *he* seals. 8. Work proper. 9. Oblong Zhenghe seal. 10. Oblong Xuanhe seal. 11. Buff-colored mounting silk. 12. Linked Zheng and *he* seals. 13. Large square "seal of the inner treasury's paintings and calligraphies." 14. Mounting paper. Based on Xu Bangda 1981a:37.

one of Gaozong's sources for what was done during Huizong's time.[44] Gaozong draws a distinction between the works of lower grade kept in the Palace Library and the more highly valued collection kept in the inner palace. Scrolls in this more select group were remounted, and given the "inner palace" seal as well as other seals with reign names on them (Daguan, Zhenghe, and Xuanhe). Huizong himself wrote out titles for them.

Besides this textual evidence of Huizong's practice, there is a substantial body of paintings and calligraphies with what purport to be Huizong's seals on them. Many of these need to be dismissed as evidence either because the work itself clearly postdates Huizong or because the seals seem odd in one way or another. Forgers learned early on that placing Huizong seals on a painting could add to its value, so many works with "Huizong" seals are not plausible as works once in his collection. Excluding such implausible works leaves thirty-five works with a reasonably high likelihood to have been in Huizong's collection.[45] Appendix 2 lists them and provides illustrations of the seals on them. Some works on this list have both genuine and fake Huizong seals, probably the result of a later collector or dealer trying to "improve" the work.[46]

Twenty of these thirty-five works show the sort of remounting, seals, and titles that Gaozong referred to in this passage (dubbed here the Xuanhe mounting set; see fig. 4.5 and plate 13). They were remounted using buff-colored silk damask immediately before and after the work (in the case of handscrolls) or above and below (in the case of hanging scrolls), followed by a sheet of coated white paper. In addition they have one or more of a set of eight seals placed in standard positions on the work, along with a title inscribed just outside the work itself. In a few cases every element of this package survives, but more often some of the seals or the title have been lost in remountings.[47]

A complete example of the program for calligraphy is the calligraphy handscroll by Du Mu in the Palace Museum, Beijing (plate 13). Reading the scroll from right to left, in the middle of the seam between the front and the mounting cloth, is a gourd-shaped seal reading *yushu*, "imperial writing," only the left half now visible. At the next seam, between the mounting silk and the work itself, are two seals. A round double dragon seal overlaps the bottom of the title strip. The title itself is today barely legible. At the bottom of the seam is a linked pair of seals reading Xuanhe. At the seam that marks the end of the work are two seals. At the top is one reading Zhenghe; at the bottom, one reading Xuanhe. At the middle of the next seam, linking the mounting cloth and the white paper, is the pair of seals reading Zhenghe. A few inches to its left, also centered top to bottom, is a large seal reading *neifu tushu zhiyin,* "Seal of the paintings and calligraphies of the inner palace."[48]

In the case of paintings, the program is similar but not identical. The main difference concerns the title. For calligraphies the title is done on an added strip of paper and is written out in gold ink. For paintings, the title is done with black ink directly on the mounting cloth, just before the painting itself (with hanging scrolls treated as though they were handscrolls; see plate 14). Then, whereas calligraphy scrolls have a round double dragon seal at the bottom of the title strip on the seam, paintings have a square one at the top of the title (fig. 4.5 shows both versions of the double dragon seal).

The full Xuanhe mounting program could not have been implemented before 1119, when the Xuanhe reign period began. Did Huizong put any seals on paintings or calligraphies before that date? In all likelihood he did. One clue here are works that have slight variations from the full Xuanhe mounting package. Three scrolls use a Daguan seal, a seal mentioned by Gaozong but not seen nearly as often as the Zhenghe and Xuanhe seals that he also mentions. The Daguan seal is found on the upper left on both Qu Ding's *Summer Mountains* in the Metropolitan Museum of Art in New York and Wang Xizhi's *Yuanhuan tie,* in the National Palace Museum, Taipei. It most likely is in the same place on Liang Shimin's *Riverbank with Reeds in Light Snow*, in the Palace Museum, Beijing.[49] These scrolls, thus, are missing the Zhenghe seal usually in that position. One possible explanation for this anomaly is that these paintings were already in the palace during the Daguan period (1107–1110), when the Daguan seal was put on them. They were given two Xuanhe seals in the lower right and lower left, so they were still in the palace after 1119.[50] Another variation from the standard Xuanhe pattern is the use of the square double dragon on two pieces of calligraphy (Wang Xizhi's *Yuanhuan tie* and Tang Xuanzong's *Jiling song*). Again, the seal may have been put on them before a firm decision was made to distinguish the seals on calligraphies and paintings.

Turning to the seals outside the Xuanhe mounting set, three are connected to halls. Eight of the paintings (but none of the calligraphies) listed in appendix 2 have the seal of the Eastern Pavilion of Sagacious Thoughts Hall.[51] The paintings with this seal include works regularly taken to be as attributed (such as the Huang Jucai), and ones seen as later, even possibly as late as Huizong's reign. These are works attributed to Five Dynasties or earlier artists, but thought by most scholars today to have been executed later, either as copies of extant works, imitations of the style of earlier artists, or even new creations that later people mistakenly attributed to famous earlier artists. Why they were in the Eastern Pavilion of Sagacious Thoughts Hall is not clear, as the purpose of this building is not explained in any extant sources.[52] In two cases, the paintings were later given the full Xuanhe mounting treatment, which may have meant that they were moved to a different hall.[53]

Two different seals were used to mark a connection to Harmony Revealed Hall. The large seal reading "Treasure of Harmony Revealed Hall" (Xuanhedian bao) is found on a hanging scroll attributed to Juran in the National Palace Museum, Taipei, a hanging scroll of a goose attributed to Huizong in the same museum, and a hanging scroll attributed to Guo Xi in the Shanghai Museum, in each case with no other seals associated with Huizong.[54] Richard Barnhart suggests that this seal may have been used on paintings mounted on screens or panels, pointing out that the seal is meant to be read vertically, not horizontally like the seals on the hanging scrolls by Wei Xian and Huang Jucai.[55]

The other Harmony Revealed seal—"Secret [treasure] of Harmony Revealed [Hall]" (Xuanhe zhongmi), is found on five handscroll paintings: the Li Gonglin copy of a Tang painting of herding horses; the Yi Yuanji handscroll, *Monkey and Cat,* in the National Palace Museum in Taipei (plate 15); the painting of Fu Sheng attributed to the Tang painter Wang Wei in the Osaka City Museum; Wang Shen's *Rivers and Mountains in Mist* (plate 9); and the Guo Xi handscroll, *Old Trees, Level Distance,* in the Metropolitan Museum of Art in New York. My suspicion is that sometime before 1119 Huizong put this seal on these paintings to mark them as ones he particularly appreciated among those he had in Harmony Revealed Hall.[56] Of these, only one (the Wang Shen) also has the full Xuanhe mounting set, which suggests the possibility that the palace had not completed remounting handscrolls when work came to a halt because of the Jurchen invasion.

This leaves us with a final subgroup of works that Huizong inscribed directly on the painting surface (not confining himself to a title strip outside the painting itself). Because two of the inscriptions bear the date 1107, most likely direct inscription was an early practice of Huizong's. From four surviving examples, it seems he wrote only on paintings, and only on rather small paintings. One example is a painting inscribed "*Monkey and Cat* by Yi Yuanji" (see plate 15). As just mentioned, this painting has the seal marking it as a secret treasure of Harmony Revealed Hall. It also

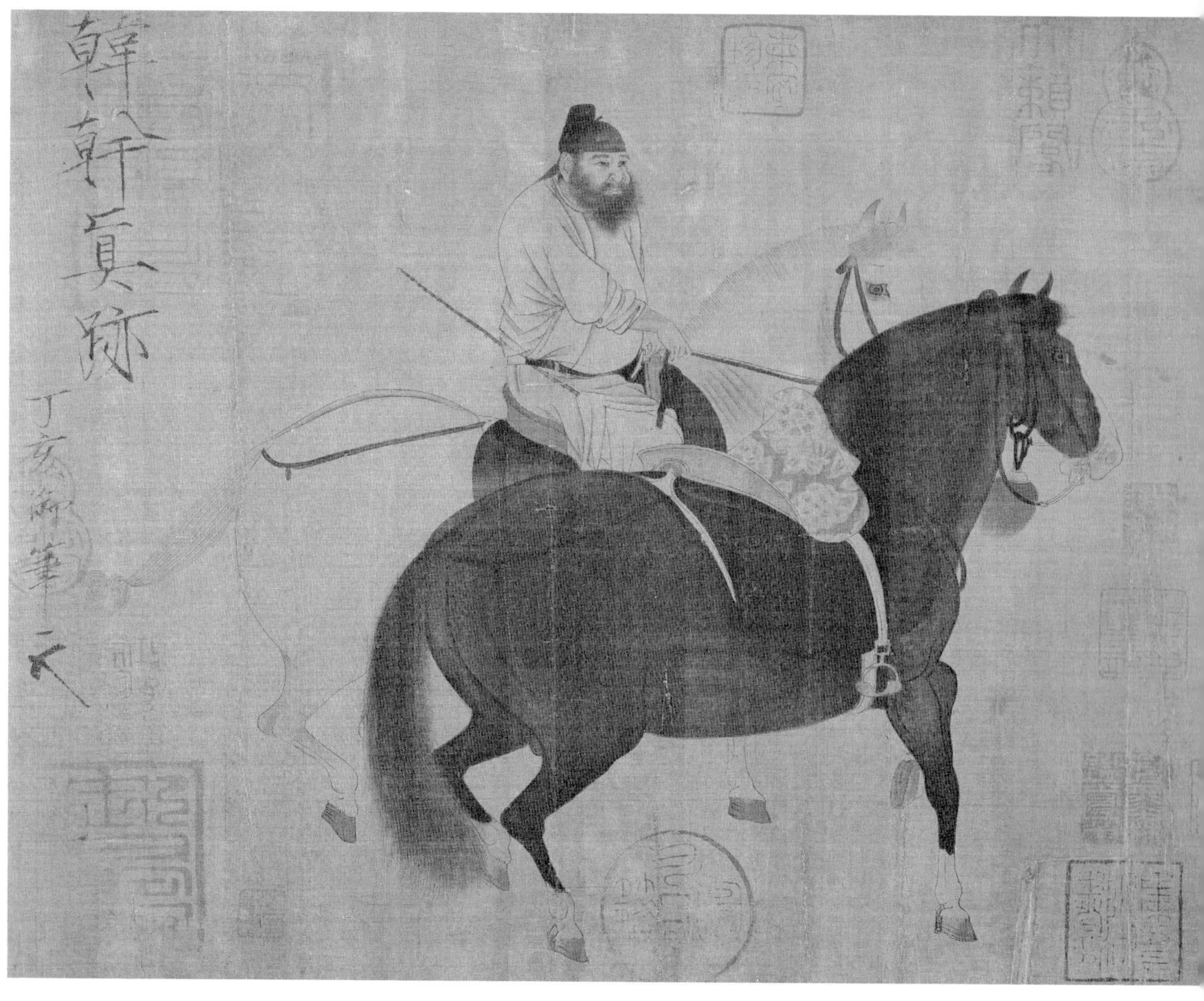

Fig. 4.6
Attributed to Han Gan (fl. 713–756), *Groom and Two Horses*. Album leaf, ink on silk, 27.5 × 34.1 cm. National Palace Museum, Taiwan, Republic of China. The inscription, by Huizong, is in two lines. The first, somewhat larger, reads "True trace of Han Gan"; the second, "imperial brush in *dinghai* (1107)." Under the words "Han Gan" is the seal of the

has a seal from the Xuanhe mounting set, but not placed in its normal position. This is the seal reading "Seal of the Inner Palace Paintings and Calligraphies," and on this painting it is directly over Huizong's inscription. One of the two dated to 1107 is an album leaf in the National Palace Museum in Taipei (fig. 4.6) which depicts a groom and two horses and is inscribed "True trace of Han Gan, imperial brush in *dinghai* [1107]." It has two seals, the Sagacious Thoughts Hall seal already discussed, and a small square seal reading "imperial writing" (*yushu*), commonly found on Huizong's own paintings and calligraphies.[57] The modern scholar Wang Yao-t'ing interprets these seals and inscriptions to mean that Huizong did the copying himself—this was a "true trace" done by the imperial brush.[58] The other is a leaf in the Boston Museum of Fine Arts (fig. 4.7) of a man and a horse, inscribed "Brush of Hao Cheng, imperially recorded in *dinghai*." Its sole seal is the same

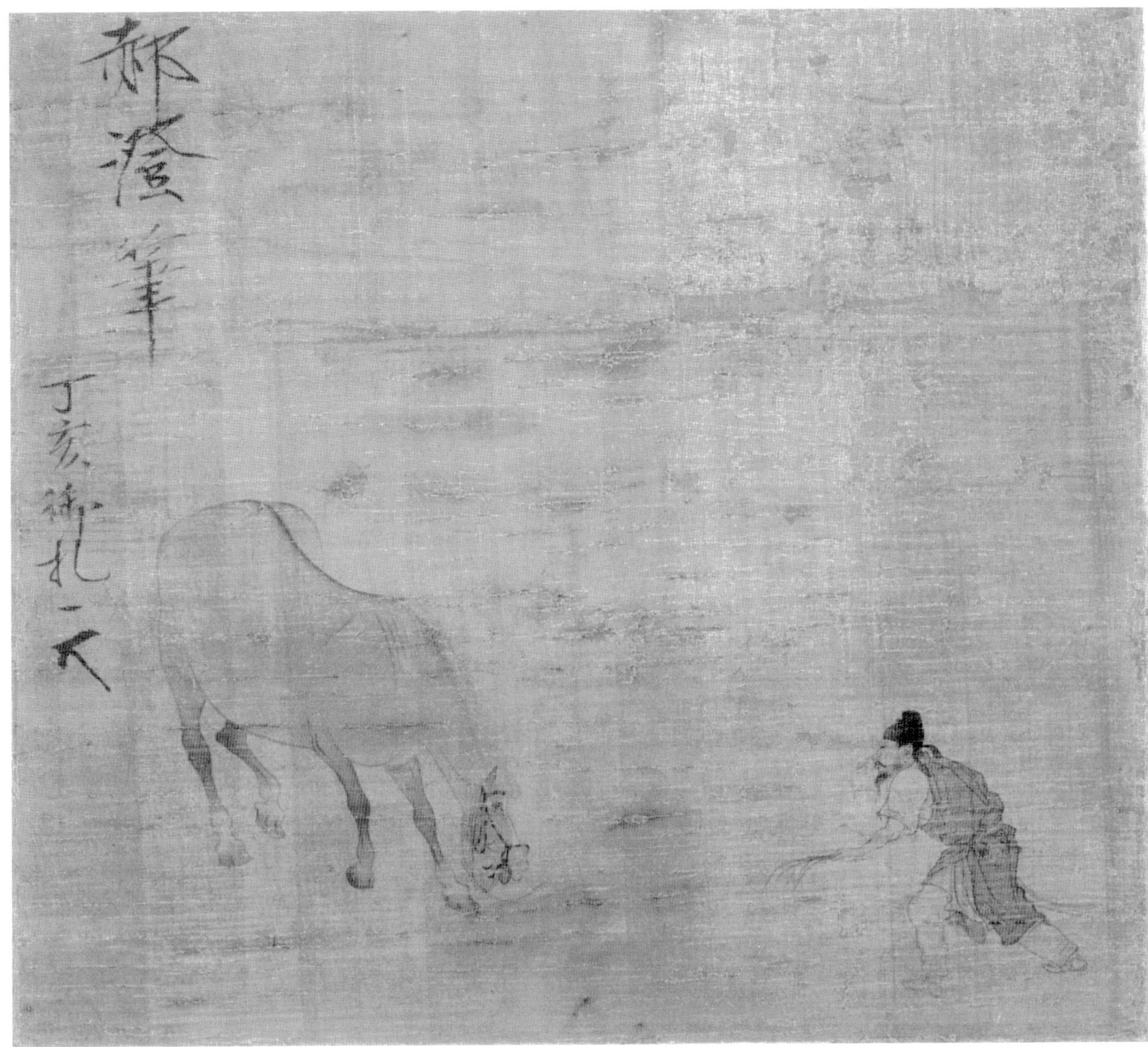

Fig. 4.6 (*continued*)

Eastern Pavilion of Sagacious Thoughts Hall. Under 1107 is the gourd-shaped imperial writing seal, which also appears in the upper right. The square imperial writing seal is in the lower left.

Fig. 4.7

Attributed to Hao Cheng (Northern Song), *Horse and Groom*. Album leaf, ink and color on silk, 33.1 × 36 cm. Photograph © 2008 Museum of Fine Arts, Boston. Denman Waldo Ross Collection, 17.741. The groom appears to be coaxing the horse to come forward by offering it fodder.

"imperial writing" seal. The Boston Museum curator Wu Tung believes in this case that Huizong was approving a copy made by a court artist.[59] These last two album leaves also have Huizong's distinctive cipher. There is also an album leaf depicting two boats with "true trace" in the inscription but no date. The inscription reads, "River Travel after Snowfall, a true trace of Guo Zhongshu."[60] The seal on it reads "treasure of imperial writing," a seal also found on one painting and two calligraphies attributed to Huizong.[61] Neither the paintings inscribed in 1107 nor those using the phrase "true trace" show a pattern in their use of seals. A list of paintings extant in 1199 includes ones with similar inscriptions by Huizong, so the variability in their inscriptions need not be taken as reason to doubt their authenticity.[62]

By and large, Huizong kept his artist seals and his collector seals separate. The Zhenghe, Xuanhe, and Inner Palace seals are rarely found on the more convincing paintings attributed to Huizong.[63] The one seal in the Xuanhe group commonly found on paintings attributed to Huizong is the gourd-shaped "imperial writing" seal. This seal is found on several fans attributed to Huizong and a few paintings as well.[64] Perhaps it was always intended as an artist's seal, marking the fact that the title slip was indeed a case of imperial writing.

Taken together, the surviving evidence suggests that Huizong's use of seals and inscriptions changed over time. Early in his reign, he had no fixed rules; he chose among seals according to his mood and put them wherever he liked. He may not yet have even clearly distinguished between artist and collector seals. He rarely inscribed works, but when he did, he wrote what came to him, following no fixed formula. Probably in these early years he handled most paintings and calligraphies himself and therefore did not need a set of rules for others to apply on his behalf. The consistency of the Xuanhe program, by contrast, suggests that remounting and marking the works had been delegated to others who were given clear instructions of what to do, with Huizong not seeing works until they were ready for him to write out the title strip (as Gaozong implied).

This shift in practice involved more than institutionalization, however. Over time Huizong shifted toward less invasive practices. In his early years he often put large seals on paintings, such as the seals associated with halls. By contrast, all but one of the seals in the Xuanhe mounting set were small and placed over the seams. The only large seal, the inner palace one, was placed at some distance from the work itself. There was a similar shift in inscriptions. The paintings that Huizong inscribed in 1107 were forever changed: it would be impossible to ever again see the painting the way it had been seen before the inscription was added. In the Xuanhe program, the only inscription was a very small one just outside the painting or calligraphy itself. Most likely this was a purposeful shift; sometime after 1107 Huizong apparently decided to minimize his impact on his most prized works.

At the same time that Huizong was adopting a minimally invasive approach to the space of his art works, he consistently began to give them titles. In cases of unsigned works, he was attributing them to a named artist. Equally often he was giving a title to a work whose author had not titled it. In the case of paintings, titles directed the viewers' interpretation of a work. As discussed in the next chapter, Palace Library officials often did the research to come up with titles for paintings, but Huizong was the one who imposed the title on the work, thus asserting intellectual authority over it.

Copying Paintings in the Collection

Copying paintings was a common practice in Song China. It was done for several reasons: as an exercise to improve one's painting technique; to make a facsimile of a work owned by someone else in order to be able to study it; to "preserve" a work that was beginning to fall apart; and to counterfeit a work in the hope of being able to sell it as an original. As seen in the last chapter, the scholar-painter Li Gonglin habitually copied paintings, sometimes borrowing works from other collectors in order to make copies of them. Zhao Lingrang and Wang Shen also at least occasionally made copies of paintings.[65]

There is scattered evidence that Huizong himself sometimes made copies of paintings in his collection. Although Cai Tao never referred to the practice, we have another contemporary reference: a document in the *Song Classified Documents* that mentions Huizong showing officials at the Palace Library a copy he had done of a painting by the Sui dynasty painter Zhan Ziqian titled *Emperor Wenxuan of the Northern Qi Visiting Jinyang*. The original painting is listed in the *Xuanhe Painting Catalogue*.[66]

After the fall of Kaifeng and the scattering of Huizong's collections, a few paintings were identified as copies made by Huizong. Wang Yun (1227–1304) referred to a copy Huizong did of a painting by Zhang Xuan titled *Palace Horsemen*, and both Tang Hou (fl. 1322) and Zhou Mi (1232–1298) referred to his copy of a painting by Li Zhaodao titled *Picking Melons,* which depicted the flight of Xuanzong from the capital during the Tang.[67] The Jin emperor Zhangzong (b. 1168, r. 1189–1208) inscribed some paintings as copies made by Huizong. As will be discussed in chapter 9, everything of value from Huizong's palace was transported north by the Jin armies, so it is reasonable to assume that copies Huizong had made would have been among the paintings Zhangzong inherited. Possibly he had access to some documentary evidence, such as an old label on the outside of the painting. It is also possible that the information about the paintings was passed on by oral tradition, as hundreds of eunuchs and women from Huizong's palace were taken north and made to serve in the Jin palace, including several of Huizong's daughters. (During the Southern Song it was rumored that Zhangzong, who imitated Huizong's calligraphy, was in fact his great-grandchild, the son of a daughter of one of his daughters.)[68]

Two paintings survive which Zhangzong labeled as copies made by Huizong, *Lady Guoguo on an Outing*, in the Liaoning Provincial Museum (plate 16), and *Court Ladies Preparing Newly Woven Silk*, in the Boston Museum of Fine Arts (plates 27 and 28).[69] Although some scholars suspect that these were done by court artists rather than Huizong himself, at the minimum they give us a sense of what would have been considered a good copy of an earlier masterpiece at Huizong's court. If any of the copies Huizong made himself were as painstakingly done as these, he must have spent many hours with paintings from his collections.

Displaying Objects to Favored Officials

According to Cai Tao, "when Huizong heard [the explanations of the primal tablet] he was pleased and ordered it to be shown to the officials. The ritual officials then prepared for it to be reverently presented using colored silk cords and ten layers of colorful silk padding. Then that winter solstice, Huizong received the tablet in Grand Celebration Hall."[70]

This was not the only occasion on which Huizong let his officials see his treasures. In another passage Cai Tao reports his display of the ancient bronzes he had acquired:

> Once Huizong issued an order that the antiquities in the collection be displayed on the two side chambers of Promoting Governance Hall and had the officials summoned to view them. At that time Huizong was attentive to government matters, concentrated and serene. He would secretly peek through the cracks in the inner doors to hear his officials discuss the objects with each other. He could recognize each one and enjoyed listening to their displays of broad knowledge; he savored the flavor of their discussions, and appreciated their eminence, all without the officials knowing he was there.[71]

Huizong also showed treasures to select groups of senior officials as part of banquets and parties. In 1112, according to the record Cai Jing wrote, Huizong arranged a grand banquet at Grand Clarity Edifice, saying he wanted it to be like the royal banquets of Zhou times mentioned in the *Book of Songs*. Four senior eunuchs took charge of the preparations and eleven senior officials were the guests. When they arrived at Harmony Revealed Hall, "paintings and calligraphy, brushes and inkstones, ancient cauldrons, libation cups, tall jars, and washpans were displayed on black lacquered tables and stands."[72]

Another occasion when Huizong displayed objects in his collection was a private party at Harmony Preserved Hall in 1119, which Cai Jing also recounted.[73] Guests included several of Huizong's own relatives—his two brothers, his third son Kai (who had passed the *jinshi* examination the year before and was skilled at painting and calligraphy), and the more distantly related clansman Zhao Zhonghu (who was a collector of antiquities). In addition, Huizong invited Cai Jing and several of Cai's sons and grandsons, including Cai Tiao, who the year before had married Huizong's fifth daughter (whether Cai Tao, then twenty-two or twenty-three, was among the guests is not clear).[74] Cai Jing had for several years been semiretired, coming to court only once every five days. Other guests included the senior official Wang Fu, who had been on the Council of State for over a year, and the eunuch military commander Tong Guan, on the Council of State since 1116. The year before, Tong Guan had proposed allying with the newly emerging power to the north, the Jurchen, who had rebelled against their overlords, the state of Liao, a plan that Wang Fu and eventually Huizong too supported.

After the guests passed through beautiful gardens and arrived at Harmony Preserved Hall, they found that preparations had been made for their visit. Huizong's seat had been placed in the center of the hall which had the side rooms holding books, bronzes, paintings, and calligraphies. Cai Jing, in his account of this occasion, portrayed Huizong as acting as tour guide:

> To our surprise the emperor personally pointed to different works of art and told us about them. Then he pointed to the studio where every one of the memorials in my hand had been stored. He ordered someone to open the case. In it was a red divider, and behind the divider a small box, and in the box was something covered in silk. That turned out to be the appointment paper I had written for the Pure Consort Miss Liu. I said to the emperor, "My calligraphy is poor and my prose is bad. I didn't think you would have kept it." Not knowing how else to respond, I bowed my head deferentially.[75]

The group then took another stroll through the gardens. When they got to the Hall of Complete Truth, Huizong made tea for them, personally holding the kettle to pour. Later Huizong made his guests perform, asking them all to write poems to inscribe on the wall of the hall. But they did not have to provide all of the entertainment, as female musicians were brought in to play for them.

At one point, Huizong had a servant pass Cai Jing the poetic lines: "At the elegant banquet, drinking wine adds to our high spirits. / Within Jade Truth Gallery one can see the Peaceful Consort." He then ordered him to complete the poem. Cai's lines were based on his assumption that he was going to get to see the consort, but it turned out that the hall only had a portrait of her. Cai promptly wrote another poem to make up for his blunder, which, when delivered to Huizong, caused him to laugh and invite the group to actually meet the consort. Cai Jing's record gives a description of the consort and the drinking and entertainment that followed. Huizong started a word game, in which the guests had to come up with poetic lines that paralleled his.

By evening Cai Jing was getting tired and tried to hint to Huizong, "Your Majesty shares his pleasures with others, making no distinction between high and low. Yet the sun has long gone down, and we are still bothering you, which makes us uncomfortable." But Huizong wanted everyone to stay and drink. Perhaps stimulated by the wine, at one point he recalled a couple of lines from a poem Cai Jing had written at a banquet held a quarter century earlier, before Huizong became emperor. Cai Jing could recall nothing of it, but Huizong gradually remembered all the lines. A bit later Huizong recalled the occasion when Cai Jing inscribed a fan for him.

Cai Jing's record of this event is fascinating in many regards. Huizong personally gave a tour of his treasures, explaining their features to his guests. All this was done in an atmosphere of refinement and cultivation, combined as it was with the composition and recitation of poems. Cai Jing as author evoked the context of banquets and literary gatherings, associating the party loosely with many similar occasions over the centuries, some involving rulers, some simply private gatherings of friends, which had been narrated in earlier literary pieces.[76] It is thus reminiscent of the painting of a Tang court gathering inscribed by both Huizong and Cai Jing (see plates 17 and 18). That painting depicts twelve guests attended to by eight servants, some of whom are warming the wine at a stove in the foreground. On a stone table below the willow tree can be seen a zither and a bronze cauldron.[77]

We have even fuller record of an occasion three years later, in 1122, when Huizong displayed items from his collection to help celebrate the completion of new quarters for the Palace Library. By then Cai Jing had fully retired, and Wang Fu, who had replaced him, had rescinded many of his policies, including the expansion of the school system and recruitment to office via the schools. By 1122, the court was deeply involved with its alliance with Jin against Liao, but had had to shift its main armies south to put down a major rebellion (the Rebellion of Fang La). Still, there was as yet no sense of impending doom or any need to scrimp on the construction of the new quarters for the Palace Library. For the opening celebration, Huizong had quite a few of the imperial treasures packed up and brought to the new Library. He invited both officials of the Palace Library and members of the Council of State and other high officials to join the viewing. Since visiting the Library now required taking the imperial carriage outside the gates of the Palace City, it was much more of a production than earlier visits.[78] The visit made so much of an impression on those present that several accounts of the occasion survive.

We can begin again with Cai Tao's account, though it is not one of the fullest:

> At the end of the Zhenghe period, the Palace Library was moved beyond the eastern hall, but construction was not complete until the middle of the Xuanhe period. Following precedent, Huizong paid it a visit. With his own hands he took a calligraphy scroll by Taizu and made a gift of it to the Three Institutes [i.e., the Palace Library], telling the officials present, "People only know that Taizu brought peace to the realm through his divine military force; they don't know that from natural endowment and study he attained such a good hand. I am now giving this piece to the Palace Library, which should treasure it always." The high officials and close attendants then got a chance to view it respectfully. Taizu's calligraphy showed some influence from Yan Zhenqing, but even more reflected the spirit of the late Tang, and occasionally there would be a few lines with words from the classics. Among [the works shown us] were also three or four short poems, all of them bold and energetic, very strikingly done, allowing us to see the spirit of a great ruler. Here and there they were signed, "Written by a soldier wearing armor." Apparently they were calligraphy Taizu did to amuse himself while his position was still humble. On this occasion Huizong also gave the Library a handscroll by General Li [Li Sixun], titled *Tang Minghuang's Journey to Shu.* From where I stood in attendance at the end of the ranks I gazed on it and thought to myself, "The palace has thousands of famous paintings by artists like Gu Kaizhi, Lu Tanwei, Cao Fuxing, and Zhan Ziqian, but he unaccountably takes out this one. How inauspicious!"[79]

Six other accounts of this occasion survive, three by participants (Cheng Ju, Wang Fu, and Wang Anzhong), two in the form of government documents preserved in the *Song Collected Documents*, and the last by the early Southern Song writer Deng Chun, relatively well-versed about Huizong's court because his grandfather had served there.[80] Taking all of these accounts together makes it possible to reconstruct the occasion in some detail.

The grand councilor Wang Fu took charge of making arrangements for the occasion, among which were the selection of documents, paintings, calligraphy, and ancient vessels to take to the Palace Library.[81] The day before the event, the grand councilors accompanied the objects and saw that they were correctly handled at the Library. Some of the Library officials stayed overnight to guard them. On the day of the visit, officials who had been especially invited for the occasion, including grand councilors, retired grand councilors, and princes, arrived at the Library. The officials of the Library and the invited guests lined up outside the gate to meet Huizong.

After Huizong arrived in his sedan chair, he visited each building in turn, giving the officials at each one the opportunity to bow to him. When he got to the Imperial Repository, the officials were summoned to view a subset of the treasures, which were all lined up at the base of the steps.[82] One of the pieces of calligraphy by Taizu was conferred on the Palace Library, as was the handscroll by the Tang painter Li Sixun titled *Tang Minghuang's Journey to Shu*.

Later, when Huizong arrived at Promoting Culture Hall in the complex, the officials were honored by being allowed to sit in Huizong's presence and drink tea with him. After further ceremonies, Huizong went to the office of the Library supervisor, Liang Shicheng. The top officials were summoned there for a second viewing of art objects. They were told not to kneel, and they responded by calling out "Blessings on the emperor." When the officials were all in the hall, "Huizong left his seat and went to the large calligraphy table where the former emperors' calligraphy was laid out along with antique paintings and calligraphies."[83] At this point the works by earlier emperors were put on display. According to Wang Fu,

> The emperor personally took out several sheets of original calligraphy from the Jianlong period [the initial years of the Song dynasty, 960–62], which was the first time that we officials saw Taizu's calligraphy. He also took out calligraphy by Taizong, Zhenzong, and Renzong. When he took out a transcription of the annotated version of *Mencius* written by Shenzong, he said, "This was done by my father when he was a prince."[84]

Because the senior officials crowded around to look and the more junior ones did not want to push through them to get a peek, Huizong had another table set up on the other side, so everyone could see something. Also on display were "copies Huizong had done himself of famous paintings, such as Zhan Ziqian's *Emperor Wenxuan of Northern Qi Visiting Jinyang*," Huizong's transcription of the *Rhapsody on the Goddess of the Luo River*, as well as paintings Huizong had made and poems he had both composed and written out. Also viewed were transcriptions Huizong had done of the *Thousand Character Essay* in ten scripts. Some of the pieces of Huizong's calligraphy that were displayed were of poems he had written, and those attending were invited to write poems that used the same rhymes.[85]

Afterwards, Huizong had paintings and calligraphies he had done himself distributed as gifts to the officials in attendance. Each of the fifty-six officials was given two pieces of calligraphy, one in cursive script and one in running script, plus a painting. Nine lower-rank officials also received gifts. The highest officials all got a booklet of the *Thousand Character Essay* in ten scripts. The *Song Classified Documents* adds that the lower officials "clamored around him, shoulder to shoulder and heel to heel, sometimes even hitting their heads together, hurrying to be the first to see the objects." In Deng Chun's description, "When the magnanimous distribution began, the officials competed to get to the front, breaking their pendants or bumping their hats, which made Huizong laugh."[86]

Besides the general distribution, Wang Fu, as a mark of special favor, was given a copy of the *Thousand Character Essay* on paper decorated with gold, along with twenty-two other scrolls of Huizong's calligraphy. (The *Thousand Character Essay* he received is probably the one currently in the collection of the Liaoning Provincial Museum. See plate 19.) It was also Wang Fu who wrote the official account of the occasion.[87]

At this celebration, four rather different sorts of objects were displayed: calligraphy by former emperors; objects from Huizong's painting, calligraphy, and antiquities collections; Huizong's copies of paintings in the collections; and Huizong's original works, including paintings, calligraphies, and poems. In other words, Huizong did not rigidly compartmentalize traces of the brush into historical documents, collectible art objects, and his own works, thus blurring his own roles as collector, artist, and emperor.

Unlike Taizu, who gave out paintings by famous artists in his collection as rewards to officials, Huizong limited his gifts to works he did himself. For Huizong such gifts made a lot of sense. Attached as he was to the objects in his collection, he was probably reluctant to part with them. His own works were a renewable resource, as he could always do more. He must have spent many hours practicing calligraphy to make all of the gifts he did for the Palace Library viewing. The calligraphy fan shown in figure 4.8 is probably typical of those he used for gifts. It transcribes a poem, probably by Huizong himself. Presumably the paintings took even more of his time, unless they were the simplest bamboo or orchid paintings. And, of course, he may have had court painters do them for him, since Cai Tao describes Huizong as willing to take credit for paintings executed by court painters at his command.[88]

Several themes run through these accounts of Huizong displaying his collections. One is the pleasure he took in observing his officials respond to the objects he showed them. This is perhaps clearest in the case of the display of bronzes, when he hid behind the door to listen to the visitors, wanting to see how they would behave out of his presence. But several observers of the 1122 showing also indicate that Huizong was pleased rather than annoyed at the unseemly eagerness of his officials to see his long-hidden masterpieces. Another theme is that Huizong knew the collection intimately. He knew exactly where Cai Jing's calligraphy was kept, he knew

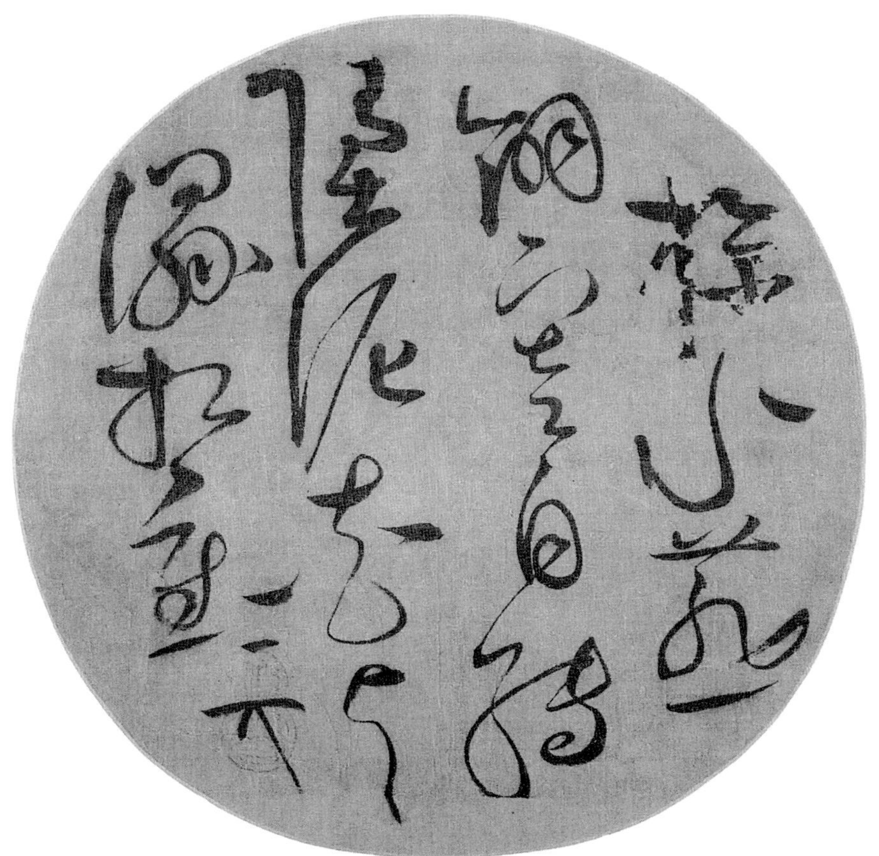

Fig. 4.8
Huizong, calligraphy fan. Ink on silk, 28.4 × 28.4 cm. Shanghai Museum. The text of the fan is a poem in seven-character lines, which can be translated as "Swallows skim and touch the lake, sending ripples shimmering. Fallen petals on the mud pile up layer on layer" (trans. Z. Shen 1983:222).

that a piece of calligraphy by Shenzong was done in his youth, and he could give a guided tour of the object in Harmony Preserved's side halls.

Models

Did Huizong model his behavior as an emperor-collector on any earlier rulers? As discussed in chapter 1, his predecessors, Taizong, Zhenzong, and Renzong, had found many occasions to entertain their officials in ways that stressed their common connections to culture and art—for instance, by composing poetry together or viewing the writings of a former emperor. Huizong may well have had some of those occasions in his mind when he planned the 1112 and 1119 parties or the 1122 celebration of the opening of the new Library buildings.

Huizong may also have had in mind some examples from Tang times. The *Xuanhe Calligraphy Catalogue* includes a very positive discussion of the Tang emperor Taizong as a collector of the calligraphy of Wang Xizhi, noting his willingness to spend generously to acquire items and to turn to Chu Suiliang to authenticate Wang's works. His devotion to calligraphy was also seen as raising the standard of calligraphy in his day.[89] Huizong may well have seen in him a model of how to collect aggressively without hurting one's image as a good ruler. Huizong's use of seals carved with the names of his reign periods may have been based on the practice of the Tang emperors Taizong and Xuanzong, who used seals of their reign periods (Zhenguan and Kaiyuan, respectively) that were written in their own hands (a fact recorded in Zhang Yanyuan's 847 *Celebrated Painters of All the Dynasties*).[90] Earlier Song emperors did not adopt this practice, so Huizong could have been consciously modeling himself on the Tang emperors in this regard.

Even more intriguing are the signs that Huizong wished to emulate Li Yu, today remembered above all as a poet, but equally notable as an artist and patron of artists.[91] Several eminent painters served at Li Yu's court at Nanjing, including Zhao Gan, Dong Yu, Gu Hongzhong, Wang Qihan, Wei Xian, Zhou Wenju, and Juran, and some of them accompanied Li Yu when he was brought to Kaifeng after submitting to Song in 975. While still in Jiangnan, Li Yu built up a large collection of paintings, which included works of his court artists and also works by other contemporary painters, such as Xu Xi, an official who became celebrated as a bird-and-flower painter.

Li Yu went further than earlier rulers in putting seals on his paintings. Guo Ruoxu described his handling of the works in his collection this way:

> The last Li prince was endowed with a lofty understanding and was widely cultivated. He set great store by paintings and calligraphy, and collected them until he had a very great number, [chosen] with the most refined taste. Large numbers of the painting scrolls now in the inner palace, as well as the calligraphies and paintings in private hands, have [his] seals on them. These will read (usually in black ink):
>
> Calligraphies and Paintings of the Inner Halls
> Seal of Union Within
> Treasure of the Jianye Reading Room
> Seal of the Palace Director of Letters
> Seal of the College of Letters of Assembled Worthies Hall
> August Writing Seal of Assembled Worthies College
>
> Sometimes he personally wrote the painter's name, or signed it, or wrote phrases of some song or poem.
>
> The weave [of the silk] used for the mounting [may be one of the patterns known as] "the large repeating luan bird," "the small repeating luan bird," "cranes in snow," "male Paradise fly-catchers," or be of black brocade. (The present Office of Silks and

> Brocades imitates these weaves.) The cord is generally a ribbon of woven silk, and the affixed label [a piece of] yellow sutra paper. On the back is usually written the name of the man who supervised the mounting, and the qualitative ranking assigned.[92]

Most of the practices here attributed to Li Yu, such as using distinctive silks for his mountings, using a variety of seals, and inscribing titles and sometimes also his own signatures, were also adopted by Huizong. We do not have surviving paintings or calligraphies which Huizong marked with rankings, but Gaozong said that Huizong had rankings put on calligraphies, so it could be that he adopted this practice as well, putting them on the back as Li Yu did. His rankings then would have been lost when the backings were removed during remounting.

The image of Huizong the collector that emerges from the pens of Cai Tao and his contemporaries is one of a man who shared many of the passions of the scholarly collectors described in chapter 3. He had scrolls remounted and put his seals on them. He expanded the space he gave over to housing his treasures. He enjoyed showing them and observing the impression they made on visitors granted the privilege of viewing them. He continued to be avid in his pursuit of new objects even after he had rooms full of acquisitions.

Of course, there were differences between Huizong and even the most wealthy and committed private collector. Huizong's resources were nearly unlimited. He undoubtedly made greater use of agents, especially to acquire objects but also to do research on them. He showed works much less frequently, and the occasions on which he showed them were much grander events.

Whether or not Huizong thought of himself as just another collector, his actions carried political meaning simply because he was emperor. By gathering into the palace so many of the objects highly valued for their connections to great men of the past, he was implicitly claiming that the throne was the proper guardian of the inherited culture.

Huizong was never in a position to devote all of his energies to his collections. There was too much else that consumed his time—not only routine government business and a very large family but also his other cultural projects, from his own practice of painting and calligraphy to his study of Daoism. Much of the research on items in his collections he entrusted to officials with appointments in the Palace Library.

CHAPTER 5

Managing the Collections at the Palace Library

On the sixth day of the fifth month [of 1122], the supervisor of the Palace Library [Liang Shicheng] said, "Ancient writing and unusual scripts of the Xia, Shang, and Zhou dynasties can be seen on bells and cauldrons. Records of historical events can also be found on surviving inscriptions on metal and stone. I would like to ask all of the circuits to do a full search for them."

—*Song hui yao*

THE GOVERNMENT AGENCY THAT HAD GENERAL OVERSIGHT OF THE palace collections of books, calligraphy, ancient bronzes, and paintings was the Palace Library (*bishu sheng*), a venerable institution with a tradition of employing erudite men and setting them to work on scholarly projects. Under Huizong, staff of the library did not devote themselves exclusively to books but also took on many curatorial tasks, such as assessing the date, subject matter, and authenticity of art and antiquities in the palace collection. They were also the ones who did much of the work on the catalogues of Huizong's collections.

The last chapter emphasized the links between Huizong's collections and the passions and political goals of one individual collector—Huizong himself. This chapter focuses on a different dimension of his collection, its institutional side. Record keeping for the collection was handled by erudite officials in one of the most prestigious organs of the government. A collection with thousands of objects (tens of thousands, if all of the books are also included) naturally calls for orderly record-keeping and systems for locating objects. The officials who worked at the Library saw that each object was properly classified and given an accurate title—necessary steps for managing such an enormous amount of information. No one would want officials concerned with creating and maintaining such institutional structures to be carried away with collectors' passions. More valuable were the habits and values of the good librarian or archivist who wants system, order, and a documentary trail.

The Palace Library

In 1105, Luo Ji, an official with strong literary credentials, submitted to Huizong a five-chapter history of the Palace Library, titled *Record of Peng Mountain*.[1] This book does not survive as an independent volume, but several dozen passages were copied into another book compiled in 1144, and these provide an indication of its contents.[2] If Huizong read through this new book, he would have been reminded of all the steps the early Song emperors had taken to build up the palace collections of books, paintings, and calligraphies. *Record of Peng Mountain* told the story of the construction of the Library buildings in 992, the fire of 1015, and the steps taken subsequently to replace the destroyed books. It described in some detail the project to catalogue the Palace Library that resulted in the *Chongwen Catalogue*. It listed some of the most famous paintings and calligraphies held in the Palace Library, such as calligraphy by major masters from Wang Xizhi to Huaisu and paintings by masters from Gu Kaizhi to Huang Quan. It also reported that some of the most famous works that Taizong had transferred to the Imperial Repository were no longer in the collection. These included a calligraphy by Huairen, Gu Kaizhi's *Vimalakirtri*, Han Gan's *Horse*, and Xue Ji's *Cranes*. The author speculated that they might have been destroyed in the fire of 1015.[3]

From perusing this book, Huizong could not have missed the honor of being appointed to the Palace Library. The prestige of these assignments was maintained in large part by limiting them to men of demonstrated talent—often based on success in special examinations. Another factor was the favor successive emperors showed Library officials. *Record of Peng Mountain* devoted much space to the times when former emperors showed favor to the staff of the Library. For instance, it mentioned that Taizong made gifts to the Library of his own calligraphy and every summer would inscribe fans to give to the officials working in the Library.[4]

Reading *Peng Mountain*, Huizong would have been reminded of the many books compiled by Library scholars, especially authoritative compilations of selected passages from books in the Library collection, such as the compendiums produced in 1036, 1057, and 1061 on geomancy, medicine, and military strategy, respectively. There were also the authoritatively collated editions of the dynastic histories produced at the Library. The most recent printing project mentioned occurred just a few years before *Peng Mountain* was written, during Zhezong's reign, when the Library printed a rare medical book that had recently been submitted by the envoy from Korea.[5]

SENIOR OFFICIALS AT THE LIBRARY

The highest three officials in the Palace Library were the director (*bishu jian*, 4a), the vice director (*bishu shaojian*, 5b), and the assistant director (*bishu cheng*, 7b). (Often there was either a director or a vice director, rather than both.) Beginning in 1117, officials could also be given the concurrent assignment of supervisor of the Palace Library (*tiju bishusheng*).[6] Some of those who held these posts during Huizong's reign were men esteemed for their literary ability and erudition, who had worked their way up from lower posts in the Library. Others seem to have been above all administrators, assigned there as often as not because a close relative held a policy-making post which barred them from other central government posts.

Luo Ji, the author of *Record of Peng Mountain*, was serving as vice director of the Library in 1106. He was highly erudite, among the five officials who had passed the special examination for literary talent in 1095.[7] One official who held leading positions in the Library for longer periods was He Zhitong. He was serving as editorial director in 1108, by 1110 he was director of the Library, and from 1111 to 1113 he had charge of one of the Library's major book projects, the *Nine Provinces Illustrated Gazetteer* (Jiuzhou tuzhi).[8] He's father, He Zhizhong (1044–1117), was on the Council of State during this period, which would have kept He Zhitong from occupying most higher-level central government positions. During this same period, Cai You, son of the even more powerful grand councilor Cai Jing, also held positions in the Library, rising through a series of appointments. In 1104 he was appointed Palace Library assistant. Later he worked on several of the Library's book projects, including the *Nine Provinces Illustrated Gazetteer* and the *Six Institutes*. In 1117 Cai You was given the newly created assignment of supervisor of the Palace Library. In the 1120s, the eunuch Liang Shicheng replaced Cai You as supervisor.[9]

During Liang's tenure as supervisor, the director of the Library was Weng Yanshen. In Weng's case, his biographer explicitly stated that his appointment as director of the Library had resulted from the need to avoid conflict with his brother's appointment as a vice censor-in-chief.[10] Weng had worked his way up the Library hierarchy. He spent six years working on the *Nine Provinces Illustrated Gazetteer* project before holding the position of assistant director, then in 1121–1122 vice director, then director until 1123/8. Weng's biographer, writing long after the death of Liang Shicheng (and long after Liang was labeled one of the Six Traitors who brought down the Northern Song), stressed that Weng kept Liang at a distance:

> When Liang Shicheng was supervisor of the Library, literary scholars rarely advanced unless they called themselves his students. This was true even for the grand councilors. Weng, though, never once called on Liang. Liang Shicheng repeatedly expressed

> his desire to see him, but Weng to the end did not go to his place. When someone told him that he was going too far, Weng, with a stern face, said, "The Three Institutes [an old name for the Library] are located next to Grand Celebration Hall. They contain the country's books. Even if a eunuch is high-ranking, he still is in direct service, nothing more than an old soldier. As the leader of the assembled talents, shouldn't I worry about bringing shame on the emperor's Institutes if I have contact with him?"[11]

Whether or not the biographer had any basis for this conversation, it does suggest some of the tensions likely to have marred administration of the Library when it had in a sense two heads—one a eunuch, and one an official whose qualifications were literary.[12] As seen in the last chapter, Huizong did not consider Liang Shicheng an outsider to the realms of books, documents, and works of art; he had him assess pieces of calligraphy, and even invited him to his art-viewing party in 1119. Scholar-officials, however, rarely seem to have shared his evaluation of Liang.

JUNIOR OFFICIALS AT THE LIBRARY

Curatorial work in the Library was largely done by officials holding the lower-ranked posts in the Palace Library. According to the *Song History*, regular staffing of the Library involved eleven officials: one editorial director (*zhuzuo lang*, 7b); two assistant editorial directors (*zhuzuo zuolang*, 8a), in charge of the daily record; two editors (*bishu lang*, 8b), in charge of the book and document collections; four editors (*jiaoshu lang*, 8b); and two proofreaders (*zhengzi*, 8b), who took charge of catching errors in the collections. In addition to these regular officials, the Library employed a larger number of clerks, copyists, and workmen. From 1106 on, only *jinshi* were to be appointed to regular Library posts, a rule not strictly followed.[13] One might think from the descriptions of their responsibilities that these officials had nothing to do with the paintings, calligraphies, and antiquities held by the Library, but, as we shall see, their job descriptions did not limit the types of assignments they were given. In addition to these standard appointments, Huizong regularly took advantage of the flexibility of book project staffing to add to the number of officials working at the Palace Library. Quite a few men who served in the Library for years began their careers there with an assignment to work on the *Nine Provinces Illustrated Gazetteer*, the *Classified Documents*, or the *Six Institutes*. Probably as a consequence, during the second half of Huizong's reign there began to be complaints that the Library was overstaffed. When Wang Fu became grand councilor in 1120, he dismissed large numbers of men working on publishing projects, reportedly closing fifty-eight projects.[14]

More than a hundred men must have served in the regular rank 7 and rank 8

Library posts during Huizong's reign. Although the names of several dozen are known, information about their careers survives for only about a dozen of them. From those cases, however, certain themes emerge consistently. Appointees were among the most learned men of their day, with remarkably retentive memories and interests that ranged widely. Huang Fu "memorized everything he read." Fu Liangyou, we are told, "when reading, with one glance knew the main arguments." Mao Sui had studied not only the classics, histories, and philosophers, but also astronomy, geography, the calendar, mathematics, and divination. Wang Zao was "widely learned with a strong memory." He had read everything from the Six Classics to the philosophers, histories, works of Confucian teachers, military treatises, genealogies, works on dialect, local histories, astronomy, the calendar, and Buddhist and Daoist doctrines.[15]

Many of these men were highly regarded for their literary style. Three of the four men later designated the best stylists of the 1111–1125 period served in the Library—Wang Zao, Zhai Ruwen, and Sun Di.[16] Sometimes such praise was taken as evidence that these men were closet followers of Su Shi, and could get them into trouble.[17] In other cases, men who had been on the lists of banned officials of 1102 or 1104, when brought back into the government were given politically innocuous positions in the Library. Cheng Ju reported that both he and Mao Sui had been on the banned list. When the ban was relaxed, Mao returned to office, soon serving in the Library, first as editor, then assistant editorial director.[18]

Many of those working in the Library got there because of special distinction in the civil-service examinations. Zhai Ruwen was only fourteen *sui* when he earned his *jinshi* in 1089.[19] Huang Fu took the top place in the 1095 special exam, along with Luo Ji. Teng Kang passed first in the special test of literary ability in 1112; his younger brother Teng Yu was one of three to pass in 1114, along with Sun Di. Mo Chou, who came in first in the *jinshi* examinations in 1113, was first appointed to the Agency for Deliberating on Ritual, then in 1114 to the Library.[20]

Several men who worked in the Library had artistic talents. Huang Bosi, Wang Zao, and Zhai Ruwen were all known as calligraphers. Wang excelled in both large and small seal script. Zhai Ruwen was also a painter and a sculptor. Ni Tao had a reputation as a painter. A few were also collectors. Zhai Ruwen had a collection of a thousand rubbings as well as Six Dynasties and Tang paintings. Dong You's family had been collectors for generations, and in his day they had books, bronzes, and rubbings. Dong You himself was said to be an expert connoisseur who could not be fooled by fakes.[21]

Even relatively low-rank curatorial officials occasionally met personally with Huizong. Zhai Ruwen, whose father had once served as director of the Palace Library, was first appointed to the Agency for Deliberating on Ritual. After giving him an audience, Huizong told Cai Jing that Zhai's knowledge of ancient vessels was profound, and had him moved to the Palace Library. A decade later Huizong gave audiences to Fu Liangyou and Teng Kang then serving in the Library.[22]

Two of the many men who served as curators in the Library during Huizong's time, Dong You and Huang Bosi, have left writings that allow us to judge where they stood on the sorts of issues debated by collectors and connoisseurs during the eleventh century. Dong You was a classicist who authored a study of the *Changes* and another of the *Book of Songs*. From his six-chapter *Guangchuan's Notes on Paintings* and his ten-chapter *Guangchuan's Notes on Calligraphy*, we can see his strong interest in inscribed ancient bronzes, rubbings of historical or calligraphic interest, and paintings. In his discussions of paintings, he showed an awareness of the difficulties of determining authenticity and an interest in the nature of artistic creativity.[23] To give an example, he wrote this note for a landscape by the tenth-century master Li Cheng:

> Xie He says that in painting depicting reality is the most difficult thing.[24] Gu Kaizhi took it all to lie in dotting the eyes. Therefore he said that conveying the spirit is found there. People who discuss painting today all miss the significance of the ideas of the ancients. They do not know that there is nothing unreal about landscape, grasses and trees, insects and fish, and birds and beasts. If, indeed, one has lost form likeness and, painting a tiger, makes it resemble a dog, can it then be said to have captured reality? Li Cheng was of the scholar class, pure and free. Therefore, his painting reached the ultimate in marvels, to the point that no traces of his brush technique can be sought, and no point of his beginning the brushwork can be recognized. Then, too, he was able to exclude any vulgar atmosphere. Where he surpassed others was not in achieving true forms. In his landscapes, trees, and rocks, with their mists and haze, the operations of divine invention and the interactions of yang and yin were all swiftly expressed in a most startling way, so that people were unable to comprehend it. That is why one says that vitality is produced by the brush, which leaves it within the image. Now, if a painter reaches the point of forgetting that he is painting, won't the forms be painted properly? Unless a man is enlightened, he cannot attain this.[25]

Huang Bosi, Dong's coworker, had a similar background. He came from an official family, and his grandfather was a prominent official. Inclined toward scholarship even as a child, he passed the *jinshi* in 1100 at age twenty-two. An accomplished calligrapher, he could write in virtually all scripts. While serving in Luoyang he got to know collectors of rubbings and ancient bronzes and studied the evolution of scripts. He wrote a detailed critique of the rubbings included in the *Chunhua Model Letters*, going beyond Mi Fu in many particulars.[26]

Huang Bosi's first appointment in the Palace Library was on the *Nine Provinces Illustrated Gazetteer* project. His next appointment was as editor (8b), and then he had a slight promotion to assistant (8a). He had a reputation for knowing all sorts of recondite subjects. Li Gang, who also worked in the Library in this period, reported that during the time Huang was in the Library, Huizong would order him to explain "the documents and cultural artifacts of earlier ages, including maps/pictures and ancient cauldrons and beakers, and make investigations into their authenticity. [Huang], from his past study and deliberations, was better able than anyone else to clarify issues. None of the other officials in the Library considered himself at Huang's level."[27] The notes he wrote were collected after his death by his son and published under the title *Further Discussions from the Eastern Belvedere.*

Huang Bosi occasionally wrote about paintings, and expressed sentiments much like Dong You's.[28] He wrote much more about calligraphy. Below is an example:

> On looking at Tang Xuandu's *Calligraphy in Ten Scripts*, I was reminded of Zhang Huaiguan's reference to flying white as entirely based on the clerical script. "It is a light version of the *bafen* style."[29] People today when using this style employ the cursive script, which means that they are galloping off in just the opposite direction as the ancients. Bao Zhao's flying white was done with a downy brush, which enabled him to form characters that were alternatively light or heavy. They might be as light as silk floss or as heavy as a mountain in fog, the dense and the thin alternating in forming the characters. It can only be done this way by using a downy brush. Now when I look at the two characters "flying dragon" 飛龍 in the *Ten Scripts*, the ones in flying white were made with a downy brush and are rather close to the clerical style, but more misty, entwined, and lofty. This piece also uses the standard script. One sees something similar in the *Record of the Wise Virtue of the Filial and Respectful Emperor* at the Tang Gong Tomb at Luoyang and at the top of the stele recording merit at Niukou. Tang Taizong's flying white was also done this way. All used downy brushes to convey the impression of being both dense and thin.
>
> Today those who continue the flying white style all write with splintered sticks that resemble lacquer brushes, and certainly do not use downy brushes. Therefore when they make characters, there are none of the changes in density and pattern. This is not the ancient way. When Cai Yong [in the Han dynasty] saw a workman outside Hongdu [library] using a whitewash brush to write, he returned home and invented flying white calligraphy. It was not that he then promptly used the whitewash brush; it was just that he imitated its effect while using a writing brush.
>
> People also use the phrases "flying but not white" and "white but not flying." It seems that they refer to the hair-like places as white and the soaring places as flying. This is vulgar and inaccurate. Others say that Cai Yong saw silk flying in the air and

modeled his characters on it, with "white" 白 a component of the character for silk 帛. This is even more unfounded.[30]

Erudite men like Dong You and Huang Bosi were naturally delighted to be able to spend their days at the Palace Library doing research on objects in its collections. They did a variety of chores, ranging from collating books to checking records, making copies of items, and deciphering inscriptions. The work they did on books is discussed next, before turning to the more complex connoisseurial responsibilities related to other objects kept in the Palace Library.

Working with Books

Work done to develop the palace book collection ranged from initiating new fields of collecting to searching for missing titles, supervising the production of copies, and preparing a catalogue, as well as routine matters such as keeping track of books that were borrowed.

When Huizong took the throne, the clerks in the Palace Library were busy working on a time-consuming project to make archival (yellow paper) copies of the books in the collection. Huizong was informed in 1103 that this project had been begun seventeen years earlier and had so far resulted in copies of 2,082 titles, but the Library's records showed that 1,213 titles as well as 289 individual chapters still awaited copying. The Library officials considered this a disappointing record and wanted to set up quotas and deadlines for copying, calculating that if thirty copyists worked on the project at a cost of 3,500 cash per month and every day copied 2,500 characters, in one year they should be able to copy more than 4,000,000 characters.[31]

Huizong not only continued this project, but soon began initiatives of his own. Three times during his reign he approved campaigns to solicit titles or chapters missing from the Palace Library. In 1103 he instructed Zhedong, Zhexi, and Chengdu circuits to search for privately-owned printing blocks of rare books and send them to the Palace Library. Seven years later, in 1110, Huizong approved the request of the director of the Palace Library, He Zhitong, to conduct a new search for books on the grounds that the Song Palace Library, according to the 1041 catalogue, was less than half the size of the Tang library and smaller even than the Han or Sui libraries.[32] Moreover, as much as a third of the titles in the Song library were missing chapters. He proposed publicizing the titles that had been in the *Chongwen Catalogue* but were now missing so that scholars would search for them. Books not in the catalogue, for whatever reason, should be acquired or borrowed for copying.

He Zhitong wanted to include recently written books, collected works, and titles printed anywhere in the country.[33]

In 1114 Cai You submitted a long memorial proposing ways to deal with books that had been borrowed but not returned, which by his records in the last ten years had reached 4,328 volumes. He proposed setting due dates to prevent the recurrence of this problem. To deal with the books currently missing, rather than make new copies of all of them, Cai proposed whenever possible replacing books missing in one collection with duplicates in another. Where printing blocks were available, extra copies could be run off. But much hand copying would still be needed, which he proposed to handle by setting quotas for each official and clerk and keeping records of how much they completed.[34]

Some of the types of responsibilities Cai had as a Library administrator can be inferred from another long memorial he submitted later that year concerning the lower level functionaries at the Library. He wanted to add four people to the staff (two of whom could read) to the six already serving. Their responsibilities would be to keep records of what was taken out or brought back and to inspect those coming in or going out, as well as to take care of cleaning, candles, and fires.[35]

In 1117 Sun Di, then an editor in the Palace Library, urged the preparation of a new catalogue, given that the *Chongwen Catalogue* was so out of date. Sun Di worked on the project with several other learned men, including Wang Zao and Ni Tao. The resulting catalogue, titled the *Palace Library Catalogue* (Bishu zongmu), added 25,254 chapters, bringing the total to 73,877 chapters.[36] Unfortunately, almost nothing of this catalogue has survived, not even quotations in other books.

Book collecting did not stop with the completion of the catalogue. In 1121, the vice director Weng Yanshen brought up the fact that the Library had the collected works of many Tang writers but had never collected Song writers' works. His proposal that these be systematically sought was approved, and rewards were offered to those who turned in needed books. The next year the supervisor of the Palace Library, Liang Shicheng, proposed to collect rubbings of inscriptions.[37] This was apparently a new field of collecting for the palace, but one that had been highly developed by private collectors over the previous century. The court collected enough rubbings for a list of them to be made. The list circulated, probably in handwritten copies.[38]

When the results of the book collection initiative were reported in 1123, the most successful official had submitted 504 chapters, of which 221 proved to be volumes that the Library needed, and the next best submitted 600 chapters, of which 162 were ones the Library lacked.[39] As new books arrived, extra copies were made for the emperor's personal use. According to Wang Mingqing, Cai You took the lead on this copying project and set to work not only with ten palace attendants but also with recent *jinshi* who had not yet received appointments but who were promised an office once they had worked as copyists for a year.[40]

Huang Bosi was probably one of those given the task of comparing editions of books so that miswritten characters would be identified before the copy was made. His *Further Discussions* includes two reports on such collations, written in similar format. They also include assessments of the book, perhaps intended for its catalogue entry. One on a Han period book begins:

> Your subject Huang so-and-so, an editor in the Palace Library (with the rank of gentleman for discussion), has collated editions of Jiao Yanshou's *Forest of Changes* [Yilin], in sixteen parts. In each part there are many cases of miswritten characters, such as *jue* 决 for *kuai* 快, and *nian* 年 for *yang* 羊. These comparisons are now complete. There are also substitutions, such as 嘉 for 喜, 鹊 for 鹳, where both are retained side by side. The book is ready to be copied.

There follows a biography of the author and a description of the contents of the book. Huang concludes:

> As for what Yanshou wrote, although books on divination emerged from the yin-yang school, the Western Han was not long after the Three Dynasties [of antiquity]. His writing is plain and elegant, worth reading.
>
> Respectfully submitted.[41]

All considered, it seems fair to say that Huizong's interests in art and antiquities did not lead him to neglect the core mission of the Palace Library to obtain, preserve, and catalogue books. During the quarter century of Huizong's reign, several searches were made for books, categories to be collected were expanded in sensible ways, copies were made of books to better assure their preservation, and the catalogue was revised for the first time in nearly eighty years.

Working with Art and Antiquities

The standard sources on Song institutions, such as the *Song History*, the *Song Classified Documents*, the *Jade Sea*, and so on, cited above as sources for the Library's work with books, do not discuss in any detail the work that the Library did with non-book, non-document objects. Information about this aspect of the work of the Library comes mostly from accounts of or by men who worked in the Library, above all Dong You and Huang Bosi.

In the notes Dong You wrote on paintings and bronzes in the Imperial Repository, he refers from time to time to his working there and his interactions with his colleagues, including Huang Fu, Luo Ji, Wang Cai, and Huang Bosi.[42] Occasionally he also mentions a date. Several times he refers to arriving at the Palace Library in 1104, and most of the dated entries range from that year to 1108, with another group from 1113, when he was apparently called back to help with the preparation of illustrations of ancient vessels. The offices he held were quite low ones: proofreader (rank 8b), editor (also rank 8b), and junior compiler (rank 8a). During the first period, he worked with all sorts of objects—paintings, calligraphies, and bronzes—and his approach to all of them shows certain basic similarities, especially a desire to place objects in a text-based context.

Below is an item from his first year at the Library:

> The Imperial Repository's painting of a dragon by Wu Huai had been placed in the inspired class [*shen pin*]. When I checked the painting record [*hua lu*], [I saw] Huai is ranked in the talented class [*neng pin*], and Chuangu [another dragon painter] is ranked one degree higher.[43] In 1103 Huai's picture of a dragon and water was shown at the Grand Clarity Edifice. In comparison to the dragons usually seen [in paintings], it is very unusual. It has a head like a pig and a shape like a donkey. Its scaly flesh, several feet long, is hidden under its hair. Its horns are curved, forking at the top. Holding on to emptiness, it rises up with the clouds. Its head has something the shape of Bo mountain, called a foot-tree. If a dragon does not have a foot-tree, it cannot ascend to Heaven. In this painting it has it. It is likely that those who evaluated the painting did not know that. The next year [1104], in the winter, the emperor sent a messenger to the Repository to fetch it along with Yan Liben's *Twenty-Eight Lunar Mansions*, Xu Xi's *Crab Apples*, and Huang Jucai's *Flowers and Bamboo*.[44] It was retained in the palace when the others were returned. My colleague, Wang Cai, had earlier made a copy of it, and it is for the copy that on his request I am writing this note.[45]

Dong You refers here to several aspects of the ways objects were handled in the Palace Library. There was a written record of objects that ranked artists and art works. Objects were brought back and forth between the Library and Huizong's quarters by messengers. Copies were made of objects in the Library. And objects were occasionally put on display. Each of these practices is also referred to in other entries in his or Huang Bosi's writings, with many entries, like this one, referring to more than one of these practices.

RECORD KEEPING

Records kept by the library about the objects in the collections are referred to in a variety of ways. From some entries it is evident that these records gave information about how and when the item entered the collection:

> The Imperial Repository has a very unusual painting of flowers. . . . When I checked the detailed list [*zhang mu*], [I learned that this painting] entered the collection in 1013. It was submitted by the capital prefecture, then sent to the Imperial Repository . . .[46]

Objects that were not considered of much importance might not be listed in the records. This is made clear in an entry that can be dated to 1103 or 1104:

> This picture of shepherds was originally among the objects that entered the Imperial Repository with the confiscation of the property of Zeng Bu's son Yu for corruption.[47] It depicts sheep and wild animals in unusual postures like the [stone] kneeling sheep and recumbent wild animals placed at graves. The shepherd is a feather-cloaked Daoist master. At first no one thought much of the painting, so it was not entered into the checking record [*jiao lu*]. The next year the vice director Luo Ji ordered a workman to mount it on rollers and entered it in the painting record [*hua lu*]. . . .[48]

The records kept on objects gave enough information about them for Dong You to sometimes conclude that parts were missing. He noted that a set of paintings by Yan Liben, *Five Stars and Twenty-Eight Lunar Mansions,* was incomplete, and suggested that the clerks in charge of storing the paintings had probably stolen the missing ones. In an item dated 1106, Dong You wrote, "Concerning the Imperial Repository's paintings of a meeting of kings, in the list record [*zhang lu*], this work has twenty-four leaves, but twelve have been lost. . . ."[49]

At least sometimes, the records included notes about the interpretation of an object. Dong You reported that the Repository's painting record listed a painting under the title *Wang Boli Presenting a Horse,* with the annotation explaining that Wang Boli was an exceptional archer during the reign of Emperor Wu of the Han.[50]

RANKING OBJECTS AND ARTISTS

For paintings, at least, the records kept by the library apparently ranked both artists and individual works. The entry about Wu Huai quoted above referred to the "inspired" and "talented" classes. Another painting is described as being placed in the "unusual rank of the talented" class.[51] By the twelfth century, these categories had a history going back several centuries. Zhang Huaiguan, in his *Calligraphy Standards* of 724–727, divided calligraphers into inspired, subtle (*miao*), and talented classes, each class subdivided into three levels. Earlier, Li Sizhen (d. 696) had referred to a top rank of calligraphers as "untrammeled" (*yi*), a term which Zhu Jingzhen also used in the late ninth century for painters. In the early eleventh century Huang Xiufu placed "untrammeled" highest. According to Deng Chun, Huizong used this order: "inspired," "untrammeled," "subtle," and "talented."[52]

Further evidence of the use of these quality classifications for Huizong's collections is found in another one of Dong You's entries, which refers to a major reevaluation of the rankings assigned to objects:

> The year after I wrote a note on the picture of the test for skills owned by Mr. Li,[53] the Imperial Repository collection of painting and calligraphy obtained a set of four paintings of the test for skills that had been confiscated from the collection of Ding Wei.[54] The inscription reads, "Made by Wang Ai." Ai had a reputation for ability and past generations put him in the inspired class.[55] In the newly set ranks of the Repository, he was entered only into the talented class. Still, this painting has a lot of brush force and is very successful in capturing the appearance of people. It is very different from what contemporary artists do. Yet it would be wrong to promote him and class him with [the major masters] Zhang, Wu, Gu, and Lu. . . .[56]

Wang Ai is omitted from Huizong's painting catalogue, most likely as a consequence of this downgrading.

HANDLING OBJECTS

Several items in Dong You's book refer to paintings being brought back and forth between the inner part of the palace (Huizong's living quarters) and the Palace Library. Messengers handled the paintings; probably these messengers were eunuchs, as eunuchs were normally the people to carry objects from the rear parts of the palace, where women could move freely, to the front part, where officials worked. Sometimes the messengers asked for information:

> The Imperial Repository has a painting by Li Zanhua of a deer. . . . In 1105 an order came down for the Imperial Repository to send the painting inside [to the emperor's quarters]. The messenger had doubts about what it depicted and sought an explanation. Previously, in similar situations, we had come up with titles to be prepared should the emperor ask questions.[57]

Within the Palace Library's own storehouses (particularly the Imperial Repository), Library officials seem to have been free to look for objects themselves. In the note below, Dong shows that he was familiar with the *Investigations of Antiquity Illustrated* before joining the Library and that as soon as he arrived there he was eager to see antiquities identified in it as belonging to the Imperial Repository:

> The *Investigations of Antiquity Illustrated* records that the Imperial Repository had seven objects, large and small, whose program [of decoration] was similar.[58] The two largest were walking animals with two heads and a body with patterns on it like a tiger and a projecting tail like a monkey, and a hole under its belly from which one could suspend something, making them tureens [*dui*]. In 1104 when I took up my post in the Library I searched for them. . . .[59]

Even if the curatorial staff could pull out objects themselves, often their interest was aroused because objects had been taken out of the storehouse to be sunned in the annual sunning of objects. Only a small portion of the objects were sunned in any given year, and particular objects might not have been widely seen for decades. For instance, Dong You wrote:

> This painting of the Feng and Shan sacrifices has been in the Imperial Repository collection for a long time. The Palace Library took it out of its box for the sunning of books in 1104. It apparently dates from the visit of Emperor Zhenzong to Taishan in 1008.[60]
>
> . . . .When books were sunned in 1104, [a painting of flowers] was brought out and I did research on what it should be titled.[61]

MAKING COPIES

Several entries in Dong You's *Notes on Painting* refer to staff of the Library copying paintings or making tracing copies of calligraphy or inscriptions on bronzes. The entry cited above about the picture of shepherds noted, "My colleague Fang Hui had a worker draw it." Presumably this worker was a skilled painting copyist. In some cases, the copies were intended as a kind of conservation, a way to extend the life of the object, "to pass it on to future generations."[62]

Copies were also done to make it easier to do research on objects. This was especially the case with inscriptions on bronzes. Dong You remarked that in one case, Luo Ji showed him a tracing he had made of an inscription from a cauldron and asked him about a word in it. In another case Dong made a tracing copy of the inscription on an ancient vessel that had just been submitted to the Library so that he could more easily do research on it.[63]

Sometimes copies were made for private purposes, because the person who did the copy wanted it for himself. This was a common practice with books—as we have seen, more than one official made copies of books in the Palace Library to increase his own collection. But those who were capable painters could also copy paintings. The entry on Wu Huai's dragon painting mentioned Wang Cai copying it. Similarly, another entry reported that in 1104 Huang Fu made a tracing copy of a painting by Li Shenwei.[64]

CLASSIFYING AND LABELING OF OBJECTS

A very common theme running through both Dong You's and Huang Bosi's writings is the need to know precisely what an object is in order to classify it correctly or give it a title. Narrative paintings whose stories were not immediately evident were one challenge. Dong You did research on a painting titled *Wang Boli Presenting a Horse,* and concluded that earlier scholars' analysis was wrong. Wang Boli had not lived in the Han period but rather had been a Turk in the early Tang period. Another time Dong You interpreted a painting of a feather-cloaked shepherd as a depiction of a Daoist story recorded in Ge Hong's *Biographies of Immortals.*[65]

The correct classification of ancient vessels was at least as great a challenge. In many cases, the officials at the Library first had to decipher any characters that were inscribed on the vessel. Not infrequently scholars disagreed on the correct modern equivalent of the ancient graphs.[66] Once the reading was settled, the next step was to determine if the inscription named the vessel type. For instance, inscriptions often contain phrases like "So-and-so made this *ding* [cauldron]. His sons and grandsons should cherish and use it." However, as Huang Bosi pointed out in a discussion of square cauldrons, even when a vessel used a specific term, one still had the problem of deciding when the term was used as a technical term for a type of vessel and when it was used as a generic term for sacrificial vessel.[67]

When bronzes were not inscribed, Library officials had to match vessels to similar ones that were inscribed or to descriptions of vessels found in ancient texts. To give an example, classical texts mention the capacity of some vessels, and Dong used that in one of his analyses. He reported that he had classified a newly discovered set of several dozen bronze vessels by their capacity. They were covered vessels with rope-shaped handles that held less than six pints in the units of his day. Based on his reconstruction of ancient measurements, he calculated that the vessels would have held one peck and two pints in ancient units, making them tureens (*dui*). In another case, Huang Bosi discussed at length the textual evidence of what the musical instrument called a *chun* was like, then asserted that a set of six instruments should be classed as *chun* rather than as bells, as they were in the "old record list" (*jiu ji mu*) of the Imperial Repository. Other scholars had also done research on these issues, and occasionally they were cited. Once Dong You cited with approval the discussion in Lü Dalin's *Investigations of Antiquities Illustrated* on the vessels called grain pans. The decoration on vessels could also be used to help classify them. In one case Huang Bosi interpreted the decoration on a beaker (*zun*) as depicting the ancient mythological figure Chiyou.[68]

Sometimes Huang and Dong studied the same object but came to different conclusions. In 1113, when "the Palace Library was investigating and categorizing the ancient vessels," both Dong You and Huang Bosi examined the same "wild cat headed raised dish," but analysis of textual references to wild cats led them in different directions. Dong took the vessel as a feasting dish, while Huang suggested that it had been used for temple offerings.[69]

Dating was an important part of the classification that Huizong's curators were called on to perform. Huang Bosi argued that because a raised dish (*dou*) was simple and plain, it was probably of Shang date. Similarly, he once argued that because a beaker (*zun*) was plainer than typical Zhou ones, it was a Shang piece. Dong You dated a bell without an inscription to the Zhou period on the grounds that its dimensions fit the scheme used in Zhou musical instruments. Huang dated a crock to the Han period rather than the Zhou because of the delicacy of the workmanship and the lack of an antique appearance. Sometimes paintings also needed to be dated. Dong You dated a painting to Tang on the basis of costumes.[70]

ASSESSING AUTHENTICITY

As discussed in chapter 3, scholarly collectors in the eleventh century often cast doubt on the authenticity of objects that had entered both private and palace collections. Perhaps because it was so widely available, the *Chunhua Model Letters* was subject to widespread criticism and thus brought into question the quality of the palace calligraphy collection. Both Mi Fu and Huang Bosi had written at length on their doubts about specific pieces included in it.

Huizong and his curators built up the palace collections so quickly that they surely acquired works that they later decided were copies or fakes. Huang Bosi claimed that many of the pieces attributed to famous early calligraphers were done by a single person at Li Yu's court. He added, "At present the Imperial Repository still has several of these pieces. They all are on paper from Pure Heart Hall and are clearly distinguished by a label reading 'Imitation calligraphy; do not transmit or copy along with authentic pieces.'"[71] On another occasion he referred to calligraphy in the palace labeled either imitation (*fang*) or fake (*wei*).[72]

In the following rather lengthy entry, Huang Bosi proceeds step by step to show that an object could not be a third-century work, as it purported to be:

> Recently it was reported that someone from Chang'an has the original of Cao Zhi's calligraphy, *Ode to the Sparrow-Hawk*.[73] After I got the rubbing from the version carved by Zhang Yunsou (fl. 1080s) and compared the two, I could see that this work is a recent fake. Note that the cursive script, like the regular and running scripts, enlarges over time. Therefore there are cursive characters in later periods that did not exist before the Tang dynasty, such as the characters *yu* 於 and *bi* 必. . . . Now on the fake *Ode to the Sparrow Hawk*, the three characters all resemble the way Tang people did them in cursive script. This is the first anomaly.
>
> At the beginning of the ode is written the title, which is capped by the character *yue* 曰 "is called." This is probably a result of foolishly recording what was in a [literary] collectanea that had Cao Zhi's *Ode*. How vulgar! The *Yiwen leiju* has this ode. This is the second anomaly.
>
> At the end [of the scroll] is a colophon by Wu Youji.[74] The characters are done in a vulgar ancient seal script of the sort done today by men in the market. It also says "to pass on forever," which is a recent expression, not used in Tang times. This is the third anomaly.
>
> There are several seals which purport to be seals of Tang people but are no different from the seals that can be bought in the market today in terms of the form of the seal script characters. At the end the two characters *jing* and *hua* were clearly copied from Wang Xianzhi's *Zhong dong jing* and *Hua xin fu*. This is the fourth anomaly.
>
> At the end there is a portrait of Cao Zhi. Its spirit is extremely common, as are the clothes and the brushwork. It resembles work done by painters in the current painting academy. Men of the past did not paint like this. This is the fifth anomaly.
>
> Not only did someone make a fake calligraphy, but also he painted a portrait and applied lots of fake seals and signatures. He probably went to all this trouble because he was afraid that people would not believe [the attribution]. He had no idea how ignorant he was. He even claimed that the calligraphy was better than the Two Wangs and worth sighing over! This shows us that it is not difficult to forge calligraphy, but it is difficult to appreciate calligraphy. The popularly transmitted stone engraving of Wang Wei's pictures of the four seasons, which has Wang Wei's and Xue Yong's seals, is a similar case. Viewing things done recently in these shallow and popular ways dulls people. And yet there are scholar-officials who collect these things. In the most extreme cases they even hang them on their walls. How lamentable![75]

PREPARING MATERIAL FOR A CATALOGUE

Dong You reported that in 1113 officials in the Library were ordered to prepare a catalogue of the bronzes kept there:

> In the Imperial Repository there is a vessel classified as a tureen [*dui*] which is really a cauldron [*ding*]. In 1113 the palace issued *Antique Objects Illustrated of Xuanhe Hall*, one hundred chapters/scrolls in all, with very full analyses of [the vessels'] shapes and decorative programs. Thereupon our Library was told to make a separate catalogue of the ancient vessels in our collection to submit. The editor, Huang Bosi, showed me a picture and said, "This plain Shang tureen is 5.5 inches tall, 4.1 inches deep, 6.7 inches in circumference at the mouth; it holds 8 pints and weighs 6.7 pounds (these are all using current measurements). The decoration consists of two monkey heads. Below the ears are ornaments, which may be the tail protruding." He also said, "The ancient tureens that have survived until today, such as . . . all are inscribed.[76] This vessel is quite unusual. I suspect that it may have been made by men of the Shang."
>
> I investigated it. Although of the simian type with the tail protruding, it is a normal ancient ritual vessel of the sort that has existed since the time of Shun of Yu. What makes this specifically Shang? Thereupon I classed it as a monkey cauldron.[77]

Quite a few other entries in Huang's and Dong's books read like the sorts of reports officials would have prepared in preparation for a catalogue. How the catalogues were compiled from these sorts of reports will be more closely examined in chapters 6, 7, and 8.

Working with books, art, and antiquities presented a variety of challenges to the officials at the Palace Library. Erudition was a great asset, whether an official was working with manuscripts, printed books, paintings, calligraphies, or ancient bronzes. Broad familiarity with both classical texts and more recent writings was used repeatedly to help distinguish subject matter, authorship, and authenticity. A desire to add to the total store of knowledge seems to have motivated work on many different sorts of objects. Careful record keeping was essential, whether one was trying to maintain the integrity of many-volume books or knowledge of how and when objects had entered the palace collection. Cai You's proposal to put in place procedures for checking out books and giving them due dates made sense. Dong You's concern for proper classification and accurate titles similarly reflected the need to manage an enormous amount of information. The curatorial staff required men who had seen many objects over the years, but it did not need men with an intense desire to possess objects that caught their fancy. Dong You and Huang Bosi made better curators than Mi Fu or Zhao Mingcheng would have.

Policies toward staffing the Palace Library can be seen as one of the ways Huizong tried to court the scholar-official class, comparable in some ways to his ambitious school system. Men who were highly respected for their learning and writing ability were assigned prestigious posts there, giving them a place in the central government even when their political commitment to the New Policies was in doubt (such as men who had been on the 1104 blacklist or men thought to be followers of Su Shi). Much the way collecting was taken to be a politically neutral activity during Shenzong's and Zhezong's reigns, working on the palace collections was considered politically innocuous. It did not require implementing the New Policies' financial policies or involve much interaction with top officials like Cai Jing. Thus the resources Huizong devoted to the study and cataloguing of his collections (and the books he had the Library compile) can also be seen as part of his strategy to win support from accomplished scholars.

Even though at least two of the senior officials in the Library, He Zhitong and Cai You, were without doubt in the reform camp, work in the Library seems to have been both pleasant and a source of pride for those who secured appointments there, whatever their political inclinations. Men who served at the Palace Library, even in the rank 7 and rank 8 posts, seem generally to have considered themselves privileged. According to his biographer, when Huang Bosi arrived at the Palace Library to take up his new assignment and saw all of the books stored there, he was elated and would linger, forgetting to stop to eat or sleep.[78] Sun Di, who was an editor at the Library in 1117, wrote effusively about the Library in his funerary inscription for one of his colleagues in that period, Fu Liangyou:

> During the Zhenghe period (1111–1117), I was favored with an editing position in the Palace Library and Mr. Fu Liangyou was also there editing the *Nine Provinces Illustrated Gazetteer*. Our offices were in the same building and we became friends. At that time the world was at peace and the emperor was organizing auspicious signs and promoting ritual and music, thus adding elegance to the peace. He had drawn together the realm's Confucian scholars and the famous literary talents of the age and placed them in the scholarly offices and agencies while they waited for regular appointments.[79]

Huizong of course also benefited from this arrangement. The Library's collections meant enough to him that he wanted the best possible scholars to work on them and produce the catalogues that would establish the splendor of his court for centuries to come.

CHAPTER 6

Collecting and Cataloguing Antiquities

Our ruler, in his divine wisdom, promotes ritual on a grand scale. He has adopted the sounds of the Ying and Jing music [of the Shang dynasty] and has investigated rituals on the basis of vessels from the Xia and Shang dynasties. A full set of vessels of the Three Dynasties has been made and has been taken out to show to the officials. In recent times, beginning with the Biyong Academy and the Hall of Enlightenment, down to the Nine Cauldrons, the Music of [Great] Brilliance, and the rituals at the Round Hill and the Square Marsh, all have been made to accord fully with antiquity. This is very different from treating the Six Classics as empty texts.

— Zhai Ruwen

By the end of his reign, Huizong had assembled a collection of antiquities that vastly exceeded anything put together before his time, either by an earlier court or by a private collector. It included bronzes, jades, engraved stones, and perhaps other objects. Some were recent discoveries; others had been in private hands for a generation or more. Among the best-known objects were the Stone Drums (see fig. 4.1). Ever since these ten large stones were discovered in the early Tang, calligraphers had marveled over the poems inscribed on them and used them to help reconstruct the evolution of Chinese scripts. Huizong had the Drums transported to Kaifeng early in his reign. The Drums were first placed in the Biyong Academy, then later brought into the palace.[1] They were among the treasures viewed at the 1119 party in the rear palace discussed in chapter 4. Huizong also acquired objects that had been in private collections. After Li Gonglin's death, all but one of his ancient jades ended up in Huizong's collection.[2] Some of them had been published in Lü Dalin's *Investigations of Antiquities Illustrated* and therefore were well known to collectors of antiquities (see fig. 6.1 for an example).

Fig. 6.1
Two views of an ancient jade belt hook in the collection of Li Gonglin, as shown in *Investigations of Antiquities Illustrated*. Li Gonglin's note, copied into the book, mentions the importance of appropriate clothing in the ritual classics and states that this jade hook dates to the Three Dynasties (that is, Xia, Shang, or Zhou); the note also states that craftsmen since Han times have not been able to carve such marvelous curvilinear designs. This jade later entered Huizong's collection. KGT 1752 ed. 8.10a.

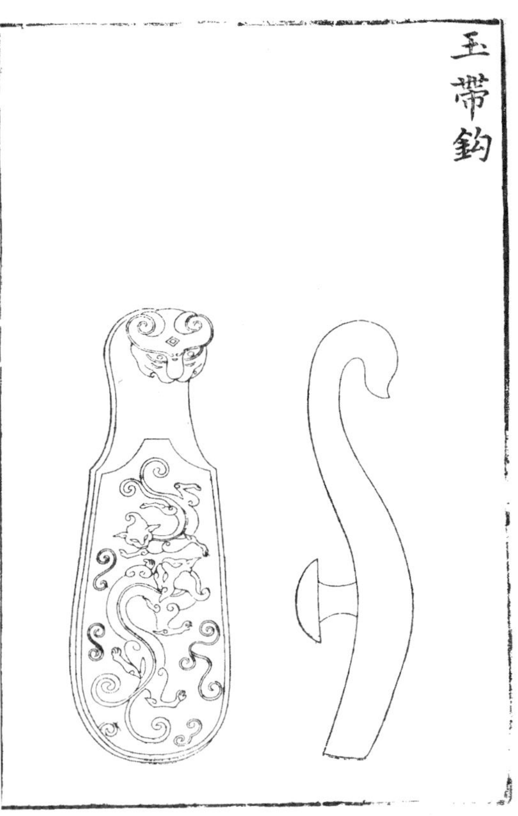

Collecting antiquities at Huizong's court was intertwined with politics at several levels. Ever since Han times, the discovery of ancient vessels had been taken as a positive augury for the court, a sign that Heaven was pleased with the ruler.[3] Consequently, the fact that hundreds of ancient objects were found during Huizong's reign and sent to the court had to be considered extremely propitious. Ancient sacrificial vessels had special meaning for the court because of their connection to rituals the emperor performed. There was thus a political side to Huizong's decision to replicate ancient bells and sacrificial vessels to use during ritual performances. He was enacting the long-recognized goal of "recovering antiquity" and honoring *The Rites of Zhou* and scholars who promoted its use. At the same time, much of the potential power of the court antiquities collection could be realized only by issuing a catalogue of them, something Huizong recognized relatively early as more than one catalogue was completed (the extant one is the "revised" one). Cataloguing the antiquities was a way the resources of the throne could be used to advance scholarship and at the same time display the court's cultural leadership.

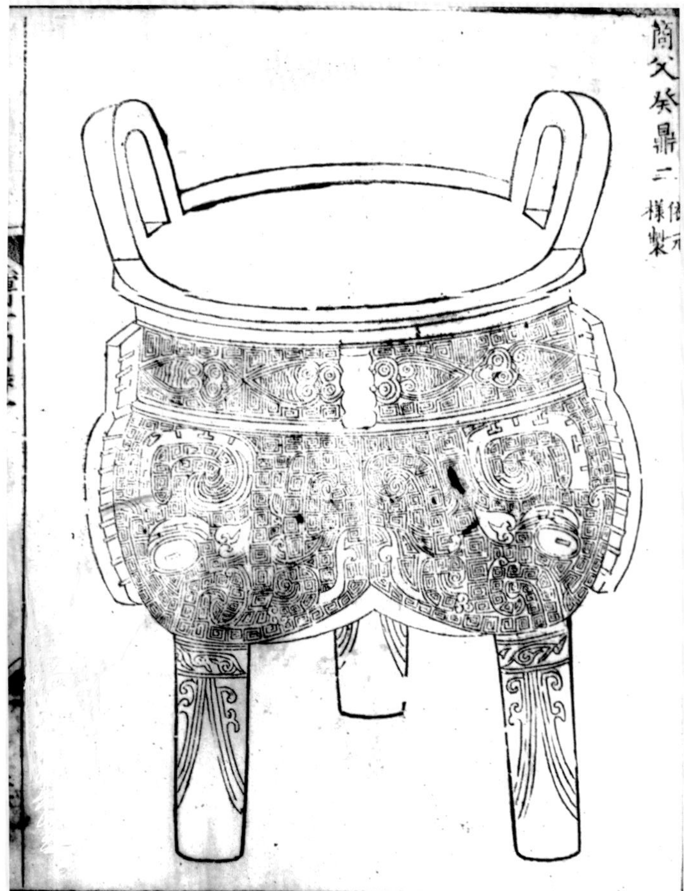

Fig. 6.2
Fugui cauldron as illustrated in *Antiquities Illustrated.* The inscription on the inside wall of the vessel also closely matches the rubbing of the inscription reproduced in *Antiquities Illustrated.* The vessel is described as 5.9 inches tall (with the handles adding another 1.4 inches) and weighing 5 pounds, 12 ounces. The first graph of the inscription is interpreted as a picture of a standing axe. BGT 1528 ed. 1.26a.

Only bronzes are documented in the surviving catalogue of antiquities. Its full title is *Antiquities Illustrated of Xuanhe [Hall or Period], Revised* (Chongxiu Xuanhe Bogu tu [lu]), but it is commonly called *Antiquities Illustrated* (Bogu tu) for short. The book has no preface, but because it includes a set of bells only discovered and submitted to the court in 1123, it could not have been completed before that date.[4] Of the 800–plus bronzes illustrated in it, only one seems to have survived until today. It is a cauldron owned by the National Palace Museum in Taipei, which matches one in *Antiquities Illustrated* so closely that it surely was once in the palace (see plate 20 and fig. 6.2).[5]

Huizong's antiquities catalogue had entries for sacrificial vessels, musical instruments, mirrors, and such miscellaneous items as crossbow mechanisms and axe heads. Huizong's collection of cauldrons was huge and highly varied. Its largest piece was more than two feet tall and weighed a hundred pounds (fig. 6.3). Some of the vessels had already gained fame when they were in private collections, such as the Jin Jiang cauldron, with its long inscription (fig. 6.4). It had been in Liu Chang's

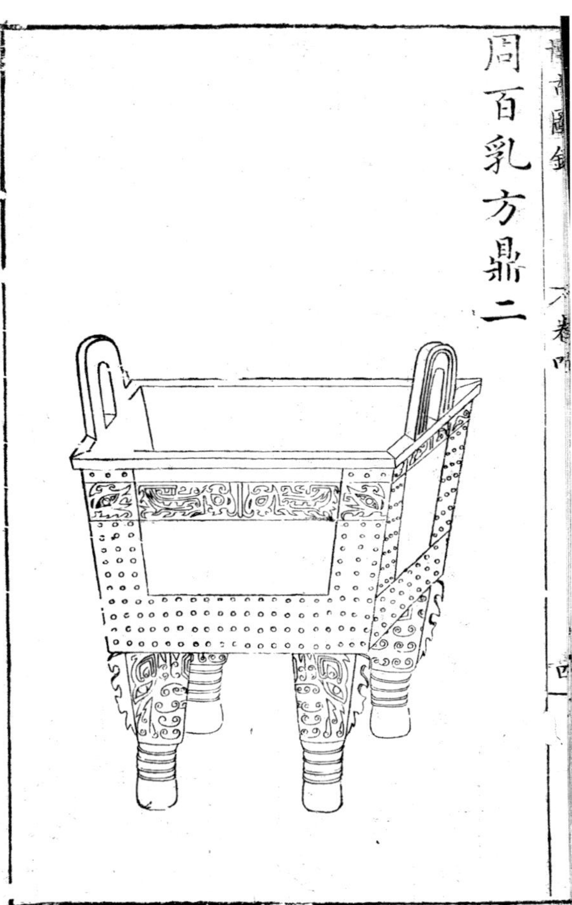

Fig. 6.3
The largest of the cauldrons in *Antiquities Illustrated.* Given the title "Zhou Cauldron with Hundred Nipples Décor," it was more than two feet tall and weighed a hundred pounds. BGT 1752 ed. 4.4b.

collection in the mid-eleventh century and had had its inscription traced and deciphered in both Ouyang Xiu's *Record of Collected Antiquities* and Lü Dalin's *Investigations of Antiquities Illustrated.* Huizong's editors in *Antiquities Illustrated* remarked that its calligraphy was the best example from its period. Other cauldrons were notable because their inscriptions linked them to famous figures of the past, such as the "King Wen of Zhou" cauldron associated with the founder of the Zhou dynasty. Huizong's collection of ancient musical instruments was just as amazing. It included five different types of bells, among which were three sets of inscribed bells. In terms of innovation, the mirror collection is impressive, as Huizong was apparently the first to collect mirrors on a significant scale. Most of the 113 Han to Tang mirrors illustrated in his catalogue were decorated with cosmic diagrams, images of gods, or auspicious messages about long life, prosperity, and progeny.[6]

Huizong's catalogue of antiquities built on but went beyond the slightly earlier *Investigations of Antiquities Illustrated* discussed in chapter 3. The format of the earlier work was largely adopted, including the provision of pictures, rubbings,

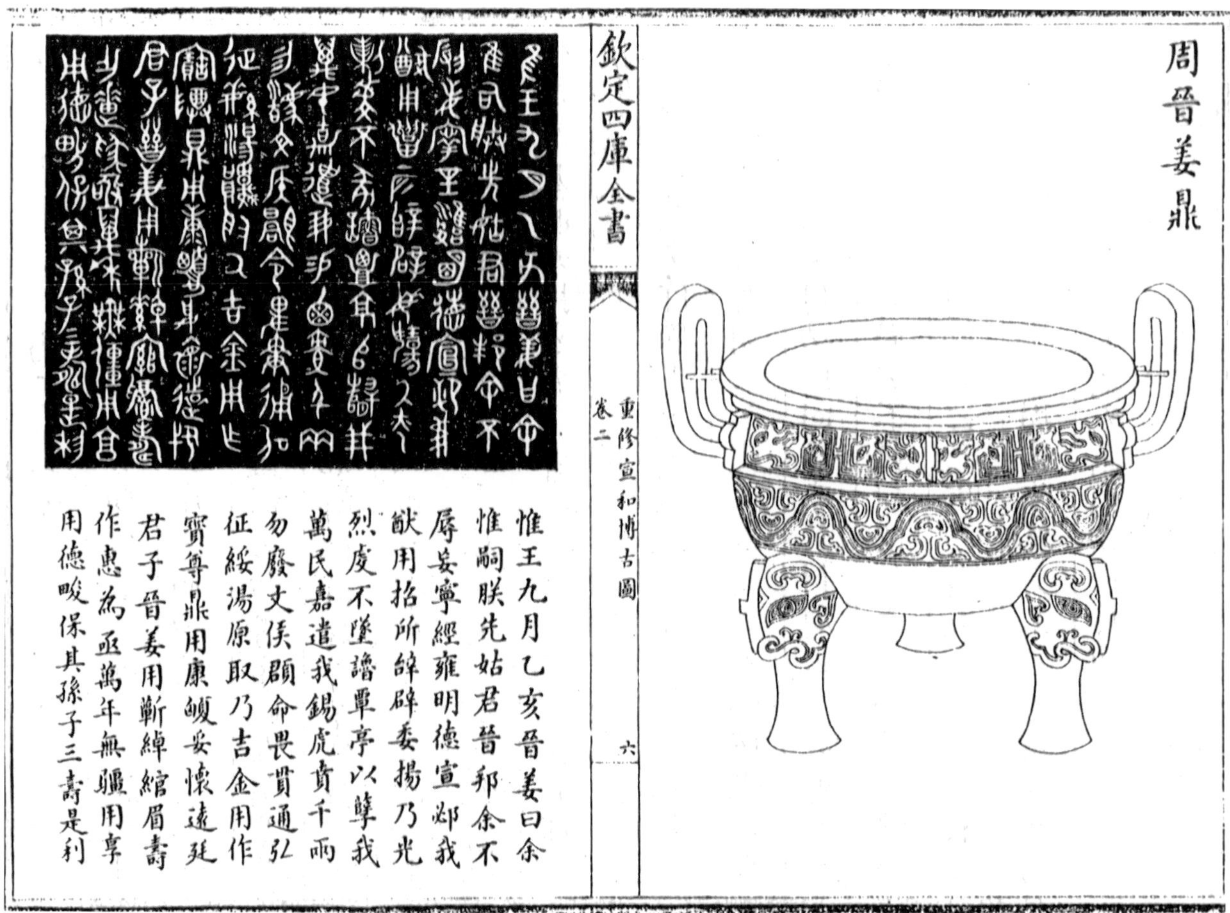

欽定四庫全書

周晉姜鼎

重修宣和博古圖 卷二 六

惟王九月乙亥晉姜曰余
惟嗣朕先姑君晉邦余不
厤妄寧經雍明德宣邲我
猷用招所辞辟妥揚乃光
烈虔不墜譇覃亭以嬖我
萬民嘉遣我錫虎責千兩
勿廢文侯顯命畏貫通弘
征綏湯原取乃吉金用作
寶尊鼎用康頗妥懷遠廷
君子晉姜用蘄綽綰眉壽
作惠為亟萬年無疆用享
用德畯保其孫子三壽是利

Fig. 6.4
Jin Jiang cauldron, with its inscription, in *Antiquities Illustrated*. This cauldron is described as 1 foot 3 inches tall and weighing more than seventy pounds. What made this cauldron important was its 121-character inscription, which refers to a woman from the state of Qi whose family name was Jiang and who married the ruler of the state of Jin. The inscription was widely discussed by eleventh-century scholars. BGT 2.6ab.

transcriptions, and notes. But Huizong's catalogue is both larger and more selective. Even though Lü published works from several dozen collectors, Lü's catalogue included only a quarter as many bronzes (210, compared to 840). Lü's catalogue illustrated twenty-five pieces that were in the palace in 1092 (two bells in the Court of Imperial Sacrifice, fifteen vessels in the Palace Storehouse, and eight vessels in the Imperial Repository). Only seven of these were included in Huizong's catalogue, most likely because the palace collection had since acquired many superior pieces (for instance, ones with longer or more interesting inscriptions) and the cataloguers were not trying to record every piece in the palace.

Antiquities Illustrated is a large book, 1,292 double pages in the edition of the *Siku quanshu* (1,262 in the 1528 ed.), divided into thirty chapters with an average of more than forty double pages each. It classified objects into fifty-nine types and dated them by dynasty, as shown in table 6.1.[7]

The fifty-nine categories into which bronzes were classified is much larger than the six script types used in the calligraphy catalogue or the ten fields of paintings used in the painting catalogue (see chapters 7 and 8), and should probably be taken as a sign of the relative immaturity of antiquities scholarship. The instinct of the scholars and curators was to respect the term inscribed on vessels and only reluctantly to group together similar vessels which had different words inscribed on them. Progress in more analytical assessment was being made, however, which we can see in the twenty introductory essays to the types or groups of types of bronze objects. These essays vary considerably, though most deal in one way or another with the problem of connecting surviving vessels to references to vessels in the classics, especially *The Rites of Zhou*, a text esteemed by Wang Anshi, considered a foundational text for the New Policies, and studied by everyone who aspired to office during the reform era.

One of the most fundamental differences between the collection of antiquities and the collection of other culturally valued objects lay in their connection to rituals, especially the rituals rulers performed. Early strains of Chinese thought, continued in Song times especially by scholars of the ritual classics, saw the performance of ritual and music as central to the role of the ruler and indeed to the maintenance of good order in the cosmos. The *Book of Music*, included in the *Record of Ritual*, contains the statement, "Ritual and music, punishments and regulations, all have the same ultimate aim. They all are means by which the hearts of the people are unified and the orderly way attained."[8] *The Rites of Zhou*, in discussing the duties of the minister of rites (*dazongbo*), similarly makes royal rituals a key element in creating and preserving the harmony of the cosmos: "Rites and music are the means to adjust the transformations of Heaven and Earth and the production of all creation, to serve the ghosts and gods, bring harmony to the myriad people, and perfect all creation."[9] Not any music or rites would do, however. Although the ancient sage kings had achieved the full potential of rites and music, over time perfection had been lost. Much of the improperly tuned music of later times was more likely to lead men astray than elevate them.[10]

As a practical matter, how could a ruler adjust court rituals and music to make them better conform to the ideal music and rituals of the ancient sage kings, or at least the Zhou period? The classics were considered the source for understanding the ancients, but interpreting them was often difficult. Consider, for instance, *The Rites of Zhou*. Among the duties it assigned to the deputy minister of rites (*xiao zongbo*) was distinguishing the names and designs of the six *yi* (彝, libation cups) and the six *zun* (尊, beakers) so that they could be used in ceremonies and the entertainment of guests. The commentary listed the six *yi* as the chicken *yi*, the bird *yi*, the *jia yi*, the yellow *yi*, the tiger *yi*, and the monkey *yi*. The six *zun* were

TABLE 6.1. Contents of Huizong's *Antiquities Illustrated*

Object and chapter number in *Antiquities Illustrated*	Shang	Zhou	Han	Later	Total
cauldrons (*ding* 鼎) ch. 1–5*	26	81	18	1	126
beakers (*zun* 尊) ch. 6–7*	14	19			33
tall jars (*lei* 罍) ch. 7		8			8
libation cups (*yi* 彝) ch. 8*	7	18			25
wine bowls (*zhou* 舟) ch. 8			2		2
covered wine jars (*you* 卣) ch. 9–11*	30	22	1		53
pitchers (*ping* 瓶) ch. 12*		1	2		3
bottles (*hu* 壺) ch. 12–13	3	18	33		54
goblets (*jue* 爵) ch. 14*	35				35
wine vessels (*jia* 斝) ch. 15*		15	1		16
wine cups (*gu* 觚) ch. 15	16	19			35
ladles (*dou* 斗) ch. 16			2		2
low cups (*zhi* 卮) ch. 16			4		4
jars (*zhi* 觶) ch. 16	3	2			5
double-mouthed cups (*jue* 角) ch. 16		1			1
cups (*bei* 杯) ch. 16			1		1
tureens (*dui* 敦) ch. 16–17*	1	27			28
grain pans (*fugui* 簠簋) ch. 18*		4			4
raised dishes (*dou* 豆) ch. 18		4	2		6
raised platters (*pu* 鋪) ch. 18		1			1
steamers (*yan* 甗) ch. 18*	7	5	2		14
pots (*ding* 錠) ch. 18			1		1
pans (*li* 鬲) ch. 19*	2	14			16
fu jars (*fu* 鍑) ch. 19		1	1		2
wine warmers (*he* 盉) ch. 19*	2	10	2		14
bowls (*an* 盦) ch. 20*		1			1
warming ladles (*jiaodou* 鐎斗) ch. 20			2		2
crocks (*pou* 瓿) ch. 20		8			8
pitchers (*ying* 罂) ch. 20			1		1
ice trays (*bingjian* 冰鑒) ch. 20				1	1
ice scoops (*bingdou* 冰斗) ch. 20			1		1

* Includes introductory essay.

Object and chapter number in *Antiquities Illustrated*	Shang	Zhou	Han	Later	Total
washbasins (*yi* 匜) ch. 20–21*	3	11	2		16
washpans (*yipan* 匜盤) ch. 21		2			2
washbowls (*xi* 洗) ch. 21		3	3		6
tubs (*pen* 盆) ch. 21			1		1
dishes (*xuan* 鋗) ch. 21			1		1
soup pots (*yu* 杅) ch. 21		1	1		2
bells (*zhong* 鍾) ch. 22–25*		109	6	3	118
chimes (*qing* 磬) ch. 26*		4			4
bronze drums (*chun* 錞) ch. 26*		19			19
handbells (*duo* 鐸) ch. 26*		2			2
gong bells (*zheng* 鉦) ch. 26		9			9
small handbells (*nao* 鐃) ch. 26			2		2
axe heads (*qi* 戚) ch. 26			2		2
crossbow mechanisms (*nuji* 弩機) ch. 27*			7		7
tube ornaments (*dui* 鐓) ch. 27			3		3
dressing cases (*lian* 奩) ch. 27			5		5
money (*qian* 錢) ch. 27			9		9
water droppers (*yandi* 硯滴) ch. 27			2		2
carriage fittings (*yuan* 轅) ch. 27		3			3
carriage decorations (*yulushi* 輿輅飾) ch. 27			1		1
stands (*zuo* 座) ch. 27		1	1		2
harness bells (*ling* 鈴) ch. 27			1		1
knife pens (*daobi* 刀筆) ch. 27			1		1
staff handles (*zhangtou* 杖頭) ch. 27			2		2
squatting dragons (*dunlong* 蹲龍) ch. 27				1	1
dove carts (*jiuche* 鳩車) ch. 27			2		2
steelyards (*tiliang* 提梁) ch. 27			1		1
mirrors (*jian* 鑑) ch. 28–30*			68	45	113
Total	149	443	197	51	840

listed as the sacrificial animal *zun*, the elephant or ivory *zun*, the bottle *zun*, the settled *zun*, the large *zun*, and the mountain *zun*.[11] But how could one distinguish them if one did not know what they looked like? In Song times, the easiest place to turn was the *Illustrations of the Three Ritual Classics*, written early in the dynasty by Nie Chongyi.[12] Nie provided pictures of these and many other objects mentioned in the classics, relying on Han or later commentators and probably sometimes his own imagination. For instance, Nie's book depicted the various *yi* as plain wooden cups with pictures on their side of chickens, birds, and tigers; the yellow *yi* has a picture of a pair of eyes, based on Zheng Xuan's second-century commentary, which linked the yellow *yi* to a reference in the *Record of Ritual* to a yellow eye vessel; the *jia yi* depicted grain, from Zheng Xuan's commentary stating that this *jia* 斝 character was borrowed for the *jia* 稼 character meaning grain. Similarly, the *zun* are depicted as nearly identical in shape to the *yi*, but in this case Nie gave alternative reconstructions, drawing on different commentators' interpretations. Thus he showed the elephant/ivory *zun* as either a large cup with a picture of an elephant on it or one decorated with three dots of ivory (see fig. 6.5).[13] The settled *zun* is shown to be shaped like a cup, with no foot (see fig. 6.6). The *Illustrations of the Three Ritual Classics* was treated as the authoritative source by the Song government, which had its pictures copied onto the walls at the Directorate of Education. Many prefectural schools followed that example, spreading knowledge of its pictures.[14]

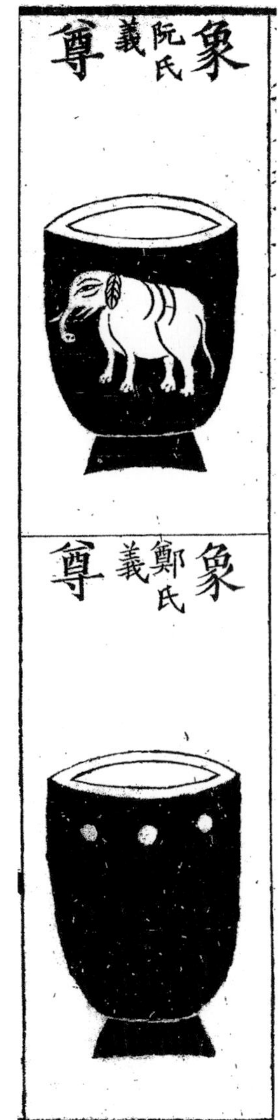

Fig. 6.5
Alternatives for "elephant beaker" in *Illustrations of the Three Ritual Classics*. SLT 14.4a–5a.

Over the course of the eleventh century, scholars began to see the importance of examining actual ancient objects to correct misunderstandings of the classics. The early Song emperors Taizong and Zhenzong had not collected antiquities when they solicited books, calligraphies, and paintings, but the court gradually accumulated a few vessels anyway. In 1051 Renzong had the ancient bronzes held by the Imperial Repository and the Ministry of Rites taken out and rubbings made of the inscriptions on them. At the time there seem to have been no more than a dozen objects, and scholars at court had considerable difficulty deciphering the writing on them.[15] Because of the progress made by scholars outside the court, however, by the end of the eleventh century, scholars were proposing corrections to the *Illustrations to the Three Ritual Classics*. The *Investigations of Antiquities Illustrated* suggested that two objects in Li Gonglin's collection were likely to be what the classics referred to as a tiger *yi* and an elephant *zun*, even though they looked entirely unlike the pictures in the *Illustrations of the Three Ritual Classics*.[16] Knowledge of this sort was only of scholarly interest to men like Li Gonglin, who were not about to cast such vessels themselves, but it was of practical importance to court officials who had to supply vessels for use in court rituals.

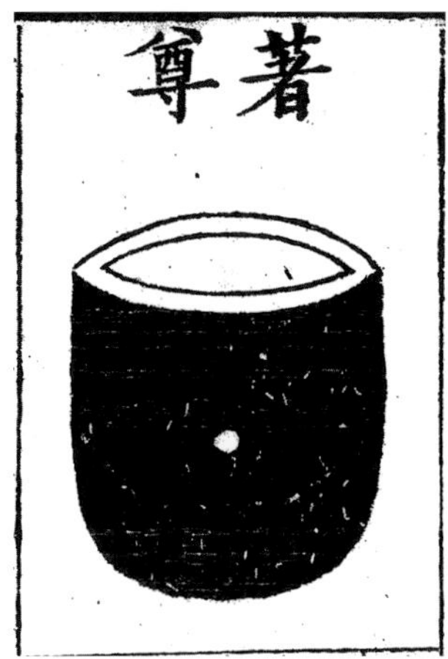

Fig. 6.6
"Settled beaker" in *Illustrations of the Three Ritual Classics*. SLT 14.4b.

Refashioning Music on the Basis of Ancient Instruments

In 1102, only two years after he took the throne, Huizong complained about the sorry state of court music. Musical instruments were broken, many of the musicians were temporary recruits unfamiliar with the music and not able to follow the notation, and government music officials argued endlessly about music theory to no effect. He called for a nationwide search for music masters whose knowledge of music came from personal transmission rather than books.[17]

Among those recommended to him was Wei Hanjin, a music expert over ninety who had helped with a music reform at court some fifty years earlier. In 1104 Wei proposed resetting the musical scale. In Chinese mythology it was the Yellow Emperor who had first set the length of the pitch pipes, and from them the tone of the tuning bell (*huang zhong*, literally "yellow bell"). By Han times, it was commonly thought that the true tone of the tuning bell had been lost, and scholars disagreed on how to recover it.[18] Wei attributed this to the burning of the books in the Qin dynasty, which cut off knowledge of the true ancient method of calculating the length of the pitch pipes. He proposed reviving the method of the great sage king Yu, who, he said, had used the length of the different fingers of the hand to set the length of the pitch pipes. Wei asked for the measurements of Huizong's middle, fourth, and fifth fingers so that he could revive this method. Once the new pitches were set, he would "first cast the Nine Cauldrons, and then the imperial big bells, the four clear-tone bells, and the twenty-four solar-term bells." On that basis, the string and wind instruments would be retuned "to make new music for this generation."[19]

Wei's theory involved a conflation of the implements most sacred to both sacrificial rites and music, that is, cauldrons and bells. Ancient texts had described in awed language the significance of the nine cauldrons that had been associated with the true ruler ever since they were fashioned by Yu, the founder of the Xia dynasty, using metal from each of the nine provinces and decorated with images of the creatures of all the regions. Bells, similarly, are presented in classical texts as the most crucial of the ruler's musical instruments. Of the lord's bells, the tuning bell was of particular importance because it set an absolute pitch that other instruments, such as stringed instruments and flutes, had to harmonize with.[20] Wei's innovation was to argue that a single object could serve as both the tuning bell and the largest of a set of nine cauldrons.

Before the first bell was cast, however, an auspicious discovery was made that greatly facilitated the design of the new bells. A local official in Yingtian prefecture recognized the significance of the discovery of a set of six bells and forwarded them

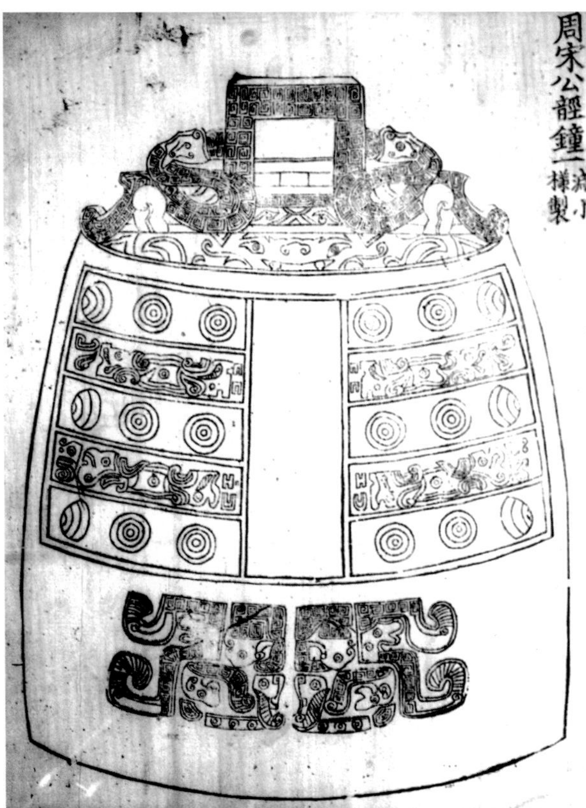

Fig. 6.7
The first of six Duke Cheng of Song bells. This, the largest of the bells, was 1 foot 3.6 inches tall and weighed 33 pounds. The smallest bell in the series was 1 foot 3 inches tall and weighed 16.5 pounds. BGT 1528 ed. 22.27a.

to the court.[21] From the drawings of them later included in *Antiquities Illustrated* (fig. 6.7), they belonged to the class of bells today called *bo*, marked by flat bottoms and elaborate hooks at the top. These particular bells, which probably dated from the fifth or sixth century BCE,[22] had opposing dragons on top as hooks and bosses with spiral designs.

These bells had special meaning for the Song dynasty. First, each bell had an inscription linking it to Duke Cheng of the state of Song.[23] And second, they were found in Yingtian prefecture, which meant "responding to Heaven" prefecture. In Tang times this prefecture had been called Song prefecture (after the ancient state in the same place). Because it was where the founder of the Song dynasty started his rise (that is, responded to Heaven's intentions for him), it was given the new name Yingtian.[24] In 1105 Huizong described the creation of the new music as resulting from the combination of Wei Hanjin's ideas on how to set the pitches and "obtaining the Ying and Jing instruments from the land where the Mandate was received." Another time he expressed the same idea but added more explicitly that the excavated bells made possible the discovery of the proportions used in their design.[25]

Both Huang Bosi and Dong You were asked to analyze these bells. Huang Bosi began in a straightforward way by describing when and where the bells had been found and their connection to Huizong's music reforms:

> To the right are the six Jing bells. Their inscriptions read: "Jing bell of Duke Cheng of Song."[26] In 1104 (a *jiashen* year), they were found at Honoring Blessings Cloister at the Southern Capital. Subsequently they were sent to the palace. From my research, the place where the Song bells were found was in the territory of [the ancient state of] Song. The imperial edict with the line "Obtaining the Ying and Jing instruments from the land where the Mandate was received" was referring to these bells.[27] At that time the emperor was creating the Music of Great Brilliance and used them as models.

Huang Bosi went on to explain how these bells gave one access to music not just of Zhou times but all the way back to a grandson of the Yellow Emperor, called here Lord Zhuan.

> Let me note that the *Illustrations and Proofs of Music Harmonization* says that Lord Zhuan's music was called the Six Stalks (*jing* 莖).[28] Song Jun's commentary glosses this as "Able to establish the root and the stalk for the Way of the Five Phases."[29] (䪫 was the ancient text form for 莖.) The transmission of the system of the Six Stalks began very far back, from the time of Lord Zhuan through Lord Ku, Yao and Shun, the Xia and Shang dynasties, to the Zhou dynasty. But the Zhou dynasty completed the music of the six eras. The music of Cloud Gate, Xian Pond, Shao, Xia, Waterfall, and Martial all survived; only the Five Ying and the Six Jing have disappeared.[30] The [ruling house of the state of] Song was descended from the Shang [ruling house]. Therefore the Duke of Song was able to pass [the music of Shang] down.[31]

In this passage Huang Bosi explained the word *jing* by connecting it to another word pronounced *jing* that an early text says was the music of Lord Zhuan. He hypothesized that the music had passed from Lord Zhuan in a direct line to the Shang Dynasty, even though it was not as famous as other music associated with the Shang. Because the ducal house of Song was descended from the royal house of Shang, it was able to preserve elements of this very ancient music. Next Huang tried to determine the identity of the Duke Cheng named in the inscription:

> Cheng was the personal name of Duke Ping. Song was founded by Weizi and after twenty-six generations reached Duke Ping. His name first appears in the tenth year of Duke Zhao of Lu [that is, 531 BCE].[323] The *Spring and Autumn Annals* says "Duke Cheng of Song," which matches the inscription on these bells. He took the throne in

> the tenth year of King Jian of Zhou, the year *yiyou* [that is, 576 BCE], which is 1680 years before [the current year of] 1104.

Huang then returned to the significance of the bells in his own day, remarking that the bells "appeared in the land where the Mandate was received just when our sagely ruler, to the glory of his heroic forebears, was honoring wise elders and enthusiastically formulating rituals and music." The discovery of the bells, he concluded, "makes visible the sage ruler's flourishing virtue and abundant merits, which are as great as that of the Five Lords. There has been nothing to equal it since the Xia and Shang dynasties."[33]

Dong You also wrote on these bells. Besides tracing the origins of the music to the Shang dynasty and earlier, he considered issues more strictly related to the music-making function of the bells. He gave six dimensions for each bell (height, length and width of top, length of sides, and length and width of bottom opening). He also gave both the name of each bell's absolute pitch and the name of its note (assuming that the tuning bell, the largest and lowest, was the note *gong*), proving that officials at the Palace Library had tried playing them. Dong You remarked that even though there were quite a few bells that had survived from the Zhou period, officials at court had not been able to cast bells that worked properly as musical instruments. Some did not hang properly on their frames, some did not give their full sound, and so on. It was only after Huizong ordered that the Jing bells be used as the model that the responsible officials were able to cast bells that could be played in tune.[34]

In 1105/7, the casting of the Nine Cauldrons was complete. According to Cai Tao, when the first one was cast in the southern suburbs, the sky was lit up with colored light visible from the palace. When ready, the cauldrons were installed in a newly built temple called the Nine Completions. A new set of sacrifices to the Yellow Emperor was performed there, using seasonal, color, and directional symbolism worked out by Wei Hanjin. Once the cauldrons were installed, an auspicious sign was observed: several thousand cranes flew above the temple. The next day Huizong visited, and more than a thousand cranes returned, flying in front of the multicolored clouds, in apparent response to the music (see plate 21).[35]

The cauldron used as the tuning bell was said to be nine feet tall and decorated with images of nine dragons.[36] Even if this bell looked like a cauldron and could stand with the other cauldrons in its temple, surviving bells were clearly modeled on the newly discovered Duke Cheng of Song bells. Recently several scholars have put together information on twenty-six extant bells cast as part of the Music of Great Brilliance.[37] The shape and decoration of these bells closely resembles that of the bells of Duke Cheng (compare plate 22 and fig. 6.7). Typically these bells have

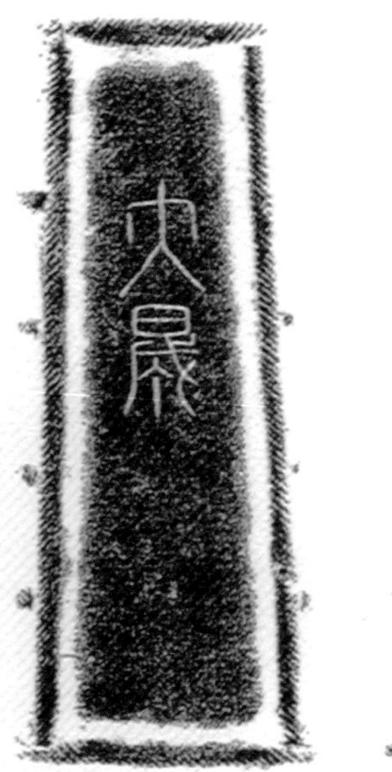

Fig. 6.8
Rubbing of the inscriptions on both sides of a Dasheng bell. Palace Museum, Beijing. The rubbing on the left reads "Dasheng," the one on the right reads "Dalü qing," indicating both the pitch and the series it belonged to.

the phrase "Great Brilliance" inscribed on one side and the name of the pitch on the other (see fig. 6.8).[38] They belong to three types of chimes, one with just the name of one of the twelve pitches, one with the name of one of the twelve pitches with "middle sound" added to it, and one with the name of one of the four "clear tones." These three series correspond to the bells Wei Hanjin had asked to have cast. Li Youping was able to carefully measure and record the pitches of eighteen of the extant bells held in China. He found that each bell has a single pitch, which corresponds well to the pitch inscribed on it. He infers that the bells were originally made in three sizes, the smallest varying from 18 to 23 centimeters in height; the middle range ones (the majority of those surviving), from 22 to 28 centimeters; and the largest, from 54 to 69 centimeters.[39] The workmanship of these bells is of a high order (see fig. 6.9). Like the ancient bells, their openings are not round, but rather pointed ovals (see fig. 6.10). Interestingly, Huizong's bells were so convincing as replicas of Zhou bells that in the eighteenth century the Qianlong emperor's curators thought that they were Zhou bells, not recognizing them as more recent imitations.[40]

In 1105/8, after the full set of bells had been cast and new music written, Huizong called on the court orchestra to demonstrate the difference between the old and new music. First, three pieces of the old music were played. Huizong interrupted the performance, declaring that it sounded like someone weeping. When the new music was then played, Huizong approved. The next month the new music formally premiered at a court banquet. As the officials offered toasts to the emperor, the *Song*

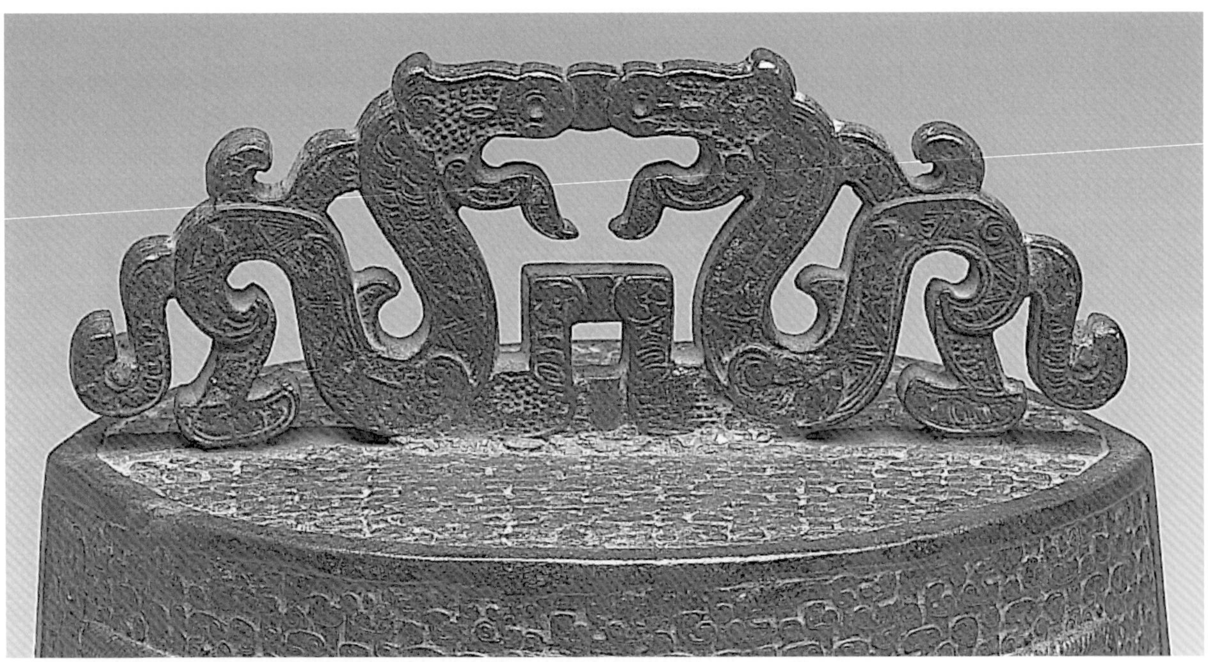

Fig. 6.9
Decoration on Dasheng bell (detail of plate 22).

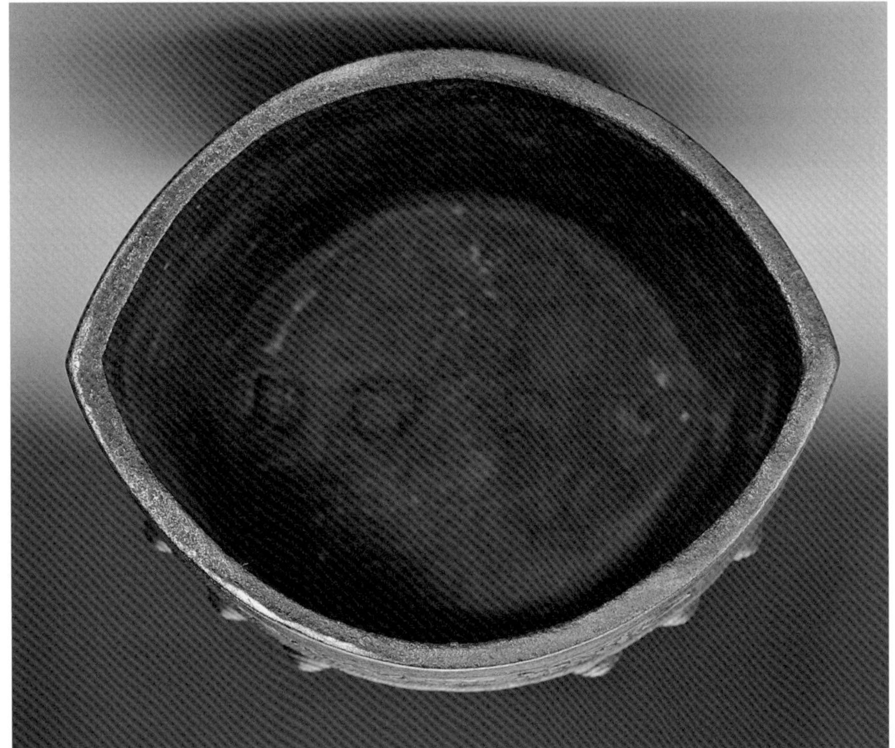

Fig. 6.10
Bottom opening of a Dasheng bell, showing its "pointed oval" shape. National Palace Museum, Taiwan, Republic of China. This particular bell (shown in plate 22) is labeled with the pitch *ruibin*.

History reports, cranes flew in from the northeast, circled over the imperial terrace where the music was being performed, and sang their approval before flying away.[41] Delighted by this auspicious omen, Huizong issued an edict explaining the reasons and goals for launching this new music. It was an opportune time to institute new music, he proclaimed, because the world had been at peace for a hundred years and there had been fortuitous discoveries:

> Recently, we found a hermit [i.e. Wei Hanjin] from the lowly ranks of foot soldiers. I also acquired instruments of the [Shang Dynasty's] Ying and Jing music from the land where the Mandate was received. As now is an opportune time, my body has been used to set the measurements. We cast the cauldrons to establish a tuning and temperament standard, on the basis of which other musical instruments were designed. . . .
>
> In the past, Yao had the Dazhang music, Shun had the Dashao music, and the kings of the Three Dynasties had musics with different names. Now, emulating their examples of millennia past, I am establishing the music of our generation, which I name Music of Great Brilliance. I will have it performed at the altars and shrines to honor the deities and spirits, to harmonize the nations, and to share it with all under Heaven. Won't this be excellent? The old music is no longer to be used.[42]

According to Li Youping, the music reform connected to the discovery of the Duke Cheng bells and the casting of the Dasheng bells had a long-lasting influence on Chinese music. Unlike the scales set in the music reforms of the eleventh century, which proved difficult for musicians to use or discordant to the ear, the scale set in this reform proved harmonious.[43]

To administer this new court music and its performers, Huizong created the Bureau of the Music of Great Brilliance. This bureau supervised the making of new instruments and the retuning of old ones (such as string instruments). It issued notated scores and illustrative diagrams to help musicians cope with the changes. Musicians in the employ of the government were ordered to follow these instructions closely and were threatened with punishment if they dared to alter the tuning or the designs of the new instruments.[44]

When the *Antiquities Illustrated* was compiled in the mid-1120s, the editors introduced the three chapters on bells with an essay that stressed the crucial role of bells in ancient music, the role of the tuning bell among bells, and the significance of the court collection of bells to the reform of music at Huizong's court. It concluded, "Now our collection of ancient bells dates from the Shang and the Zhou dynasties to the Qin and the Han dynasties, meaning that the ancient ways of making music still survive. We thus have been able to explore the tones through the extant bells, and to perform music using these tones. It is truly excellent that the once-lost musics of [the founders of the Shang and Zhou dynasties] Tang and Wu are sounding again in our day!"[45]

The impression one gets from reading the chapters on music in the *Song History*, however, is rather different. There it would seem that Wei Hanjin's theorizing was considered to be by far the most important stimulus to the music reforms. If the new music in fact owed much more to the discovery of ancient instruments, why would the *Song History* make much more of Wei Hanjin's numerological theories than of the discoveries? One reason is simply bureaucratic: Memorials from officials versed in music theory discussed Wei's theories at length, giving later historians plenty of documents to summarize or quote. The actual casting was probably entrusted to master craftsmen who did not write documents. Instead, they tested the discovered bells to see what pitches they sounded, made careful measurements of them to figure out the system of proportions, then designed models for other bells needed to complete the pitch sequence.

A second reason for historians to stress numerology over ancient artifacts is that a redesign of court music on the basis of abstruse theories fit better with their view of the downfall of Huizong's government. Careful study of actual artifacts from the past was considered fully legitimate among leading intellectuals of the eleventh century, such as Ouyang Xiu and Sima Guang. It would be hard to fault Huizong for casting new bells on the basis of true ancient bells, or for retuning string and woodwind instruments to harmonize with these bells. Both steps would qualify as sincere efforts to recover antiquity. But if Huizong's new music was based on what seemed to some to be mumbo jumbo, any harmony achieved must have been illusory. If properly harmonized music could bring about harmony in society, it followed that improperly harmonized music would endanger society and might well have been a factor in the fall of Kaifeng to the Jurchens.

Huizong recognized the potential of the new bells to help his court establish its credentials as a true seeker of the ancient way, committed to restoring antiquity in both music and rites. He even saw their potential in international relations. In 1116 Huizong had a full set of the Dasheng bells sent to Korea as part of a larger gift of 428 musical instruments.[46] Reportedly, they still survive at the Confucian temple in Seoul.[47]

Casting Ritual Vessels on the Basis of Ancient Ones

Perhaps because copying the newly discovered bells proved to be a musical success, soon after they were cast the court began thinking about the possibilities of making comparable use of ancient sacrificial vessels. In 1107 a new Agency for Deliberating on Ritual was established.[48] In 1108/11, one of the officials serving in it, Xue Ang (who appeared as an educational official in chapter 2), submitted a memorial stating that ancient vessels could be used as a source for returning ritual to its ancient forms:

> The ritual vessels used by government agencies, such as beakers, goblets, grain pans, and the like, differ from the ancient vessels in scholar-officials' collections, which mostly came from ancient sites or tombs. After one to two thousand years, styles have inevitably changed; it is not that [the ones in collections] are forgeries. It is said that when the ritual has been lost, one should search for it in remote places.[49] Since the court now wishes to correct the ritual texts, it should widely seek ancient vessels as evidence. I request that counties and prefectures be ordered to inquire about scholar-officials or commoners who have ancient vessels, then send someone to their homes to make drawings of them to be sent to the Agency for Deliberating on Ritual.[50]

This request was approved, and soon the palace was receiving not merely pictures of vessels in private hands but also many vessels themselves. The Agency for Deliberating on Ritual, though, spent most of its energies preparing revised liturgies for court rituals, in time producing first a 231-chapter ritual compendium for the Daguan period (1107–1110), then a 220-chapter one for the Zhenghe period (1111–1117); the latter survives. Because of the weight given to *The Rites of Zhou,* the *New Rituals for the Five Categories of Rites of the Zhenghe Period* includes a list of the vessels needed for sacrifices, based on that classic. For instance, the *New Rituals* specifies that at higher-ranked sacrifices wine be offered in five large beakers and five mountain beakers, but that at lower-ranked ceremonies the wine should be poured into five, four, or three offering beakers and elephant beakers.[51]

Once the *New Rituals* was issued, the Agency for Deliberating on Ritual was abolished and a new agency created, the Agency for Instituting Rituals. This new agency took on the task of reconciling the ancient vessels and court rites. Two experts on ancient vessels, Zhai Ruwen and Liu Bing, were appointed to the new agency. Both Zhai and Liu received their *jinshi* in 1100, Huizong's first year on the throne. A learned scholar with interests in books, paintings, calligraphy, antiquities, and medicine, Zhai had a rich collection of Six Dynasty and Tang paintings and a thousand rubbings.[52] Liu Bing was an expert on music and had been involved in the Music of Great Brilliance project. His *Song History* biography reports that he was summoned to examine ancient vessels whenever they arrived at Huizong's court and that he helped in the production of new vessels modeled on them. Scholars working in the Palace Library were also drawn into this project, including Huang Bosi and Dong You.[53]

Ancient vessels steadily arrived at the palace, including one that scholars identified as a "yellow eye *zun*."[54] By 1113/7 Huizong announced that more than 500 ancient vessels had been found, that pictures had been drawn of them, and that studies had been made of their design and imagery. "None of the vessels used today in the sacrifices to Heaven and Earth and in the ancestral rites is anything like the ancient vessels. We are far removed from the past, so the rites have lost connection to antiquity. . . . Let the responsible officials make new ones on the model [of the ancient ones]." Three months later, in 1113/10, Huizong wrote out an edict that Liu Bing had drafted which proclaimed that the design of ancient vessels was integral to the way rituals reached the spirits and Heaven and Earth. Now that the court had been able to fashion vessels on the basis of authentic ancient ones, they claimed, "We have no reason to be ashamed before the ancients." Four days later (1113/10/18), Huizong visited Promoting Governance Hall to view the new ritual implements made by the Workshop for Fabricating Ritual Implements (*zhizao liqi suo*), along with the ancient vessels on which they were based. On this occasion he invited his officials to view them as well.[55] As discussed in chapter 4, Cai Tao reported that after leaving his officials to inspect the vessels on their own, Huizong lingered just outside the door to listen to their conversations.[56]

In 1113 Huizong issued a three-chapter book illustrating the new vessels made for the sacrifices to Heaven and Earth, the Supreme Shrine, and the Hall of Enlightenment. The next year he issued a one-chapter book depicting the twenty-eight vessels used at the winter sacrifice to Earth in 1114. Neither of these books has survived. In accounts Huizong wrote for the winter sacrifices in 1113 and the summer sacrifices in 1114, he mentioned the use of the new vessels based on research into ancient bronzes. In 1115 an official at the Palace Library proposed that the pictures from the *Illustrations of the Three Ritual Classics* that had been painted on the walls of the Directorate of Education be destroyed and replaced by ones that accorded with the newly made vessels.[57]

Sacrificial vessels continued to be made over the next several years, probably reaching into the hundreds.[58] In 1115 Zhai Ruwen wrote sixteen inscriptions for new vessels in a literary style imitating inscriptions on ancient vessels. For instance, the inscription for a "mountain tall jar" (*shan lei*) read, "The emperor has investigated antiquity to make vessels for the Song, using metal supplied by the nine governors. He first uses this mountain tall jar to make a fine offering. His descendants should treasure it forever." In 1116, responding to a query from the Workshop for Fabricating Ritual Implements, the Agency for Instituting Rituals proposed increasing the numbers of vessels used at the Supreme Shrine to correspond to the numbers specified in *The Rites of Zhou*.[59]

Vessels were also made for use outside the court. In 1116 Zhai Ruwen proposed that high officials be granted sacrificial vessels on the model of royal grants to feudal lords in Zhou times. He argued that living with such symbolically meaningful objects would allow people to gain an understanding of the mysteries of ritual in the course of their daily activities. Zhai's request was approved, and eight officials, including Cai Jing and Tong Guan, were given vessels in numbers varying by rank. For instance, they would each get one goblet, two cauldrons, two or four grain pans, and eight to twelve raised dishes.[60]

Another recipient of newly cast vessels was the Korean royal court. In 1117 twenty-four sacrificial vessels were sent as a diplomatic gift. The inscriptions on them referred to Korea's position on the eastern frontier and said the vessels should be used for ancestral rites and passed down to later generations.[61]

The court did not supply sacrificial vessels for use by local officials, but did encourage them to undertake the task themselves. In 1119 an official reported that the vessels that local officials used during sacrifices to Confucius differed markedly from the new ones introduced at court. Huizong approved his request to have colored pictures of the new vessels sent to all circuits and prefectures to enable the officials there to make more authentic-looking vessels. However, rather than fashion the vessels from expensive bronze, the localities were to make them of lacquered wood.[62]

Only two bronze vessels made by Huizong's court seem to have survived. One, now in the Palace Museum, Beijing, is a beaker in a standard ancient style, inscribed "mountain *zun*," showing that it was intended to be used in the rites where *The Rites of Zhou* specified that the mountain *zun* be used (see figs. 6.11 and 6.12). Its inscription, dated 1121, states that it was made by the emperor on the basis of studying antiquity. The other surviving vessel is a cauldron that was conferred on Tong Guan (see figs. 6.13 and 6.14). The inscription, dated 1116, says that it was conferred on Tong Guan, then in charge of the Bureau of Military Affairs, to use in sacrificing to his ancestors. Its main decoration is a large animal mask (*taotie*) above each of the three legs, and in general style it is closest to late Shang or early Zhou cauldrons. However, it does not seem to be copied from a particular cauldron recorded in *Antiquities Illustrated* (though it could have been copied from one of the thousands not recorded in that book). The vessels made at Huizong's court were so convincing that until the mid-nineteenth century they were regularly taken as Shang or Zhou vessels.[63]

Huizong's initiatives to reform music and ritual to make them accord with antiquity correspond to many of his initiatives to expand the government school system, discussed in chapter 2. Both were presented in the spirit of "recovering antiquity," in particular the idealized antiquity of *The Rites of Zhou*. Making impe-

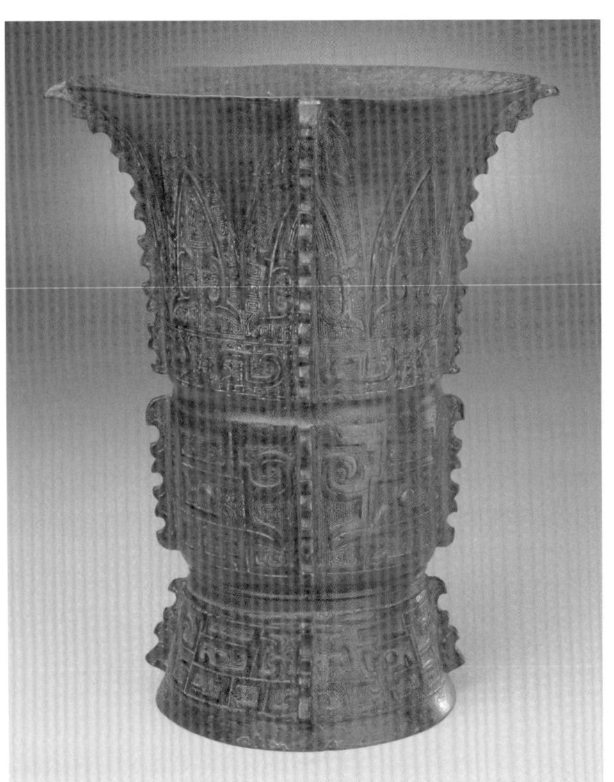

Fig. 6.11
Mountain beaker made at Huizong's court, dated 1121. 29 × 17.4 cm (at its mouth), weight 5.4 kg. Palace Museum, Beijing.

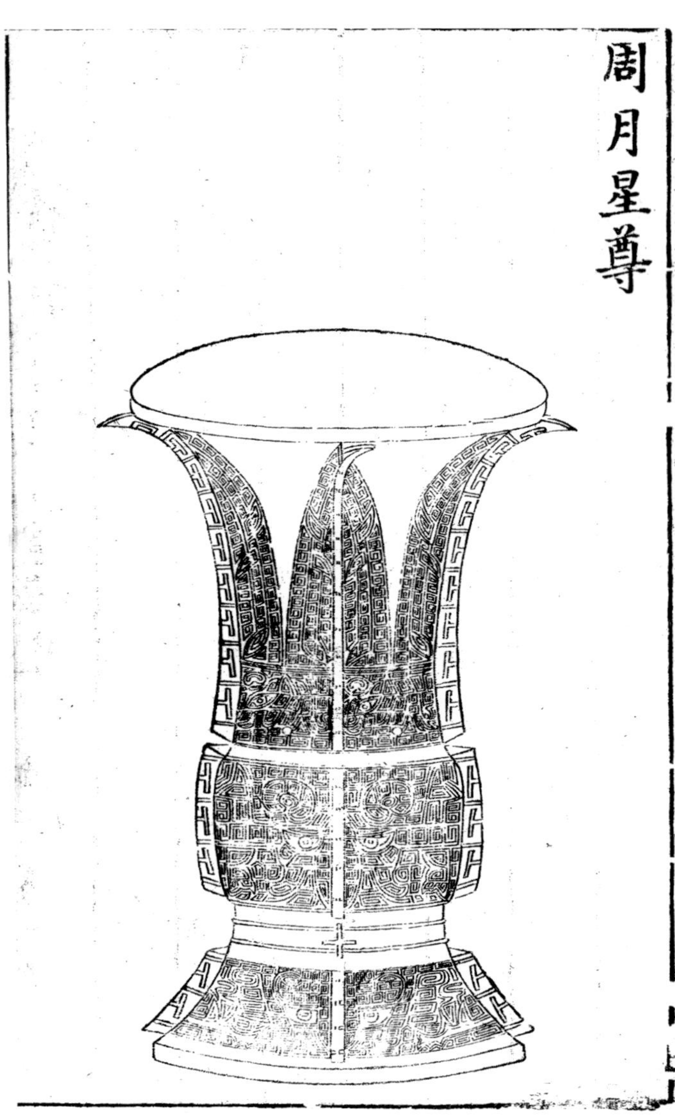

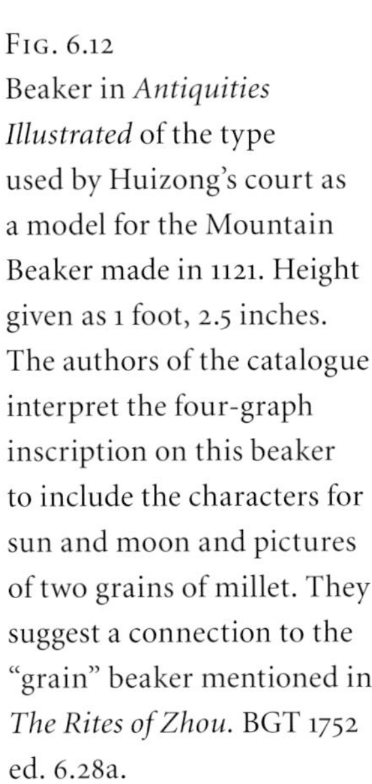

Fig. 6.12
Beaker in *Antiquities Illustrated* of the type used by Huizong's court as a model for the Mountain Beaker made in 1121. Height given as 1 foot, 2.5 inches. The authors of the catalogue interpret the four-graph inscription on this beaker to include the characters for sun and moon and pictures of two grains of millet. They suggest a connection to the "grain" beaker mentioned in *The Rites of Zhou*. BGT 1752 ed. 6.28a.

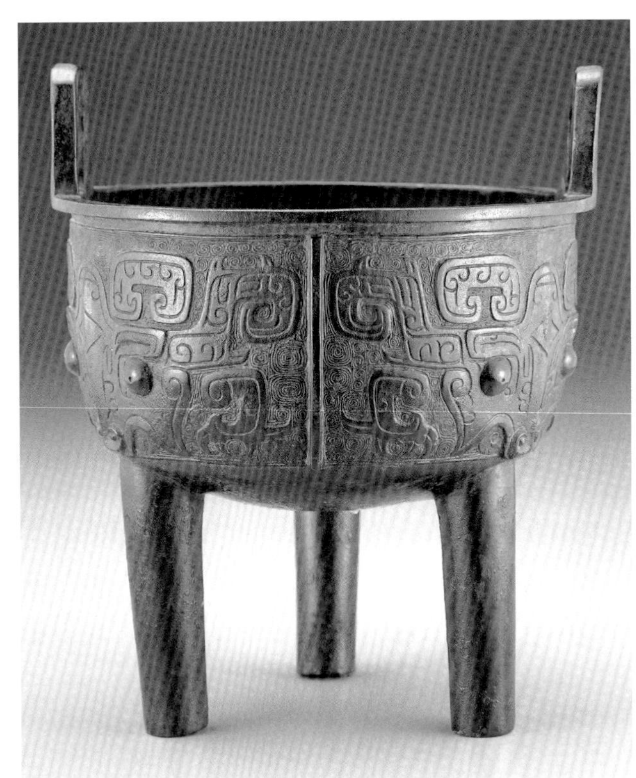

Fig. 6.13
Cauldron given to Tong Guan in 1116. Height 23.2 cm, 18.9 cm in diameter, weight 2.4 kg. National Palace Museum, Taiwan, Republic of China.

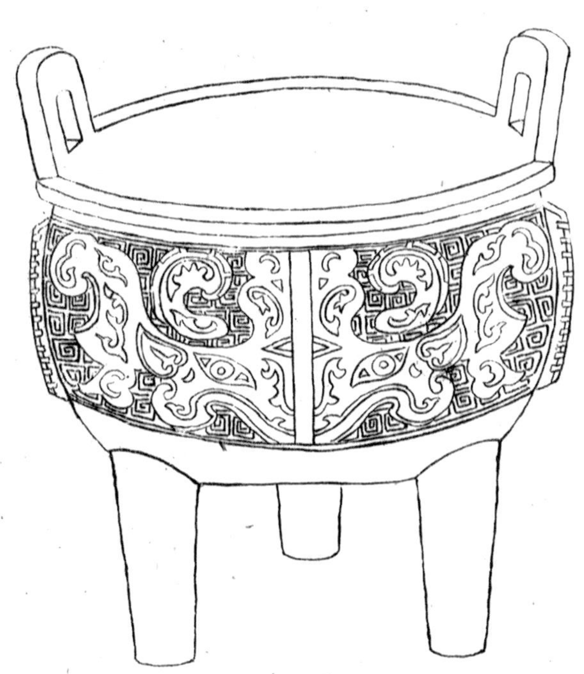

Fig. 6.14
Cauldron in *Antiquities Illustrated* of the type that served as a model for the cauldron given to Tong Guan. Height given as 5.7 in., weight as 3 pounds, 9 ounces. From GJTSJC Kaogong 199.25a, corresponding to BGT 1.42a.

rial rituals and ritual music more authentically ancient had been advocated by Confucian scholars since early times, so these gestures, like the expansion of the school system, could be presented as efforts on the part of the court to support Confucian learning and Confucian scholars. Zhai Ruwen explicitly linked the reforms of the school system and the casting of new bells and sacrificial vessels in an examination question that he wrote. Both the educational and ritual institutions had been in decline for centuries, he asserted, until the current ruler had revived the ancient school system and cast new bells and sacrificial vessels, with the result that, "In terms of the completion of music and rituals, there has never been an age more successful than our own."[64]

Compiling the Catalogue as a Scholarly Project

Many scholars have noted the degree to which Huizong's antiquities catalogue is indebted to the advances in deciphering ancient inscriptions and analyzing vessels associated with such scholars as Liu Chang, Ouyang Xiu, Li Gonglin, and Lü Dalin. Much less notice has been taken of how, under Huizong, a massive imperial push to gather, study, and document antiquities served to advance knowledge further.[65] Assembling thousands of ancient vessels gave scholars in government employ—men like Dong You, Huang Bosi, Zhai Ruwen, and Liu Bing—the unprecedented ability to compare vessels. Never before had anyone had the opportunities these men had. The size of Huizong's collections allowed them to make major advances in typology—in deciding which vessels belonged to which distinct types and matching them to ancient texts. Having hundreds or thousands of pieces also allowed them to begin the complex and difficult process of putting vessels in chronological sequence, a task not attempted in *Investigations of Antiquity Illustrated.* The possibility of drawing on the staff of the Palace Library made it possible for the research presented in Huizong's catalogue to be more thorough than that in Lü's catalogue—for instance, by giving more dimensions for each piece and providing fuller discussion of possible interpretations of the piece in relation to ancient texts. On the other hand, Huizong's catalogue dropped one of the most valuable features of Lü's catalogue—the listing of the places where antiquities had been found.

A sample entry can serve to illustrate the style of the catalogue. This entry is for a vessel titled "Shang period covered wine jar [inscribed] Qu Grandfather Ding" (see fig. 6.15).

> With its cover, this vessel is 6.4 inches tall, 4.4 inches deep. At the mouth it is 3.1 inches across, 2.3 inches wide. At the widest point it is 4.8 inches across, 3.5 inches wide. It

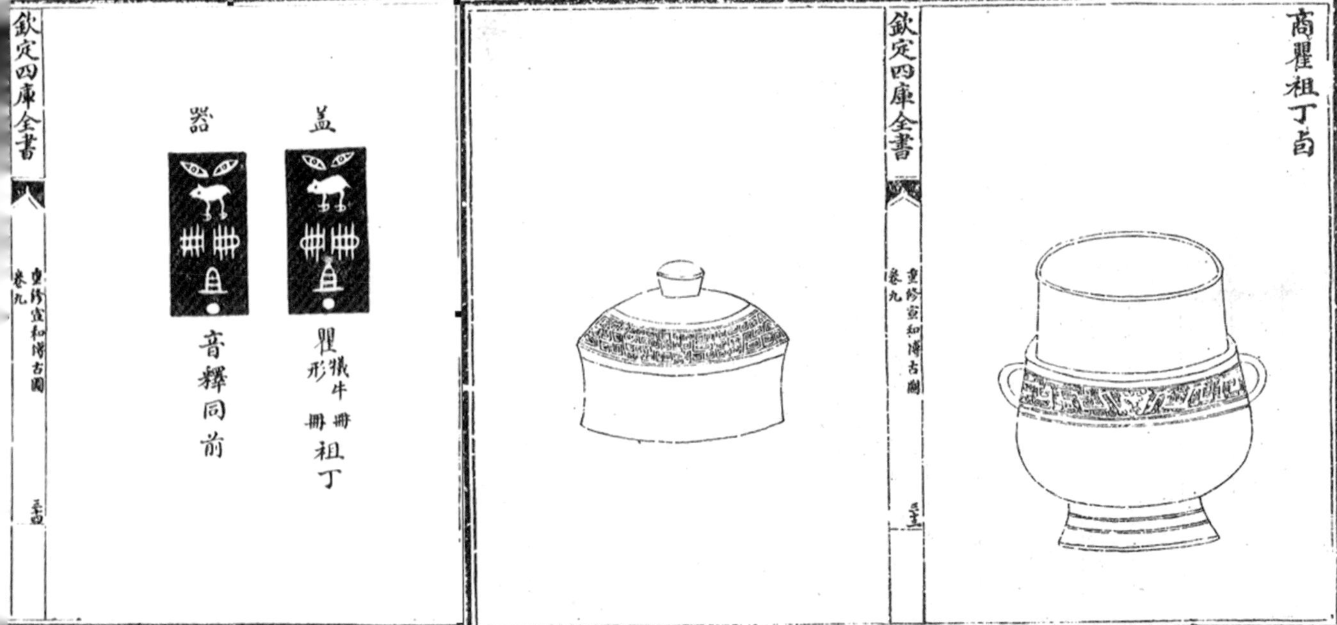

Fig. 6.15
Qu Grandfather Ding wine jar and its cover and the rubbing of the inscription on it. Its height is given as 6.4 inches, including the cover. The two inscriptions are identical. Under the one on the right is given the modern reading, with one graph explained as a picture of a sacrificial ox, rather than a word. BGT 9.33a–34a.

holds 1.5 pints. The two parts together weigh two pounds, ten ounces. There are two loops for handles. The cover and the vessel have an inscription of twelve characters total.

With regard to the character "Qu" 瞿, it is not seen in the classics, but there is a Shang period "Qu fu" cauldron which also has a "Qu" made up of two "eyes" 目 next to each other, just like this one.[66] They must have been made in the same period. As for "ancestor Ding" [mentioned in the inscription], he is the son of the fourteenth Shang ruler, Ancestor Xin. In the middle [of the inscription] is the shape of a sacrificial animal, below which are two *ce* 冊 [characters meaning records], all three of which take their shape from the object, as drawing and writing had not yet diverged. *The Offices of Zhou*, under "managing the beaker vessels," says to decorate the sacrificial animal beaker with a sacrificial ox,[67] which probably preserves some of the meaning of the Shang practice. The pictures of the two sets of strips means "appoint him with a written charge," which is like King Kang giving an order to Duke Bi and saying "appoint Bi." Meaning is conveyed in this way in vessels that honor images.[68]

Many inferences about how *Antiquities Illustrated* was compiled can be made simply by reading entries like this one. There must have been files or dossiers assembled on each of the items finally included in the catalogue, dossiers that included several dimensions (at a minimum, height, diameter, volume, and weight, but often additional dimensions, such as height and width of handles, depth of a container on legs, diameter at both opening and widest place, and so on). Rubbings were made of inscriptions and these were transcribed into modern characters. In cases where scholars disagreed on readings, a single, best reading was offered, consistently converted to modern characters (that is, where the ancient graph had omitted radicals, they were supplied, which was an act of interpretation). After coming up with a reading, researchers searched ancient literature for anything that might help illuminate the inscription or identify the people mentioned in it. Interest in the types of vessels mentioned in the classics, especially *The Rites of Zhou,* was pervasive. In addition, before they were finished, the authors of the catalogue had to come up with a unique name for each item. The first part of the name was the date by dynasty (that is, in most cases, Shang, Zhou, or Han). For inscribed objects, the name normally made use of a distinctive phrase from the inscription. In the case of uninscribed objects, it is clear that the curatorial staff tried to sort them into meaningful sub-groups, generally on the basis of variations in shape or decorative scheme.

Li Gang's epitaph for Huang Bosi reported that before he died in 1118 he had prepared 426 discussions of ancient objects in the palace collections which were eventually incorporated into *Antiquities Illustrated.*[69] Many of the items in Dong You's *Guangchuan shuba* could also have been notes he made on objects in the Palace Library that the final editors of *Antiquities Illustrated* drew on. Presumably other officials, including Zhai Ruwen and Liu Bing, also helped prepare material for the catalogue entries.

CLASSIFYING OBJECTS AND ASSIGNING THEM NAMES

Huizong's curators assigned names to every object, not uncommonly giving them names different from the ones used in earlier writings.[70] The normal practice used to assign names to objects was to look for similarities and differences among vessels so that their names would reflect some distinctive characteristic. For instance, three cauldrons of Zhou date are grouped together because their legs were similar in size and design, leading to the three being labeled "Zhou animal leg cauldron 1, 2, and 3." In another case five bottles were grouped together because of the similarity in the shape of their tube-shaped handles even though the author of the entry recognized differences in the patterns of their decoration (see fig. 6.16).[71]

Because of the many comparisons they made, the scholars working on the catalogue decided to classify objects by their shape and function, not the term used in

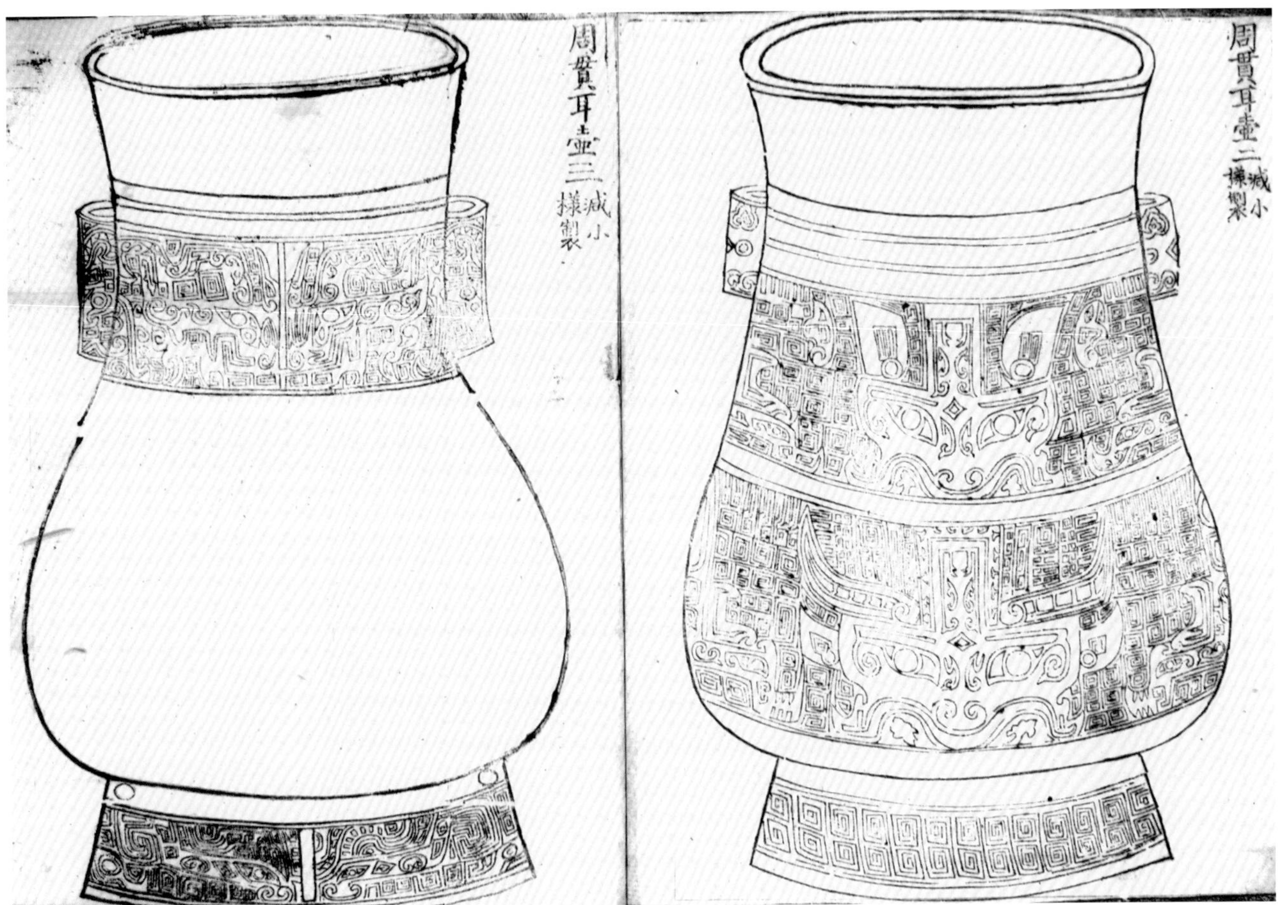

FIG. 6.16
Two bottles grouped together because of the shape of their handles. Height is given as 1 foot 1 inch for the one on the right, and 1 foot 5 inches for the one on the left. BGT 1528 ed. 12.18b–19a.

the inscription. Thus, in contrast to *Investigations of Antiquities Illustrated,* which called everything an *yi* (libation cup) that called itself an *yi* in its inscription, no matter what it looked like, Huizong's editors recognized that *yi* could be a generic term for vessel and classified vessels that looked like cauldrons as cauldrons, no matter what was inscribed on them. In some cases, objects classed as *yi* in the earlier book were reclassified by their shape in *Antiquities Illustrated.*[72] As the authors noted, "Since the word *yi* basically means 'constancy,' all vessels with meanings lodged in them can be called *yi*. For instance, the characters *zun-yi* [beaker-vessel] were inscribed on the Bobao covered wine jars [*you*] of the Zhou dynasty, and 'precious *zun-yi* of father Yi' was inscribed on the Shao duke beaker also of the Zhou dynasty."[73]

Classifying objects and assigning them names thus forced the editors to compare and group vessels, practices that then influenced how they dated them.

DATING

In much the same way that the editors chose a single reading for each character in an inscription, they explicitly labeled every item by dynasty, even when the scholars working on them were not entirely sure. In the case of dating, however, the entries often provide rationales for the choices made or admit to a degree of uncertainty.[74]

Several criteria were used to judge the date of objects. Vessels mentioned in *The Rites of Zhou* were generally assumed to be Zhou in date. The length of inscriptions was taken into consideration. In one entry the author distinguished Shang inscriptions, which are often only a few characters long, or even one character, from Zhou ones, which could go on at length. The author of an entry on a goblet wrote, "The inscriptions on vessels of the Three Dynasties vary, but in general the simpler, the older, the more detailed, the more recent. This is a way to distinguish Xia, Shang, and Zhou dates." Another principle frequently evoked was that plainer vessels were older than more ornate ones and that Shang vessels were plainer than Zhou ones. Vessels were compared to others that looked similar, with the assertion that they were probably of the same period.[75] Shape and ornamentation were regularly considered as well. Sometimes the decoration was described as typically Shang. Sometimes the author compromised on the date—in one case, for instance, saying that the calligraphy style seemed Shang but that it was more heavily decorated, making it likely early Zhou. In another case a vessel dated to the Zhou period that strongly resembled Shang vessels was explained by positing that the Zhou casters had tried to copy Shang vessels.[76]

Objects were generally assigned to the Han period when they could not be matched to anything earlier in date. For instance, a pair of bottles (*hu*) were described as much like Zhou bottles in shape, but the cord decoration on them did not correspond to anything found in Three Dynasties pieces, so they had to be Han pieces. In another case, three "flattened" bottles were assigned a Han date on the grounds that bottles mentioned in the classics were either round or square, and the idea of "flattened" bottles was probably an unfounded invention of Han scholars (see fig. 6.17).[77] In this last case, the editors were likely overly cautious, as Warring States vessels of this shape have been discovered in more recent times (see fig. 6.18).

CLARIFYING *THE RITES OF ZHOU*

A theme running through many of the antiquities catalogue's entries and introductory essays is the value of actual ancient vessels for interpreting obscure references to vessels in *The Rites of Zhou* (also called *The Offices of Zhou*). This is seen especially clearly in the introductory essay on libation cups (*yi*):

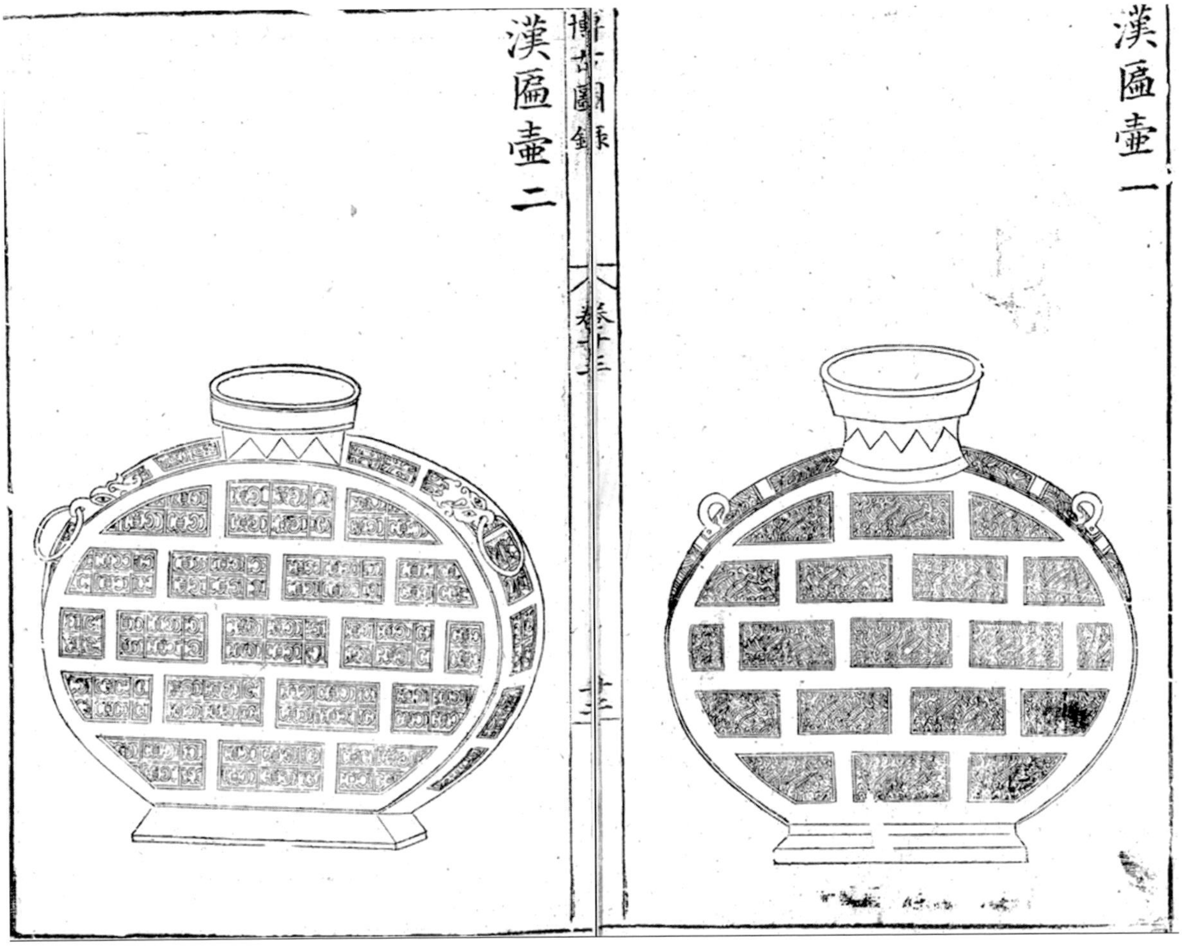

漢匾壺一

博古圖錄

漢匾壺二

Fig. 6.17
Two of three "flattened bottles" dated to the Han period because earlier examples were not known. The first one (on the right) is listed as 1 foot 2 inches in height, the second as 1 foot 5 inches. BGT 1752 ed. 13.12a–b.

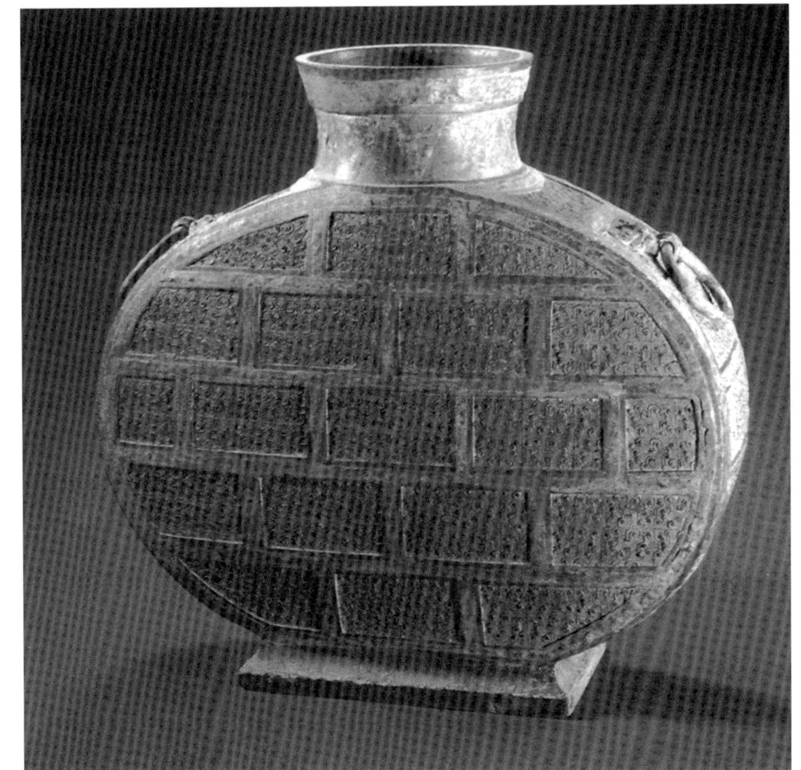

Fig. 6.18
A "flattened bottle" dated to the mid-to-late Warring States Period, excavated in 1975 in Henan. Height 34 cm. After Li Xueqin 1986:2:111.

The six categories of libation cups [*yi*] recorded in *The Offices of Zhou* are chicken cup, bird cup, crop cup, yellow cup, and those of the tiger and the monkey. The commentary says that those vessels were used to hold either sacred water or sacrificial wine. Chicken cups, crop cups, and tiger cups hold water, whereas bird cups, yellow cups, and monkey cups hold wine. All six kinds of libation cups are set with wine bowls. Both libation cups and wine bowls are sacrificial vessels, used in the drinking and pouring of wine at the seasonal sacrifices.

Those vessels are the vehicles of the rituals, the means by which the rituals are carried out. The functions of the rituals are revealed through the vessels. However, the vessels as material objects cannot last forever. As time passed and ancient vessels disappeared, scholars made far-fetched statements and disagreed with each other. False assumptions could not be corrected.

Now our dynasty has been accumulating virtue and promoting ritual and music for more than a century. As we gathered the traces of the former dynasties, hundreds of bronzes, including bells, cauldrons, beakers, and bottles, were found in the remote countryside and presented to the court from all directions.

We studied and discussed the meanings of those pieces thoroughly in our leisure time, learned a lot from the inscriptions on them, and as a result the forms and functions of libation cups and wine bowls could be identified in detail. We came to recognize the mistakes of our predecessors, who did not realize the relationship between libation cups and wine bowls, and how it is similar to the relationship between beakers and bottles, pitchers, and tall jars. They thought that wine bowls were saucer-like vessels on which libation cups were placed, carrying them like a boat [the common meaning of *zhou*, the word here translated as "wine bowl"].[78] This is not true. If we look at the shape of the extant wine bowls, such as the Dunzu wine bowl and the Chuihua wine bowl, which have roughly the same shape as libation cups, it is clear that wine bowls and libation cups are related vessels of similar shape. . . .[79]

When referring to vessels used in rites, however, the six types named in *The Rites of Zhou* are the only correct ones.[80]

In this passage, the editors demonstrate their conviction that the best way to deal with confusing passages in *The Rites of Zhou* is to examine actual ancient vessels. From their survey, they found no significant difference in size, shape, or function between *yi* and *zhou* vessels. Scholars who thought that the modern meaning of *zhou* as "boat" gave a hint of what a vessel called a *zhou* was like were sorely mistaken. In the end, however, even if the excavated vessels do not use the vocabulary of *The Rites of Zhou*, that vocabulary must be maintained.

Another way the editors contributed to the understanding of *The Rites of Zhou*

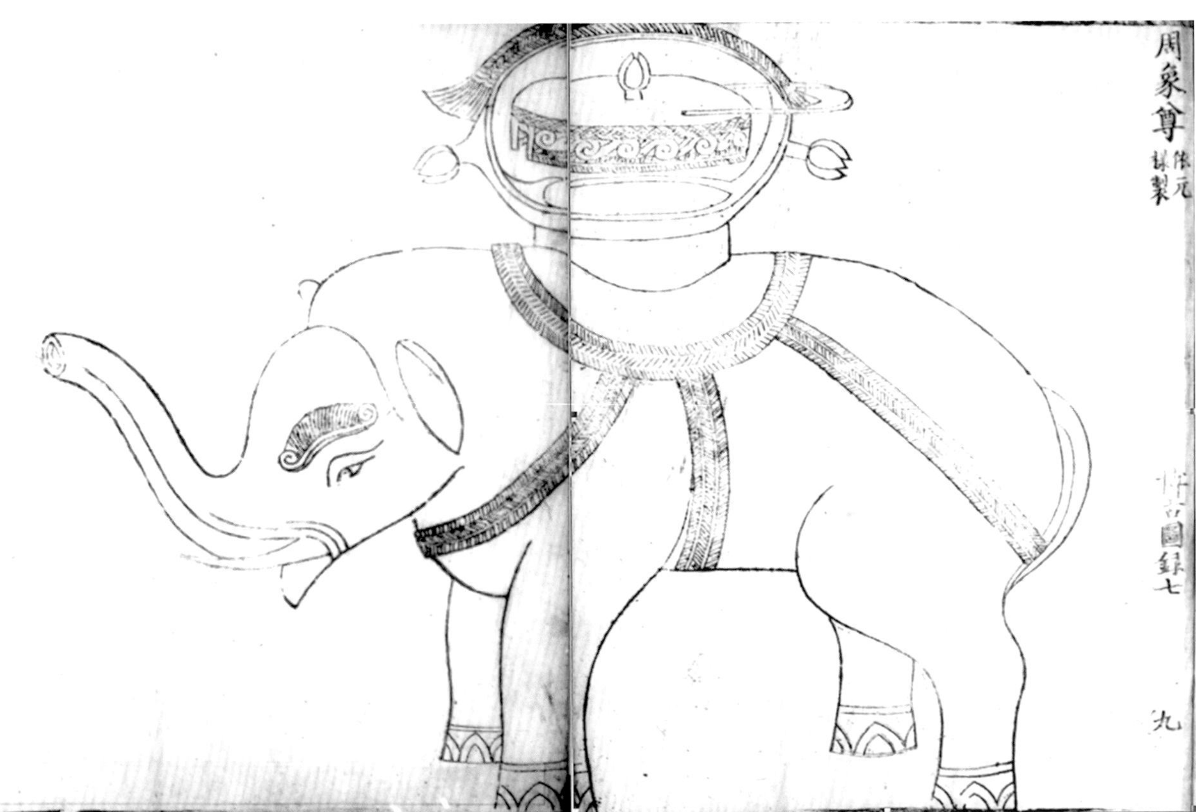

FIG. 6.19
Elephant beaker. Height with cover is given as 9.8 inches. BGT 1528 ed. 7.9a–b.

was by searching for vessels that would match ones mentioned in the text. For instance, the chapter on Zhou dynasty beakers (*zun*) included two identified as sacrificial animal beakers, one identified as an elephant beaker, two as settled beakers, and two as bottle beakers (all terms used in *The Rites of Zhou*). The two sacrificial animal beakers were shaped like cattle with openings in their backs where wine could be poured. The note stressed the functions of these beakers in *The Rites of Zhou* and remarked that as early as the Taihe period of the Wei dynasty (227–232) an example of this sort of vessel had been unearthed, leading the eminent classical commentator Wang Su to correct the errors of Han commentators.[81] The example of the elephant beaker is even more striking (fig. 6.19), especially when compared to the depictions of it in the *Illustrations of the Three Ritual Classics* (fig. 6.5). Again the note discussed the uses of this beaker in *The Rites of Zhou* and cited Zheng Xuan's and Ruan Chen's mistaken views of its shape, attributing their errors to the fact that Qin had destroyed Zhou traditions and that later scholars "knew the names but did not know the vessels," so that unfounded theories filled the gaps and guesses were passed on.[82] The vessels identified as "settled" beakers look like jugs (fig. 6.20).[83] The reason these particular vessels were selected as most likely to be examples of

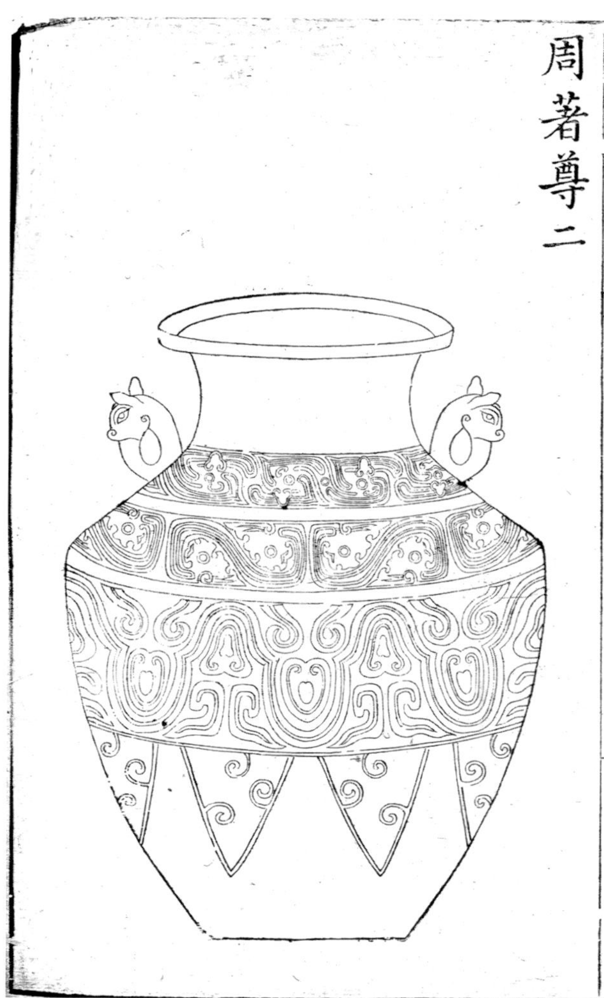

Fig. 6.20
One of the "settled beakers." Height given as 1 foot .4 inches. BGT 1588 ed. 7.18b.

"settled" beakers is that commentators described them as being settled on the ground and having no feet (thus in this case the cataloguers drew on the commentators). After describing the dragon, cloud, and thunder imagery on the vessels, and asserting that since they sat flat on the ground they were truly "settled beakers," the authors went on, "Settled beakers were a Shang beaker type, and thus should be plain without decoration. So why do these vessels bear this decoration? It is probably the case that men of Zhou, in making the *chao* offerings, also used two settled beakers, which would be this sort of beaker. Isn't this a case of Zhou basing itself on Shang vessels but adding more decoration?"[84]

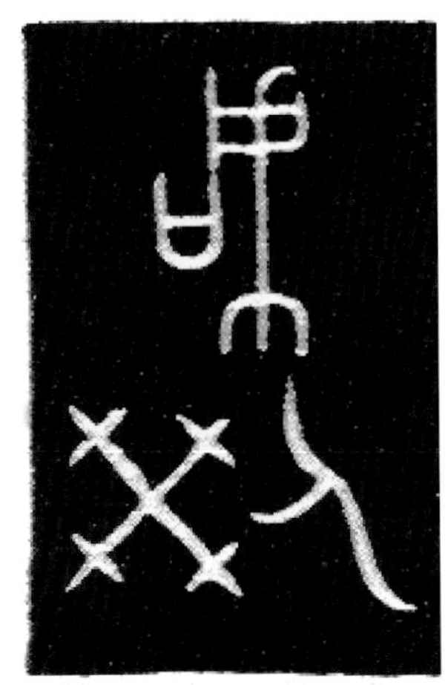

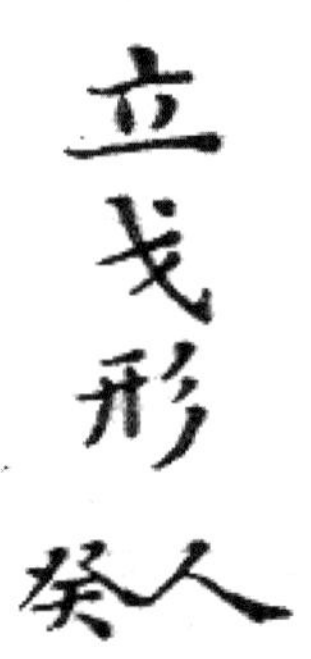

FIG. 6.21
Rubbing of the inscription on Standing Axe Gui Beaker. BGT 6.19b.

IMPUTING MORAL MEANING TO DECORATION

Following a long tradition of scholarly analyses of the decoration on ancient vessels, Huizong's curators and editors tried to infer the moral meaning of decorative motifs. Robert Harrist's study of Li Gonglin as an antiquarian emphasized this side of his studies and credited him with being the first to identify animal masks with the term *taotie* used in a passage in the *Zuo zhuan* and to consequently conclude that decorating a vessel with these masks should be interpreted as a warning against eating or drinking too much.[85] In the passage below, the editors propose several ways to find moral meaning in the picture-like character for battle axe found on the three preceding cauldrons (see fig. 6.21):

> Men of Shang made many vessels showing the image of the battle axe. Thus there are standing axe goblets, standing axe steamers, the Standing Axe Gui beaker,[86] and the Grasping Axe Father Gui Wine Jar.[87] All of these vessels decorated with axes are Shang pieces. Wang Anshi's *Explanations of Characters* [Zi shuo] says that battle axes and halberds are weapons for piercing. One uses the battle axe when one wants the smaller [weapon]. Choosing the small symbolizes the need to be sparing in drinking and eating. The purpose of axes is to pierce things. Therefore this must be a warning on harmful things. Nevertheless, axes are a weapon for overcoming others. The reason the word "I" 我 has the battle axe as part of it is that "I" oppose other things. If one does not have knowledge that surpasses other things, then one cannot oppose things. If I did not have knowledge to establish myself, I would end up losing myself. The way the ancients instilled meaning here is profound.[88]

This entry is not exceptional in citing Wang Anshi's *Explanation of Characters*, which is cited more often than any other Song period book, though still less than half as often as *The Rites of Zhou*.[89] The cataloguers may have been adhering to political correctness in citing Wang Anshi's etymological work. But it is also possible that they did so because they knew the work well; it had been a part of the curriculum for those seeking office during most of their adulthood.

REFUTING THE *ILLUSTRATIONS OF THE THREE RITUAL CLASSICS*

The chief value of collecting actual ancient vessels was seen by the authors of the catalogue to lie in correcting the long tradition of making up descriptions of ancient vessels on little or no basis. As a result, the *Illustrations of the Three Ritual Classics* comes in for repeated criticism. For instance, the introductory essay on goblets concludes, "If you seek them in the *Illustrations of the Ritual Classics*, then they are described as wood carved to make sparrows with cups on their backs, which does not reflect the ancient system. It is based entirely on the unfounded opinions of Han Confucian scholars. If [those scholars] could view these vessels from the Three Dynasties, could they make such mistakes?"[90] We have already seen the corrections made in the case of elephant beakers. Many other examples could be given.

PROVIDING INTRODUCTORY SURVEYS

Even if individual entries could be largely constructed from the files kept on each piece, at some point those putting together the catalogue had to step back and try to synthesize what had been learned from a larger group of objects. In writing the introductions, the compilers of the catalogue seem also to have had in mind catalogues of the books in the Palace Library, which had been produced since Han times and regularly began sections with essays that summarized a genre of books. There were, however, no models for the authors to rely on in writing about bronze vessel types, and the essays themselves are quite varied, perhaps because several different scholars authored them.[91] Much of the introductory essay on libation cups has already been cited, and later in this chapter the essay on mirrors will be examined closely. The first of the introductory essays, on cauldrons, is also worth analyzing.

This essay begins at a high level of abstraction with a discussion of symbols, their connections to the sages and to the objects found in Heaven and Earth, and the deep meanings they carry. It then gives some examples: "Round symbolizes yang, square symbolizes yin; three legs symbolizes the Three Ducal Ministers, and four legs symbolizes the Four Districts [of the capital]." Other associations listed include the *taotie* mask as a warning against gluttony and dragons as symbols of unanticipated changes. This brings the authors to ox, sheep, and pig cauldrons, which are decorated with what they symbolize. Some discussion of special words for particular types of cauldrons follows. The authors also cite the classical specification of differences in the numbers of cauldrons allowed by rank and differences in the material they were made of. Thus gentlemen could have three cauldrons made of iron, great officers five of bronze, feudal lords seven of silver, and the Son of Heaven nine of gold.[92]

After this broad introduction to cauldrons, the authors offer an overview of the types of cauldrons in the collection:

> Over the centuries the shape of cauldrons has not remained constant. There are ones with *taotie* on their bellies with thunder motifs interspersed, such as the Father Yi and

> Father Gui cauldrons.[93] There are ones where the color of the metal is golden and the decoration is beautiful in its simplicity, such as the Xin cauldron and the Gui cauldron.[94] There are ones with twisting flower designs that are attractive in their unusual antique style, such as the Elephant Form cauldron and the Crosswise Battle Axe Father Gui cauldron.[95]

After giving examples of variation in style, the authors also mention the large variation in size of cauldrons and differences in the ways the legs connect to the body.

The authors then take up the inscriptions on the cauldrons. They note that Shang inscriptions often use the ten stems to refer to ancestors, but add that Zhou inscriptions occasionally also continued this practice. The authors mention the problem of cauldrons whose inscriptions called themselves *zun* or *yi*, and cite specific inscriptions to argue that *zun* in these cases means "honored," not "beaker," and *yi* means "vessel," not a specific type of vessel. The essay concludes with a discussion of the importance of the careful study of the writing on unearthed vessels.[96] Not all introductory essays followed the same format, though most at some point discussed passages from the classics that bear on the type of vessel under discussion.

The advances made by Huizong's curators should not be exaggerated. As early as the mid-twelfth century, Hong Mai criticized the tendency (by no means new to *Antiquities Illustrated*) of identifying people mentioned in inscriptions with people mentioned in the classics.[97] Not surprisingly, modern scholarship has gone beyond Song scholarship in many ways. An unusual three-legged vessel with a long spout was thought by Huizong's curators to be a late version of the wine vessel (*jia*), and so was given a Han date. Modern scholars, however, classify it as a wine warmer (*he*) and date it to late Shang, about a thousand years earlier. There are also cases where modern understanding of the reading of the early script is different. Thus tureens classified in the *Antiquities Illustrated* as *dui* are now called *gui*, based on a different interpretation of the evolution of Chinese scripts. And scholars no longer see the character *yi* as having both a generic and a specific meaning (needed to make sense of both *The Rites of Zhou* and inscriptions on bronzes) but solely as a generic term.[98]

On the other hand, it should be recognized that *Antiquities Illustrated* set the standard for the next six or seven centuries. It was frequently cited, and treated as the prime source of reference. In the eighteenth century, when the Qianlong emperor prepared a catalogue of his antiquities collection, he not only adopted the format of Huizong's catalogue, but also largely kept its terminology and sequential order. His catalogue still has *yi* as libation cups, in fourth place, and also still had the reading of *dui* rather than *gui* for tureens.[99]

Cultural Politics of the Catalogue: The Case of Mirrors

All three of Huizong's surviving catalogues can be analyzed in terms of the choices that the editors/compilers made concerning what to include and exclude and what sort of hierarchical arrangement to impose on the material. In many instances, the choices they made were conventional for the period, but in other cases they were pursuing strategies that were less common or even counter to the dominant trends. Often, political motives for the choices can be inferred.

In the case of the antiquities catalogue, most of the choices the editors made followed established practice. The sequence of objects owes much to the classics. Vessels used in sacrifices are treated as the most important ones, and the catalogue begins with the vessels most frequently mentioned in the classics as being central to sacrificial rituals. In terms of selection, the editors clearly preferred Shang and Zhou pieces to more recent ones and inscribed objects to uninscribed ones, attitudes widely shared by Song scholars. Privileging early, inscribed ritual vessels can be viewed as vaguely supporting Confucian culture, but was not an effort to change how scholars thought.

Two choices made by the cataloguers, most likely with Huizong's support, should be viewed as more political. The first is the pervasive attention to *The Rites of Zhou,* already discussed. Less expected, perhaps, is the inclusion of mirrors of Han to Tang date, which makes that decision worth some analysis.

Eleventh-century collectors paid little if any attention to mirrors. The *Investigations of Antiquities Illustrated* included no mirrors, nor were inscriptions on mirrors among the thousands of inscriptions in Ouyang Xiu's *Record of Collected Antiquities* or Zhao Mingcheng's *Record of Metal and Stone [Inscriptions]*, even though both books included inscriptions as late as the Tang. This earlier neglect is not difficult to understand. Mirrors played no role in the rituals described in the classics; they were not ritual implements that could shed light on obscure points in the ritual classics. Although made of bronze, their decoration shows little carryover from the decoration on Shang or Zhou bronze vessels. Unlike stone inscriptions of Han to Tang date, the inscriptions on mirrors rarely add to the store of historical knowledge or allow scholars to correct errors in the dynastic histories. Moreover, there was no tradition of scholarly writing about mirrors (though mirrors with miraculous powers figure in some stories of the strange and supernatural).[100] The late-eleventh-century polymath Shen Gua wrote about "magical mirrors" that could reflect the designs on their backs and the use of mirrors to start fires.[101] But this interest in the physical properties of mirrors did not stimulate a desire to collect them.

What sort of a collection of mirrors did Huizong assemble? To the extent that the 113 mirrors featured in *Antiquities Illustrated* is representative of Huizong's mirror collection, he seems to have valued older mirrors over more recent ones (sixty-nine Han mirrors, to forty-three Tang ones). Nearly half (48 percent) of the Han mirrors were inscribed, as were a third (33 percent) of the Tang ones. Only one mirror is listed from the four centuries between the Han and the Tang. In all likelihood, this lack of mirrors attributed to the Period of Division (220–589) reflects the relatively crude dating of mirrors and the lack of dated mirrors. The curators had ideas of what Han and Tang mirrors were like, but were unsure of the transition between them.[102]

Mirrors regularly carried positive messages, sometimes even about political success (see fig. 6.22).[103] Five of the Han mirrors have an inscription that can be rendered "may you have sons and grandsons forever" or "forever fitting for sons and grandsons."[104] In some cases the designs on these mirrors are rather simple and geometric, as seen in the mirror in figure 6.23 and the nearly identical surviving mirror, shown in figure 6.24.

Seventeen of the Han mirrors were the "cosmic" ones we now refer to as TLV mirrors, thought to depict the square earth surrounded by the circular heavens (see figs. 6.25 and 6.26). These mirrors have a square around the central knob, often marked with the twelve "earthly branches" that correspond to the directions, the Chinese zodiac, and the twelve celestial stations of Jupiter. Four marks resembling Ts come out from the square, with marks that resemble Ls and Vs beyond them, connecting to the next circle. The design of TLV mirrors is now usually interpreted in terms of the board used for the game of *liubo* and a similar diviner's board, thus connecting the decoration of these mirrors to both cosmology and divination.[105]

Gods and divine creatures are often depicted on mirrors (see figs. 6.27, 6.28, 6.29, 6.30, and 6.31).[106] The inscription on the mirror in figure 6.30 reads:

> I have made this bright mirror, refining the three *shang* elements in seclusion.[107] On it I have suitably depicted the ten thousand regions and followed all the proper norms and orderly principles. I respectfully present the mirror to the wise and virtuous. The carvings cover the entire surface. May all people have everlasting joy. May in all matters the yang force preponderate. May your wealth and rank be perfect and bright. May your sons and grandsons be numerous and prosperous. May the wise [possessor of the mirror] be high-ranking and illustrious, his position reaching the highest court posts. May [the mirror's] maker be long-lived.[108]

Among Tang mirrors without inscriptions, depictions of dragons are not uncommon (see figs. 6.32 and 6.33). Another common theme on uninscribed mirrors was labeled "sea creatures and grapes," and probably reflects Persian influence (see figs. 6.34 and 6.35).[109]

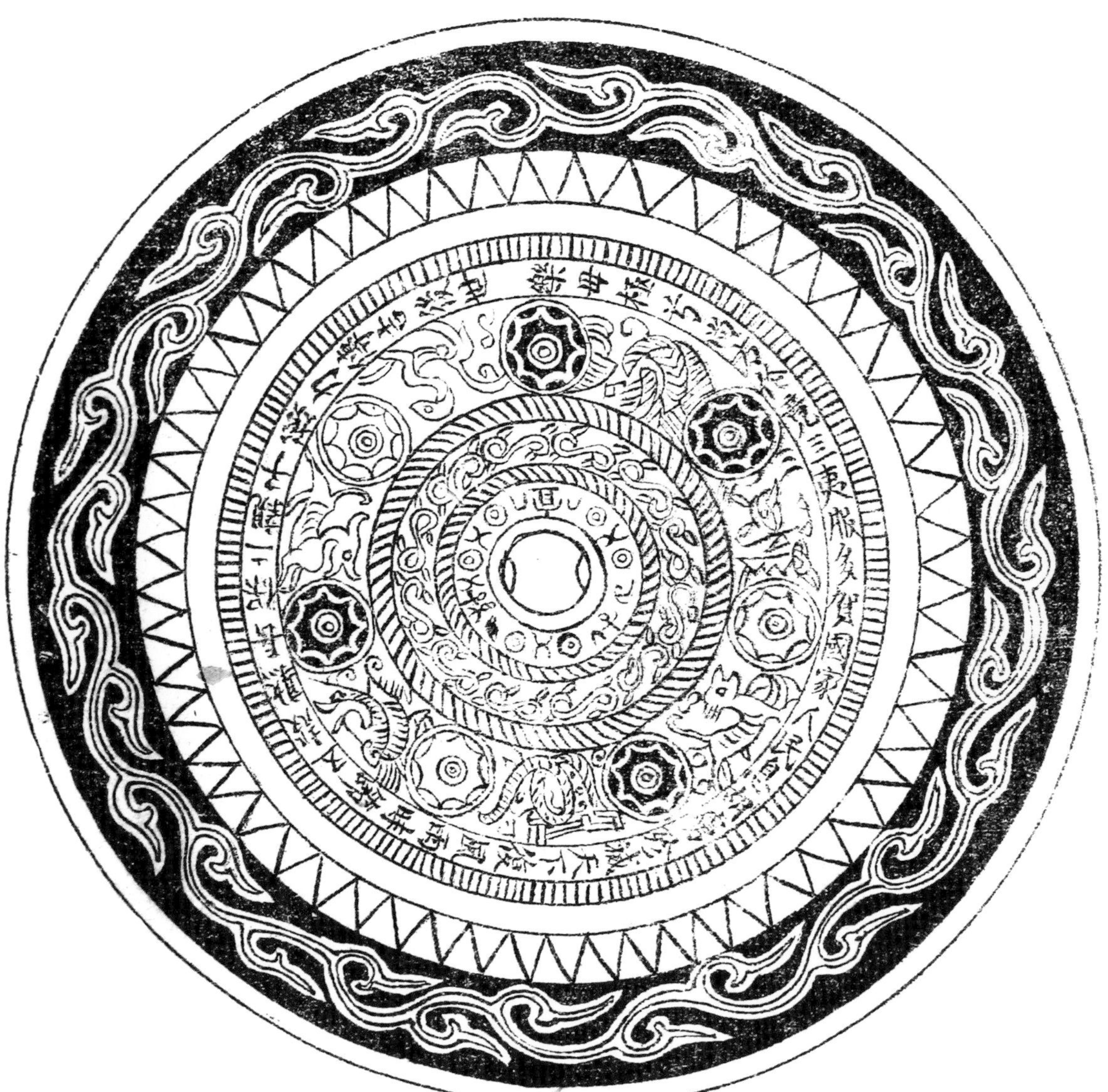

Fig. 6.22
Han Palace Workshop May You Have Sons and Grandsons Forever Mirror. Diameter given as 5.8 inches. The verse inscription on the mirror reads: "The palace workshop made this mirror. The barbarians of the four directions have submitted. Great is the blessing of the dynasty, and its people are at rest. Destroying the northern barbarians has made it possible for the realm to be restored. May wind and rain come in due season and the five grains ripen. Long may you preserve your two parents, and may your children and grandchildren be strong. May this be handed down to inform posterity, and may your joy have no end." From GJTSJC Jingji Kaogong 225.5b, which corresponds to BGT 29.7a–b.

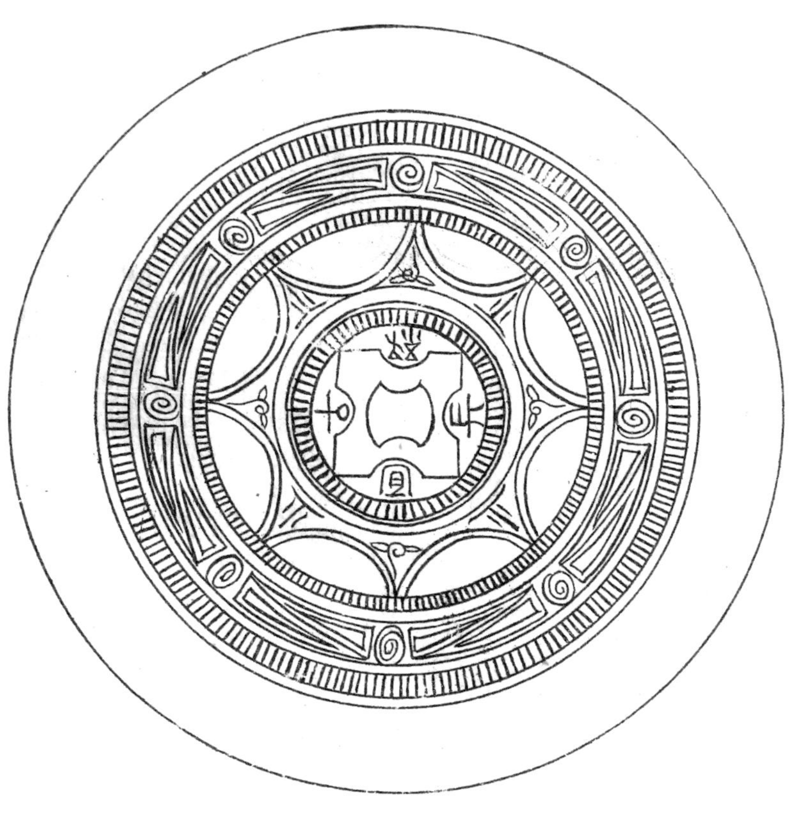

Fig. 6.23
Han May You Have Sons and Grandsons Forever Mirror. Diameter given as 5.9 inches. From GJTSJC Jingji Kaogong 225.24a, which corresponds to BGT 29.10a–b.

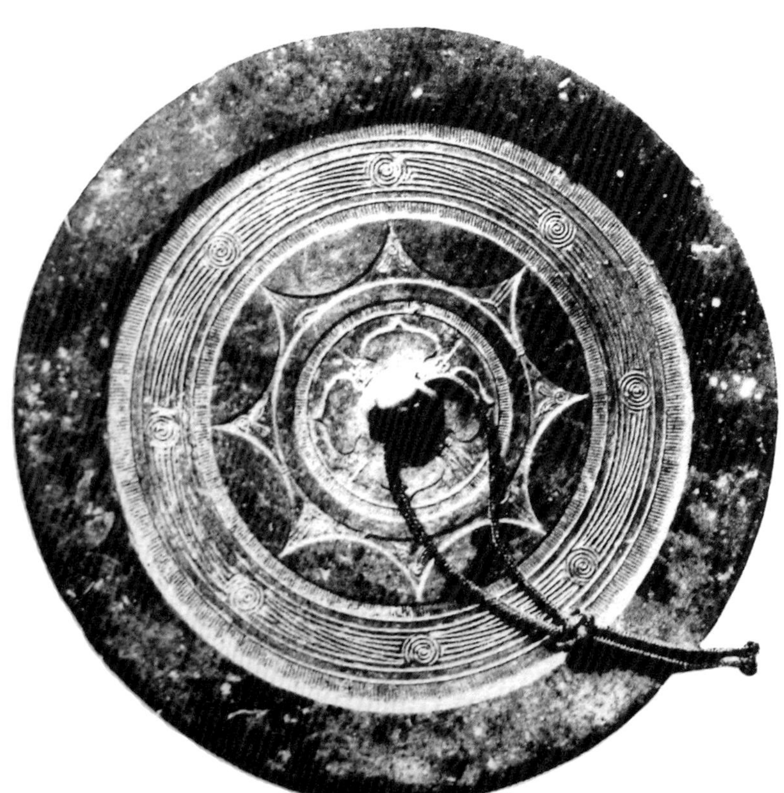

Fig. 6.24
Sons and Grandsons Mirror. After Swallow 1937 frontispiece.

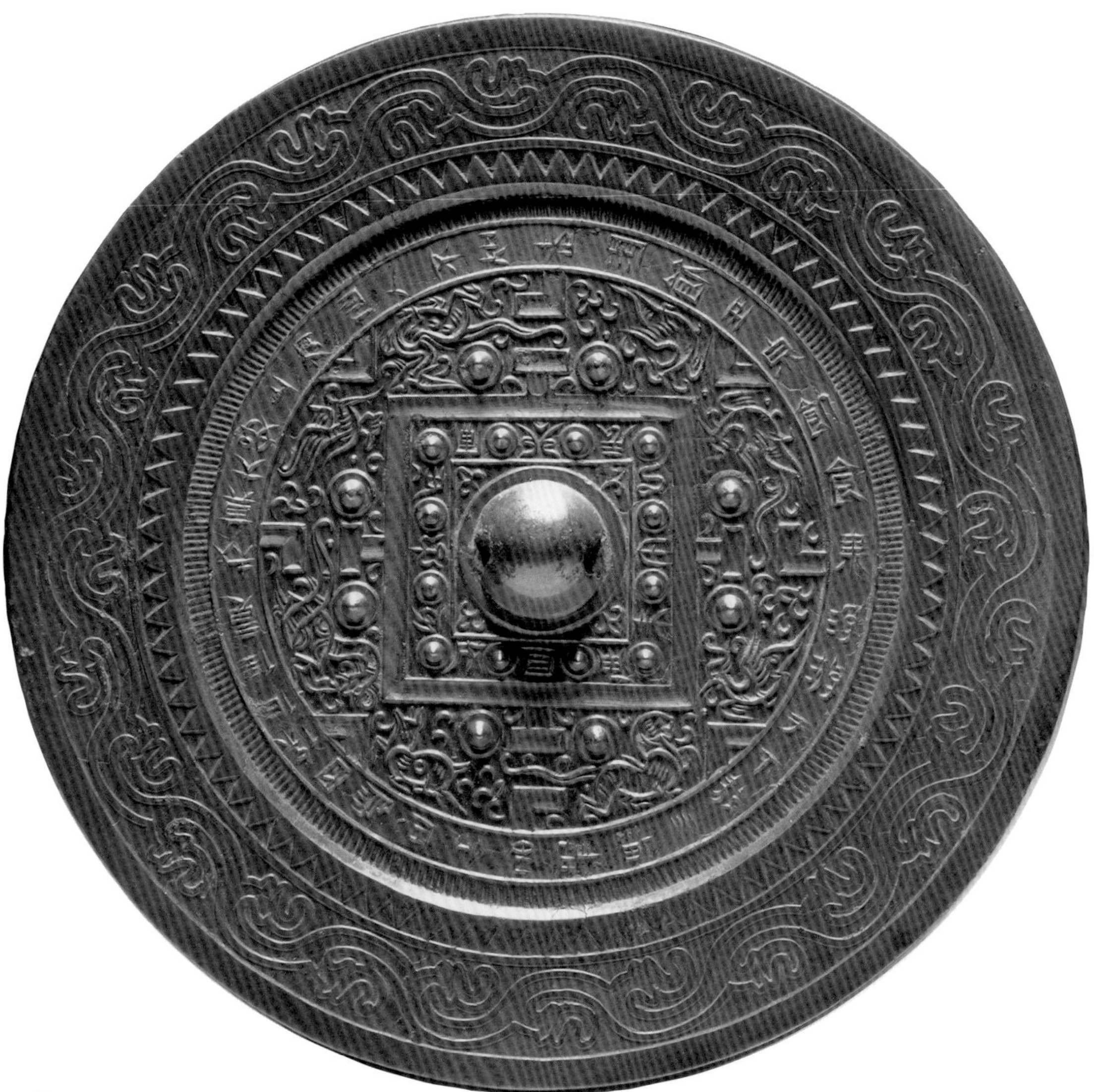

FIG. 6.25
TLV Mirror with Multiple Nipples, Xin dynasty, first century CE. Bronze. Diameter 16.9 cm. © The Cleveland Museum of Art. Gift of Drs. Thomas and Martha Carter in Honor of Sherman E. Lee, 1995.298. Commonly between the Ls and Vs are depictions of eight animals. Four of these are the four directional animals (blue dragon, red bird, white tiger, and the tortoise-snake combination called the dark warrior) and four are other animals needed to fill out the rest of the eight spaces created by the T, L, and V pattern.

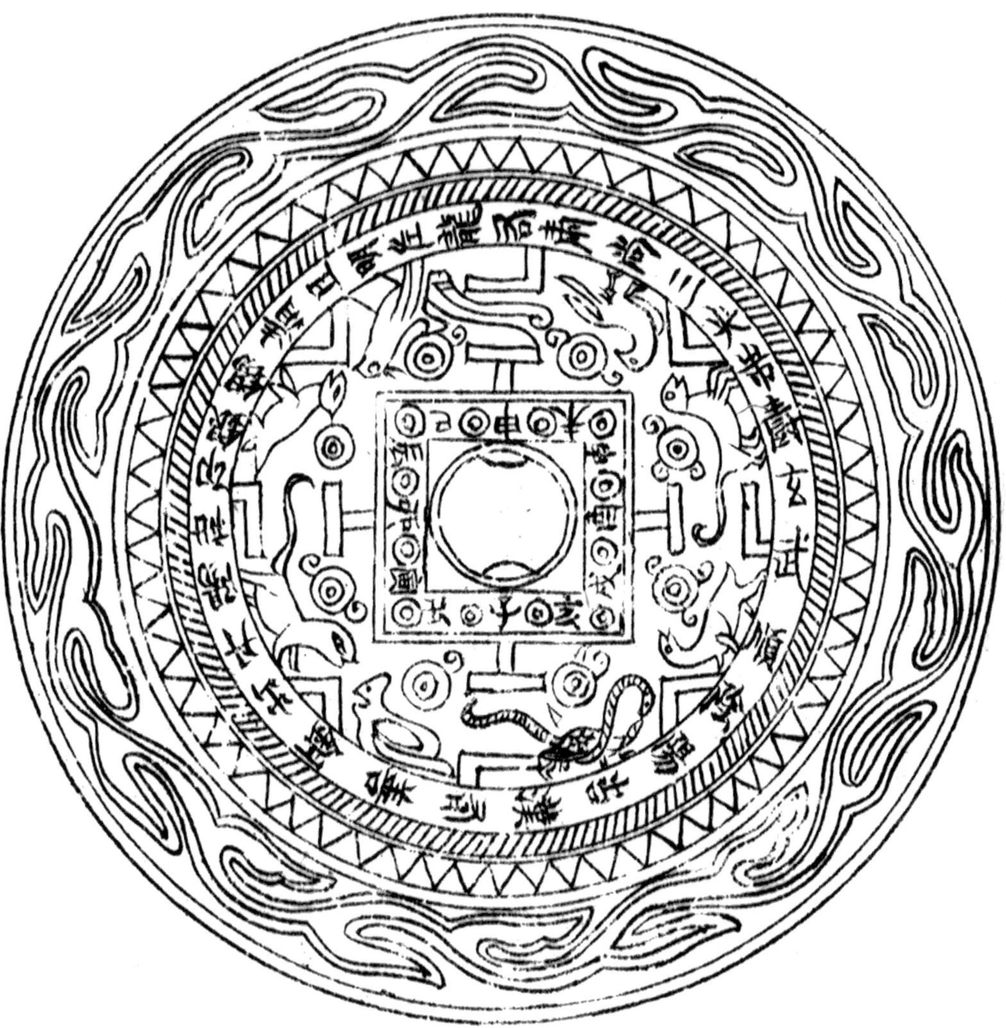

Fig. 6.26
Han Pure and Bright Mirror Number 1. Diameter given as 4.8 inches. The verse inscription reads, “The Han has good copper mines in Danyang. I have mixed copper with silver and tin to make it pure and bright. The dragon on the left and the tiger on the right honor the sun, moon, and stars. The red bird and the dark warrior harmonize yin and yang. How auspicious!” From GJTSJC Jingji Kaogong 225.18a, which corresponds to BGT 28.35a–b.

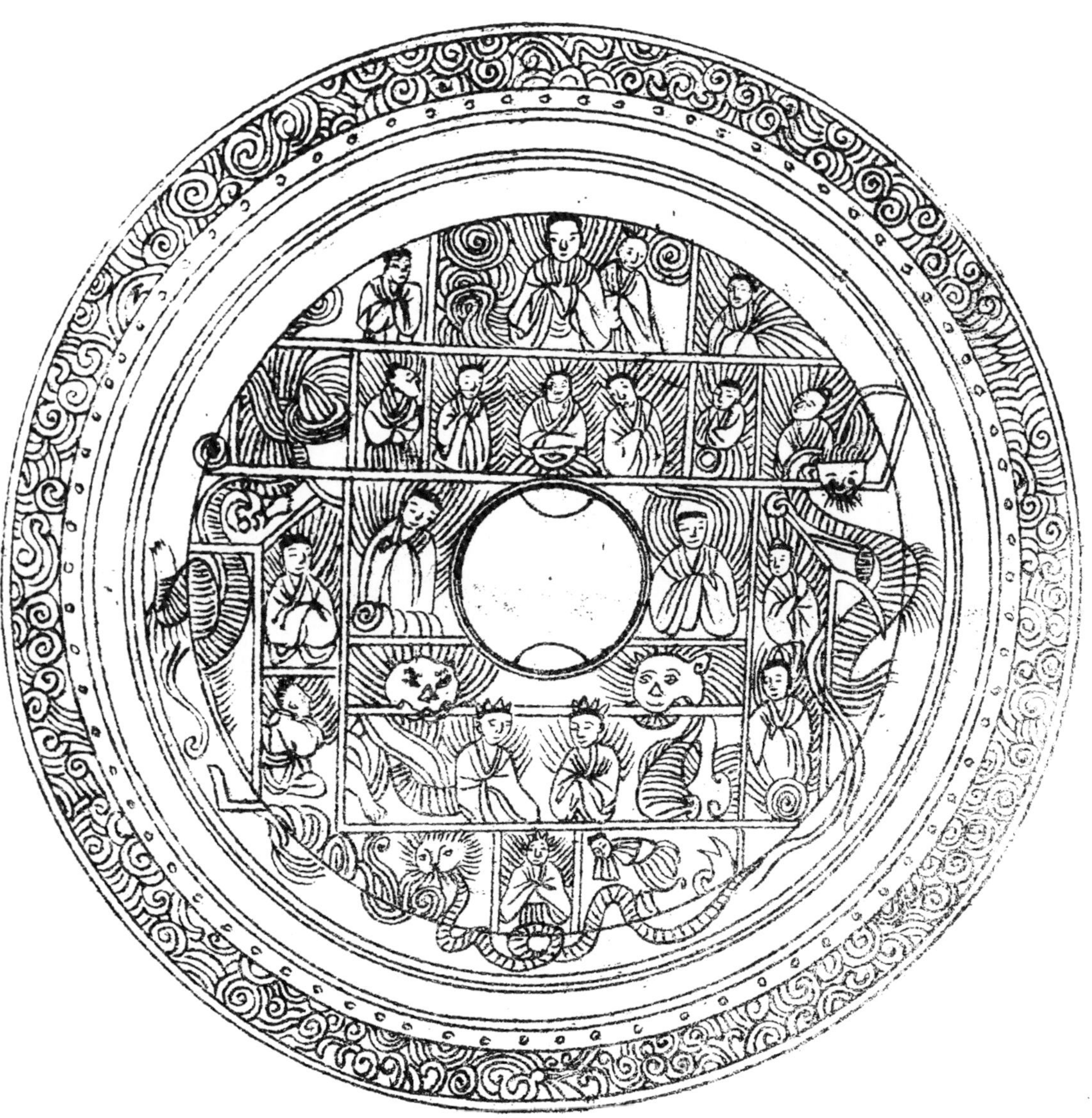

FIG. 6.27
Han Hundred Deities Mirror.
Diameter given as 5.5 inches. From GJTSJC Jingji Kaogong 225.17b, which corresponds to BGT 28.17a.

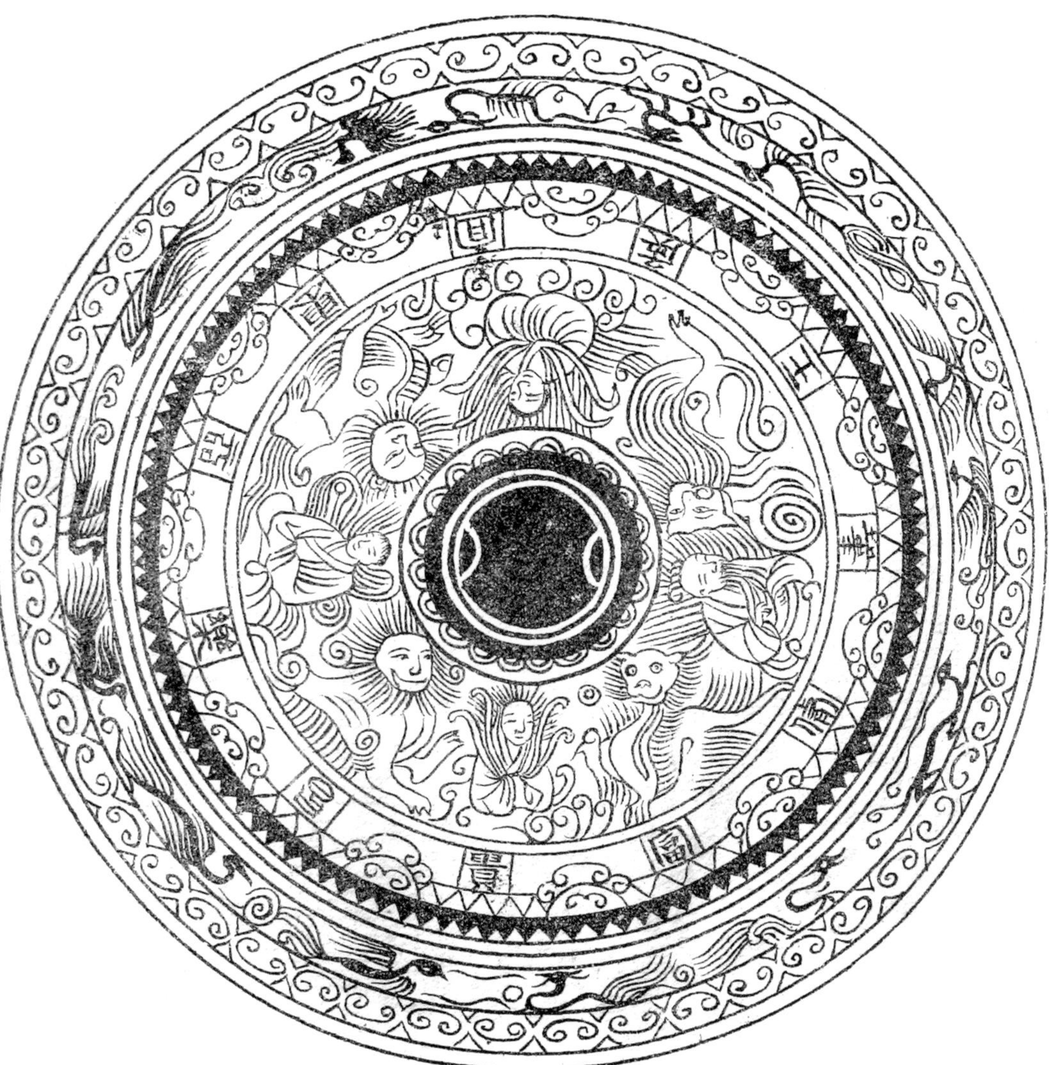

Fig. 6.28
Han Fitting for Nobles and Kings Mirror. Diameter given as 4.4 inches. On this mirror the gods are presented in the inner circle, with fabulous creatures between them. From GJTSJC Jingji Kaogong 225.26a, which corresponds to BGT 29.14a–b.

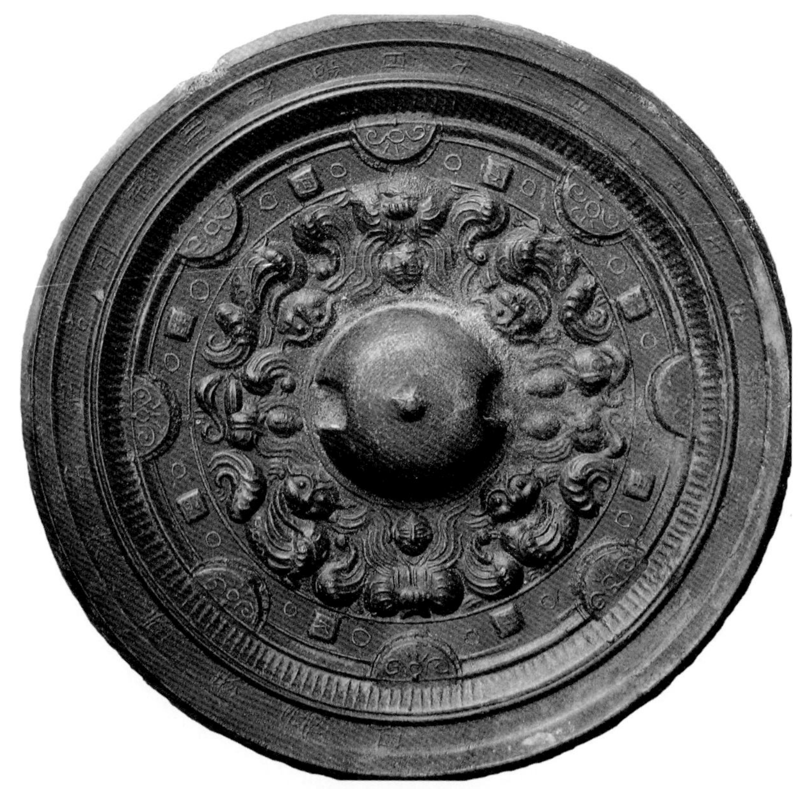

Fig. 6.29
Mirror with Deities and Animals. Diameter 12 cm. National Museum of China. Dated 262, from the Kingdom of Wu in the southeast during the Three Kingdoms period.

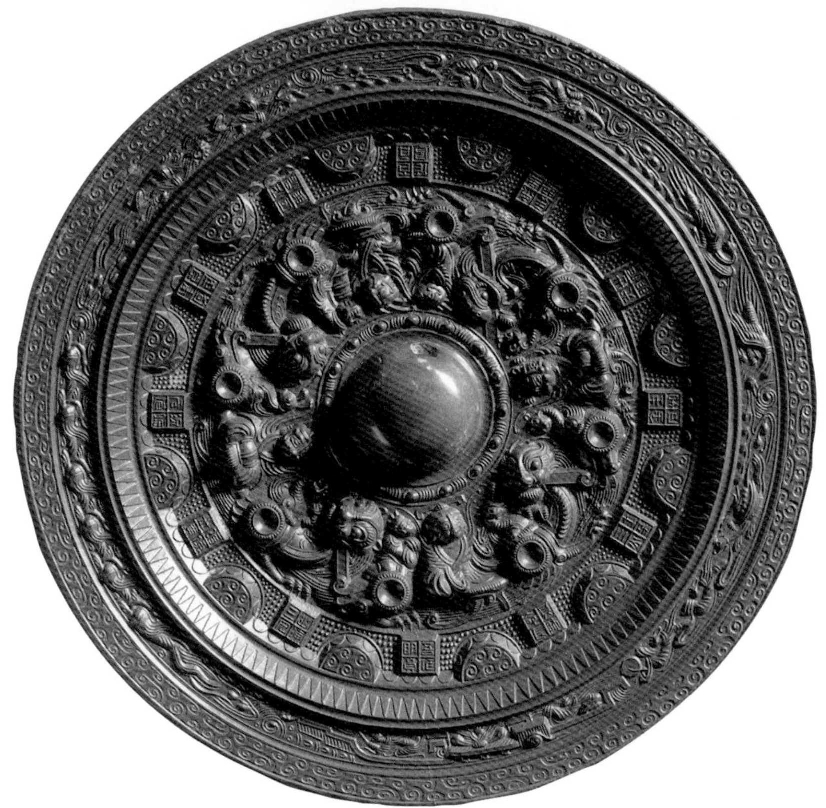

Fig. 6.30
Mirror with Deities and Surrounded by Rings of Squares and Semicircles, Eastern Han dynasty, late second century. Bronze. Diameter 15 cm. © The Cleveland Museum of Art. Gift of Drs. Thomas and Martha Carter in Honor of Sherman E. Lee, 1995.333. Among the figures on this mirror are the Queen Mother of the West, the King Father of the East, and the Yellow Emperor.

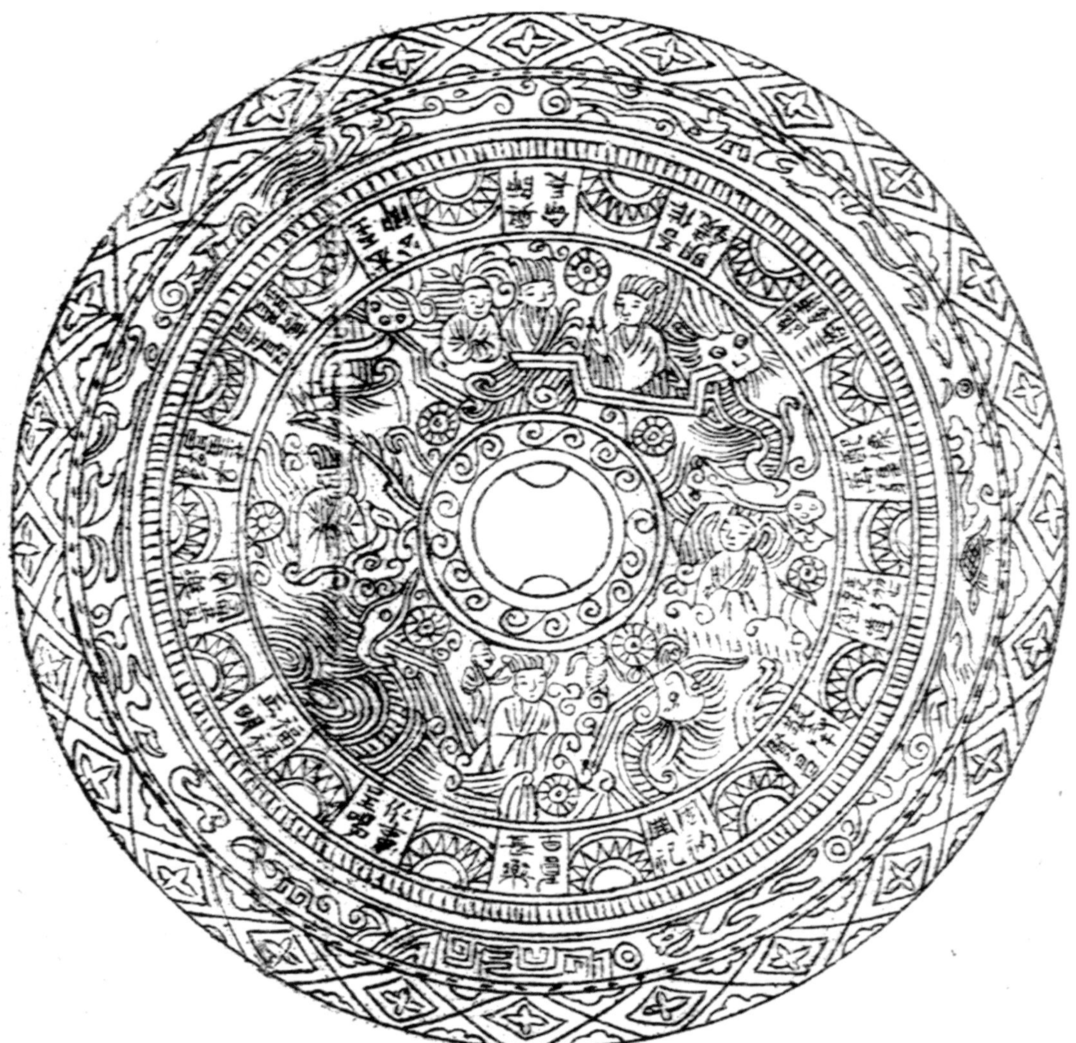

Fig. 6.31
Han Three Spirits Mirror. Diameter given as 5 inches. From GJTSJC Jingji Kaogong 225.5b, which corresponds to BGT 28.13a–b. This mirror, like the extant one in 6.30, has its fifty-seven-character inscription in four-character blocks, each resembling a seal, placed along an outer circle. Within the inner circle are six deities in human form and several divine animals. Beyond the inscription are three decorative bands.

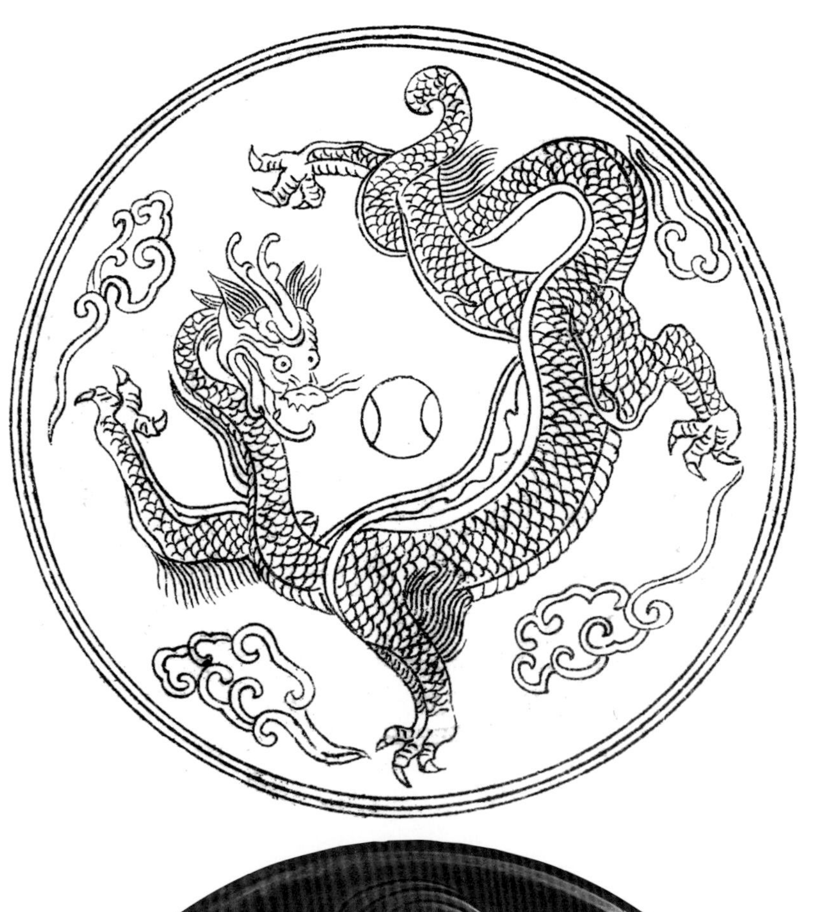

FIG. 6.32
Tang Dragon Mirror.
Diameter given as 3.8 inches. In both this mirror and the surviving one (fig. 6.33), a scaly, horned dragon twists around the round knob, which comes to function as the pearl long associated with dragons. Each pair of the dragon's legs is stretched wide, and the tail twists around one of the rear legs. The background is plain except for four stylized clouds. From GJTSJC Jingji Kaogong 226.12a, which corresponds to BGT 30.4b.

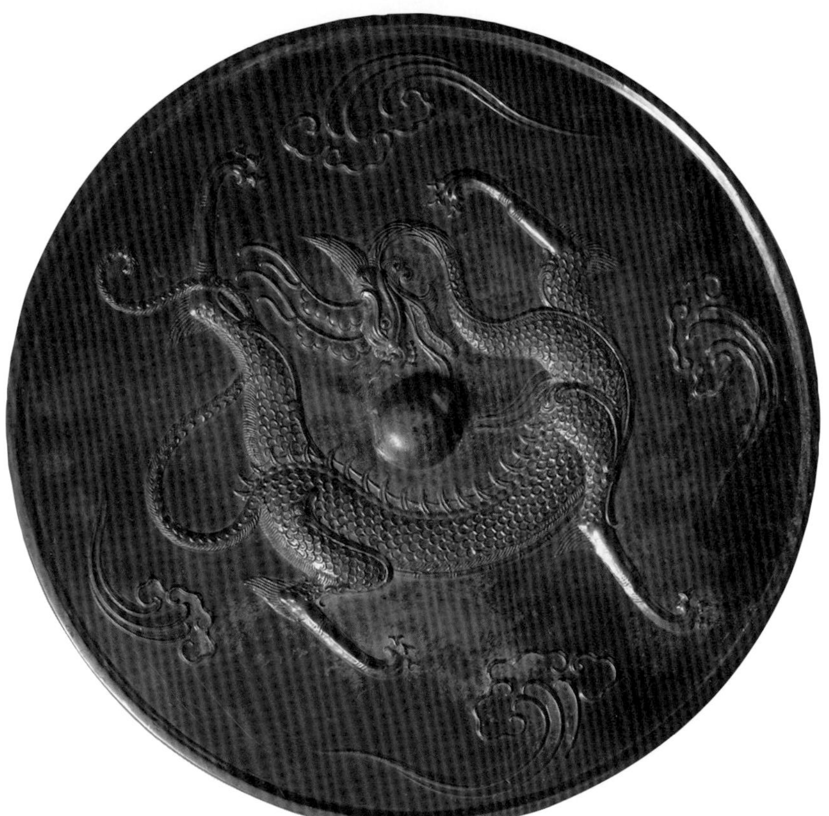

FIG. 6.33
Mirror with a Coiling Dragon, Tang dynasty (618–907). Bronze. Diameter 10.2 cm. © The Cleveland Museum of Art. Gift of Drs. Thomas and Martha Carter in Honor of Sherman E. Lee, 1995.367.

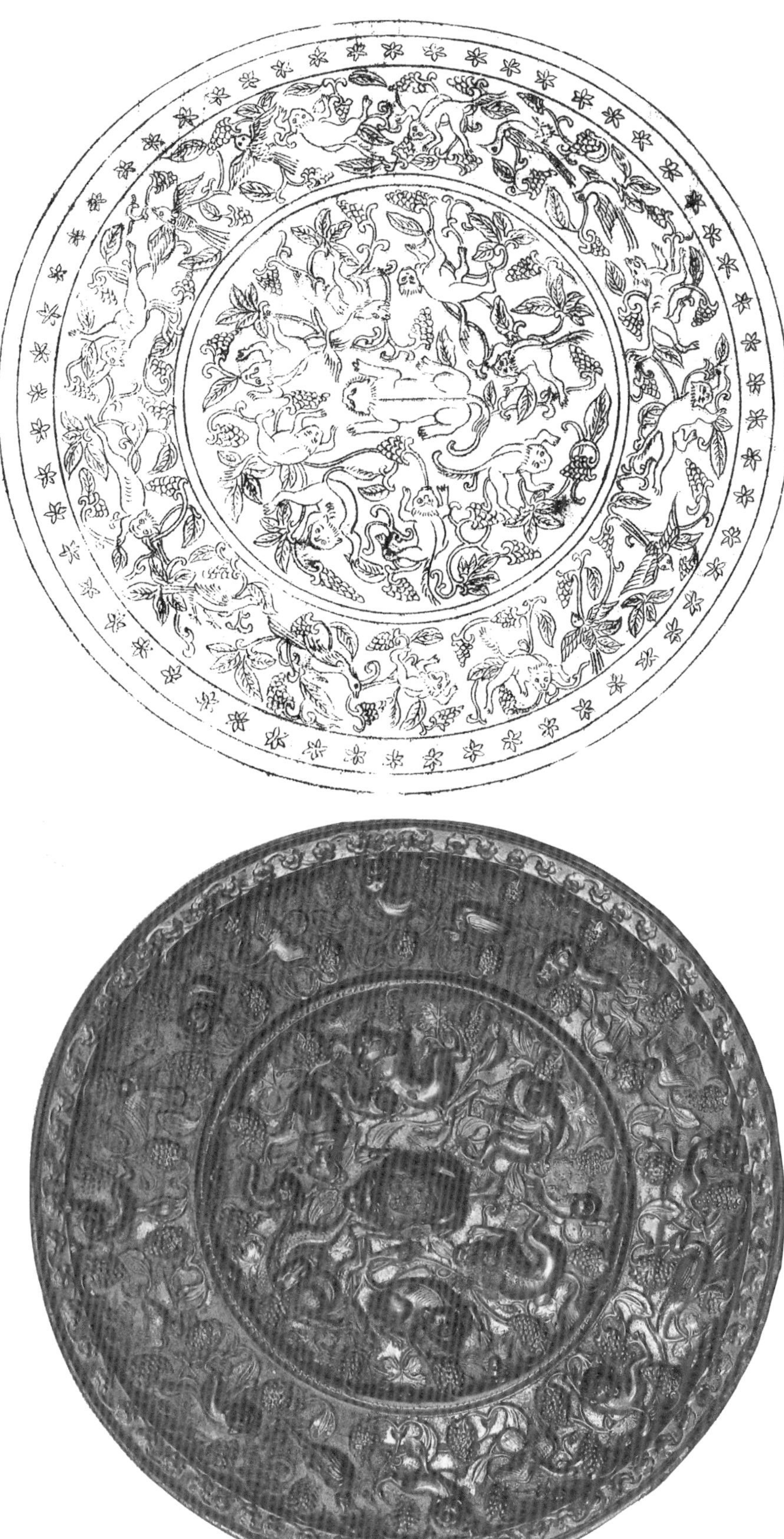

Fig. 6.34
"Han" Sea Creatures and Grapes Mirror. Diameter given as 7.7 inches. Huizong's curators thought these mirrors were of Han date, though today they are considered Tang products and the animal is identified as a lion, not a sea creature. From GJTSJC Jingji Kaogong 226.8a, which corresponds to BGT 29.31b.

Fig. 6.35
Tang Sea Creatures and Grapes Mirror. Diameter 20.8 cm. Found near Luoyang, this mirror depicts eight birds and eight animals in the outer band. After Luoyang bowuguan 1988:8.

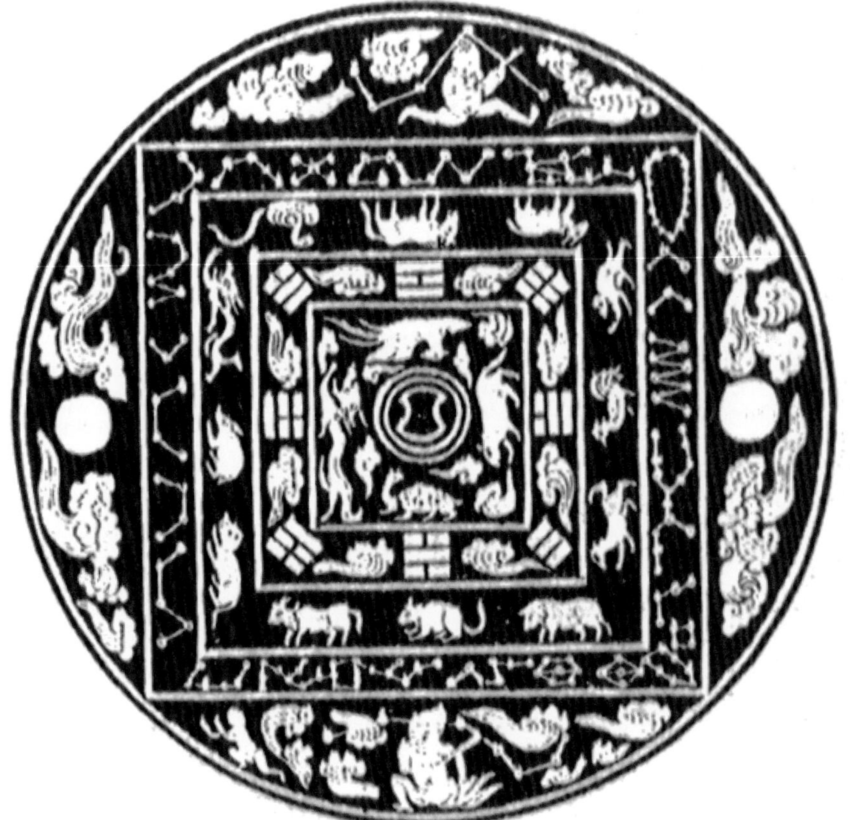

Fig. 6.36
Tang Sun and Moon Iron Mirror. Diameter given as 5.8 inches. The innermost square has the four directional animals, the next one the eight trigrams among clouds, then the twelve animals of the zodiac, followed by star maps (probably representing the twenty-eight lunar mansions). In the four outer slices of the circle, on the left is the sun and on the right the moon, with what appear to be star gods at the top and bottom, all surrounded by clouds. BGT 30.16b.

Iron mirrors are rare in modern collections, probably because iron objects rust, but Huizong's catalogue includes twenty-two—one of Sui date, the rest Tang. Most often cosmic symbolism dominates these mirrors, as in figure 6.36, which shows four nested squares within the circle of the mirror. By depicting the sun, moon, and stars, the directional animals, the eight trigrams, and the animals of the zodiac, this mirror links all of the phenomena of the sky with the eight trigrams. There is also a mirror with Daoist talismanic writing (fig. 6.37) and another with images of auspicious phenomena (fig. 38).

Even this small sampling of the 113 mirrors featured in Huizong's catalogue offers clues as to why he would have decided to take the unprecedented step of collecting and cataloguing mirrors. Both the imagery on the mirrors and the sentiments expressed in the inscriptions on them fit well with two long-standing and interlinked interests of Huizong's: auspicious signs and Daoism. Huizong delighted in auspicious signs such as the clearing of the Yellow River and the arrival of cranes at the palace. He not only let his officials congratulate him and write effusive praise on such occasions but mentioned these events in his own poems and commissioned visual documentation of them in the form of both flags and paintings.[110] Huizong's

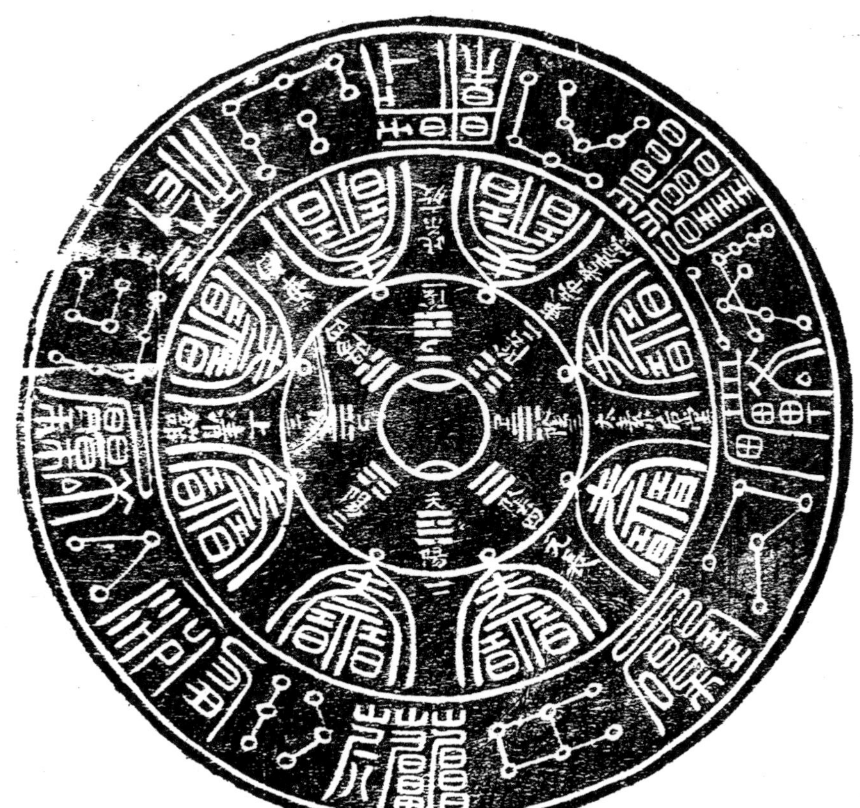

Fig. 6.37
Sui Sixteen Talismans Iron Mirror. Diameter given as 7.9 inches. Depicted on this mirror are talismanic writing, star maps, and trigrams. BGT 1588 ed. 30.14a.

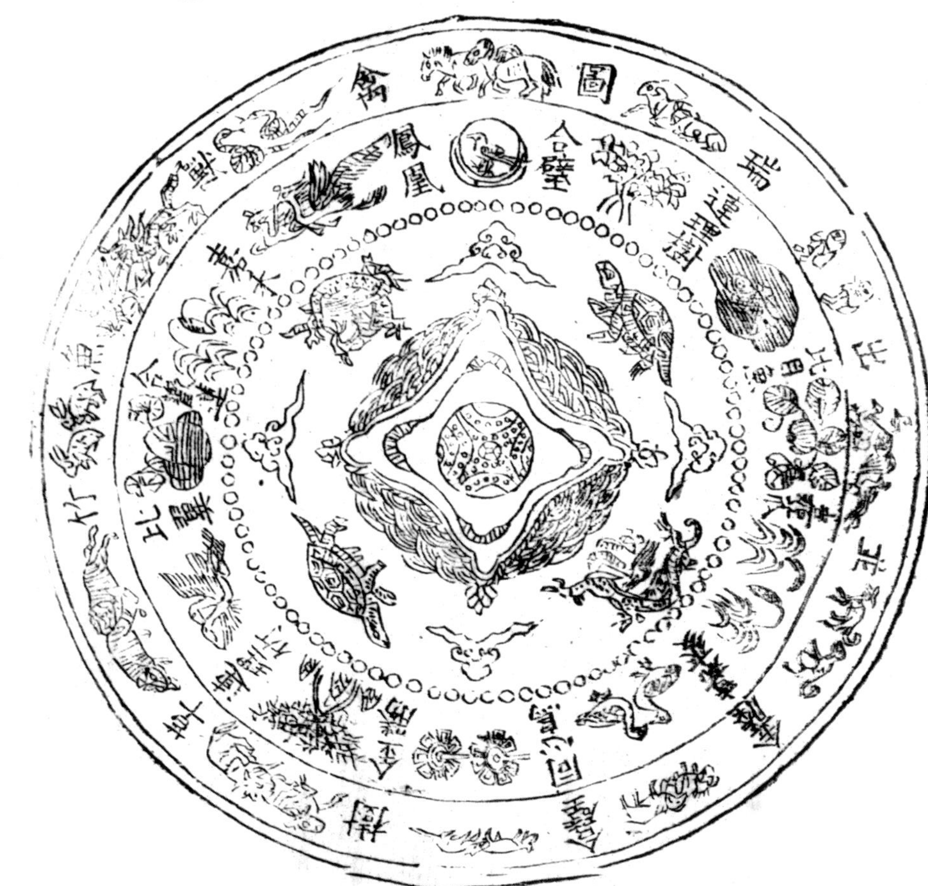

Fig. 6.38
Tang Auspicious Pictures Mirror. Diameter given as 6.5 inches. The outer circle has a series of paired animals inserted between the words in an inscription that reads, "Birds, animals, and fish, bamboo, grass, and trees, joined disks and golden gears all produce auspicious pictures." The next circle has images of particular auspicious phenomena, such as joined trees, phoenixes, auspicious grain, and birds that mate for life. BGT 1528 ed. 30.11b.

long involvement with Daoism is also well documented. As mentioned in chapter 2, Huizong patronized Daoist clerics, built Daoist temples, sponsored the collection of Daoist texts, set up schools for Daoist clergy (complete with examinations), and issued under his name commentaries on key Daoist texts.

Mirrors have an aura of auspiciousness because they regularly evoke the wish for positive outcomes: progeny, long life, health, wealth, joy, and high office. Besides the phrases already seen in the inscriptions cited above, some common wishes include "May your sons and grandsons be complete in number and occupy the center," "May you become a noble or a king," and "May your life last as long as metal and stone."[111] In Song times most Han mirrors had probably not been handed down continuously since Han times but rather had been found when Han graves were disturbed, as mirrors were commonly placed in coffins in Han times. The inauspiciousness of association with death, however, seems to have been largely overlooked, probably because of the frequency of these auspicious messages.[112]

The relationship between mirrors and Daoism is more complex. Certainly in Han or Tang times one did not in any sense have to be a Daoist to have a mirror with cosmic imagery or depictions of gods or immortals. In Han times, cosmic mirrors were part of a broad shared culture. But it is also true that by Song times such imagery came to play a large role in Daoism.[113]

The earliest extant text to tie mirrors to Daoism was written by the fourth-century Daoist Ge Hong. After discussing the risks involved in entering the mountains—ranging from rock slides, tigers, and wolves, to demons capable of taking on human form—he advised bringing along a mirror, which would reflect the true form of disguised spirits:

> This is why, since ancient times, Daoists who go into the mountains always carry a nine-inch mirror [a solar number] on their backs; in this way, the ghosts of old things dare not go near them. If by chance they come to provoke the adepts, the latter will have only to turn around and look into the mirror; if they are Immortals or true mountain gods, they will keep their human aspect even in the mirror, but if they are perverse animals or ghosts of old things, then the mirror will reflect their true appearance.[114]

By Tang times, if not earlier, mirrors were also used by Daoists as aids to meditation and visualization. One Tang text provides seven illustrations of cosmic mirrors, some with talismanic writing, like that shown in figure 6.37.[115] Several Daoist texts available in Huizong's day describe ways Daoists could use mirrors for spiritual exercises. The 122-chapter compendium put together in 1032 by Zhang Junfang, titled *Cloudy Bookcase with Seven Labels* (Yunji qiqian), has a section on mirrors.[116] In Pauline Koffler's words, "From resolute self-visualization in one or several mirrors, the adept progresses to the technique of the four discs. These discs are implanted at cardinal points by the four emblematic animals, each bearing a looking glass. In this way the adept may perceive his personal gods as well as the nine transformations of Laozi according to the hours of the day."[117]

A few more of the inscriptions found on mirrors in Huizong's catalogue should help convey the appeal of these mirrors to ardent Daoists.

> An excellent mirror from the palace workshops, truly very fine. On it are immortals oblivious to old age. They drink in springs of jade when thirsty and eat dates when hungry. They roam through the realm, wandering the four seas. May your life be as lasting as metal and stone, and may you be a protector of the land.[118]
>
> The palace workshop made this mirror. The gods [depicted on it] eat flowers of jade, drink from the thirst-quenching springs, ride the colored dragon, and float to Heaven.[119]
>
> I have refined and regulated copper and tin and filtered off the lees. [This mirror] wards off evil and is fitting for the market. Long may you preserve your two parents, and may profit come to your children and grandchildren. May all the people have joy without end. May your life last as long as metal and stone and the Queen Mother of the West. It was after she flew here and told us about this that I made this record.[120]

Once Huizong made the decision to collect mirrors and include them in his catalogue, his curators had much to do. A basic and challenging task was deciphering the inscriptions on mirrors. Even though the forms of the characters were not as old as those on Shang and Zhou vessels, many still perplexed scholars. Indeed, even after the major advances in epigraphy of the eighteenth century, scholars continued to come up with divergent readings, even of the more common formulas on Han mirrors.[121] Somewhere along the way Huizong and his curators had to form a sense of what a good collection of mirrors would be like—what kinds of mirrors it would have—so that they could judge whether they needed to seek out particular types of mirrors to help complete the collection. This, of course, required notions of types of mirrors. Once they decided on the types of mirrors, they needed to agree on a sequence for them, as the catalogue regularly put items in a hierarchical order. And in order to conform to the rest of the catalogue, it would be necessary to write an introductory essay about mirrors that put them in a broad cultural framework. Most of the essays in the antiquities catalogue relate the objects to the classics and classical ritual. Thus, a decision had to be made on whether to highlight or to obscure the connections between mirrors and Daoism.

Neither Huang Bosi nor Dong You left much in the way of discussion of mirrors, so we do not have the musings of Huizong's curators on these issues.[122] The introductory essay itself, however, is highly revealing of the decisions that were made on how to think about and present the mirror collection. It begins by linking mirrors to the Yellow Emperor, esteemed in both the Confucian and Daoist traditions, then quickly moves to the cosmological and evil-averting properties mirrors possessed:

> In the past, the Yellow Emperor cast metals to make divine objects, among which were fifteen mirrors.[123] Those mirrors absorbed the essence of yin and yang, and took from the five odd and even numbers of *qian* and *kun*.[124] They were thereby able to join the light of the sun and the moon and penetrate the thoughts of ghosts and gods, allowing them to protect people against demons and cure them of illness. They last for thousands of years and endure while all other materials vanish.

The editors next list in a straightforward way the most common cosmic decoration found on mirrors:

> Mirrors were created so long ago that we cannot know everything about them, yet we can infer their principles by examining the ones found today. They are [decorated with] the Four Spiritual Animals guarding the four directions, the Eight Trigrams fixing the eight farthest places, the Twelve Hours on the outer circle, and the Twenty-Four Solar Terms arrayed inside it.

The editors then return to the magical and mystical side of mirrors, showing no inclination to obscure this dimension of mirrors:

> Mirrors' potency to pierce the secrets of the whole creation and to drive the ultimate power lies beyond those forms and numbers. Hence, as an object, a mirror is limited by its form, yet its power is not exhausted by its form; it is ruled by numbers, yet it goes beyond numbers. It varies dynamically and is on friendly terms with the Creator of Things.

The cataloguers next relate several items in the lore of mirrors, some of which do not seem to be preserved in other sources:

> In the Zhou dynasty, thirteen mirrors were cast. The number thirteen took the intercalary month into consideration. Twelve of them were situated in the twelve outlying districts, while the other one protected the central province. It is said that those mirrors' images included the Five Mountains, the Seven Deities, the Fifteen Animals, the Fourteen Directions, and four seal script characters. Yet there are no records [in

ancient texts] suggesting how those mirrors were used, except for *The Offices of Zhou*, which says "mirrors absorbing the sacred water from the moon" were used in sacrificing to gods.[125]

The next two stories had strong Daoist overtones:

During the Kaiyuan period of the Tang dynasty, a man called Li Tai presented the Water Heart Mirror, which had a dragon curling like a tongue in relief on its back. Li also presented a memorial saying that Dragon Hu had made it and the soul of a real dragon lived in it. Time passed, then in a year with a terrible drought, Emperor Xuanzong had [the Daoist priest] Ye Fashan pray to the mirror. Clouds then emerged from the mouth of the dragon on the mirror and it rained for seven days afterwards, ending the drought.[126] How miraculous!

When Emperor Gaozu of the Western Han dynasty first ascended the throne, he entered Xianyang, where he acquired a square mirror that reflected the image of one's intestines and stomach.[127]

These are cases of how miraculous [mirrors] shielded and sustained emperors. Reliable records have transmitted these truths from generation to generation.

After these proofs of the miraculous powers of mirrors, the editors turned to interpreting the decoration found on mirrors. They associated the roundness of mirrors with Heaven, and the squares often depicted on them with Earth. They pointed to the common representation on mirrors of the four directional animals and other markers of space and time, including the twelve hours in the day and the twenty-four solar periods in the year. They also mention depictions of the Jade Maiden, the gods of the Five Mountains, and dragons, as well as a host of fantastic creatures and auspicious plants.

The editors then turned to the words inscribed on mirrors. Clearly they had collected many inscriptions and had tried to divide them into meaningful categories.

As for the inscriptions on the back of mirrors, some use four-character lines in the style of the official histories, and others use seven characters per line in the Boliang [verse] style. Some have barely a single word, while others have more than enough. Names and dates are sometimes recorded. Those inscribed "palace workshop" or "jade hall" were for imperial use. Those inscribed "May you become an official" or "May you become a noble" were used by officials. Those inscribed "may you have sons and grandsons" were owned by families. One inscribed phrases such as "A thousand autumns, ten thousand years" to express good wishes. Using sixteen talismanic seal script characters was done to ward off evil.

TABLE 6.2. Types of mirrors in *Antiquities Illustrated* (by date)

	Han inscribed	Han uninscribed	Sui	Tang inscribed	Tang uninscribed	Total
cosmic	11	7		1		19
strange substance		1				1
verse good wishes	12			4		16
prose good wishes	11			2		13
nipples		6				6
dragons and related creatures	2	18			15	35
plain		1				1
iron			1	7	14	22
Total	36	33	1	14	29	113

Finally the editors explained the principles they used to divide mirrors into categories and put the categories in order:

> We have established a way to order the mirrors. In the sequence of the Five Metals, gold is first, silver is second, copper is third, iron and tin are fourth and fifth. Based on this order, in this catalogue the copper/bronze mirrors come before the iron ones. Since nothing was created before Heaven and Earth, we start with the motif of Heaven [*qian*]. Heaven is the master of the hundred deities, so the motif of hundred deities is appended to that of Heaven. Participating in the work of creation and mastering the hundred deities, Heaven could therefore create objects, so these objects come next, such as objects made of unusual materials like insects [*tuixing*] and floating water [*fushui*].[128] With such objects, good wishes can be expressed in verse, so verse comes next. Verse gives rise to enjoying blessings, so good wishes are next. Good wishes are connected to nurturing, so the mirrors with nipples come next. Nipples are a means of nurturing people; when all animals and plants are nurtured, auspicious creatures appear, so the category of dragons, phoenixes, colorful birds, and sea creatures comes next. However, the most ingenious appears to be dull, and the colors are applied last in the process of painting. We therefore know that plain mirrors are the most basic ones; this catalogue ends with mirrors without any decoration on them. This is the sequence used in this catalogue.[129]

The order outlined here is the order followed in the catalogue. The rationales offered for the order, however, seem rather forced. More likely the usual preference for early over later objects and inscribed over uninscribed ones explains the sequence. The number of mirrors falling into each type is shown in table 6.2.

Huizong undoubtedly had complex motivations for greatly expanding the palace collection of antiquities. He was a great admirer of Li Gonglin and could have collected antiquities in imitation of him. Aesthetic attraction probably played a role, as many ancient vessels are striking to look at. The auspicious implication of the discovery of ancient vessels all over his realm had to please Huizong. From his many pronouncements, we know Huizong saw the potential of these objects to help his court establish its credentials as a true seeker of the ancient way, committed to restoring antiquity in both music and rites. Court ritual had long been a central concern of Confucian scholars, who insisted that the early Zhou period rituals, recorded in the ritual classics, should be kept alive through imperial performance. Huizong was aware that there was cultural capital to gain from using genuine ancient vessels as a basis for reforming the performance of rites at his court.

Huizong also seems to have recognized that the value of the collection could be enhanced by cataloguing it. Preparing a catalogue of the antiquities collection was a major undertaking. It involved selecting the objects to be included, dividing them into categories, ranking the categories, preparing drawings of every object and rubbings and transcriptions of every inscription, as well as entries that gave both basic facts and interpretive discussion. The cultural power of the completed catalogue made this effort worthwhile. As the largest and most comprehensive work on ancient bronze artifacts to its date, the catalogue set standards that lasted six centuries. By bringing together so many rubbings of inscriptions along with readings of them, it became a book no one interested in ancient scripts could overlook. The categories it developed for analyzing vessel types and decorative elements similarly came to dominate discussion. Although the scholars assigned to work on the catalogue strove to maintain high standards of scholarship, they also saw ways to advance Huizong's political goals. The pervasive concern with *The Rites of Zhou* needs to be seen in the context of Wang Anshi's promotion of that text. Similarly, the inclusion of mirrors into the category of collectible antiquities should be seen in relation to Huizong's goal of reuniting the Dao of the Daoists and the Confucians.

CHAPTER 7

Collecting and Cataloguing Calligraphy

Because Emperor Taizong of the Tang loved calligraphy, his successors were able to maintain the tradition of calligraphic excellence. They set up and filled the office of court calligrapher, with the result that generation after generation there was no lack [of great calligraphers].

—*Xuanhe Calligraphy Catalogue*

PERHAPS THE MOST VALUED OF THE EXTANT CALLIGRAPHIES THAT were once in Huizong's collection is Sun Guoting's transcription of the first part of his own essay, *On Calligraphy*, now in the National Palace Museum in Taipei (fig. 7.1). Dated 687, *On Calligraphy* is a large work (nine meters long), and its content is directly relevant to the appreciation of calligraphy. We know that it entered the palace during Huizong's reign because until then it was in private hands. Mi Fu saw it at the home of Huizong's uncle Wang Shen and he expressed admiration for Sun Guoting's faithfulness to the tradition of Wang Xizhi.[1] Today it is more common to praise it for giving visual expression to the points that it articulates. Wen Fong, for instance, describes Sun as capturing emotion "through dots and strokes" and creating "forms with the turning of the brush," just as he advised his readers to do.[2]

Sun's *On Calligraphy* was one of more than 1,200 pieces of calligraphy listed in the catalogue of Huizong's calligraphy collection, the *Xuanhe Calligraphy Catalogue* (Xuanhe shupu), completed in 1122 or later.[3] The catalogue is a rich source for the sort of calligraphy collection Huizong and his curators put together and for how they wished it to be understood. The catalogue is much more than a record of calligraphy held by the palace. It is at the same time a critical history of calligraphy, a list of calligraphers worth collecting, an effort to impress other connoisseurs with the breadth and depth of the emperor's collection, and an attempt to promote and demote particular calligraphers in critical opinion. The catalogue reveals not only

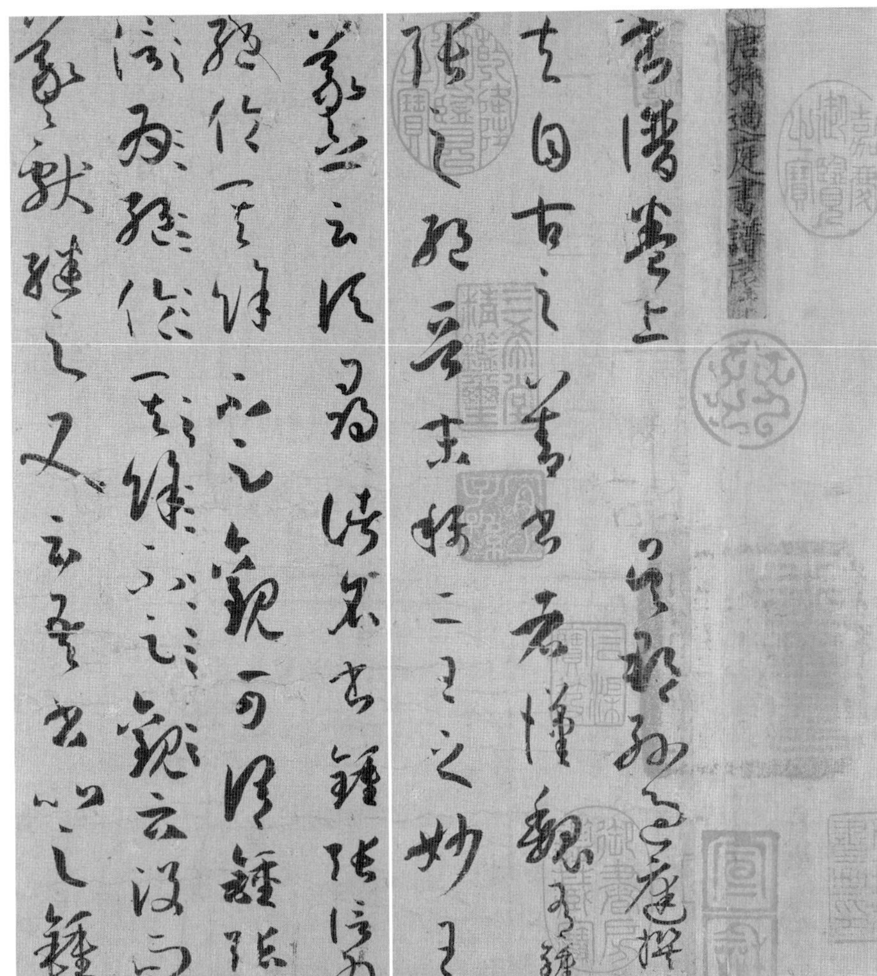

FIG. 7.1
Sun Guoting (646–691), *On Calligraphy* (detail). Handscroll, ink on paper, 26.5 × 900.8 cm. National Palace Museum, Taiwan, Republic of China. The cursive script Sun used in this piece is in the tradition of Wang Xizhi.

Huizong's favorite calligraphers but also how he responded to the many advances in connoisseurship during the eleventh century.

Updating and cataloguing the palace calligraphy collection posed challenges to Huizong's curators quite unlike the ones they faced in building and cataloguing the antiquities collection. One fundamental difference is that they did not in any sense have to start from scratch. Whereas antiquities was the newest field of scholarly collecting, calligraphy was the oldest. Beginning in the Later Han period (25–220 CE), members of the educated class gained reputations as talented calligraphers, with the result that people saved their writings for their aesthetic qualities.[4] Calligraphers were not anonymous craftsmen like bronze workers, but prominent members of the educated elite whose lives left many traces in the written record.[5]

Because calligraphy had been collected for about a thousand years, a large critical literature about it already existed. Huizong's curators did not need to invent for themselves meaningful categories into which to divide the calligraphy they found in the palace collections; the tradition of framing calligraphy in terms of a series of script types was well established, as was a critical vocabulary closely related to the vocabulary used to discuss literature.[6] Huizong's curators had ample resources to consult when considering which calligraphers the collection should contain, as lists of the most eminent calligraphers of the past had been compiled for centuries.

The problem of copies and forgeries further distinguished calligraphy from bronzes as objects of collection. In Northern Song times the collecting of bronzes was a sufficiently new activity that detecting replicas and forgeries does not yet seem to have been much of a problem for collectors; Song collectors of bronzes were not on the lookout for recent replicas or imitations.[7] By contrast, the major challenge for a collector of autograph calligraphy (as opposed to rubbings or other copies) was distinguishing between originals, acknowledged copies (often still desired when originals did not survive), and forgeries. Already in the Southern Dynasties tracing and freehand copies of the calligraphy of the masters of the previous centuries were in circulation, sometimes identified as such, sometimes mistaken for originals. By Song times it is likely that the large majority of the works attributed to pre-Tang masters were copies rather than originals.[8] Huizong's curators would have had to spend many hours comparing alternative versions of famous pieces to select the one most likely to be the original.

For the antiquities collection, many tasks, such as taking measurements, deciphering inscriptions, and searching through ancient texts for relevant material, could be delegated to erudite men in the Palace Library with the expectation that any one of them would come up with similar answers. That was not the case in the selection of the best of the thousands of versions of the calligraphy of the great masters. No doubt Ouyang Xiu, Zhu Changwen, Mi Fu, and Huang Bosi would all have made different selections if asked to select the fifty best out of all the works attributed to Wang Xizhi in the palace collection. To put this another way, the subjective nature of the criteria for evaluating calligraphy made routinization and institutionalization much more difficult. What made personal collecting of calligraphy extremely attractive in Northern Song times hampered institutional collecting.

When Huizong's curators and editors set out to write the catalogue of the calligraphy collection, they undoubtedly were aware that they were undertaking the largest and most ambitious book on calligraphy since Zhang Huaiguan wrote the *Calligraphy Standards* (Shuduan) more than three centuries earlier. The challenge of cataloguing the bronze collection was made easier for Huizong's editors because they could adapt the format of Lü Dalin's and Li Gonglin's illustrated catalogues of antiquities. No annotated catalogue of an autograph calligraphy collection was in existence. Huizong and those he assigned to the task had to decide what sort of book to write. If the model was to be Ouyang Xiu's catalogue of rubbings, the key organizing principle should be to organize the rubbings chronologically by work, not by script type or artist. If the model was to be book catalogues, categories equivalent to book genres would need to be identified and synthetic essays about them prepared. Moreover, the works of an artist who did works in different categories would be dispersed rather than listed together. If the model was to be critical histories of calligraphy, such as Zhang Huaiguan's eighth-century *Calligraphy Standards*, capsule biographies would need to be written and artists classified by rank and script type. In the end, Huizong's authors came up with their own design. They used script types as the first-level organizing principle, comparable to genres in book catalogues, but included capsule biographies as well. They listed all works by an artist after his capsule biography, placed under a single script, no matter how many of his pieces were in other scripts.[9] Although calligraphers were not in any sense treated equally—the number of calligraphies listed for each varied from 1 to 243—no formal ranking of artists or objects was given.

The Need to Update the Palace Calligraphy Collection

As seen in chapter 1, the early Song rulers had put together a sizable collection of calligraphy. Their immediate heirs, however, did not pay much attention to it. During the reigns of emperors Yingzong, Shenzong, and Zhezong, in the mid- to late eleventh century, connoisseurs of calligraphy frequently belittled objects held by the palace, declaring them to be copies rather than originals. By Huizong's time, upgrading the palace collection could not be done simply by adding new works; it would also require weeding out inferior pieces.

Recent scholarship has demonstrated the intellectual liveliness of calligraphy criticism during Tang and Song times. A common approach has been to examine reassessments of particular calligraphers.[10] Scholars have been able to draw not only on book-length works on calligraphy—such as Zhang Huaiguan's eighth-century *Calligraphy Standards,* Zhu Changwen's 1074 *Continued Calligraphy Standards* (Xu shuduan), and Mi Fu's *Calligraphy Chronicles* (Shu shi)—but also on shorter essays and on the notes or colophons that connoisseurs such as Ouyang Xiu, Su Shi, Mi Fu, Huang Tingjian, and Huang Bosi wrote about works that they viewed. Modern scholarship has identified broad trends in calligraphy criticism. Tang critics such as Sun Guoting and Zhang Huaiguan believed that calligraphers first needed to gain mastery of technique, then leave the rules behind and create their own styles.

They saw calligraphy, much like poetry, as expressing the calligrapher's fleeting emotional reactions. Song critics, too, regularly praised calligraphers' ability to go beyond conformity to a model; however, they placed new emphasis on the expression of ideas, plainness or simplicity (*pingdan*), and "ancientness."

One stimulus to the development of calligraphy criticism in the Northern Song period was the circulation of a set of reproductions of calligraphy that allowed men to discuss the same piece without being physically together. This was the imperially issued *Model Letters from the Imperial Repository Issued in the Chunhua Period* (Chunhua bige tie), called here *Chunhua Model Letters* for short. As mentioned in chapter 1, in 992 Wang Zhu was instructed by Emperor Taizong to select the best pieces of calligraphy from the palace collection and to acquire others from private collections as needed to prepare a ten-chapter book of rubbings. Each of the 419 pieces selected was traced, then carved onto woodblocks, from which rubbings were made. The rubbings were assembled into books, sets of which were given to officials. Soon these books circulated widely.[11] Over half the works in the *Chunhua Model Letters* were by the Two Wangs; Wang Xizhi had 160, and his son Wang Xianzhi had 73. The *Model Letters* also included many works by former rulers and early masters, especially of the Southern Dynasties. The book was, however, weak on the work of Tang calligraphers, containing only twenty-eight pieces by eleven Tang artists.[12]

The dominant place of the Two Wangs in the *Model Letters* owed much to imperial patronage beginning in the Southern Dynasties. The Tang court, especially under Tang Taizong (r. 626–649), not only collected calligraphy by the Two Wangs on a large scale but appointed as court calligraphers men who saw themselves in a direct line of transmission from the Wangs.[13] By promoting the calligraphy of the Two Wangs and their early followers via the *Chunhua Model Letters*, Song Taizong probably wanted to be compared to Tang Taizong. As a calligrapher himself, however, he did not confine himself to the style of the Two Wangs. As seen in chapter 1, he often wrote in the decorative flying white style, and made gifts to his officials of works in this script.

The original blocks used to produce the *Chunhua Model Letters* were apparently destroyed in a palace fire in the 1040s, but demand for the book continued strong, so private individuals produced reproductions by engraving plates on the basis of the copies still in circulation. As the popularity of the *Chunhua Model Letters* grew, critics began to lament its influence. Ouyang Xiu thought it gave too much space to Jin dynasty masters Wang Xizhi and Wang Xianzhi. Because calligraphy reflects character, he thought one should model one's calligraphy on upstanding men. To him, Southern Dynasties aristocrats like the Wangs were much less worth copying than upright Tang officials like Yan Zhenqing. According to Amy McNair, Ouyang Xiu's promotion of Yan Zhenqing in place of the Two Wangs should be seen as part of a campaign of the early neo-Confucian reformers to "counter imperial styles in all areas of art and literature, in pursuit of their political goal of greater influence in government affairs."[14] Ronald Egan, by contrast, associates his advocacy of Yan Zhenqing more with the commitment of Ouyang Xiu and his friends to the plain "ancient text" (*guwen*) style in literature rather than the allusive, ornamented modern style; to them the rugged, block style of Yan was plainer than the enticing grace of the Wang style. This moral dimension meant that "Collectors were praised not so much for their aesthetic judgment as for their ability to recognize and appreciate the worthiness of past masters."[15]

As a follower of Ouyang Xiu, Su Shi maintained the stance that it was politically correct to use Yan Zhenqing as a model (though he personally could not rid his work of the influence of the Two Wangs).[16] Many calligraphers, of course, valued both the Two Wang tradition and Yan Zhenqing's model. Huang Tingjian, for instance, gave high standing not only to the Two Wangs and Yan Zhenqing but also to the Tang cursive master Zhang Xu and the Five Dynasties calligrapher Yang Ningshi. Other critics, especially Mi Fu and Huang Bosi, used the search for the ancient to return to Wang Xizhi. Mi Fu saw Yan Zhenqing's regular script as stiff and unwieldy, lacking in naturalness. Mi Fu preferred cursive and running scripts to the regular script. For regular script, both he and Huang Bosi found the style of the early master Zhong You to come closest to the plain and unaffected (*pingdan*) ideal.[17]

Mi Fu's admiration for Wang Xizhi did not, however, make him a fan of the *Chunhua Model Letters* as a copybook. He believed firmly that calligraphy should be studied from originals, or at least copies traced onto paper, not from rubbings, since carving on stone or wood is a very different act than using a brush to write on paper. Moreover, he did not have a high opinion of the choice of items that were included in the collection, believing many of them to be inferior copies rather than originals. Huang Bosi (who, as discussed in chapter 5, became one of Huizong's curators), expanded on Mi Fu's critiques, often reattributing particular letters. McNair calculated that between them, Mi Fu and Huang Bosi declared nearly half the items in *Chunhua Model Letters* to be fakes or misattributed. Dong You, another of Huizong's curators, in his critique of the *Chunhua Model Letters* brought up the fact that any transfer to carved blocks requires first making a copy. To his eyes, Wang Zhu's hand could be seen in all of the *Model Letters.* Dong You had the opportunity to inspect the originals in the Imperial Repository and found them quite different from the reproductions, not only because works on paper can show differences in the heaviness of the ink, but also because the copies had similarities in brushwork that the originals lacked.[18]

What sort of an impact did all of this discussion of calligraphy have on Huizong as a calligraphy collector? We should remember that as a young man his relationships with Wang Shen and Zhao Lingrang had allowed him to participate in the world of connoisseurs and collectors active in Kaifeng. He would have known about the criticisms of the *Chunhua Model Letters*, the fear of forgeries, and questions about the relative merit of different calligraphers. He would have learned that the palace calligraphy collection was no longer a source of prestige for the court. It would hardly be worth expending energy and resources on upgrading the collection or publicizing it unless he was confident that these actions would earn the court respect, not derision. Since neither Shenzong nor Zhezong had initiated a campaign to add to the calligraphy collection, Huizong was under no obligation to fulfill their intentions.

Nevertheless, Huizong does not seem to have hesitated more than a couple of years before setting out to expand the palace collections. As seen in chapter 4, Huizong involved both Mi Fu and Cai Jing in work on his collection early on. In 1109 Huizong had a new version of the *Chunhua Model Letters* produced, later dubbed the *Daguan Model Letters* (Daguan being the name of the reign period 1107–1110). Huizong had the original pieces of calligraphy retrieved from the Imperial Repository so that they could be recopied more accurately and new engravings could be made. Errors of one sort or another were corrected, such as misattributions or inaccurate chronological orders. Cai Jing wrote out the labels identifying each artist and at the end of each chapter added the date.[19] One of the Wang Xizhi pieces in the *Daguan Model Letters* that was later listed in Huizong's catalogue but is no longer extant on paper is illustrated in figure 7.2.

Patterns of Collecting

Although the list of each artist's calligraphies in the *Xuanhe Calligraphy Catalogue* is regularly prefaced with a phrase such as "those currently collected in the imperial quarters" 今御府所藏, the works listed cannot be read as an inventory of all the calligraphy held in the palace during Huizong's reign. Evidence that items were left out is strong. In a few cases later model letter writers include rubbings of works with Huizong's seals that are not in the *Xuanhe Calligraphy Catalogue*, suggesting that even some pieces that were impressed with Huizong's seals were later excluded from the catalogue.[20] Only about a fifth of the items that had been in the *Chunhua Model Letters* also appear in Huizong's catalogue, presumably because the others were no longer judged authentic or important.[21] That is a very high rate of exclusion, but it is exceeded by the rate implied by Cai Tao. Cai claimed he once saw a catalogue of Huizong's collection that listed over 3,800 Tang copies of calligraphy by the Two

Wangs and more than 800 pieces by Yan Zhenqing.[22] In the final catalogue only about one-twentieth (forty-two) of the Yan Zhenqings were included, and only a handful of the Tang copies of the Two Wangs (only ones that could be attributed to particular artists such as Chu Suiliang).

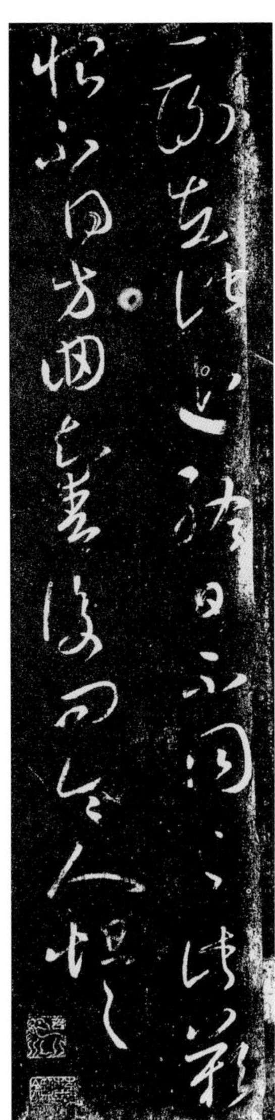

Fig. 7.2
Wang Xizhi (309–ca. 365), *Er Xie tie*. After *Daguan Taiqing lou tie* (DGTQLT 6).

Recognizing that the catalogue is a select list does not diminish its value as a source for the preferences, values, and goals that shaped the formation of Huizong's calligraphy collection. One can weigh what the catalogue says about particular masters, periods, scripts, and styles, and one can count how many works of each sort are listed. Given that most of those listed in the catalogue are described positively, the numbers have an attractive precision that allows comparisons. They are summarized in table 7.1.

As seen in this table, the catalogue lists 1,220 works by 245 artists.[23] In terms of script types, the catalogue heavily favored cursive and running scripts, each of which accounted for more than a third of the items. Seal, clerical, and *bafen* scripts made up a very minor portion of the works listed. Regular script, a script Huizong himself developed into a distinctive personal style, accounts for a tenth of the items listed.

Why the strong interest in running and cursive scripts? One reason surely is that the catalogue is a catalogue of autograph calligraphy, and does not include rubbings, collected by many literati of the period. Much of the interest among Song collectors in seal, clerical, regular, and *bafen* script was based on the rubbings they had been able to collect of early bronze and stone inscriptions. Huizong's curators did not disparage such rubbings, and they cite them with some frequency in discussions of script types and individual artists, but the collection being catalogued was not a rubbing collection.[24] As seen in chapter 5, the palace had started collecting rubbings by the late years of Huizong's reign and might well have produced a catalogue of them if the Jurchens had not invaded.

In terms of periods, the catalogue is strong in both pre-Tang and Tang works (see fig. 7.3). If we consider both the number of works and the number of artists, it is clear that Huizong and his curators shared the common view that the greatest age for calligraphy had been the Six Dynasties and the Tang; 36 and 45 percent of the pieces in the catalogue came from those periods, respectively. Calculating per year, the first 150 years of the Song was only about half as well represented as the Tang in the number of artists or objects of art.

For the pre-Tang period, the *Calligraphy Catalogue* includes an extraordinary number of calligraphies by Wang Xizhi and Wang Xianzhi, but then falls off very rapidly. Only three calligraphers had more than ten works, and only eight had four or more:

TABLE 7.1. Artists and items in the *Xuanhe Calligraphy Catalogue* (by period and script type)

	Two Wangs		other pre-Tang		Tang		Five Dynasties		Song		Total artists		Total items	
	Artists	Items	Artists	Items	Artists	Items	Artists	Items	Artists	Items	no.	%	no.	%
emperors 帝王			1		8		3				12	5%		
seal script 篆書					4	9			3	9	7	3	18	1%
clerical script 隸書					1	6					1	0%	6	>1%
regular script 正書		9	5	7	34	73	8	11	10	27	57	23%	127	10%
running script 行書		72	23	37	41	191	11	26	11	125	86	35%	451	37%
cursive script 草書	2	251	38	68	30	223	3	7	5	8	78	32%	557	46%
bafen script 八分書					4	10					4	2%	10	1%
gov. documents 制詔誥命						41		10					51	4%
Total artists	2	1%	67	27%	122	50%	25	10%	29	12%	245	100%		
Total items	332	27%	112	9%	553	45%	54	4%	169	14%			1220	100%

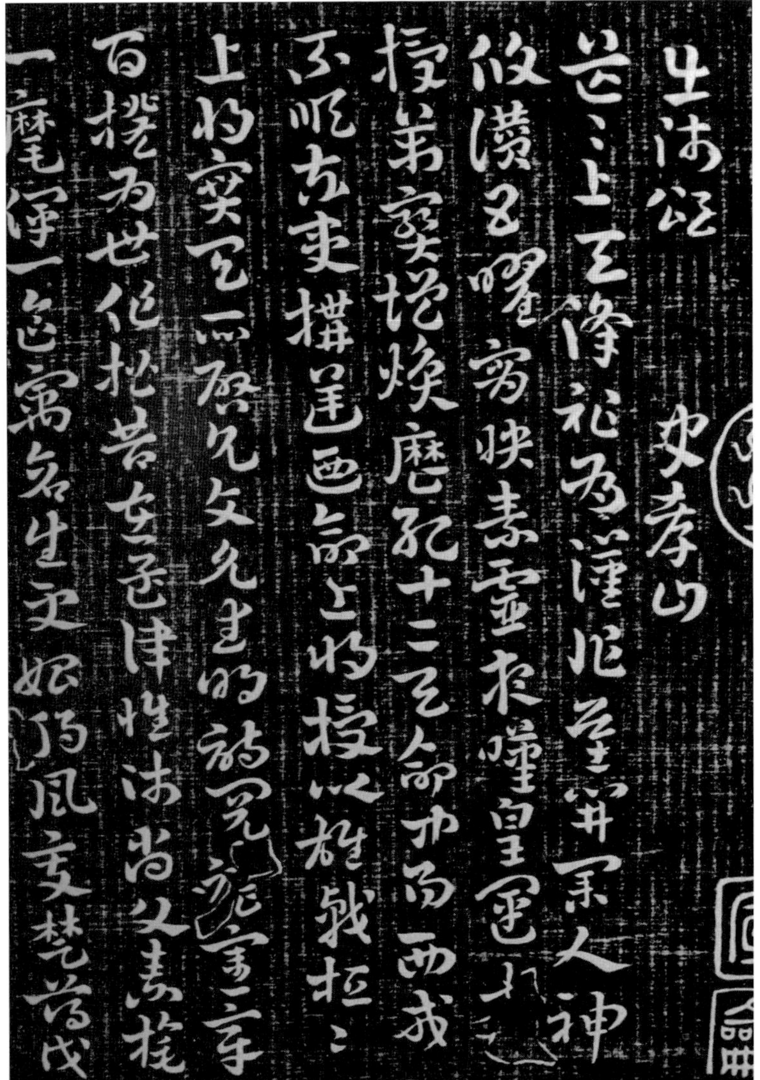

FIG. 7.3
Suo Jing (239–303), rubbing version of *In Praise of Going Out to Study with a Teacher* (*Chushi song*), from *Linsu yuan fatie* (1892). The original of this calligraphy was in Huizong's collection. Not only is it listed in Huizong's calligraphy catalogue but Huizong's seals are reproduced in the rubbing. After Nakata 1977–95 1: plate 12.

Wang Xizhi	王羲之	243
Wang Xianzhi	王獻之	89
Zhiyong	智永	23
Tao Hongjing	陶弘景	6
Suo Jing	索靖	4
Wang Huizhi	王徽之	4
Wang Yi	王廙	4
Wang Qia	王洽	4

Nearly half the items in the catalogue were Tang works, with 122 artists represented. In terms of number of works included, Huizong's favorites were as follows:

Huaisu	懷素	101
Ouyang Xun	歐陽詢	40
Yan Zhenqing	顏真卿	28
Emperor Xuanzong	唐玄宗	25
Zhang Xu	張旭	24
Emperor Taizong	唐太宗	14
Yu Shinan	虞世南	13
Wu Cailuan	吳彩鸞	13
Chu Suiliang	褚遂良	11
Liu Gongquan	柳公權	11
Xue Daoheng	薛道衡	11
Li Yong	李邕	10

The greater number of items per artist for Tang than earlier periods need not reflect a greater admiration for Tang calligraphers; more likely it reflects the greater availability of these works (the relatively small size of the collection of Song calligraphy will be discussed below in terms of cultural politics).

The calligraphers included in Huizong's catalogue can be compared to the many lists of eminent calligraphers that had been compiled since the early fifth century, when Yang Xin made a list of sixty-nine calligraphers from the Qin through the Eastern Jin dynasties, categorized according to the scripts they excelled in. Over the next century, further lists were made by Wang Sengqian, Wang Yin, and Yu Jianwu.[25] The last list ranked 123 calligraphers from Han to Liang times into nine grades, with Zhang Zhi, Zhong You, and Wang Xizhi the only ones ranked in the highest grade. The second grade had five calligraphers, the third nine, the fourth fifteen, and so on.[26] Although quite a few leading calligraphers were on all four of these early lists, the lists were by no means identical, and sometimes some of the shorter ones have calligraphers not included on longer lists. In the first century of the Tang, Li Sizhen took the idea of classification a step further and added a tenth rank at the top, called the "untrammeled class" (*yipin*). At the same time, he was more selective, reducing the list to eighty-two names, even though it covered an additional century. One of the most ambitious lists was compiled by Dou Ji, who wrote a *Rhapsody on Calligraphy* (Shushu fu), which characterized in verse 207 calligraphers from ancient times until Suzong's reign (756–62) in the Tang.[27]

Although these lists were undoubtedly still consulted in Huizong's time (and most of them had been included in Zhu Changwen's late-eleventh-century compendium of texts on calligraphy, *Mochi bian*), they were largely superseded by the fuller treatment of Zhang Huaiguan, who in 724–727 wrote the three-chapter *Calligraphy Standards* (Shuduan).[28] Chapters two and three of Zhang's book divide calligraphy into ten scripts, then assign calligraphers to the "inspired" (*shen*), "subtle" (*miao*), and "talented" (*neng*) categories under each script type. After the listings, brief characterizations of each calligrapher are given, with longer entries for those ranked highest. Altogether 174 calligraphers were ranked, but many are ranked more than once, as one might be talented in one script and subtle in another. Zhang's work, however, only covered calligraphers through the first century of the Tang. In the generation before Huizong, Zhu Changwen wrote a continuation of it, titled *Continued Calligraphy Standards* (Xu Shuduan). It brought the list and ranking to the middle of the eleventh century, adding sixty Tang and twenty-four Song calligraphers. By Zhu Changwen's time there was also an implied list in the form of the 76 pre-Tang and 14 Tang calligraphers whose works were included in the *Chunhua Model Letters.*

How does the *Xuanhe Calligraphy Catalogue* compare to these earlier works as a list of eminent calligraphers? None of the Tang or earlier lists was the catalogue of a collection, so it was possible for them to list early calligraphers whose works did not survive, something Huizong's curators could not do. Thus, of the couple dozen Qin and Han names found in the early lists, Huizong's catalogue includes only one, Zhang Zhi. For the Jin and Southern Dynasties, earlier lists were also considerably longer. The *Calligraphy Standards* lists ninety-seven calligraphers, of whom only thirty are in Huizong's catalogue. The *Chunhua Model Letters* had calligraphy by fifteen rulers of the pre-Tang period, only one of whom was included in the *Xuanhe Calligraphy Catalogue.* Of the forty-one Jin dynasty calligraphers in *Model Letters*, only twenty-four were also in the *Xuanhe Calligraphy Catalogue.*

Certainly a major reason Huizong's list of pre-Tang calligraphers was much shorter than those of the *Model Letters* and the *Calligraphy Standards* was that by his time connoisseurs doubted that there were any authentic works extant by many of the great names. For the Tang, however, Huizong and his curators were more successful in gathering items by those ranked highly by earlier authorities. The list of Tang calligraphers in the *Xuanhe Catalogue* is much shorter than the list in the *Calligraphy Standards* and *Continued Calligraphy Standards* combined, but it does include all but one of those ranked in the higher two grades ("inspired" and "subtle").[29]

At the other extreme, Huizong, like many collectors in other times and places, wanted to have at least one item by every famous calligrapher. More than 40 percent of the artists given entries (103 out of 245) are represented by a single work. It is easy to imagine that those who chose the calligraphy to be included in the catalogue often selected the best work they had of each famous artist, even if the best one was still not especially good (or even of doubtful authenticity).

The authors of the *Xuanhe Calligraphy Catalogue* employed a wide range of evaluative standards. They shared Sun Guoting's contention that successful calligraphers leave the rules behind as their hand responds automatically to their heart, and Zhang Huaiguan's view that those who create their own style are more worthy of praise than those who merely replicate an existing style faithfully. But an attitude that Egan identifies as distinctly Song—praising a calligrapher or a piece of calligraphy for its "ancientness"—was also very common.[30]

Although some have proposed that Mi Fu was a major influence on the shape of Huizong's calligraphy collection, the catalogue includes quite a few calligraphers that Mi Fu disparaged. Mi Fu called the calligraphy of the Tang emperor Xuanzong "fat and vulgar" and lamented its influence in his day. He criticized the Tang calligrapher Xu Hao and the early Song calligrapher Shi Yannian for forcing all of their characters to be the same size. He also wrote negatively of the wild cursive scripts of Zhang Xu and Gaoxian. Yet all of these men are treated as excellent calligraphers in the *Xuanhe Catalogue*.[31]

What about Huizong's antipathy toward Su Shi and his circle? Did the editors of the catalogue consciously or unconsciously try to counter their critical influence? It is true that they included quite a few calligraphers that Su Shi had denigrated. Su Shi called the calligraphy of Li Yu exceptionally weak. Su also did not like the work of the early Song calligrapher Li Jianzhong, concerning whom he wrote, "At the beginning of our dynasty Li Jianzhong had a reputation for being a talented calligrapher, but the character of his calligraphy is mean and turbid, continuing the wasted and lowly spirit that had been perpetuated since the late Tang."[32] Su also criticized another earlier Song calligrapher, Zhou Yue, for writing cursive slowly and painstakingly. Huang Tingjian criticized the calligraphy of Ouyang Xun, Chu Suiliang, and Xu Hao as "too restrained by methods and principles."[33] On the other hand, the authors of the catalogue by no means argued against all of Su Shi's views. Not infrequently when they mentioned "critics" they were referring to Su Shi or

Huang Tingjian.[34] In other words, rather than argue against Su's and Huang's opinions, the authors of the catalogues made them seem like widely shared attitudes.

At the same time it should be recognized that most Song criticism of calligraphy was implicitly concerned with the issue of which calligraphers or pieces of calligraphy one should use as models in one's own calligraphy practice, not which pieces of calligraphy were worth collecting for other reasons. Scholars with small collections of original calligraphy may have looked on each piece as a potential model. The palace collection, with over a thousand pieces, had different purposes. Certainly Huizong did not acquire only pieces that he wanted to copy or which he thought would make good copying material for his many sons. Rather he aimed at a comprehensive collection, one that went as far back in history as possible, covered all styles and script types, and had works by all the major masters, not just those that Huizong personally used as models. For the pre-Song period, the compilers of the catalogue tried to be inclusive, to include artists that at least some critics liked, whether or not others dismissed them. Huizong's may be the first such comprehensive collection in Chinese history.

All considered, the accomplishment of Huizong's agents and curators in shaping the collection represented by the catalogue is impressive. Agents located large numbers of works, which the curators winnowed stringently—rejecting a large majority of the pieces in the case of the most famous artists. Not only did the curators reevaluate many of the works that Huizong had inherited from earlier emperors, but they infused the collection with hundreds of new pieces. Many works that had been in private hands in the late eleventh century entered the palace collection. By the time the catalogue was completed, the palace had a collection that was both broad and deep, with especially remarkable coverage of the Tang period. They did this with constant changes in personnel at the Palace Library and without narrowing their scope to a few periods or artists, but rather aiming at a broad collection spanning a period of nearly a thousand years.

The Connoisseurship of Huizong's Curators

How good was the connoisseurship of Huizong's curators? This question is probably best approached by distinguishing the two sides of connoisseurship: detecting fakes and recognizing great works.

The catalogue does not have a preface or any explicit statement that it contains only original works. Did the curators think that the 243 pieces of calligraphy listed in Wang Xizhi's entry were all originals? Or did they list works they believed to be faithful copies when they had concluded that no original existed? The evidence can be read both ways. First, there is the fact that 243 is such a large number. Only eighty-four of the calligraphies could have come from the collection Taizong had assembled in the early Song, if those with the same titles as pieces in the *Chunhua Model Letters* are in fact all the same pieces (and not other versions of the same title). It is true that in the early seventh century, Tang Taizong's vigorous search had turned up 2,200 pieces of calligraphy attributed to Wang Xizhi, but Chu Suiliang gave his full approval to only 266 of them.[35] It seems implausible that Huizong's agents had located almost all of them, especially given that Mi Fu described seeing only twenty-three, less than half of which he considered originals.[36]

On the other hand, Huizong's curators certainly did reject many attributions to Wang Xizhi. They did not include the most famous of Wang Xizhi's pieces, the *Preface to the Orchid Pavilion Poetry Collection*, presumably because they knew that the original had been buried with Tang Taizong, and that therefore all extant versions were copies. Moreover, they excluded three-quarters of the pieces in the *Chunhua Model Letters* and more than half of the twenty-three works by Wang mentioned by Mi Fu. One plausible explanation of this conflicting evidence is that some of those working on the catalogue thought that good copies of early works belonged in the catalogue and others did not.

We know something of how the winnowing was done. Chapter 4 cited Gaozong's description of the procedures followed in his father's day to try to assure that copies were identified as such. When calligraphies arrived at the palace, the responsible officials sorted them into originals and copies. The originals were further graded, with those of lower grades kept in the Palace Library, and those of higher grades in the inner palace, where they were remounted and impressed with Huizong's collector seals.[37] Chapter 5 cited Huang Bosi's reference to calligraphy in the palace collection that was labeled either "imitation" or "fake." He also reported that there was a group of works that the curators had concluded had all been done by a single person at the court of Li Yu in the tenth century, which had since been labeled "imitation calligraphy" as distinct from copies and authentic works.[38]

Still, one must admit that many copies escaped the detection of Huizong's curators. Appendix 3 lists extant pre-Song calligraphies considered by scholars today to be important works. It includes twelve items attributed to Wang Xizhi, all of which are now regarded as copies (even if faithful, early copies).[39] In the case of the set of three letters mounted together called *Ping'an, Heru, Fengju tie*, in the collection of the National Palace Museum in Taipei, the use of a microscope allows one to see traces of the "outline and fill" technique used by the copyist (see fig. 7.4). Because no originals survive, copies of Wang Xizhi's calligraphy are today evaluated largely according to the skill of the copyist. For instance, the modern expert Shen Fu describes the copyist of *Xingrang tie* (fig. 7.5) as masterful and praises his ability to reproduce the slightest irregularities in the original and to capture differences "in

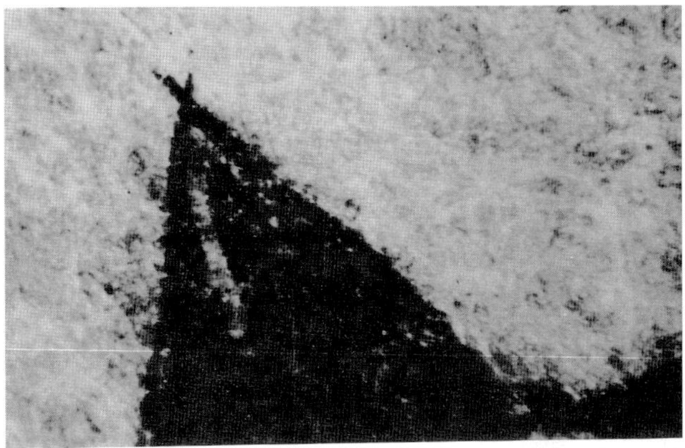

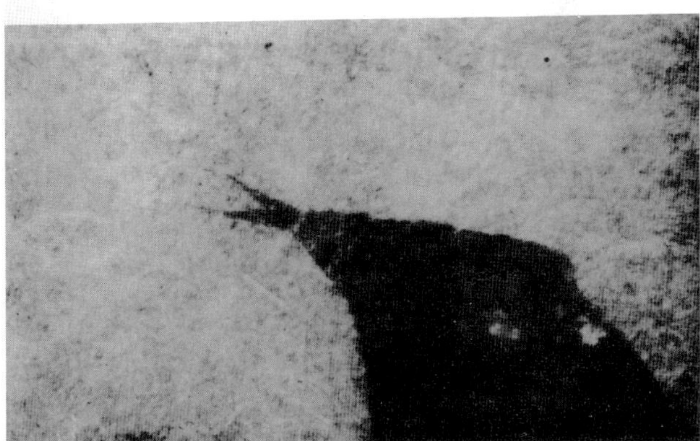

Fig. 7.4
Magnification of tips of two characters in Wang Xizhi, *Ping'an, Heru, Fengju tie.* National Palace Museum, Taiwan, Republic of China.

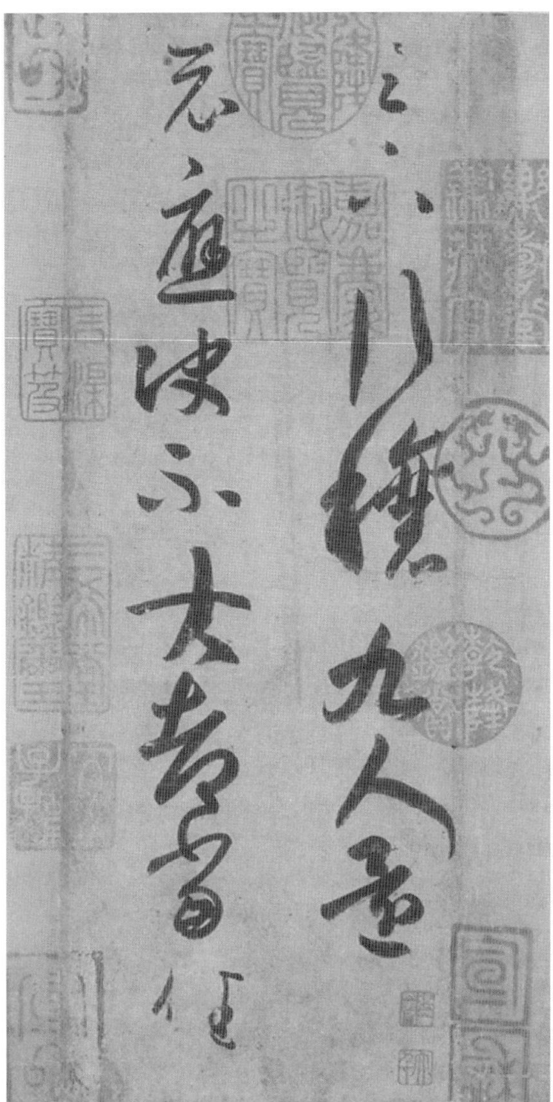

Fig. 7.5
Wang Xizhi (309–ca. 365), *Xingrang tie*. Letter mounted as a handscroll, ink on paper, letter alone 24.4 × 8.9 cm. Princeton University Art Museum.

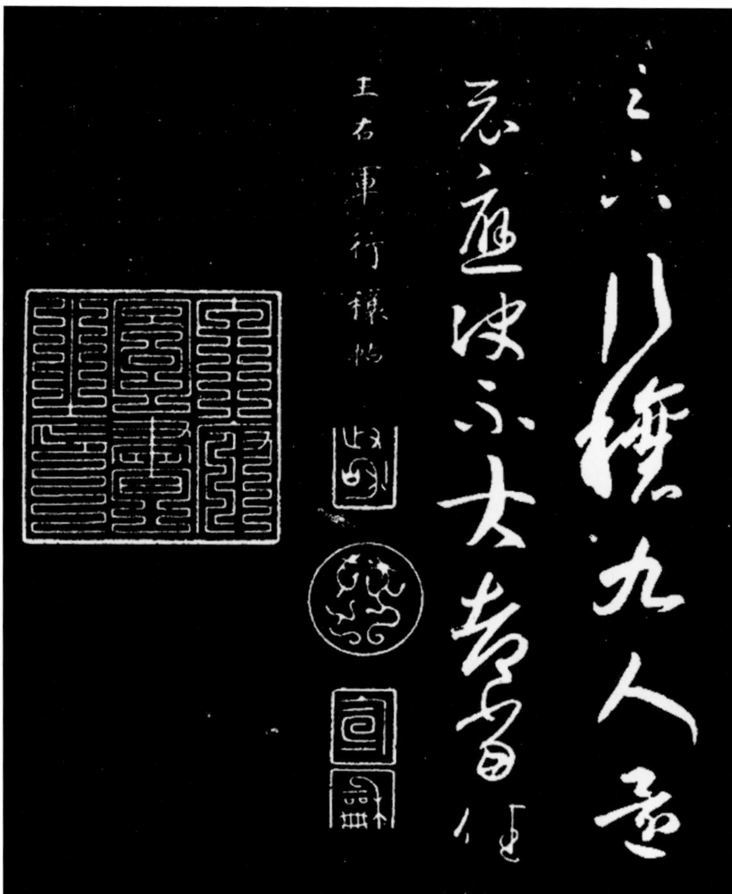

Fig. 7.6
Rubbing of Wang Xizhi (309–ca. 365), *Xingrang tie*, in Qianlong's *Sanxi tang fatie* (SXTFT). Four of Huizong's seals are placed after the title of the work, moved from their normal position (cf. fig. 7.5).

pressure, speed, or slant of the brush." Robert Harrist writes that the copy "recreates the buoyant, energetic flow of Wang's characters, which seem fully three-dimensional and are enlivened by constant changes in thickness in the brushstrokes that resemble twisting wire."[40]

Of course, it is anachronistic to expect Huizong's curators to be able to detect copying to the degree that modern scholars using powerful magnifying lenses can. Even centuries after Huizong, leading connoisseurs accepted works that had once been in Huizong's collection that today we know are copies. For instance, Dong Qichang, one of the most highly respected Ming connoisseurs, acquired the *Xingrang tie*, wrote colophons on it, and let a friend reproduce it. In the eighteenth century, this piece entered the collection of the Qianlong emperor, who in 1747 had a rubbing of it included in his *Model Calligraphies from the Hall of Three Rarities* (Sanxi tang fatie, see fig. 7.6).[41]

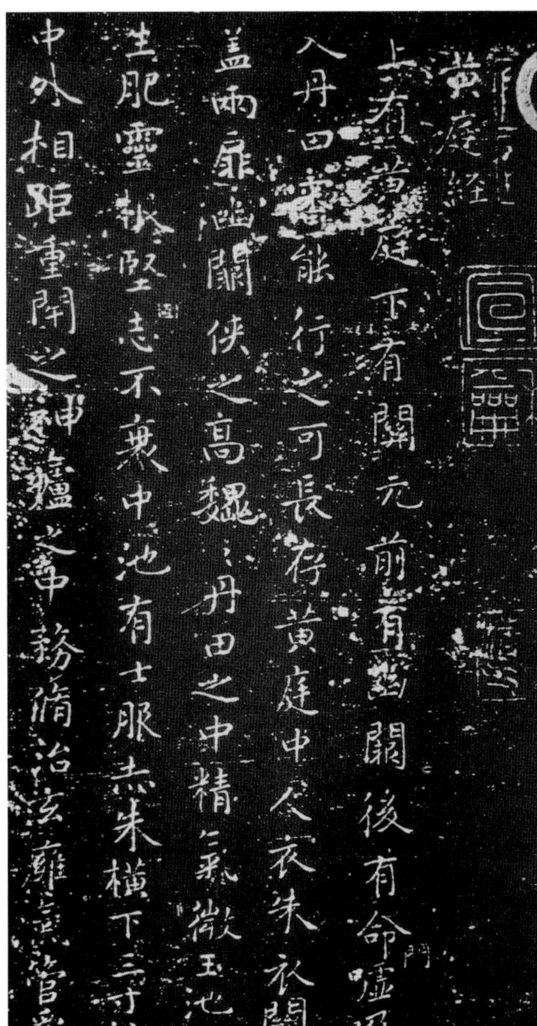

Fig. 7.7
Rubbing of Wang Xizhi (309–ca. 365), *Classic of the Yellow Court* (detail). From *Yuqingzhai tie*. Notice the linked Xuan and *he* seals below the title. They are unlikely to have been in this position on the paper original, but were moved to make the rubbing more compact.

How good were Huizong's agents and curators at spotting masterpieces? Appendix 3 distinguishes works listed from works not listed in Huizong's catalogue. Generally speaking, those familiar with Chinese calligraphy would agree that the works listed in the catalogue are at least as good as, and in many cases clearly better than, the works not listed. For instance, of the twelve "important" works by Wang Xizhi in the appendix, the seven that were listed in Huizong's catalogue as a group are more frequently discussed as good examples of Wang Xizhi's work than the five that were not listed in his catalogue. This would be even more true if we added works that had been in Huizong's collection but are today known only through rubbings (which, in the case of Wang Xizhi, would include the *Yellow Court Classic*, *On Yue Yi*, and *Wang Lue tie*; see fig. 7.7).[42]

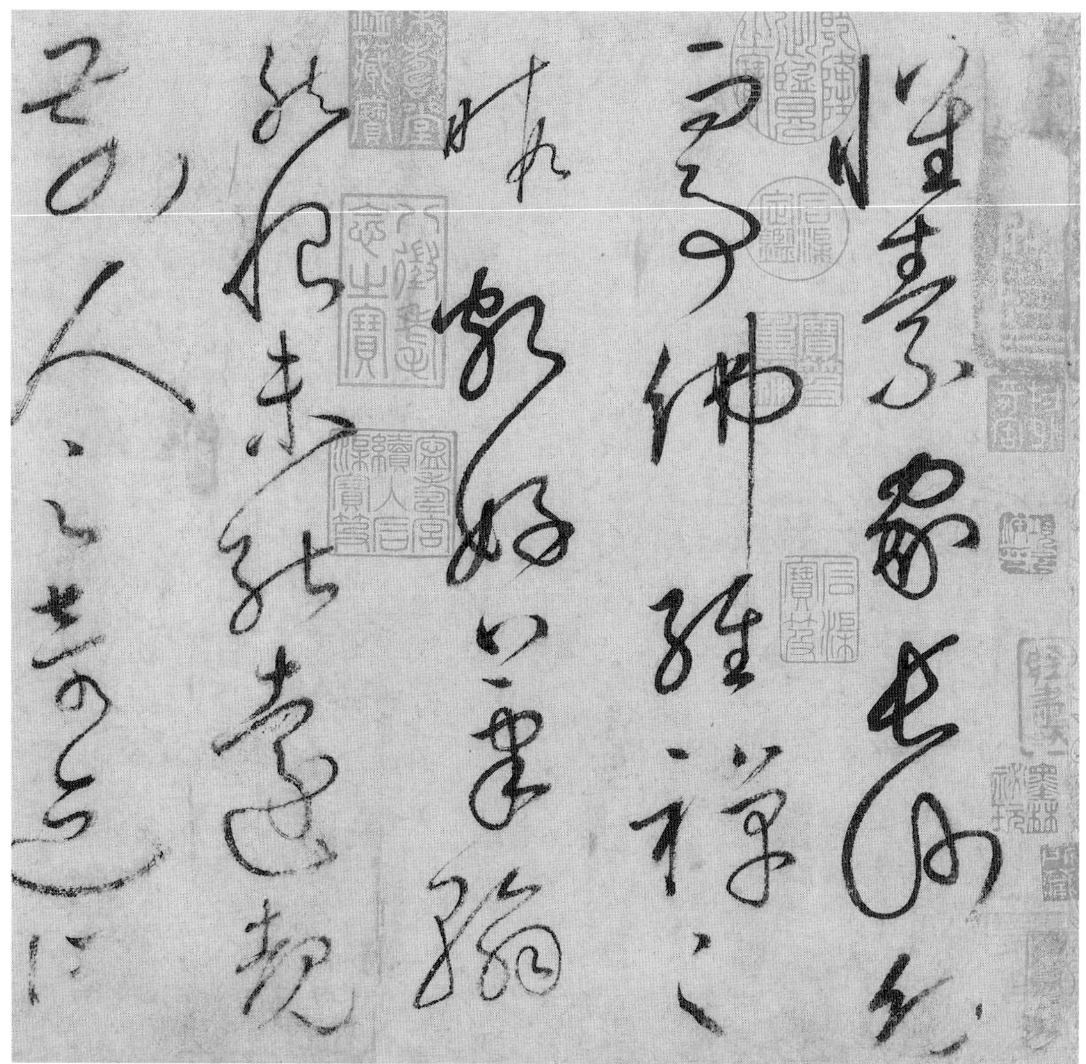

The Two Wangs should perhaps be considered a special case, since by Huizong's time calligraphers had been making copies of their writings for seven centuries. Huizong's collection of Tang calligraphy also holds up well. As can be seen in appendix 3, of thirty-five pieces of Tang calligraphy that are today highly regarded, over half (twenty) were listed in Huizong's catalogue. There are scholars who consider particular items on this list to be copies rather than originals.[43] Still, the list includes many of the works most valued today, including Huaisu's *Autobiography* (fig. 7.8) and Yan Zhenqing's *Draft Eulogy for His Nephew.*[44]

Neither of the last two works have Huizong's seals on them (compare appendix

2). Since we know that Gaozong had Huizong's seals cut off paintings before his own were put on, and it seems likely that the Jin emperor Zhangzong did as well,[45] there is a strong possibility that works listed in Huizong's catalogue with either Gaozong or Zhangzong seals were in fact the same objects that had once been in Huizong's collection (and there is no reason to think that the trimming of old seals was limited to these two emperors).

The institutional context in which Huizong's curators worked should be kept in mind in assessing their work. Working in the Palace Library would have made research easier but connoisseurship more problematic. Because several men could be assigned to search through relevant writings, the catalogue's authors could draw on more varied sources in their entries than could independent scholars like Zhu Changwen. But judgments about the quality or authenticity of works would have been constrained by political realities. Like collectors in other times and places, Huizong undoubtedly preferred positive reports on his objects to negative ones. Men like Zhai Ruwen, Huang Bosi, and Dong You could probably cast doubts on works newly acquired by eunuch agents before they were shown to Huizong, but would have avoided dismissing objects they knew Huizong liked. If they knew Huizong wanted a particular artist represented in the catalogue, or was proud of the depth of the collection on a certain calligrapher, they probably considered it prudent to make compromises with their own judgments, much the way curators in modern museums try to avoid offending major donors. Mi Fu recorded his doubts about many of the objects he saw in friends' collections, but he does not seem to have told his hosts to their faces what he thought of their treasures. No one would have expected Huizong's curators to be bolder.

Fig. 7.8
Huaisu (725–782+), *Autobiography* (detail). Handscroll, ink on paper, 28.3 × 755 cm. National Palace Museum, Taiwan, Republic of China. In the eleventh century more than one version of this work was in circulation, so, although listed in Huizong's calligraphy catalogue, this surviving version may not be the one Huizong owned.

Writing Entries

After decisions were made about which calligraphies to include in the catalogue, the compilers had to prepare entries. Probably they began by assembling dossiers on each artist, copying out what had been written about him by earlier authors. Most entries include critical comments, some of which are marked with phrases like "critics have said." The modern Japanese translators of the catalogue identified numerous cases of this sort.[46] The work most cited is Zhang Huaiguan's *Calligraphy Standards*, cited over twenty times, and next are Dou Ji's *Rhapsody on Calligraphy* and Yuan Ang's *Ancient and Modern Evaluations of Calligraphy.*

To demonstrate that the catalogue entries do not deserve their reputation for being mostly derivative, let me show how two entries were put together. For Huaisu, one of Huizong's favorite calligraphers, the authors could draw not only on Zhu Changwen's entry in *Continued Calligraphy Standards*, but also on poems by several

Tang poets, a biography written in Tang times by Lu Yu (732–804), and Huaisu's own writings, especially his *Autobiography*, which they had in the collection in Huaisu's own hand. The source closest in time to the *Xuanhe Catalogue* would be the entry in Zhu Changwen's book, which can be translated as follows:

> The monk Huaisu (styled Zangzhen) was a native of Changsha. He said of himself that he had attained the Samadhi of cursive script. In the beginning he worked hard at copying and made a grave to bury his old worn-out brushes.[47] He once looked at the summer clouds transforming as they moved, which led to sudden enlightenment.[48] Afterwards, his work became marvelous, like a strong knight wielding a sword, moved by spiritual forces.[49] Yan [Zhenqing] once wrote, "Formerly Zhang Xu's actions led people to call him Crazy Zhang; now Huaisu's behavior leads people to call him Wild Monk. Can anyone deny that the one's wildness is a continuation of the other's craziness?"[50] Famous people promoted him in this manner.[51]

Much of Huaisu's entry in *Continued Calligraphy Standards* is drawn from earlier authors. The authors of *Xuanhe Calligraphy Catalogue* drew on many of the same stories, but added further evaluations and anecdotes:

> The monk Huaisu (styled Zangzhen), whose secular family name was Qian, was a native of Changsha. He moved to the capital, where he became a disciple of Xuanzang "Tripitaka."[52]
>
> At first Huaisu studied monastic rules, then later he concentrated on calligraphy. He so continuously copied previous models that worn-out brushes were piled up like a grave mound. One summer night he saw the clouds floating with the wind and was suddenly enlightened about the meaning of the brush. He himself said he had attained the Samadhi of cursive script.[53] It is thus clear that he could focus his mind and concentrate his spirit. Contemporary celebrities such as Li Bo, Dai Shulun, Dou Ji, and Qian Qi all wrote poems to praise his work.[54] Such comparisons as "as vigorous as a stunned snake, a running viper, a sudden shower, and a wild wind" are not exaggerations.[55] Critics also said, "Zhang Changshi's writing is crazy, while Huaisu's is wild. Can anyone deny that the one's wildness is a continuation of the other's craziness?"[56]
>
> In his old age Huaisu's calligraphy advanced further, and critics declared that he was in an endless competition with Zhang Zhi [for status as the sage of cursive script].[57] Assessments of him only became more and more favorable. Research reveals that drinking often inspired him.[58] He then liked to see his characters fly and his curving strokes become mysterious as though they had their own souls, much to others' admiration.[59]

Comparing these two accounts shows that Huizong's authors kept four of the six statements by Zhu Changwen, corrected his inaccurate citation of Yan Zhenqing, and introduced a new error by checking for Huaisu in the *Song Biographies of Eminent Monks*. They also doubled the length of the entry by adding other statements, drawn from such sources as Tang poetry, Huaisu's *Autobiography*, Mi Fu's colophons, and Lu Yu's biography of Huaisu. In this way they expanded considerably the proportion of the entry that can be considered evaluation rather than biography.

The second example is the account of the early Song calligrapher, Song Shou (seen in chapter 3 as a book collector). Because Song Shou was a high official, a draft biography of him would have been available in the History Office. Zhu Changwen also had given him a brief entry:

> Song Shou (styled Gongchui) served in the Hanlin Academy under Zhenzong and participated in an exemplary way in the Council of State during Renzong's reign. He was particularly skilled in brushwork. Since the beginning of our dynasty those who discuss calligraphy have praised him along with Li Jianzhong.[60]

The entry on Song Shou in the *Xuanhe Calligraphy Catalogue* is much fuller, especially on his calligraphy:

> The civil official Song Shou (styled Gongchui), a native of Zhao, rose to vice grand councilor and was given the posthumous title Xuanxian. His deeds and achievements are well documented in the histories. Shou was refined and had a powerful memory. He once took the examination for novices and recited the *Lotus Sutra* for ten days without omitting a word. It would seem that his inborn nature was way beyond that of ordinary people.[61]
>
> Shou's calligraphy was highly esteemed in his day and he himself also liked it. When working [as a drafter] in the Hanlin Academy, he never wrote a stroke without carefully preparing and he preserved every draft he made because he wanted his calligraphy to be passed down to later generations along with his writings. He practiced the small regular script, which was impressively neat and followed the style of [Wang Xizhi's] *Yellow Court Classic* and *On Yue Yi*. During the Tiansheng and Mingdao reign periods (1023–33), Empress Dowager [Liu] Zhangxian Mingsu, hearing of Song's talent for calligraphy, ordered him to transcribe the *Thousand Character Essay* in regular script as an aid to Renzong's education. Song Shou's transcription of this text in the collection is in fact the one kept today in Heavenly Emblems Pavilion. This paved the way for Song Shou's later service to Renzong as grand councilor.

> The only two figures excelling in calligraphy in the early years of our dynasty were Li Jianzhong and Song Shou. Li's writing was thick, heavy, and turbid; contemporaries therefore sometimes criticized it for continuing the degenerate style of the Five Dynasties.[62] However, there has been no unfavorable criticism of Song. Rather it was said of him that his calligraphy was rich in technique, slender and delicate, but not weak, to the extent that even the ancient calligraphers could hardly compete with him.[63] Critics also remarked that while other calligraphers failed in balancing the left and the right halves of a character—which would be either withered or too slender—Song could lay out both perfectly.[64] Only a calligraphy adept finds this easy to do.[65]

The *Xuanhe Calligraphy Catalogue* entry owes virtually nothing to the biography of Song in the *Song History*.[66] It expands on Zhu Changwen in part by adding an anecdote about Song Shou's youthful ability to memorize (from Ouyang Xiu), but much more by expanding the discussion of his calligraphy. The authors compare Song Shou favorably to a somewhat earlier calligrapher, Li Jianzhong, juxtaposing negative comments Su Shi had made about Li to positive ones Huang Tingjian had made about Song Shou (without, of course, mentioning either Su or Huang by name).[67] The authors also cite another source (that does not seem to survive) on his skills in balancing the left and right sides of characters.

In a fair number of cases, the authors of the *Xuanhe Calligraphy Catalogue* had no biographical information about a calligrapher. In those instances, they used the piece of calligraphy to make inferences about the man.[68] Practically all they knew about a monk calligrapher named Yingzhi was what they could infer from the two pieces in the collection. The authors observed that Yingzhi used the style of Liu Gongquan, then proceeded to compare him unfavorably to Liu, commenting at the end that Yingzhi's piece allowed one to appreciate Liu's comparative excellence.[69] In the case of a man from the Southern Dynasties named Chen Shuhuai, the only source for understanding him was the single piece of calligraphy in the collection titled *Plum Blossoms*. From this they were willing to speculate that he was a man of the Huai or Jiangnan area, as plum trees were common there. In addition, because of the connections between literary and calligraphic expression, the editors were willing to see Chen as a sensitive man. They generalized, "In times past, whenever a man wrote something it was always based on his feelings coming forth. Once he felt them in his heart, his hand would respond without him being conscious of it."[70]

Negative evaluations are not rare in the catalogue, but are limited mostly to lesser-known figures or are placed in other people's entries. Consider, for instance, the entry for Li Xiaoyuan, who lived in the early Tang period:

> There is no record of Li Xiaoyuan's career, but his calligraphies were often seen in later periods, so he seems to have been someone with a reputation for calligraphy in his day. Xiaoyuan enjoyed doing cursive script calligraphy in the style of the monk Yaqi. Yaqi was highly regarded in Tang times, and students of calligraphy without deep knowledge often modeled themselves on him. They did not realize that from the time when the Wang Xizhi and Wang Xianzhi styles declined, only Zhang Xu did cursive in a way that attained marvelous passages by learning the rules but then leaving them behind. The decline of calligraphy really began with Yaxi. Since Xiaoyuan is a follower of Yaqi, it makes sense that he concentrated on being untrammeled like the wind and the clouds and moving with nearly no pauses. This is the style that the vulgar adore, but it cannot escape the condemnation of those who understand calligraphy.[71]

This entry not only denigrates its subject, Li Xiaoyuan, but is very harsh toward Yaqi, the monk whose style Li Xiaoyuan employed. Yaqi is treated much more positively in his own entry, where he is said to have attained Zhang Xu's brushwork.[72] One cannot rule out the possibility that the different views of Yaqi reflect sloppy editing, but there are enough cases of harsher judgments being placed in other people's entries to think that this was a purposeful strategy, reflecting a common practice of the compilers of the dynastic histories.

The Catalogue as a Narrative of Calligraphy's Development

When Huizong's curators and editors began work on the calligraphy catalogue, they must have known that they were attempting a more comprehensive treatise on calligraphy than anyone had in centuries. Like Zhang Huaiguan, the author of the *Calligraphy Standards,* Huizong's authors related the history of calligraphy in terms of the development of script types. However, as the table below shows, the stories told by the two works differ in significant ways. The *Xuanhe Catalogue* distinguished fewer script types, was less inclined to see them as having been invented by particular people, and disagreed on such particular facts as the dates of Wang Cizhong and the period when the *bafen* script appeared.

The *Xuanhe Catalogue*'s introductions to script types trace their historical development. The introduction to seal script begins this way:

> Seal script originated in the distant past. The ancient tadpole script already appeared on bronze and stone antiquities such as cauldrons and libation cups. Ancient script is often pictographic and not well developed as a writing system. After tadpole script was abandoned, the large seal script gained currency. It was invented by Shi (Historian)

TABLE 7.2. Origins of script types in two works

Calligraphy Standards		*Xuanhe Calligraphy Catalogue*	
Script type	Founder/period	Script type	Founder/period
ancient script	Cang Jie/high antiquity	seal	gradual
large seal	Shi Zhou/W. Zhou		
Zhou script	Shi Zhou/W. Zhou		
small seal	Li Si/Qin		
bafen	Wang Cizhong/Qin		
clerical	Cheng Miao/Qin	clerical	Cheng Miao/Qins
		regular	Wang Cizhong/E. Han
zhang cursive	Shi You/W. Han		
running	Liu Desheng/E. Han	running	Liu Desheng/E. Han
flying white	Cai Yong/E. Han		
cursive	Zhang Zhi/E. Han	cursive	lots
		bafen/Tang	gradual

> Zhou. Zhou was the official historian during the reign of Xuan [r. 827–782 BCE] in the Zhou dynasty. His calligraphy still survives on the Stone Drums. The large seal script is also named "Zhou script" or "historian's script" after its inventor.[73]

In this opening, Huizong's editors offer a distinctly different narrative than Zhang Huaiguan had offered some three centuries earlier. They make no mention of the mythical inventor of writing, Cang Jie. They were aware of the evolution of early scripts visible on inscribed ancient bronzes and did not give credence to the idea that one man had invented writing. They did credit large seal script to Shi Zhou but did not distinguish two scripts that Shi Zhou had invented, arguing that one script was referred to by two different terms:

> As for the small seal script, it follows the basic method of the large seal script but abbreviates some of the strokes. The founding father of the script was [the Qin prime minister] Li Si. However, if we examine *Cursing Chu*, done during the [much earlier] reign of Duke Mu of Qin [r. 660–621 BCE], we see that it was already written in small seal script, so it would seem that the small seal script was developed in ancient times without anyone inventing it, and that Li Si simply claimed authorship. In fact, when the Qin unified the realm and Prime Minister Li Si proscribed all types of script differing from Qin's, if writing at that time had included no scripts other than the ancient

> writing and the large seal script, what would have been the point of Li Si making a different small seal script? Moreover, after Li Si, there was Xu Shen in the Han dynasty and Wei Dan in the Wei dynasty whose stylish calligraphy continued ancient traditions and made them famous in their day.[74]

In this passage, although the editors admit Li Si's status as the patriarch of the small script, they devote more space to undermining the meaning of that label, saying that the script had clearly existed before Li Si as one of many scripts before the unification of scripts under Qin, and that other calligraphers also played important roles in establishing the script. Moreover, they cite the evidence of *Cursing Chu,* an inscribed stone discovered during the Northern Song and discussed in Ouyang Xiu's *Collected Antiquities,* which dated well before Li Si.[75] Next they brought the story to more recent times:

> Truly the appearance of the Li Si style of seal script was good for calligraphy, and during the thousand years from Han and Wei through Tang, several masters appeared. During the three hundred years of the Tang dynasty, the greatest figure was Li Yangbing, who wrote exceptional seal script and called himself Cang Jie reincarnate. Looking at his writing, one can admit that he truly did not bring shame on the ancient masters. In the Five Dynasties, the pretender Li Yu of the Southern Tang held an area south of the Yangzi River, his authority as slight as a feather. Yet [at his court] there was the calligrapher Xu Xuan, who wrote such elegant and "ancient" seal script that people's opinion of the script changed. It is a fact that the rise or fall of seal script has depended on the emergence of masters. Today both Prince Yiduan Xian and Zhang Youzhi are famous for their seal script, each bravely establishing his own style.[76]
>
> Below we list seven figures from Tang on, none of whom was put in just to fill the space and all of whom were talented. As for Mengying and his followers who acquired reputations in later periods by inventing strange scripts—such as the "bending leek seal script" said to have been made [in Shang times] by Wu Guang the Immortal—scholars despise their fantastic characters and they are not included here.[77]

In the concluding section of this introduction, the editors argue for the significance of individual masters to the history of the script, but more for their role in maintaining interest in it as an art than as founders. They also hint at the processes involved in drawing up the list of artists to include under seal script by mentioning a group purposely left out: those like the early Song monk Mengying who went too far in striving for originality.[78] One possible scenario is that Huizong himself said something negative about Mengying. If Huizong, looking over a list of artists to be included, said not to include Mengying because he went too far in inventing new scripts, the authors would have felt bound to explicitly exclude him.

The introductions to the other scripts follow this general format. The account of the clerical script presents two alternative theories of when and how the script was created, both of which were also found in *Calligraphy Standards*. Like Zhang Huaiguan, the cataloguers doubted the view first expressed in the *Annotated Classic of Rivers* (Shuijing zhu) that the inscribed coffin of a Zhou lord proved that clerical script dated back to Western Zhou times.[79] They again placed more emphasis on the appearance of masters of the script than on its original invention, and saw the two key masters as Cai Yong and Zhong You, whose styles could still be seen through rubbings of stone inscriptions.[80]

The opening line of the introduction to the regular script asserts its modernity: "The evolution of scripts reached a high point with the clerical script, which still had something of the ancient to it. The regular script has nothing ancient about it."[81] The cataloguers associate the creation of the script with a man named Wang Cizhong, whom they dated to the Eastern Han period, specifically 76–83 CE. *Calligraphy Standards* had credited Wang Cizhong with the invention of a different script, the *bafen* script, but had accepted an alternative account of him, which made him an immortal who presented the script to the First Emperor of Qin. The *Xuanhe Catalogue* strongly rejects that interpretation, largely on the grounds that it came from the tradition of stories of the strange and fantastic, not from historical sources. Again, more emphasis is placed on the masters who brought the script to perfection. Here attention is drawn to Zhong You, specifically to one of his pieces in the palace collection, and to Wang Xizhi, whose two masterpieces, *On Yue Yi* and *Classic of the Yellow Court*, were in the collection. Thus, even though Wang Xizhi's entry is in another section of the catalogue (cursive script), his role in the development of regular script is not neglected.[82]

The introduction to the running script presents it as developing to fill the gap between the constrained regular script and the free cursive script. The authors did not dispute the *Calligraphy Standards* account of Liu Desheng inventing the script in the Han, but put more emphasis on the role of his key followers, Zhong You and Hu Zhao, who respectively developed the slender/tense and the fat/heavy versions of running script. Wang Xizhi and Wang Xianzhi were seen as the culmination of the development of the script, bringing it to its full potential. Still, they noted, the collection included examples by dozens of men who had excelled in the script in subsequent dynasties.[83]

The introduction to the cursive scripts gets somewhat bogged down in discussing the meanings of the terms used to refer to the script, in both its earlier form, called *zhang cao*, and its later form, simply called *cao*. The authors argue against those who date the script to the Qin period, and instead linked it to Emperor Zhang (r. 75–88) in the Eastern Han period.[84] They cite many views of the meaning of *cao*, and contend that those who saw it as meaning "draft" were closest to the truth. After listing key figures whose works were in the collection, the authors mention that they were deliberately excluding men like Zhong Yi who wrote in a debased version of the copyist style (*yuanti*) of the late Tang.[85]

The introduction to the *bafen* script takes a strong stance on the mistakes of earlier scholars:

> There are many theories about the *bafen* ["eight-part"] script. One is that in the Eastern Han period Wang Cizhong of Shanggu transformed clerical script into regular script, then transformed regular script into *bafen*. This is the theory of [the Tang author] Cai Xizong.[86] Another theory is that it refers to the fact that it rejected eight tenths and took two tenths from clerical script, and rejected two tenths and took eight tenths from small seal script. This is the view that Cai Yan claimed was held by her father Cai Yong. In prior generations, those fond of calligraphy were all familiar with these texts. Yet, all of the inscriptions that survive from the thousand years from Han to Tang are in seal, clerical, running, or cursive script, never *bafen*. It is not until the Tang period that *bafen* became prominent. It was modeled on the clerical script but changed to be more square and broad, with its wave shape neither ancient nor strict. Most likely this occurred in Tang times. Du Fu wrote the "Song on the *Bafen* Style," which prominently mentions Li Chao, Han Zemu, and Cai Youlin, all of whom were masters of the Tang period. Moreover, all pieces extant today are from the Tang period. In that case, what were Cai Xizong and Cai Yan talking about? In all likelihood, the meaning of the terms has changed since their day. What we today call regular script, in olden times was called clerical. What we today call clerical, in olden times was called *bafen*. In Tang times, people made a new script from clerical and called it *bafen*. Thus what was called *bafen* in Tang times is not what was called *bafen* in olden times. Now the palace collection of *bafen* calligraphy includes works by four men, Zhang Yanyuan, Bei Lenggai, Yu Senghan, and the monk Linggai. These four are all men of Tang times, which supports the view that modern *bafen* began in the Tang. We needed to clarify this for the sake of later generations.[87]

This introduction clearly shows the authors of the catalogue reading what earlier scholars had written, but thinking through the issues themselves and offering their own interpretation of the stages and connections of the scripts. There is nothing intrinsically implausible about changes in the meanings of the terms used to refer to scripts. For instance, Zhang Huaiguan used *li* ("clerical") to refer to what others in his day called regular script.[88]

The introductions to script types were not the only places the authors of the *Xuanhe Calligraphy Catalogue* discussed the history of calligraphy. The biographies of individual masters provided the editors with many opportunities to expand on their explanations of how calligraphy had developed. For instance, several entries help explain the mechanics of the spread of Wang Xizhi's style. The entry for the Tang monk Yuanya discusses the importance of a composite work used for copy material: "Since Emperor Wu of the Liang had Zhou Xingsi write out the *Thousand Character Essay* by reordering a thousand words from Wang Xizhi's calligraphy, this text has been commonly used for practice material, and Zhiyong made 800 transcriptions of it."[89] The entry for the early Tang monk Huairen, after discussing his commitment to mastering the Wang Xizhi style, discusses Huairen's role in spreading the style through another composite work: "Two versions of [Tang] Taizong's *Preface on the Sagely Teaching* circulated, one in Chu Suiliang's calligraphy, one done by Huairen by assembling characters in running script copied from Wang Xizhi's works." Both versions, we are told, were used by later students as models to copy from, but Huairen's was more successful in conveying the otherworldliness of Wang's style.[90]

Cultural Politics of the Catalogue

Because the palace was not nearly as constrained by resources as private collectors were, a list of objects in its collection could be taken to define the canon of great artists or objects. Moreover, so long as the list did not seem eccentric, it had the potential to revise the canon. Huizong exploited this potential; he used his power of list-making to promote some artists and downgrade others.

The political side of acts of inclusion, exclusion, and sequencing is more evident in the calligraphy catalogue than in the antiquities catalogue. Of most interest here are the choices that bear most directly on the relationships between the throne and the educated class. These include the treatment of rulers as calligraphers, the ways calligraphic excellence is linked to standing as a literatus, the inclusion of Buddhist and Daoist clerics, and the identification of individuals close to the court as the Song dynasty's best calligraphers.

RULERS AS CALLIGRAPHERS

Beginning in the Southern Dynasties, rulers had played an important role as connoisseurs and promoters of the art of calligraphy, and some took to ardent practice of the art themselves. Both Zhang Huaiguan and Zhu Changwen had discussed emperors as calligraphers and promoters of calligraphy before treating other calligraphers, a precedent Huizong's editors adopted. The first chapter of the *Xuanhe Catalogue* covers twelve rulers, as summarized in table 7.3.

The entries for rulers express recurring themes. Strong personalities have strong calligraphy. Calligraphy should in no way be associated with bookish men; some of the best calligraphers were men with real military talents and accomplishments. Similarly, a passion for calligraphy need not interfere with devotion to successful management of government affairs. Indeed, some of the best calligraphy by emperors is found in the comments they wrote on the memorials submitted by their officials. On the other hand, despicable rulers (the one example is Emperor Taizu of Liang) not surprisingly had poor calligraphy.

Emperor Taizong of the Tang has the longest and the most exuberant entry. His contribution to quelling the disorder of the end of the Sui is compared to that of the founders of the ancient Shang and Zhou dynasties. Once peace was achieved Taizong put his mind to calligraphy. By commissioning agents to search out Wang Xizhi's works, he acquired 2,200 of them and in his spare time would copy them. He had an attractive humility about his own ability as a calligrapher and studied with major masters, first Yu Shinan, then Chu Suiliang. Taizong wrote essays on calligraphy and once compared his own approach to calligraphy to his approach to battle tactics. Besides Wang Xizhi's styles, he practiced flying white and once gave pieces he had done in it to the high officials he was entertaining. He allowed calligraphy in his collection to be taken out to aid the education of calligraphers-in-training at his court. Eight of the fourteen pieces by Taizong in Huizong's collection were edicts, mostly in running or cursive script. None of these survives as an original, but one of the letters that had earlier been included in the *Chunhua Model Letters* later was included in Huizong's collection (see fig. 7.9). From it, Taizong's debt to Wang Xizhi is evident.

Empress Wu may have caused some wavering on the part of the cataloguers. Although one earlier work on calligraphy had listed her, it had concentrated on her good deed of returning the Wang family's album of calligraphy by twenty-eight ancestors after having it carefully copied.[91] Huizong's editors certainly knew that history had condemned Empress Wu as a usurper and linked the negative evaluation of her to her perverse insistence on using alternate forms of nineteen common characters (all included in the entry as an aid to those reading stelae from her period). On the other hand, they admitted finding her calligraphy attractively forceful (albeit unfeminine).[92]

Huizong's collection had more works by Xuanzong than by any other ruler. In the entry, the authors gave him credit for reviving the *zhang* cursive script and the *bafen* script. To bolster their high evaluation of the emperor as a calligrapher, they extensively cited the opinions of earlier critics:

> With regard to his pieces such as *Notes on Zhang Jiuling's Memorial, Poem Granted to Pei*

TABLE 7.3. Rulers with entries in the *Xuanhe Calligraphy Catalogue*

Ruler	Listed in earlier works?[1]	Number of items in each script type				Comments from entry
		regular	running	cursive	clerical	
Jin Wudi 晉武帝 (r. 265–290)				2		Unified the country, and his calligraphy reflected his valor and strength. But love of calligraphy could not compensate for political mistakes, which set the stage for later political failures (1.1–2).
Tang Taizong 唐太宗 (r. 626–649)	SD, XSD, SSF, CHGT	1	9	4		Due much of the credit for Tang military and political successes. Once the realm was at peace, he applied himself to calligraphy, and expended great sums to acquire works by Wang Xizhi. He took as a teacher Yu Shinan, who carried on the Wang Xizhi tradition via his study with the monk Zhiyong. After Yu died, he appointed Chu Suiliang, who authenticated Wang Xizhi's works for him. Taizong was good at flying white and gave some of his pieces in it to his top officials. He promoted the study of calligraphy at court, to great effect. His own calligraphy was superb (1.2–3).
Tang Xuanzong 唐玄宗 (r. 712–756)	SD, SSF, XSD		21		4	An accomplished ruler, he devoted his spare time to literature and calligraphy. Dissatisfied with the conventional court styles, he began writing in the *zhang* cursive and *bafen* styles. His calligraphy was praised as vigorous and imposing (1.3–4).
Tang Suzong 唐肅宗 (r. 756–762)			7			Performed heroically during the rebellion, selecting good generals and saving the dynasty. Under his father's influence, he became a fine calligrapher in several scripts (1.4–5).
Tang Daizong 唐代宗 (r. 762–779)			7			Intelligent with a good memory, he carried on the family tradition in calligraphy. His brushwork, while not as good as Taizong's or Xuanzong's, still had attractive traits (1.5–6).
Tang Dezong 唐德宗 (r. 779–805)			1			A quick learner, Dezong proved an attentive ruler who promptly commented at length on his officials' memorials in flowing calligraphy. His running script was particularly good (1.6).

(r. 846–859)						personnel decisions and wrote out edicts himself. During his day major calligraphers continued to appear, and imperial clansmen perpetuated the devotion to calligraphy initiated by Taizong (1.6–7).
Tang Zhaozong 唐昭宗 (r. 888–904)			1			Intelligent and fond of calligraphy, he tried to curb the regional warlords and restore Tang power. His determination can be seen in his one piece of calligraphy in the collection (1.7).
Tang Empress Wu 唐武后 (r. 689–705)	SSF		1			Although a woman of impressive abilities, Empress Wu missed the chance to go down in history as a worthy consort when she usurped the throne. Her egotism and love of calligraphy led her to invent strange forms for nineteen characters that people had to use during her period of domination. A descendant of Wang Dao submitted twenty-eight of his ancestor's calligraphies, which she had copied. She used the copies for practice material, leading to a vigorous running script, much like a man's (1.7–8).
Liang Taizu 梁太祖 (r. 907–912)			1			His inelegant, mediocre calligraphy reflected his despicable character as a man who rebelled against the Tang, then accepted office under it, only to usurp the throne and search vainly for signs that he was responding to a mandate from Heaven (1.8).
Liang Modi 梁末帝 (r. 913–923)			1			An attractive and cultivated man who served as an official during the Tang and associated with Confucian scholars. Not long after his father founded the Liang dynasty, he succeeded to the throne, but had no talents other than calligraphy. His calligraphy in the style of the Two Wangs was better than that of most court calligraphers (1.8–9).
Zhou Shizong 周世宗 (r. 954–959)			1			Able military commander who intimidated his rivals and expanded the Zhou realm. His brushwork reflects his military valor (1.9).
Total		1	53	6	4	

1 The abbreviations used here are SD = *Shuduan;* SSF = *Shu shu fu;* CHGT = *Chunhua ge tie;* XSD = *Xu Shuduan.*

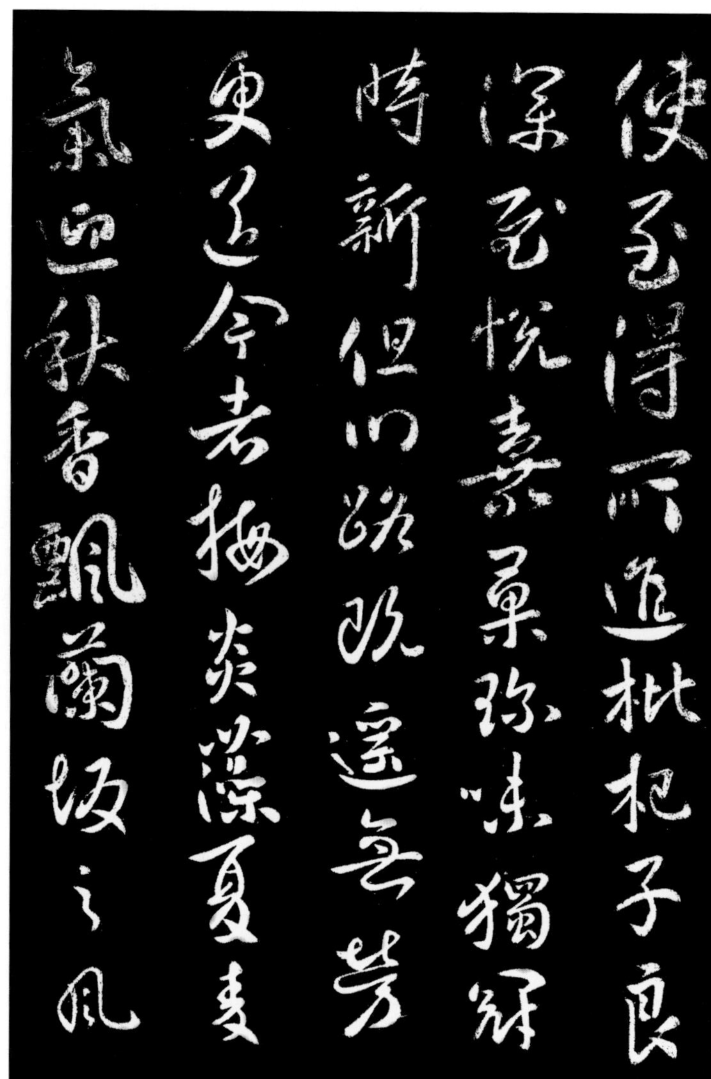

FIG. 7.9
Rubbing of Tang Taizong (r. 626–649), *Pipa tie*. Rubbing from *Chunhua Model Letters* (CHGT). The paper original on which the rubbing was based was one of the fourteen pieces by Tang Taizong in Huizong's collection.

Yaoqing, Edict on "Fine Guest," and *Appreciation of the Five Princes,* critics described them as luxuriant and bold, features generated from his own genius.[93] As for the *bafen* script pieces such as the *Stele for the Ritual Hall at the Northern Capital* and the *Stele for Enfiefing the Spirits at the Eastern Marchmount* [not in Huizong's collection but known through rubbings], although their transmission is based on the copies made by contemporary scholars, much of the original style remains. Dou Ji referred to Xuanzong's calligraphy in his *Rhapsody on Calligraphy*: "His vigorous and magnificent style is outstandingly inscribed on stelae. His ideas bubble up like a spring issuing forth

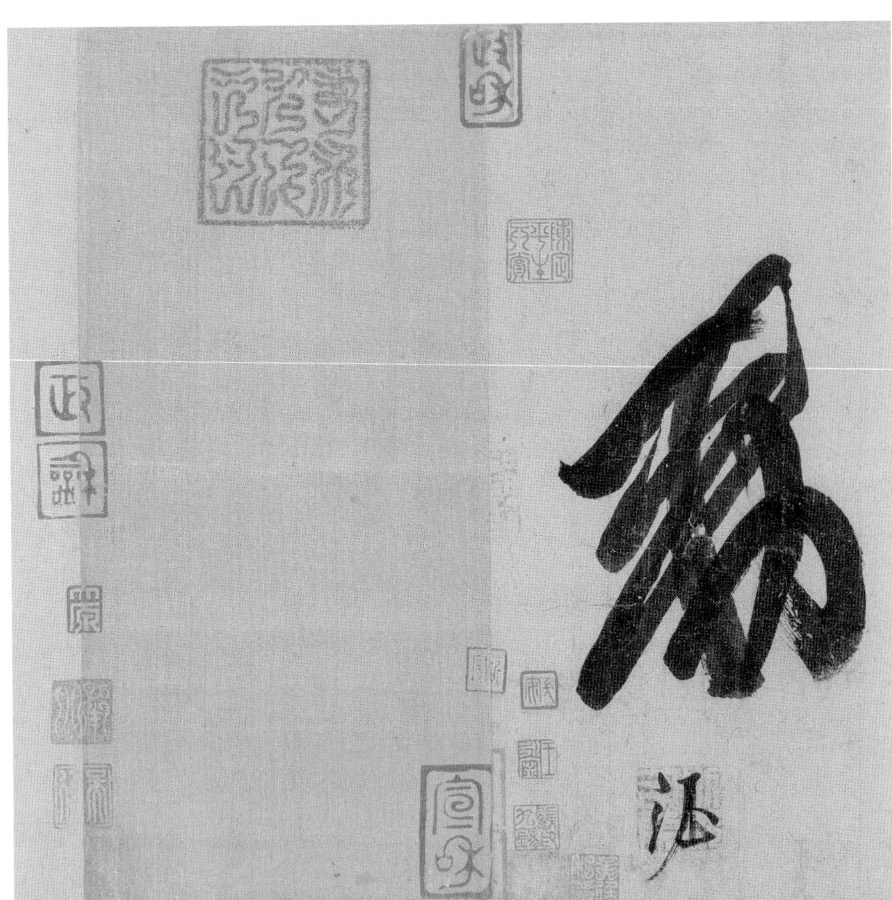

Fig. 7.10
Tang Xuanzong (r. 712–756), *Ode to the Pied Wagtails* (detail). Handscroll, ink on paper, 24.5 × 184.9 cm. National Palace Museum, Taiwan, Republic of China. This is the concluding section. The large character, *chi*, means "decreed." Below it is the cipher that Xuanzong used to sign his works, made up of the two characters of his personal name.

> phoenixes; his brushwork resembles the sea swallowing a whale."[94] Such comments aptly describe Xuanzong's great achievements in calligraphy.[95]

One of the twenty-five pieces of Xuanzong's calligraphy listed in the catalogue is still extant (see fig. 7.10). Held by the National Palace Museum in Taipei, it is the transcription of a rhapsody Xuanzong had written on a type of bird (the pied wagtail). The text celebrates Xuanzong's congenial relations with his five brothers, with whom he enjoyed spending his leisure time. On one occasion when they were partying, thousands of pied wagtails had landed on trees in the palace, which he took as an auspicious omen. Xuanzong's calligraphy, in running script, is bold and fluid, in the tradition of the Two Wangs. The characters vary in size, with no fixed number of characters per line. The work is marked at the beginning, end, and each seam with a seal reading "Kaiyuan," the name of one of Xuanzong's reign periods. This

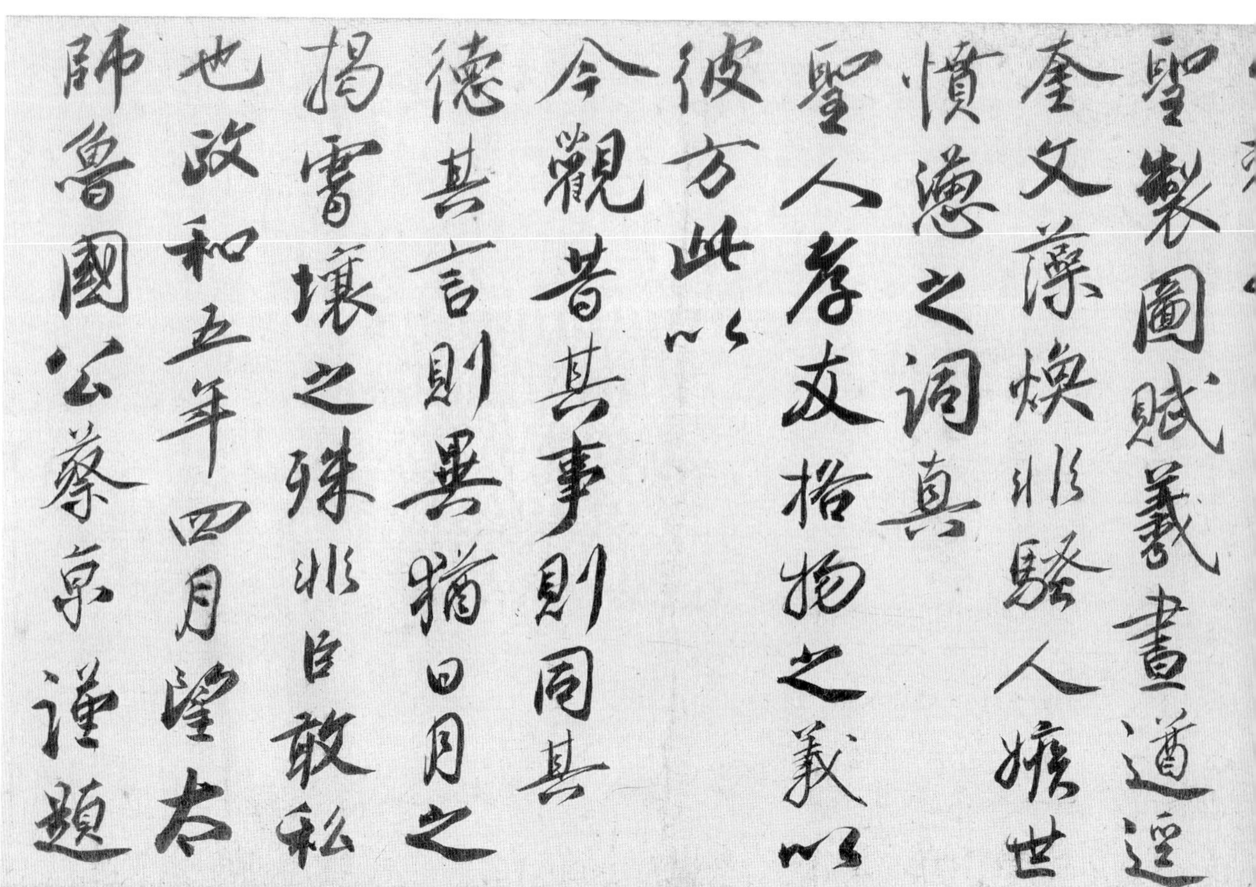

Fig. 7.11
Cai Jing (1047–1126), colophon to Xuanzong's *Ode to the Pied Wagtails* (detail). National Palace Museum, Taiwan, Republic of China. In the colophon, dated 1115, Cai Jing tells Huizong he compares positively to Xuanzong in the Tang.

piece had been in private hands in Ouyang Xiu's times, and Mi Fu had also seen it, so most likely it entered the court collection during Huizong's reign.[96]

It is easy to imagine that Huizong would have found this piece of calligraphy personally meaningful, as he also had several brothers whom he would entertain in the palace and he also was intrigued by the auspicious implications of flocks of birds descending on the palace. Attached to the calligraphy are two colophons, one written by Cai Jing and the other by his brother, Cai Bian, with Cai Jing's dated 1115 (fig. 7.11). Since Cai refers to himself in the colophon as "your subject" (*chen*), Huizong most likely asked Cai Jing to write the colophon after they looked at the piece together. Cai Jing's colophon states that the reign of Xuanzong is considered the height of Tang, and this piece among his best calligraphy, and yet it is not as good as a painting and rhapsody recently done by Huizong on the same subject of brotherliness. Cai Bian, too, uses his colophon as an opportunity to flatter Huizong,

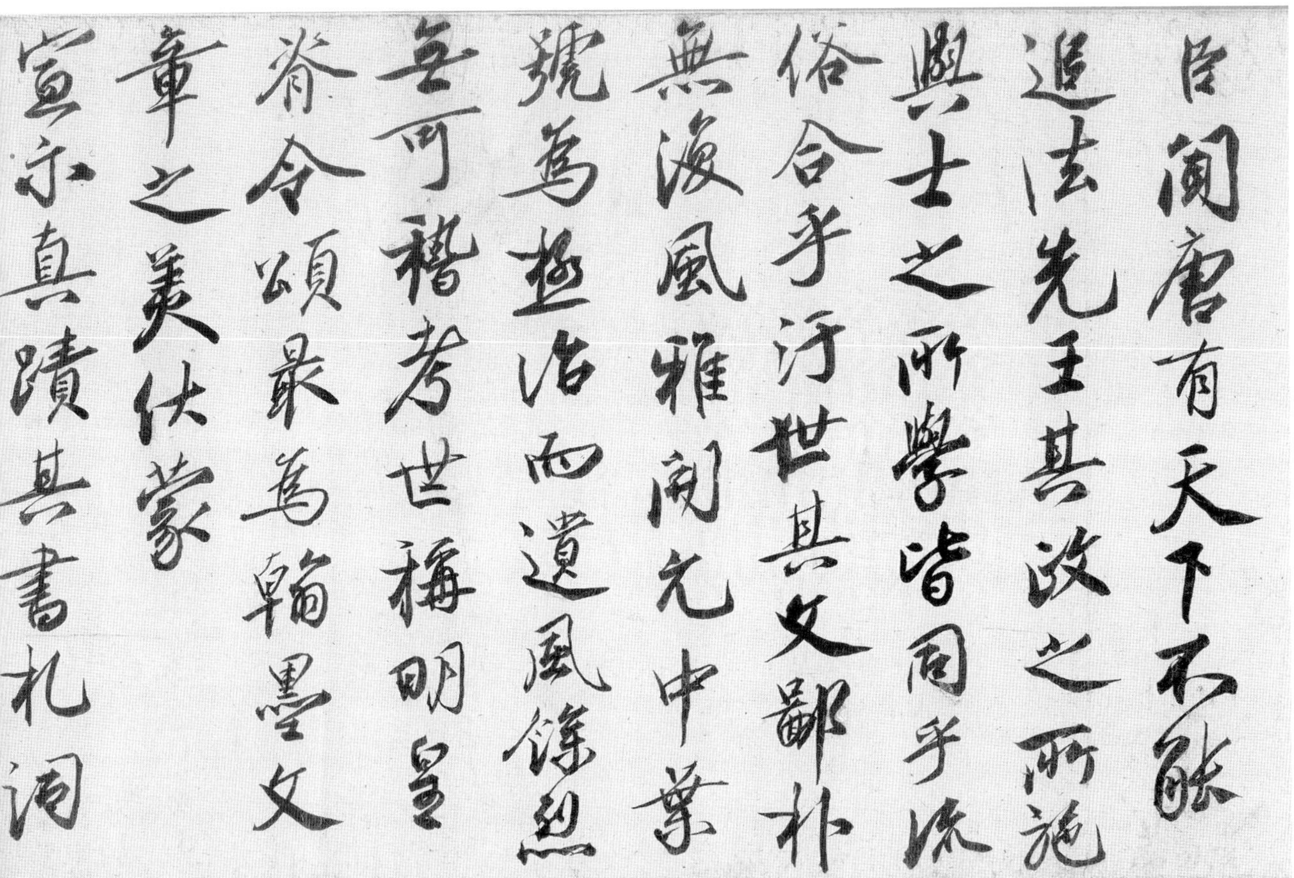

mentioning a time when tens of thousands of wagtails had gathered in his palace. The painting and poem he made to commemorate it, Cai Bian says, are more impressive than Xuanzong's.[97]

It was not solely in the special chapter on rulers that the catalogue's authors cited the role of Tang rulers in fostering calligraphy. For instance, the introduction to clerical script mentioned the contribution Xuanzong made when he commissioned a forty-chapter compendium of clerical script out of concern that knowledge of the script was dying out. In the entry for the Tang monk Linggai, the authors added the comment that because Xuanzong encouraged his officials to study the *bafen* style, the style flourished: "What the ruler likes, his subordinates will carry to extremes." The introduction to the section on government documents credits the general excellence of Tang calligraphy to the Tang rulers' support of culture, to "Taizong paying attention to the study of scripts," to his successors continuing these policies, and to the many leading officials who were expert calligraphers.[98] The entry for Lin Zao, a Tang man otherwise unknown, associated his ability as a calligrapher to the period in which he lived:

> For the three hundred years of the Tang, calligraphy flourished. Even students, when they lowered their brushes, produced work worth looking at. The calligraphy of the Tang began with Taizong establishing the Institute for Advancement of Literature as an educational institution. In that age practice was honored and flourished. Even later literati who pursued their own styles were all successful in their own way.[99]

Ouyang Xiu and other Northern Song literati frequently referred to the Tang as a flourishing age for calligraphy, much better than their own.[100] Huizong's authors gave the Tang emperors credit for the greatness of calligraphy in their day.

CONNECTING CALLIGRAPHY TO MORAL CHARACTER AND LITERATI TRADITIONS

Despite the prominent place given to rulers, in no sense does the catalogue downplay the connections between calligraphy as an art and the scholarly and literary traditions of the literati. Over and over again entries refer to the connections between a man's calligraphy and his learning, character, and political or literary achievements. It was because men were successful as literati that they were successful as calligraphers. Some examples from less-well-known calligraphers can be used to illustrate this.

The entry on the Tang official Li Xi begins by noting that after entering officialdom through the examinations he rose to the high post of prime minister. His family had collected books and he himself liked to write commentaries and was called a true Confucian minister. The success of his calligraphy was explained this way:

> In general, highly learned Confucian scholars do not write even a dot that is common. Their ability to conform to the rules of calligraphy comes naturally from the quality of their minds. When someone works hard at calligraphy but his style is weak or vulgar, the fault lies in the quality of his mind, not in his failure to master technique. Someone like Xi who pored over ten thousand books would never in his calligraphy emphasize the trivial aspects of technique, but would attain a resonance of spirit.[101]

The courage needed to take political stands was also seen to reveal itself in men's calligraphy. Pei Lin, a successful Tang official, is described as "fond of straightforward talk and pointed critiques in the manner of the loyal royal advisor." Even though his talents were not put to full use, people admired his sincere loyalty. It was because "his sincerity flowed to the tip of his brush that his brushwork was flawless and he achieved a natural and elevated resonance."[102]

The emotional sensibility needed to write good poetry was similarly seen as contributing to expressive calligraphy. The late Tang official Zhang Ji was a follower of Han Yu in literary matters and "all the worthy literati of the period competed to make friends with him." His poetry was the best among Han Yu's disciples, and the elegance of his calligraphy was simply the counterpart or other side of his literary abilities.[103] In another entry the authors generalize that when literature declines, as it did during the last decades of the Tang and the subsequent Five Dynasties, calligraphy deteriorates as well.[104]

There was nothing original about the sorts of associations that Huizong's editors made between the qualities that made a man admirable as a scholar and those that made his calligraphy admirable. As discussed earlier, these sorts of points had been made from the beginning of calligraphy criticism in China. But it is also worth noting that Huizong's editors do not take a narrow view of literati excellence. They saw many ways to be an admirable literatus, and all of them—Confucian scholarship, loyal political service, and literary talent—contribute to a man's calligraphy.

The belief that literary and calligraphic ability go together can also be seen in the large number of men known today primarily for their literary writings who were included as calligraphers, all but two of whom no earlier authority had listed as eminent calligraphers. These entries are summarized in table 7.4.

One of the pieces of calligraphy by these literary men survives, the transcription of a poem by Du Mu believed to be in Du Mu's own hand (plate 13). Now in the collection of the Palace Museum in Beijing, this work consists of a preface dated 835 and a set of poems. It is done in running script, with characters that vary considerably in size but are usually taller than wide, with many extended vertical strokes. While writing this piece, Du Mu gradually became looser and less restrained. Occasionally he continued using the brush after it was nearly out of ink, for a flying white effect.[105]

It is not at all unlikely that Huizong wanted calligraphy by famous men of letters more for the fame of the man than for the aesthetic appeal of his writing. That is, calligraphies were also autographs, valued for their connection to their author. Those who loved a poet's work could not own a poem of his but they could own a transcription of one of his poems in his own hand. The blurring of autographs and autograph calligraphy is clearest in the case of these famous writers, but would also have applied to emperors and anyone else who was famous independently of his standing as a calligrapher.

TABLE 7.4. Literary figures in the *Xuanhe Calligraphy Catalogue*

Name	Listed in earlier works?[1]	Number of items in each script type			Comments from entry
		running	regular	cursive	
Lu Ji 陸機 261–303			1	1	Born into an aristocrat family. His calligraphic ability was overshadowed by his genius in literature. For ten years he devoted himself to Confucian learning, and calligraphy was only a leisure interest (14.107–8).
Xie Lingyun 謝靈運 385–443	SD miao SSF			1	A nephew of Wang Xianzhi. His poetry is pure, fluent, and full of energy. He vividly imitated Wang Xianzhi's script to the extent that few people could tell the difference (16.128).
Shen Yue 沈約 441–513				1	A diligent historian, poet, phonetician, and calligrapher, especially skilled in cursive script. His bold calligraphy testified to the truth that the calligraphy of a learned man is never vulgar (17.130–31).
Li Bo 李白 701–762			2	3	Fond of sword play and drinking. Some called him an immortal. His poetry could almost rival that of Du Fu, the best poet of the Tang. When Emperor Xuanzong gave him an audience although he was a commoner, he came down the steps to greet him. He is famous not only in poetry but also in calligraphy and painting, in all three of which he had an especially free and flowing style (9.72).
Xue Tao 薛濤 768–831			1		A courtesan famous for her poetry. Whenever she wrote a poem, people eagerly passed it around. Her calligraphy is unfeminine, sturdy, and energetic, and at its best could capture the style of Wang Xizhi. She liked to transcribe her own verses, which were quite moving (10.82–83).
Bo Juyi 白居易			5		A talented official and perceptive writer, famous for his satiric poetry. He

772–846					remained tranquil during the ups and downs in his political life. Although most famous for his prose and poetry, his calligraphy and painting were also good. The depth of his mind is revealed through his brush. Those who view his calligraphy can imagine his spirit (9.75).
Yuan Zhen 元稹 779–831		1			An official who rose to grand councilor, Yuan Zhen's official essays changed the style of the time, as did his lyric poems. His regular script is elegant, flowing, and moving. His poems contain calligraphic rhythm, and his calligraphy has poetic traits. Both are expressions of his mind (3.26–27).
Du Mu 杜牧 803–852			1		After passing the exams and being recommended for his character, Du Mu served in both the provinces and capital. A man of integrity and courage, he dared to make political criticisms in front of the emperor. His poems are energetic and unconstrained, and his rhapsody on the Afang Palace admonishes in splendid language. His grand and vigorous running script is the other side of his literary performance (9.73–74).
Li Shangyin 李商隱 813?–858		1	1		After success in the exams, he attracted attention for his skill in writing memorials. Though somewhat away from his true mind, the calligraphy of his *Siliu Gaocao* is still beautiful and soars with energy (3.27).
Sikong Tu 司空圖 837–908			2		After passing the exams and serving in the central government, he withdrew to live in the mountains. His father had a screen with calligraphy on it by Xu Hao and impressed on Tu the connection between the man and his writings, once saying "A person with stern appearance must have a strong mind. When you look at someone's writings, you see what sort of a person he is." His excellent calligraphy reflects his integrity (9.76–77).
Su Shunqin 蘇舜欽 1008–1048	XSD		4	1	He had a majestic appearance, excelled in literary composition, and gained a reputation for political service and courage. His writings were highly expressive and his running and cursive script were classed by critics as subtle. His calligraphy was described as "as beautiful as blossoms in the imperial garden and the moon reflected on the Huai River" (12.91).
Total		2	17	7	

BUDDHIST AND DAOIST CLERICS AS CALLIGRAPHERS

Although the early stages of calligraphy as an expressive art were closely tied to the early stages of Daoism as a scriptural religion,[106] lists of eminent calligraphers written before Huizong's time rarely devoted much space to religious professionals as calligraphers (with the notable exceptions of the Sui monk Zhiyong and the Tang monk Huaisu).[107] In the late Tang period, Han Yu even questioned the capacity of Buddhist monks to become great calligraphers because great calligraphy depended on expressing strongly felt emotion, and monks practiced emotional detachment.[108] In Song times neither Zhu Changwen nor Mi Fu wrote much about clerics as calligraphers, even though there were many well-educated clerics in Song times, men who frequently interacted with literati and exchanged poems with them.[109]

Table 7.5 shows that Huizong's catalogue gave extensive coverage to Buddhist and Daoist clerics as calligraphers. Although Huizong was personally more attracted to Daoism than to Buddhism, this list of calligraphers has more Buddhists than Daoists, most likely reflecting the many Tang monks whose calligraphy had survived, particularly in cursive script. The catalogue itself credits Zhiyong and Huaisu for making cursive script popular among Tang monks.[110]

Both Buddhist and Daoist clergy were described very positively in the catalogue. A good example is the Daoist master Chen Jingyuan, mentioned in chapter 3 as a generous book collector. His entry mentions that he had been at court during Shenzong's reign and had exchanged poems with Wang Anshi and discussed calligraphy with Cai Bian. He not only copied over five thousand chapters of texts in his regular script (modeled on Wang Xizhi's), but was the author of a half dozen works on Daoism.[111]

In the entries for both Buddhist and Daoist clerics, we are repeatedly told that their ability to transcend the mundane world improved their calligraphy, much the way that scholarship, political integrity, and poetic talent enhanced the calligraphy of secular literati. In the entry for the Daoist priest Liang Yuanyi, for instance, we are told that his calligraphy reflected his concentration on purity and transcendence. The authors asserted that if one looked at his transcription of the *Inner Canon of the Supreme Elder*, which he had done in excellent small regular script, "one would know that people of the mundane world cannot reach the level of those who wander in the realms beyond."[112] Practicing calligraphy could also be a useful tool in attaining spiritual goals. The entry on the Tang monk Yuanya remarks on the powers of transcribing the *Thousand Character Essay*: "It is said that while learners govern their mind by reading the *Thousand Character Essay*, to transcribe it in calligraphy helps them harmonize their hands with their minds and therefore enter the realm of the Dao/Dharma."[113] Sometimes Daoist ideas are used to analyze the calligraphy of Buddhist monks. For instance, in the entry for the monk Xingdun, the authors explain that although he worked hard at the Wang Xizhi style, his success was limited because effort alone is not enough: "critics placed Xizhi's regular and running scripts in the inspired class. It was just like the skill of Cook Ding and the carving of Wheelwright Bian [both discussed by Zhuangzi]: the hand and heart are in accord and nothing can disturb them from outside. This is not something people can attain by assiduous effort."[114]

Although religious sensibility may have helped these men become outstanding calligraphers, the pieces in Huizong's collection by them were not scriptures. Only two of the Buddhist monks had even a single sutra transcription listed. Instead, the collection listed their poems and letters written in running or cursive script (sutras were usually transcribed in standard script). Even in the case of the Daoist clerics, where Huizong might have had more interest in the content, scriptures were rare.

THE CENTRALITY OF THE COURT IN SONG CULTURE

So far most of the discussion has focused on the pre-Song calligraphers listed in the *Xuanhe Catalogue*. One reason for this is that only about an eighth of the catalogue was devoted to Song calligraphers. Another, equally important, reason, however, is that the editors used different criteria in deciding whom to include in the catalogue the closer they came to their own time. Their selection of Song calligraphers seems to have been guided by the desire to demonstrate the cultural centrality of the Song court.

Zhu Changwen did not rate any Song calligraphers as "inspired," and only four as "subtle." These four were all later given entries in Huizong's catalogue. By contrast, only seven of the twenty Song calligraphers that Zhu ranked as "talented" are in the *Calligraphy Catalogue*. Most of those Huizong or his curators substituted lived after Zhu's time, but that is not the entire story. As table 7.6 shows, Song men who served in high court posts or had other connections to the Song court are especially well represented.

Several themes recur on this list of twenty-four men. Six served on the councils of state of Renzong, Shenzong, Zhezong, or Huizong. Four served in the Palace Library, the central government organ most closely associated with cultural accomplishment, indicating that while the men in question may not have had the political talent to serve in more substantive posts, the court recognized their literary talent and gave them appropriate appointments. Several did calligraphy for the emperor of the time. Two of the four religious clerics interacted with the court (the entries of the other two mention no connection with the court). Two were former

TABLE 7.5. Buddhist and Daoist clerics in the *Xuanhe Calligraphy Catalogue*

Cleric	Listed in earlier works?	Number of items in each script type					Comments from entry
		seal	regular	running	cursive	clerical	
Zhiyong 智永 Sui Buddhist monk	SD miao				23		A descendant of Wang Xizhi, he practiced calligraphy in the style of Wang, wrote with unrestrained vigor, and was skilled both in regular and cursive script, just like his ancestor. His works were in great demand. His versions of the *Thousand Character Essay* in regular cursive circulated widely and were regularly used as models for practice (17.135–36).
Huairen 懷仁 7th century Buddhist monk				1	1		Studied the calligraphy of Wang Xizhi for years, and made a copy of Tang Taizong's composition using Wang Xizhi's characters. Still, he never fully attained the inner basis of Wang's style (11.84–85).
Xingdun 行敦 8th century Buddhist monk				1			Wrote in running script on the model of Wang Xizhi. His calligraphy and paintings are alluring and conform to the rules, and look roughly similar to Wang's works; yet Wang's inner energy and spirit could never be captured by him even with his extreme efforts (11.85).
Huaisu 懷素 725–782+ Buddhist monk	CHGT, XSD miao				98		His spiritual concentration allowed him to gain insight into the cursive script, and many contemporaries praised him extravagantly. He often wrote after drinking, and was described as wild in his style (19.146–47).
Liang Yuanyi 梁元一 Tang Daoist priest			1				Reclusive by nature and detached from ordinary life. In his pare time saway from alchemy, he especially loved calligraphy. At first he studied the regular script of Zhong You and Wang Xizhi, and eventually was able to free himself from relying on their models. Yet his principles were rigorous, his spirit was unfettered, and his manner was lucid

					and pure. His calligraphy reflects his concentration on purity and his transcendence of the mundane world (5.41).
Tanlin 曇林 Tang Buddhist monk		1			From his transcription of the *Diamond Sutra*, it is evident that he wrote forceful small regular script that is highly legible. On the other hand, it is overly constrained and lacks individual style (5.41).
Yu Youxuan 魚又玄 Tang Daoist priest			1		Skilled in running script, he could grasp the idea of Wang Xizhi's calligraphy. His script is pure and vigorous, able to escape the vulgar style, soaring with the spirit and temperament of immortals. His profundity can be inferred from the text in the collection (10.83).
Yuanya 元雅 Tang Buddhist monk	1				Diligently worked on the ancient scripts—tadpole, seal, and clerical—and did versions of the *Thousand Character Essay* in each (2.14).
Qiji 齊己 Tang Buddhist monk		2	7		Aside from his Buddhist studies, he was also interested in poetry and calligraphy. His script is clear, tailored, and in accordance with the rules, quite unlike the typical monk's. He had a noble personality and behaved like a Confucian (11.85–86).
Guanxiu 貫休 832–912			1	2	Good at lyrics, painting, and cursive script. His painting style is strange, ancient, and not alluring. His cursive script is especially strange and flamboyant, which reflects his personality (19.150–51).
Du Guangting 杜光庭 850–933 Daoist priest		1			Educated in the Confucian classics and literature before turning to Daoism. He became a prominent Daoist priest who held high rank at the imperial court. He liked to transcribe his own literary works in regular script, which people eagerly sought. Although not able to rival the Two Wangs, his calligraphy transcends the ordinary (5.40–41).
Gaoxian 高閑 9th century Buddhist monk			2	1	Devout in Buddhist discipline and skilled in cursive script. He was bestowed the purple robe and a noble title by the emperor. His friend Han Yu insightfully noted that his calligraphy is similar to Zhang Xu's in its origins in his mind, and has as many permutations as a ghost, with no beginning or end (19.149).

TABLE 7.5. (continued)

Cleric	Listed in earlier works?	Number of items in each script type: seal	regular	running	cursive	clerical	Comments from entry
Jingyun 景雲 9th century					1		Especially fond of cursive script, he started by learning Zhang Xu's calligraphy and later could grasp the subtlety beyond normal ideas, which comes from the depth of his mind. His calligraphy piece *Exhorting the General* uses Wang Xizhi's metaphor of calligraphy as a battle (19.150).
Wenchu 文楚 9th century					1		Quiet by nature and fond only of cursive script. After working hard to master the model of Zhiyong, he developed his own style, which is light and clear, without the slightest sense of vulgarity, as light as the pure moonlight reflected on the floating clouds. While Yaxi and Chongguang egged each other on to be unusual, Wenchu formed his unique style, which was pure and elegant (19.151–52).
Linggai 靈該 9th century						1	Known for his *bafen* script. Although his hands and brush harmonized with each other, there is still a gap between his calligraphy and the ancients'. The *bafen* script was encouraged in the reign of Tang Xuanzong and therefore became popular among literati at that time (20.161).
Bianguang 䛒光 10th century Buddhist monk					2		Exalted by his contemporaries for his cursive script. Poems described his calligraphy as "striking in a sudden flying movement and awaking the dragons and snakes" and likened it to Li Bo's and Gao Shi's poetry. Though his calligraphy is not as good as Zhiyong's and Huaisu's, he created a unique style (19.149–50).
Menggui 夢龜 10th century					10		His wild cursive script can be bizarre; though not as rapid as the stunned snake and the flying bird, it is fairly vigorous and original (19.151).

Yingzhi 應之 10th century Buddhist monk			2			Wrote vigorous running script on the model of Liu Gongquan. Yet he is criticized for lacking a free and unfettered style. While Liu developed his own style out of imitating Zhong and Wang, Yingzhi could capture only formal similarity, not the inner spiritual core (11.88).
Yaqi 亞栖 10th century				15		In his spare time from Buddhist study and practice, he was fond of calligraphy and could capture the idea of Zhang Xu's cursive script. He had been bestowed the purple robe by the emperor twice for his cursive script performance at court (19.148–49).
Chen Jingyuan 陳景元 fl. 1067–1099 Daoist priest		6	2			A diligent Daoist scholar, he was fond of books and had a large collection of them. He was invited to court by Shenzong and was on friendly terms with leading court officials such as Wang Anshi and Cai Bian. Not liking the cursive script, he imitated the regular script of Wang Xizhi and Ouyang Xun (6.50–51).
Zhongli Quan 鍾離權				1		An immortal who claimed to be born in Tang times. The piece of calligraphy in the collection was a set of poems written in 1092 that discussed Daoist topics such as longevity and alchemy (19.154).
Pu Yun 蒲云 Song hermit		2				Interested in the supernatural world since childhood. Especially fond of calligraphy, he practiced regular script in an ancient style. He once transcribed the *Laozi* with commentaries in outlined characters that are as slender and continuous as the gossamer floating on the river and a single thread of smoke in a soft wind, bringing forth a feeling of walking on clouds (6.51–52).
Fahui 法暉 fl. 1110s Buddhist monk		1				In 1112 he presented a sutra pagoda to the emperor, made up of transcriptions of ten sutras in extremely small regular script. By putting an incense burner inside the pagoda, the characters would shine and fly before one's eyes. It was his piety that enabled him to accomplish this task (6.52).
Total	1	14	17	155	1	

TABLE 7.6. Song Calligraphers included in the *Xuanhe Calligraphy Catalogue*

Artist	Rank in XSD[1]	Number of items	Connection to court
Xu Xuan 徐鉉 916–991	subtle	7	Came to court with Li Yu. He served under Taizong and had a positive effect on court calligraphy (2.15–16).
Qian Chu 錢俶 929–988	talented	2	Former ruler of Wuyue, who submitted to Song and was given noble titles. Taizong asked for his cursive calligraphy (19.154–55).
Li Yu 李煜 937–978	talented	24	Former ruler of Jiangnan who submitted to Taizu (12.89–90).
Li Jianzhong 李建中 945–1013	talented	4	Submitted a piece of calligraphy done in ancient tadpole script, which the emperor appreciated highly (12.90).
Du Yan 杜衍 978–1057	talented	1	High official, from eminent family (19.155–56).
Song Shou 宋綬 991–1040	talented	8	Grand councilor under Renzong. Empress Dowager Liu had him write out the *Thousand Character Essay* for the child Renzong to use for practice (6.46–47).
Shi Yannian 石延年 994–1041	subtle	1	Served in Palace Library (6.48).
Zhou Yue 周越 fl. 1030s	talented	3	Held office (19.156).
Su Shunqin 蘇舜欽 1008–1048	subtle	5	Served in Palace Library (12.91).
Cai Xiang 蔡襄 1012–1067	subtle	3	Renzong admired his calligraphy and asked him to copy out an epitaph, but later did not insist when he did not want to do calligraphy on command (6.47–48).
Zhang Youzhi 章友直 11th century	talented	1	Transcribed classics in seal script for inscription at the Directorate of Education during Renzong's reign (2.16).
Lu Jing 陸經 fl. 1040s–60s	recent	4	Served in Palace Library (6.49).
Cen Zongdan 岑宗旦 fl. 1040s–70s	—	4	Court eunuch, Renzong to Shenzong. Yingzong had him do calligraphy on ten fans (12.97–98).
Wang Anshi 王安石 1021–1086	recent	1	Grand councilor to match the sagely Shenzong (12.91–92).
Wang Zishao 王子韶 fl. 1070s	—	1	Vice Director of Palace Library (6.49–50).

TABLE 7.6. (continued)

Artist	Rank in XSD[1]	Number of items	Connection to court
Chen Jingyuan 陳景元 fl. 1070s	—	8	Honored by Shenzong and appointed to office supervising religion (6.50–51).
Cai Jing 蔡京 1046–1126	—	77	Extraordinary grand councilor under Huizong (12.92–94).
Mi Fu 米芾 1051–1107	—	2	Served as erudite of the calligraphy and painting schools under Huizong and did calligraphy for him (12.96).
Zhao Jun 趙頵 1056–1088	—	1	Shenzong's brother (2.15).
Zhongli Quan 鍾離權 fl. 1090s	—	1	None (19.154).
Cai Bian 蔡卞 1058–1117	—	6	Shenzong learned of his talent from Wang Anshi and gave him appointments. Later held top posts [Grand Council under Zhezong] (12.94–95).
Liu Zhengfu 劉正夫 1062–1119	—	2	Council of State under Huizong (12.95–96).
Pu Yun 蒲雲 11th century	—	2	None (6.51–52).
Fahui 法暉 fl. 1110s	—	1	Submitted a pagoda made of tiny transcriptions of ten sutras to the court on Huizong's birthday in 1112 (6.52).

[1]XSD used these ranks: *shen* ("inspired"), *miao* ("subtle"), and *neng* ("talented"). At the end the book mentions some good calligraphers of the recent several decades, listed here as "recent."

rulers of small states in the south that submitted to the Song and came to live in Kaifeng; another came in the entourage of one of these former rulers.

Not all of those listed were government officials. Besides the monks and priests, there is a close relative of Huizong's, his father's brother. There also is a court eunuch named Cen Zongdan, whom Huizong may possibly have known as a child. His entry is remarkably long and interesting. Cen does not have a biography in the *Song History*, and he is not mentioned in collections of Song documents or the collected works of Song authors.[115] His entry in the *Xuanhe Catalogue* thus is nearly the only source we have about him. Zongdan may have been the adopted son of the high-ranking eunuch Cen Shousu, because his entry reports that because of his father's posthumous memorial in about 1041–1042, he was registered as a palace eunuch able to pass through the palace gates. At seventeen, however, he gave up his post and traveled through the southeast. In 1054–1055, Renzong was giving appointments to the descendants of meritorious officials, and Cen Zongdan returned to office, serving seven terms, until about 1080. During Yingzong's reign, the emperor once asked him to do calligraphy on ten fans, and he responded by writing his own poems on them. He was later recommended to Shenzong, but since he did not like the humble way palace eunuchs had to behave in front of the mighty, he did not take up the appointment. Instead he spent his time acting like a Daoist, enjoying himself with friends and with wine. In his old age he gave all of his books and other property to a grand nephew, who then looked after him. One of his poems is quoted, as is a longer passage from a text he wrote evaluating eleven major calligraphers. Concerning his highly sought calligraphy, we are told that he was best at running script, which had sharp hooks and was not at all ingratiating.

At the opposite extreme from Cen are Cai Xiang and Mi Fu, both of whom were considered major calligraphers by their contemporaries. They are not particularly well represented in the collection (Cai Xiang has only three works, Mi Fu only two). Cai Xiang's entry devotes much of its space to a summary of his political career, which could have been drawn from material assembled for the dynastic history, as most of the incidents are also in Cai Xiang's later *Song History* biography.[116] He is portrayed as an exemplary official who early in his career stood up for the reformers associated with Fan Zhongyan. He and Renzong are both portrayed positively in an anecdote in the *Calligraphy Catalogue* later also included in his dynastic history biography:

> Renzong deeply loved [Cai Xiang's] calligraphy. Once the emperor composed an epitaph for his uncle Li Yonghe, the Prince of Longxi, and ordered Xiang to write it out. Some time later academicians wrote the epitaph for his empress Wencheng, and again he told Xiang to write it out, but Xiang declined, saying, "That is a job for a [Hanlin] editorial assistant. A Confucian scholar works at his calligraphy simply for his own recreation." Renzong did not force him.[117]

In this brief anecdote, it is undoubtedly significant that Cai Xiang did not refuse the honor of writing out the emperor's own composition, but made it clear that he did not want to do routine calligraphy that he thought could just as well be done by entry-level officials in the Hanlin Academy. Renzong had enough respect for scholar-officials' dignity not to press him.

In analyzing Cai's calligraphy, the authors of the catalogue stressed his versatility. He could do characters several feet large or so tiny that the strokes were as slender as hairs. Moreover, he could write in all scripts, including tadpole, seal, clerical, flying white, running, cursive, and wild cursive. The authors of Cai Xiang's entry also went on to allude to Su Shi's statements that Cai Xiang's calligraphy was the best in the dynasty and that it was not an exaggeration when Cai Xiang described his own writing as resembling soaring dragons and dancing phoenixes.[118]

The entry on Mi Fu gives a sketch of his personality, mentioning his compulsive cleanliness and his eccentricity, his large collection of paintings and calligraphies, and his ability to copy calligraphy in others' collections so well that the original and the copy could not be distinguished. The authors of the entry also took the opportunity to put Huizong in a good light:

> During the Chongning period (1102–1106), the realm was at peace and government affairs were proceeding in an orderly fashion, with ritual and music undergoing brilliant renewal. The only exception was that calligraphy and painting had not yet surpassed prior ages. As [Mi Fu] was uniquely qualified, he was appointed erudite of both the calligraphy and painting schools, an appointment which met the approval of the literati.[119]

The entry also mentions that on Huizong's request Mi Fu wrote out the *Thousand Character Essay* in the small regular script of Wang Xizhi's *Yellow Court Classic.* Curiously, this piece is not listed as part of the palace collection, though two other versions in running script are.

The Song calligrapher represented by the most pieces in Huizong's calligraphy collection was his own grand councilor Cai Jing. With seventy-seven pieces, Cai Jing had three times as many pieces as the next highest Song calligrapher (and more than any Tang calligrapher except Huaisu). His entry, one of the longest in the book, is filled with superlatives. After a highly complimentary summary of his political career, the entry turns to his cultural accomplishments:

> Cai Jing enjoys writing prose and verse and is a very talented poet. He can do regulated verse on Du Fu's model. His edicts and memorials are to the point, detailed, clear, elegant, and refined. When writing on imperial order he moves his brush promptly and never has to add a dot or do a second draft. By nature he is especially fond of calligraphy, practicing with the diligence [of Zhang Zhi] who wrote by the side of the pond [to have ample water]. At first, he worked in the style of Shen Chuanshi, but later he deeply absorbed the brush ideas of Wang Xizhi and formed his own style.[120] His characters are stern but not restricted; they are relaxed but do not violate the rules. His standard script is like a great official wearing hat and sword debating policy in court. His cursive script is like a young aristocrat, full of spirit and brilliance who reflects glory on those around him. His large characters surpass anything ancient or modern. He has made uncountable inscribed plaques for our dynasty. The two characters he wrote,

"Gui Mountain," are linked and imposing, the brushwork vigorous. They are as massive as the giant tortoise carrying Mount Kunlun, yet soar as lightly as the great Peng bird flying over the vast oceans. Whether they can understand the characters or not, all those who see them are moved by them. This is one of the great sights of our time.[121]

Calligraphers have secrets about using the brush, which since antiquity have been passed down orally, from person to person, with no gaps in the transmission. During the Tang dynasty, these essential methods were honored and the attainments correspondingly marvelous, but during the Five Dynasties the transmission was interrupted and calligraphy declined.

Cai Jing's cousin Cai Xiang (1012–1067) became deeply aware of the secret essentials, and his calligraphy is the best of our dynasty.[122] Cai Jing alone fully caught his spirit. When writing, his hand responds to the feelings in his heart, putting him on a par [with Cai Xiang]. Critics say he exceeded Xiang in gracefulness. People compete for even fragments of paper with his ink on them. He enjoys inscribing fans. Those who get them don't consider them inferior to Wang Xizhi's six plantain fans,[123] so highly is he evaluated by contemporaries.[124]

Cai Jing was without doubt respected as a calligrapher in his own day, and the surviving examples of his calligraphy in running script are forceful and elegant (see fig. 7.11).[125] Still, it seems clear that Huizong is attempting to use the catalogue to promote Cai Jing to the pinnacle of calligraphers. We know from the account of the 1119 banquet discussed in chapter 4 that Huizong had the highest possible regard for Cai Jing as a calligrapher and that he had preserved a large number of Cai Jing's state papers for their calligraphy. It is easy to imagine Huizong personally selecting the pieces of Cai Jing's calligraphy to be listed in the catalogue and also working closely with the drafters on the wording of his entry.[126]

Which Song calligraphers did Huizong leave out of the catalogue? Of the twenty Song calligraphers in Zhu Changwen's *Continued Calligraphy Standards,* the Xuanhe catalogue left out twelve. Probably the most celebrated as a calligrapher was Wang Zhu, who had helped Song Taizong develop the Song calligraphy collection and had made the selections for the *Chunhua Model Letters.* The next most prominent would be the monk Mengying, who was mentioned in the introduction to the seal script as being purposely omitted because of his pernicious practice of inventing idiosyncratic scripts.

More striking than these omissions, however, were the omissions of Zhu Changwen's contemporaries (not covered in his book) Su Shi, Su Che, and Huang Tingjian. All three were recognized as talented calligraphers in their lifetime, and their reputations had not diminished in the years since their deaths. It would have been easy to find a few of their memorials in the archives to transfer into the collection if Huizong had wanted them there. The politics underlying their exclusion were discussed in chapter 2, but it is worth noting that even in the 1120s Huizong had not let up on his efforts to undo their fame.

Putting together a more comprehensive collection of calligraphy than anyone had in China before him was a bold act on Huizong's part. Unlike Tang Taizong, whose passion for Wang Xizhi overshadowed his interest in the work of other calligraphers, Huizong tried to assemble a collection that would give due recognition to all styles, periods, and artists. Such a comprehensive collection has much more potential to influence judgments of artists and works than a specialized collection could. Before Huizong's time, association with the imperial calligraphy collection did little to assure critics of the authenticity of a piece of calligraphy, and doubt about works published in the *Chunhua Model Letters* was widespread. By contrast, having been in Huizong's collection added an aura to a work, which it retains to this day (and which also, unfortunately, encouraged forgers to add fake Huizong seals).

Much of the cultural power of assembling these art works came from the text that recorded them, the *Xuanhe Calligraphy Catalogue*. The *Catalogue* documented how many works the palace had acquired by the acknowledged masters of the Southern Dynasties and Tang. No private collector came anywhere near the record of the court in this regard. Because the text of the catalogue for the pre-Song period avoided taking contested stands or siding with one group of critics, the work as a whole gained credibility as a reference work—a list of the greatest calligraphers, coupled with assessments of their work and a sampling of their calligraphies. That allowed Huizong to use the catalogue to present his own vision of the role of the court in the culture of his day. Viewed broadly, the *Xuanhe Calligraphy Catalogue* depicts a cultural realm where the court draws together the enormous talents of its subjects—especially literati, but also Buddhist and Daoist clergy, and even court eunuchs. This is a court-centered picture, but far from an exclusive one. There is room for everyone who masters artistic traditions and develops an individual style. The generous treatment of Tang rulers can be read as a statement that rulers have enormous potential to be a positive force in the culture of the brush. This is, however, treated as being complementary to, not in tension with, the primacy of literati as the practitioners of calligraphy. At the same time Huizong made one more attempt to get his contemporaries to lower their opinions of Su Shi and Huang Tingjian. Even though both men had been dead for more than a decade, Huizong still found their fame among the educated class sufficiently disturbing that he was willing to risk discrediting his other selections by conspicuously excluding them. Here he overreached himself, overestimating his cultural power.

Three of the individuals represented in the calligraphy catalogue—the tenth century monk Guanxiu, the ruler of Southern Tang Li Yu, and Huizong's Uncle Jun—were also given entries in the painting catalogue. This is a relatively small number, given that many of the scholar-painters featured in Huizong's painting catalogue were good calligraphers as well. It is just one of the indications that, despite the material qualities shared by paintings and calligraphies in Huizong's collections, the issues that surrounded their collection diverged in interesting ways.

CHAPTER 8

Collecting and Cataloguing Paintings

In the old days most painters were not common fellows. The way they depicted things was like the way men of letters expressed their ideas in writing; both involved similar deep analysis.

—from the entry for Cao Zhongyuan in the *Xuanhe Painting Catalogue*

HUIZONG'S PAINTING COLLECTION INCLUDED DOZENS OF WORKS THAT he believed predated the Tang dynasty. One that survives is a short handscroll, *Spring Outing*, which Huizong in his title strip attributed to Zhan Ziqian, a court official in the period from 550 to 600 (see plates 23 and 24).[1] On what basis Huizong or his curators attributed this painting to Zhan is unclear. Zhan is described in his entry in the *Xuanhe Painting Catalogue* as especially good at depicting near and far vistas of mountains and rivers and at using the same techniques as poets to convey things difficult to show.[2] Certainly *Spring Outing* has features that would have seemed archaic by Huizong's time. The landforms are neatly outlined in thin lines, and the ripples on the surface of the water are drawn in, only fading in the far distance. As the detail in plate 24 shows, the painting is full of people, horses, buildings, fences, a bridge, and a waterfall. Trees on distant hills are made nearly as large as ones in the foreground, and the people and horses too are about the same size everywhere in the painting, another feature that would have seemed primitive by Huizong's time.

Spring Outing is one of a few dozen extant paintings that hint at the enormous riches of Huizong's painting collection. Huizong's painting catalogue lists more than five times as many pieces as his calligraphy catalogue, a total of nearly 6,400. The large size of the catalogue undoubtedly reflects Huizong's assessment of his collection: He believed that he had thousands of excellent paintings, well worth recording.

Huizong's painting catalogue is a rich source for his ideas about painting. It is simultaneously a list of painters worth collecting, a theoretical treatise on painting, and an attempt to promote and demote particular painters in critical opinion. From the catalogue we can infer not only which painters Huizong admired but also how he responded to trends in Northern Song painting and painting criticism.

Collecting paintings had more in common with collecting calligraphy than with collecting antiquities or books, but there were some significant differences as well. Calligraphy as an art grew out of the routine activity of the educated class: writing. Consequently, sought-after calligraphers were invariably members of the educated class. The history of painting as an art was more complex, with much stronger ties to craft traditions. Through the Tang period even the most renowned painters, such as Wu Daozi and Han Gan, did much of their work on temple or palace walls, not a form of the art that could be collected. Through the eleventh century, as Mi Fu's *Painting Chronicles* attests, many of the painters whose works commanded high prices were not scholar-officials but professional painters. Works of high quality but unknown authorship were not rejected by collectors.

The vitality of both painting as an art and painting criticism in the eleventh century probably seemed to Huizong reason enough to undertake a major upgrading of the palace painting collection. In Deng Chun's undoubtedly exaggerated assessment, Huizong expanded the palace painting collection "a hundred fold."[3] Although Huizong must have inherited many paintings, especially paintings made by court painters during earlier reigns of the dynasty, he also added to the palace collection many types of paintings that had only come to be appreciated in the second half of the eleventh century.[4] Even though Huizong had strongly negative attitudes toward Su Shi as a political actor and tried his best to limit Su Shi's cultural influence, he did not let Su Shi's celebration of scholar painting dim his own enthusiasm for it.

Writing about Painting

Writing about painting as a fine art had a long history in China before Huizong's day. Critics drew on the vocabulary used to analyze poetry and calligraphy but also developed terminology specific to painting. Two essays on painting attributed to the Eastern Jin scholar-official-painter Gu Kaizhi (c. 345–c. 406) introduced key terms such as *chuanshen* (transmit spirit). In the early sixth century Xie He (fl. 479–501) wrote *Record of Rankings of Ancient Paintings* (Guhua pin lu), which classified twenty-seven painters back to the third century into six ranks. It included a very influential discussion of the Six Laws of painting, which introduced perhaps the key term in Chinese painting criticism, *qiyun* (variously translated as "spirit resonance," "spirit consonance," "vital resonance," "vitality," "spirit harmony," "spiritual tone," and so on). Writing on landscape painting also went back to the Southern Dynasties, when the scholar-painter Zong Bing associated it with Buddhist and Daoist connections to mountains, nature, and withdrawal from everyday life.[5]

Probably influenced by books that gave sketches of calligraphers, Tang writers wrote comparable books on painters—most notably Zhang Yanyuan, who wrote *Celebrated Painters of All the Dynasties* (Lidai minghua ji) in 847. After several essays on the history of painting, painting theory, and temples with paintings on their walls, he gave brief biographies of major painters, arranged chronologically. In contrast to Zhang's book on calligraphy, discussed in the last chapter, which presented the greatest figures as men of earlier ages (such as the Two Wangs), his book on painting extolled Tang artists, whom he saw as having achieved new heights of representational ability, referred to as *xingsi* (form likeness).[6]

In Northern Song times, two authors modeled themselves on Zhang Yanyuan. Liu Daochun's *Evaluations of Song Dynasty Painters of Renown* (Songchao minghua ping) covered the century 950 to 1050, but was organized first by subject matter, then quality rankings ("inspired," "subtle," "talented," and so on), much the way earlier works on calligraphy had been organized in terms of script type and rank.[7] Similar material was covered a couple of decades later by Guo Ruoxu in his *Experiences in Painting* (Tuhua jianwen zhi). Guo's book did not employ rankings, but added social status as part of his organizational scheme, placing the emperor first, then nobles and scholar-official painters, then other painters divided by subject matter. Guo, like his Tang predecessors, admired painters who got the details right. He wrote that pictures of plants had to take into account the season and the age of the plant. For birds, painters had to understand all of the different types of feathers—for instance, that "the wing as a whole has at its top the large and small joints and the large and small covering feathers, leading out to the six tips." In addition, there were the feathers of the head, the "rain cape" on the back, the fanning feathers of the tail, the tail point, and so on.[8]

The Northern Song was also the period when paintings by educated men attained special standing. Literati had painted before the Song; Gu Kaizhi, Zhan Ziqian, Yan Liben, Wang Wei, and many other highly esteemed early painters were officials. But critics did not identify a distinctly scholarly way to paint until the eleventh century. Ouyang Xiu wrote that in both poetry and painting, one must "abandon form to realize ideas," and Su Shi praised literati for achieving heights artisan-painters could never reach. He claimed that the "wholly divine and brilliantly fresh" brushwork of the eminent Song official Yan Su had "left behind the calculations of the artisan-painter and achieved the poet's purity and beauty." To Su, the concern for "form likeness" missed the point of painting, which was to capture the spirit or meaning of a scene, not its mere physical appearance. In this painting was said to resemble poetry. In another place Su wrote that looking at scholars' paintings was "like judging the best horses of the empire: one sees how spirit has been brought out." The work of artisan-painters was different, however: "One usually just gets whip and skin, stable and fodder, without one speck of superior achievement. After looking at a few feet or so, one is tired."[9]

Northern Song scholar-painters took the lead in developing monochrome painting of bamboo and plum blossoms, easier to master than figure painting by those already familiar with the calligraphy brush. In this type of monochrome painting, the effect depends much more on brushwork, and was therefore seen as particularly expressive of the taste, values, and momentary feelings of the painter. In Maggie Bickford's words, "Scholars allied the methods and materials of calligraphy and the purposes of poetry with the art of painting, formulating a monochromatic approach that stressed the expression of the painter above the depiction of a subject." But literati painters did not confine themselves to these more calligraphic genres. Mi Fu, Wang Shen, Li Gonglin, and Zhao Lingrang were all connoisseurs and collectors who at the same time became successful landscape painters. They did not disdain technical mastery (any more than calligraphers or poets did), though they did avoid large-format paintings, probably because they were too closely associated with professional painters.[10]

Patterns of Collecting

Much like the antiquities and calligraphy catalogues, the *Painting Catalogue* was a select list, not a full inventory of the paintings in the palace. Not only did it omit imperial ancestor portraits and paintings by Huizong's court painters but it omitted all paintings that could not be attributed to particular artists. In addition, before starting work on the catalogue, specific artists were excluded on the grounds that their work was of inferior quality. The introduction to each field of painting generally ends with a reference to this selection process. For instance, the introduction to Buddhist and Daoist paintings ends with an explanation of the exclusion of two established painters, one because of his slavish imitation of another painter, the other because of his lack of significant accomplishment.[11] The introduction to landscape painting concludes, "As for Shang Xun, Zhou Zeng, Li Mao, and their like, although they also have reputations for landscape, Shang Xun errs in awkwardness, and Zhou Zeng and Li Mao lack skillfulness. None of them is capable of the ancients' combination of strengths, so they are not recorded here."[12] Besides excluding specific artists, in all likelihood specific paintings were culled as well. Huizong clearly did not include every one of the works by eleventh-century court artists that he had inherited.[13] That the list in the catalogue is selective adds to its historical value, as it does not list everything Huizong inherited, but only those works he valued highly.

What types of paintings did Huizong collect? The simple answer is all types. As can be readily seen from table 8.1, Huizong collected ancient, old, and contemporary paintings and believed that all of the established fields of painting (conceived in terms of subject matter) included works worth owning. Evidently his goal was a comprehensive collection. Just as the Palace Library ought to have all books in all fields, the painting collection ought to have all types of paintings and works by all masters of merit. The ambition of this goal set the palace collection apart from even the most extensive private collection of the era.

Whereas the calligraphy collection was heavily weighted toward Tang and pre-Tang pieces, the painting collection was over 80 percent post-Tang (and 58 percent Song). It is not that Huizong had few Tang paintings—he had more Tang paintings than Tang calligraphies—but that he had so many Five Dynasties and Song paintings. Much of the difference in painting and calligraphy in this regard reflects the shift in the material form of paintings from walls and screens to the more collectible format of scrolls. But this difference also reflects Huizong's judgment of the high quality of more recent painters. As the accounts in the catalogue of each field and artist confirm, Huizong and his curators saw Song painting as superior to the painting of earlier eras. Huizong's appreciation of recent paintings was especially strong in bird-and-flower and landscape paintings; the collection had twenty times as many Song bird-and-flower paintings as Tang ones, and four times as many Song landscape paintings.

In his esteem for Song paintings, Huizong had a lot of company. Whereas calligraphy critics bemoaned a decline in calligraphy since the Tang dynasty, Song painting critics confidently asserted that in several fields, painters of their own day were superior to painters of former times. Guo Ruoxu granted that the greatest masters of figure, horse, and cattle painting were men of the past, but considered Song painters unsurpassed in landscape, forest, rock, flower, bamboo, bird, and fish paintings.[14] A large majority of the paintings Mi Fu mentioned as owned by contemporaries were Song paintings, not earlier ones.[15] This is in contrast to Mi Fu's high esteem for early calligraphy, especially by the Two Wangs.

Another difference between the ways Huizong catalogued his paintings and his calligraphies lies in the number of works by each artist. Whereas over half of those in the calligraphy catalogue were represented by a single piece, only 18 percent (41 of the 231) of the painters featured had only one work listed.[16] Apparently, in the case of painting, Huizong or his curators did not feel so compelled to have at least one work by every highly rated artist.[17] On the other hand, Huizong clearly had

TABLE 8.1. Painters and Paintings in the *Xuanhe Painting Catalogue* (by period and field)

	Pre-Tang		Tang		Five Dyn.		Song		Total			
	Artists	Items	Artists	Items	Artists	Items	Artists	Items	Artists	Percent	Items	Percent
religious 道釋	5	56	19	422	12	413	13	289	49	21%	1180	18%
figures 人物	4	16	13	205	6	52	10	232	33	14%	505	8%
architecture 宮室			1	4	2	33	1	34	4	2%	71	1%
northern border people 番族			2	109	3	24			5	2%	133	2%
dragons/fish 龍魚					2	50	6	67	8	3%	117	2%
landscape 山水			10	187	2	95	29	826	41	18%	1108	17%
animals 畜獸	1	3	14	169	4	49	8	103	27	12%	324	5%
birds/flowers 花鳥			8	89	8	681	30	2016	46	20%	2786	44%
ink bamboo/ small scenes 墨竹小景附					1	1	11	147	12	5%	148	2%
vegetation 蔬果葯品草蟲附	1	1			2	4	3	20	6	3%	25	1%
Total painters	11		67		42		111		231	100%		
%	5%		29%		18%		48%		100%			
Total paintings		76		1185		1402		3734			6397	100%
%		1%		19%		22%		58%			100%	

TABLE 8.2. Painters with fifty or more paintings in the *Xuanhe Painting Catalogue*

Painters of people and religious subjects		Landscape painters		Painters of plants and animals	
Lu Lengqie 盧楞伽 (T)	150	Li Cheng 李成 (S)	159	Huang Quan 黃筌 (5D)	349
Wang Qihan 王齊翰 (S)	119	Juran 巨然 (S)	136	Huang Jucai 黃居寀 (S)	332
Li Gonglin 李公麟 (S)	107	Xu Daoning 許道寧 (S)	138	Xu Xi 徐熙 (S)	249
Wu Daoxuan 吳道玄 (T)	93	Wang Wei 王維 (T)	126	Yi Yuanji 易元吉 (S)	245
Zhang Yuan 張元 (5D)	88	Guan Tong 關仝 (5D)	94	Wu Yuanyu 吳元瑜 (S)	189
Zhu You 朱繇 (5D)	83	Dong Yuan 董元 (S)	78	Zhao Chang 趙昌 (S)	154
Zhou Wenju 周文矩 (S)	76	Fan Kuan 范寬 (S)	58	Guo Qianhui 郭乾暉 (5D)	104
Zhou Fang 周昉 (T)	72			Tang Xiya 唐希雅 (S)	88
Hu Gui 胡瓌 (T)	65			Zhong Yin 鍾隱 (5D)	71
Li Sheng 李昇 (5D)	52			Cui Que 崔慤 (S)	67
				Zhao Jun 趙頵 (S)	70
				Teng Changyou 滕昌佑 (5D)	65
				Han Gan 韓幹 (T)	52
				Zhao Shilei 趙士雷 (S)	51

T = Tang 5D = Five Dynasties S = Song

favorite painters. Below are lists of artists who were represented by fifty or more paintings, divided by classification

Again, we see differences according to time period. Only one Song painter, Li Gonglin, was among the figure and religious painters with more than fifty paintings, but all but one of the favored landscape painters were Five Dynasties or Song. Five Dynasties and Song artists dominate painters of birds, animals, fish, and various types of plants as well.[18] These differences undoubtedly reflect both the availability of different kinds of paintings and Huizong's own preferences in ways that can no longer be fully disentangled.

The titles of paintings listed under each entry, especially when coupled with surviving works that seem to match them, offer further insight into the sorts of paintings in Huizong's collection. For religious paintings, we can take the case of the first painter listed in the book, treated almost as the founding father of painting, the scholar-official Gu Kaizhi (c. 345– c. 406). Although Gu is classed under religious paintings, only one of the nine works listed under his entry (*Vimalakīrtri*) is a religious work. The rest were secular subjects, including pictures of shepherds, dragons, and ancient sages. One of the listed paintings, *Admonitions of the Instruc-*

tress, is in the collection of the British Museum (plate 25).[19] In the scene shown there, two well-dressed women peer into mirrors as they attend to their toilette, one seen from behind, so that we see her face only in the mirror.[20] Scholars agree on the importance of this celebrated painting, but not its date; some think it may have been done in Gu Kaizhi's time, others see it as a later painting or copy, even as late as Song times.[21]

Some of the painters listed under religious paintings did in fact specialize in that genre. From the titles listed, Buddhist works predominated in Tang times, especially images of Buddhas, bodhisattvas, arhats, and eminent monks. No Tang or Five Dynasty Buddhist painting with Huizong's seals has survived, but there are a few paintings that could have been copies of these earlier works made at his court. A good example is the work attributed to the Tang master Lu Lengqie in the Palace Museum, Beijing (see plate 26).[22] Lu's entry in the catalogue describes him as a student of Wu Daozi who eventually earned Wu's respect. It listed 150 works by Lu Lengqie, many of which were probably originally intended for hanging in temples. Five were of Śakyamuni, two of Guanyin, and one each of Mañjuśrī (Wenshu) and Samantabhadra (Puxian). Arhats and eminent monks were also popular subjects.[23] Some of the arhats in the painting illustrated here appear to be Chinese, others are clearly meant to be Indian or Central Asian.[24]

In the sequence of the catalogue, figure paintings followed religious paintings. Painters identified by earlier authorities as major masters were well represented. For instance, there were forty-seven paintings by the Tang painter Zhang Xuan, praised especially for his ability to capture the appearance of women and children.[25] No original works by Zhang Xuan survive, but two copies done at Huizong's court are extant. *Court Ladies Preparing Newly Woven Silk,* in the Boston Museum of Fine Arts, is shown in plates 27 and 28.[26] Wu Tung sees this painting as a selective copy of a few scenes from a larger Tang original, which would have illustrated more of the steps in silk making as described in a fifth-century poem.[27]

The *Xuanhe Painting Catalogue* lists fewer Song figure painters than Tang ones, but one of those listed—Li Gonglin—was perhaps Huizong's favorite painter. An extant figure painting attributed to him is the *Illustration of the Classic of Filial Piety,* in the Metropolitan Museum of Art in New York. The scene shown in figure 8.1 illustrates the need for subordinates to offer honest but respectful criticism when they think that their superiors are making a mistake. The plain, slightly archaistic outline style was probably thought best for conveying the moral message of the text—the call for restraint and sincerity.[28]

Only four artists were classified under architectural painting in the *Xuanhe Painting Catalogue*, but two extant paintings, both with Huizong's seals, have been attributed to one of them, Wei Xian (fl. 937–975). Wei Xian had been a court painter

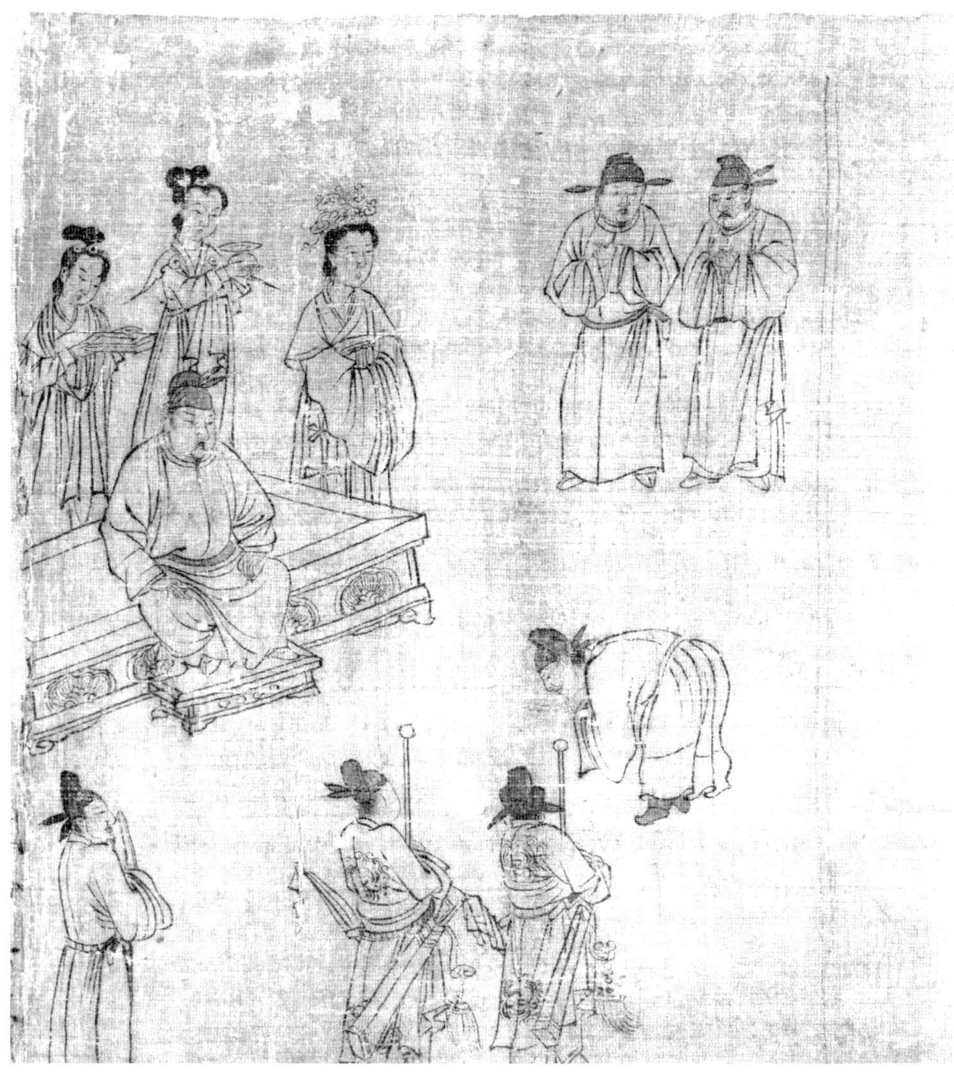

Fig. 8.1
Li Gonglin (ca. 1041–1106), *Illustration of the Classic of Filial Piety* (detail). Handscroll, ink on silk, 21.9 × 475.5 cm. Image © The Metropolitan Museum of Art, New York. Ex Coll.: C. C. Wang Family, from the P. Y. Kinmay W. Tang Family Collection, Gift of the Oscar L. Tang Family, 1996 (1996.479a–c). The scene shown here depicts how the filial son makes a good official. An official who thinks his superior is making a mistake is respectfully pointing this out, much as a filial son should caution his parents.

at Li Yu's court in Nanjing, and the Xuanhe catalogue praises his skill in depicting figures, buildings, and trees.[29] The short handscroll *Waterwheel* (fig. 8.2) depicts the busy activity around a water-powered mill for grinding grain.[30] The other Wei Xian painting, *Lofty Scholar,* is a long hanging scroll showing a scholar at work in his mountain retreat (plates 14 and 29). Above him tower mountains. Huizong attributes the unsigned painting to Wei Xian and gives it both a general title, *Lofty Scholar,* and identifies its subject, the Han scholar Liang Hong and his deferential wife, who, the histories tell, always raised a tray she was offering to her husband to eyebrow level.[31]

FIG. 8.2
Attributed to Wei Xian (fl. 937–975), *Waterwheel* (detail). Handscroll, ink and color on silk, 53.3 × 119.2 cm. Shanghai Museum. In this painting, the buildings, boats, carts, and machinery are all drawn in meticulous detail.

Only five artists were listed under the category of peoples of the northern border, a category that was new with Huizong's catalogue. Of them, Hu Gui of the Five Dynasties period had the most paintings listed (sixty-five). These were primarily scenes of animal husbandry and other dimensions of nomadic life.[32] A couple of works with titles that match these may possibly have been in Huizong's collection (either as originals or as copies), though none of them have Huizong's seals. A good example is *Drinking Party* (plate 30), in the Palace Museum, Beijing.[33] Given the enormous importance to the Song of peaceful relations with its northern neighbors, especially the Khitans' Liao dynasty (907–1125), it is not surprising that depictions of the way of life of the herders of the steppe attracted interest at the Northern Song court.

Of the eight painters classed under dragons and fish in the catalogue, the two with the most paintings listed are the Five Dynasties monk Chuangu, with thirty-one paintings of dragons, and Liu Cai, still living when the catalogue was compiled, with thirty paintings of fish. Liu Cai was an official who was praised for his talent as a poet and for depicting fish as they looked in the water, moving freely about, which is how they appear in the long handscroll by Liu in the St. Louis Art Museum (plate 31).[34]

Extant works by the forty-two artists classed under landscape are relatively plentiful. A pre-Song example is Zhao Gan's *Along the River at First Snow* (fig. 8.3).[35] This long handscroll of fishermen at work was listed in the catalogue and has seals of the Jin emperor Zhangzong (an indication that it likely came from Huizong's collection; see chapter 9). In the *Xuanhe Painting Catalogue*, Zhao Gan's painting is said to capture the scenery of the Jiangnan region: "Even though you may be distracted by all the petty annoyances of the court or marketplace, once you look at his paintings, you are transported to the Yangzi River."[36] A good example of a Song landscape once in Huizong's collection is Wang Shen's *Light Snow over a Fishing Village* (fig. 8.4).[37] The entry on Wang Shen in the catalogue describes him as well-read and multitalented, able to create atmospheric landscapes that captured what could not be put into words.[38]

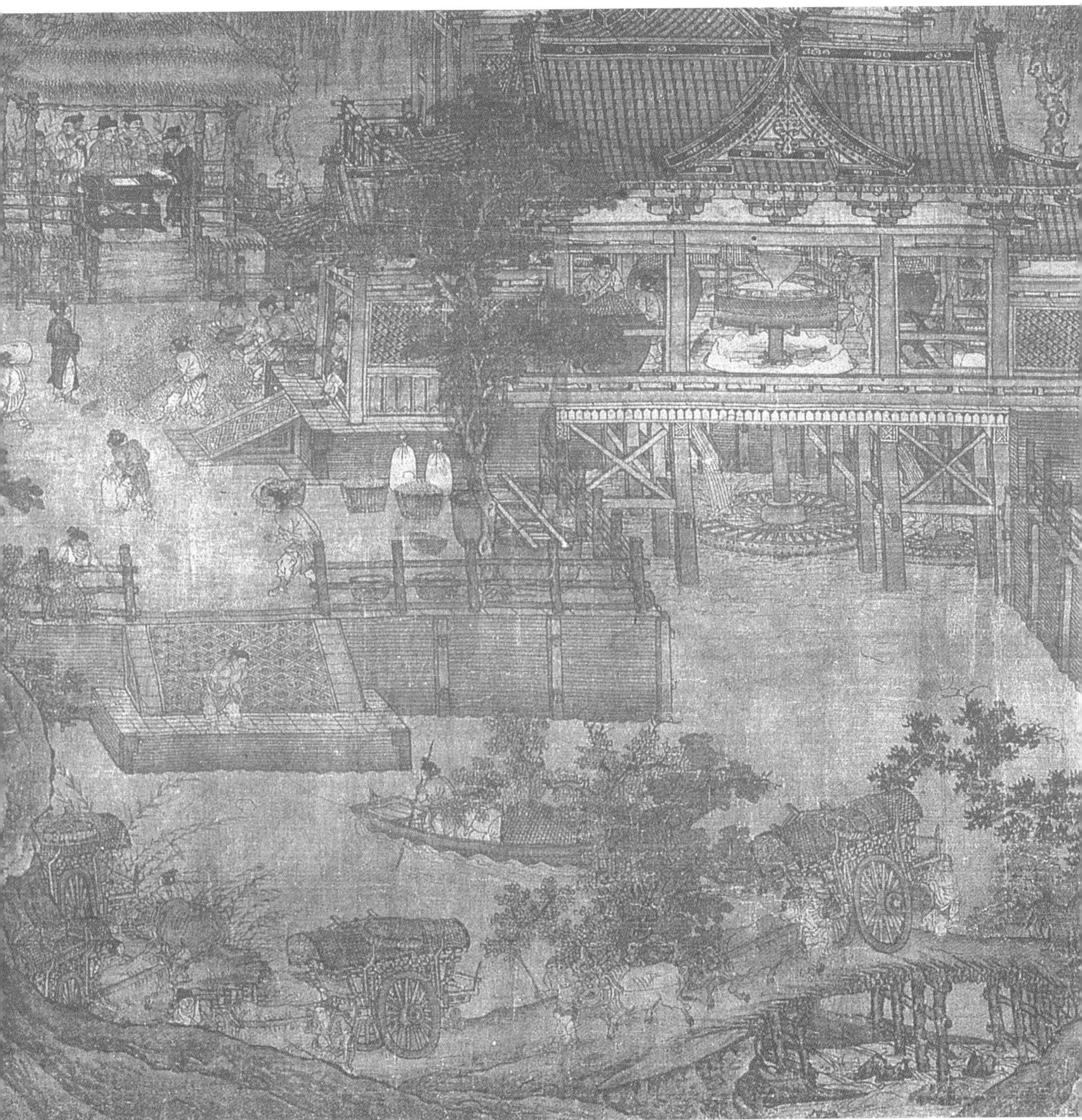

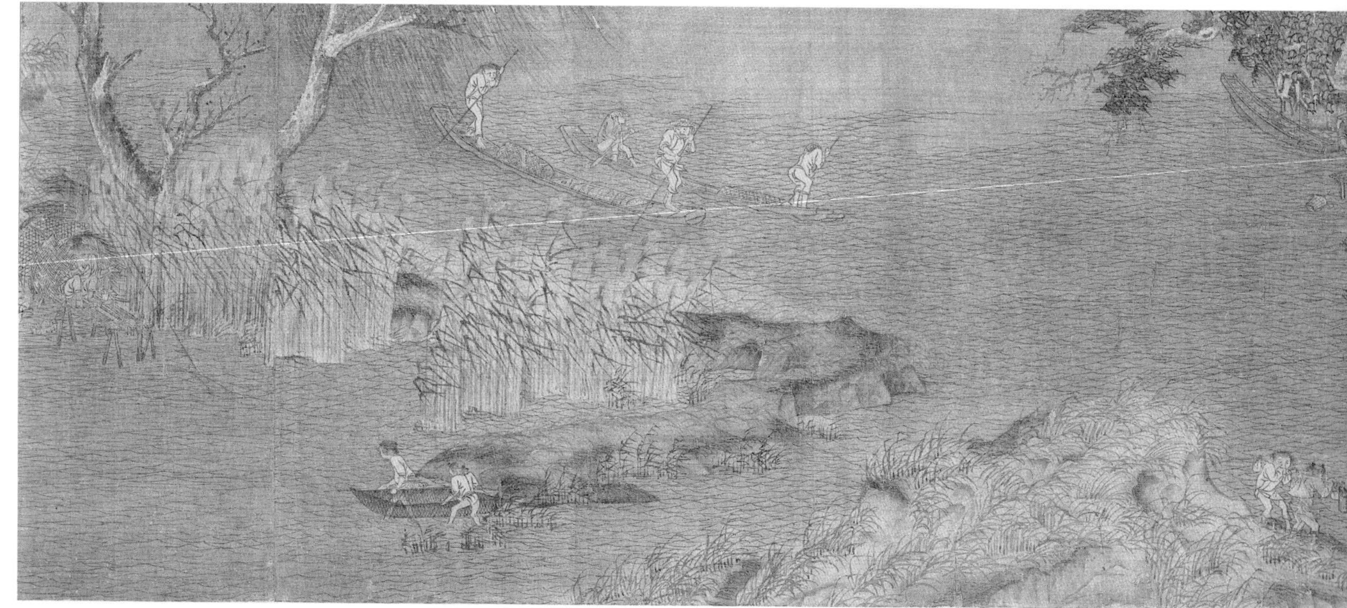

FIG. 8.3
Zhao Gan (fl. 960s), *Along the River at First Snow* (detail). Handscroll, ink and color on silk, 25.9 × 376.5 cm. National Palace Museum, Taiwan, Republic of China. This long handscroll depicts fishermen at work, with attention to the ripples on the water and the reeds blowing in the wind, but also the details of everyday life—their nets, shelters, and boats. Snow is conveyed by a light spattering of white paint and its chill by the people in the boats or shelters huddling together and sticking their hands in their sleeves.

Of the twenty-seven artists classified as animal painters in the *Xuanhe Catalogue*, just over half lived in Tang times. By far the most common subject was horses, but there were also painters who specialized in cattle, cats, and tigers. The best evidence of Tang horse painting comes from Song copies, such as Li Gonglin's copy of Wei Yan's *Pasturing Horses* (plate 11), a work with Huizong's seals.[39] An example of a specialist in water buffaloes is Qi Xu. The *Xuanhe Painting Catalogue* lists twenty-two paintings by him, one of which, *Pasturing Water Buffaloes*, has survived (fig. 8.5). It depicts a pleasant bucolic landscape where boys get to amuse themselves by the edge of a stream while tending to the family's animals.[40]

Bird-and-flower painting was the category with the second-largest number of artists (46) but by far the most paintings (2,786). In this category, Song artists dominated, especially Song court artists. A good example from the early Song is the hanging scroll by Huang Jucai in the National Palace Museum in Taipei (plates

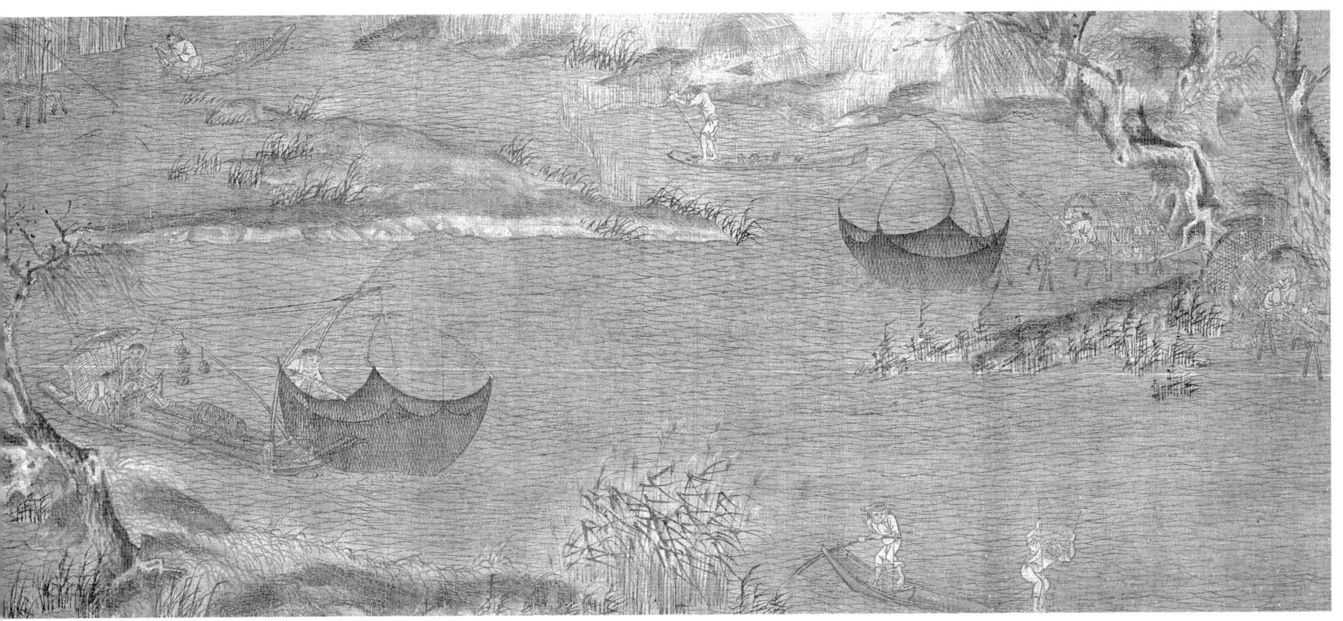

32 and 33).[41] Huang Jucai served first in the Sichuan court of Meng Chang, then in the Song court under Taizong.[42] Titled by Huizong *Partridges by a Thorny Bush,* the painting depicts a long-tailed bird, several rocks, a variety of plants (including bamboo), and six smaller birds, each caught at a different angle, suggesting that the small flock was in motion. The long-tailed bird, by contrast, seems still, its eyes fixed on something in the water.

After bird-and-flower painting in the catalogue is another new category, ink bamboo and small scenes, with twelve artists. Only one painting by these artists from Huizong's collection seems to have survived, the handscroll Huizong titled *Riverbank with Reeds in Light Snow,* by Liang Shimin (fig. 8.6).[43] The catalogue described Liang as an official from an official family, who had studied poetry before learning to paint, and praised him for his ability to negotiate successfully between the poles of technical polish and free expression.[44] The painting is one of the few in Huizong's collection inscribed by the artist. From his inscription, we know that Liang presented the work to Huizong, probably hoping that it would help him secure his monarch's favor.

The final field of painting in the catalogue is another new one, literally "vegetables and fruit with herbs, grass, and insects appended," or "vegetation" for short. Sixteen of the twenty-five titles listed in this category are by a single Song artist, the Song official Li Yanzhi, ten of them titled *Grass and Insects Drawn from Life.* Li was said to be good at insects, fish, grass, and trees; to have attained the manner of a poet; and to have been able to convey the particular nature of every species of living

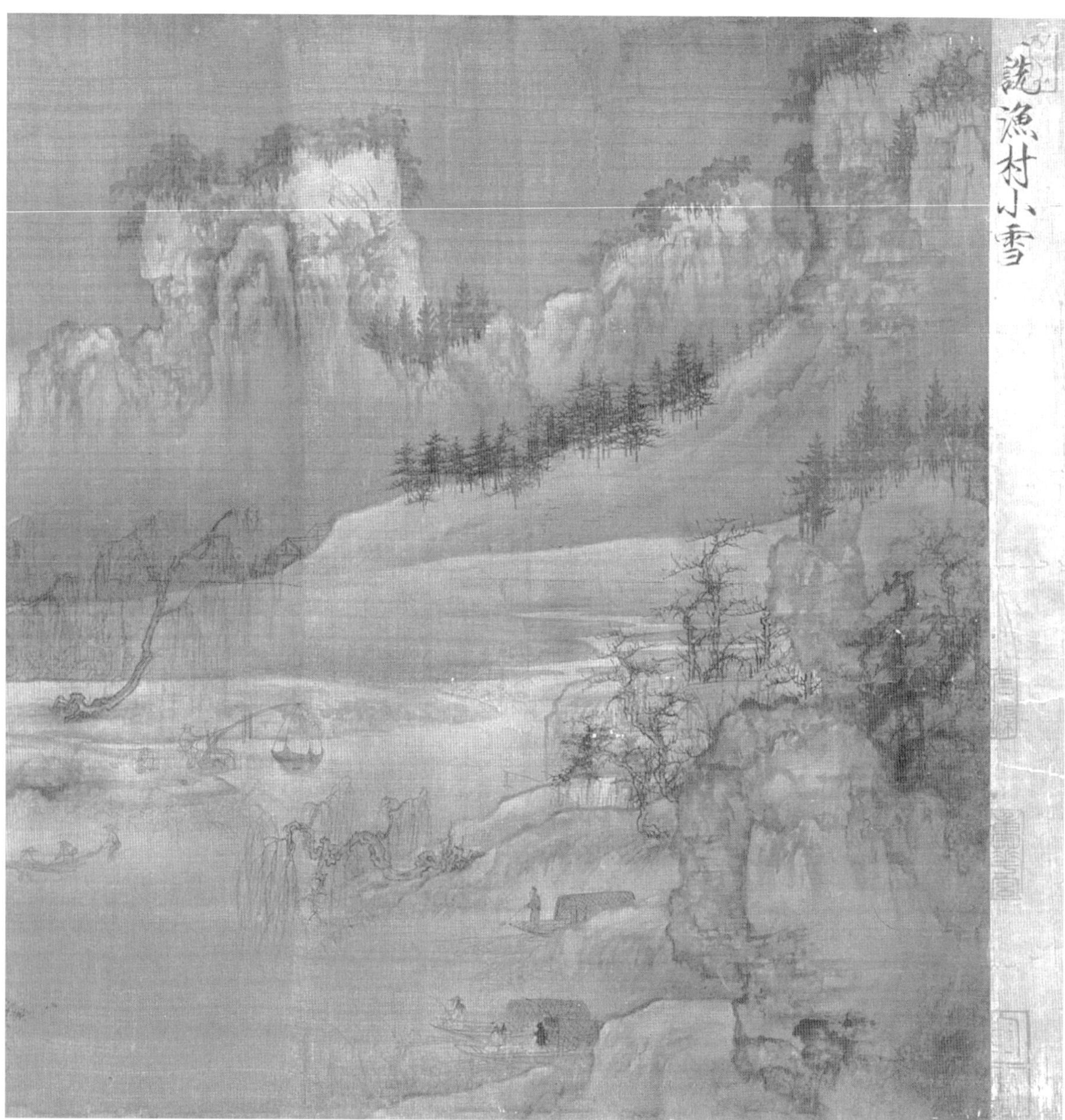

FIG. 8.4
Wang Shen (ca. 1048–ca. 1103), *Light Snow over a Fishing Village* (detail). Handscroll, ink and color on silk, 44.4 × 219.7 cm. Palace Museum, Beijing.

Wang Shen was an amateur painter, but strongly influenced by the brushwork and compositions of the contemporary court painter Guo Xi.

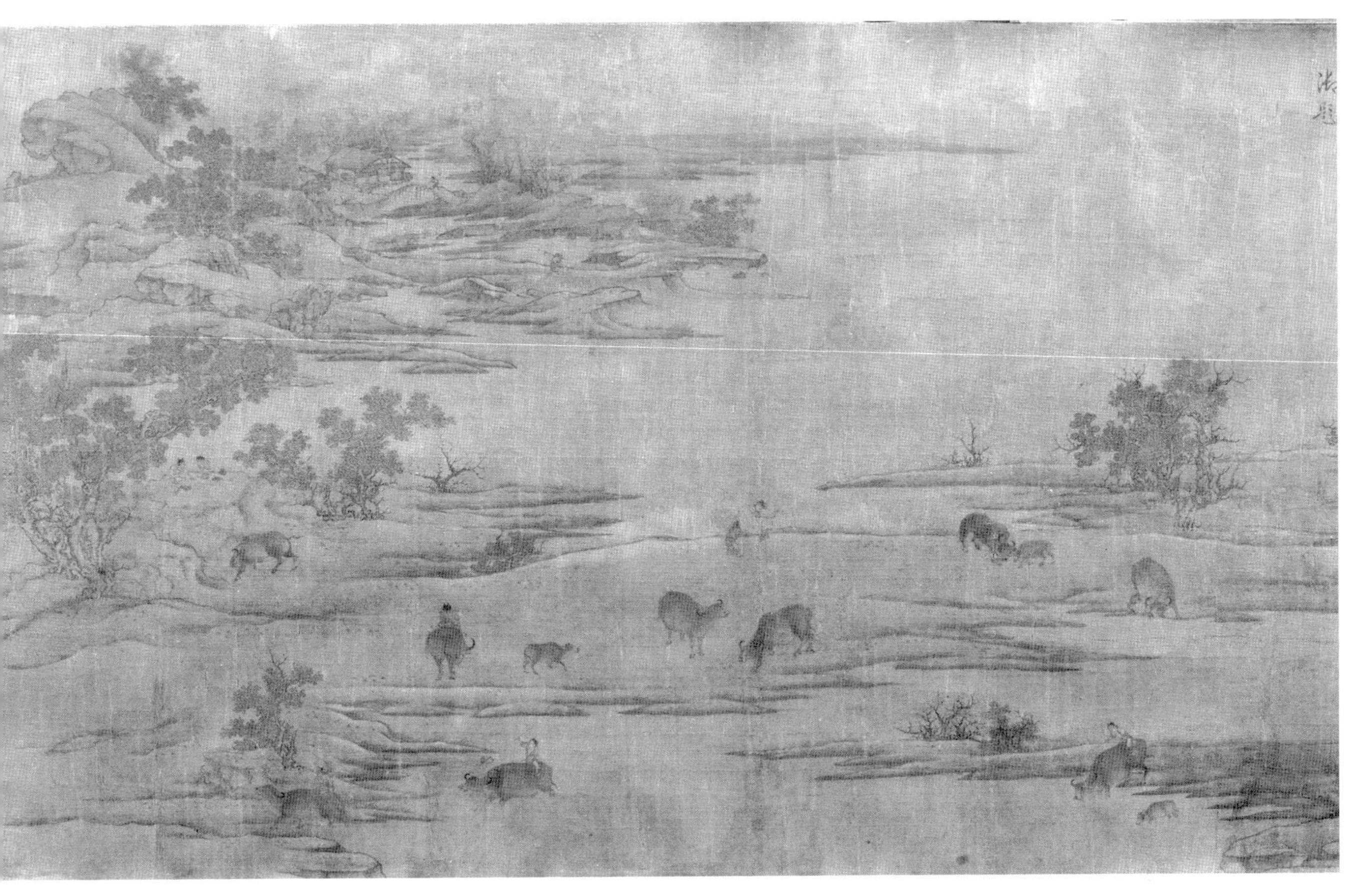

Fig. 8.5
Attributed to Qi Xu (eleventh century), *Pasturing Water Buffaloes* (detail). Handscroll, ink and color on silk, 47.3 × 115.6 cm. Palace Museum, Beijing. The dozen-odd water buffaloes depicted in this painting are shown in a wide range of postures and from many different angles.

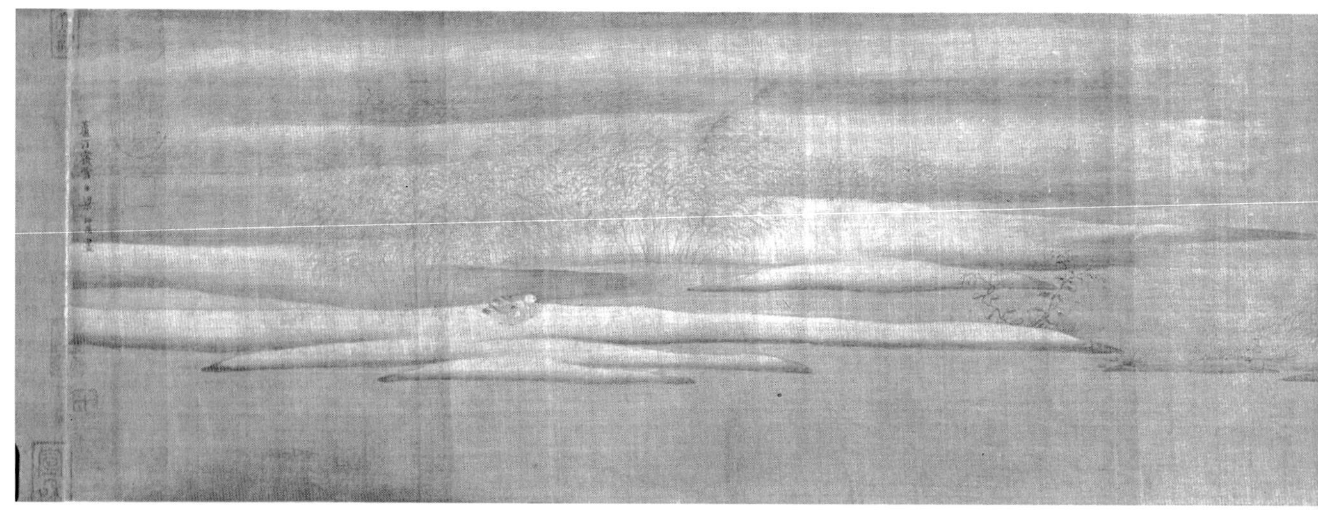

Fig. 8.6
Liang Shimin (early twelfth century), *Riverbank with Reeds in Light Snow.* Handscroll, ink and color on silk, 26.5 × 145.6 cm. Palace Museum, Beijing. This painting is an example of the type of "poetic" painting Huizong admired, combining sensitively drawn birds and trees with sketchy land forms that recede into an undefined distance.

thing. He was said to "draw skillfully from life without descending to the habits of contemporary painting masters."[45] Unfortunately, no paintings survive by Li or by the other five painters classed under "vegetation."

Collected Paintings as Models for Court-Produced Paintings

As discussed in earlier chapters, Huizong used antiquities and calligraphies that he had collected as models for works produced at court. Ancient bronze vessels and bells were the basis for the replicas cast for use in imperial rituals. Calligraphy held by the palace was copied to produce a set of rubbings designed to serve as an improvement on the model letter collection issued over a century earlier by Taizong (*Chunhua Model Letters*). Evidence suggests that the court collection of paintings was used in a similar manner as the basis for a fairly extensive production of paintings—both close copies and free reinterpretations. Two paintings survive that were labeled by the Jin emperor Zhangzong as copies made by Huizong: the copy of Zhang Xuan's *Court Ladies Preparing Newly Woven Silk* (plate 27) and *Lady Guoguo on an Outing* (plate 16). In addition, quite a few paintings attributed to earlier artists are now thought to have been painted during the Northern Song, quite possibly at Huizong's court.[46]

Certainly there is evidence that copies were made with some frequency at Huizong's court. As discussed in chapter 5, Dong You referred several times to copies being made of paintings while they were in the Palace Library, sometimes

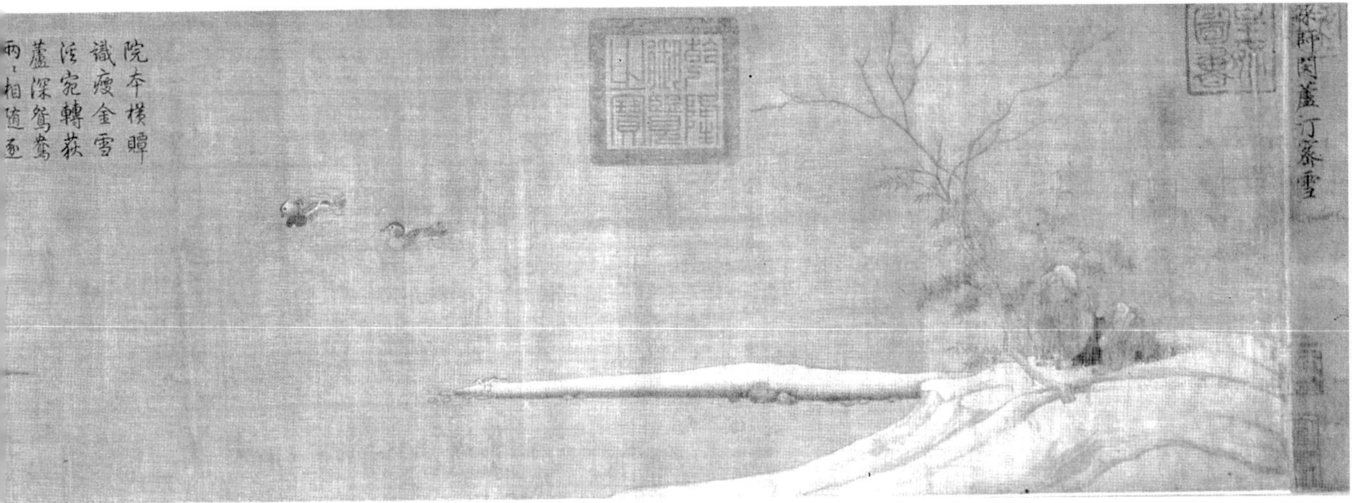

by court painters, sometimes by the staff of the Library themselves. There are also references to Huizong making copies of paintings in the collection and showing them to officials. At the grand ceremony held to commemorate the completion of new buildings for the Palace Library in 1122, among the paintings Huizong displayed to the gathered officials was his own copy of Zhan Ziqian's *Emperor Wenxuan of Northern Qi Visiting Jinyang.*[47] Another painting that may well be a copy made at Huizong's court is *Literary Gathering* in the National Palace Museum, Taipei (plates 17 and 18).[48] This painting was long attributed to Huizong himself because both he and Cai Jing inscribed it, but it is now commonly thought to have been done by one of Huizong's court artists. It appears to depict the scholars favored by Tang Taizong, and might well be based on a Tang work, though probably rather freely reinterpreted.

Huizong himself looked on the making of copies as a positive act. The entry in the *Xuanhe Painting Catalogue* for Li Gonglin highlighted his practice of making copies of paintings. We are told of Li, "Whenever he obtained a painting, ancient or modern, he would make a close copy, thus accumulating reproductions. Consequently his home had many famous paintings, and was lacking nothing."[49] Huizong considered these copies collectible. The 107 paintings by Li Gonglin listed in the catalogue include 23 explicitly said to be copies of earlier works, including Wang Wei's *Viewing Clouds*, Lu Hong's *Thatched Hut*, Wu Daozi's *Four Protectors of the Dharma*, and Li Zhaodao's *Seascape*. The one copy done by Li Gonglin that survives, his copy of Wei Yan's *Pasturing Horses* (plate 11), shows that he was willing to lavish many hours on making a copy. Huizong also collected copies made by other painters he esteemed, including Wang Wei, Yan Su, Wang Shen, Zhou Wenju, and Wu Yuanyu.

Huizong also considered making copies to be good training for his court artists. Deng Chun tells us that Huizong had paintings from the collection regularly shown to his court painters:

> After the disastrous departure [i.e., the Jurchen invasion and the move of the court to the south in 1127], two or three painters who had worked in the Painting Academy made their way to Sichuan. They told me that when they were in the Academy, every ten days two cases of paintings from the palace collection would be brought out and the emperor would order a high-ranking palace functionary to take them to the Academy to show to the painters. Military guards accompanied them to assure that they were all returned undamaged. Therefore the artists of that time developed a fine mastery, enabling them to comply with the emperor's wishes.[50]

There is another intriguing passage in Deng Chun's *Painting Continued* that may refer to the making of copies. After mentioning Huizong's talents as an artist and his assembling of a collection of paintings much greater than his predecessors', Deng went on, "He also took paintings by ancient and modern masters from Cao Fuxing to Huang Jucai and collected them to make one hundred books, divided into fourteen categories, containing a total of 1,500 items, which was titled, *The Xuanhe Collection for Imperial Perusal*."[51] Since Huizong's total collection was much larger than 1,500 items, and since many of the items were large scrolls that could not have fit into these sorts of albums, one possible explanation of this passage is that it refers to album leaves, perhaps not considered important enough to have been listed in the catalogue. An alternative possibility is that these albums were comparable to the copies of books made specifically for imperial perusal, that is, that they consisted of copies made of paintings in Huizong's collection in a format convenient for Huizong to use for quick reference (serving the same purpose as the photographs and Xerox copies that those studying painting today use to remind themselves of a composition).

Of course, copies made by Song artists were not in fact replicas. Richard Barnhart says of Li Gonglin's copy of *Pasturing Horses,* "He transformed his antique model into a very modern picture." Wu Tung believes it likely that Huizong's court painters, in making *Court Ladies Preparing Newly Woven Silk,* may have imitated selectively a few sections from the more comprehensive original by Zhang Xuan. Wu Hung describes the two copies of Zhang Xuan compositions as "at best Song reinterpretations of Zhang Xuan's works. Their composition may follow the originals, but the painting style—the opaque coloring, flat images, and especially the meticulous neatness of the ornamental details—reflects the distinctive taste of Huizong's Academy of Painting."[52]

From the perspective of today's art historians, the production of copies at Huizong's court has both its positive and its negative sides. The production of copies there preserved traces of the development of painting in China that would not have survived otherwise. On the other hand, surviving works are not labeled in ways that distinguish originals, close copies, imaginative reconstructions, and fabrications. Since fabrications do not provide evidence of earlier compositions, no one wants them as place holders in the history of Chinese painting. Some of the confusion between originals and copies and between copies and fabrications may not be the fault of Huizong and his staff—it could well be that later collectors removed labels identifying paintings as copies, since a work was worth more when it was believed to be an original. Gaozong and Dong You both reported that calligraphy in Huizong's collection was clearly marked "copy" or "original," and paintings probably were as well.

Preparing the Catalogue

Once Huizong decided to commission a catalogue of his painting collection, the officials assigned the task had to do at least a half dozen things. They had to decide how the catalogue would be organized—that is, what categories would be used to classify artists or objects and in what order they would be listed. They had to select the artists to be included in each category, then the paintings by that artist to list. They had to make sure that all the paintings to be considered were attributed to particular painters and that each had a title. They had to write biographical sketches that evaluated each artist. And they had to prepare synthetic introductions to each of the sections of the book, placing that field of painting in a larger cultural context. At many points the officials involved must have sought Huizong's guidance or at least approval, as they would not have wanted to omit a painter he greatly admired or praise highly one he dismissed as mediocre.

Like the other two catalogues, the painting catalogue is organized in a hierarchical way, with objects sorted by category, and the categories placed in order. The cataloguers had several examples of sequences in earlier treatises on painting that they could consider adopting. Gu Kaizhi described a scale of difficulty, with figures the most difficult, followed by landscapes, dogs and horses, and buildings. Zhang Yanyuan divided paintings into more divisions: figures, buildings, landscapes, horses, spirits, and birds and flowers. Liu Daochun, who used the categories to organize his book, began like the others with figure paintings, then differed in his order: landscapes, domestic animals, birds and flowers, spirits, and buildings. Guo Ruoxu used a somewhat simpler scheme: figure, landscape, bird-and-flower, and miscellaneous paintings.[53] In all these books, paintings of Buddhist and Daoist deities were treated as figure paintings. The *Xuanhe Painting Catalogue* divided figure paintings in two, making religious paintings a separate category (see table 8.1). The catalogue also introduced four new categories, notably people of the border regions, dragons and fish, ink bamboo and small scenes, and vegetation. In putting religious and figure paintings first, the cataloguers were following convention, as they were in putting most plant and animal pictures after landscapes. But convention was not yet settled on whether architectural paintings should precede or follow landscapes. People of the border regions could be thought of as a kind of figure painting, but it is not placed immediately after figure painting but rather after architectural painting (which, admittedly, also often include figures). Most likely putting dragons and fish before other animals, and even before landscapes, reflects their connection to Daoist ideas (the general elevation of Daoist art is discussed below under "cultural politics"). The cataloguers ended up placing ink bamboo and small scenes and vegetation last rather than insert them between more established categories, but do not seem to have held them in low esteem.

As discussed in chapter 5, basic work on attributing paintings to particular artists and giving them titles was done by men like Dong You and Huang Bosi as part of their responsibilities in the Palace Library. These tasks were certainly more challenging for painting than for calligraphy. It was easy to come up with titles for calligraphy by taking a phrase in the first line, but painting titles usually reflected the subject, which was often unclear. Was this a painting of a generalized lofty scholar, or a particular one? Was a famous incident being portrayed? Giving an artist and a title to a work is not a trivial act, because it encourages the viewer to look at the painting with some preconceptions in mind. Alfreda Murck, in a study of the titles given to paintings in the Northern Song, draws attention to the poetic qualities of the titles in the *Xuanhe Painting Catalogue*.[54] Not only do many allude to specific poems, but they often contain evocative words such as "misty" that are common in poetry. That is, rather than a title like *Bird and Rock*, the cataloguers assigned a title like *Mountain Partridge Nesting in Rocks*, or, rather than *Autumn Mountains*, they gave the name *Auspicious Vapors over Autumn Mountains*.

Paintings also presented more intractable problems of authorship than calligraphy did. Virtually all of the calligraphy that was collected had a traditional attribution (even if some of these were questioned), and many had signatures. But paintings had often been passed down without attributions.[55] Attributions written on the back of the painting could be useful, but careful curators would want to keep an open mind and consider the possibility of errors. Many surely knew

Mi Fu's caustic comments on the prevalence of attributing paintings on little or no grounds.

Did Huizong's curators include only paintings they felt confident about attributing? Did they assign an artist to every painting considered of high enough quality or interest to be listed in the catalogue? Did they work from a list of famous painters they wanted represented in the collection, attributing at least one work to each? There is no way to answer these questions with certainty, nor any reason to assume only one approach was followed.

Access to thousands of paintings should have helped Huizong's curators' connoisseurship. A connoisseur like Mi Fu saw hundreds of paintings in his lifetime, but he rarely had the opportunity to place several works attributed to the same artist next to each other. It seems only reasonable that the opportunity to make careful comparisons would advance Huizong's curators' connoisseurship. However, there is no body of earlier attributions to which they can be compared in order to judge whether or not advances were in fact made. Although we know that Mi Fu made many attributions, we cannot match them to extant works. The attributions made by Huizong and his curators stand alone in that regard.[56]

With regard to writing the artists' entries, the cataloguers probably began by making files for each artist. They clearly checked what had been written about each by earlier authors, and often repeated their stories, though normally they added some new material and evaluations. The entry for the Tang figure painter Zhang Xuan can serve as an example. He was discussed in two ninth-century works, Zhu Jingxuan's *Celebrated Painters of the Tang Dynasty* (Tangchao minghua lu) and Zhang Yanyuan's *Celebrated Painters of All the Dynasties* (Lidai minghua ji). Alexander Soper translated Zhu's entry as follows:

> Zhang Xuan, a native of the capital, used to paint young bloods, saddle-horses, screens, palace gardens, and gentlewomen, and in those subjects was the most renowned artist of his day. He excelled in rough sketches and in bringing things out with a touch. The layout of his scenery, with kiosks, terraces, trees, flowers, and birds, was carried out to perfection. He illustrated the poem cycle of *Grievances in the Changmen Palace*, letting his imagination play with views of winding balustrades, kiosks and terraces, golden wells, and wutong trees. He also did pictures of *Young Bloods on a Night Outing*, *Palace Women Praying for Skill on the Seventh Night*, and *Looking at the Moon*. To all of these he lent a wealth of study that made them far exceed earlier versions. In doing gentlewomen he ranks with Zhou Fang; his young bloods, palace gardens, and saddle-horses are all first class. Hence he is assigned to the excellent class.[57]

Zhang Yanyuan, writing a little later, had less to say:

Zhang Xuan loved to paint women and babies. *Singing Girls, A Nursing Mother Picking up a Baby, Patting the Deerskin Drum, Woman on a Swing*, and *Lady Guoguo on an Outing* are all still extant.[58]

The entry in the *Xuanhe Painting Catalogue* repeats some of the information in these earlier works, but discusses Zhang's artistry at greater length and with more attention to its connections to poetry:

Zhang Xuan, a native of the capital, was good at figure painting, and was particularly skillful at depictions of young bloods and the women's quarters. He also depicted flower paths and bamboos and trees in an exceptionally lovely way. Extremely affecting is his painting *Grievances in the Changmen Palace,* based on the poetic line, "By the golden well the leaves of the wutong tree in autumn are yellow."[59] He was also very talented at depicting children, which is very hard to do, since children's bodies and postures are alike enough so that their age has to be shown through their facial features and hairdos. Most painters err either by making them look like smaller versions of adults or err in making them look like women. In addition, it is important to convey clearly differences in social class and personality. A poem by Du Fu has the line "The child of five had enough energy to eat an ox, making all the guests in the hall turn their heads."[60] Such a child should hardly be depicted like an ordinary one. A painter needs to put thought into these kinds of issues. In the past it was said that Xuan painted *Young Bloods on a Night Outing, Palace Women Praying for Skill on the Seventh Night, A Nursing Mother Picking up a Baby, Patting the Deerskin Drum*, and other paintings.[61]

The last sentence in this entry clearly refers to the two Tang texts, which list these paintings, but most of the entry is devoted to analyzing Zhang's skill in depicting children in varied ways, a feature of his talent not emphasized by either earlier author.[62]

In cases where no earlier authors had discussed a long-dead painter, the cataloguers seem to have used the paintings to make inferences about the painter, much as the compilers of the calligraphy catalogue had done for obscure calligraphers. For instance, the palace had two paintings by Yan Yun, both of Heavenly Kings, but knew nothing else about him. The cataloguers therefore wrote:

Yan Yun's original place of residence is unknown. He was skilled in painting Heavenly Kings. In brushwork he followed Zhou Fang, attaining marvelous effects. Yet no painting of his of subjects other than the Heavenly Kings has survived. Isn't it because faith in the Heavenly Kings flourished during the turmoil of the Five Dynasties, leading to

> the popularity of paintings of them? In addition, the Heavenly King also helped our generals attain victory at Tanyuan [in 1004]. Thus their contribution [to our state] is significant and it is reasonable that people worship them. Yan therefore deserves praise for becoming a master of such paintings.[63]

To give another example, the palace had a single painting by Wu Shen, depicting Xiao Yi using deception to secure Wang Xizhi's famous *Preface to the Orchid Pavilion Poetry Collection* from the monk who owned it. Apparently knowing of no other paintings by Wu, the catalogue authors used the one painting to write the entry on Wu:

> Wu Shen's original place of residence is unknown. His level distance paintings of streams and rocks and people fishing by the river bank all have a subtle and secluded feeling. The surviving painting of his titled *Xiao Yi Acquiring the Orchid Pavilion Preface* depicts the differences in bearing and character of the individuals. As soon as one unrolls the painting, one can vividly imagine the historical event. Truly the connection between the transmission of painting and calligraphy goes far back.[64]

In the case of Zhang Fu, the palace had three paintings they assigned to him, all of water buffaloes. His entry reads:

> Zhang Fu's original place of residence is unknown. He was good at painting water buffaloes and rather skilled in brushwork. He absorbed much from Han Huang and probably is a follower of his. His *Tending Water Buffaloes* focuses on the charm of the isolated village, where the breezes blow away the fog and boys lie on the grass and play their flutes. He depicted a herd boy wearing a straw rain cape and a bamboo hat, capturing the way the boy and the water buffalo ignored each other. Such expressiveness with the brush must have come from his marvelous sensibility improving his technique.[65]

In one case the palace had twelve paintings all attributed to the same man, Sun Keyuan, but knew nothing of his biography. The four paintings titled *Lofty Recluse, Tao Qian Returning Home, Spring Clouds Emerging from the Mountains*, and *Fishing and Singing in the Hills* may well have formed the basis for this entry:

> Sun Keyuan's original place of residence is unknown. He loved to paint the landscapes in the area of Wu and Yue. Although his brushwork is not especially vigorous or unconstrained, the spirit resonance of his paintings is lofty and antique. He loved to depict the pleasures of lofty scholars who live in the mountains and hermits who fish

alone. Contemplating the meaning of his painting titled *Spring Clouds Emerging from the Mountains*, one can detect his detachment from the mundane world and the way he enjoyed playing with the brush. The primary difference between him and men like Tao Qian and the Elder Qi is that he is not recorded.[66]

Besides writing 231 biographical entries, the authors of the catalogue had to write introductory essays for each of the ten fields of painting. No earlier text on painting, even those arranged by subject matter, had synthetic essays of this sort, so the cataloguers had to invent their own model. The introductions they wrote generally began by relating the subject of the paintings to the Confucian or Daoist classics or to the cosmology that the two traditions shared. Normally the names of major masters of the field were mentioned, along with some reference to the number of painters whose entries followed. The final discussion was of popular painters omitted because of specified flaws. The introduction to dragons and fish can serve as an example:

Under the hexagram *qian* in the *Book of Changes*, the dragon is said to appear in the fields, in the depths, and in the heavens in order to explain its far-ranging transformations. It does not know restriction or restraint; thus the comparison [in the commentary on this hexagram]: "It furthers one to see the great man."[67] In the poem "Fish and Water Plants" of the *Book of Songs*, it is said, "Beautifully streaked are their heads," "very pliant are their tails," and "snuggling close to the reeds" to describe their deep and distant roaming and swimming.[68] "Forgetting each other in the rivers and lakes" [in *Zhuangzi*] refers to the difficulty in gaining the services of virtuous men.[69] In the writing of the *Changes* and the editing of the *Songs*, the early sages did not neglect to speak of dragons or fish. Painting may be a lesser Dao, but it still has its value. The painting of dragons and fish is the outer expression of the inner meaning of the *Changes* and *Songs*.

Although dragons are not visible, because the Duke of She was fond of them [and had many pictures of them], a true dragon appeared.[70] Thus the painting of dragons has a long tradition. Cao Fuxing, of the state of Wu [in the Three Kingdoms], once saw a red dragon emerge from a stream. He drew it and submitted it to Sun Hao. People of the time thought it was an inspired work.[71] Afterward the tradition of painting dragons was lost until the Five Dynasties when Chuangu appeared. His untrammeled style went beyond what people of the past had been able to achieve. Dong Yu of the present dynasty was next to gain fame for his dragons and water; truly, he is the incomparable master of recent times.

As fish are a delight to the senses, there should be many masters of fish painting. But painters often portray them as if they were lying on the kitchen table, failing

> entirely to convey their ability to ride the wind and break the waves. This point has not escaped notice in contemporary criticism. In the Five Dynasties Yuan Yi pursued a reputation entirely through painting fish and crabs. In our dynasty, the literatus Liu Cai also gained fame in that way, so there has been no shortage of followers. Here we arrange in chronological order eight men from the Five Dynasties to the present. We have appended at the end paintings of some creatures that can be classed as marine life. As for painters such as Xu Bai and Xu Gao, although they gained fame in their day for their paintings of fish, their pictures do not show fish moving about or opening and closing their mouths, so they do not belong in this catalogue.[72]

Most of the introductions follow this pattern quite closely, though in a few cases the opening puts more emphasis on the wonders of nature than on citations of the classics. For instance, the introduction to landscape painting begins this way: "The mountain peaks are protective and the rivers, numinous; the ocean submerges and the earth supports. The divine grace of creation, the light or darkness of yin and yang, a distance of a thousand miles—all this can be captured in the space of a foot." The introduction to bird and flower painting includes both: it begins with a discussion of the splendors of creation as seen in the wonderful variety of flowers, then turns to the many references to birds and animals in the *Book of Songs*.[73]

The work of compiling the painting catalogue was comparable to that of compiling the calligraphy catalogue, but some distinctions can be noted. First, the introductions to script types are fundamentally more historical in thrust than those for fields of painting. Second, painters whose overall evaluation was negative were not included in the painting catalogue, in contrast to the calligraphy catalogue which included some masters even though the authors had little good to say about them. Third, the calligraphy catalogue much more often cited earlier books on calligraphy either by name or by such expressions as "critics say" or "those who evaluate calligraphy say."[74] Given these differences, it seems unlikely that the final editing teams of the two books were identical.

The Catalogue as a Work of Painting Criticism

As passages already cited reveal, the *Xuanhe Painting Catalogue* has much in it that can be read as painting criticism.[75] Some of this is found in the introductions, but much more is in the individual entries. The authors of the catalogue were certainly familiar with earlier painting criticism, ranging from the biographically rich books by Zhang Yanyuan, Liu Daochun, and Guo Ruoxu, to the more scattered writings by Su Shi, Huang Tingjian, and Mi Fu.

For political reasons, Su Shi was never cited by name, though, as in the calligraphy catalogue, some passages paraphrase or quote things he had written.[76] In some cases, Su's ideas may have seemed like common ideas to Huizong and his editors, not ideas they associated narrowly with Su Shi. Mi Fu was not politically taboo, and had worked at Huizong's court, but, as Hironobu Kohara notes, Huizong's *Xuanhe Painting Catalogue* makes very little use of Mi Fu's writings on paintings, citing him only twice—and once to correct him.[77] Certainly the *Painting Catalogue* did not adopt all of Mi Fu's prejudices, such as his condemnation of the Song painters Xu Daoning and Cui Bo, both treated as major artists in Huizong's catalogue. Mi Fu saw Li Yu as a popular painter of little worth, sarcastically saying that every collector had a half dozen or so of his pictures of birds done with a fine brush. Mi wrote that Huang Quan's paintings were not worth collecting since they were easily imitated and that Zhao Chang was untalented but eager to please, making him detestable.[78] Perhaps disagreement about the merit of such painters was one of the reasons Huizong dismissed Mi Fu from his post as head of the painting and calligraphy schools after he had served only a matter of months.[79]

Painting theory in the *Xuanhe Painting Catalogue* is discussed below in terms of four traits that were highly valued—magical power, poetic allusiveness, literati status, and antiqueness—and two that were disparaged—excessive attention to form likeness and service as a court painter.

VALUING THE UNCANNY SKILL OF GENIUSES AND AMAZING POWERS OF VERISIMILITUDE

The *Xuanhe Painting Catalogue* reiterated many long-established ideas about the extraordinary ability of such rare geniuses as Han Gan and Wu Daozi. Born with natural talent, such geniuses did not need formal study. With amazing speed and without preliminary sketches, they could paint people or animals that seemed alive. Even paintings by lesser artists, if they were realistic enough, could magically come to life. In several of the entries in Huizong's catalogue, we encounter dragons that fly off from a painting or bring rain, or Heavenly Kings that emerge from paintings to engage in battle, the accounts sounding much like miracle tales.[80]

One example should suffice. The entry in Huizong's catalogue for the Tang horse painter Han Gan retold two stories of his uncanny abilities. The first reported that one evening a man in a red robe and black hat knocked on Han Gan's door and said he was a messenger from a ghost who had heard of Han Gan's fame for painting fine horses and wished to acquire one. Han Gan quickly painted a horse and burned it to send it to the spirit world. A few days later Han Gan received a gift of a hundred pieces of silk as thanks. The other story concerned a veterinarian who was surprised by the appearance of a lame horse brought to him to treat. He showed the horse to

Han Gan, who immediately identified it as a horse he had painted. Perplexed by its lameness, Han Gan looked through his pictures of horses until he found the right one, which indeed was missing a stroke on its leg.[81]

LIKENING PAINTING TO POETRY

Repeatedly the authors of the painting catalogue compare painters to poets. Like poets, painters draw from their well of feelings. We are told of the monk-poet Juran, "Because there was so much within his breast, there was no end to what he could do when he lowered his brush."[82] When a painter was not appreciated in his day, he could be compared to a writer who complained that people did not understand his work and preferred his most mediocre or routine efforts, not his best ones. When a painter took a long time to complete a work, he could be compared to similarly painstaking writers, such as Zuo Si, who spent three years writing three rhapsodies. Painters could also use their paintings as subtle forms of admonishment in the same way that poets did. The entry for the Five Dynasty figure painter Chang Can cited a line from the Great Preface to the *Book of Songs* on indirect admonishment to explain the subtle but effective criticism of Chang's highly evocative paintings of parties with elegantly made-up women dancing and singing.[83]

When a painter was also a poet, doing paintings in a poetic way was presented as a natural outgrowth of his ability to compose poems. The brief entry for Hu Zhuo, a Five Dynasties bird-and-flower painter, can serve as an example:

> Hu Zhuo's original place of residence is not known. He was broadly learned and a talented poet, whose spirit resonance was way beyond the ordinary, as he soared with his mind on the beyond. Once he said to his younger brother, "My poetic thoughts are like the reverberation of the screeches of monkeys in the Three Gorges," which shows the sort of lofty and detached feelings he had. Whenever he encountered a scene difficult to describe in words, he would put it in a painting. Thus the way he made grass, trees, and birds had a poet's responsiveness to things.[84]

The fullest discussion of the comparability of poetry and painting is in the entry for Li Gonglin. It was the infusion of ideas and the subtlety of the poet that made Li Gonglin so exceptional:

> Generally speaking, Gonglin put his emphasis on expressing ideas, and made composition and decoration secondary. Ordinary painters might be able to master his fine colored style, but they can never come close to his sketchy, simple style. This is probably because he applied Du Fu's way of creating poems to the creation of paintings.

> For instance, when Du Fu wrote "Trussed Chickens," he did not concentrate on the competition between chickens and insects, but on the moment when he stares at the cold river while leaning against the pavilion in the hills.[85] Similarly, when Li Gonglin painted the picture of Tao Qian returning home, he did not focus on the fields, gardens, pines, or chrysanthemums, but on the place where he stood looking down at the flowing water.[86] When Du Fu wrote "My thatched roof was hit by the autumn wind," even though his quilts were torn and his roof leaked, he did not look for pity but rather he wanted "to provide cover for all the poor scholars of the realm and see their happy faces."[87] Similarly when Li Gonglin painted *Yang Pass,* he considered the sadness of parting as too conventional, so focused on the fisherman at the bank sitting alone, forgetting the phenomenal world, unconcerned by the feelings of sorrow and joy. His other paintings are similar; it is up to the viewer to grasp their meaning.[88]

Huizong's cataloguers were not the only ones who thought Li Gonglin painted in a poetic way. Su Shi wrote that Li achieved marvels because in his paintings he was basically a poet. The *Xuanhe Catalogue* quoted Li himself as claiming, "I make paintings as a poet composes poems, simply to recite my feelings and express my nature."[89] Huizong's cataloguers went further by analyzing Li's technique and showing specific similarities to Du Fu's methods.

The emphasis that the cataloguers placed on composing paintings in a poetic way fits well with what is known of Huizong's expectations for court painters, who were selected through examinations that involved composing paintings cleverly suggesting the activity implied by a poetic line rather than directly illustrating it.[90]

EXTOLLING LITERATI AS THE IDEAL PAINTERS

Given that painting was so much like poetry, literati are portrayed in the catalogue as ideal painters. Although those who have written about the development of literati painting have often presented it as oppositional, an act of protest aimed vaguely at the court, clearly Huizong and the officials he assigned to work on his painting catalogue did not read it that way. It was to the glory of the Song dynasty that so many of its men of letters and government officials excelled at painting.

One sign of the support the *Painting Catalogue* gave to literati painting was making a separate category of monochrome bamboo and plum paintings (which had appended to it "small scenes," described as the sorts of landscapes often done by literati).[91] The introduction to this section stressed that it was not professional artists but poets and writers who favored doing bamboo "in light ink with strokes, now upright, now slanting, which do not emphasize formal likeness but simply succeed in what lies behind the image." Wen Tong, one of the best-known of those listed in that chapter, owed his fame in no small part to the extravagant praise given to him by Su Shi and Su Che. Su Che's prose poem on ink bamboo quotes Wen Tong as saying, "In the morning the bamboo were my friends; in the evening they were my companions. . . . At first, I looked and enjoyed them. Now I enjoy them without consciousness of doing so. Suddenly, forgetting the brush in my hand and the paper in front of me, I rise up instantly and make bamboo in quantities. How is the impersonality of Creation itself different from this?"[92] Su Shi concurred in seeing in Wen Tong an almost sage-like ability to penetrate to the underlying meaning or principle of things:

> In bamboo and rocks and leafless trees, Wen Tong can truly be said to have grasped their principles. Now they are alive and now dead; now they are twisted and cramped, and now regular and luxuriant. Their roots and stems, joints and leaves—sharp and pointed or veined and striated—have innumerable changes and transformations. They are never once repeated, yet each part fits in its place, in harmony with divine creation and accord with man's conceptions.[93]

The *Xuanhe Painting Catalogue* conveys much the same message without mentioning the Su brothers: Wen Tong gained insight into bamboo by living surrounded by them. "When he depicted them alone by a pavilion in the moonlight, swaying gracefully, it seemed like the wind could move them." "Once his light ink was laid down, even the most marvelous of the painters using colors would not be able to convey what he conveyed."[94]

The high evaluation for paintings done by literati was not confined to this special section of the catalogue, but permeates the book. Li Gonglin, listed under "figure painting," was described as a scholar-painter par excellence.[95] So were many landscape painters. Table 8.3 lists passages in the biographies of landscape painters that highlight their standing as officials or men of letters.

EXTOLLING THE ANTIQUE SPIRIT IN PAINTINGS

In 1976 Alexander Soper wrote, "Unquestionably, the *Xuanhe huapu* is more deeply permeated by respect for the past than any previous work on painting." Soper had surveyed earlier writings on painting, most of which took pride in the progress the art had made in recent times. Liu Daochun, for instance, praised the figure painter Wang Guan because he "discarded the shortcomings of men of old and created a new excellence for the future," and said of Fan Kuan, "Antiquity gave him no rules. His creative ideas were his own: his achievements were like those of Creation itself."[96]

TABLE 8.3. Landscapists presented as literati or sharing literati approaches in the *Xuanhe Painting Catalogue* (with number of paintings listed)

Name	No.	Comments
Li Sixun 李思訓	17	Member of Tang imperial family, of high military rank, highly regarded as a marvelous painter in his time. His ability to convey a sense of ease in remote realms was not hindered by his wealth and status (10.166).
Li Zhaodao 李昭道	6	Li Sixun's son, a court official and military officer who "played" with brush and ink. Admonished Empress Wu by means of a painting (10.167).
Wang Wei 王維	126	Passed the exams, served in court, attained fame as a poet, and was given a biography in the histories. His poems and his paintings were basically similar. He was not ashamed of being called a painter, but was equally famous as a poet (10.169–70).
Lu Hong 盧鴻	3	Declined office, preferring to live in the mountains (10.168).
Zhang Zao 張璪	6	An official, famous for his cultivated appearance. Wrote an essay on painting skills (10.175).
Jing Hao 荊浩	22	"Broadly cultivated and loved the ancient." Wrote *Landscape Secrets* (10.176).
Li Cheng 李成	159	Official family, good writer, painted for self amusement. He emptied out his heart through his brush, like Meng Jiao calling out through poems and Zhang Xu being crazy with cursive calligraphy. Refused commissions, not wanting to be classed with artisan painters (11.182–83).
Wang Shiyuan 王士元		Official from official family (11.195).
Yan Su 燕肅	37	Good writer, court official (11.195–96).
Song Dao 宋道	1	Passed exams, lodged meanings in his paintings, did not sell them (12.198).
Song Di 宋迪	31	Passed exams (12.198–99).
Wang Gu 王穀	3	An official, who used methods from poetry in his paintings (12.199–200).
Fan Tan 范坦	6	"Those who discuss paintings say scholars often come up short in adhering to standards, they are often weak, with no bones. Tan, being old and firm, did not err either in being too restricted or too soft" (12.200).

TABLE 8.3. (continued)

Name	No.	Comments
Huang Qi 黃齊	4	Passed exams, served in office. His paintings were like poems (12.201).
Li Gongnian 李公年	17	Official, whose paintings were like poems (12.202).
Li Shiyong 李時雍	1	From official family, served as a teacher at the calligraphy school. A poet who lodged meaning in his paintings. Did ink bamboo (12.202–3).
Wang Shen 王詵	35	Good calligrapher, poet, and painter. Painted when scenes were hard to describe in words. A major collector (12.203–4).
Juran 巨然	136	Although a monk, painted like a scholar (12.211).

The *Xuanhe Painting Catalogue*, by contrast, referred positively to painters who "love antiquity" (*haogu*) and used "lofty and ancient" (*gaogu*) as a form of high praise. Throughout the book antiquity is imbued with strongly positive associations. In discussing the bird-and-flower painter Cui Bo, the cataloguers wrote, "His finest passages were not inferior to the ancients'. . . . Had he not been a lover of the past and broadly cultivated, so that he could master what the men of the past conveyed from mind to brush point, this would not have been possible for him."[97]

As Soper points out, since Huizong collected what were considered "ancient" paintings (Tang and earlier), it is not unreasonable that he saw value in the ancient. We have also seen that he built up a collection of bronze vessels valued for their connection to ancient rulers and ancient rituals. And we should not forget that the catalogue was probably written in large part by men holding offices in the Palace Library, who would have been familiar with the critical language used to discuss literature and calligraphy. Ever since the late Tang literary movement to "reattain antiquity" (*fugu*), antiquity had been treated as a source of value. In the calligraphy catalogue, "ancientness" was a frequent term of praise. In calligraphy criticism, the term "ancients" usually referred to the great masters of the pre-Tang period, and saying that a work had an ancient elegance, or an ancient air, was strong praise. To those compiling the painting catalogue, painting could also benefit from spiritual connection to the past.[98]

DISPARAGING ATTENTION TO FORM LIKENESS

The painting catalogue reinforced its praise of certain ways of painting by disparaging opposed approaches. The catalogue frequently stressed the dangers of placing too much attention on form likeness at the expense of conveying spirit or vitality. Perhaps the fullest discussion of this issue is in the entry for the Song painter of grass and insects Guo Yuanfang. Guo Ruoxu had praised him as "an excellent painter of grasses and insects, who made an exhaustive study of the way they fly and crawl, and had a deep understanding of the processes of Creation," who however sometimes was too meticulous.[99] The *Painting Catalogue* went considerably further in criticizing his preoccupation with form likeness:

> The official of military rank Guo Yuanfang was a resident of the capital. He was good at painting grasses and insects. Even drawing freehand, he made things seem alive, as he was able to convey the appearance of flying and crawling. In his day he was rather appreciated by scholar-officials. However, he was more successful when he was most abbreviated. When he added detail and sought to be striking, the harder he tried, the worse he failed, what [Zhuangzi] referred to as when the external is emphasized the inner will be poorly done, like when the prize is gold.[100] Critics have used this to disparage him. Generally speaking, nature does not begin with a conception of the larger whole but gives each element its appropriate form and color, to make each right. But if you chisel and polish till each is pretty, how can you capture the whole? Therefore gentlemen are not interested in the highly skilled carver who devotes three years to carving one leaf.[101] One cannot force naturalness through assiduous effort.[102]

For centuries anecdotes have circulated about Huizong's insistence that his court painters get every detail right in the murals they painted for palace halls or temples. Since several of the best-known paintings attributed to Huizong (such as the *Five-Colored Parakeet*, plate 4) were also in an exactingly descriptive style, he has been taken as the last supporter of the old court style of painting, the last to insist on representational truthfulness in painting.[103] Whether or not the stories of Huizong's interaction with his court artists have any basis in fact, as a collector Huizong was anything other than narrow-minded. The *Xuanhe Catalogue* shows conclusively that he did not put form likeness above other qualities in judging paintings.

DOWNPLAYING SERVICE AS A COURT ARTIST

A less expected negative sentiment frequently found in Huizong's catalogue is a low opinion of service as a court painter. This is all the more surprising since Huizong took steps to raise the status of painters at his court.

Court painting was given a lesser place in several ways. First of all, most of those who had served as court painters under earlier emperors were not included in the catalogue. When the catalogue is compared to the two earlier works on Song painters, Liu Daochun's *Evaluations of Song Dynasty Painters of Renown* and Guo Ruoxu's *Experiences in Painting*, the shift in emphasis away from court painters is striking. Of the ninety-one Song painters given biographies in Liu's work (covering the period 950 to 1050), a third are explicitly referred to as holding court painting appointments, and a few others were known primarily for undertaking major court commissions. Guo's work covers another twenty-five years, to 1074, and adds the names of another seventeen court artists. Thus, from these two works we know the names of forty-eight court artists active from 950 to 1074, only a fifth of whom are listed in the *Xuanhe Painting Catalogue*. To give an example, Liu ranked six painters in his highest "inspired" class for figure painting. Among them was Wang Ai, who had served first under the Later Liang dynasty, and later the Song. He was given commissions to do portraits of members of the imperial family and also did wall paintings for Buddhist temples.[104] Guo also listed him, but did not seem to hold him in such high esteem.[105] Yet Wang Ai does not appear with even one painting in the *Xuanhe Catalogue*. To mention a painter better known today, both Liu and Guo wrote highly of Yan Wengui, but he does not figure in the *Xuanhe Catalogue*. Liu listed him under three genres, as a talented-class figure painter whom Taizong himself admired for his refined brushwork, and a subtle-class architectural and landscape painter who created his own style and produced paintings other painters considered perfect. Guo described him as having developed his own style, and mentioned that scroll paintings by him were in circulation.[106] None of these paintings, however, made Huizong's select list. Yan Wengui is known today primarily through two paintings, one a landscape handscroll in the Osaka City Museum, the other a landscape hanging scroll in the National Palace Museum, Taipei. From these paintings, Yan has been described as a polished master in the tradition of Li Cheng and Fan Kuan (see figure 8.7).[107] The only place the *Xuanhe Painting Catalogue* mentions Yan Wengui is at the end of the introduction to the architectural section, where he is listed with two other painters who were excluded for lack of originality.[108]

Sometimes the *Xuanhe Catalogue* did not mention service at court in its entry for a painter described as a court artist by earlier authorities. A good example is Goulong Shuang. Both Liu Daochun and Guo Ruoxu wrote that Goulong Shuang served as a painter-in-waiting at the Painting Academy.[109] His account in Huizong's catalogue, by contrast, makes no mention of any service at court, and instead elaborates on his skill in depicting ancient worthies: "He enjoyed doing ancient gentry, portraying them as solid and unwilling to flatter. These paintings are the equivalent of the seal script found on cauldrons and other vessels from the Three

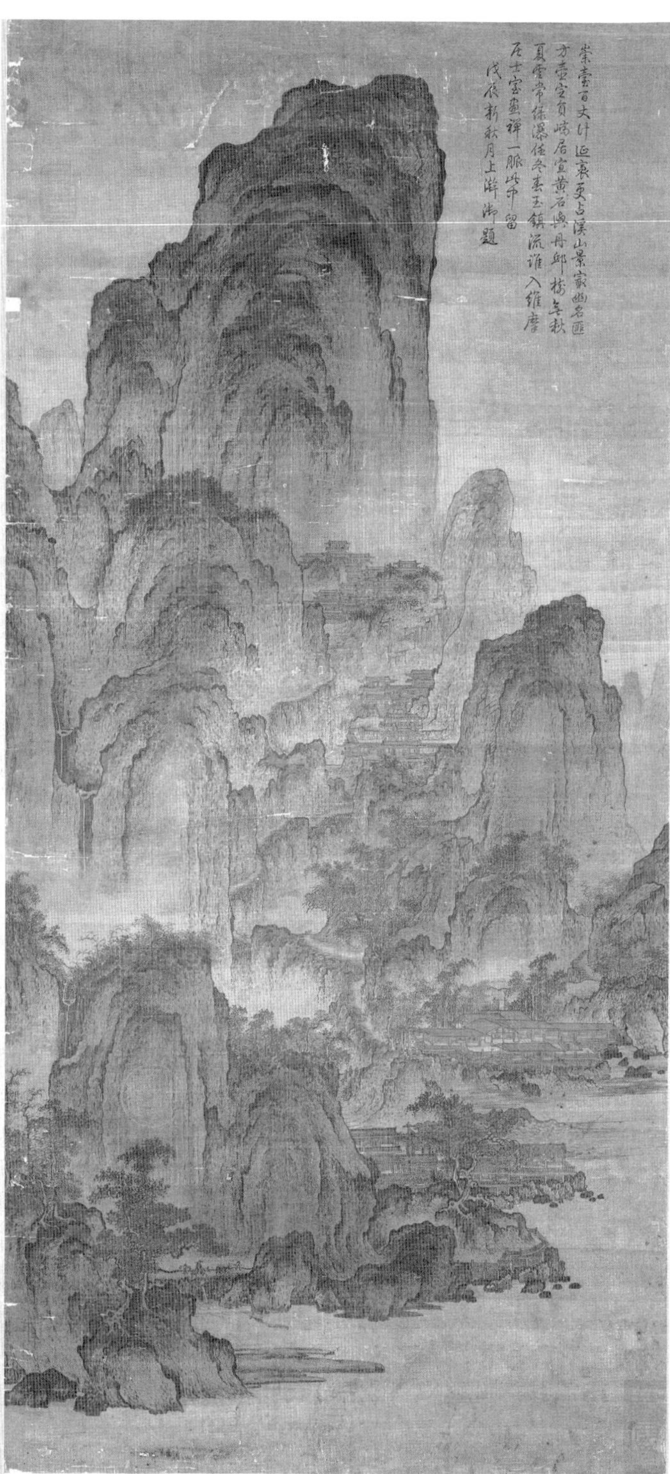

Fig. 8.7
Yan Wengui (967–1044), *Temples amid Mountains and Streams.* Hanging scroll, ink on silk, 103.9 × 47.4 cm. National Palace Museum, Taiwan, Republic of China. As very few paintings survive by Yan Wengui, it is difficult to determine why he was rejected when the *Xuanhe Painting Catalogue* was compiled.

Dynasties; that is, they make one recognize the recent decline in customs and long for the return to simplicity."[110]

What of the painters who are described as Song court painters? It is difficult to find cases where their service at court is celebrated in any way. Sometimes the *Xuanhe Painting Catalogue*'s evaluation of a court painter is much harsher than that of Liu Daochun or Guo Ruoxu. Perhaps the best example is Chen Yongzhi. Liu Daochun classed him as "subtle" in figure painting and "talented" in both landscape and animal painting and had nothing negative to say of him. Chen Yongzhi followed Hu Gui in painting foreign horses but also developed his own ideas, and "his understanding of proportion and his knowledge of pictorial depth were very accomplished." Guo Ruoxu admitted that he sometimes went too far: "In fineness of details and in cunning effects he was well-nigh unsurpassable; but in striving so hard for comprehensiveness he lost something of purity." The authors of the *Xuanhe* catalogue developed this criticism further using terms common in calligraphy criticism: "Although his exhaustive detail is done exquisitely, he is entirely lacking in freedom, as he sticks strictly to the models. With regard to what lies beyond the rules, he entirely lacks soaring or untrammeled passages."[111]

In some cases, the point was made that painters who served at court should not be seen as men who simply worked for money. Of a landscapist who served under Zhenzong and Renzong, we are told that when "contemporaries tried to use their influence or wealth to get paintings from him, he would not comply, but he happily gave works to friends who wanted them."[112] In other cases court service is treated as something to be explained away. For instance, the biography of Cui Bo recounts:

> He was good at painting flowers, bamboo, birds, lotus flowers, ducks, Buddhist and Daoist images, spirits, mountains, forests, and wild creatures. He was especially good at drawing from life, and could do geese with consummate skill. Whatever he painted always captured the essentials, expressing his thoughts with the lowering of his brush. He did not waste time with a ruler, but could do perfect freehand squares and circles. During the Xining period (1068–1077) he came to Shenzong's attention, and the emperor had him along with Ai Xuan, Ding Kuang, and Ge Shouchang paint the screen for Hanging Hem Hall, which depicted bamboo, crabapples, and cranes. Because Bo was considered the best of them, he was appointed assistant at the Hanlin Painting Academy. Because Bo was by nature easy-going and unambitious, he insistently declined the appointment. As a special favor he was allowed to take only assignments made by the emperor himself, and with these assurances he reluctantly took up the post.[113]

In terms of fields of painting, the turn against court artists was more severe with regard to landscape painting than with bird-and-flower painting. Of the thirty Song landscape painters, only four are said to have served at court for at least part of their careers. If all of the paintings listed for them were done at court, forty-three (about 5 percent of the 827 Song landscape paintings) were done at court. A much higher percentage of the bird-and-flower paintings were done by court painters, however. Six court painters did slightly over half of the 2,016 Song bird-and-flower paintings.[114] Moreover, the tone of their entries rarely disparages professional skill. Even bird paintings by scholar-officials, such as the early Tang official Xue Ji, are praised for their ability to rival professional painters in close observation and accurate depiction of the fine differences between species:

> Xue Ji excelled in painting birds and flowers, figures, and various other miscellaneous subjects, but he was particularly skilled in painting cranes. Therefore, when one thinks of cranes, one also thinks of Xue Ji. Because there are many people who raise cranes, it is easy to gain a thorough understanding of their appearance when flying, calling out, drinking, or eating. However, there are very few people who can paint cranes well. There has not been one who can accurately depict every detail: the shape of the head, the hue of the down, the length of the beak, the thickness of the legs, and the position of the knees. Indicating the sex of the cranes is also particularly difficult. Although there are famous artists who are skilled in painting, when they paint cranes their weakness is revealed in the feet. Therefore, it is fitting that Xue Ji should be famous among past and present artists because his paintings of cranes are truly magnificent.[115]

Even in the case of court bird-and-flower painters, however, the cataloguers might add comments implying that a painter's focus on certain kinds of flowers was a drawback. The entry for Xu Chongsi notes that he normally painted flashy subjects like peonies, peach and apricot blossoms, and butterflies, which associated him with aristocratic taste. He lacked the "hills and ravines" which a literati painter would have had in his breast.[116]

How much of the art criticism and theory in the *Xuanhe Painting Catalogue* is Huizong's and how much that of men like Dong You and Huang Bosi who worked for him in the Palace Library? As early as 1936, Osvald Sirén described Dong You as holding ideas about painting quite close to those of Su Shi on such issues as the sources of creativity or the importance of going beyond form.[117] Still, a comparison of Dong's items in his *Guangchuan huaba* and entries in the *Xuanhe Painting Catalogue* shows little verbal overlap; if Dong You drafted entries for the imperial catalogue, he did not later include them in his own book of notes on paintings. All that one can say for sure is that Huizong was content to have men like Dong You write entries for the catalogue.

Cultural Politics of the Painting Catalogue

Much of the organization and content of the *Xuanhe Painting Catalogue* can be read as political in one sense or another. Certainly never mentioning Su Shi by name was politically motivated. More subtle messages are also significant. In the catalogue, Song painters are characterized by their ritual relationship to the throne as a clansman, civil servitor (*wenchen*), military servitor (*wuchen*), or inner servitor (*neichen*), categories corresponding to the ways in which those who were privileged to enter the emperor's presence were divided at audiences and other ceremonies. Imperial clansmen lined up on the south; officials of civil rank, the bulk of whom had passed the *jinshi* exams, lined up on the east; officials of military rank, the bulk of whom had entered through hereditary privilege, lined up on the west.[118] Those without the rank to attend audiences are merely listed by name—even members of the court painting academy, such as Guo Xi and Cui Bo. For instance, among the eight Song bird-and-flower painters, two were military servitors and four were inner servitors. Of the eleven Song painters listed under "ink bamboo," five were imperial relatives, two were civil servitors, one was a military servitor, and one was a monk. Those we today classify as literati painters were framed as imperial servitors, not independent men of letters.

The influence of politics on the *Xuanhe Painting Catalogue* is also apparent in the attention given to Daoist paintings and to works by those with close connections to the throne as either imperial relatives or court eunuchs. Although one could speculate that the emphasis on the links between poetry and painting or painting and literati status owed more to the officials who did the actual work on the catalogue than to Huizong, the decisions to highlight Daoism, imperial relatives, and court eunuchs surely must have had the active support of Huizong himself.

DAOIST PAINTINGS

Huizong's commitment to Daoism is reflected throughout the *Xuanhe Painting Catalogue*. As Xiao Baifang has shown in a detailed study, this catalogue was compiled and edited in a way that gave Daoism a more elevated position than it occupied in any earlier work on painting.[119] First, and perhaps most importantly, it included more than 350 paintings on Daoist subjects, the majority in the Daoist-Buddhist

TABLE 8.4. Daoist paintings listed in the *Xuanhe Painting Catalogue*

Period	Listed under Daoist and Buddhist paintings	Listed under figure paintings	Listed under other categories	Total
pre-Tang	6	0	0	6
Tang	86	31	1	118
Five Dynasties	71	1	12	84
Song	125	19	24	168
Total	288	51	37	376

section, but a large number also listed for artists who were classified under figure, landscape, architecture, or other subjects. As seen in table 8.4, nearly half of the Daoist paintings dated from the Northern Song period.

Typical of the Daoist paintings listed in the *Painting Catalogue* are depictions of major deities such as the Three Pure Ones, the Venerable Celestial of the Primal Beginning, Laozi, astral deities, immortals, and Perfected Ones. For instance, there were fifty-seven paintings of star gods, eight of the Nine Sources of Brightness (Jiuyao), thirty of Laozi (mostly called the Supreme Superior), and twenty-nine of the Three Officials (of Heaven, Earth, and Water).

Another way the catalogue elevates Daoism is by giving religious paintings top ranking in the catalogue and, within religious paintings, giving Daoism priority. Neither Liu Daochun nor Guo Ruoxu separated figure and religious paintings. Moreover, when they mentioned religious paintings, they used the more common term "Buddhist and Daoist" (Fo-Dao), not the term used in Huizong's catalogue, "Daoist and Buddhist" (Dao-Shi), which reverses the order. In addition, in the list of paintings by each individual artist under his entry, Daoist paintings are generally listed first, before Buddhist paintings and before secular subjects.[120] Moreover, Daoist language and Daoist ideas are found throughout the work. The death of the painter Guo Zhongshu, for instance, is referred to as his "becoming an immortal." The preface justifies the inclusion of paintings of vegetables and fruits in terms of "nourishing life" (*yangsheng*), a term with a long history in Daoist thinking. It also alludes to a passage in *Zhuangzi* in which a gardener bests a disciple of Confucius in his understanding of the Dao.[121]

Not surprisingly, status as a Daoist master is given more attention in the *Xuanhe Painting Catalogue* than in earlier works on painting. The Tang master Zhang Suqing, for instance, had been described by Guo Ruoxu as a Daoist adept attached to a

FIG. 8.8
Attributed to Zhang Sengyou (sixth century), *Five Planets and Twenty-Eight Lunar Mansions* (detail). Handscroll, ink and color on silk, 27.5 × 489.7 cm. Osaka Municipal Museum of Art. The twenty-eight lunar mansions are the constellations through which the moon passes as it crosses the sky. They have links to Western astrology, as they incorporate the twelve Western zodiac figures. The figure on the right depicts the Lunar Mansion named Woman, who corresponds to Capricorn, shown here with a goat head. The next, on the left, is called Emptiness, and corresponds to Aquarius, shown inside a water jar.

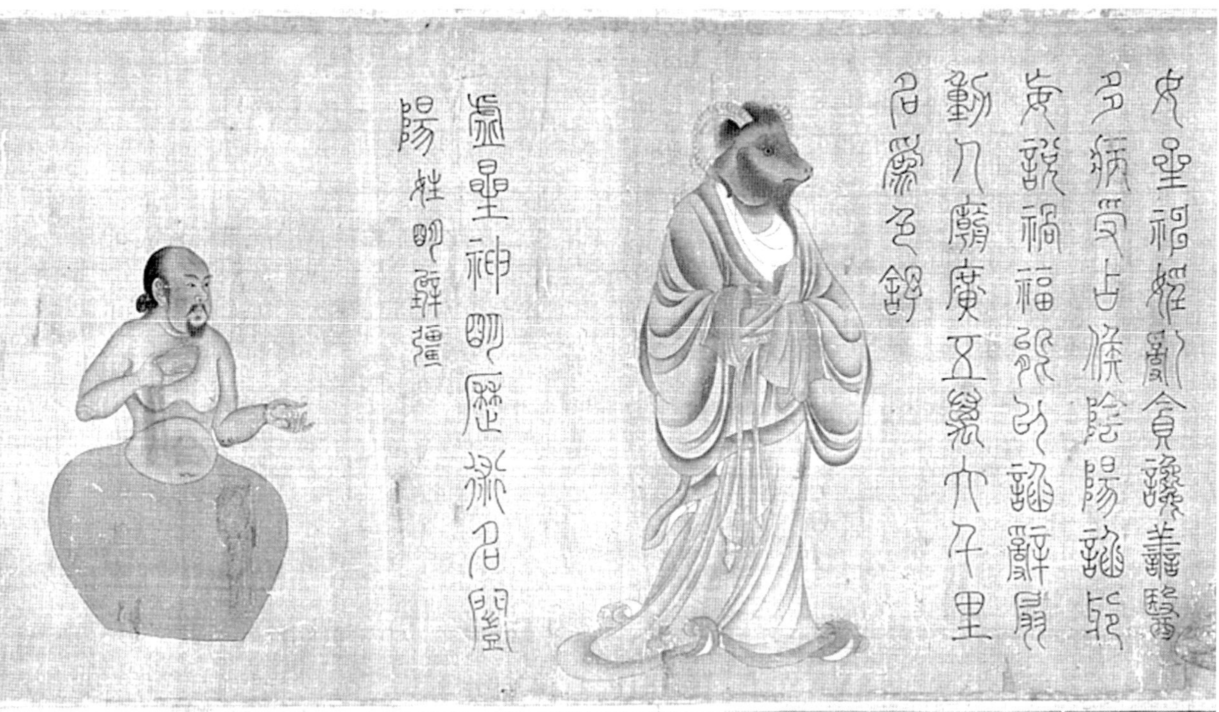

temple, but nothing more is said of his Daoist status. In the *Xuanhe Painting Catalogue*, however, his status as a priest is highlighted by citing the effort of a Tang emperor to confer honors on him.[122]

The *Five Planets and Twenty-Eight Lunar Mansions*, attributed to the sixth-century painter Zhang Sengyou, can serve as an example of the sort of Daoist paintings Huizong had in his collection (fig. 8.8).[123] This painting is not an icon meant to be hung in a temple, but rather a handscroll that would have functioned as an illustrated book, both describing and depicting Daoist divinities. Some are depicted as people, others as animals, and a few as hybrid creatures. Scholars today do not believe the work dates to the sixth century; Stephen Little and Shawn Eichman think it may be a Tang work or perhaps a Song copy of a Tang work. Each picture of a god is accompanied by a text written out in fine-line seal script that gives its attributes, the types of vessels and food to be used in offerings to it, and the location of its shrine. Although the divinities depicted in the scroll had by Tang times been absorbed into the Daoist pantheon, they did not originate with Daoism but with early Chinese cosmological beliefs combined with Western astrology, probably absorbed via Central Asia, as Sogdians had a similar system.[124]

In much the way that Buddhist religious experience was said to lie behind the success of Buddhist paintings in earlier treatises on painting, Daoist religious experience was given similar powers in the *Xuanhe Painting Catalogue.* The palace had a painting titled *Tableaux from the Daoist Classics* (Daojing bianxiang) that was attributed to the Sui official Dong Zhan. His entry in the late Tang *Celebrated Painters of All the Dynasties* refers to his paintings of figures, buildings, and horses, and mentions one Buddhist painting, *Maitreya's Paradise,* but says nothing of any interest in Daoism or paintings of Daoist subjects. Dong Zhan's entry in the *Xuanhe Catalogue,* by contrast, refers to his painting in this way: "*Tableaux from the Daoist Classics,* which Zhan painted, was highly appreciated by his contemporaries. If it had not been for his feeling outside the painting, his contact with the numinous and marvelous, his ability to enter into the dream of the land of Huaxu, and his journeys with magicians, how could he have painted this?"[125] The entry alludes to two passages in the *Liezi,* one in which the Yellow Emperor dreams of traveling to the land of Huaxu, where there were no leaders or teachers and the people were without desires and never died before their times, the other in which a magician took the Yellow Emperor on a trip into the sky from which even the most splendid palace on earth seemed paltry.[126]

Several Daoist priests are featured as painters in Huizong's catalogue. The ninth-century master Zhang Suqing is described as becoming a Daoist priest because he was orphaned young and faced poverty. He once did a set of paintings of the Twelve Perfected Lords that showed them engaged in such activities as selling divinations, trading in cinnabar, and writing out talismans. Among the fourteen paintings listed for him were ones of the Three Officials, the Nine Sources of Brightness, the Longevity Star, and ten portraits of historical figures (including Dong Zhongshu) imagined as Daoist Perfected Ones.[127] Zhang Suqing's follower, Chen Ruoyu, was best known for the wall paintings he did at Daoist temples in Chengdu. The one painting by him in Huizong's collection, a depiction of the Eastern Floriate Lord, is described as even better than the temple paintings and as evidence of his deep knowledge of Daoist teachings.[128]

Two Daoist priests still active when the catalogue was compiled were also given entries in the *Painting Catalogue.* Xu Zhichang, a prominent official who was said to have been the one to introduce Lin Lingsu to Huizong, was described as a skilled musician able to cure illnesses without the use of drugs. At the same time he was said to have the "style of a literati gentleman." Knowledgeable in both Daoist and Confucian texts, he was assigned by Huizong to work on the canon editing project. As a painter, his portrayals of gods and immortals were said to be right in every detail. Still, the imperial collection had only a single scroll by him.[129]

Many more paintings were included by Xu's contemporary, Li Derou, who was also employed on the Daoist canon project. Li was said to have had a natural talent for painting and to have been especially good at capturing likenesses. The twenty-six paintings by him in the palace collection included pictures of the Mao lords, Zhuangzi, Lü Dongbin, Tao Hongjing, Sun Simiao, Wang Ziqiao, Liezi, and many other key figures in Daoist traditions.[130]

IMPERIAL RELATIVES AS PAINTERS

Even though the authors of the painting catalogue did not overrepresent Song court painters, they found other ways to convey the message that the court was central to culture. They did this by selecting for inclusion in the catalogue men who had close connections to the Song court, such as imperial relatives, court eunuchs, and high court officials. Imperial relatives appear in many sections of the catalogue, as summarized in table 8.5.[131]

Quite a few of the listed clansmen listed in the catalogue (and one of the two clanswomen) did the sorts of poetic paintings that were associated with literati. In fact, five of the twelve painters profiled in the section on ink bamboo and small scenes were Huizong's relatives: one was his uncle (Shenzong's brother), one was that uncle's wife, two were imperial clansmen, and one was an imperial son-in-law. Moreover, one of the fullest explications of literati painting is in the entry for the clansman Zhao Lingbi:

> There are a great many people in the world who paint bamboo, but it is rare to find one who does not seek form likeness but rather exhausts the beauty of their exceptional appearance. . . .[The usual painters] are skillful [in depicting bamboo in varied circumstances], but are too constrained by rules. Therefore their style is ordinary, their life-force weak, and they do not attain marvels of naturalness. However, literati are not like this. They are not necessarily able to attain form likeness through technique, but they express ideas and their compositions are elegant. To capture sparse twigs and flourishing leaves does not depend on doing a lot. When one lowers the brush for horizontal or vertical strokes, they move unimpeded. The excellence of bamboo can be adequately expressed in simple strokes. Ordinary painters put their efforts into novelty and ingenuity rather than expression of ideas. The more they strive for fineness, the more belabored their work becomes. Exceptional painters put their efforts into free expression, resulting in an abundance of meaning. The more they abbreviate, the more they capture the essence. These two approaches proceed in opposite directions.[132]

Paintings by several clansmen survive, so there is no reason to doubt that some were accomplished painters, but it also is apparent that Huizong decided to err on

TABLE 8.5. Song imperial relatives with entries in the *Xuanhe Painting Catalogue*

Genre	Name	Status	No. of paintings	Evaluation
dragon and fish	Zhao Kexiong 趙克敻	clansman	1	Painted to amuse himself; regretted never getting to see the sea (9.157–58).
	Zhao Shunuo 趙叔儺	clansman	17	He did paintings to match poems, including one by Wang Anshi that is cited (9.158).
landscape	Wang Shen 王詵	princess's husband	35	Well-read and an able writer, friends with many of the scholars and teachers of the day. Skilled in many fields, from chess to painting. Depicted landscape scenes hard to capture in words. Also a calligrapher in all scripts. Had a hall at his house called "Treasured Paintings" to store his calligraphy and paintings. Liked to hang paintings on all his walls. Once presented a poem to Shenzong, who appreciated it. After the princess died, Shenzong chastised him, but he reformed himself (12.203–4).
animals	Zhao Lingsong 趙令松	clansman	4	Just as good a reputation as his elder brother Zhao Lingrang (see below). Good at monochrome flowers and fruit, but some criticize him for depicting too many maggots. Especially known for painting dogs (14.233).
bird and flower	Zhao Zonghan 趙宗漢	clansman/ prince	8	Never put on airs, preferred poetry and calligraphy to dogs and horses. Painted to amuse himself. Often rewarded for the paintings he presented at court. Did an atmospheric picture of eight geese (16.260–61).
	Zhao Xiaoying 趙孝穎	clansman/ cousin	22	Impressed people with how well he could depict things he had never seen but only imagined. At the sacrifices to Heaven in 1119, Huizong gave him one of his own paintings of wagtails, which conveyed the poetic meaning of good relations between brothers. Alive (16.261–62).
	Zhao Zhongquan 趙仲佺	clansman	14	Main interest the literature of the Han and Jin periods. Did poetry in the style of Bo Juyi. In his pictures there were poems, even his paintings of grass, trees, animals, and birds, something highly skilled professional painters could not attain (16.262–63).
	Zhao Zhongxian 趙仲僴	clansman	7	Loved to paint and kept practicing even in the coldest or hottest weather. Every year when the scholar-officials in the capital opened their gardens to let others see the blooming flowers, he would join, bringing along his paints, and when he saw an unpainted screen or wall, would paint something on it for fun. Once he did a painting

Genre	Name	Status	No. of paintings	Evaluation
				of mandarin ducks at Wang Shen's house, using very little color. Everyone who saw it admired it, and someone added a poem (which is quoted; 16.263).
	Zhao Shitian 趙世腆	clansman	5	Good at painting trees along river banks, paintings that make you feel you are seeing vast emptiness. He did a very thoughtful painting to match a poem by Su Shunqin. He also did bamboo and rocks. Alive (16.264).
	Zhao Shilei 趙士雷	clansman	51	Famous as a painter. He did very poetic water birds by the water. He also did flowers and bamboo, usually in the wind or snow. He had none of the habits of the high-ranking, and his painting was totally unlike that of artisan painters. Alive (16.264–65).
	Miss Cao 曹氏	clansman's wife	5	Her paintings were not soft and charming women's paintings. They make you feel that you are traveling among the mountains and streams. Someone inscribed a poem on one of her paintings, showing the esteem in which her work was held (16.266).
ink bamboo and small scenes	Prince Jun 端獻王趙頵	prince/ uncle	70	Shenzong's younger brother, whom Shenzong refused to let leave the palace. Main pleasure in painting and calligraphy. Good at several scripts and several genres of painting, such as ink bamboo, flowers and fruit, old trees, and reeds along the river (20.304–5).
	Zhao Lingrang 趙令穰	clansman	24	Although he grew up among the high-ranking, he devoted himself to the classics and histories and amused himself with painting. He collected old calligraphy and paintings, seeing the special features of any piece that he glanced at. Achieved impressive effect even though limited by only seeing scenery in the vicinity of the capital. He once submitted a painting to Zhezong, who conferred on him in return a piece of calligraphy saying "national treasure" (20.306).
	Zhao Lingbi 趙令庇	clansman	1	A follower of Wen Tong, who painted highly abbreviated monochrome bamboo. Alive (20.307).
	Miss Wang 王氏	uncle's wife	2	Amused herself with paintings and histories, also did calligraphy. The quality of her ink bamboos is evidence of what was in her heart (20.307).
	Li Wei 李瑋	princess's husband	2	Painted bamboo when inspiration struck him, but didn't let others know. Also wrote poetry and did calligraphy in several scripts. Appreciated by Renzong (20.308).

the side of listing too many rather than too few.[133] One of the clansmen, Zhao Lingrang, is today still well known as a painter, and a couple of fine paintings by him are extant, including *Summer Mist along the Lake Shore*, dated 1100, in the Boston Museum of Fine Arts (fig. 8.9, plate 12).[134] The scene depicted has nothing of the grandeur of the central mountain hanging scrolls for which the Northern Song is noted, but fits rather well the description of Zhao's paintings in the *Xuanhe Catalogue:* "His paintings offer wide views over low embankments and lakes, or represent shady groves in a misty atmosphere with ducks and geese; they have an air of quiet repose which is very pleasant and which has made them highly appreciated by connoisseurs."[135]

None of the surviving paintings by Zhao Lingrang have Huizong's seals, and it may be that none of them were among the twenty-four paintings by him listed in the catalogue. A clansman with even more paintings in Huizong's catalogue (fifty-one), Zhao Shilei, is less well known today, although his entry describes him as a famous painter. A handscroll by him in the Palace Museum, Beijing, was apparently in Huizong's collection (fig. 8.10). About 2.3 meters long, this scroll also depicts a river scene. On the mounting just before the beginning of the scroll is the inscription in Huizong's Slender Gold calligraphy: "*Small Scenes of the Xiao and Xiang Rivers* by clansman Shilei," a title recorded in the *Xuanhe Painting Catalogue.*[136] The painting seems more staged than the other two river scenes shown here, by Zhao Lingrang (fig. 8.9) and Liang Shimin (fig. 8.6). But certainly if Zhao Shilei did this painting, he would have impressed his contemporaries with his ability to portray birds in flight.

In a few cases, Huizong had close personal knowledge of relatives who were painters. His Uncle Jun (Shenzong's younger brother) was one of only three men to be recorded in both Huizong's painting and calligraphy catalogues.[137] The *Calligraphy Catalogue* describes him as good-looking, well read, interested in medicine, and adept at both flying white and seal script calligraphy.[138] The painting catalogue lists seventy of his paintings, mostly bamboo or small scenes. He was praised for his skill in depicting bamboo in different circumstances. "He was also good at shrimp, fish, rushes, old trees, and river reeds. His interests lay in the distant rivers and clouds, quite unlike what painter-artisans can glimpse through the walls."[139]

Uncle Jun's wife, Princess Wang, also painted. After she married the prince at sixteen, she interested herself in painting and literature, we are told, not jewelry or other luxuries:

> Her seal and clerical style calligraphies followed the styles established since the Han and Jin periods, and she wrote short poems as refreshing as streams flowing through forests. She painted bamboo in light ink, catching the appearance of both the straight

and the slanted. Those who saw them wondered if the shadow had fallen onto the silk. Unless she was exceptional inside, how could she have accomplished this?[140]

One of the sons of Uncle Jun and Princess Wang, Zhao Xiaoying, also is listed as a painter. Born in 1084 or 1085, he was a first cousin of Huizong, less than three years his junior. Huizong's collection contained twenty-two of Xiaoying's paintings, including monochromes of flowers and birds, but also scenes of birds in ponds, bamboo in snow, flowers in color, and so on. Zhao Xiaoying was particularly praised for his ability to catch a likeness.[141]

EUNUCHS AS PAINTERS

Mi Fu had drawn attention to collectors who were imperial clansmen and imperial relatives. It is not surprising that the *Xuanhe Painting Catalogue* took pains to show how many were creditable painters as well. There is much less precedent for drawing attention to the talents of eunuchs.[142]

Although in Song times palace eunuchs were not as numerous or politically powerful as they were in late Tang or late Ming times, they still were a key element in the imperial system. Eunuchs had their own bureaucracy and career paths, involving promotion from one rank to another. The most important eunuchs were much more than messengers; they could be sent outside the palace city or even the capital city, and given tasks such as checking on military operations or tax collection in the provinces. A few eunuchs even became military commanders. Eunuchs kept track of and audited the many storehouses in the palace complex, including the Inner Palace Treasury, which was under the direct control of the throne for palace use, the privy purse as distinct from the state treasury. They also had charge of storehouses that held objects for the use of palace residents and for gifts, such as the tea and charcoal warehouse, the oil and vinegar warehouse, the ritual dress warehouse, and the import warehouse with spices, medicines, and ivory received from tribute missions. Perhaps the involvement of eunuchs with court paintings grew out of their responsibilities for the storehouses.[143] As seen in chapter 4, eunuchs took on many responsibilities connected to palace art. They were sent as agents to travel to other parts of the country to purchase art works, and they were put in charge of palace construction projects, which would have involved supervising painters decorating buildings.

Several of the nine eunuchs in the *Xuanhe Painting Catalogue* would have been known personally to Huizong, as they were active during Zhezong's reign or later. Three were still living when the catalogue was compiled. Five were listed as landscapists, including the general Tong Guan. Nine paintings were attributed to Liu

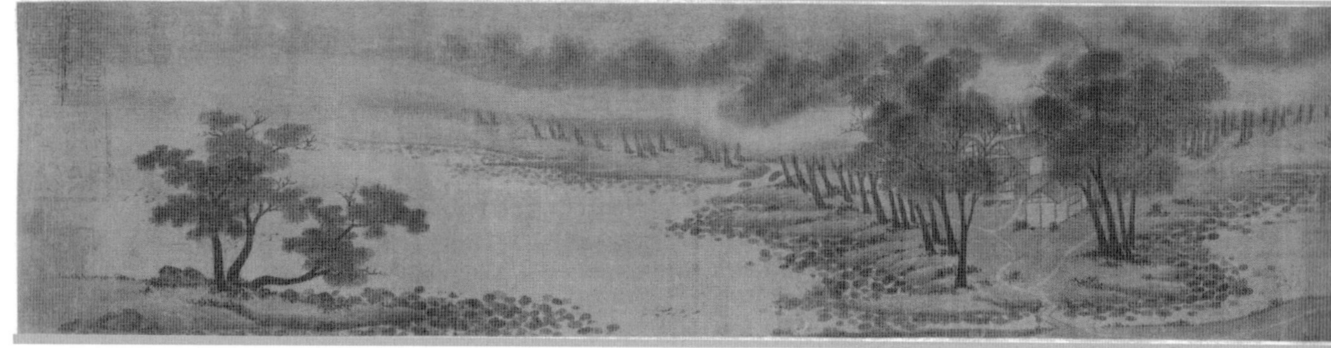

FIG. 8.9
Zhao Lingrang (ca. 1070–ca. 1100), *Summer Mist along the Lake Shore*. Handscroll, ink and color on silk, 19.1 × 161.3 cm. Photograph © 2008 Museum of Fine Arts, Boston. Keith McLeod Fund, 57.724. The painting shows a path leading from a cottage surrounded by trees, over a bridge and through a grove largely obscured by mist, toward another small settlement. Lotuses grow along the banks, and ducks swim in the river. See also the detail, plate 12.

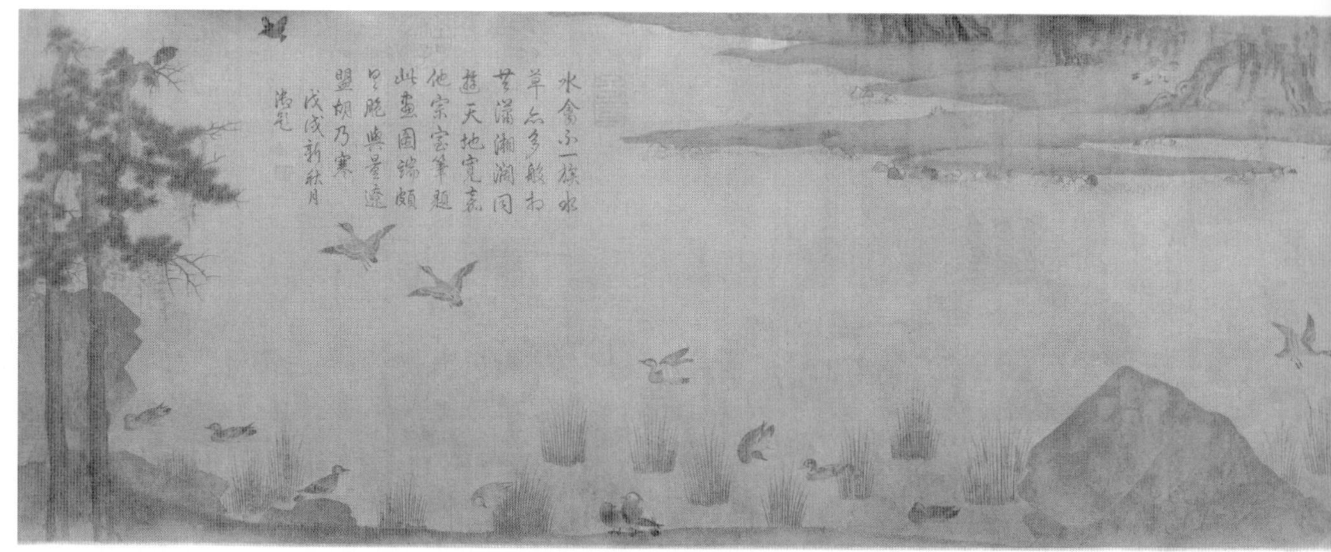

FIG. 8.10
Zhao Shilei (ca. 1100), *Small Scenes of the Xiao and Xiang Rivers* (detail). Handscroll, ink and color on silk, 43.2 × 233.5 cm. Palace Museum, Beijing. The painting opens with a pair of pine trees in the foreground, then moves to the water, where reeds grow and several kinds of ducks are swimming, taking flight, or landing. On the far shore we see the gnarled lower trunks of willow trees as well as two pairs of birds.

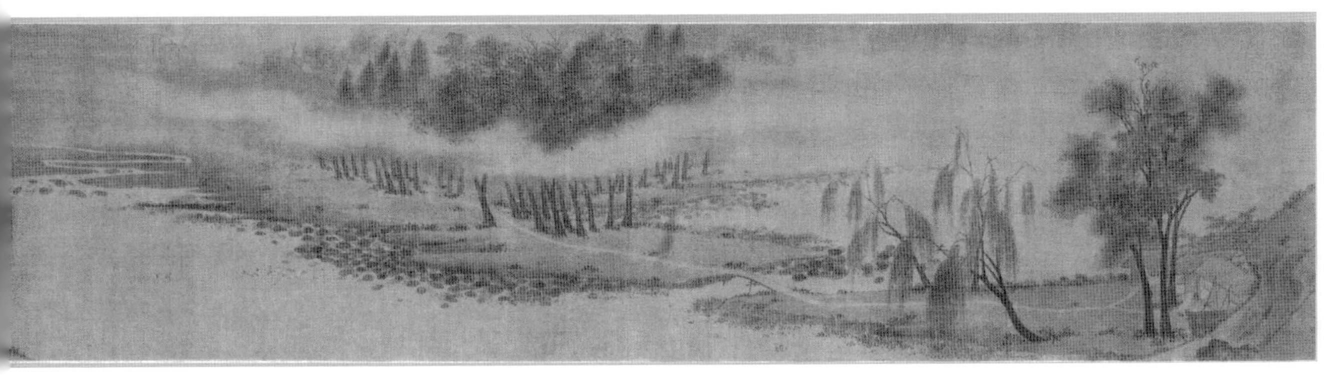

Yuan, who served in the palace for five decades and was considered by both those inside and outside the palace as an expert in identifying and authenticating paintings (see table 8.6).

Some of the eunuch painters are described as amateurs, much like the imperial relatives, especially those listed in the section on landscape painters. A few, however, seem to have been closer to professional painters. This would seem to be the case with Yang Riyan, who did portraits, and Jia Xiang, placed in charge of the painters when Harmony Preserved Hall was built and decorated. Their entries are translated below.

> The palace eunuch Yang Riyan's family had lived in Kaifeng for generations. He was a good student as a youth and enjoyed the histories and classics, especially the *Spring and Autumn Annals*. He wrote eloquently, and literary men were all willing to interact with him. His seal, clerical, and *bafen* script calligraphy is not inferior to the ancients'. He was especially good at using a fine brush, to marvelous effects, but his portraits were even more exquisite. When he was still in a low position, Emperor Shenzong recognized his talent, promoted him to personal attendant, and had him paint portraits of former worthies and Empress Qinsheng Xiansu [Xiang]. In 1101, [Huizong] wanted someone to paint a portrait of [his long deceased mother, now titled] Empress Qinci [Chen], but none of the painters in the court remembered what she looked like, so he commanded Yang to paint it from memory. Once Yang began painting, people surrounded him and watched, putting their hands on their foreheads and weeping because it was so lifelike. This is how refined and exceptional his skill was. His landscapes and figure paintings are lofty and otherworldly, with spirit resonance of a high order, far beyond ordinary works.[144]

> The palace eunuch Jia Xiang was from Kaifeng. He was interested in craft from his youth and attained marvels as a painter. Whenever he gave a high evaluation to a contemporary painter, it would make him famous. When Harmony Preserved Hall was completed, dragons in water were supposed to be painted on the screens, but none of the work by the painting masters satisfied Jia Xiang, so Huizong had him paint them himself. He was calm and collected as dragons emerged from his brush. He painted without planning and yet the dragons flew splendidly through the sky. The style and composition were novel and made people's hair stand up when they looked at it; everyone admired its subtlety. He was also good at painting bamboo, rocks, grass, trees, birds, and animals. Contemporaries who obtained his works treated them as treasures. He was also skilled in wood and clay sculpture . . .[145]

There was of course a huge difference in the social standing of imperial relatives

TABLE 8.6. Song eunuchs with entries in the *Xuanhe Painting Catalogue*

Genre	Name	No. of paintings	Evaluation
figure	Yang Riyan 楊日言	4	Enjoyed the histories and classics, especially the *Chunqiu*. Interacted with literary men. Did seal and clerical calligraphy. Shenzong recognized his talent, and had him paint portraits of former worthies and the empress. Excellent at catching a likeness. Did a portrait of Huizong's mother in 1101 (7.137).
landscape	Tong Guan 童貫	4	Court painters had frequented his father's house. He would play at painting when brush and ink were handy. Paints in a simple and natural way. Also an accomplished general. Living (12.205–6).
	Liu Yuan 劉瑗	9	Father a collector, with 10,000 scrolls of paintings, calligraphies, and books. Learned to recognize authentic ones, so often asked to inspect objects. He painted simply to express his ideas and did not save his work (12.207–8).
	Liang Kui 梁揆	2	Likes to carve and paint since young. Able to convey people, flowers, and bamboo. Alive, serving in Sagely Thoughts Hall (12.209).
	Luo Cun 羅存	2	Likes to paint, especially small pieces. Able to let his mind travel to the rivers and seas while his body is in the capital. Unrolling his scroll is like climbing a tall mountain, letting you accompany the fish and birds. Since he is still young, he will likely have even greater accomplishments in time. Living (12.209).
	Feng Jin 馮覲	13	He did paintings of the four seasons in the streams and mountains, showing the rising or setting sun as well as clouds and mist. His painting *The Ten Thousand Sounds in the Golden Wind* makes you feel you can hear the rustling of the tree branches. His ability to convey profundities is comparable to Ouyang Xiu's in his prose poem on the sounds of autumn (12.210).
bird and flower	Jia Xiang 賈祥	17	Good at crafts from his youth, he attained marvels in painting. He painted the dragons on the walls at Harmony Preserved Hall on Huizong's orders. He was also good at painting bamboo, rocks, grass and trees, birds, and animals. He even was a talented sculptor (19.297–98).
	Yue Shixuan 樂士宣	41	In middle age became interested in Daoism and devoted himself to poetry and writing. Even before that he liked painting and took Ai Xuan as a model, but after he learned to read he realized the limitations of his old model and attained higher levels, especially in bird-and-flower paintings, some of which corresponded to lines from Du Fu. Scholar-officials admired his work. The paintings that he submitted to Shenzong were the best done by eunuchs. He also proved courageous in the campaign against Xia (19.298–99).
	Li Zhengchen 李正臣	6	Made the birds and flowers he painted seem alive. Didn't do vulgar peach or plum blossoms or finely carved railings, preferring to express the ideas in his breast, not to seek the showy and beautiful (19.300).

and eunuchs. Imperial relatives, in Song social life and in the *Xuanhe Painting Catalogue,* were treated as quasi-nobility, people whose birth entitled them to deference as well as visible privileges, such as standing in the southern ranks at court audiences. Eunuchs, by contrast, did not participate in capital social life and were in general looked on by officials as menials. Mi Fu did not mention ever consulting a eunuch painting expert or looking at paintings together with a eunuch. Although it was generally recognized that palace eunuchs could have great political influence, most scholar-officials considered their power regrettable and did their best to act as though they did not exist. The *Xuanhe Catalogue*, by listing eunuchs after military rank officials, recognizes their relative rank. Still, the catalogue lists them before Buddhist and Daoist clergy, even though in the pecking order of literati social life monks and priests had much more standing than eunuchs, and no one's reputation was endangered by interacting with clerics.

Some scholars have speculated that eunuchs compiled the *Painting Catalogue*,[146] but even if that were the case, they would have had to have Huizong's approval before including so many eunuchs in the catalogue. More likely, Huizong, having grown up among eunuchs, perhaps having even learned something about painting or painting connoisseurship from palace eunuchs, did not share most literati's contempt for them. Early in his reign Huizong gave the eunuch general Tong Guan his transcription of the *Thousand Character Essay*.[147] In 1116 he took the unprecedented step of making Tong Guan a member of the Council of State. In 1122 he made Liang Shicheng the supervisor of the Palace Library, and in his essay commemorating the completion of the Genyue Garden, he heaped lavish praise on Liang.[148] Since Huizong was willing to make his respect for particular eunuchs so public, he had no reason not to draw attention to eunuchs' talent as painters in his catalogue.

In the first two decades of his reign, Huizong assembled an unprecedented collection of paintings. It easily surpassed any earlier collection in scope and size. Although it contained more than a thousand works that had been produced at the Song court by court artists, these were not its heart. What made the collection so strong was the types of paintings sought by Northern Song collectors, from works by old masters to those of living artists, from religious icons to pictures of kittens, from landscapes of imposing mountains to intimate scenes of ducks swimming in rivers, from brightly colored pictures of peonies and butterflies to chaste monochrome sketches of bamboo or plum blossoms.

How was Huizong able to put together so huge a collection of paintings in so short a span of time? Chinese authors, beginning well before Huizong's time, used language which suggested that fine works would find their way to an emperor who appreciated them. Still, the speed with which Huizong's collection grew suggests that he did not passively wait for objects to arrive. There are no records of massive confiscations during his reign; Huizong did not seize the art collections of the men he banned from office or cashiered.[149] Rather, as discussed in chapter 4, the collection was built up bit by bit as agents made purchases and owners made gifts. Of course, those who presented paintings to the court expected some reward, whether money, office, or influence.

We know of the depth and riches of Huizong's painting collection only because he decided to have a catalogue of it compiled. The act of cataloguing is interesting in and of itself. In reality, the composition of the collection would have reflected a series of historical accidents—whether it was a collector who died during Huizong's reign, making his possessions available for purchase, or an official sent to a particular prefecture who knew enough about painting to recognize a masterpiece in a local collection and try to acquire it for the palace collection. The job of the cataloguers, however, was to obscure these chance factors and make the collection seem like a perfect microcosm of the larger whole of valued paintings. They did this by writing an overview of the art of painting that found merit in all the types of paintings Huizong collected.

In framing the collection in this way, the cataloguers necessarily engaged many of the issues that had been discussed by art critics in the eleventh century. Some of the most influential critics, such as Mi Fu and Su Shi, wrote about painting mostly in terms of particular paintings that they had viewed. Huizong's officials were asked to attempt something more ambitious. The catalogue format required essays on each type of painting that would explain its larger cultural significance and sketch key features of its historical development.

A catalogue of an imperial collection helps establish a canon of great works. The overall standing of Huizong's collection was unassailable—who else had so many of the great masters? This gave Huizong the opportunity to use the catalogue to draw attention to lesser-known painters. Most of those he chose to promote in this way had close ties to the throne. Huizong did not include works by himself, his children, his consorts, or his own court painters (that might have seemed immodest) but he did not hesitate to include one or two paintings by quite a few people not recorded in any other source as painters—above all, imperial clansmen and court eunuchs. Thus, like the calligraphy catalogue, the painting catalogue was written in a way that highlighted the cultural prowess and centrality of the court. Cultural accomplishment and proximity to the throne went together.

A noteworthy feature of Huizong's painting catalogue is its strong support for the relatively new theory of literati painting. Clearly Huizong did not use the *Paint-*

ing Catalogue to try to undermine Su Shi's critical opinions on painters, no matter how much he resented Su Shi and opposed his politics. On the issue of literati painting, the catalogue took a stand entirely consistent with Su Shi's, and, other than leaving out Su himself, did not reject people because Su had admired them.

This strikes modern observers as odd, not only because they know the stories of Huizong insisting that his court painters paint in an exactingly descriptive style, but also because it has become conventional to view literati painting theory as an act of resistance against the court. Wai-kam Ho, in a short but influential essay, describes the emergence of scholar-official painting as a response to the artistic rigidity of the court Painting Academy: "One cannot help but be convinced that the rise of scholar official painting was directly caused, stimulated, and conditioned by the conspicuous presence of the Academy. It was an inevitable antithesis in such a dialectical historical development."[150] Perhaps influenced by Ho, many art historians treat the opposition of court and literati painting as an established fact. In Martin Powers's view, "The competition between court and literati for hegemony in the cultural arena must have strongly encouraged the literati to place their own pictorial ideals in opposition to court painting." Maggie Bickford writes, "The omnipresent influence of the Imperial Painting Academy seems to have served as the critical irritant that provoked the scholars into forcefully articulating their contrary views."[151]

Assuming that Su Shi had court painters in mind when he talked of painter-artisans makes it possible to read Su's stance as an act of political opposition. Richard Barnhart sees political intentions behind both court art and literati art. In contrast to the "colorful, handsome, and dramatic art" common in the period which glorified "the political, religious, and economic rulers of China," the new art had "the capacity to criticize, reject, exhort, and subvert, as well as to flatter and glorify the powerful." Alfreda Murck places specific paintings done in the late Northern Song by literati in the context of the bitter political disputes of the time and shows ways they can be read as covert political protest.[152]

The flaws of an overly rigid division between court and literati have already been pointed out by other scholars. Robert Harrist disabuses us of the notion that literati painters invariably looked down on craft and training. He points out that Li Gonglin had "technical skill with brush and ink [that] approached that of a professional artist," and that he would paint almost any subject matter, from birds and flowers to Buddhist icons and horses. James Cahill, in discussing the early stages of the development of poetic painting, notes that some of the most important artists had close connections to the throne through marriage or kinship and deserve to be called aristocrat-artists. In reference to the same men, Richard Barnhart says that some of those most central to the development of the scholar-painter tradition "stood just beside the imperial structure—sometimes in fact just within it—and found the authority to comment on it." Ping Foong shows that Guo Xi, although a court painter known for large landscapes with imposing central mountains, also painted landscape handscrolls for literati patrons, paintings which literati viewers could interpret in terms of typically literati concerns of farewell from office and protest against retirement or exile. Maggie Bickford, in a study of late Southern Song flower painting, argues that the visual evidence does not support a bipolar view of the art world but rather a fluid one with much mutual influence between amateur and court painters.[153]

Perhaps it is time to reconsider the basic assumption that the target of literati art theory was court art, and that the court would have had to see it that way. First, the term Su Shi uses to refer to the painters he disparages is painter-artisans, not painters-in-attendance, or any other term he could have used to refer to court painters if that is what he wanted to say. The meaning he wanted to convey was probably something more like "hack painter," not the cream of the crop of professional painters who had secured appointments at court. Certainly men at court could have read his target as bad art, not court art. After all, Su Shi had good things to say about particular court painters. He owned a painting by the court bird-and-flower painter Huang Quan that he liked enough to invite a friend to view with him. When Shenzong had Guo Xi paint a screen for the newly built quarters for the Hanlin Academy, Su was among those enthusiastic in their response.[154] There is no evidence that Su assumed that court painters were more likely to be hacks than painters who worked outside the court. And Su and his friends had certainly seen many more paintings by professional painters in friends' homes or for sale in the market than works done at court by court artists.

Not only should we abandon the notion that Su Shi was specifically targeting court painters, we should probably also abandon the idea that Huizong stood staunchly on the side of a fine-style court aesthetic. True, a handful of anecdotes circulated in the Southern Song or later that depicted him as insisting on highly naturalistic forms of painting. These anecdotes make him seem the defender of everything Su Shi opposed in painting. But isn't it likely that the anecdotes were told for precisely that reason? Why should they be given more weight than the book-length catalogue that Huizong himself commissioned?

Anyone who reads the catalogue carefully would have to agree that Huizong did not see any fundamental opposition between the court and men of letters. Literati, in their capacity as his officials, were very much a part of court life. Officials lined up for almost all court ceremonies. Officials had for centuries produced poetry at court and for court purposes; they also were of course the creators of the calligraphy the court collected. If scholar-officials expanded their artistic repertoire to include paintings that could be considered the visual equivalent of poems, there was no reason why the court should not also want this product of their creativity. Rather than look at these paintings as an alternative to the screen paintings and murals done by court painters, it was perfectly reasonable to think of them as yet another product of the brushes of literati, as worth collecting as their calligraphy and as worth appreciating as their poems. Some literati could assert that a painting by a poet was better than a painting by a professional artist, but the palace had the means to acquire both; it did not have to choose one over the other. Another way to think about this is that the culture Huizong sought to be the center of was Chinese culture, not some fragment of Chinese culture defined negatively by the literati as what they did not like.

CHAPTER 9

The Fate of Huizong's Collections

To the right is a genuine trace of Lu Ji. It has Huizong's title strip as well as the small Xuanhe and Zhenghe seals. These few lines are all that survive from the period from Zhang You to Wang Xizhi, making it a rare treasure. The colophon I wrote for it in the spring of 1591 was done for Han Jishi (Zongbo), who at the time was a tutor, so I would get to see this masterpiece from time to time. I ranked it in the top grade. I was very sorry that there were no good copies of it in circulation, so I wanted to have it carved for the *Xihong tang Model Letters*, but I was no longer able to get hold of it. Written on the first day of the twelfth month of 1604 by Dong Qichang.

—Colophon attached to Lu Ji's calligraphy

When the grand viewing took place at the newly constructed Palace Library in the third month of 1122, the Song state's international situation had taken a dramatic turn. The Khitans' Liao dynasty, for a century and a half the Song dynasty's main worry, was close to being destroyed by its erstwhile vassals, the Jurchens, who had proclaimed their own Jin dynasty. Earlier that year Jin had taken the Liao Central Capital, the third of its five capitals to fall. The Western Capital at Datong was on the point of falling as well. At the Southern Capital (Yanjing), Liao officials, out of contact with the Liao emperor, tried to negotiate an accommodation with Jin that would allow them to set up a vassal state with a Liao prince as ruler. This offer had no appeal to Jin, since they already had an agreement with Song for a joint attack on Yanjing.

Five years later, in the third month of 1127, the Song dynasty was close to extinction itself; the capital had been thoroughly looted and most of the people and treasures of the palace were in the Jurchens' camps outside the city walls. The events that led to this fate are worth relating in some detail to convey the contingency of what happened to Huizong, his relatives, and his treasures. The outcome was not foreordained by Huizong's love of art and luxury—as traditional historians have often implied—but resulted from a concatenation of situations, events, and decisions. At many points in the story, another outcome was possible if a different decision had been made.

To understand these events, it must be remembered that the founders of the Song dynasty had not been able to secure control of all of the territory that the Tang dynasty had held at its height, and in particular had not been able to regain sixteen prefectures in the northern parts of modern Hebei and Shanxi provinces, around Beijing and Datong. This territory had been held by the Khitan state of Liao since the mid-tenth century. The Song founders had tried to push the Khitan out of it, but had found themselves unable to do so and had opted for a peace agreement instead. Since 1004 the Song and Liao had lived by the rules of a treaty that had involved the Song making large annual payments to the Liao and the Liao agreeing not to invade Song. By Huizong's day, the annual payments amounted to 200,000 ounces of silver and 300,000 bolts of silk, which was less than 5 percent of the annual revenues of the Song state, but still sounded very large. Although this agreement had kept the peace, it was widely viewed as a humiliating concession of military weakness. Moreover, the Northern Song government still had to spend about half its revenue to maintain a million-man army.

Then, in 1115, after Huizong had been on the throne for fifteen years, it appeared that Song might get the opportunity to rectify this situation. That year a defector from Liao told Song officials about the success the Jurchens were having in their battles against Liao and recommended that Song contact them. By 1120 Song had agreed to join the Jurchens in attacking Liao in exchange for the return of the sixteen prefectures. Then a massive rebellion in the southeast preoccupied the Song armies, and it was Jin armies acting on their own that destroyed Liao. Jin still let Song take the city they cared the most about, Yanjing, but now realized that they did not need Song help and that Song was not much of a military threat.[1] During 1124 and 1125, the Song court celebrated the recovery of Yanjing, but many officials were uneasy about Jin ambitions.

The Jin Invasions

In the last month of 1125, Jin invaded. Two separate armies entered Song territory, one led by Wolibu, going through Hebei toward Kaifeng, the other led by Nianhan, aiming first to take Taiyuan (in Shanxi). The territory north of Taiyuan fell fairly quickly, but Taiyuan itself settled in for a long siege. In the east, defense of Yanjing was entrusted to Guo Yaoshi, a Bohai general who had switched from Liao to Song two years earlier and had been handsomely rewarded by Huizong. Unfortunately for Song, when Jurchen troops defeated Guo in battle, rather than retreat, Guo switched sides again and turned his troops against the armies of other Song commanders. The next day, Yanjing fell, less than three years after Jin had turned it over to Song.

Huizong's court was thrown into a panic. Calls were issued to bring grain to the capital to prepare for a siege. Armies were summoned to come to the capital to help with defense. Envoys were sent to the Jin commanders to try to negotiate a truce. What to do was discussed by court officials both in open court sessions and in the corridors and offices where they gathered. Among the ideas discussed was giving over responsibility for safeguarding the capital to the heir apparent, then twenty-six, while Huizong and a small group of senior officials set up another base in a safer place, perhaps in the Yangzi Valley, perhaps in Chang'an, the capital during the Han and Tang dynasties. Although some considered leaving tantamount to running away, others saw it as prudent. When the Tang dynasty was threatened by the rebellion of An Lushan, Xuanzong and his court evacuated the capital, heading west into Sichuan, and as a consequence when the capital fell, the dynasty did not fall with it. Moreover, the Jurchens might simply be raiding deep into the country, the way the Khitan had done in the tenth century, when they had taken Kaifeng then left after a few months.[2]

Some officials, including Li Gang and Wu Min, thought Huizong should abdicate as a gesture to the Jurchens. After talking the situation over with Li Gang, Wu Min bravely sought an audience with Huizong to urge him to abdicate. Huizong was persuaded, and a few days later the very reluctant heir apparent, Qinzong, took over as emperor and Huizong became the senior, or retired, emperor.[3] When Li Gang urged Wu Min to talk to Huizong about abdication, he said that if Huizong abdicated, Jin would withdraw its armies. Wu Min, when he met with Huizong, told him that if he abdicated, the central plains would remain part of China for centuries to come. Their arguments were persuasive, but their predictions proved false. When Song envoys reached the Jurchen camp to report the abdication and request a truce, Guo Yaoshi urged the general to turn them down and to continue south, assuring him that Kaifeng was a much richer prize than Yanjing.[4]

The first day of the new year, 1126, Qinzong promulgated a new reign name, Jingkang, "secure and vigorous." The new name was soon belied when the Jurchens crossed the Yellow River. Some officials urged Qinzong to withdraw to Chang'an, arguing that he could raise an army there to defeat Jin. Huizong also thought that strategy made sense. Other advisors urged Qinzong to stay, including Huizong's youngest brother, who argued that no place was better fortified than the capital. Another who pleaded with Qinzong to stay was the scholar Li Gang, who had become a close advisor. Impressed with Li Gang's passion, Qinzong put him in charge of defense of the capital even though he had no military experience. Altogether about 96,000 troops were available to defend the capital. Li Gang positioned 12,000 troops armed with crossbows and catapults on each of the four walls. Another 10,000 were assigned to defend the Yanfeng storehouse with its 400,000 piculs of stored grains and beans. He also put 8,000 soldiers by one of the gates, and held about 24,000 in reserve.[5]

The Jin army under Wolibu reached the walls of Kaifeng on 1126/1/7. After a returning envoy reported that the Jin could not be defeated, Qinzong sued for peace. By 1126/1/10 his envoys had reached a tentative agreement to an increase in the annual tribute of 2 million strings of cash and a special indemnity of 5 million ounces of gold, 50 million ounces of silver, and 2 million lengths of silk, as well as 10,000 horses, oxen, and mules, and 1,000 camels. In addition, the three prefectures of Taiyuan, Zhongshan, and Hejian would be turned over to the Jin and an imperial prince and a grand councilor would serve as hostages. On 1/15 Wolibu agreed to a relatively token change in the amount of the annual payments, and the treaty was signed.[6]

Although relieved that they would not have to endure a long siege, the capital was thrown into an uproar trying to raise the truly huge sum of gold and silver, equal to 180 times the annual payments that Song had been paying to Liao. Government warehouses had only about half the sum needed; the rest had to be requisitioned from the populace. There were promises of later compensation and rewards, but it was still not easy to secure enough gold and silver. People were ordered to turn over everything they had within two days. Informers who turned in people concealing wealth were promised two tenths of the concealed gold and one tenth of the concealed silver as a reward. By 1126/1/20, the besieged Song court sent to the Jin camp more than 500,000 ounces of gold and 8 million ounces of silver. On 1/26, they sent the equivalent of another 500,000 ounces of gold and 8 million ounces of silver, much of it made up of jewelry, clothing, utensils, and money. There was reason to rush; on 1/27 it was reported that the Jurchens were excavating the tombs of imperial consorts, princes, and princesses. Finally, on 2/10 the last of the gold and silver was delivered to the Jurchen army camp, and the next day the Jurchens departed, unexpectedly taking Huizong's son Prince Su with them.[7] The pressure on Kaifeng was lifted, but not the pressure on the Song, since these negotiations made no mention of the second Jurchen army still surrounding Taiyuan, which occasionally struck south toward the city of Luoyang.

Once the Jurchens were gone, Qinzong presided over a major change in administration. Huizong's leading officials were demoted one after the other. At the same time, honors were restored to leading conservatives, including the long-deceased Sima Guang.[8] In the seventh month, eighty-year-old Cai Jing died on the road in

Tanzhou, on his way to his site of banishment. On the same day, it was ruled that no future amnesties would lighten the exiles of twenty-three of Cai Jing's sons and grandsons. From then through the tenth month, a series of officials who had worked closely with Huizong were executed, including Tong Guan and Cai You.[9]

Qinzong's advisors included both hawks and doves, both those who believed that the best hope lay in showing Jin that Song could not be pushed around, and those who thought it would be possible to reach a stable peace with the Jurchens through negotiation and adherence to treaties. The appeasers had held sway as long as the Jurchens were at the gates of Kaifeng, but after the Jurchens left, the hawks gained dominance at court. Yang Shi, the chancellor of the National Academy, reproached the court for so readily turning over territory that had been central to the rise of the Song dynasty. Because Jin had violated the treaty by taking Prince Su with them, he argued, Song had no obligation to fulfill their part of the bargain and should not turn over the three prefectures. Rather, the Song should go on the offensive. Li Gang took a similar tough stand and urged that the Song send troops to "accompany" the Jin troops on their return home, the intention being both to harass them and to reduce the damage they did on their trip north. Qinzong consented, believing that the Jurchens, returning home heavily laden, "with many carts and countless captive women," could be successfully attacked. Huizong was not a party to these discussions but told associates that he was convinced that the Jurchens would return, and proposed that he go to Luoyang to organize an army there. Wu Min convinced Qinzong to reject this idea.[10]

Jin armies did return before the end of the year. By then Taiyuan had fallen, so both Jin armies could join the attack on the capital. In 1126/10 the Song court once again had to summon armies from other parts of the country to defend the capital. As the situation worsened, the leading general, Chong Shidao, urged Qinzong to relocate the court to Chang'an. Qinzong recalled him for consultation, but the seventy-six-year-old Chong died of illness before reaching the capital.[11]

Early in the eleventh month officials at court bitterly argued over whether or not to grant the Jurchens their demand for the three prefectures north of the Yellow River, which the court had refused to turn over up to then. Seventy-one officials were in favor of ceding them, and thirty-six were opposed; Qinzong went with the majority. Qinzong sent his 20–*sui* brother Prince Kang as an "envoy to cede land and request peace." The day before he left, however, Jin forces crossed the Yellow River. Prince Kang ended up behind their lines in Hebei.[12]

The Jurchen general Nianhan, once he got to the suburbs of Kaifeng, made his own offer: he would withdraw if the Yellow River were made the border between the two countries. Soon Qinzong was sending envoys to agree to this proposal, but he also took the precaution of bringing those who lived in the suburbs into the walls of the city and closing its gates. On 11/25 the first Jin cavalry arrived outside the walls of Kaifeng. Inside, almost anyone willing to fight was put to work, including Guo Jing, who gained the confidence of the high official Sun Fu for his plans to recruit 7,777 soldiers and use magical techniques to make his soldiers invisible. Some of the fiercest critics of Huizong's administration, including Hu Shunzhi and Sun Di, now agreed that Qinzong should flee (euphemistically called "moving the capital").[13] Whether or not this plan would have succeeded the year before, at this late date most court officials considered it unworkable.

By the end of the eleventh month, the armies of both Wolibu and Nianhan were camped outside Kaifeng with about 100,000 troops. The year before, Nianhan's army had been held up at Taiyuan, so this time, with both armies at the city's gates, the situation was bleak. Still, this time the Song court was determined to fight the enemy rather than appease them. Real combat began in the intercalary month between the eleventh and twelfth months of 1126. Song concentrated on defending its walls, using recently recruited civilians, and only rarely sent out sorties to disrupt Jin preparation of siege equipment. Both sides initially employed fire as a weapon. The Jurchens set fire to eleven of the gates to the city, and the Song sent out troops to burn the Jurchen stockades. Catapults were widely employed to rain stones on the other side. To keep the catapults supplied, on 1126/i11/8, residents were told to take the stones from Huizong's Genyue garden for launching at the attackers.[14]

As combat moved from one gate to another, both sides sent a stream of envoys to the other. Jin urged Qinzong to come in person, saying that if he came immediately he would be treated with courtesy, something he could not expect after the city fell. A few days later, Jin offered to reopen negotiations if Qinzong would send as hostages his father Huizong, his son the heir apparent Prince Chen, an uncle, and a brother. Qinzong refused to send his father but did send Huizong's brother Si, the King of Yue.[15]

The Fall of Kaifeng and the Emptying of the Palace

Battles for the walls grew fierce as negotiations stalled. On 1126/i11/25, with snow swirling about, the doors of Transformation Revealed Gate were opened, and Guo Jing's magical army surged out to engage the Jin forces, followed by several thousand Kaifeng residents hoping to help them. Rumors spread that Guo achieved great victories, whereas in fact his troops were mowed down.[16]

When the outer walls fell, many of the defenders died in the final onslaught, and others fled the city with tens of thousands of residents. The Jurchens set fire to the gate towers and defense works along the wall, and soon much of the city was aflame. Fleeing Song soldiers began looting. Near several of the gates, Jurchen soldiers entered the city and began killing people and pillaging. Panic ensued. The well-to-do changed into poor people's clothes and hid. Thousands committed suicide by jumping into the rivers or wells or by hanging themselves, especially women.[17]

Once he heard that the outer walls had fallen, Huizong had his guards bring him to the more secure palace complex. That same day Qinzong appeared at the tower of the southern gate of the palace complex to speak to the soldiers and the people. A group of several hundred soldiers willing to try to break out climbed onto the roof of a nearby building and shouted that Qinzong should immediately leave, that the city was no longer a safe place for him. Qinzong said that it would be necessary to first prepare food and money, and issued orders to begin preparations. The next day Jin sent a Song official into Kaifeng to tell Qinzong not to attempt to leave, since Jin controlled everything within 500 *li*. The idea of breaking out was then abandoned.[18]

After the Jurchens occupied the walls, they began negotiating with the Song court to get it to turn over everything they wanted from the city in exchange for a promise not to let their soldiers loose on the population. Their first demand was that Huizong come to their camp as a hostage, along with a long list of other people, including relatives of officials in Hebei and Hedong, who would serve as guarantors that those officials would not resist turning over their prefectures. In addition, the Jurchens wanted the relatives of a long list of officials who had been involved in Song policy making—from Cai Jing to Li Gang, Wu Min, and more minor figures. When He Li protested that he could not carry such a message, Nianhan said, in effect, that Qinzong had a choice: he could turn over either his father or his wife and daughters. Song sources relate that Qinzong offered to go himself rather than hand over Huizong. At the same time, he sent a messenger appointing his brother Prince Kang as Grand Marshal of Hebei and ordering him to mobilize an army.[19]

On 1126/i11/28, placards were posted in the city telling the elders and ordinary people to go to the Jin camp and offer gold, silk, meat, and wine as rewards for their soldiers. People responded, and soon the streets were crowded with people carrying signs giving their names, addresses, and the objects they were offering to Jin in thanks for their sparing the population. The city itself, however, was descending into disorder. The markets were by now selling human flesh without hiding the fact. Song soldiers, whose rations had run out, were escaping from their camps and seizing what they could find in the city. To try to get the situation under control, the court allowed those who caught such thieves to execute them, leading to even more deaths. By the next day, young men in the city had organized themselves into patrols, which brought robbery under control.[20]

On 1126/i11/30, Qinzong went to Wolibu's camp, accompanied by two of his uncles and four hundred other men, imperial clansmen and officials, all of whom, according to Jin sources, "called themselves subjects of Jin." The Jin generals demanded a formal surrender. The draft written by Qinzong's officials had to be revised several times before the Jin commanders accepted it. For instance, Song was not allowed to refer to two emperors, one of Great Jin and one of Great Song; only the Jin could be said to have an emperor. When Qinzong finally met with Wolibu and Nianhan, he asked the Jin commanders to withdraw their troops, volunteering to submit treasures for generations and present gold and silk from the imperial treasuries. Nianhan replied, "Is there a person or object that is not already mine?"[21]

A few days later, after Qinzong had returned to Kaifeng, Jin informed Qinzong of their basic demand: ten million bolts of both silk and satin, five million bars of gold (each bar fifty ounces), and ten million bars of silver.[22] This was impossibly high—fifty times the gold demanded after the first invasion, and ten times the silver. Moreover, Song authorities had not been able to raise the sums demanded then and had not had time to replenish the government storehouses. Jin also sent a letter to Prince Kang, demanding his return, but Qinzong sent a secret message reiterating the need for him to raise troops.[23]

Jin officials now entered Kaifeng and opened the Song government warehouses, which were found to have even more bolts of plain silk than demanded, but only a tiny fraction of the gold and silver. Song officials were assigned the responsibility of searching specific quadrants of the city and confiscating all gold and silver. Every few days, the Jurchens demanded something else from the Song government. For instance, on 12/5 Jin demanded 10,000 horses. Ranking officials were allowed to keep one horse, but all others were seized, over 7,000 altogether. The next day, 12/6, Jin demanded weapons, many of which people had taken after the soldiers had abandoned them. Qinzong issued an order that all weapons in Kaifeng, both government and private, be turned over to the Jin authorities.[24]

A few days later, on 12/10, all the money in the storehouses was distributed to the Jin soldiers as their reward. On 12/13, a call was issued for twenty painters, fifty wine-makers, and 3,000 bottles of wine. Ten days later Jin demanded a long list of books and documents by name, including Sima Guang's *Comprehensive Mirror* and works by Su Shi and Huang Tingjian. In some cases, the Kaifeng prefectural authorities had to buy the works from bookshops to fulfill the orders. A few days after that, the books from the Directorate of Education were taken (though, as an insult, works by Wang Anshi were discarded). Just before the Lantern Festival, Jin demanded all the lanterns usually used not only by the palace but also by temples and shops, then held their own ceremony outside the walls of the city. Not long afterward, they demanded the full set of procession paraphernalia, then took such objects as the Nine Cauldrons, the Primal Tablet, ancient vessels, books and documents from the Palace Library, old paintings, the Dasheng bells and other musical instruments, consorts' headgear, the blocks for printing books (including those for the Buddhist and Daoist canons), and maps and diagrams of all sorts. From time to time, the Jurchen commander requisitioned specific craftsmen or specialists, such as doctors, musicians, astronomers, weapon makers, masons, gardeners, jade carvers, clerks, painters, story tellers, professors, Buddhist monks, and so on. Lists of objects taken from the palace are often staggering: 25,000 ancient bronze vessels, 1,000 ox carts, 2,000 oil carts, 1,000 parasols, 28,700 pills from the imperial pharmacy, 1,000,000 pounds of silk thread, and 1,800 bolts of a certain type of silk made in Hebei.[25]

The crucial element in the Jin demands, however, was gold and silver. Jin repeatedly warned Song that if they did not want the Jurchen soldiers to be set loose to find what they could in the city, they had to raise the indemnity as quickly as possible. Court officials knew that the quota of gold and silver demanded was impossibly high, but were divided on how to cope with that fact. Some urged going to the Jurchens and pleading with them to lower the quota on the grounds that it was impossible to fill, but the view that prevailed was to do as thorough a search as possible and then present the Jurchens with the results, a strategy that had worked eleven months earlier. On 12/14 the goods in pawnshops and in silk, gold, and silver shops were all confiscated. On 12/24, placards were posted in the marketplaces explaining that the government treasuries had enough plain silk, but not enough gold, silver, or satin. Valuables in the homes of officials and the palaces of the imperial family, from Huizong and the heir apparent on down, had already been confiscated; thus it was time to search the homes of rich families. Specified officials were given charge of different sections of the city. Compliance was again encouraged by rewarding informers.[26]

Although the city had fallen, the Jurchen forces kept the gates closed, enforcing, in a sense, a reverse siege to keep up the pressure on the city until all its demands were met. Food and firewood, therefore, were in very short supply. On 12/21 the court allowed government office buildings to be demolished for firewood; the next day, after a snowfall aggravated the situation, approval was given for people to enter Genyue Garden to chop down the rare trees planted there. A few days later, with another snowfall, people were also allowed to break up the hundred-odd buildings in the garden for fuel. So many rushed there that people were trampled to death. On 12/25 placards were posted in the city informing families who had had members abducted by Jin soldiers to go to the eastern and western pagoda temples to file reports so that ransoms could be arranged. When twenty or thirty thousand people showed up at the western pagoda temple, the officials were overwhelmed and had no way to deal with them all.[27]

Early in the new year, 1127, the Jurchen commanders pressured Qinzong to return to their camp. Before going, Qinzong named his eldest son, the heir apparent Prince Chen, as regent, with two officials to assist him, as he was only a little over nine years old.[28] On 1127/1/10, when Qinzong proceeded through the city to leave by the Gate of Southern Infusion, he reassured the people lining the road that he would return the next day. Once in the Jin camp he was pressed to agree to make the Yellow River the boundary; to allow the marriage of a Song princess to a Jurchen prince; to turn over 2,000 items of court paraphernalia, 500 commoner women, and 500 female musicians; and to send a long list of named individuals to serve as hostages. Soon the city was posted with placards stating that Qinzong would not be allowed to return until the quota of gold and silver had been met.[29]

Song officials tried every means to collect gold and silver. There was a steady line of soldiers and people from the Gate of Virtue Revealed to the Gate of Southern Infusion carrying objects from the palaces and princes' mansions. On 1/14 Huizong added his consent to an order that all of the sacrificial vessels used in the ancestral sacrifices at the Supreme Shrine or the homes of princes be handed over. This would have included all of the vessels cast as replicas of ancient vessels. By 1/18 ten thousand people were employed in the transportation of goods to the southern gate. By 1/19 Kaifeng prefecture had delivered 160,000 ounces of gold and 2,000,000 ounces of silver.[30]

Life in the city kept getting more and more difficult. Because people could not leave the city, bodies were piled everywhere, mostly of people who had died of starvation, frozen to death, or succumbed to the epidemics raging through the city.[31] On 1/23 the Song government began selling rationed grain and firewood at about 10 to 20 percent of the market price. The demand was so great that at first only the strongest (usually soldiers) were able to get to the front to buy the grain, so soldiers had to be banned from the markets and alternate days designated for men and women, to make sure that the weak were not deprived of the chance to purchase food. Outside the city Jurchen soldiers with time on their hands dug up graves, large and small, to get the grave goods buried in them.[32]

After more than ten days in captivity, on 1/22, Qinzong had to countersign a new agreement worked out by Nianhan and Wolibu, which had several significant provisions. Huizong would not have to go north, but six hostages, including the heir apparent, Prince Kang, and a grand councilor, would have to serve as hostages until all agreements had been fulfilled. All the treasures in the palaces would be turned over to Jin. Two princesses, eight clanswomen, 2,500 palace ladies, 1,500 female musicians, and 3,000 craftsmen would be turned over. The annual payments would be increased to 5 million units of silk and silver. If the required sum for rewarding the soldiers (the one million bars of gold and five million bars of silver) was not turned over within ten days, the quota would be filled by the sale of women. Each princess or consort of a prince would be assessed at 1,000 bars of gold; each close clansman's daughter or wife, at 500 bars; each distant clansmen's daughter or wife, at 200 bars; and daughters of nobles, at 100 silver bars. To make sure Song did not just send the old and ugly, the Jurchen authorities retained the right to select the women they wanted.[33]

The Song had no choice but to fill most of the quota through women—over 5,000 all told, ranging from princesses and imperial consorts to low status performers and prostitutes. Within days, all the women of the entertainment quarters were rounded up, along with all the women who had been palace ladies during Huizong's reign and later dismissed, even if they had already been married. Wives, daughters, and concubines of disgraced officials were also seized. When the women were delivered, the Jurchen soldiers, in order of rank, got to make their choices; Nianhan took several dozen; senior generals, several; and other officers, one or two. More than a thousand women were rejected and sent back because they were not in good enough health; the Song had to send substitutes.[34]

While their houses were being ransacked and their daughters seized, the populace of Kaifeng remained remarkably loyal to the Song imperial family. Every day hundreds of thousands would line the Imperial Way, showing their solidarity with Qinzong and waiting for his return. In the end, however, the Jurchens not only did not release him but forced him to order Huizong and all the other residents of the palace to join him in the Jurchen camp.[35]

At the same time that Huizong was being told that he had to leave within hours, the Jurchens sent more than a hundred eunuchs into the palace to help make arrangements for moving the consorts and princesses. Soon Huizong's consorts, young children, palace ladies, maids, wet nurses, and the like were leaving the palace. When the party got to the gate, the soldiers had the eunuchs identify each person. One baby son of Huizong had been taken by his wet nurse to hide among the common people, but the Jurchens had good enough records to discover that he was missing and gave an official one day to find him and turn him over. On 2/11, after both Qinzong and Huizong were forced to write letters requesting that Prince Chen and his mother be sent, they also entered the Jurchen camp. Next, members of the imperial clan were rounded up and moved to the Jurchen camps. People went around the city calling out, "Do not hide Zhao family members. If you have hidden any, produce them immediately or suffer the consequences."[36]

On 1127/2/18, Wolibu hosted a feast for Nianhan and other leading Jurchens and forced Huizong, Qinzong, and their empresses to attend, probably as part of the entertainment for his men. Wine was served by fifty-two of the confiscated women—twenty consorts and princesses and thirty-two singing girls. Huizong, Qinzong, and their empresses, mortified at seeing them, wanted to leave, but were not allowed to. After the meal, Wolibu told Huizong that Nianhan's son Sheyema liked Huizong's daughter Princess Fujin and that he wanted Huizong to give her to him. Huizong replied, "Fujin is already married. In China this is very shameful; one does not take two husbands. We are not like your esteemed country in having no taboo against it." To this Nianhan replied, "Recently we ordered the distribution of the prisoners. How can you resist this command? Let each guest take two."[37]

Jin made no attempt to oust or replace the Song officials who ran the government in Kaifeng, but they tried to make them understand who their real masters were. They sent in soldiers to thoroughly search the palaces, assigning former palace eunuchs to show searchers where treasures were kept. During these searches they found all sorts of valuables, ranging from pearls and gems to musical instruments, screens, old books, fine paintings, and jade and gold seals. Whether the Jurchens took every one of the paintings and calligraphies Huizong had accumulated is unclear, as no numbers are given and some items soon entered general circulation (which could have happened because Jurchen soldiers who got them sold them or because residents of Kaifeng had looted them before or after the Jurchens left). But we should not assume that the Jurchens left them behind because they weighed too much, for they transported the ten ancient Stone Drums as far as Yanjing.[38]

After devoting more than three months to stripping Kaifeng of its assets, the Jurchens were nearly ready to leave. On 1127/3/4 a commander was dispatched with 1,050 carts of books and ritual implements. Places outside the city walls were more thoroughly searched. Last-minute searches of a temple turned up paintings and calligraphies owned by Zhu Mian's family. On 3/12 and 3/13 the temples devoted to the Song imperial ancestors were looted—the soldiers even took the clothing off the statues of imperial ancestors. On 1127/3/23, the Jin declared that the gold and silver quota was to be considered filled, with much of the total made up through women. Five days later the Jin soldiers finally came down from the walls of Kaifeng, which they had occupied for nearly four months. Transport of the nearly fifteen thousand captives was organized into seven separate convoys.[39]

Conditions on the march north were difficult, and many of the captives did not survive. Of the 6,592 in the sixth convoy, 1,892 (28 percent) failed to make it to Yanjing, some dying on the way, others, especially young children, abandoned along the road when they could not keep up. Most were city dwellers not used to walking long distances, and if they fell behind they were beaten or killed, so that bodies littered the fields they passed. Practically every one of Huizong's relatives that the Jurchen invaders were able to find—including all of the Song imperial clansmen in Kaifeng or the vicinity and all of his daughters who had married, along with their husbands—was transported north at the same time that he was. A great many died of abuse or neglect over the next couple of years, especially the clansmen, who were of little use to the Jurchens.[40] Huizong himself lived until 1135, his son Qinzong until 1161.

In terms of humiliation, the failure of the Song dynasty to protect its sacrificial vessels was a much greater blow than its failure to protect its books, paintings, or calligraphies. In the classics, the preservation of a state was often spoken of in terms of the protection of its altars, giving both the altars and the objects associated with them great symbolic meaning. Huizong and Qinzong, however, consistently put preserving life above preserving buildings or objects, even the material symbols of the dynasty. The emperors made every effort to raise the gold and silver demanded because they hoped in that way to spare the population of the capital from indiscriminate slaughter. When Huizong, his empress, or Qinzong made special pleas, it was always for the release of people, such as Huizong's married daughters or Empress Zheng's relatives, and never for material objects.

With hindsight, it is clear that if only one of the many proposals to move the capital south or west had been adopted, there is a good chance that Huizong, the Song imperial family, and the palace collections would all have survived. As it turned out, because of the great reservoir of loyalty to the Song ruling family, the dynasty was preserved by the enthronement of the closest relative of the imperial line not taken captive by the Jin, Qinzong's younger brother Prince Kang, known as Gaozong (r. 1127–1162). After more than a decade of dodging Jin attacks, Gaozong established a capital at Hangzhou and reached a peace settlement with Jin that included the return of his mother and Huizong's remains, but none of his brothers or nephews nor, of course, any of the ritual vessels or other objects in Huizong's collections. Just as the Song founders had seized the collections of the states they vanquished a century and a half earlier, its conquerors took its collections.

The Dispersion and Destruction of Huizong's Treasures

None of the sources on the fall of Kaifeng describe the specific fate of objects in Huizong's collections. We do not know which bronzes or paintings went to the various palaces in Jin's five capitals, which were given out as rewards to generals, officials, or soldiers, and which were left behind. Over the next couple of centuries, many objects disappeared one way or another, casualties of war and dislocation, with attrition probably especially high in the years immediately after the fall of Kaifeng and in the early thirteenth century when Jin suffered its own military disaster at the hands of the Mongols.

SOUTHERN SONG AND JIN

Once Huizong's son Gaozong had stabilized his court in the south, he made vigorous efforts to rebuild the palace collections. According to Julia Murray, he rebuilt the palace painting and calligraphy collections to "demonstrate that the dynasty had not lost favor with Heaven despite the loss of the ancient homeland in the North."[41] In an essay he wrote on calligraphy, Gaozong referred proudly to the work Huizong and his curators had done to assemble the collections, classify and rank objects, and remount them, and then described his own efforts. "Since [the move south] across the Yangzi, genuine works by Zhong [You] and Wang [Xizhi] [from the former palace collection] are rarely seen. When I have heard that one has been found, I have offered generous rewards to obtain it. [Huizong's] mountings, rollers, and calligraphy can still be examined."[42]

One of those who helped Gaozong find objects that had been in his father's collections was Bi Liangshi. Bi had been a dealer in paintings, calligraphies, and ancient vessels in Kaifeng. After Kaifeng's fall, Bi went back when circumstances allowed (such as in 1139–1140) to search for objects that had been left behind. When Gaozong learned of Bi's abilities to distinguish genuine from fake objects, he put him on a retainer. Bi soon recruited many associates who helped him in the search for art and antiquities. At one point, Bi submitted fifteen bronzes, seven of which had been illustrated in Huizong's catalogue, including one of the Duke Cheng of Song bells. In time, regular markets developed on the Song-Jin border, and art and antiquities could sometimes be acquired there. The Jin government became concerned enough about the loss of antiquities through trade with the south to ban their sale in 1157, but this ban probably simply moved the trade to the illegal markets rather than the legal ones.[43]

Once Gaozong made it known that he would reward those who presented famous art works or antiquities, many people came forward. In 1151, the high official Zhang Jun feasted Gaozong and other guests and presented the emperor with ten Shang and Zhou vessels and nineteen paintings that had been in the imperial collection, as evidenced by Huizong's seals or titles.[44]

Gaozong had Huizong's seals taken off works that had been in his father's collection, relatively easy to do to those with seals only on the margins. As a consequence, today one rarely sees scrolls with good seals of both Huizong and Gaozong. Works listed in Huizong's catalogue with good Gaozong seals but no Huizong seals consequently may well be ones that had originally come from the Kaifeng collection. An example here would be Dong Yuan's *Awaiting a Crossing at the Mountain Pass in Summer*, a handscroll in the Liaoning Provincial Museum, which has Gaozong seals plus Yuan imperial seals and an inscription by Dong Qichang linking it to a painting listed in Huizong's catalogue.[45]

Sometimes, undoubtedly, works presented to Gaozong as being from Huizong's collection actually had no connection to it. Especially in the case of Tang and earlier calligraphy, competing copies had circulated for centuries.[46] Even if Huizong acquired several versions of a famous piece, others remained in private hands. Probably at times Gaozong was presented with copies that an enterprising person had "improved" by adding Huizong's seals, to make it seem as though the work had come from Huizong's collection. That, at least, would seem to be the explanation of works that have authentic Gaozong seals but dubious Huizong seals, such as Wang Xizhi's *Fengju tie*.[47] Others who had versions of works in Huizong's catalogue that lacked his seals could have claimed that the version in Huizong's collection was not in fact as good as the one that had remained outside it.[48]

At times Gaozong sought reassurance from his curators that the objects he had acquired were indeed the best versions. In the case of calligraphy, from the mid-1130s on, pieces were often shown to Mi Youren (1074–1151), Mi Fu's son, with requests that he authenticate them.[49] According to Deng Chun, Gaozong for a while had Mi Youren in constant attendance.[50] Mi was naturally considered the best qualified to authenticate his father's calligraphy, but he also vouched for other works, such as Huaisu's *Bitter Gourds,* a work with dubious Huizong seals and not listed in the *Xuanhe Catalogue*.[51]

Sometimes Gaozong wrote on works himself. A surviving example is the Shanghai Museum's *Yatou wan*, a piece of calligraphy attributed to Wang Xianzhi. It was listed in Huizong's catalogue but the only Huizong seals on it seem doubtful. The Gaozong seals, however, seem fine, as does his inscription dated 1140.[52] Women in Gaozong's palace also sometimes acquired works that had been in Huizong's palace, including Empress Wu (1115–1197). Her seal is found on one of the most famous pieces by Yan Zhenqing, his *Draft Eulogy for His Nephew.* In the Yuan period, this work still had Huizong's seals on it, but they were removed by a mounter in about 1300.[53] Empress Wu also put her seal on *Admonitions of the Instructress* (plate 25), a painting attributed to the early master Gu Kaizhi, which was listed in Huizong's catalogue.[54]

In 1199, after several reigns, the Palace Library made a list of its 215 calligraphies, 458 bronzes, and 1,098 paintings. From the names of the artists and titles of the works, it is evident that the early Southern Song rulers sought much the same sorts of works that Huizong had, with strong representation of Tang calligraphy and bird-and-flower and religious paintings. They were not able, however, to gather proportionally as much pre-Tang calligraphy.[55]

Although many people seem to have felt that objects that had been in Huizong's collection should be turned over to Gaozong and his successors, there are also occasional reports of pieces from Huizong's collection that were acquired in the twelfth century by private collectors. Wang Mingqing (1127–1214+) saw a painting by Zhou Wenju at the home of Lou Yao (1137–1213), who had recently acquired it. Wang reported that Huizong had written the title *Double Screen* on it and also inscribed a poem by Tang poet Bo Juyi on it.[56]

One reason Southern Song collectors were able to acquire objects that had been in Huizong's collection was that none of the Jin emperors before the sixth emperor Zhangzong (r. 1189–1208) had much interest in the paintings and calligraphies they acquired from the Song palace. In all likelihood, during the seven decades between the fall of Kaifeng and Zhangzong's reign, many objects left the Jin palace collections. In 1158, the mentally unstable Jin ruler Hailing ordered the destruction of all the ancient vessels acquired from Liao and Song on the grounds that being very old, they might well be ill-omened or have demonic powers. Zhang Linsheng sees this order as responsible for the destruction of most of Huizong's antiquities.[57]

Zhangzong's predecessor, his grandfather Shizong (r. 1161–1189), was a strong ruler proficient in both Jurchen and Chinese cultural traditions.[58] As a youth Zhangzong received a good education in both traditions and developed strong interests in the Chinese arts of poetry, calligraphy, and painting. When he came to the throne at twenty, he turned to Chinese scholar-officials to prevent two of his uncles from taking the throne away from him. He took a Chinese empress and allowed her relatives to occupy prominent places at court.[59]

In 1192, Zhangzong had Wang Tingyun and another official "grade the finer works of calligraphy and painting," 550 scrolls altogether. Zhangzong seems to have modeled his handling of these scrolls on Huizong's. Like Huizong, he had a set of seven seals that he placed in a consistent pattern on paintings.[60] He also, quite conspicuously, modeled his calligraphy on Huizong's—so successfully, in fact, that his inscriptions have often been taken as Huizong's (see fig. 9.1). Like Gaozong in the south, Zhangzong removed Huizong's seals and inscriptions before applying his own. Several of the oldest copies of Wang Xizhi's calligraphy listed in Huizong's catalogue have Zhangzong seals (e.g., *Kuaixue shiqing tie* and *Yuanhuan tie*).[61] A couple dozen paintings survive with Zhangzong's seals on them, most of which can plausibly be matched to paintings listed in Huizong's catalogue.[62] These include a painting now in the Palace Museum in Beijing, attributed to Yan Liben, titled *Taizong in the Sedan Chair* (plate 34), Zhao Gan's *Along the River at First Snow* in the National Palace Museum, Taipei (figs. 1.3 and 8.3), and *Admonitions of the Instructress,* in the British Museum (plate 25).[63] Zhangzong also had an interest in the antiquities he inherited. He once asked a scholar to explicate the inscription on

Fig. 9.1
Zhangzong (r. 1189–1208), title strip. National Palace Museum, Taiwan, Republic of China. The Jin emperor Zhangzong wrote this title on a painting of a man leading a long-horned goat-like animal with a leash. It reads "picture of a barbarian bringing tribute by Zhou Fang."

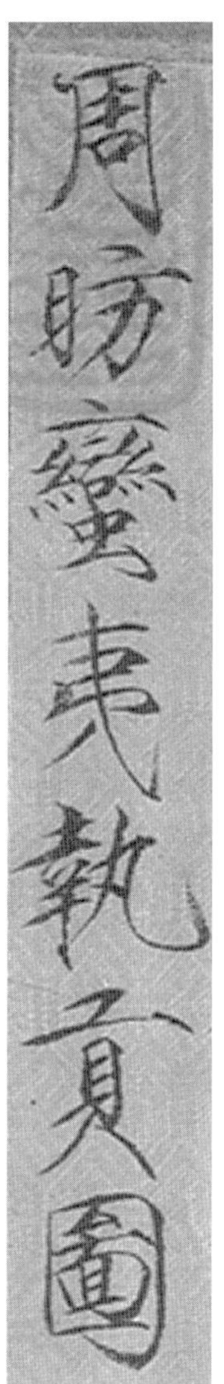

a basin. In 1199 he had new quarters built for the National Academy (Taixue), with wings that housed ancient and modern books on one side and ancient bronze vessels on the other.[64] He had his officials study the Dasheng bells he had inherited from Huizong, and on their recommendation searched out Chinese craftsmen who could cast new bells to fill out the sequence so that the bells could be used at court ceremonies.[65]

Objects from Huizong's collection that survived to the thirteenth century soon faced new dangers from the Mongols. In 1210 the Mongols ceased recognizing Jin as their overlords and began an all-out campaign against them. They took the Jin Western Capital (Datong) in 1211, the Eastern Capital (Liaoyang) in 1212, and looted territory throughout north China. In 1214, after the Mongols temporarily left Yanjing, the new Jin emperor Xuanzong (r. 1223–1234) moved his main capital south to Kaifeng. He is said to have taken 30,000 carts loaded with documents and court paraphernalia as well as 3,000 camels loaded with treasure, and so may have been able to move all or most of Zhangzong's collections. Anything not transported was most likely scattered or destroyed in the subsequent leveling of Yanjing by the Mongols. Kaifeng itself fell in 1232 and was extensively looted.[66]

Many items from Zhangzong's collection entered general circulation in the years after the fall of Kaifeng. Jia Sidao (1213–1275), a wealthy high official in Hangzhou with a passion for art, acquired quite a few pieces.[67] A listing of the titles in his collection stated that he had a thousand scrolls, including many that had been in Huizong's collection. Some of these still had Huizong's seals and titles. Three examples are Wang Shen's *Rivers and Mountains in Mist* (plate 9), Wang Xizhi's *Yuanhuan tie*, and Du Mu's inscription of his own poem (plate 13).[68]

YUAN DYNASTY

When the Southern Song capital of Hangzhou surrendered in 1276, the Mongols had been in China for more than half a century and were much better prepared to take charge of Chinese scholarly treasures than they were at the fall of Yanjing in 1214 or Kaifeng in 1232. Yuan officials urged preserving the books, printing blocks, maps, calligraphies, and paintings confiscated in the south, whether from the palace or private hands. Large numbers of works were sent north to the Palace Library in Dadu (Beijing). After they arrived, Wang Yun was able to view 228 newly acquired works (147 calligraphies and 81 paintings). He made a list of works that he saw, several of which came from Huizong's collection, such as Sun Guoting's *On Calligraphy* (fig. 7.1).[69]

The Mongols found so much in the way of art works in Hangzhou that they did not send it all north. The surplus they disposed of in markets they set up for that purpose.[70] They also gave away objects. Zhao Mengfu received Wang Xizhi's *Kuaixue shiqing tie* (fig. 4) from the Yuan emperor Renzong.[71]

The best witness to the circulation during Yuan times of art objects that had once been in Huizong's collection is the scholar Zhou Mi (1232–1298). Zhou suffered the Mongol conquest of the Southern Song and lost his own large collection of books and art works when the Mongols captured Wuxing.[72] Then forty-seven, he spent most of the rest of his life in Hangzhou. One of his favorite activities was to visit art collectors, especially collectors of paintings, and one of his books is a lightly annotated list of the works he saw in the collections of forty-seven men living in Hangzhou.[73] Sixteen of these collectors had works with Huizong's titles or seals. To give an example, Zhou Mi listed twenty-seven paintings owned by Si Jin. These included a small Wang Wei hanging scroll inscribed by Huizong and impressed with three of his seals as well as several of Zhangzong's seals, showing that the scroll had come from the Jin imperial collection. Other works inscribed by Huizong included religious paintings (*Personified Deity of Mars,* attributed to Wu Daozi; *Sixteen Lohans,* by Lu Lengqie; and *The Yellow Emperor Casting Mirrors,* by the Song painter Tang Zisheng). All four of these painters are represented in the *Xuanhe Painting Catalogue,* and plausible identifications can be made to paintings listed in it. Si Jin, however, also had a Huizong-inscribed figure painting by the early Song painter Wang Rui, who is not listed in Huizong's catalogue.[74]

Other collectors Zhou Mi visited had only a single scroll that had been in Huizong's collection. An example would be Xianyu Shu, a prominent calligrapher himself, who had a very early calligraphy by Emperor Wu of Jin (r. 265–290) that had been in Huizong's collection. Xianyu Shu also had pieces that had been listed in Huizong's catalogue that Zhou Mi did not link to Huizong, such as Suo Jing's *Monthly Greetings,* which had seals of Gaozong and Han Tuozhou (d. 1207), and Wu Cailuan's *Dictionary of Rhyme Schemes.*[75]

The first member of the Yuan royal house to take an active interest in Chinese painting was Princess Sengge (ca. 1283–1331), the sister of emperors Wuzong (r. 1308–1312) and Renzong (r. 1312–1321). She avidly sought objects once in Huizong's collection. Two that she acquired were Zhan Ziqian's *Spring Outing* (plates 23 and 24) and Liang Shimin's *Riverbank with Reeds in Light Snow* (fig. 8.6).[76]

The Yuan emperor who took the greatest interest in the imperial art collections was Princess Sengge's nephew and son-in-law, Wenzong (Tugh Temür, r. 1328–1329, 1330–1332). Like Huizong, he did both calligraphy and painting himself, and during his short reign he took active steps to add to the court collections. In 1329 he set up the Pavilion of the Star of Literature, which had one room for storing art objects, another for exhibiting them, and a central room for his scholars to use. Quite a few

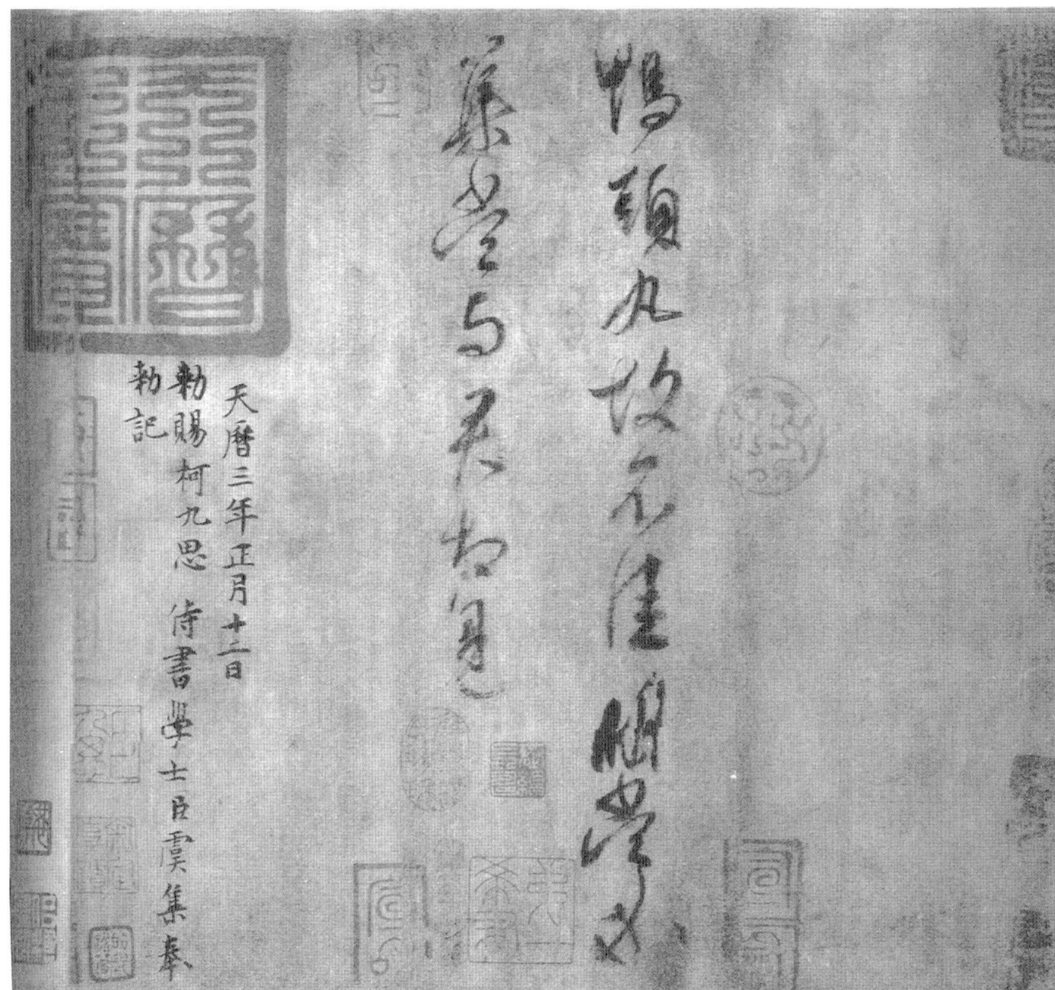

FIG. 9.2
Yu Ji (1272–1348), colophon for Wang Xianzhi's *Yatou wan*. Handscroll, ink on silk, 26.1 × 26.9 cm. Shanghai Museum. The colophon is dated 1330 and records that Yu Ji inscribed the work on the command of the emperor, who conferred the calligraphy on Ke Jiusi.

paintings survive with inscriptions or colophons by these scholars, often drawing links between their subject matter and benevolent rule.[77] After conferring with two of these officials, Ke Jiusi and Yu Ji, Wenzong classified Zhao Gan's *Along the River at First Snow* (fig. 8.3) as "divine" and put his seal on it, as he did on *Waterwheel* (fig. 8.2).[78] Wenzong also made gifts of paintings and calligraphies. In 1330 he asked to see Ke Jiusi's early copy of Wang Xizhi's *Preface to the Orchid Pavilion Poetry Collection*, but after putting his seal on it, he returned it to Ke and also gave him a piece of calligraphy by Wang Xianzhi, the still extant *Yatou wan* (fig. 9.2).[79]

Like Zhangzong in Jin times, Wenzong seems to have admired Huizong. He owned several paintings by Huizong, including one titled *Feting Cai Jing in the*

Chengping Hall, which hung in the Pavilion of the Star of Literature. His officials, however, sometimes warned him against following Huizong's example of paying excessive attention to the arts.[80]

Yu Ji, one of those who worked on Wenzong's collections, recorded the history of the Stone Drums (fig. 4.1). After the Jurchens had transported them to Yanjing, they were stored in a private house. They seem to have been largely ignored until Yu Ji noticed them amid mud and thistles at what was by then a school. He stood them up and cleaned them and arranged for them to be moved inside the main gate of the National Academy, where they were put on brick pedestals and protected with fences.[81]

By the end of the dynasty, the Yuan imperial collection certainly exceeded either the Jin or the Southern Song collections—and perhaps both of them put together (even though many items from those collections had entered general circulation). In 1342 the Palace Library tallied its possessions as part of an inventory project. It had 3,163 paintings and calligraphies, many of which would have dated from the two centuries since Huizong's time, so clearly it had only a small part of the nearly 7,600 works that had been in Huizong's catalogues.[82]

MING AND QING COLLECTORS

The Ming government took over the Yuan collections (and in 1382 the agency responsible for them put its seal on the paintings and calligraphies it had acquired), but no Ming emperor was particularly active in searching for lost masterpieces. Moreover, several Ming emperors were generous in making gifts of objects in the palace collections to favored officials and imperial relatives, leading to attrition out of the palace. Several Ming princes were given important works. When the huge collection of the high official Yan Song (1480–1565) was confiscated, rather than absorbing it into the palace collection (as was done in comparable Song cases), it was auctioned off to raise revenues. Near the end of the dynasty, because of fiscal distress, the court not only sold some of its treasures but also melted down Shang and Zhou bronzes, some of which may have been passed down from Huizong's collection.[83]

Perhaps because the Ming throne did not pursue old paintings and calligraphies, the private market for them flourished. Most of the great collectors in the Ming and Qing periods acquired some paintings or calligraphies that they believed had once been in Huizong's collections. Although many items recorded in Yuan times disappeared, others that had not been recorded since their listing in Huizong's catalogue reappeared (undoubtedly sometimes by forgery). By the late Ming, collectors and connoisseurs were compiling detailed catalogues of paintings and calligraphies that they had seen or acquired, making it possible to trace the history of art works much more fully.

Most extant paintings and calligraphies from Huizong's collections survived the transition from Ming to Qing in the major private collections of the period, such as those of Dong Qichang, Xiang Yuanbian, Sun Chengze, Liang Qingbiao, Song Luo, Gao Shiqi, and An Qi.[84] Of these collectors, Liang Qingbiao seems to have garnered the largest number of works once in Huizong's collection. One of more than a dozen examples is *Studies from Nature,* attributed to Huang Quan (plates 36 and 37).

The works that the painter, calligrapher, connoisseur, and collector Dong Qichang saw can be traced through the innumerable colophons or inscriptions he wrote on works that he viewed—some in his own collection, but many in the collections of his friends and acquaintances. He was particularly active in identifying paintings and calligraphies that had earlier been in Huizong's collection.[85]

Early in the Qing dynasty, objects that the Manchus had confiscated from the Ming were often given to favored officials and generals. Officials would also make comparable gifts to the emperors. A piece of calligraphy by Wang Xizhi once in Huizong's collection, *Kuaixue shiqing tie* (fig. 4), was given by the chancellor of the Directorate of Education to the Kangxi emperor. Another official, Gao Shiqi, compiled a list of paintings with the prices he had paid for them. One section, labeled "Gifts to the emperor," had many items annotated "not authentic" or "fake."[86]

As mentioned in the introduction, the fourth Qing ruler, the Qianlong emperor (r. 1735–1796), collected on a scale that exceeded even Huizong. A very high proportion of the works today considered most likely to have been in Huizong's collection were acquired by Qianlong, most of them previously gathered together by Liang Qingbiao and a few other collectors. In some cases, Qianlong put several inscriptions on the work. A good example here would be *Five Oxen*, attributed to Han Huang (plate 35). Qianlong wrote out a title for the handscroll, placed an inscription before the painting itself (which mentioned the *Xuanhe Painting Catalogue*), dated 1752, wrote another inscription in the middle of the painting, dated 1753, and two after it, dated 1754 and 1753.[87]

Not infrequently Qianlong and his curators were mistaken in their belief that a work they had acquired had once been in Huizong's collections, as they rarely questioned the authenticity of inscriptions or seals purporting to be Huizong's. A good example is a hanging scroll attributed to the tenth-century painter Li Cheng (fig. 9.3). It has a large inscription in the upper right reading "Trees on a Plain in Winter," which Qianlong's cataloguers identified as being in Huizong's hand,

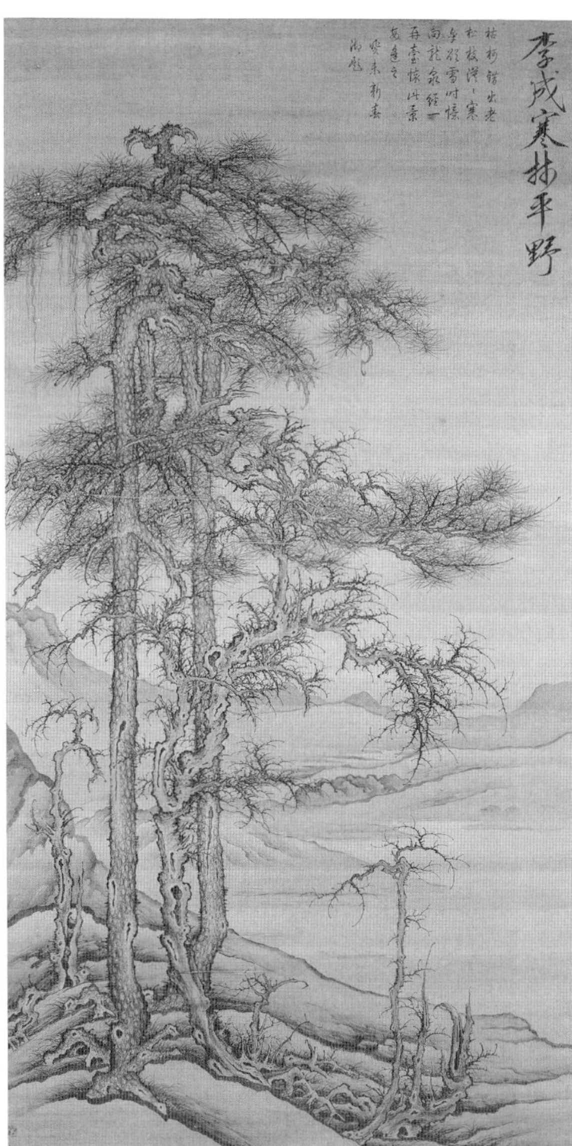

FIG. 9.3
Painting in Qianlong's collection that he believed Huizong had titled as a work by the tenth-century artist Li Cheng. National Palace Museum, Taiwan, Republic of China. The large inscription on the right margin is the putative Huizong inscription. Qianlong's own inscription follows it.

matched with a seal reading "imperial writing" alongside the inscription, and a seal at the bottom right reading "Xuanhe." Qianlong liked this painting enough to write a poem on it and impress it with five of his seals.[88] Since there is little evidence that Huizong inscribed paintings in this fashion, in all likelihood this inscription was added by a forger to associate the work with Huizong and thus "prove" that it was painted before the twelfth century.

Some Disparate Fates

The afterlife of the objects in Huizong's collections varied enormously. A few examples can serve to convey something of the diversity of their fates.

NEVER HEARD FROM AGAIN

This is true of the large majority of the items in Huizong's three catalogues.

PASSED FROM ONE PALACE COLLECTION TO ANOTHER, UNTIL THE PRESENT

One work which apparently went from Huizong's collection to subsequent palace collections, without spending much time in private collections, is the early Song painting by Huang Jucai titled *Partridges by a Thorny Bush* (see plates 32 and 33). The only seals on it are a late Southern Song imperial seal (reign of Lizong, r. 1224–1264), a seal of the early Ming imperial collection, and Qing imperial seals. The colophons are by the Qianlong emperor and three of his officials.[89]

HEARD OF FROM SOUTHERN SONG ON

Li Gonglin's copy of the Tang painter Wei Yan's *Pasturing Horses* (plate 11) has seals of Song Gaozong and Jia Sidao, as well as three Huizong seals. By the early Ming the painting was in the hands of a general, who had probably seized it as booty in the wars. In 1370 he presented it to the founder of the Ming, who wrote a colophon for it (fig. 9.4). Ming Taizu soon gave the painting to his heir apparent, as the painting has his seal (and does not have the half seal put on works in the Ming imperial collection in 1382). During the Ming-Qing transition, the painting was in the collections of Sun Chengze and then Liang Qingbiao, and also has seals of two other owners named Xu and Huang. Eventually, like so many other paintings, it entered Qianlong's collection. In 1751 Qianlong wrote a poem on it and also added comments immediately after Ming Taizu's colophon. Qianlong also wrote out a title for the painting and placed numerous seals on it in many different places.[90]

HEARD OF IN SOUTHERN SONG, BUT NOT LATER

The 1199 list of paintings in the Southern Song Palace Library includes fourteen paintings by earlier painters that Huizong had inscribed. None were ever heard of again. One of these was a painting of a horse by the Tang painter Wei Yan on which

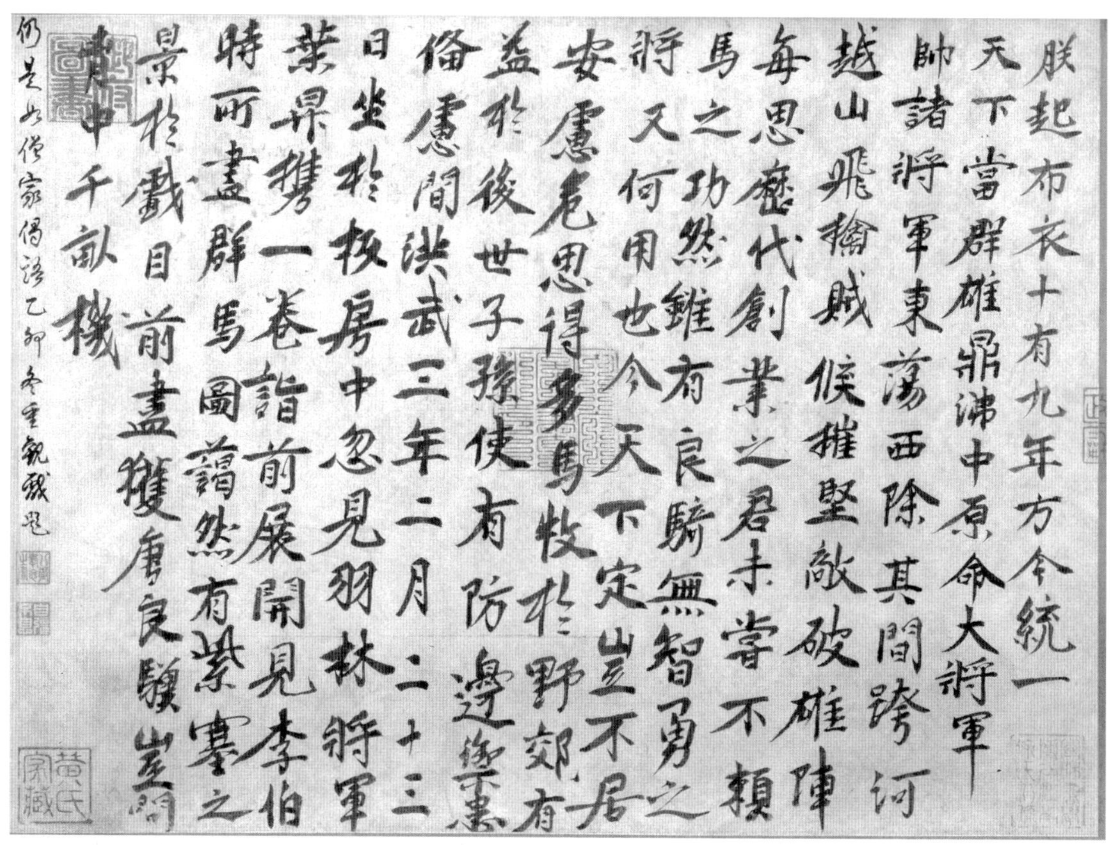
朕起布衣十有九年方今統一
天下當群雄鼎沸中原命大將軍
帥諸將軍東蕩西除其間跨河
越山飛擒賊候摧堅敵破雄陣
每思歷代創業之君未嘗不賴
馬之功然雖有良騎無智勇之
將又何用也今天下定豈不居
安慮危思得多馬牧於野郊有
益於後世子孫使有防邊塞
備慮間洪武三年二月二十三
日坐於板房中忽見羽林將軍
葉昇携一卷詣前展開見李伯
時所畫群馬圖藹然有紫塞之
景於戲目前盡獲唐良驥豈
非中千畝機

Fig. 9.4
Ming Taizu (r. 1368–1398), colophon for Li Gonglin's copy of Wei Yan's *Pasturing Horses* (see plate 11). Palace Museum, Beijing. Taizu's colophon shows that he was attracted to the depiction of horse raising, which he saw as central to maintaining defense readiness.

Huizong had written, "Wei Yan of Tang painted this horse. His brushwork is fine and marvelous, his use of color is truly amazing, a very admirable work. Inscribed by the emperor in 1105."[91]

HEARD OF IN YUAN, BUT NOT LATER

Zhao Mengfu's collected works includes a poem he wrote after he acquired one of the bronzes illustrated in Huizong's *Antiquities Illustrated.* It was a very small four-legged cauldron of Zhou date with a six-character inscription. According to *Antiquities Illustrated,* it was only 3.2 inches tall. Zhou Mi saw this bronze vessel when he viewed Zhao Mengfu's collection and recorded the poem.[92] This bronze disappears from the record soon thereafter.

In Yuan times the painter Guo Bi described a painting with Huizong's seals by Huang Jucai, called *Birds in Snow,* which he saw in a private collection.[93] It, too, is not mentioned later.

NOT HEARD OF UNTIL YUAN TIMES

Zhou Mi recorded a pair of paintings by the Five Dynasties painter Wei Xian titled *Lofty Scholar*, one depicting Lu Tong, the other Liang Hong, both of which had been in Huizong's catalogue. The second of these has survived and is presently in the Palace Museum, Beijing. It was recorded in the late Ming and early Qing by Zhang Chou, Sun Chengze, and An Qi in their catalogues, and has seals of Liang Qingbiao and An Qi. It entered Qianlong's collection and he not only impressed it with a dozen seals but also inscribed it in two places, once on the painting itself, and once on the lower mounting (see plates 14 and 29). This Wei Xian was one of the paintings that left the palace collection in the early twentieth century with the abolition of the monarchy. It entered the painting market in Beijing and changed hands a couple of times, but eventually was given to the Palace Museum, Beijing, by the collector Jin Bosheng.[94]

NOT HEARD OF UNTIL MING TIMES

Nothing is known of the whereabouts of Wang Xizhi's *Xingrang tie* before 1603, when Dong Qichang mentioned that it was in his collection. The next year he wrote a long colophon for it in which he described this piece as one of the 143 works by Wang in Huizong's collection. In 1609 he added another colophon marking an occasion when he viewed it in the company of his friend Chen Jiru and the work's new owner, the collector and art dealer Wu Ting (see fig. 9.5). Subsequently it entered the collections of An Qi (b. 1683), Qianlong, and Zhang Daqian (1899–1983). In 1970 it was acquired by the American collector John Elliott, who gave it to the Princeton University Art Museum in 1998.[95]

NOT HEARD OF UNTIL QING TIMES

In the eighteenth century, *Scholars,* attributed to the Tang artist Sun Wei, was in the collection of Liang Qingbiao, and from there it entered the Qianlong collection. It is not mentioned in any earlier catalogues, and the one earlier inscription on it, dated 1489, is of unclear authorship. The painting left the palace collection in the twentieth century, but is now in the Shanghai Museum.[96]

SURVIVED INTO THE EIGHTEENTH CENTURY, BUT THEN LOST

Zhang Xuan's *Court Ladies Playing the Qin* was one of the thirteen paintings from Huizong's and Zhangzong's collection that Zhou Mi in Yuan times reported were

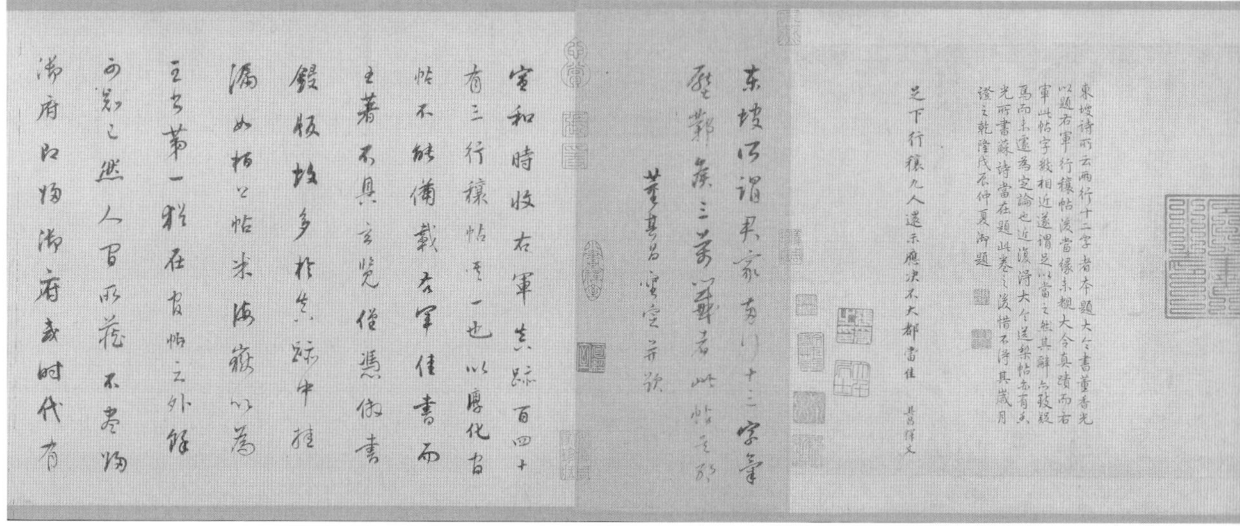

Fig. 9.5
Inscriptions and seals on Wang Xizhi, *Xingrang tie* (see fig. 7.5).

owned by Qiao Kuicheng. Before Qiao obtained this painting it had been in the collection of Jia Sidao, who had acquired many paintings after the dispersal of the Jin collections with its fall. Several centuries later, in 1636, Wu Qizhen acquired it. Subsequently it was described in the 1712 catalogue by Wu Sheng, the *Daguan lu*, which gives its size, Zhangzong's title, and the connection to Huizong. Although several versions of this composition survive, none have Zhangzong's title or seals, so presumably this work has been lost.[97]

SURVIVED TO THE PRESENT WITHOUT GETTING QIANLONG'S SEALS

One of the handful of works from Huizong's collection that never had any Qianlong seals impressed on it is the oldest of them all, Lu Ji's *Pingfu tie*, in the Palace Museum, Beijing (plate 3). In the seventeenth century the work had attached to it a colophon dated 1285 written by four men who viewed it. Later Dong Qichang wrote a colophon for it. In the late Ming (Wanli period), several scholars recorded seeing this piece and commented on its quality. It was owned by Han Shineng (*jinshi* 1568), then his son Han Fengxi, then Zhang Chou, who wrote about it in his *Qinghe shuhua fang* of 1616. He recorded Dong Qichang's colophon, which mentioned seeing the piece at Han's home in 1591. According to Wu Qizhen, he saw it in 1660 when the dealer Ge Junchang showed it to him. Ge had removed the colophon by the Yuan writers and sold it to another dealer who attached it to a forged painting. Lu Ji's piece then was treated as worthless. Later it passed to the well-known mounter Wang

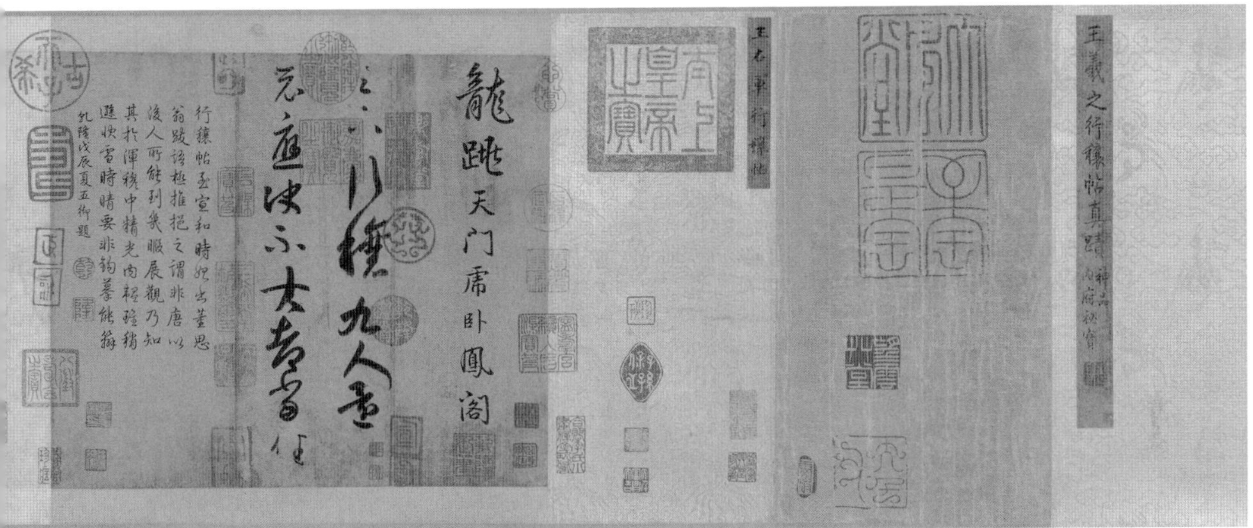

Jizhi, who took it north and sold it to the high official Feng Quan for 300 strings of cash.[98]

Once in the north, the fame of the piece grew and it passed to such well-known connoisseurs as Sun Chengze and Liang Qingbiao. Liang had a rubbing of it made and included in a set of model letters he issued. He also put several of his seals on it. Wu Sheng recorded it in his *Daguan lu* of 1712. Next it passed to An Qi, who recorded it in his catalogue as well. When An Qi died in 1746, it entered the Qing palace. It seems Qianlong gave it to his mother as a birthday gift, and she left it at her death to Qianlong's son, Yongxing (1752–1823), who was a calligrapher himself. It passed down in the imperial family for the next century and a half. In the mid-nineteenth century it was owned by the politically important Prince Gong (1833–1898); in the early twentieth century by the well-known painter Pu Ru (1887–1963). In 1910 Pu Wei (Pu Ru's older brother) wrote a record of its transmission in the imperial family, and in 1938 Pu Zengxiang recorded its sale the year before to the collector Zhang Boju (1898–1982). Zhang eventually passed it to the Palace Museum, Beijing.[99]

SURVIVED INTO THE TWENTIETH CENTURY, THEN LOST

A piece of calligraphy by the Five Dynasties artist Yang Ningshi titled *Jiuhua tie* was known to collectors until about 1945.[100] It was listed in Huizong's catalogue and had Gaozong seals. Two Yuan-period colophons by Zhang Yan dated 1302 and 1304 reported that he had bought it from a traveling merchant and had brought it to the

Jiangnan area. The scroll also had seals of Zhao Mengfu, who may have been the next owner. A Ming colophon of 1512 reported that the piece had entered the Pavilion of the Star of Literature in Yuan times and later was given to Wang Shi. Chen Jiru wrote a colophon in 1637 which reported that he and Dong Qichang had viewed the piece together. Dong Qichang published a copy of it in one of his model letter compilations and also apparently wrote a colophon that later was removed. Zhang Chou recorded it in his *Qinghe shuhua fang,* and Xiang Yuanbian put his seals on it. There are also several other colophons and recordings in the first century of the Qing period. Where the calligraphy was for the next century and a half cannot be traced, but in the early twentieth century the famous scholar Luo Zhenyu acquired it. He published a reproduction of it in 1938. His family had it in Changchun in 1945, but lost it in the confusion of the end of the war, and it has not been seen since.[101]

IDENTIFIED IN RELATIVELY RECENT TIMES

Probably the object most recently identified as from Huizong's collection is a small Shang period cauldron (plate 20) in the National Palace Museum in Taipei. In the Southern Song, Wang Houzhi (1131–1204) reproduced its inscription and reported that Emperor Xiaozong (r. 1162–1189) had given the piece to Hong Mai. After that it disappeared from record (although many later epigraphers continued to discuss its inscriptions). It is not listed in any of Qianlong's antiquities catalogues. In 1987 the National Palace Museum in Taipei published it, for the first time identifying it as the same cauldron published in Huizong's catalogue.[102]

The initial dispersal of Huizong's collections was a direct consequence of the failure of his foreign policies. Certainly this fate was not preordained. It is easy to imagine different outcomes at every step in the history of the fall of Kaifeng. Not only might the Jurchen never have become a problem (because Liao was able to suppress them), but even granting their attack on Song, Huizong and Qinzong had many opportunities to leave the capital with the most valued of their treasures.

Contingency also shaped the fate of particular objects. The objects that have survived until today are not necessarily the ones most valued by Huizong, or even most valued by later generations of collectors. Which ones had their seals cut off seems also to have depended very much on chance.

Tracing the history of objects in Huizong's collections raises questions about the long-term cultural consequences of Huizong gathering together so many culturally valued objects. Were the objects he concentrated in the palace less likely to survive than ones in private hands? Attrition seems to have been at its worst in the aftermaths of the Jurchen and Mongol victories. Certainly many private collectors also lost treasured objects in this period—Li Qingzhao's description of how she struggled to preserve the collection she and her husband had put together is a case in point.[103] Still, the palace had much more symbolic meaning to the conquerors, and for that reason alone was subject to much more systematic looting. The differences, however, do not seem to be as large as one might expect. Very few paintings survive that were listed in Guo Ruoxu's *Experiences in Painting*, written about a half century before Huizong's catalogue. Of the 492 paintings mentioned by Zhou Mi in his *Records of Clouds and Mist Passing before One's Eyes*, written nearly two centuries after Huizong's catalogue and recording only works that survived both the Jurchen and Mongol conquests, Ankeney Weitz is confident of the survival of only six.[104]

The ways Huizong had handled his collection had an impact on the survival and later history of objects from it. Although both Song Gaozong and Jin Zhangzong removed Huizong's seals (perhaps copying Huizong's practice in that regard), by Yuan times it was common to leave them on, and indeed to treat the seals as important documentation, increasing the value of the work by giving it an interesting provenance.

What about the consequences of cataloguing the collection? By Ming times collectors and connoisseurs regularly checked Huizong's catalogues when researching pieces, in the hope that they would be able to give imperial provenance to the work, to show that it was one long missing. They also used the catalogues as reference books that documented the types of works an artist did. One probably unforeseen consequence of the circulation of the catalogues was their use by forgers who knew that people would pay more for pieces that seemed likely to have once been in Huizong's collection. Forgers would use the titles listed in the catalogues and add imitation Huizong seals. Thus facilitating forgery is a long-term outcome of the cataloguing process.

Gathering related objects together did cultural work: it allowed a much more systematic comparison of similar art works. A connoisseur can recognize the style of a painter or calligrapher much more accurately from seeing thirty works than he can from seeing three; he can sort out the differences in shape and design of ancient bronzes much more accurately when he has hundreds of examples to work with than when he has a dozen.

Dispersal also does cultural work. In periods when the palace absorbed much of the art work on the market—as in Huizong's, Gaozong's, and, later, Qianlong's reigns—the art market is altered, and works do not circulate in the way they do in a market dominated by numerous medium-sized collectors, whose collections are often dispersed at their deaths. Royal collections in China, unlike modern museums, were less accessible than private collections, so that works that entered imperial collections were seen less often after they entered the collection than before. Dispersing them stimulates the art market by making it possible for private collectors to acquire masterpieces.

Reflections

HUIZONG WAS A SINGULAR INDIVIDUAL, AND CHANCE PLAYED A LARGE role in the formation and dispersal of his collections. Still, his story has much to tell us about imperial collecting and the cultural side of emperorship in China. These larger issues are brought to the fore when Huizong is placed in broad historical perspective.

Huizong in Chinese Comparative Perspective

Most Chinese emperors were indifferent collectors. A handful of emperors before Huizong are described as avid collectors who amassed thousands of calligraphies or paintings, but none of them issued catalogues. After Huizong, too, few emperors attained his stature as collectors. His son Gaozong did his best to put together a collection modeled on his father's, but the Southern Song collections never rivaled Huizong's in size. Later emperors, too, sometimes emulated Huizong—at a minimum, Zhangzong in the Jin, Renzong in the Yuan period, Wenzong in the Ming period, and Qianlong in the Qing—but only Qianlong truly matched him.

Huizong might well have had more imitators had his example not been treated as cautionary by imperial advisors. Since Huizong's reign did not come to a good end, advisors discouraged later emperors from doing anything that would prompt comparison to Huizong. When the Yuan emperor Wenzong praised a painting by Huizong in his collection, his advisor Kangli Naonao told him that it did not matter how much talent Huizong had had, since his loss of his country proved that he did not have the one talent crucial to a ruler, the talent for governing.[1] In the sixteenth century, when the ten-year-old Emperor Shenzong (r. 1572–1620) took an interest in practicing calligraphy, his councilor-cum-tutor Zhang Juzheng warned him not to let his interests in the arts go too far, evoking Huizong's example.[2]

Most likely, megacollecting also became more difficult with the passage of time.

In Northern Song times, there was still a degree of unity among the fields of scholarly collecting. Some private collectors, such as Li Gonglin and Zhao Mingcheng, collected in all of them. As each of the fields of collecting grew larger over time—as there were more books, more painters and calligraphers, more discoveries of ancient objects—greater specialization set in. The great collectors of paintings in Ming and Qing times did not even necessarily collect calligraphy, much less ancient vessels. Thus it progressively became more difficult for the court to gather together and synthesize the diverse forms of cultural production appreciated by the educated class.

The only emperor to exceed Huizong as a collector was the Qianlong emperor (r. 1735–1796).[3] Huizong and Qianlong had similar ambitions. Both strove for comprehensive collections. Both produced catalogues of their collections that were major scholarly undertakings and matched or exceeded the standards of private connoisseurs of their day. When differences in the size of their realms are taken into account, the two are seen to have collected on a comparable scale. Huizong had on the order of 100 million subjects, Qianlong on the order of 300 million. Qianlong collected in more categories, but when they both collected the same things, Huizong sometimes had more objects. Qianlong's four catalogues of his paintings and calligraphies listed 509 religious pieces and 3,349 secular ones, for a total of 3,858—considerably fewer than the 7,617 in Huizong's two catalogues. (Even if we include the second supplement to the catalogues, issued in 1816 after Qianlong's death, his total reached only 5,628 paintings and calligraphies.)[4] Even in the case of books, Qianlong's famous *Four Treasuries* project was not on an entirely different scale than Huizong's. Huizong's book initiative led to a catalogue of 6,705 titles in 73,877 chapters; two extra copies were made of each book. Qianlong's book project resulted in a catalogue of 10,680 titles. A smaller group of 3,593 titles in 36,078 chapters formed the basis for a copying project that made seven copies of each.[5] Qianlong's project thus was larger, but not on a different order of magnitude, and not larger in proportion to the population of the country or the growth in the number of extant books. Qianlong's collection of antiquities was considerably larger than Huizong's—his four catalogues included 4,115 items, compared to 840 in Huizong's—though Qianlong's catalogues also included many more forgeries.[6] The Qing antiquities catalogues are less impressive as works of scholarship, however, because they entirely lack introductory essays and for a great many pieces give only dimensions, with nothing in the way of analysis of inscriptions, decoration, or comparison to other objects.

One can posit many reasons why Huizong and Qianlong initiated such ambitious collecting projects. Both came to the throne in periods of unprecedented material prosperity. By their reigns, both dynasties were well established; Huizong and

Qianlong were not rulers trying to establish the legitimacy of their dynasties. At the personal level, both collected paintings even before they came to the throne and had genuine personal interests in art and learning. Both derived pleasure and satisfaction from their collections. Both also had other cultural interests that associated them with the educated class of their day—both also wrote poetry, practiced calligraphy, and painted.

There are also similarities in their relationships with the world of private collecting. In the late Northern Song and in the mid-Qing, art markets were well developed, and connoisseurship and collecting were important markers of cultivation among the educated class. Both Huizong and Qianlong can be thought of as catching up with developments in collecting and connoisseurship outside the court. Just as Huizong's *Antiquities Illustrated* can be seen as building on the catalogues of antiquities produced by private scholars in the decades before he came to the throne, Qianlong's *Shiqu baoji* catalogue of paintings and calligraphies can be seen as adopting the meticulous way of recording all the seals and colophons on each work pioneered by connoisseurs like Wu Sheng, whose *Daguan lu* of 1712 is similarly exhaustive in its documentation. The job of gathering together cultural treasures was made easier for both Huizong and Qianlong by the prior generation of collectors. That is, both acquired many objects wholesale from the major collectors of the previous generation—in Huizong's case, from Mi Fu and Wang Shen; in Qianlong's case, from An Qi and Liang Qingbiao. Both also, however, welcomed gifts from subjects and used agents to acquire additional works. Both also treated the works in their collection much as private collectors did, remounting them, adding seals and inscriptions, and having cases made to hold them.

Both Huizong and Qianlong had complex relationships with the intellectual elites of their day. Both commissioned numerous books and employed scholars on many projects, among which were studying and cataloguing the objects in their collections. The scholars were in both cases erudite men who tended to approach objects, whether paintings or ancient bronzes, from a textual point of view. At the same time, both emperors banned certain books and ordered the blocks for printing them destroyed. In Huizong's case, the main target of his censorship was the writings of Su Shi and his circle; in Qianlong's case, the main target was any work with passages that could be construed as insulting to the Manchus or their forebears.

The similarities between Qianlong and Huizong are interesting because they suggest circumstances in which aggressive collecting is likely to appeal to an emperor. They also suggest ways that imperial resources and institutional structures foster certain practices and approaches. The differences between the two emperors as collectors are also telling.

The intellectual frameworks of Huizong's and Qianlong's catalogues are very different, undoubtedly reflecting intellectual changes during the intervening centuries. Huizong's catalogues include synthetic essays that, taken together, offer an overview of the field of collecting, an intellectual framework that encompasses everything and gives everything its appropriate place in the larger scheme of things. His catalogues are all hierarchical, the organization of the catalogue meant to reflect the value structure of the subject. Qianlong's catalogues of his paintings and calligraphies were organized in an entirely different way and made no attempt to assess an entire field. They were arranged not by the sorts of categories Huizong used but by the hall in which the objects were stored. This strategy made the catalogue useful to those who wished to know what was in a given hall, but did not help much when looking for works by a particular artist or in a particular genre. Probably reflecting the intellectual trends toward evidential research, Qianlong's catalogues focus on objective facts about individual works of art, such as their dimensions, seals, and inscriptions. Qianlong and his cataloguers were much less willing to attribute unsigned works than were Huizong and his cataloguers.[7]

Although both Huizong and Qianlong had an interest in religious art, they treated its relationship to nonreligious art in fundamentally different ways. Huizong tried to overcome the separation between religious and secular art; Qianlong increased it by putting religious paintings and calligraphies in a separate catalogue. Huizong included many more Buddhist and Daoist clerics as artists than any earlier author writing on painting or calligraphy, and he highlighted the value of religious art by putting it first in the painting catalogue. His larger thrust was to encompass religious artists and religious art within his larger structure. Qianlong presided over a multiethnic empire and found it most effective to speak to his different audiences separately. Probably because his religious art included so much that was Tibetan, he did not try to integrate it with the sort of art collected by Chinese literati.

For an emperor to become a megacollector clearly did not require a certain personal style or personal taste, as in such regards Huizong and Qianlong were rather far apart. Qianlong matches (or perhaps establishes) most people's notion of Chinese court style and court taste. The palace museums in Beijing and Taipei still have thousands of objects made for use in Qianlong's court. His court produced in large quantities not only paintings and ceramics but also embroidery and tapestry, cloisonné, enamelware, carved jade, ivory, bamboo, and rhinoceros horn. The style of most of these crafts reflected the court's vast resources and its capacity to be lavish in its use of expensive materials and craftsmen's time.[8]

In Huizong's case, he came to the throne believing that the court often overdecorated buildings. He complained that one of the last buildings built during Zhezong's reign looked as gaudy as jewelry. Later, when he commissioned buildings himself, he insisted on simpler styles—for instance, with unpainted beams and rafters and wall paintings in monochrome. The styles of ceramics associated with his court are also understated, in muted colors, not elaborate in any way. Huizong certainly was not stingy with court resources, but he did not use them to produce especially elaborate or intricate craft. It is true that Huizong appreciated finely descriptive bird-and-flower paintings made by Northern Song court artists. From the small number that survive, combined with the discussions of them in the *Xuanhe Painting Catalogue*, what Huizong found compelling in them was their ability to capture all the differences between the species of birds and flowers and between birds' many different types of motion. There is no sign that what he liked about them was the evidence that many hours had been lavished on making them.

Both Qianlong and Huizong commissioned works by court artists that can be seen as glorifying their reigns, but Huizong's penchant for small pictures of the auspicious signs of his reign does not seem quite as egocentric and grandiose as Qianlong's love of large portraits of himself. Huizong did not include any of his own paintings or calligraphies in his catalogues, or even works by his own court artists. Qianlong, by contrast, was not restrained by modesty from including his own works. The initial catalogue of religious art had thirty-two pieces of his calligraphy (transcriptions of the *Heart Sutra* and other religious texts), and the supplement had twenty-three. In his second catalogue of paintings and calligraphies, about half the works were by his court artists or himself. In addition, the catalogue of Qianlong's paintings meticulously recorded every word the emperor inscribed on them. Over time Qianlong wrote more and more on the paintings and calligraphies in his collection, while Huizong intruded less and less, shifting away from writing directly on works of art and choosing smaller and less obtrusive seals that were confined to the margins of the art work or outside it. By the late years of his reign, Qianlong was putting large seals on his paintings which congratulated himself on his longevity. One seal even read, "Seal of the Old Man of the Tenfold Perfection."[9] It is difficult to imagine Huizong acting in a similar manner.

The Resources of the Throne

Both Huizong and Qianlong made use of the powers of the throne to acquire objects for their collections. Both emperors found that subjects readily gave or sold works to them. There may be some who sold their prized possessions solely because the throne made the best offer—they were simply selling to the highest bidder. But I do not think that either Huizong or Qianlong would have been able to assemble such enormous collections so quickly if market forces were all that was involved. Since it was viewed as proper for the finest works to enter the palace collections, collectors gained honor from having their objects chosen by the emperor or his agents. Beyond that, the consequences of the immense patronage powers of the throne must be recognized. The emperor directly or indirectly could do much to help individual subjects. Officials certainly knew that they would be more likely to gain the sort of posts they wanted if the emperor felt positively about them. And people who were not officials also stood to benefit from the court's favor. After all, the court was an enormous consumer and contractor. Merchants and other businessmen knew that the court could direct business their way.

Given the manner in which valued objects flowed toward the court, the emperor as an individual made a major difference in how rapidly his collection would grow. High officials could manage tax collection quite successfully even if the emperor did not want to hear anything about it. But the top officials of the Palace Library could not run as successful an acquisition campaign if the emperor appeared indifferent. The dynamics of imperial collecting worked best when potential donors saw themselves as making a bargain with the emperor himself. If they thought he was unlikely to even look at what they submitted, they would have much less incentive to part with their treasures. Thus, imperial megacollecting required an emperor who was willing to get personally involved and show his appreciation of subjects who cooperated.

Once objects entered the palace in large numbers, institutional logics came into play in both Huizong's and Qianlong's courts. Officials had to figure out how objects should be labeled so that they could be readily located. They also had to find ways to organize records and keep track of objects that were moved or borrowed. In Huizong's case, he largely accepted the institutional arrangement established early in the dynasty, and gave the Palace Library general charge of the objects. He did, however, move the objects that he valued most highly to the inner palace, putting them in specially constructed halls where he had easy access to them. Probably eunuch officials took charge of those objects. The men in the Palace Library who worked with art and antiquities were regular civil-service officials, recruited from among the most esteemed of those who passed civil-service examinations. Much of their time was spent working with books. They compiled books to be issued by the Library, collated books to be printed, and wrote entries for the catalogue of the books. The mindset they acquired during their literary educations, their service in other administrative posts, and their work with books carried over to their work with antiquities, calligraphies, and paintings.

The work of these scholar-librarians on the antiquities collection excelled in many ways. They were good at taking measurements, deciphering inscriptions, looking for similarities and differences among objects, and coming up with ideas on how to date them. They were too close to texts, however, to see the many ways that texts could trip them up. Like many other Song students of antiquities, they often rushed to identify a person mentioned in an inscription with a person mentioned in a classical text, without pausing to consider the possibility that the inscription might refer to someone else. For paintings and calligraphies, where a major challenge was distinguishing originals from copies, years poring over books were probably of little help. The advantage men working in the Palace Library did have was an enormous number of examples to compare. As long as there were a few experienced connoisseurs such as Mi Fu, Dong You, and Zhai Ruwen to teach them the basic principles, these curators' access to the Library collections should have speeded the learning process.

Political realities naturally intruded into the work of Huizong's curators. Officials working in the palace had to take into account political policies, such as the sacrosanct status of *The Rites of Zhou*. Thus they gave priority to searching for vessels that could possibly represent the ones referred to in that classic. They also likely took into account Huizong's views, when they knew them. If his curators knew that Huizong wanted a particular artist represented in the catalogue, or was proud of the depth of the collection on a certain calligrapher, they probably prudently withheld their own judgments when they were at odds with the emperor's.

The Cultural Power of Cataloguing

Gathering together large numbers of highly valued objects such as books, antiquities, paintings, and calligraphies has cultural impact even if the collection is not catalogued. Concentrating the culturally most valued objects in the political center is a strong statement about the throne's place in the larger culture. Those who get to view or use the collected objects will be able to attain insights that would not be possible if the collection had never been formed. Other collectors will also find that their perspectives and opportunities change when the court becomes a major force in the market. For irreplaceable objects in limited supply—such as paintings and calligraphies from the pre-Tang period—the market may dry up as the court removes everything it can find. Ordinary collectors will likely respond by expanding the range of objects they are willing to collect, for instance, by reconsidering the desirability of works done in more recent times.

Still, a major way Huizong (and later Qianlong) attempted to gain cultural power through his collections was by cataloguing them. Huizong's catalogues were addressed to the same sort of audience who read Ouyang Xiu's *Collected Antiquities*, Zhu Changwen's *Calligraphy Standards Continued*, Mi Fu's *Painting Chronicles*, or Lü Dalin's *Investigations of Antiquities Illustrated*, but they were broader in scope. Huizong used the resources at his disposal—the highly educated men who served in his literary organs—to compile texts that people would want to use because they were so much more comprehensive than anything anyone had written before. Northern Song authors on painting and calligraphy had not tried to write new comprehensive histories but rather had confined themselves to writing supplements to the work of Tang authors. Lü Dalin's *Investigations of Antiquities Illustrated* included no synthetic essays. Su Shi and Huang Tingjian commented on many paintings and calligraphies, especially in the poems or inscriptions they wrote for them, but they did not organize their ideas and present them in coherent essays.

Huizong's catalogues, by contrast, were comprehensive and coherently organized. Although their editing was sometimes imperfect, much effort was put into giving artists and works comparable treatment. If the catalogues had been intended only for internal purposes, there would have been no reason to construct quasi-biographies of artists about whom nothing was known, or to have written all of the synthetic introductory essays.

Once the decision was made to issue selective catalogues rather than full inventories, the cultural power of the catalogues was significantly enhanced. Because Huizong was able to secure so many of the very best objects, lists of his finest objects had the potential to be read as lists of masterpieces. No other Northern Song writings on art or antiquities equaled his catalogues in this regard.

Producing catalogues of his collections offered Huizong the chance to frame the stories of his collections the way he wanted them framed and to make them tell the stories he wanted told. One story that they told concerned the centrality of the court to the arts closely associated with the educated class. Huizong's painting and calligraphy catalogues depict a cultural realm in which the court plays the leading role but fully appreciates the talents of its subjects. Men of letters are prominent among those subjects, but there is room also for Buddhist and Daoist clergy, imperial clansmen, court painters, and court eunuchs. Song court painters were fully appreciated for their marvelous bird-and-flower paintings, paintings that excelled in catching likeness, mood, movement, and fine details of feathers. But that did not mean there was no place for painters who took very different approaches, such as depicting green bamboo leaves with single strokes of black ink.

At the same time, of course, the catalogues did not in fact provide a place for all artists of talent and originality. The most important exclusions were of Su Shi and his circle. Even though Su Shi and Huang Tingjian had been dead for more than a decade when the catalogues were compiled, Huizong did not want his catalogues to honor them in any way. Huizong's goal was not to confirm the opinions of leading literati of his day but rather to persuade them of his vision.

Probably because of the crisis that engulfed the government in the mid-1120s, the painting and calligraphy catalogues were not printed during Huizong's reign (whether the antiquities catalogue was printed is not entirely clear; see appendix

1). As a consequence, there is no direct evidence of how Huizong's subjects would have read the catalogues, and most of the cultural impact of Huizong's catalogues was long delayed.

In the past, scholars have often assumed that Huizong's passion for art adequately explains why he gathered so many paintings and calligraphies into his palace. At the same time, they have treated the catalogues of his collections as handy summaries of Northern Song critical opinion, or excellent quantitative evidence for the popularity of particular styles, approaches, or subject matters, as though the personal and political side of the collections and the catalogues could be neatly bracketed. This is risky, as the catalogues are not books without agendas, or agendas that can be clearly cordoned off. At Huizong's court, both collecting and cataloguing involved the personal, the political, and the institutional in ways that are very difficult to disentangle.

Huizong's Historical Moment and the Politics of Collecting

Since megacollecting was not, in fact, especially common in Chinese history, Huizong's decision to invest heavily in upgrading and then cataloguing the palace collections needs to be seen in the context of his historical moment. The tradition of Northern Song emperors presenting themselves as patrons of culture certainly made collecting culturally valued objects appropriate for their successors. But beyond that, two developments made the time right for Huizong to make a big push to upgrade the palace collections: a decline in the cultural capital of the court collections, and a pressing need to find new bases for emperor-literati relations.

After the completion of the *Chongwen Catalogue* in 1041, the Song emperors treated the palace collections as basically complete. This provided space for private collectors to become more active. Collecting books, calligraphies, paintings, rubbings of inscriptions, ancient vessels, ancient jades, and even inkstones progressed so much in this era that by the end of the eleventh century, the imperial collections had lost much of their luster. The court had little to gain from collections of calligraphy considered fake or of inferior quality. Its antiquities were even more pitiful when compared to those gathered by men like Li Gonglin and Zhao Mingcheng. Even its paintings—which were undoubtedly more impressive—needed an infusion of new works to catch up with the creative developments that had occurred outside of the court in the eleventh century. It was not unreasonable for Huizong to try first to catch up with the advances that had occurred beyond the palace walls and then to attempt to go beyond them to reassert cultural leadership.

Many of the advances in private collecting occurred in the last third of the eleventh century, a period when the political atmosphere was poisoned by factional strife. Much of the good will that had marked relations between the emperors and the educated class in the early reigns of the dynasty disappeared in the New Policies era. Yet, through all of this bitter political factionalism, the arts, especially painting, calligraphy, and antiquities, had remained an arena in which politics did not have to separate people. The painter and collector Li Gonglin was able to maintain friendships with both Wang Anshi and Su Shi. The collector and calligrapher Mi Fu similarly maintained good relationships with Cai Jing, Su Shi, and several imperial clansmen and sons-in-law. It was not far-fetched for Huizong to suppose that art-related activities offered an escape from political bitterness and a good way to relate to the educated class.

One way Huizong made political use of his collections was by displaying items to select audiences. In 1112 he had a recently acquired ancient jade tablet shown to officials. That same year, at a banquet for eleven senior officials, Huizong took them to Harmony Revealed Hall, where paintings, calligraphies, and ancient vessels were laid out for them to view. In 1113, he had ancient vessels set out in the same hall with replicas so that his officials could compare them. In 1119 he held another banquet that involved displaying selected items from the halls in which he kept his most prized possessions. In 1122 he had objects put on display to celebrate the construction of new quarters for the Palace Library. The authors who described these occasions presented Huizong as having feelings much like those of private collectors—he wanted to astonish viewers and enjoyed observing their reactions. At the same time, however, those who saw the objects with Huizong there to explain them felt immensely privileged. The emperor was honoring them by treating them as worthy of seeing his most valued possessions. Clearly Huizong recognized the political value of his collections and the ways he could use them to build positive feelings in his officials and tie them to him and his dynasty.

Did Huizong's massive efforts to draw the cultural treasures of the realm to the political center in fact have a positive impact on his relationships with the educated class? It probably did not earn him as much good will as the school system did, but neither did it arouse resentment. Authors as varied as Cai Tao, Gaozong, and Deng Chun looked on the collections as a remarkable accomplishment, something to the credit of the dynasty.

One way to judge more general reactions to Huizong's collecting efforts is to consider what happened during the crisis of the Jurchen invasion. Huizong, in trying to rally support, admitted that he had been wrong on many things, but did not list building up his collections among them. When life became desperate in the city, people were given permission to tear down everything associated with Huizong's pleasure park, but there is no discussion of offering his treasures for sale. Nor did Qinzong offer them for sale after the first invasion, when the court needed to recover from the huge ransom it had just paid. Gaozong very publicly renounced many of Huizong's policies, such as support for Divine Empyrean Daoism, but did his best to reestablish the Palace Library and the collections of art and antiquities. He treated restoring the collections as something very basic, like restoring court rituals and the principal organs of the government.

Was Huizong pursuing a rearguard action, trying to regain cultural power for the court long after momentum had shifted?[10] With the advantage of hindsight, we can see that already by Northern Song times the court was losing its preeminence in Chinese culture. The Chinese classics, reflecting a much earlier age, provide strong validation for the preeminence of the court. The Son of Heaven should be a perfect exemplar of all the virtues, and his court should be a center for music, poetry, art, and every form of refinement. Nevertheless, over the course of time, in China as elsewhere, the court became a less dominant element in higher culture. The Southern Dynasties and Tang were perhaps the high points of court culture in China, and by Northern Song times cultural circles relatively independent of the court had gained significant ground in the largely unspoken competition for cultural leadership. The eventual decline in the cultural preeminence of the court is a complex phenomenon connected to such developments as changes in the technology of transmitting culture, new forms of wealth and ways of hanging on to it, the resulting emergence of great cities far from the capital, and so on. Emperors had limited powers to slow these changes.

Huizong, however, is unlikely to have recognized those larger historical trends. Building up court collections would have seemed to him a reasonable strategy for helping the court strengthen itself as the center of culture. The utility of collections, however, would have varied from one field of culture to another. In many fields of culture, people are the key resource. For the court to be the creative center of poetry, it has to attract or train poets. Collecting poetry books gives it relatively little advantage. For classical scholarship and history writing, however, books are more crucial. Until the spread of printing, court scholars and historians with access to the palace book collections had a tremendous advantage over other scholars. Thus until late Tang times much of the best work in classical scholarship and history was done by scholars in the employ of the government. By Song times, however, there were enough books in circulation that excellent histories were written by scholars acting independently of the government. The palace certainly still needed books, but their possession offered less and less advantage.

In other fields of culture, objects other than books could still greatly aid creative endeavor. Only those admitted to Huizong's palace could look at the paintings and calligraphies kept there. But this made more of a difference for painting than for calligraphy because the technologies of reproduction were better for calligraphy.

Even before printing, tracing copies and rubbings of stone inscriptions circulated widely. The court, in Tang and in early Song, was a major source for the distribution of copies of calligraphy, but its very success meant that calligraphy reproductions were widely available outside the court. With painting, however, copying was done by hand and on a much smaller scale. As a consequence, the court's collection of paintings was much more difficult to equal outside of it, giving the court a larger advantage in the training of painters. The court had an even greater advantage in the case of antiquities, because its resources allowed it to assemble so much larger and more diverse a collection than any private collector could manage. Just as Tang court historians could write more successful histories because of their access to the books and documents at court, so during Huizong's reign students of ancient scripts or ancient bronze design and typology who had access to the court's collections were able to accomplish much more than those less privileged.

What was the legacy of Huizong's massive collecting project? As seen in chapter 9, the objects that he had gathered into the palace and Palace Library were eventually scattered, and fewer than a hundred pieces are still extant today. But many of those that do survive are today considered masterpieces. Because they are so securely dated, they have provided modern scholars a relatively solid foundation on which to build their analyses of period styles and artists' styles.

Even if only 1 or 2 percent of the objects once in Huizong's collection are known today, three of the catalogues he commissioned did survive intact. These three catalogues—all in wide circulation from Yuan times on—probably in the long term had more impact than the surviving objects. They offered a huge store of information and opinion. Art and antiquity lovers could turn to them to look for comparative material when they came across an ancient bronze cauldron or a piece of calligraphy that purported to be by a minor Tang master. The catalogues provided not only long lists of masters and works, but also dozens of essays that placed objects in larger cultural contexts. They provided pictures of hundreds of ancient bronzes, along with rubbings of inscriptions, readings of the rubbings, and analyses of styles and periods. With the passage of time, the political agendas of the catalogues mattered less and less to readers. It was not a problem for Dong Qichang that the painting catalogue had entries for many imperial clansmen and eunuchs, so long as it also included painters and calligraphers that interested him. Thus, while Song politics help explain why the catalogues were written the way they were, they have little to do with how people made use of the catalogues in later centuries.

Much of the impact of the catalogues was delayed for centuries. Consider, for instance, the case of mirrors. *Antiquities Illustrated* was the first book to treat mirrors at length. There is little evidence, however, that the initial circulation of *Antiquities Illustrated* did much to promote the collection of mirrors by literati collectors. Ming texts on collecting rarely say much about mirrors.[11] In the early Qing period, however, people began to turn to Huizong's catalogue as the fullest source for understanding mirrors. The circulation of Huizong's catalogue made it easier for later people to take up collecting mirrors, as it gave them a lot of comparative material and an analysis of the categories into which mirrors could be divided. A late-seventeenth- or early eighteenth-century encyclopedia included an eighteen-page chapter on mirrors, much of it direct quotation from Huizong's catalogue.[12] The Qing encyclopedic compilation, the *Complete Collection of Ancient and Modern Books* (Gujin tushu jicheng), completed in 1726, included four chapters on mirrors, large chunks taken directly from Huizong's catalogue, including all of the pictures of mirrors.[13] The two chapters in Qianlong's antiquities catalogue devoted to mirrors were based closely on Huizong's catalogue in format, for instance, reproducing the inscriptions and transcribing them in the format in which they appear on the mirror, and adopting many of the labels for types of mirrors that Huizong's catalogue had pioneered.[14] By the end of Qianlong's reign, mirrors were attracting more interest from collectors. In the early nineteenth century a major compilation of inscriptions included rubbings of 177 inscribed mirrors, complete with transcriptions and comments.[15]

On the whole, the sort of sequencing and list-making seen in the case of mirrors seems to have had the greatest long-term impact. By contrast, acts that were immediately recognizable as politically based cultural interventions did relatively little to change people's thinking. Thus, the sequence of ancient bronze vessels devised by Huizong's cataloguers seemed by the time of Qianlong's cataloguers simply to be the way one organized this material, and they adopted the categories and ordering without analyzing their significance or how else one might organize antiquities. By contrast, no later lists of paintings put Daoist paintings before Buddhist ones. Perhaps the listing of quite a few Song imperial clansmen as painters helped spread their reputations and thus contributed to the preservation of paintings by them. However, the inclusion of eunuchs as painters did not lead to the preservation of many paintings by them. Huizong's most blatant act of exclusion probably backfired. Unlike many European courts, the Song court did not dominate taste or critical opinion. Leaving Su Shi and Huang Tingjian out of the calligraphy catalogue in no way damaged their standing as artists and may have even helped their reputations by confirming that they were men who stood up to power.

Did Huizong's collecting have an impact on later emperors or the imperial institution? Because of the tragedy that befell Huizong and his court, the story of his collection and its fate provided perfect material for those who wished to temper emperors' cultural ambitions. Certainly some emperors were persuaded of the dangers of devoting too much attention to the pursuit of material things and aesthetic pleasures. Yet this view never became totally dominant. There remained room for emperors to see the cultural power that comes from gathering into the political center as much of the accumulated cultural treasures as possible.

Authorship and Editions of the Catalogues

Each of Huizong's three catalogues was the longest work yet written in its field, and each has been published numerous times in the ensuing centuries, probably above all because each came to be recognized as a useful reference work. Many issues surround the writing and publishing of these catalogues, but verbal discrepancies between editions are minor. Quite possibly all extant editions derived from single Yuan-period printed texts. Here I have cited the three most widely available editions: for the antiquities catalogue, the *Siku quanshu* edition; for the painting catalogue, the 1964 punctuated and annotated edition which also has translations into modern Chinese, issued by Renmin meishu chubanshe in Beijing; and for the calligraphy catalogue, the 1984 punctuated edition issued by the Shanghai shuhua chubanshe. In the case of the painting catalogue, I have also consulted the 1999 edition put out by the Hunan meishu chubanshe, with punctuation, annotation, and translation into modern Chinese. For the calligraphy catalogue, I have consulted the 1999 edition in the same series as well as the Japanese 1978 annotated edition, with translation into Japanese, published by Nigensha.

One issue that involves all three catalogues is how much of a role Huizong played in the writing or editing of the catalogues. Throughout this book I have referred to Huizong's curators, editors, compilers, or cataloguers as doing the work. I never say that Huizong himself did any of the writing, but I also suggest that Huizong was involved in key decisions and that those doing the actual work would have consulted him from time to time to get his approval for what they were doing. In a note on the antiquities catalogue, Zhai Qinian (fl. 1120–1140), the son of Zhai Ruwen (1076–1141), one of those who worked with Huizong's antiquities, attributed the catalogue to Huizong. He cited the work Huizong did to collect antiquities and to gather officials knowledgeable in ancient scripts to study them, and also said that Huizong personally debated with these officials some of the interpretations.[1] This matches what we know of Huizong's involvement with the revision of the ritual code. In that case, the correspondence between Huizong and the officials entrusted with the revision was preserved and placed at the front of the book. This correspondence shows that the officials working on the book brought a long series of issues to him, and he repeatedly expressed opinions on them.[2] If in 1111 he was interested enough to state an opinion on whether dogs should be eliminated from the list of sacrificial animals, it is also likely that a few years later he participated in the choice of paintings, calligraphy, and bronzes to be listed in the catalogues.[3]

In the case of the painting and calligraphy catalogues, some scholars have gone so far as to argue that Huizong deserves to be listed as the author of the catalogue. Chang Bide points to wording in several of the entries in the painting catalogue that seems more appropriate for Huizong to have used than for one of his subjects. Ni Genfa argues that no one but Huizong himself would have omitted Huizong from the list of esteemed painters.[4] More commonly, however, scholars interested in the issue of authorship have concentrated on trying to identify the man whose name was on the book when it was first completed. Books issued by the government often appeared under the name of a senior official, whether or not he did any actual writing. For instance, in the early Song, Li Fang's name was listed as author of the *Taiping guangji* and *Taiping yulan*, encyclopedic works he surely did little more than supervise from a distance, and in Huizong's reign the Zhenghe ritual code was issued under the name of the supervising official, Zheng Juzhong. Scholars largely assume that the catalogues would have had names associated with them that were either accidentally lost or purposely removed. For my part, I do not see a need to identify such an author, and am comfortable considering each of the catalogues to have been produced at court by multiple authors as part of their official assignments. I consider how the books were written to be a more interesting question than who held the highest office while they were being assembled.

ANTIQUITIES ILLUSTRATED

The current versions of the antiquities catalogue have thirty chapters and the title *Antiquities Illustrated of the Xuanhe [Hall or Period], Revised* 重修宣和博古圖. Current versions can be traced back to a copy with this name printed in the Zhida period of the Yuan dynasty (1308–1310). No author is listed on this edition. This Yuan printing was not the earliest version of the book to circulate, as several Song book catalogues list the book, often with slight variations in the title or length.[5] Writing before 1147, Cai Tao, in a passage translated in chapter 5, referred to a work titled *Antiquities Illustrated of Xuanhe Hall* that was at least begun in the Daguan period (1107–1110). Zhai Qinian (fl. 1120–1140), who listed Huizong as the author, did not use the phrase "revised." Chao Gongwu (1105–1180) left out Xuanhe as well as "revised," listed the work as twenty *juan* in length, and attributed it to Wang Chu 王楚, a man of the period known to have worked on ancient scripts. Zheng Qiao

(1104–1162), You Mao (1127–1193), and Chen Zhensun (1183–1261) all left out "revised" and listed no author. Zheng, however, gave the book's length as sixty *juan*.[6]

The seventeenth-century bibliophile Qian Zeng (1629–1699+) wrote that the Song edition in his possession listed Wang Fu as author. Wang Fu was grand councilor from 1120 to 1124, so if the book was issued then, his name would be a natural one to attach to it. Moreover, Wang Fu is quoted by name four times in the book, generally on issues concerning the reading of inscriptions. Qian Zeng argued that the publishers of the Yuan edition had removed Wang Fu's name because he had come to be despised for his role in the fall of the Northern Song. The eighteenth-century authors of the *Siku quanshu* accepted Qian's argument and listed the catalogue under Wang Fu's name. A long series of scholars since then have disputed these inferences on one ground or another.[7]

The scholar who has done the most to sort out the discrepancies in the evidence is Ye Guoliang. He argues that Chao Gongwu was referring to a different book with the name *Bogu tu*, a book that did in fact have twenty *juan*, and shows one Southern Song author who cites both books. The other cataloguers, who used the term "Xuanhe" and listed thirty *juan*, could be referring to either the first or the revised version, the first probably done in 1113, when both Dong You and Huang Bosi refer to orders to work on a catalogue (see chapter 6), the revised one between 1123 (when a set of bells in the catalogue were discovered) and 1125 (the end of the Xuanhe period). The time frame for the revised version can probably be narrowed down to 1123–1124 if it appeared under Wang Fu's name, because 1124 was his last year as grand councilor.[8]

Ye does not discuss the printing of the antiquities catalogue. Chang Lin-sheng argues against the idea that *Antiquities Illustrated* was printed in Song times, saying it would have been too large and complex for Song printers. Chen Mengjia and Wang Shimin, by contrast, take it for granted that it was printed in the Song.[9] Although no edition before 1308 has survived, I find it hard not to conclude that it was printed during Huizong's reign or early in the Southern Song, as so many Southern Song and early Yuan scholars were able to consult it. Handwritten copies of books often circulated for centuries, but hand copying illustrations is much more difficult, and there is no sign that copies without illustrations circulated.

Let me summarize the evidence that copies of the catalogue circulated widely before 1308. The early Southern Song court had a copy, and in 1143 Emperor Gaozong instructed that it be used to design new sacrificial vessels. Xue Shanggong (d. 1144) cited the catalogue five times in his own study of inscriptions on ancient vessels. Zheng Qiao (1104–1162) not only listed the catalogue in his book list but also gave a list of items in it. Luo Bi, in a work written in 1170, cited it with reference to ancient vessel types. Hong Mai (1123–1202) had access to a copy, as he wrote a long critique on some of the errors he found in it. So did his brother Hong Gua (1117–1184), who cited it in his discussion of a mirror in his work on Han antiquities. Zhou Hui (1127–1198+) saw a copy when visiting the home of a descendant of Zhai Ruwen, who pulled it out to compare a picture in it to a cauldron in his collection.[10] Zhu Xi (1130–1200) mentioned it several places. His recorded conversations include a discussion of Wang Anshi's etymological theories which cites *Antiquities Illustrated.* A letter he wrote refers to borrowing a copy of *Antiquities Illustrated.* He also cited it in his guide to the sacrifices to Confucius held by prefectural schools, which includes illustrations very clearly based directly or indirectly on *Antiquities Illustrated* (see fig. A.1). As one might expect of a scholar of the classics, Zhu Xi wanted people to use vessels that more accurately reflected the vessels the authors of *The Rites of Zhou* specified, rather than to continue to draw on the fanciful pictures in the *Illustrations of the Three Ritual Classics.*[11] Zhao Yanwei (1140–1210) argued against *Antiquities Illustrated*'s position that wooden and bamboo vessels had not been used in ancient times. Tang Shichi (ca. 1180–ca. 1240) wrote a preface for *Antiquities Illustrated of Xuanhe Hall,* probably for a printing of it. Wang Yinglin (1223–1296) cited the catalogue more than forty times, in one case listing all the items in it. Other examples could be cited.[12]

The numerous citations of the antiquities catalogue during the Southern Song is in striking contrast to the absence of citation to the other two catalogues. Clearly the only copies of the painting and calligraphy catalogues were taken by the Jurchen and were not available in the south. If the antiquities catalogue had been printed, even in a small run of one hundred or two hundred copies, some of them could easily have made their way out of the palace before the Jurchen invasion and ended up in the south.

The earliest surviving edition, known as the Yuan or the Zhida 至大 edition (from the reign period, 1308–1310), is physically much larger than any of the later editions, with the book itself 40 centimeters tall, and the printed portion 30 by 24 centimeters each half page. Whenever possible, items were illustrated full size, but when they were too large, the illustration was clearly marked as reduced in scale (fig. A.2). Small objects use only part of the page (see fig. A.3). Wide objects were reproduced across a folded page, suggesting that the book was originally bound butterfly style (fig. A.4). At the same time, space was conserved in two ways, by putting the rubbing either on the same page as the illustration or on the same page as the notes (fig A.2). The original Yuan-period blocks continued to be used for a couple of centuries, so that the "Yuan" edition was often actually printed in Ming times. The copy of this book in the Gest Collection at Princeton was printed with very worn blocks, which led Qu Wanli to argue that it likely was printed in Ming times from Yuan blocks.[13] In 1528 Jiang Yang had the blocks recut, but kept the name

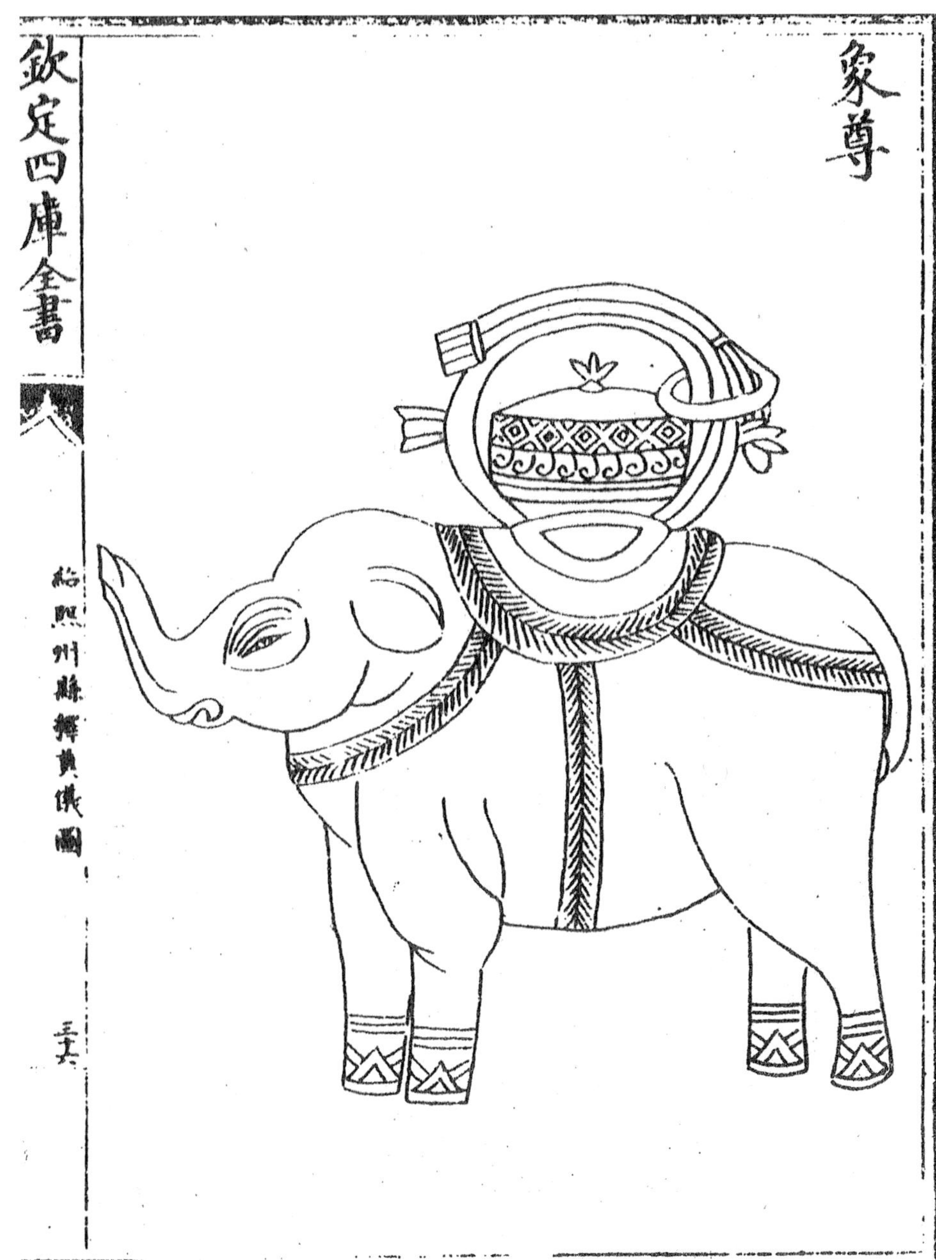

Fig. A.1
Illustration of the elephant beaker in Zhu Xi's liturgies for rites to Confucius for government schools. Compare to figure 6.19 for the comparable illustration in BGT. After SXZXSDTY 36a.

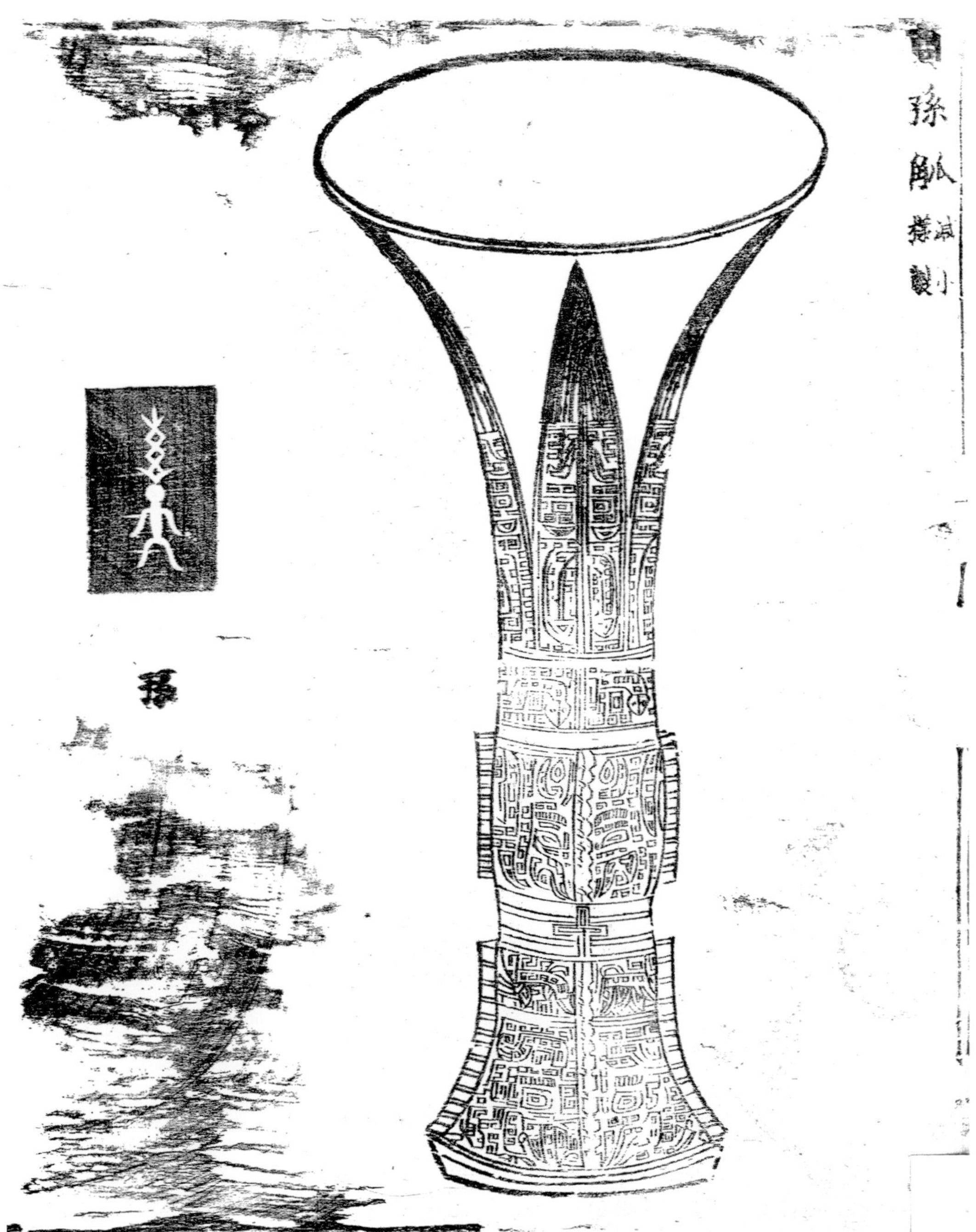

Fig. A.2
Wine glass from Yuan edition of *Antiquities Illustrated* (BGT Yuan ed. 15.36a). This picture is said to be smaller than the object. Notice the rubbing and transcription of the one-character inscription on the same page. Notice also the signs of worn blocks.

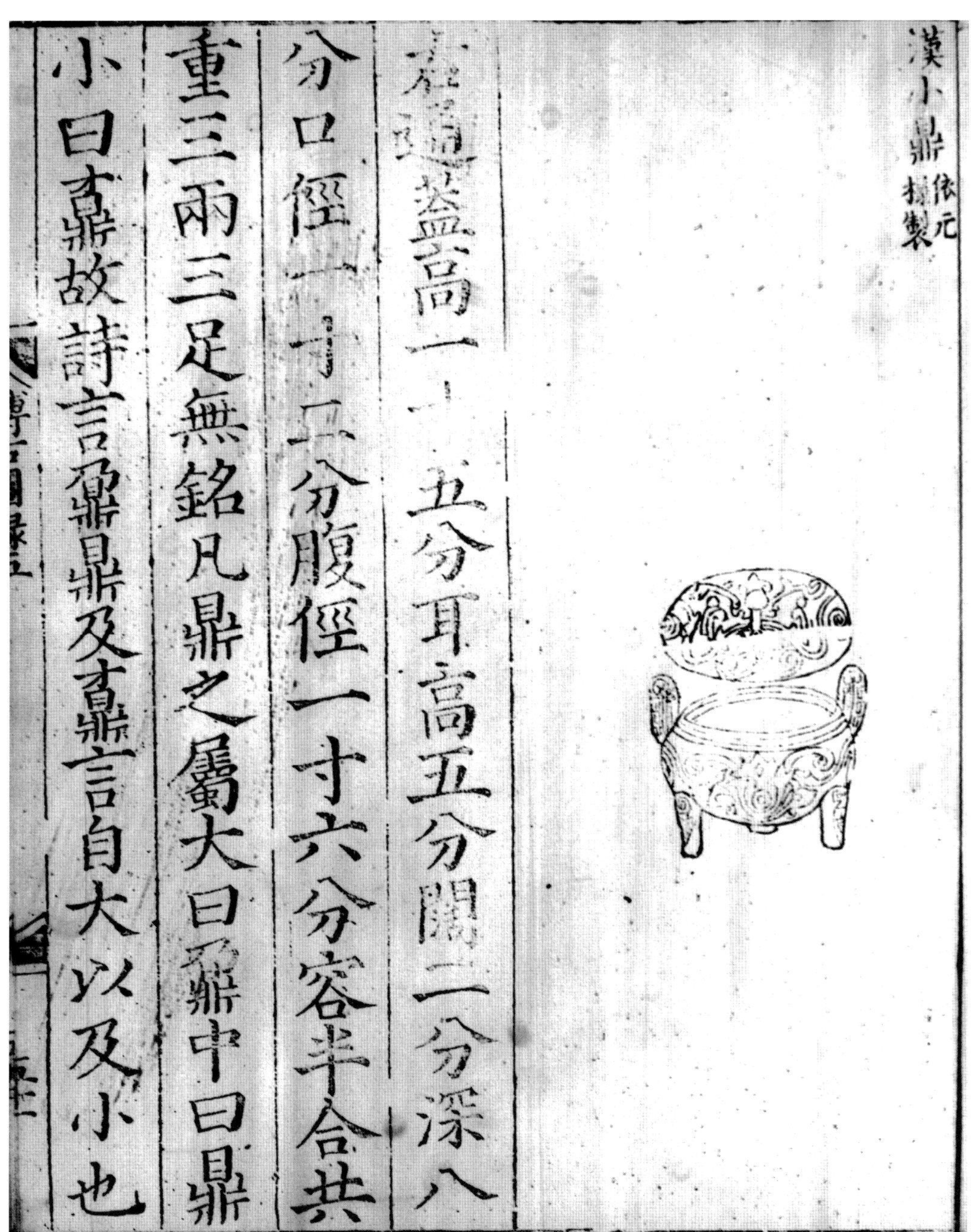
漢小鼎 依元樣製

通蓋高一寸五分耳高五分闊二分深八
分口徑一寸五分腹徑一寸六分容半合共
重三兩三足無銘凡鼎之屬大曰鼐中曰鼎
小曰鼒故詩言鼐鼎及鼒言自大以及小也

Fig. A.3
Small Han-period covered cauldron. The entry reports that this vessel is 1.5 inches tall. In the upper right, under the title it says that this image reproduces the original form, and it does take up much less space than most others, but the scale is not perfect, as this vessel is shown larger than 1.5 inches. BGT 1528 ed. 5.51a.

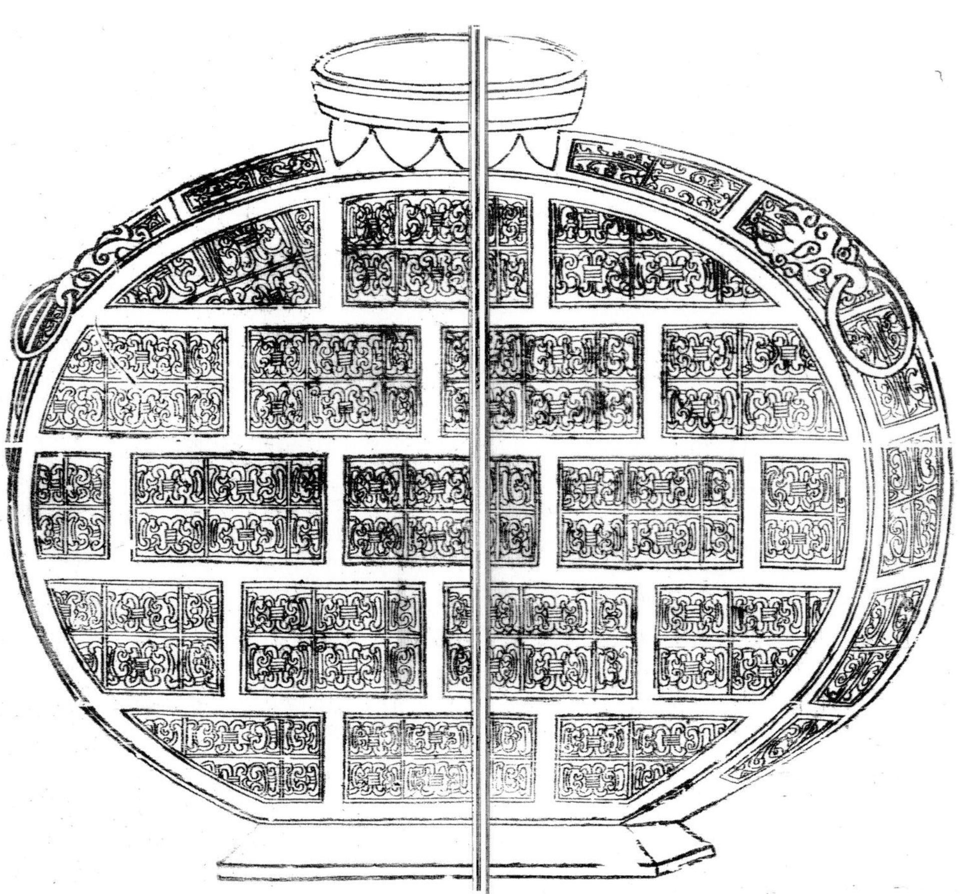

Fig. A.4
Flattened Bottle Number 2 from Yuan edition of *Antiquities Illustrated* (BGT Yuan ed. 13.13a–b). This image goes over the fold of a page, which suggests that the original binding was butterfly style.

Zhida, and copied the earlier edition closely (with indications of whether illustrations were reduced in size, with pictures that went over the fold of the page, and so on). The quality of the drawing in the original and recut Zhida editions (that is the Yuan and the 1528 editions) is high. The illustrators were quite effective in conveying three-dimensionality and such details as covers that could be removed (see figs. A.5 and A.6).

Beginning in the late Ming, *Antiquities Illustrated* was printed in new formats. These later editions fall into two distinct groups, which can be thought of as the fine and the economical versions. The fine editions include the 1588 edition, the 1603 edition based on it, and the 1752 edition based on the 1603 edition, all of which contain nearly identical illustrations.[14] Although the pages of the 1588 edition are not as large as in the Yuan or 1528 editions, the carving is so fine that virtually all detail is preserved (see figs. A.7 and A.8.). The illustrations maintain some distinction between large and small objects, but do not make any attempt to reproduce objects full size. As in the Zhida editions, space is conserved in two ways. Sometimes the rubbing is on the same page as the illustration, sometimes on the same page as

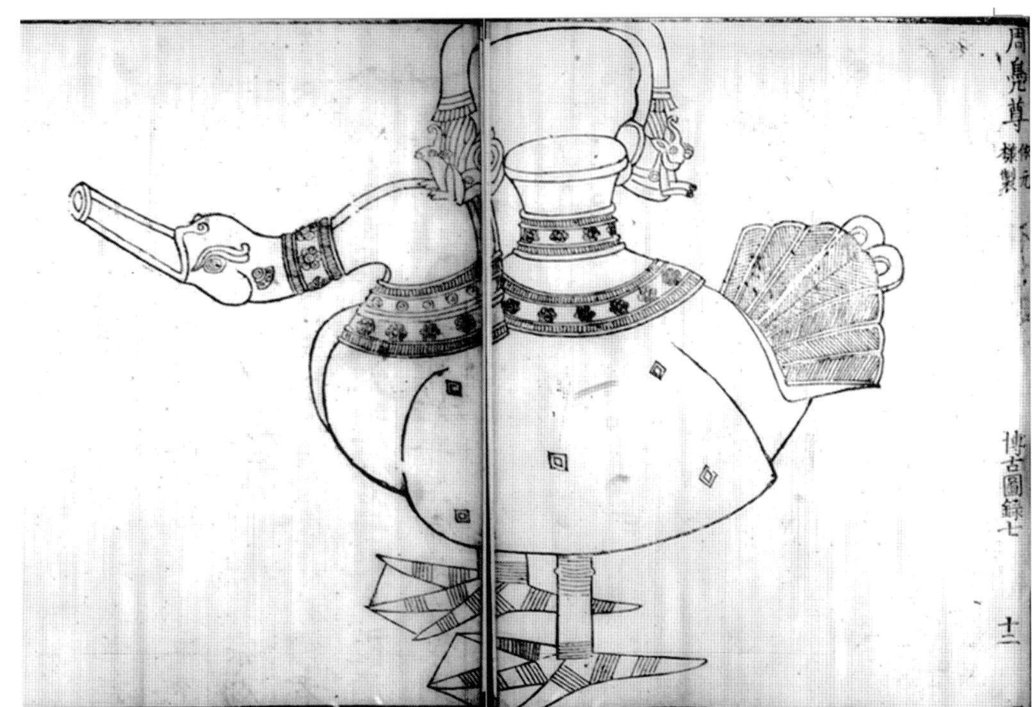

Fig. A.5
Han duck beaker. Notice how the angle effectively conveys the three-dimensionality of the vessel. BGT 1528 ed. 7.12a–b.

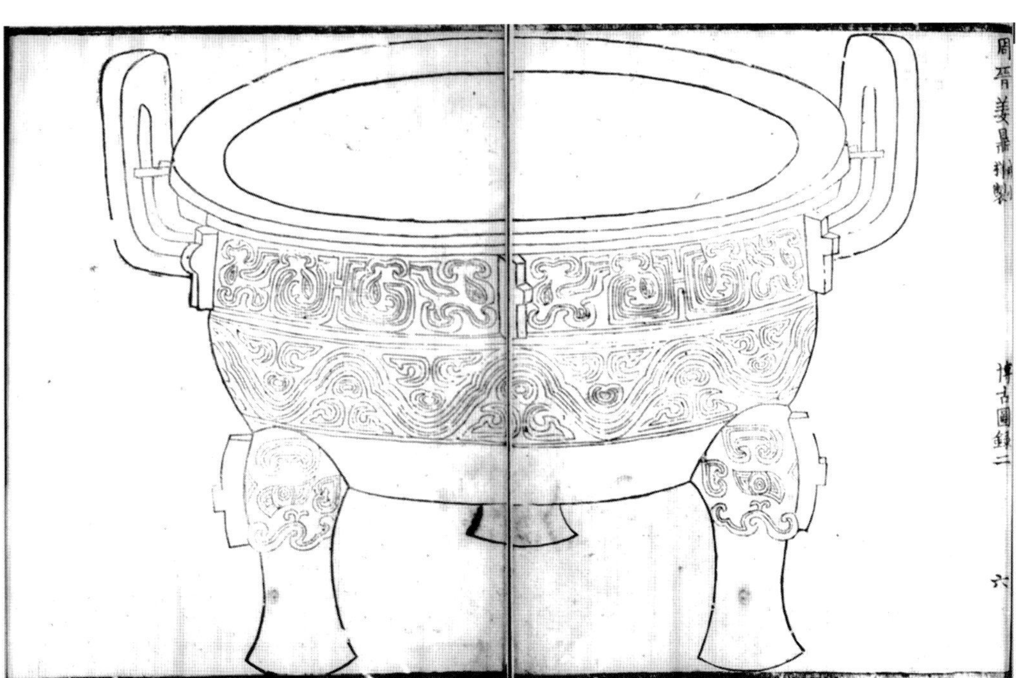

Fig. A.6
Jin Jiang cauldron in 1528 ed. After BGT 1528 ed. 2.6a–b.

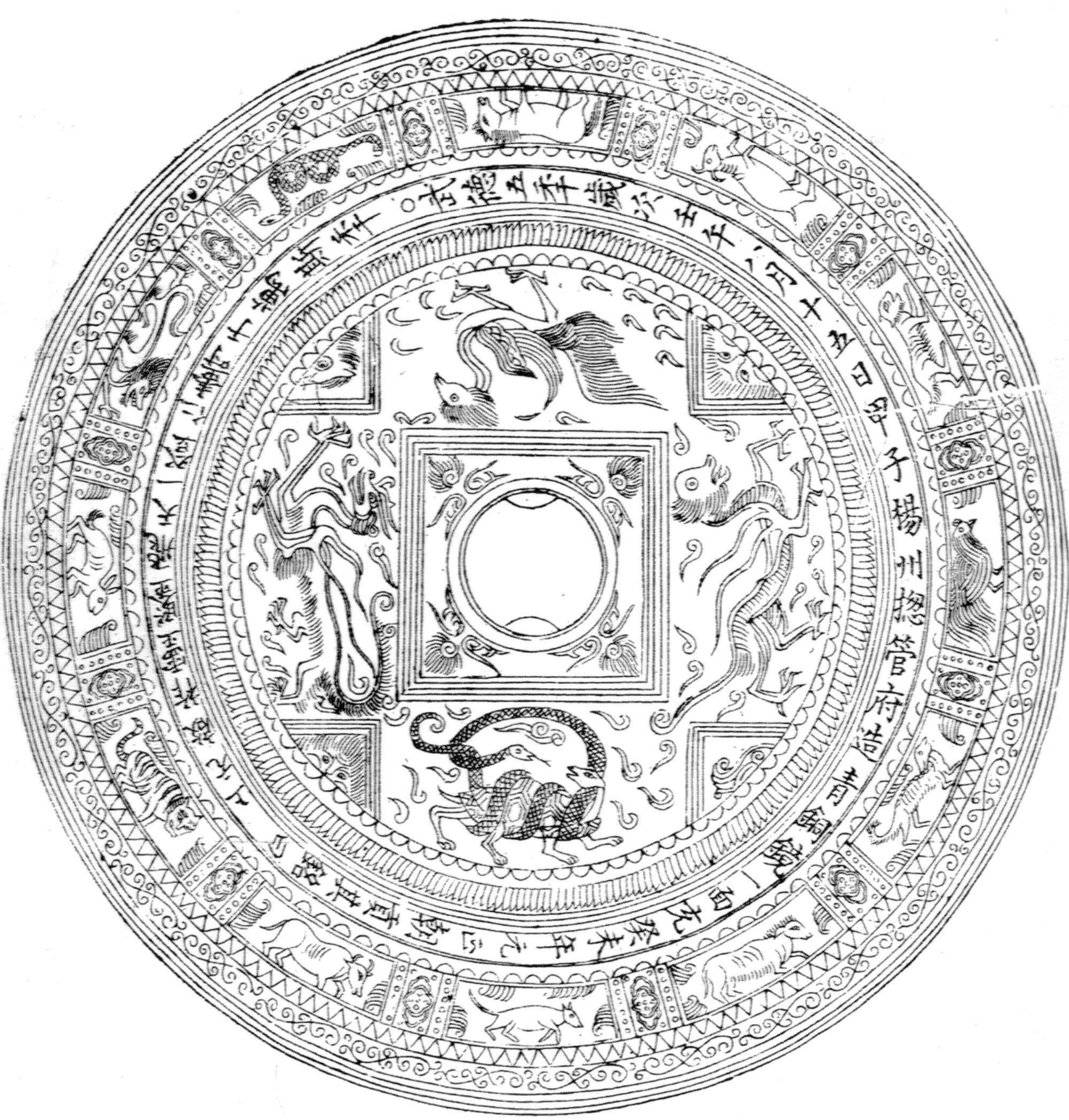

Fig. A.7
Dated mirror in 1588 ed. (BGT 1588 ed. 29.15a). Notice how fine the drawing is.

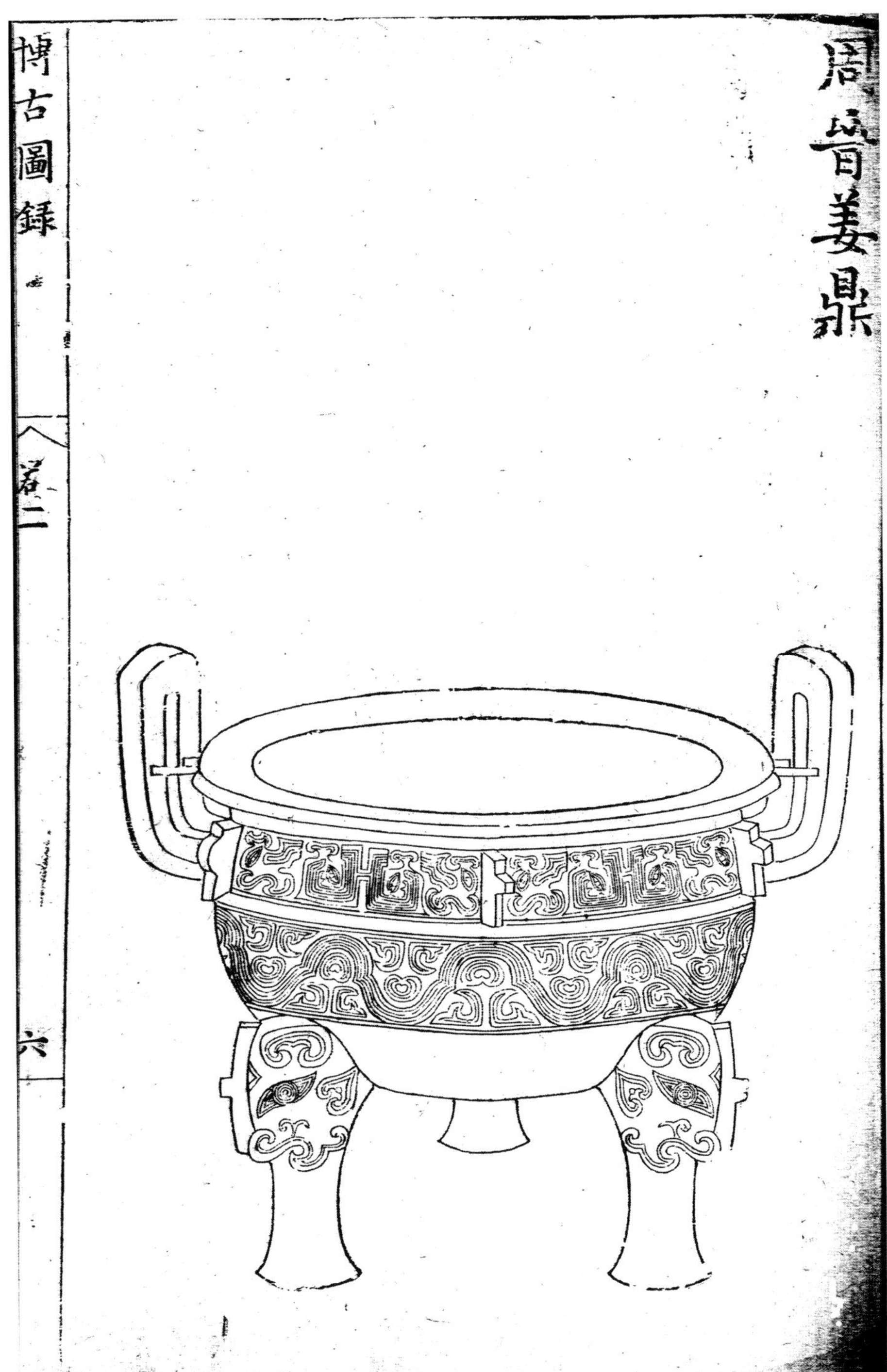

Fig. A.8
Jin Jiang cauldron in the 1588 versions of BGT. BGT 1528 ed. 2.6a.

the notes. The illustrations in the 1726 encyclopedia commissioned by the Kangxi emperor, the *Gujin tushu jicheng* 古今圖書集成, were based on the 1588 or 1603 version (see fig. A.9).

The economical editions include the 1596 "corrected" edition and the 1599 edition and its 1636 reissue. Not only are the pages smaller, but details of decoration are sometimes just suggested rather than carefully drawn (see figs. A.10 and A.11). Probably because the pages are relatively small, the images are all scaled to make full use of the page and do not reflect the size of the original objects. Rubbings are not reproduced on the same page as the object, but are sometimes combined with the notes.[15]

The version of *Antiquities Illustrated* reproduced in the *Siku quanshu* of 1782 draws on the illustrations in the "fine" versions, but generally scales illustrations to fill the page, which means that many had to be redrawn and could not simply be traced. In terms of layout, the *Siku quanshu* version is the most wasteful of space, never putting the rubbing on the same page as the illustration or the notes. See figure 6.16 and elsewhere in this volume.

Below is a list of extant editions, with libraries holding them indicated when known (asterisks indicate copies personally viewed).[16]

1308–1310 Zhida 至大 ed. Full copy at Princeton. Taipei Academia Sinica has an edition missing *juan* 1–4. The union catalogue of rare books in China lists sixteen copies, some incomplete, including ten printed in Ming times from Yuan blocks that had been repaired.[17] Several of these are in the Beijing National Library of China. Pages are 30 × 24 cm. Objects are reproduced full size when possible. Originally bound butterfly style.

1528 ed. Jiang Yang's 蔣暘 recarving of the Zhida ed. National Library of China, Taipei Academia Sinica, National Palace Museum, Taipei. Library of Congress Microfilm of Beiping Library Rare Books reel 544–45.* Pages are approximately the same size as the Yuan edition, on which it is closely modeled.

1588 Boruzhai 泊如齋 ed. Preface by Cheng Shizhuang 程士莊, blocks carved by Huang Deshi 黃德時 (b. 1566). Pages 25 × 15.5 cm. Princeton,* Berkeley, Washington University, U.S. Library of Congress, Chinese University of Hong Kong,* Beijing National Library of China, Taipei Academia Sinica.

1596 Zheng Pu's corrected ed. 鄭樸考正 ed. Book 28 cm tall. Freer/Sackler, U.S. Library of Congress, Beijing National Library of China, Taipei National Palace Museum, University of Hong Kong,* Tokyo University, Tokai University.

1599 ed. of Yu Chengzu 于承祖. Pages 21 × 13 cm. Freer.

1600 reprint of Boruzhai 1588 ed. issued by Wu Wanhua's 吳萬化 Baogutang 寶古堂. Used same blocks cut by Huang Deshi 黃德時. Beijing National Library of China, Taipei Academia Sinica.

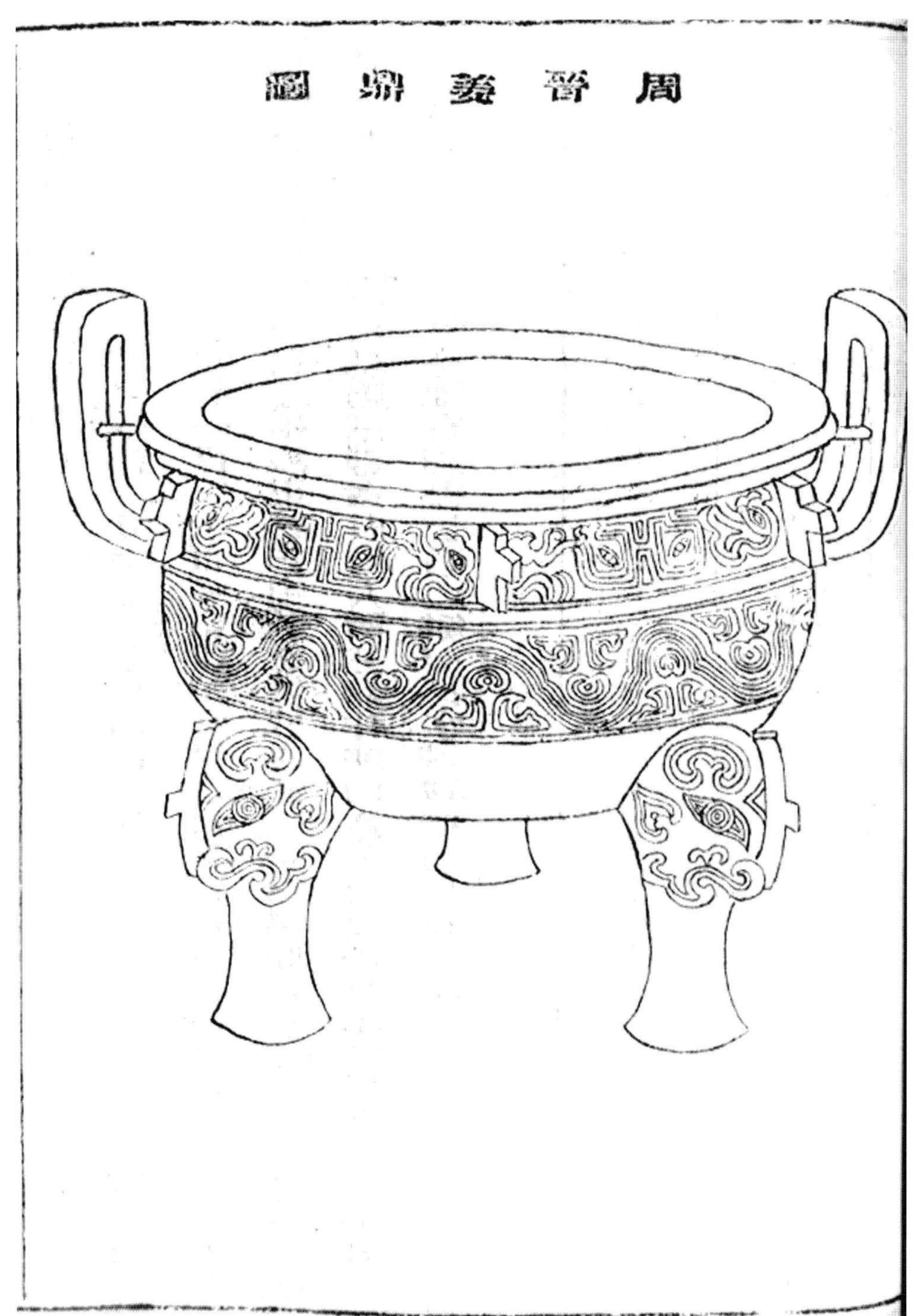

Fig. A.9
The Jin Jiang cauldron as illustrated in the *Gujin tushu jicheng.* After GJTSJC Jingji 200.23a.

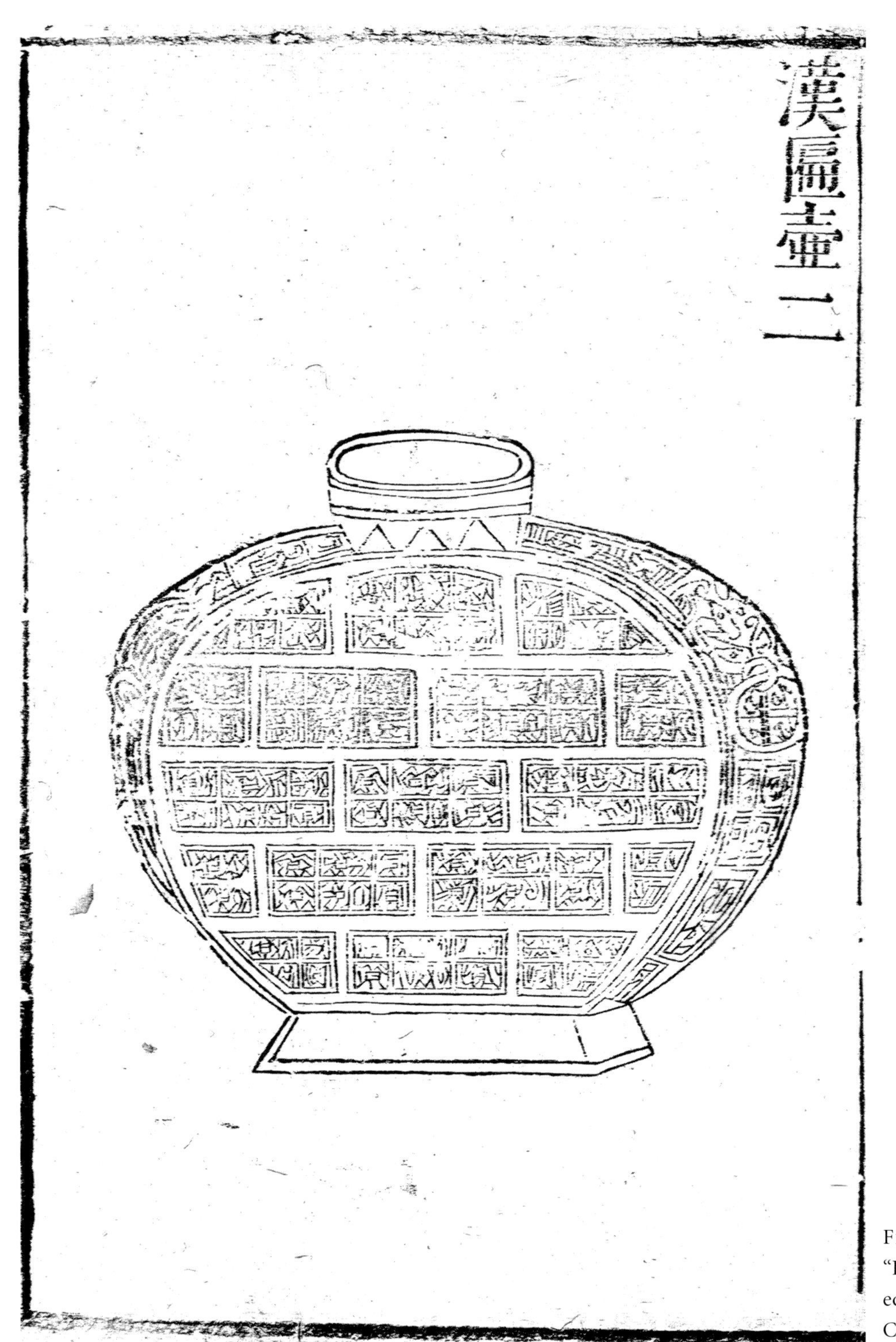

Fig. A.10
"Flattened bottle" in 1599 ed. (BGT 1599 ed. 13.12b). Compare to figure A.4 above.

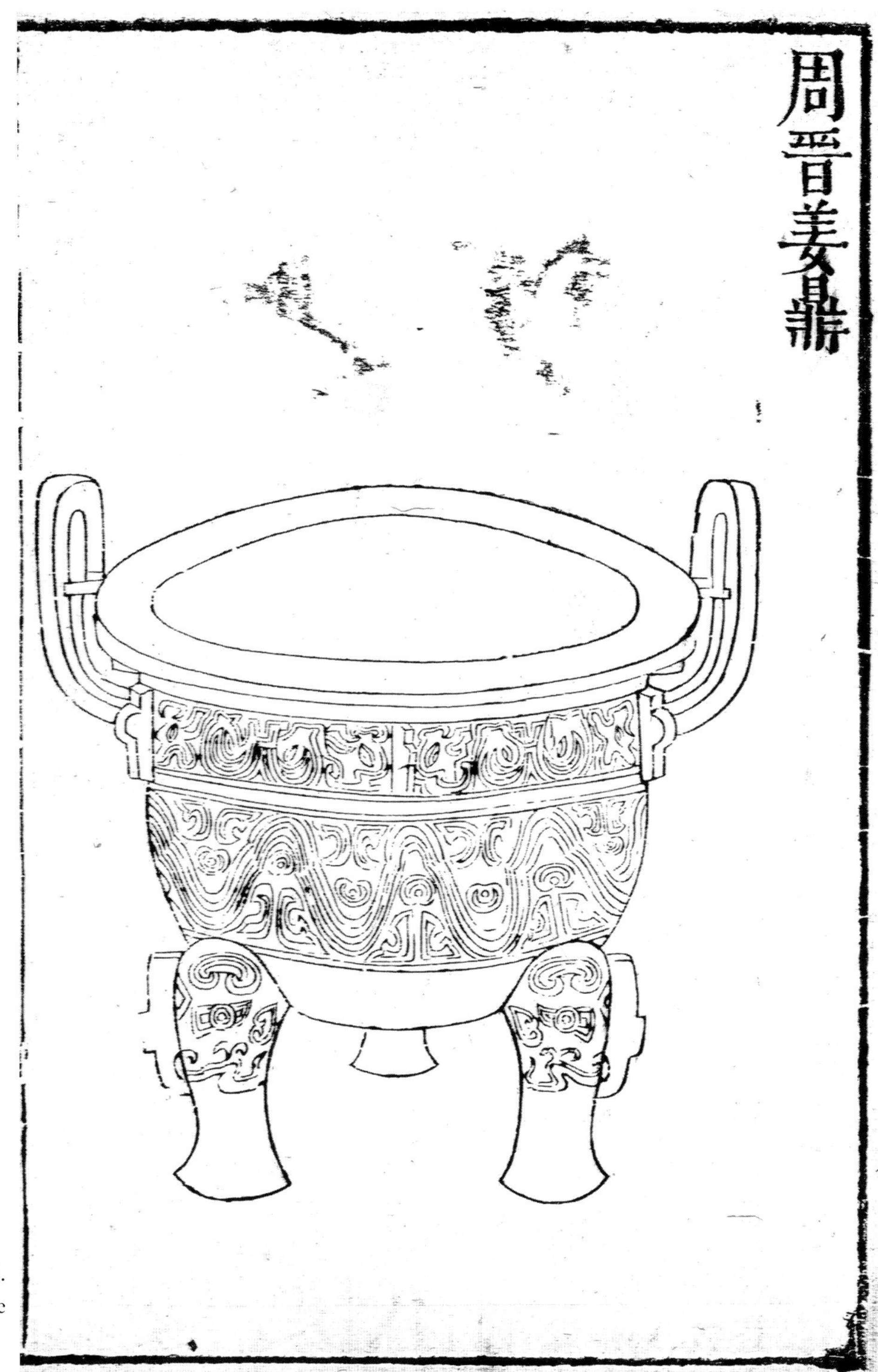

Fig. A.11
Jin Jiang cauldron in 1599 ed. (BGT 1599 ed. 2.6a). Compare to figures A.6, A.8, and A.9, above.

1603 reissue of Boruzhai /Baogutang edition, issued by Wu Gonghong 吳公弘 of the Yizheng tang 亦政堂. Part of a larger work called *Sangu tu* 三古圖. Preface by Hong Shijun 洪世俊, postface by Wu Wanhua 吳萬化 dated 1600. Pages ca. 24 × 15 cm. Harvard,* University of Pennsylvania, UCLA, Victoria and Albert Museum, Beijing National Library of China.

1636 ed. Yu Daonan's 于道南 reissue of Yu Chengzu 于承祖 1599 ed. Also includes 1528 preface of Jiang Yang, undated preface of Chen Zhenyang 陳震陽, undated preface by Yu Chengzu, 1636 preface by Yu Daonan. Blocks cut by Wan Shixu 萬師蓄. Pages given as 20.5 × 13.1 cm, or 21 × 14 cm. First two *ce* (fascicles) devoted to detailed table of contents. Harvard,* Princeton (catalogued as 1599),* Berkeley, Nelson-Atkins Gallery of Art, Kansas City.

1752 ed. Reprint of the 1603 Boruzhai ed. by Huang Sheng 黃晟. As in 1603, part of the larger *Sangu tu*. Pages 24.1 × 15.8 cm. Harvard,* Princeton (catalogued as 1603),* Berkeley, University of Southern California, UCLA, Ohio State, University of Michigan, University of London, Beijing National Library of China, Tianjin Library, Chinese University of Hong Kong, University of Hong Kong, Taiwan University, Taipei Academia Sinica, Taipei National Central Library, Taipei, National Palace Museum. See also 1969 reprint below.

1782 *Siku quanshu* ed. (Reprint; Taipei: Commercial Press, 1983.) Illustrations resemble the 1588/1603/1752 versions, but vary less in size, filling available space.

1969 reprint of 1752 ed. Taiwan Xinxing shuju.

1987 reprint of the *Siku quanshu* ed. Shanghai: Shanghai guji chubanshe.

1991 reprint of the 1603 Boruzhai ed. by Jiangsu Guangling guji keyinshe.

2002 reprint of the *Siku quanshu* ed. Hefei: Anhui jiaoyu chubanshe.

2004 reprint of 1752 ed. by Hong Kong Mingshi wenhua guoji chuban youxian gongsi, as part of *Zhongguo guwenzi daxi* 中國古文字大系.

2005 reprint of Zhida ed. by Beijing tushuguan chubanshe, in the series Zhonghua zaizao shanben 中華再造善本.

The Xuanhe Painting and Calligraphy Catalogues

The *Xuanhe Painting Catalogue* has a preface dated 1120, and those still alive when the two catalogues were written have their titles of 1120–1121 listed, suggesting that both books were begun by 1120 and finished within a few years.[18]

The transmission of the painting and calligraphy catalogues is relatively straightforward. The books were not available in the south during the Southern Song, apparently because the Jurchen army had taken all copies when they stripped the Kaifeng palace of its valuables. Some Jin and early Yuan scholars did see them, however. Wang Yun (1227–1304) reported seeing a copy of the *Xuanhe Calligraphy Catalogue* in the Yuan Palace Library in the 1260s.[19]

The first printing of the catalogues came in Yuan times, and there were many subsequent reprints. The issue that has attracted the most attention of scholars has been who wrote the books. Perhaps because most major works of painting and calligraphy criticism before that date were written by single authors, scholars have wanted to attribute these books to particular authors as well. Over the centuries many candidates have been proposed, including Mi Fu, Tong Guan, Cai Jing, Cai Tao, Cai You, and unidentified palace eunuchs.[20] Scholars have justified their choices through analysis of wording, ideas, or opportunities, but in no case is the evidence for a particular candidate conclusive.

As I have made clear throughout this book, in my view it is pointless to try to identify a single author or editor, as these works were put together as part of official responsibilities, by more than one person, and probably over a long enough span of time that there were also changes in personnel. More interesting questions concern how the books were written. Were those doing the writing officials in the Palace Library, as I have argued, or eunuchs working in the inner palace? The strongest argument in favor of the inner palace is that some of the objects were kept there, giving eunuchs better access to them than regular officials, who would have had to request them (but eunuchs would also have had to request works held in the Library). Huizong had entrusted eunuchs with responsibilities in several other areas, and he knew that some eunuchs were both good artists and good judges of painting and calligraphy. Thus, there is no reason to think he would have objected to them taking part in this project. Moreover, if a senior eunuch were to have acted as editor-in-chief, rather than a senior official like Cai Jing or Cai You, it is easy to understand why his name was not attached to the work. Since eunuchs were in a real sense the emperor's personal servants, they were merely doing what he directed them to do and would not have expected to have their authorship be recognized, especially if they were copying a great deal from files put together by a series of officials over a couple of decades. On the other hand, during the period in question the leading eunuch with expertise in calligraphy, Liang Shicheng, was supervisor of the Palace Library. If he was in fact the person in charge, the Palace Library could well have been the agency responsible. I would not rule out some eunuchs playing a role in compiling material for the catalogues, but if they did so, I suspect that they were working with officials of the Palace Library.

The textual transmission of both the painting and calligraphy catalogues is relatively straightforward. Both books were copied in their entirety into several Qing compilations, including the *Gujin tushu jicheng*, the *Peiwenzhai shuhuapu* 佩文齋書畫譜, and the *Siku quanshu*. Since discrepancies among editions are not a significant problem with the painting and calligraphy catalogues, and as illustrations are not an issue, for most purposes there is little need to consult early editions.

Below I list only the most commonly available editions of the two books.[21]

1303 Wu Wengui 吳文貴 published both books. Palace Museum, Taipei, has copies and issued facsimile reprints in 1971.

1540 ed. of XHSP and XHHP published together by Yang Shen 楊慎 (1488–1559).

1608 ed. by Gao Hong 高拱.

Ming, no date. Several undated Ming editions of both books, available in the National Library of China.

1621–1644 Mao Jin's 毛晉 (1599–1659) Jiguge 汲古閣 published XHHP in his *Jindai mishu* 津逮秘書.

1628–1644 *Tang Song congshu* 唐宋叢書 ed. of XHHP.

1782 *Siku quanshu* 四庫全書 ed. of both catalogues.

1805 *Xuejin taoyuan* 學津討原 published by Zhaokuangge 照曠閣, includes both XHSP and XHHP.

1922 Shanghai Hanfenlou 涵芬樓 reprinted *Xuejin taoyuan*.

1923 Shanghai Boguzhai 博古齋 reprinted *Jindai mishu*.

1936 Both texts included in Commercial Press's *Congshu jicheng* 叢書集成, reproducing Mao Jin's *Jindai mishu* ed.

1962 Taipei Shijie shuju included both books in its *Yishu congbian* 藝術叢編 (reprinting the *Congshu jicheng* ed.).

1964 Beijing Renmin meishu chubanshe published a punctuated ed. of XHHP, with annotation and translation into modern Chinese.

1965 Taipei Yiwen yinshuguan reprint of *Xuejin taoyuan* ed. of XHSP and XHHP in its *Baibu congshu jicheng* 百部叢書集成.

1971 National Palace Museum, Taipei, reprint of Yuan Zhida edition of both XHHP and XHSP.

1971 Taipei Commercial Press included XHHP in *Renren wenku* 人人文庫, using *Congshu jicheng* ed.

1974 Taipei Wenshizhe chubanshe included XHHP in *Huashi congshu* 畫史叢書, using *Xuejin taoyuan* ed.

1978 Tokyo Nigensha published Japanese annotated translation of XHSP as part of Nakata Yujirō's 中田勇次郎 *Chūgoku shoron taikei* 中國書論大系 series.

1983 Taipei Commercial Press reprint of SKQS.

1984 Shanghai shuhua chubanshe published XHSP, punctuated, as part of *Zhongguo shuxue congshu* 中國書學叢書.

1990 Jiangsu Guangling guji keyinshe reprinted *Xuejin taoyuan* ed. of XHHP.

1999 Hunan meishu chubanshe published punctuated editions of both XHSP and XHHP, with annotation and translation into modern Chinese.

Paintings and Calligraphies with Huizong's Collector Seals

As DISCUSSED IN CHAPTER 4, HUIZONG'S USE OF SEALS PROBABLY changed over time. This appendix reproduces Huizong's collector seals, identifies which painting or calligraphy each example comes from, and lists the more plausible paintings and calligraphies with these seals on them. Most of the seals were photographed from books and in many cases have been significantly enlarged so that they could be reproduced original size. The source of each example is found on the list of calligraphies and paintings that comes after the seals (c1 is the first of the calligraphies, and so on).

Even a quick glance at this chart shows many cases where the seal impressions from different works seem to have been made from the same seal and others where they clearly were not. It is possible that over the course of his reign Huizong had new seals made that closely copied earlier ones, a practice well documented in later times. But I cannot rule out the possibility that some of the seals whose impressions are shown here were forged.[1]

1. For an incomplete list of works with forged Huizong seals, see Barnhart 1983. For a study that tries to rigorously distinguish different versions of the same seal, see Niu Kecheng 2005.

SEALS

1. The eight seals used in the "Xuanhe mounting" set, in the order used, right to left:

1a. Small gourd-shaped *yushu*, "imperial writing" (4.3 cm tall)

c2

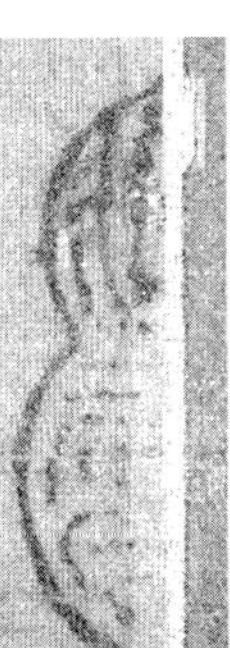

c6

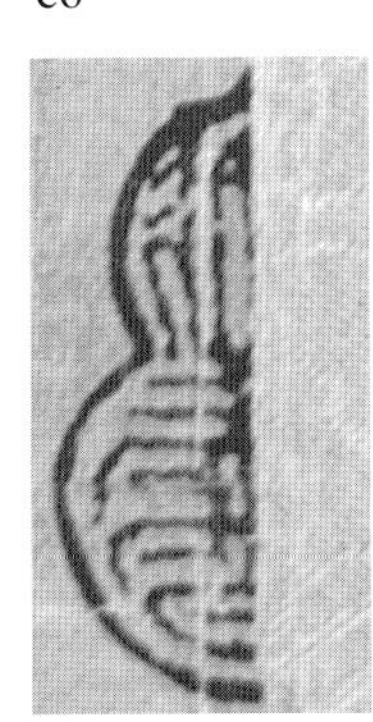

c8

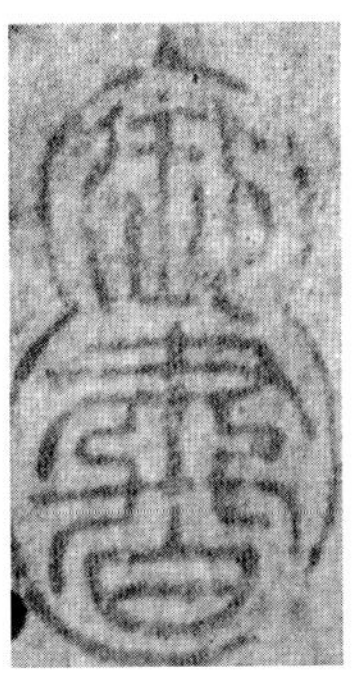

c10

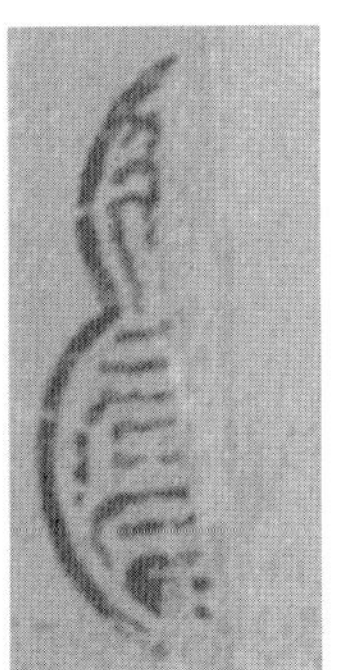

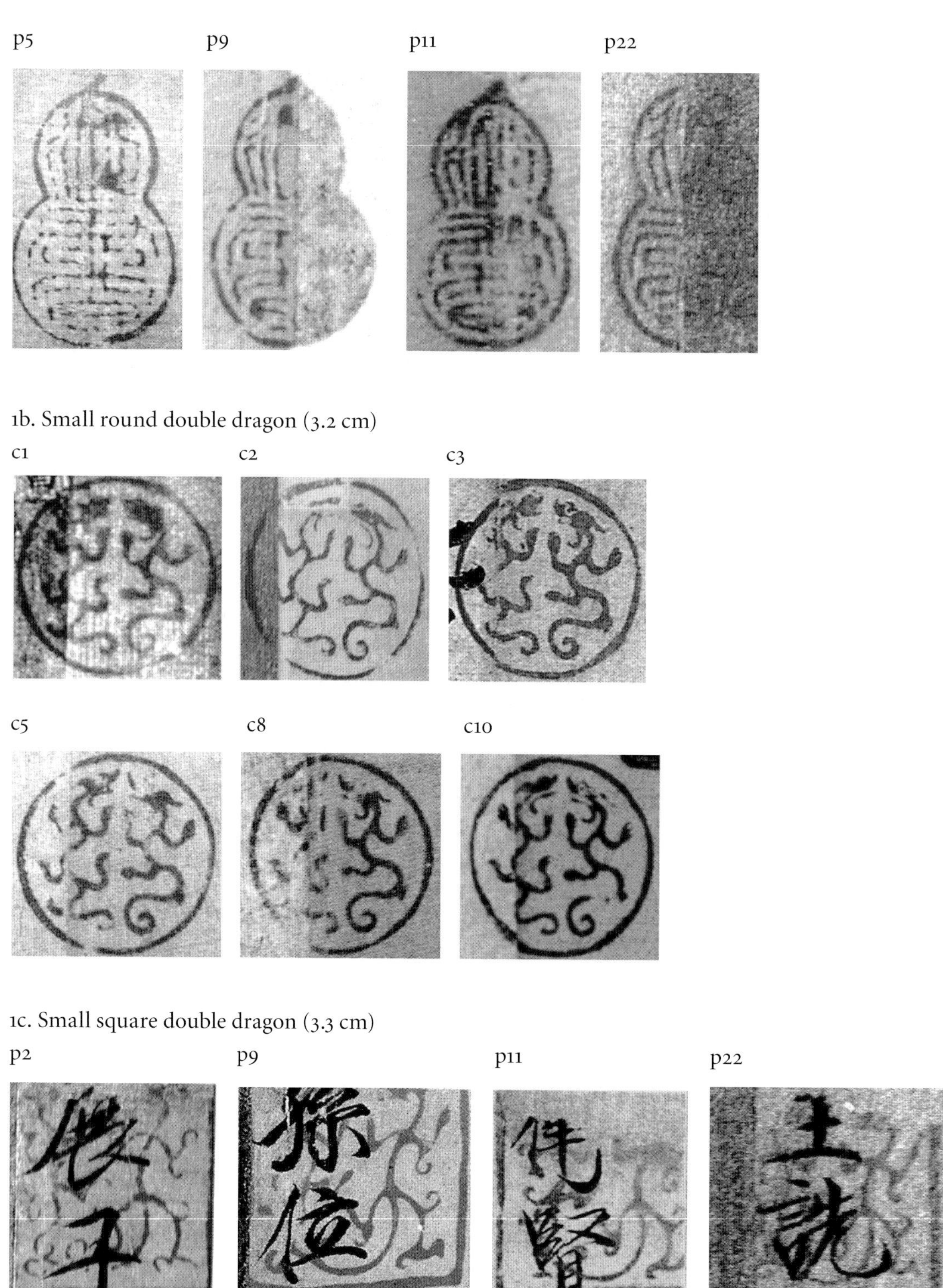
p5
p9
p11
p22
1b. Small round double dragon (3.2 cm)
c1
c2
c3
c5
c8
c10
1c. Small square double dragon (3.3 cm)
p2
p9
p11
p22

1d. Linked square seals *xuanhe,* “Xuanhe [reign name]” (4.3 cm)

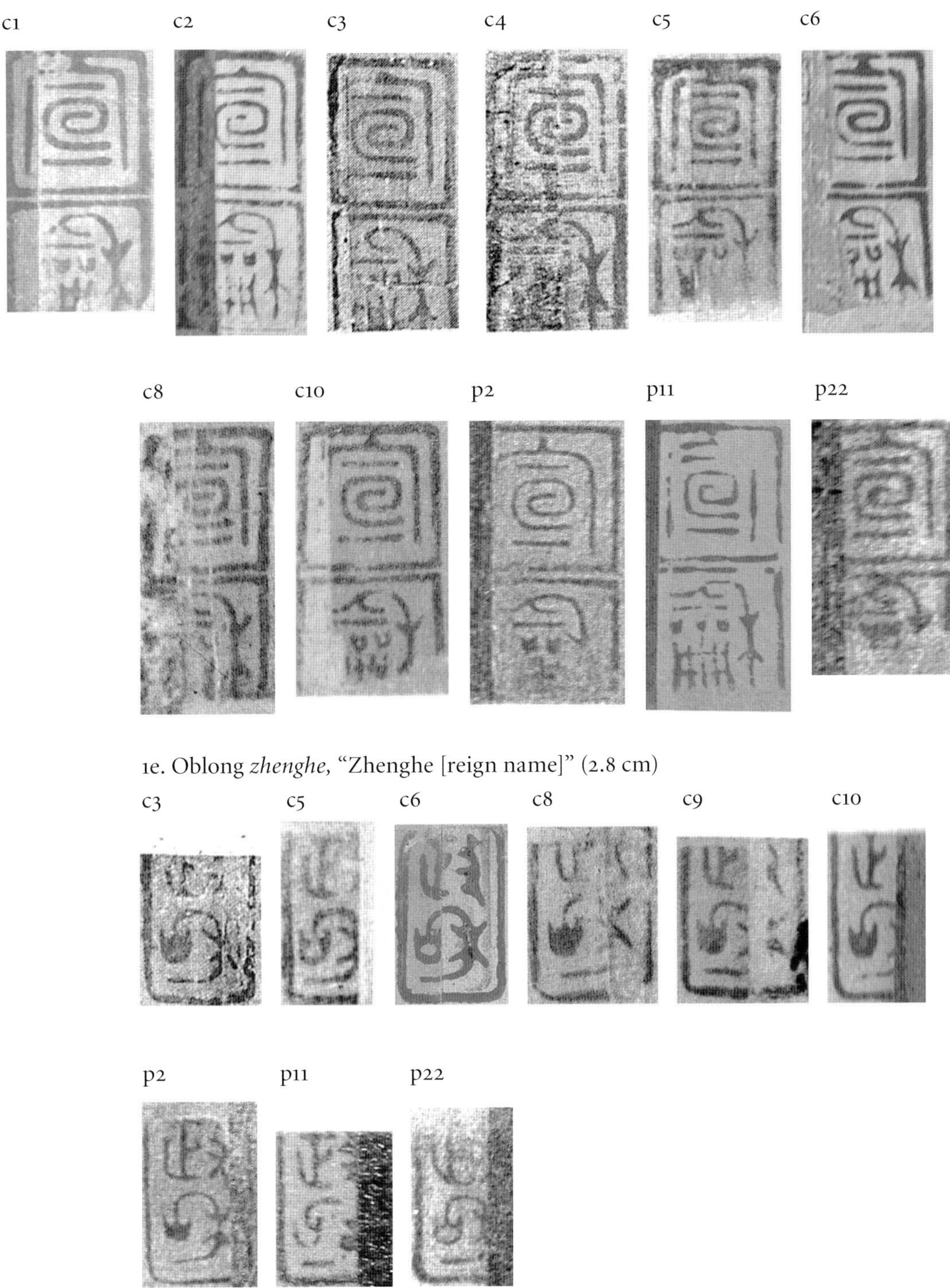

1e. Oblong *zhenghe,* “Zhenghe [reign name]” (2.8 cm)

1f. Oblong *xuanhe*, "Xuanhe [reign name]" (3.7 cm)

c1 c2 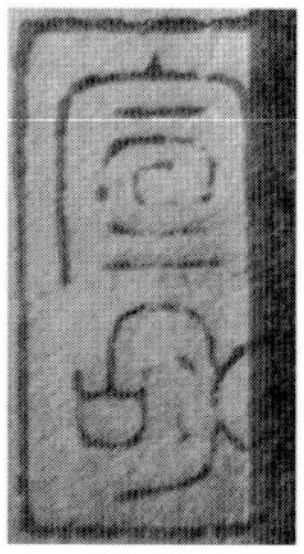 c4 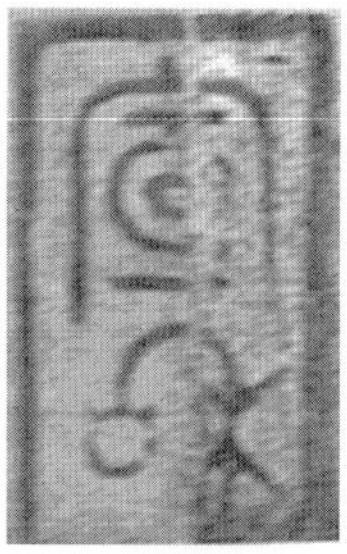 c5 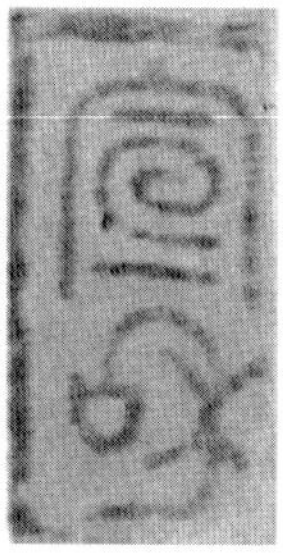 c8 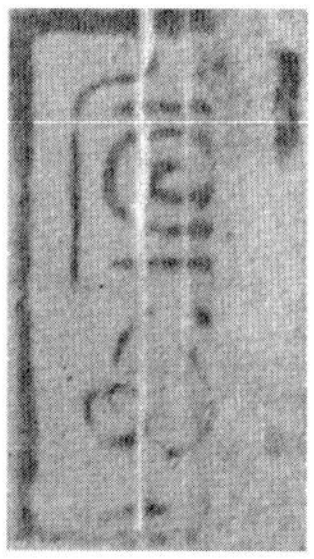 c9

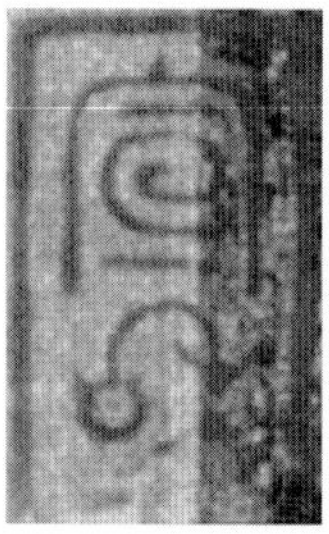

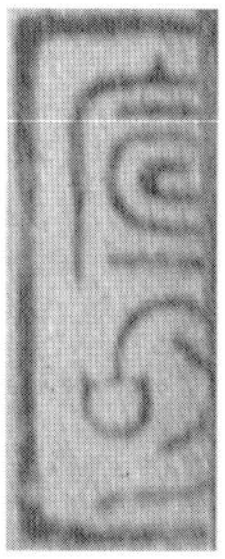

p11 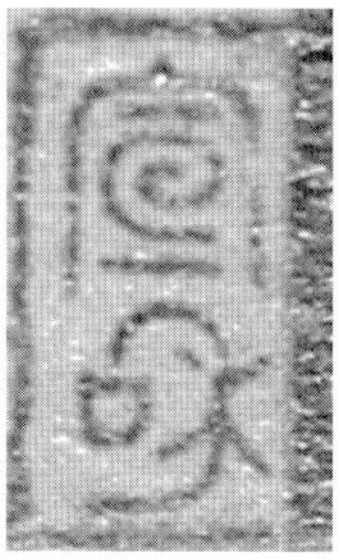 p17 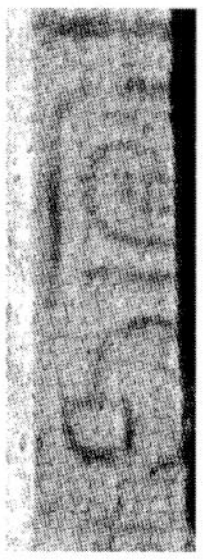 p2 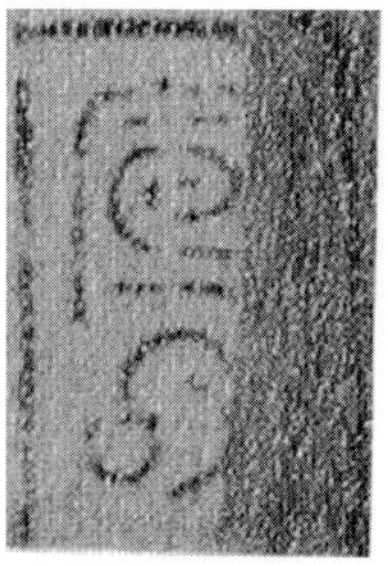 p22

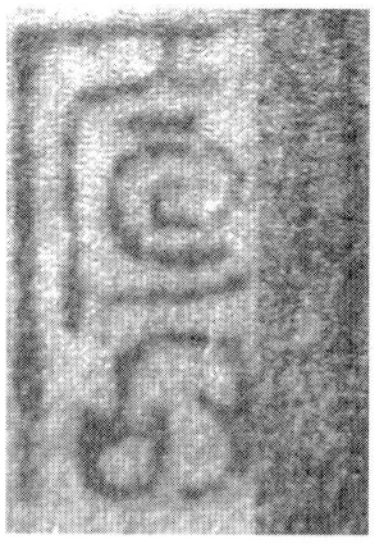

1g. Linked square seals *zhenghe*, "Zhenghe [reign name]" (4.4 cm)

c1 c2 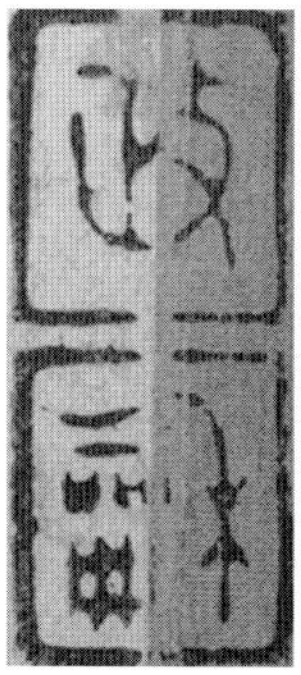 c3 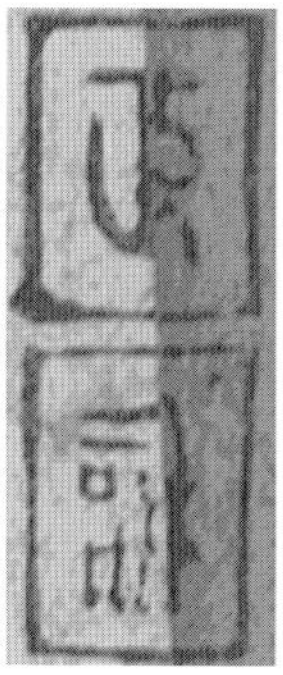 c6 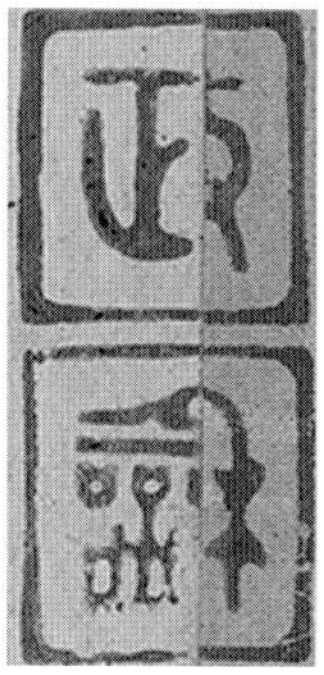 c8 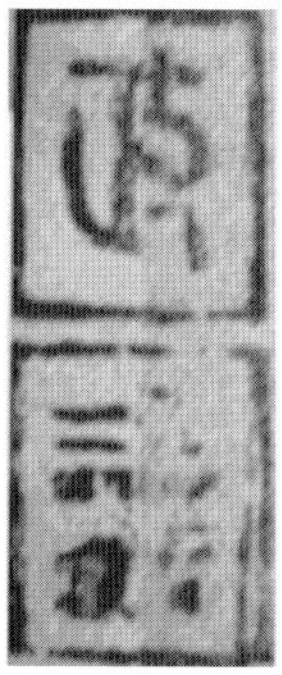 c10

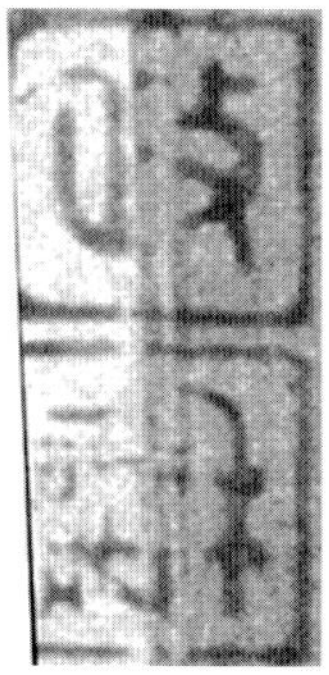

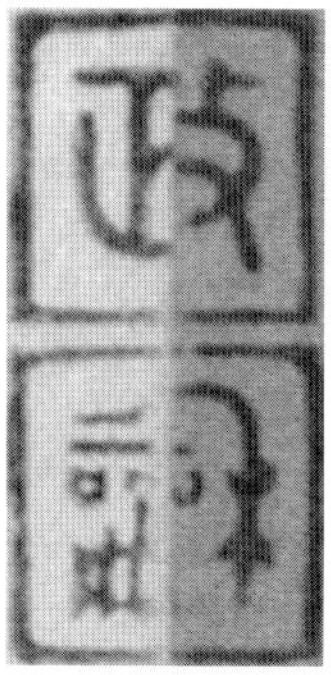

p11 p21 p22 p23

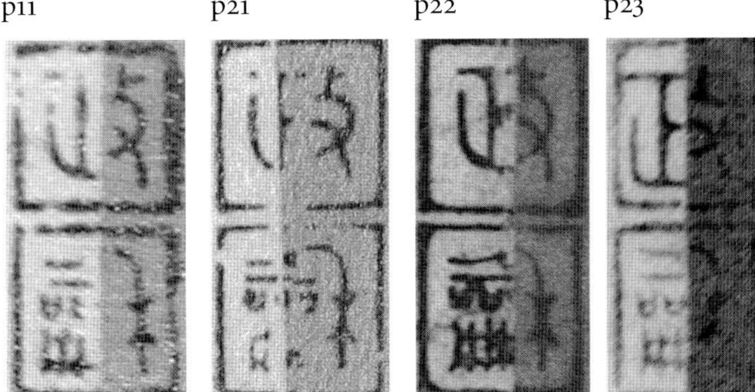

1h. Large square *neifu tushu zhiyin,* "Seal of the inner treasury's paintings and calligraphies" (7.1 cm)

c2 c10

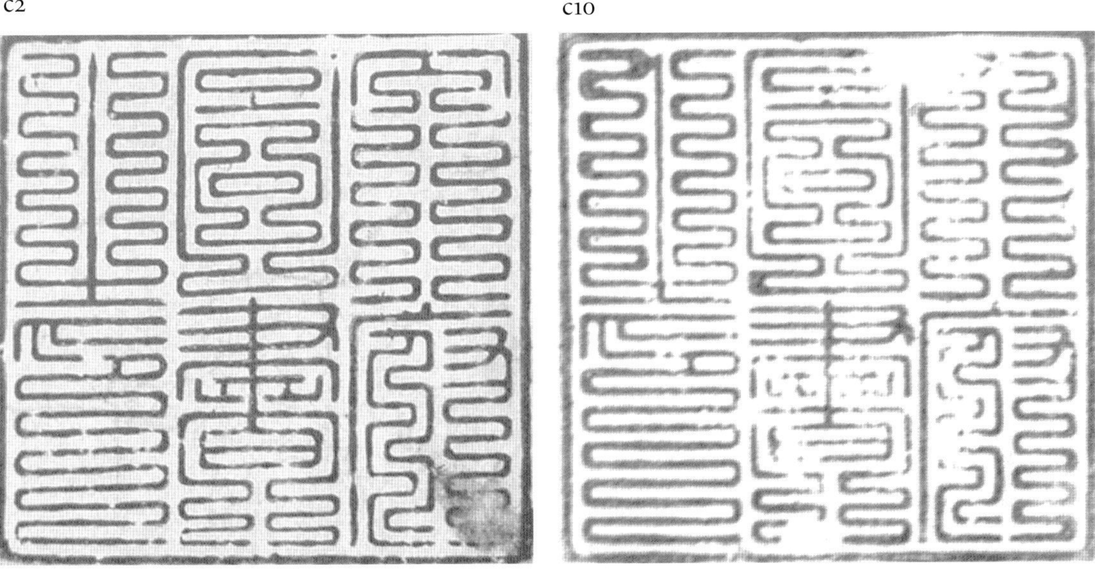

p18

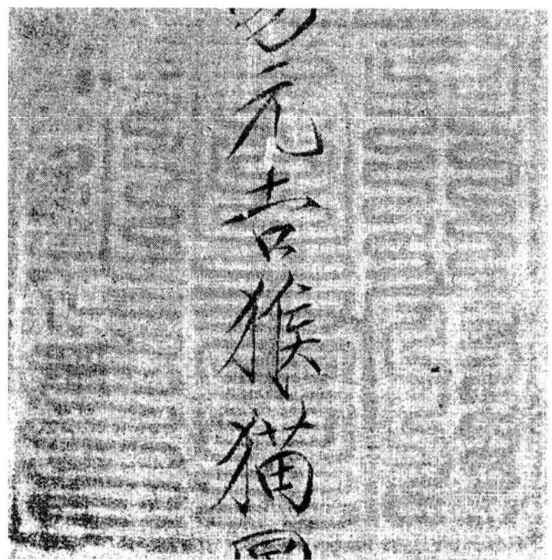

p22

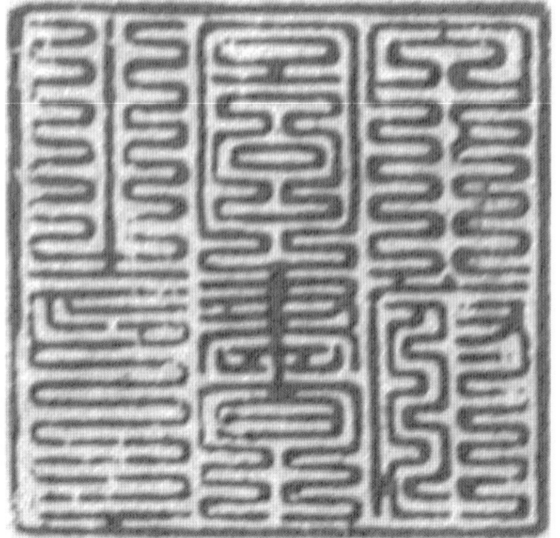

p23

2. *Seals that name halls in the palace*

2a. Large square *ruisi dongge*, "Eastern Studio of Sagacious Thoughts [Hall]" (7.4 cm)

p1

p5

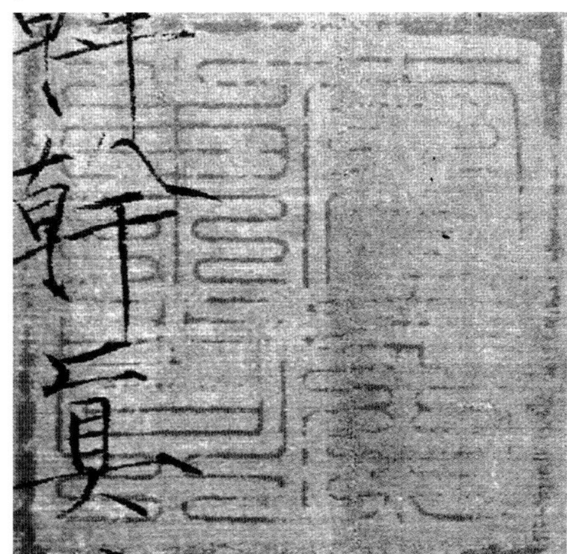

p6

p7

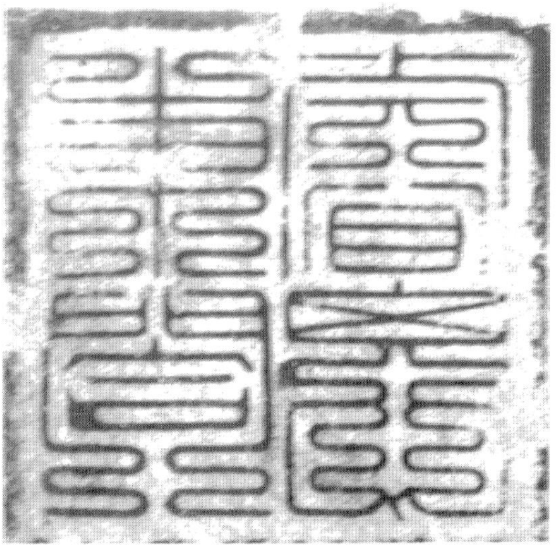

p15

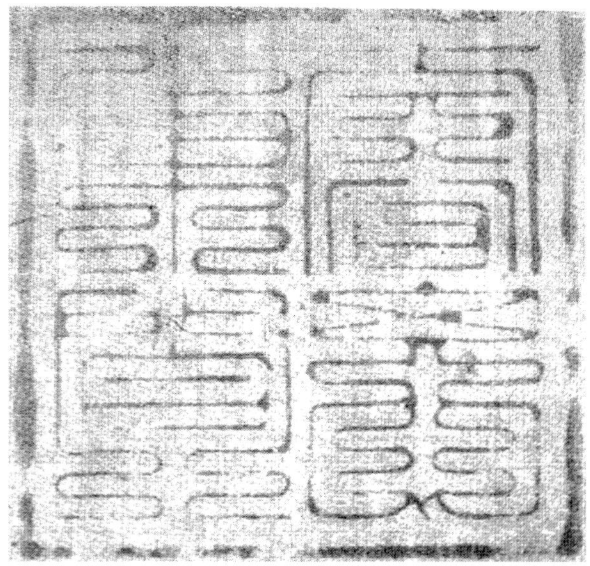

2b. Large square *xuanhedian bao,* “Treasure of Harmony Revealed Hall” (8.9 cm)

p3

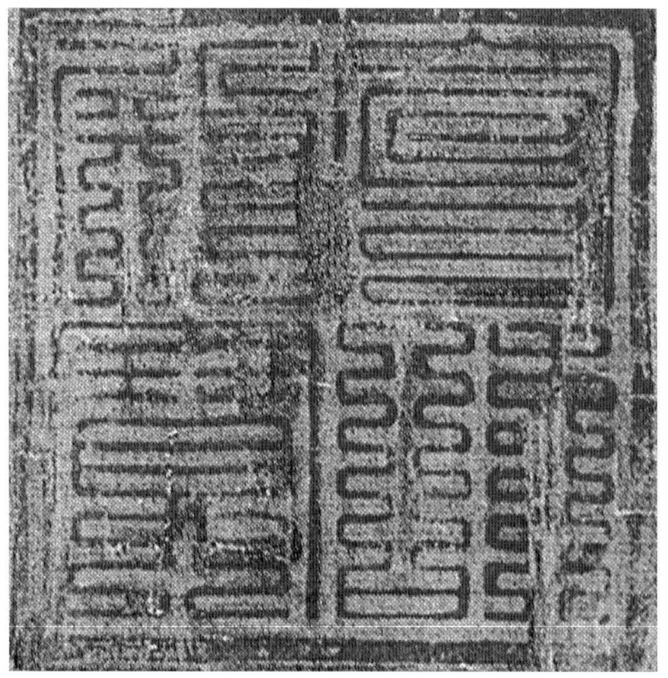

p26

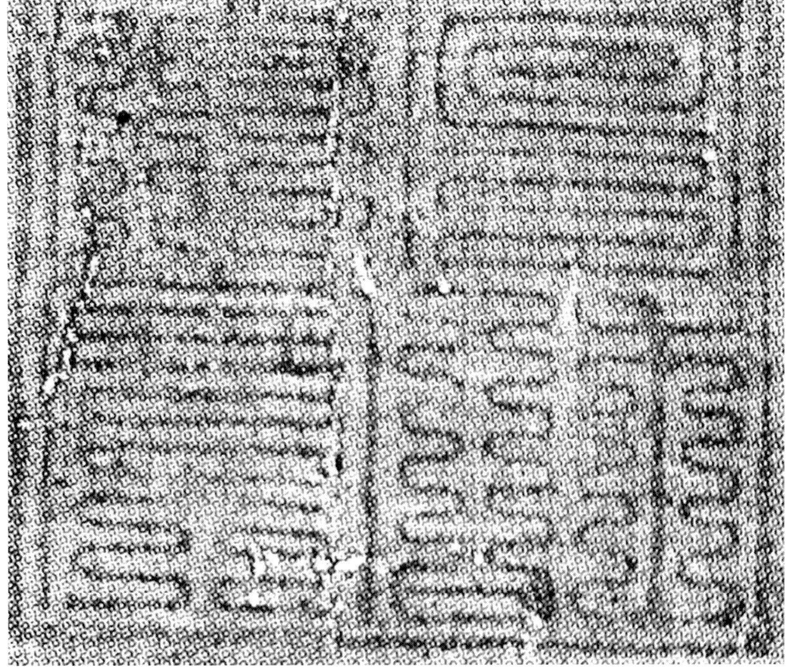

2c. Oblong *xuanhe zhongbi,* "Secret [treasure] of Harmony Revealed [Hall]" (5.7 cm)

p4 p18 p20 p23

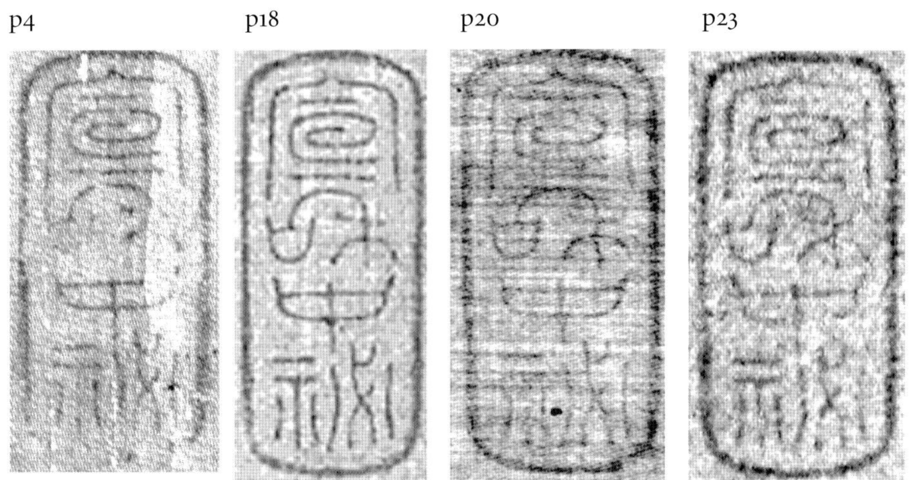

3. Seals that refer to imperial writing

3a. Small square *yushu*, "imperial writing" (5.3 cm)

p5

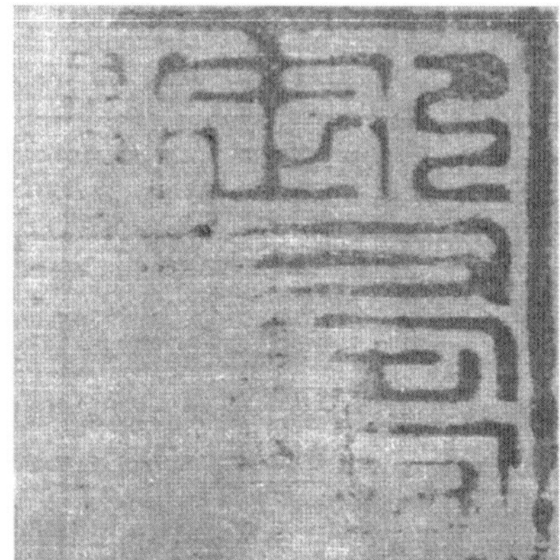

p8

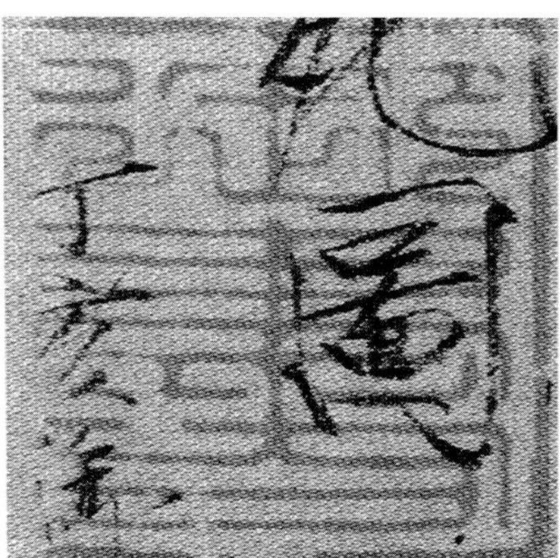

3b. Large square *yushu zhi bao*, “treasure of imperial writing” (14.9 cm)
p13

4. Miscellaneous seals

4a. Small oblong *daguan*, "Daguan [reign name]" (2.6 cm)

c4

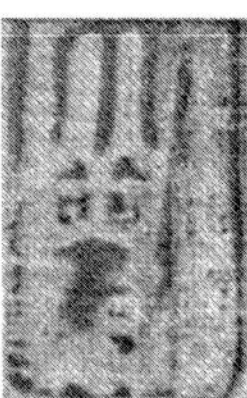

CALLIGRAPHIES (IN CHRONOLOGICAL ORDER)

1. Lu Ji, *Pingfu tie*. Seals: 1b, 1d, 1e, 1f, 1g. Palace Museum, Beijing. Illustrated: Zhang Guangbin 1984 1:10–12. Has title.
2. Wang Xizhi, *Shangyu tie*. Seals: 1a, 1b, 1d, 1e, 1f, 1g, 1h. Shanghai Museum. Illustrated: Zhang Guangbin 1984 1:14–15; *Yiyuan duoying* 1978:2; Gugong et al. 2002:48–49. No title.
3. Wang Xizhi, *Xingrang tie*. Seals: 1b, 1d, 1e, 1f, 1g, 1h. Princeton University Art Museum. Illustrated: Harrist and Fong 1999:93, 242–43. Has title.
4. Wang Xizhi, *Yuanhuan tie*. Seals: 1c, 1d, 1f, 4a. National Palace Museum, Taipei. Illustrated: Jiang Zhaoshen 1989:16–17. Has title. From this illustration, the seals look good, though it has the square rather than the round double-dragon seal and Barnhart 1983 lists this piece among those with spurious seals. Jiang, however, says that it has good seals as well as a Xuanhe mounting with Huizong's inscribed title. Y. Wang 2003:193–96 also sees its seals as good. From the illustration, the inscription looks plausible.
5. Sun Guoting, *Shupu*. Seals: 1b, 1d, 1e, 1f, possibly more. Taipei National Palace Museum. Illustrated: Yang Renkai 1989:94–97; Chang and Frankel 1995:33–77. Has title.
6. Tang Xuanzong, *Jiling song*. Seals: 1c, 1d, 1e, 1f, possibly more. Taipei National Palace Museum. Illustrated: National Palace Museum 1981: plate 2; Kunst- und Ausstellungshalle 2003:171. No title.
7. Liu Gongquan, *Lanting shi*. Seals: 1a, 1b, 1d, 1e, 1f, 1g. Palace Museum, Beijing. Illustrated: Zhang Guangbin 1984 1:194–209. Has title.
8. Huaisu, *Lunshu tie*. Seals: 1a, 1a misplaced, 1b, 1e, 1e misplaced, 1f, 1g, 1h. Liaoning Provincial Museum. Illustrated: Zhang Guangbin 1984 1:188–90; Yang Renkai 1989:164–65. No title.
9. Zhang Xu, *Gushu si tie,* "Four ancient poems." Seals: 1b, 1e, 1f, 1g. Liaoning Provincial Museum. Illustrated: Zhang Guangbin 1984 1:128–37; Yang Renkai 1989:112–17. No title.
10. Du Mu, *Zhang Haohao shi*. Seals: 1a, 1b, 1d, 1e, 1f, 1g, 1h. Palace Museum, Beijing. Illustrated: Zhang Guangbin 1984 1:218–25; Gugong et al. 2002:154–59. Has title.

TABLE A2.1. Huizong's collector seals on calligraphy

seal artist	1a yushu gourd	1b dragon round	1c dragon square	1d xuanhe linked	1e zhenghe	1f xuanhe	1g zhenghe linked	1h neifu tushu	2a ruisi dongge
1 Lu Ji		X		X	X	X	X		
2 Wang Xizhi, *Shangyu*	X	X		X	X	X	X	X	
3 Wang Xizhi, *Xingrang*		X		X	X	X	X	X	
4 Wang Xizhi, *Yuanhuan*			X	X		X			
5 Sun Guoting		X		X	X	X			
6 Tang Xuanzong	X		X	X	X	X			
7 Liu Gongquan	X	X	X	X	X	X			
8 Huaisu	X	X		X	*	X	X	X	
9 Zhang Xu		X			X	X		X	
10 Du Mu	X	X		X	X	X	X	X	

seal artist	2b xuanhedian bao	2c xuanhe zhongbi	3a yushu square	3b yushu zhi bao	4a daguan	Title?	Inscription?	full Xuanhe program?	minor variations?
1 Lu Ji						X		X	
2 Wang Xizhi, *Shangyu*								X	
3 Wang Xizhi, *Xingrang*						X		X	
4 Wang Xizhi, *Yuanhuan*					X	X			X
5 Sun Guoting						X		X	
6 Tang Xuanzong									X
7 Liu Gongquan						X		X	
8 Huaisu									X
9 Zhang Xu								X	
10 Du Mu						X		X	

PAINTINGS (IN CHRONOLOGICAL ORDER OF TRADITIONALLY ATTRIBUTED ARTIST)

1. Gu Kaizhi, *Admonitions of the Instructress.* Seals: 2a (also fake versions of other seals). British Museum. Illustrated: McCausland 2003: plates 1–13, seal plate 10.1.
2. Zhan Ziqian, *Spring Outing.* Seals: 1a, 1c, 1d, 1e, 1f, 1g. Palace Museum, Beijing. Illustrated: Gugong 1978 1:33–35 or *Yiyuan duoying* (1985) 29:10; Gugong et al. 2002: 58–61. Has title.
3. Zhang Sengyou, *The Five Planets and the Twenty-Eight Lunar Mansions.* Seals: 1c, 1d, 1g, 2b. Osaka Municipal Museum. Illustrated: Little and Eichman 2000:132–37. (Seals from Osaka shiritsu bijutsukan 1975 2:9.)
4. Wang Wei, *Fu Sheng.* Seal: 2c. Osaka Municipal Museum. Illustrated: Osaka shiritsu bijutsukan 1976 1: plate 2; Miyagawa 1983: plate 39.
5. Han Gan, *Groom and Two Horses.* Seals: 1a, 1a misplaced, 2a, 3a. National Palace Museum, Taipei. Illustrated: National Palace Museum 1973:2; Shanghai shuhua chubanshe 2003a:4–5. Inscribed 1107.
6. Zhou Fang, *Barbarians Bringing Tribute.* Seals: 2a, possibly 1e. National Palace Museum, Taipei. Illustrated: National Palace Museum 1973:3.
7. Han Huang, *Five Oxen.* Seal: 2a. Palace Museum, Beijing. Illustrated: Gugong et al. 2002:98–105.
8. Han Huang, *Literary Gathering.* Seals: 1a (misplaced), 1c, 1d, 1f (misplaced), 1g (misplaced), 2a, 3a. Palace Museum, Beijing. Illustrated: Gugong 1978 1:44–45; Shanghai shuhua chubanshe 2003b:17–19. Inscribed.
9. Sun Wei, *Lofty Scholars.* Seals: 1a, 1c, 1d, 1e, 1f, 1g, 2a. Shanghai Museum. Illustrated: Jin Weinuo 1984:80–83; Gugong et al. 2002:130–31; Shanghai shuhua chubanshe 2003b:2–16. Has title.
10. Hao Cheng, *Groom and Horse.* Seals: 3a. Museum of Fine Arts, Boston. Illustrated: Wu Tung 1997:58. Inscribed.
11. Wei Xian, *Lofty Scholar.* Seals: 1a, 1c, 1d, 1e, 1f, 1g, 1h. Palace Museum, Beijing. Illustrated: Gugong 1978 1:94–95; Gugong et al. 2002:264. Has title.
12. Wei Xian, *Waterwheel.* Seals: 1e, 1f, 1g, 1h. Shanghai Museum. Illustrated: Jin Weinuo 1984:156–57.
13. Guo Zhongshu, *Traveling on the River in Clearing Snow.* Seal: 3b. National Palace Museum, Taipei. Illustrated: National Palace Museum 1989:127–28. Illustration inadequate to see seal.
14. Juran, *Layered Cliffs and Clumped Trees.* Seals: 2b. National Palace Museum, Taipei. Illustrated: National Palace Museum 1989:99–100.

15. Huang Quan, *Studies from Nature*. Seals: 2a. Palace Museum, Beijing. Illustrated: Jin Weinuo 1984:104; back cover of *Yiyuan duoying* 15 (1982); or (best) Zhu Jia Jin 1986:86–89.
16. Huang Jucai, *Partridges by a Thorny Bush*. Seals: 1c, 1e, 1f, 2a. Taipei National Palace Museum. Illustrated: National Palace Museum 2000:112–13. Has title.
17. Qu Ding, *Summer Mountains*. Seals: 1f, 4a. Metropolitan Museum of Art, New York. Illustrated: Fong 1992:88–91; Fong 1975:52–53.
18. Yi Yuanji, *Monkey and Cat*. Seals: 1h, 2c. National Palace Museum, Taipei. Illustrated: National Palace Museum 1995a:15:245–47.
19. Guo Xi, *Hidden Valley*. Seal: 2b. Shanghai Museum. Illustrated: Fu Xinian 1988:56; Gugong et al. 2002:296.
20. Guo Xi, *Old Trees, Level Distance*. Seal: 2c. Metropolitan Museum of Art, New York. Illustrated: W. Fong 1992:94–95.
21. Wang Shen, *Light Snow Over a Fishing Village*. Seals: 1a, 1c, 1d, 1e, 1f, 1g. Palace Museum, Beijing. Illustrated: Gugong 1981:46–51; Gugong et al. 2002:300–305. Has title.
22. Wang Shen, *Rivers and Mountains in Mist*. Seals: 1a, 1c, 1d, 1e, 1f, 1g, 1h, 2c, 3a. Shanghai Museum. Illustrated: Fu Xinian 1988:66–67; Gugong et al. 2002:308–11. Has title.
23. Li Gonglin, *Copy of Wen Yan's Pasturing Horses*. Seals: 1e, 1f, 1g, 2c. Palace Museum, Beijing. Illustrated. Gugong 1981: 24–43; Gugong et al. 2002:348–67.
24. Liang Shimin, *River View in Winter*. Seals: 1c, 1d, 1f, 1h, 4a. Palace Museum, Beijing. Illustrated: Gugong 1981:52–59. Has title.
25. Anon., *Portrait within a Portrait*. Seals: 1e, 1f. National Palace Museum, Taipei. Illustrated: National Palace Museum 1995b:171–73
26. Anon., *Goose*. Seals: 2b. National Palace Museum, Taipei. Illustrated: Yiyuan duoying 42 (1992):24; Shanghai shuhua chubanshe 2005:8–9.
27. Anon., *Buddha Preaching the Law*. Seals: 1b, 1d, 1g, 1h. National Palace Museum, Taipei. Illustrated: National Palace Museum 2000:82–83 (these seals are listed, but not all are visible and placement is unclear, could be anomalous).

Table A2.2. Huizong's collector seals on paintings

seal / artist	1a yushu gourd	1b dragon round	1c dragon square	1d xuanhe linked	1e zhenghe	1f xuanhe	1g zhenghe linked	1h neifu tushu	2a ruisi dongge
1 Gu Kaizhi									X
2 Zhan Ziqian	X		X	X	X	X	X		
3 Zhang Sengyou			R	*			R		
4 Wang Wei									
5 Han Gan	*								X
6 Zhou Fang									X
7 Han Huang, *Oxen*	*								X
8 Han Huang, *Literary*	*		X	X		*	*		X
9 Sun Wei	X		X	X	X	X	X		3
10 Hao Cheng									
11 Wei Xian, *Lofty*	X		X	X	X	X	X	X	
12 Wei Xian, *Water*					X	X	X	X	
13 Guo Zhongshu									
14 Juran									
15 Huang Quan									X
16 Huang Jucai			X		X	X			X
17 Qu Ding						X			
18 Yi Yuanji								X	
19 Guo Xi, *Valley*									
20 Guo Xi, *Trees*									
21 Wang Shen, *Village*	X		X	X	X	X	X		
22 Wang Shen, *Mist*	X		X	X	X	X	X	X	
23 Li Gonglin						X	X		
24 Liang Shimin			X	X		X		X	
25 *Portrait*					X	X			
26 *Goose*									
27 *Buddha*			R	R			R	R	

* Marks cases when the seals 1a–1h are placed in ways that vary from the Xuanhe mounting standardized system.

"R" refers to seals that are reported in the notes on a painting but are not visible in the illustration. In such cases the position of the seal cannot be verified.

2b xuanhedian bao	2c xuanhe zhongbi	3a yushu square	3b yushu zhi bao	4a daguan	Title?	Inscription?	full Xuanhe program?	minor variations?
					X		X	
X								
	X							
		X				X		
		X				X		
					X			X
		X				X		
					X		X	
							X	
			X					
X								
					X			X
				X				X
	X					X		
X								
	X							
					X		X	
	X	X			X		X	
	X							X
				X	X		X	
X								
							?	

Appendix 3. Major Extant Pre-Song Calligraphies Listed in the *Xuanhe Calligraphy Catalogue*[1]

Artist	Piece[2]	Listed in XHSP?	Huizong or other seals[3]	Current location[4]	Books that illustrate the piece[5]
Lu Ji 陸機	Pingfu 平復帖	yes	good	Beijing	*Shodō zenshū; Shodō geijutsu; Chinese Calligraphy; Five Thousand Years; Zhongguo meishu quanji, shufa* 2; *Four Thousand Years; History of Chinese Calligraphy*
Wang Xizhi[6] 王羲之	Pingan etc. 平安何如奉橘帖	yes	spurious, Gaozong	Taipei	*Shodō zenshū; Masterpieces; Shodō geijutsu; Chinese Calligraphy; Zhongguo meishu quanji, shufa* 2; *Four Thousand Years; History of Chinese Calligraphy; Embodied Image*
	Xingrang 行穰帖	yes	good	Princeton	*Shodō zenshū; Shodō geijutsu; Zhongguo meishu quanji, shufa* 2; *Embodied Image*
	Shangyu 上虞帖	yes	questionable	Shanghai	*Five Thousand Years; Zhongguo meishu quanji, shufa* 2; *Chinese National Treasures*
	Hanqie 寒切帖	no	Gaozong	Tianjin	*Shodō geijutsu; Five Thousand Years; Zhongguo meishu quanji, shufa* 2
	Yuanhuan 遠宦帖	yes	good, Zhangzong	Taipei	*Shodō geijutsu; Zhongguo meishu quanji, shufa* 2
	Yimu 姨母帖	no	Shenyang		*Shodō geijutsu; Zhongguo meishu quanji, shufa* 2
	Chuyue 初月帖	yes	Shenyang		*Shodō geijutsu; Zhongguo meishu quanji, shufa* 2
	Kuaixue shiqing 快雪時晴帖	yes	Gaozong	Taipei	*Shodō geijutsu; Zhongguo meishu quanji, shufa* 2
	Zhanjin 瞻近帖	yes		Japan	*Shodō zenshū; Shodō geijutsu*
	Hanshi 漢時帖	no		Japan	*Shodō zenshū; Shodō geijutsu*
	Qiyue 七月帖	no	Gaozong, Zhangzong	Taipei	*Shodō geijutsu*
	Dadao 大道帖	no	none	Taipei	*Shodō geijutsu*

Artist	Piece[2]	Listed in XHSP?	Huizong or other seals[3]	Current location[4]	Books that illustrate the piece[5]
Wang Xianzhi 王獻之	Yatou wan 鴨頭丸帖	yes	odd	Shanghai	*Shodō geijutsu; Five Thousand Years; Zhongguo meishu quanji, shufa* 2; *Four Thousand Years; Chinese National Treasures*
	Zhongqiu 中秋	no	dubious, Zhangzong	Beijing	*Shodō zenshū; Shodō geijutsu; Five Thousand Years; History of Chinese Calligraphy*
	Dihuangtang 地黃湯帖	yes	questionable	Tokyo	*Shodō zenshū; Shodō geijutsu; Chinese Calligraphy*
	Nianjiuri 廿九日帖	no	dubious	Shenyang	*Shodō geijutsu; Zhongguo meishu quanji, shufa* 2
Wang Huizhi 王徽之	Xinyue 新月帖	no		Shenyang	*Zhongguo meishu quanji, shufa* 2
Wang Xun 王珣	Boyuan 伯遠帖	yes	none	Beijing	*Shodō zenshū; Five Thousand Years: Zhongguo meishu quanji, shufa* 2; *Chinese National Treasures*
Wang Hui 王薈	Jiezhong 癤腫帖	no entry		Shenyang	*Zhongguo meishu quanji, shufa* 2
Wang Sengqian 王僧虔	Taizi sheren 太子舍人帖	no		Shenyang	*Zhongguo meishu quanji, shufa* 2
Wang Ci 王慈	Debozhou etc. 得伯酒等帖	no entry		Shenyang	*Zhongguo meishu quanji, shufa* 2
Wang Zhi 王志	Yiri wushen 一日無申帖	no entry	Gaozong		*Zhongguo meishu quanji, shufa* 2
Zhiyong 智永	Qianzi wen 千字文	yes	none	Japan	*Shodō zenshū; Chinese Calligraphy; Zhongguo meishu quanji, shufa* 3; *Four Thousand Years; History of Chinese Calligraphy; Embodied Image*
Lu Jianzhi 陸柬之	Wenfu 文賦	no		Taipei	*Shodō geijutsu*
Ouyang Xun 歐陽詢	Meng dian 夢奠帖	no	Gaozong	Shenyang	*Shodō geijutsu; Five Thousand Years; Chinese National Treasures*
	Qianzi wen 千字文	yes	Gaozong	Shenyang	*Shodō geijutsu; Five Thousand Years*
	Zhang Han 張翰帖	yes	Gaozong	Beijing	*Five Thousand Years; Zhongguo meishu quanji, shufa* 3
	Bushang 卜商帖	yes	none[7]	Beijing	*Zhongguo meishu quanji, shufa* 3
Yu Shinan 虞世南	Runan gongzhu 汝南公主墓誌	yes	none	Shanghai	*Shodō zenshū; Shodō geijutsu; Zhongguo meishu quanji, shufa* 3
	Lanting xu 蘭亭序	no	Gaozong	Beijing	*History of Chinese Calligraphy; Chinese National Treasures;*

Artist	Piece[2]	Listed in XHSP?	Huizong or other seals[3]	Current location[4]	Books that illustrate the piece[5]
Sun Guoting 孫過庭	Shupu 書譜	yes	yes	Taipei	*Shodō zenshū; Shodō geijutsu; Masterpieces Supplement; Chinese Calligraphy; Zhongguo meishu quanji, shufa* 3; *Four Thousand Years; History of Chinese Calligraphy; Embodied Image*
	Qianzi wen 千字文	yes	none	Shenyang	*Chinese National Treasures*
	Jingfu dian fu 景福殿賦	no	none	Beijing	*Five Thousand Years*
Chu Suiliang 褚遂良	Lanting xu 蘭亭序	no		?	*Shodō zenshū; Embodied Image*
	Ni Kuan zhuanzan 倪寬傳贊	no		Taipei?	*Shodō zenshū; Shodō geijutsu*
	Yinfu jing 陰符經	no		Kansas City	*Four Thousand Years*
He Zhizhang 賀知章	Xiaojing 孝經	yes	none?	Japan	*Shodō zenshū; Shodō geijutsu; Chinese Calligraphy; Zhongguo meishu quanji, shufa* 3
Xu Hao 徐浩	Zhu Juchuan 朱巨川告身	yes	none?	Taipei	*Shodō geijutsu; Masterpieces; History of Chinese Calligraphy*
Xuanzcng 玄宗	Jiling song 鶺鴒頌	yes	good plus odd	Taipei	*Shodō zenshū; Shodō geijutsu; Masterpieces Supplement; History of Chinese Calligraphy*
Zhang Xu 張旭	Four poems 古詩四帖	yes	good	Shenyang	*Five Thousand Years; Zhongguo meishu quanji, shufa* 3; *Four Thousand Years*
	Ziyan 自言帖	no		Japan	*Shodō zenshū*
Li Bo 李白	Shang Yang tai 上陽臺帖	no	none	Beijing	*Five Thousand Years; Zhongguo meishu quanji, shufa* 3
Yan Zhenqing 嚴真情	Eulogy to nephew 祭姪文稿	yes	Gaozong?	Taipei	*Masterpieces; Shodō geijutsu; Zhongguo meishu quanji, shufa* 3
	Zhushan tang 竹山堂聯句詩	yes	Gaozong	Beijing	*Chinese Calligraphy; Five Thousand Years; Zhongguo meishu quanji, shufa* 3

Artist	Piece[2]	Listed in XHSP?	Huizong or other seals[3]	Current location[4]	Books that illustrate the piece[5]
	Huzhou 湖州	yes	Gaozong?	Beijing	*Chinese National Treasures*
	Liu Zhongshi 劉中使帖	yes	none	Taipei	*Masterpieces Supplement*
	Zishu gaoshen 自書告身	no		Japan	*Shodō geijutsu*
Huaisu 懷素	Autobiography 自敍帖	yes	Zhangzong	Taipei	*Masterpieces*; *Chinese Calligraphy; Zhongguo meishu quanji, shufa* 3; *Four Thousand Years; History of Chinese Calligraphy; Embodied Image*
	Kushun 苦筍帖	no	odd, Gaozong	Shanghai	*Five Thousand Years; Zhongguo meishu quanji, shufa* 3; *Chinese National Treasures*
	Lunshu 論書帖	yes	good, Gaozong	Shenyang	*Five Thousand Years; Zhongguo meishu quanji, shufa* 3
	Shiyu 食魚帖	no	none	Qingdao	*Zhongguo meishu quanji, shufa* 3
Wu Cailuan 吳彩鸞	Shu Tangyun 書唐韻	yes	questionable	Taipei	*Masterpieces*
Liu Gongquan 劉公權	Lanting poems 蘭亭詩	yes	full set, questionable	Beijing	*Shodō geijutsu; Five Thousand Years; History of Chinese Calligraphy*
Du Mu 杜牧	Zhang Haohao 張好好詩	yes	good	Beijing	*Five Thousand Years; Zhongguo meishu quanji, shufa* 3; *Chinese National Treasures*
Gaoxian 高閑	Qianzi wen 千字文	no	none	Shanghai	*Five Thousand Years; Zhongguo meishu quanji, shufa* 3; *Chinese National Treasures*
Yang Ningshi 楊凝式	Xiare 夏熱帖	no	none	Beijing	*Five Thousand Years; Zhongguo meishu quanji, shufa* 3; *Chinese National Treasures*
	Jiuhua 韭花帖	yes	Gaozong	Wuxi	*Five Thousand Years; Zhongguo meishu quanji, shufa* 3
	Shenxian qijufa 神仙起居法帖	no	Gaozong	Beijing	*Zhongguo meishu quanji, shufa* 3

1. This list includes only calligraphies that survive in ink on paper, not as rubbings, and which could conceivably have been in Huizong's collection (that is, excluding works that entered Korea or Japan in earlier centuries, are copies made after Huizong's time, or have been excavated in recent centuries). The list was compiled by examining which works were published in major books on Chinese calligraphy (see note 5 below). Because authors often regularly illustrate works from their own institutions or country, here I have tried to balance such books with others that drew more broadly.

2. All of these pieces are treated as major treasures by the institutions that own them, but in quite a few cases they are considered to be tracing copies rather than originals. In many cases scholarly opinion is divided on how good the pieces are, but at a minimum the institution owning them considers them important works.

3. Seals that are good enough matches to be listed in appendix 1 are listed as "good," though in a couple of cases there is also an oddly placed seal (see appendix 2 for the seals on each of these works). Seals that look unconvincing or are placed in unusual places are marked as "dubious" or "odd," respectively. Seals that Barnhart 1983 rejects but look all right to me in reproduction or that I have not been able to see, I have marked as "questionable." Because Song Gaozong (and probably also Jin Zhangzong) removed Huizong's seals from works in their collection, when their seals are on a piece of calligraphy, it is also mentioned as a possible reason why Huizong's seals are missing, adding to the probability that the extant work was the one once in Huizong's collection. In some cases I have not seen an illustration of the full work and therefore cannot be sure if there are any relevant seals. In these cases the box is left blank. Where none of these apply and there are no Huizong seals, "none" is put in this column.

4. The cities refer to the major museum there, that is, the National Palace Museum (Taipei), the Palace Museum (Beijing), the Shanghai Museum, the Liaoning Provincial Museum (Shenyang), the Qingdao City Museum, the Wuxi City Museum, the Nelson-Atkins Museum (Kansas City), the Princeton University Art Museum, and the Museum of Calligraphy, Tokyo.

5. As a convenience to readers, the books are listed here under their titles, but full bibliographical information is found in the bibliography under author and year, as follows:

Chinese National Treasures = Gugong et al. 2002

Embodied Image = Harrist and Fong 1999

Five Thousand Years = Zhang Guangbin 1984

Four Thousand Years = Chang and Miller 1990

History of Chinese Calligraphy = Y. Tseng 1993

Masterpieces = National Palace Museum 1970

Masterpieces Supplement = National Palace Museum 1981

Chinese Calligraphy = Nakata 1983

Shodō geijutsu = Nakata 1979–82

Shodō zenshū = Onoe et al. 1954–68

Zhongguo meishu quanji, shufa 2 = Wang Jingxian 1986

Zhongguo meishu quanji, shufa 3 = Yang Renkai 1989

Above, the titles are listed alphabetically, but in the table they are given chronologically by date of publication.

6. I have not included here copies of the *Preface to the Orchid Pavilion Poetry Collection*, which some books list under Wang Xizhi, since in Huizong's day it was known that no original of this work survived.

7. SXTFT shows a linked Xuanhe seal, but it is not visible in the illustrations reproduced in the books listed.

Notes

INTRODUCTION

1. Alsop 1982:175–211; Mayo 2005.

2. See Ledderose 1979:1–44; and Harrist 2004.

3. LDMHJ 190; trans. Acker 1954:212.

4. Huizong's personal name was Zhao Ji; Huizong is his posthumous name, not used during his lifetime. As is customary when writing in English, in this book Song emperors are referred to consistently by their posthumous names.

5. See Brown 1994:126–45.

6. Zhang Guangbin 1984:265–67. See also Y. Tseng 1993:247–50.

7. XHSP 14.107–8.

8. Brown 1994:107.

9. Kahn 1985:291.

10. For Huizong as a painter, see Rowland 1951; Sirén 1956 2:74–86; Ecke 1972; Li Huishu 1984; Sturman 1990; Chen Baozhen 1993; Wang Zhenghua 1998; Bo Songnian 1998; and Bickford 2002–3, 2006. Broader studies of Huizong and his era include Ren Chongyue 1998, Ihara 2004, and Ebrey and Bickford 2006.

11. For recent discussions of this painting, see T. Wu 1997:140–41; and Bickford 2002–2003:79–81.

12. On Huizong's calligraphy, see S. Chuang 1967; Ecke 1972: 58–80; Yang Renkai 1988; Shui Laiyou 1995; Sturman 1997:189–93; and Ebrey 2006a.

13. For Huizong as a patron of court artists, see Sirén 1956 2:76–89; Li Huishu 1984; She Cheng 1988; and J. Cahill 1996a:160–68. On his linking of poetry and painting, see Hartman 2001, esp. pp. 481–82.

14. Even most modern historians have not escaped the assumptions implicit in the traditional historiography. For examples, see Ren Chongyue 1998 and Zhang Bangwei 2005:177–286.

15. Only one of these novels has been translated into English. See Hennessey 1981.

16. Acker 1954:111–31; Zürcher 1955:144–43.

17. On objects that survive from Qianlong's collections, see the catalogues of recent exhibitions devoted to Qianlong, such as National Palace Museum 2002; H. Zhang 2002; and Ho and Bronson 2004. On the vicissitudes of the Qing palace collection, see Elliott and Shambaugh 2005.

18. Guy 1987:119, 79.

19. Berger 2003:68; L. Chang 1996:21; Kahn 1985:295.

20. Ho and Bronson 2004:233; Holzwarth 2005:45; H. Kohara 1988.

21. Ledderose 1978–79 (quote page 34). See also Ebrey 2007.

22. On the interstate audience for European magnificence, see Kaufmann 1994 and Brown 1994. On court culture and magnificence more generally, see Elias 1983, Asch and Birke 1991, Duindam 1994, and Adamson 1999.

23. Keene 2003: 104–9, 126–27.

24. On the civil-service recruitment system, see especially Kracke 1947, 1953; Chaffee 1985; W. Lo 1987; and J. Liu 1957, 1959, 1962. For recent studies of the Song scholar-official elite, see Hartwell 1982, Hymes 1986, and Bossler 1998, most of which concentrate on the social background of officials or how they gained office, rather than what they did in office. On factional strife during the Northern Song, see J. Liu 1959, Freeman 1973, Hartman 1990, Egan 1994, Levine 2002, X. Ji 2005, Chaffee 2006, and Smith n.d.

25. I am thinking of work by Guy 1987; Fisher 1990; Crossley 1992, 1999; Zito 1997; Rawski 1998; Berger 2003; and Ho and Bronson 2004; among others.

26. See in particular J. Cahill 1960b; Bush 1971; Barnhart 1976, 1983; Bush and Shih 1985; Bickford 1996a; Sturman 1997; Harrist 1998; McNair 1998; and Murck 2000.

27. The Song court as a site for the production of paintings is one aspect of the court that has received considerable attention. See Murray 1989; Jang 1992; H. Lee 1994, 2004; and H. Liu 2002, 2003.

28. Pearce 1995. See also Kaufmann 1994.

29. On Ouyang Xiu, see J. Liu 1967; and Egan 1984 and 2006b.

CHAPTER 1

LTGS 1.38.

1. Worthy 1976:42–70.

2. SHY Chongru 1.29a; T. Lee 1985:58–62. In this period, what I am calling the Palace Library was literally called the Three Institutes (Sanguan), following Tang practice, but in 1082 its name was changed to Bishu sheng, which I translate as Palace Library. For simplicity's sake I will use the term Palace Library throughout the book, as the institution and its functions did not change, only its name.

3. On the Palace Library in Tang times, see McMullen 1988:21–22, 71–88, 211–20; and Drège 1991:70–86.

4. XZZTJ 7.171, 8.184.

5. Chaffee 1985:48.

6. See C. Chang 1968:13–24 for the full story. On Song succession practices, see Ebrey 2006c.

7. Chaffee 1985:50; Bol 1992:52.

8. Bol 1992:156–57; C. Ho 1996:69–70; Kurz 2001.

9. YH 63.21a–b, 43.15a–b.

10. Kurz 2001:303. On Song government printing, see also M. Poon 1979:113–44; and Cherniak 1994:57–65.

11. SCSSLY 2.20–21, with some passages from the shorter version found in CB 24.559. See also Haeger 1968:401–2. The appearance of cranes is an auspicious omen.

12. YH 30.1a–11b, 28.4a, 5a–b, 7a. Taizong's collected works reached 214, then 336, then 1,414 chapters. SHY Chongru 6.5a–6a has even longer lists of his writings. The QSS has eighteen chapters of his poetry, more than any other Northern Song emperor, possibly because two substantial collections of his poems were preserved in the Buddhist canon (QSS *juan* 22–39). The QSW, in addition to edicts not necessarily authored by Taizong, has twenty-one pieces, including rhapsodies, prefaces, and inscriptions, six of which are explicitly labeled "imperially composed" (QSW 60.292–96, 74.653–68).

13. Huang Chaozong 1973:78. On the Imperial Repository and its history over the course of the Song (especially the Southern Song), see also Peng Huiping 2005.

14. YH 33.9b–20a, 27.18a; SHY Chongru 6.4a–b; LTGS zanben 2B.258; SCSSLY 2.22.

15. SHY Chongru 6.4a–b. See also C. H. Ho 1996:64.

16. SHY Zhiguan 18.47a–48b; LTGS 1.18–26.

17. SHY Zhiguan 18.48b; CB 33.739–40; THJWZ 1.9; Soper 1951:6–7. See also LTGS 1.38; and Canben 2B.255.

18. SHY Chongru 6.4a; LTGS 1.39–40. Several Song local histories record that Buddhist temples in their prefecture had pieces of Taizong's calligraphy, perhaps from this donation. See, for instance, SSZ 33.7974, 33.7975, 33.7986, 36.8027, 37.8056; SMTJ 2.5a; WJTJXJ B.12a; and YZTJ 2.17a. See also Ebrey 2002.

19. C. H. Ho 1996:61–62.

20. SCMHP 20; trans. Lachman 1989:30.

21. Chaffee 1999:34–35. In this case the prince housed his books in a specially constructed garden with an artificial mountain. When his court-appointed tutor criticized him for wasting farmers' hard-earned tax monies on such extravagances, Taizong ordered the mountain destroyed. It was fine for princes to collect books, but not to spend lavishly on such pleasures as gardens.

22. SS 283.9570; THJWZ 6.235–36; Soper 1951:95.

23. Chaffee 1985:51.

24. YH 43.18a–b; LTGS 2.52–53.

25. YH 30.11b–34a, 28.9a–10b, 11a–b, 32.1b–6a, 31.15a–16a; BQS 88.1a–2b; QSW 263.142; JSCB 127.1a-7b; JSWZJ 6.2b-3b. Zhenzong's Daoist texts are available in QSW *juan* 264–66.

26. CB 78.1788; Chaffee 1999:37–38.

27. SDJK 2.35; SHY Zhiguan 7.13a; YH 163.20a–b. The term "Dragon Diagram" refers to the dragon-horse that emerged from the Yellow River with diagrams on its back, from which Fuxi derived the eight trigrams and milfoil divination, making these diagrams the progenitor of all writing and painting.

28. CB 78.1781, 78.1785.

29. CB 114.2662; SHY Chongru 2.3b–4b; T. Lee 1985:62–64.

30. For examples of their memorials, see SCZCZY, passim.

31. SHY Chongru 6.6b–7a. There must have been a demand for the pieces of calligraphy he gave away, since in 1055 an edict threatened serious punishment for anyone who duplicated imperial calligraphy in order to sell it (SHY Chongru 6.8b).

32. SHY Chongru 6.7b–8a , 6.9a–b. In 1060 Renzong was so tired of doing them that he issued an edict stating that from then on families of his officials should not request imperially written seal-script titles for funerary stelae (SHY Chongru 6.8b–9a).

33. ZS 1.10b–11a.

34. YH 28.13a–b. See YH 30.34b–37b for examples from 1030 to 1063. Thirteen poems,

from scattered sources, have been published in QSS 4398–402. For surviving prose pieces, see QSW 984.391–402.

35. Chaffee 1999:39–40.

36. THJWZ 3.99; trans. Soper 1951:41, modified.

37. C. Huang 1994:149–55, 158–61.

38. See S. Cahill 1980; YH 31.15a–16a; SHY Li 5.19a; and C. Huang 1994:161–67.

39. SHY Zhiguan 18.47b–48a; SCSSLY 31.390–91. Cf. McMullen 1988:212–13 on comparable efforts in the early Tang.

40. On the persistence of manuscript books after the introduction of printing, see Cherniak 1994:33–35; and Pan Mingshen 1971:215–18. The term *juan* originally referred to the rolls on which a book was written, but with the spread of books bound with pages it came to refer to what can be simply called chapters. Here I generally translate *juan* as "chapter," even though in some cases the books may still have been on rolled rather than folded paper. On the development of books with either butterfly or stitched pages, see Cherniak 1994:36–40.

41. Reportedly very little was acquired from the Song's immediate predecessors, the rulers of the Five Dynasties (SHY Chongru 4.15a).

42. LTGS Canben 2B.251; SHY Chongru 4.15a; YH 43.15b; cf. Kurz 2001:296–97; Yao Yingting 1992:36–39.

43. THJWZ 6.251; Soper 1951:101–2; P. Chen 1999; Chen Baozhen 1999.

44. SHY Chongru 4.15b; SS 249.8801–2; P. Chen 1999:155–57; and Chen Baozhen 1999: 90–92.

45. THJWZ 6.235; Soper 1951:95. See also SCMHP 3.77 and Lachman 1989:76 for a painting of a goldfish given to Ding Wei by a court painter that was later among those confiscated.

46. SHY Chongru 4.15a–b; CB 7.178; THJWZ 1.8–9; Soper 1951:6–7. At about this time 114 paintings and calligraphies were transferred from the History Institute to the Imperial Repository (LTGS Canben 2B:257–58).

47. SHY Chongru 4.15b–16b.

48. SHY Chongru 4.16a–17b; LTGS 1.40; CB 25.571; YH 43.13b.

49. SHY Chongru 4.16b–17a.

50. SCMHP 1.20; trans. Lachman 1989:30, slightly modified. The story goes on to say that Taizong had the painting sent to the Painting Academy to be appraised by Gao Wenjin, who, not getting along with the painter, classed the painting as inferior. In the other case, Taizong himself unrolled the painting to inspect it and was so impressed that he had the painter, Gao Yi, immediately appointed painter-in-attendance. See SCMHP 1.13; Lachman 1989:23–24; and Sullivan 1982:168–69.

51. THJWZ 6.223; Soper 1951:90–91.

52. SHY Zhiguan 18.48b–49a; THJWZ 1.9; Soper 1951:6.

53. SHY Chongru 4.17a; LTGS Canben 2B:257; THJWZ 6.221; Soper 1951:90. Taizu also easily parted with his newly acquired treasures. When one of his commanders asked for some of the paintings from the court collection of the recently defeated Li Yu, he let him have one hundred scrolls. See THJWZ 6.220; and Soper 1951:89–90.

54. SCSSLY 2.23; SHY Zhiguan 18.48b; LTGS 1.38.

55. YH 27.10a–13a records visits in 1001, 1002, 1005, 1010, 1012, 1018, 1020, and 1021.

56. YH 27.10a–b, 52.36a–b.

57. CB 65.1447.

58. See also YH 52.33b–35a. Cary Y. Liu 1999:102–3 argues that this painting was done in the mid-eleventh century, or is a later copy of a painting of that date.

59. CB 19.422.

60. YH 52.36b. Different totals are given in CB 65.1447 for a slightly later date. The figures for paintings and calligraphies seem to be for the objects kept in the lower floor of Dragon Diagram Pavilion, as YH 163.20b and 52.36b give the same numbers of the paintings and calligraphies kept there. The paintings were said to include antique paintings of the top and middle ranks and modern paintings of the top rank.

61. McNair 1994; McNair 1998:5; C. Ho 1996; Rong Geng 1980:1–11. This compendium is discussed in more detail in chapter 7.

62. YH 52.36b; LTGS Canben 2B:259.

63. SHY Zhiguan 7.14a.

64. LTGS Canben 2B.266; SHY Chongru 4.17b–18a (which mistakenly has 10,754 books). For the conflicting evidence about the location of the new building in the palace compound, see the annotation in LTGS 1.29–30. By this point the government had become wary of fraud—of people who arbitrarily divided works into more chapters or changed the author or title of a work so that it would seem to be something that the Library lacked.

65. LTGS Canben 2B:269; YH 52.39a–b.

66. Zeng Yifen and Cui Wenyin 1991:54–56; Teng and Biggerstaff 1971:14. YH 52.38a gives the number of chapters as 36,069, but most other sources, including CB 134.3206; SS 202.5032; SSQW 14.801; and WXTK 174.1509A give it as 30,669.

67. They survive in OYXQJ Chongwen zongmu xushi 997–1004.

68. CWZM 2.48. This citation was reconstructed from the *Wenxian tongkao.*

69. SDZLJ 158.

70. YH 52.40b; LTGS Canben 2B.271–72; Zeng Yifen and Cui Wenyin 1991:57.

CHAPTER 2

SHY Xingfa 6.21a–b.

1. Cf. the discussion of "opinion power" in J. Liu 1962.
2. See Hartman 2006.
3. SS 313.10255; CBSB 1.1, 1.11–12, 2.46–48. See also Sariti 1972:62; and Smith n.d.
4. For an abridged translation, see de Bary and Bloom 1999:612–16. A full translation is available in Williamson 1935, 1:48–84.
5. WLCQJ 42.242–43; CBBM 59.8b–9a; CB 214.5206–7.
6. On the New Policies, see J. Liu 1959 and Smith n.d.
7. T. Lee 1985:239; Bol 1993:216–18.
8. On this classic, see Loewe 1993:24–32.
9. J. Liu 1959:31–32.
10. T. Lee 1985:64–65.
11. CBSB 4.178–80; Freeman 1973:21–25.
12. This sketch is based primarily on X. Ji 2005.
13. See Fisher 1987.
14. Freeman 1973:109.
15. Cf. Freeman 1973:30–78.

16. This sketch of Su Shi is based primarily on Egan 1994.
17. For a sample, see de Bary and Bloom 1999:621–25.
18. SDPQJ xuji 2.58.
19. Egan 1994:47.
20. CB 282.6908.
21. SSWJ 32.912; Egan 1994:48–49.
22. Hartman 1990:23.
23. Ibid., 20–21.
24. Egan 1994:52.
25. X. Ji 2005:165–74; CB 368.8849–51, 367.8818–20. Fan Chunren (1027–1101) pointed out the likelihood that those meting out this punishment could suffer it themselves one day. Cai Que did indeed die in Lingnan (CB 426.10298, 427.10323–26).
26. Egan 1994:92–93.
27. SSWJ 16.491, 17.512–13; cf. CB 387.9415; X. Ji 2005:180.
28. Egan 1994:104–5; CB 485.11531; CBSB 12.489.
29. CBBM 102.1a–5b; CBSB 14.549–50.
30. Egan 1994:216–18.
31. See Levine 2002 on their careers. Liu Zijian 1987:122–42 discusses Zeng Bu's career.
32. ZBYL 7.52a–b, 8.32a, 7.16b, 8.25b–26a.
33. On Huizong's succession, see Ebrey 2006c.
34. ZBYL 8.46b–47a; FXJ 26.310.
35. ZBYL 9.20b.
36. ZBYL 9.38a.
37. ZBYL 9.33a–b; SHY Zhiguan 76.21b–22b.
38. ZBYL 9.35a–36a.
39. ZBYL 9.41a.
40. ZBYL 9.48a–49b.
41. ZBYL 9.53b–54a.
42. ZBYL 9.55a–b.
43. Interestingly, this memorial was selected in the Southern Song as a model memorial. See SCZCZY 35.350–51.
44. ZBYL 9.78b–79a.
45. ZBYL 9.81a–82b.
46. SHY Zhiguan 67.34b–35a.
47. CBBM 130.12b–13a.
48. CBBM 130.13a–b.
49. CBSB 18.647–50.
50. See Ebrey 2006b.
51. CBBM 121.1a–b. Levine 2006:151–52 views this memorial as likely by Cai Jing.
52. CBBM 121.1b–6a; SHY Xingfa 6.21a–22a; SDZLJ 241.800–801.
53. CBBM 60.6a–7b; SHY Chongru 2.7b–9a; WXTK 46.432C–433C. For discussion of these measures, see also Chaffee 1985:77–84; Kracke 1977:6–30; and T. Lee 1985:290–92.
54. SS 157.3663; SHY Zhiguan 28.15a–b; Kracke 1977:17–18.
55. CBBM 123.3b–9b lists all those on the list. See also SHY Zhiguan 68.1a–3b, 68.4b–5a.
56. SHY Xingfa 2.43a.
57. CBSB 21.735, 21.736–37, 21.738, 21.743; SHY Zhiguan 28.15b; SHY Chongru 2.10b.

58. SHY Zhiguan 68.6a–b; CBSB 21.741. One source reports that an order was also issued to destroy stelae done in Su Shi's calligraphy. NGZML 11.327.

59. CBSB 22.773–74; SHY Zhiguan 68.7a, 68.9a–b.

60. CBBM 122.9b–13a. For a full analysis of this list, see Vittinghoff 1975.

61. SHY Zhiguan 76.25a–b; CBBM 122.13b–14a. Most of the people on this 1104 list who had not been on the earlier lists with 117 or 98 names were lower-rank officials, but there were also some like Zeng Bu and Zhang Dun who, while opponents of Cai Jing, were better classed as reformers than anti-reformers.

62. JSCB 144.1a–b.

63. YH 113.8b; CBSB 24.827; SZJSZ 17.30b; DYJ 12.15a–b. Also as a result of Huizong's visit, thousands of congratulatory verses and essays were submitted to the court by scholars from all over the country. Huizong told the Secretariat to rank them. The work that was ranked highest was a rhapsody (*fu*) by Ge Shengzhong, whose piece was several thousand words long (DYJ 24.4b–5a).

64. SZJSZ 17.29a–30a; BQS 109.26b, 109.28a; SHY Chongru 6.10a–b. See also Ebrey 2006a.

65. LZJSZ 7.12b–16b: or SZJSZ 17.30a–32a.

66. SS 20.374; SHY Xingfa 6.22a, SHY Zhiguan 76.25a–b; SDZLJ 217.829; CBBM 122.15b; CBSB 25.846, 25.855–58.

67. SDZLJ 217.829–30, 155.581; CBSB 25.861, 26.868, 26.870–74.

68. For the classical reference, see ZL 10.24b–26a.

69. WXTK 46.433A–B dates this to 1104, which has been followed by several authors, but CBBM 126.1a and SS 157.36666–67 more plausibly date it to 1107.

70. SDZLJ 157.591.

71. SDZLJ 179.649. Huizong again used his calligraphy to make his presence felt at the local level by writing out the name plaques for these halls, at least in one prefecture. See SSZ 8.6a (p. 7,697).

72. See SHY Chongru 2.18b–120b; and CBSB 32.1053, 32.1056, 32.1060, 32.1064.

73. SHY Chongru 2.24a.

74. See YDJSL 4.2a–5b; SZJSZ 18.15a–18a; QYT 15.11a–12b; and JSXB 17.30b–34a.

75. Overviews of Huizong's relations with Daoist masters are provided by Sun Kekuan 1965:93–122; Jin Zhongshu 1966, 1967; Miyakawa 1975b; Yang Huarong 1985; Xiao Baifang 1990a; and Ebrey 2000.

76. CB 498.6a, 491.1a, 500.1b; HZL hou 2.72; LSZX 552.1b (DZ 5:400C); CBBM 127.12a–b. On Shangqing teachings, see Robinet 1997:114–48.

77. MSZ chaps. 3, 4 (DZ 5:562A–70B). On Huizong's correspondence with Liu, see also Gyss-Vermande 1995.

78. MSZ 3.6a (DZ 5:563A), 3.7b (DZ 5:563B), 3.19a–b (DZ 5:567B); HYSJ 9 (DZ 17:881B–C); CBBM 127.12b.

79. MSZ 3.12a–b (DZ 5:565A).

80. MSZ 26.10b (DZ 5:667C), 4.1b (DZ 5:568C), 4.4b (DZ 5:569C). The Third Mao Lord was the youngest of the three Mao brothers during the Han dynasty who were later deified.

81. SS 20.380; CBBM 127.1a.

82. Strickmann 1978:341–42.

83. CBBM 127.1b, 2a; Strickmann 1978.

84. Strickmann 1978:336. CBBM 127.9b and HYSJ 9 (DZ 17.883A) describe these projects under 1121, perhaps when the work was nearing completion. Neither work survives.

85. CBBM 127.1a–b.

86. The most important primary sources on Lin Lingsu are CBBM chap. 127; LSZX chap. 53; SS 462; and BTL 1.4–6. There are many contradictions among these sources, even on basic matters like dates. Besides the scholarly works mentioned in note 75, see Miyakawa 1975a; Tang Daijian 1992; E. Davis 2001:26–28, 35–37; and S. Chao 2006.

87. Robinet 1997:180. Robinet sees Shenxiao Daoism as an offshoot of Lingbao Daoism, giving it a distinct genealogy from the Maoshan Daoism Huizong had learned from Liu Hunkang. On thunder rites, see Boltz 1993, especially pp. 272–86.

88. A surviving text in the Daoist canon records this revelation, "Formulary for the Transmission of Scriptures According to the Patriarchs of the Most Exalted Divine Empyrean" (Gaoshang shenxiao zongshi shoujing shi; Harvard-Yenching 1272). On Shenxiao texts, see Boltz 1987:26–30.

89. SHY Li 5.2b, 5.4a–b; CBBM 127.4a, 127.10a; Tang Daijian 1994; S. Chao 2006. For evidence that Buddhist temples were taken over, see LXABJ 9.115; YJZ 3 Si 7.1352–54; YJZ Zhiding 1.972.

90. XZZTJ 93.2412. CBBM 127.3a–4a, 127.11b–12a. One of these stelae survives in Putian in Fujian. See Zheng Zhenman and Ding Hesheng 1995:9–10; and Ebrey 2006a:254–55.

91. *Song Huizong yujie daode zhenjing* (Harvard-Yenching 680), in four *juan*. This text, which has been preserved in the Daoist canon, cites a range of authorities, including Confucius and Mencius, but draws most heavily on the *Zhuangzi* and the *Yijing*. Liu Ts'un-yan, who studied the commentary in depth, finds in it evidence that Huizong looked on the text as a guidebook for rulers on how to govern. See T. Liu 1974; see also his much longer Liu Cunren 1991.

92. CBBM 127.9b–11a. The Daoist canon contains two commentaries written for it, one by a low-ranking official, the other by a student at the National Academy (Boltz 1987:214–15).

93. CBBM 127.5a–6a; SS 157.3690. As S. Chao (2003) notes, the *Mencius* was probably chosen because Wang Anshi had promoted it.

94. CBBM 127.5a–b.

95. CBBM 127.4b–5a, 127.7b–8b.

96. BTL 1.4–5; LSZX 53.4–5 (DZ 5.409B–10C); Schmidt-Glintzer 1988.

97. YH 204.22b; DYJ 24.4a–5a, 24.7b–8b.

98. DYJ 1.2b–4b. The expenditures are given as 2,678,787,000 cash and 337,944 *piculs* (*dan*) of rice, while the income was substantially larger: 3,058,872,000 cash and 640,291 *piculs*. See also T. Lee 1985:132. Numbers for the year 1104 were somewhat larger. See CBSB 24.828.

99. SKTB 41.97, 41.96, 41.91 (the last transcribed in JSCB 143.9a–11a); HBJSZ 10.15a–16b.

100. E.g., SCZCZY 45.473.

101. ZZYL 130.3127.

102. On Zhao, see Chaffee 1990–92. His remarks are translated in T. Lee 1985:256.

103. S. Chao 2006:345–48; E. Davis 2001:37.

104. YJZ bu 20.1737. See also Inglis 2006:132–135.

105. SCBM 25.247–48.

106. E.g., GXJ 12.8a–11a; SMCYXL hou 13.12a–23a.

CHAPTER 3

ShuS 5.

1. See Akin 1996 for comparative perspectives on the passions of collectors.

2. The richest literature is on book collecting. See Yuan Tongli 1928; Pan Mingshen 1971; Pan Meiyue 1980; Yao Yingting 1992:36–45; T. Lee 1995; and Xu Lingzhi 2004. On private book collecting in Tang and earlier times, see Drège 1991:143–73. On the collection of paintings and calligraphy, see Ledderose 1979; Sullivan 1982; Li Huarui 1993; H. Liu 1997; Sturman 1997; and Egan 2006b:162–236. On the collection of antiquities, see Wang Guowei 1968:1924–34, 3823–87; Rudolph 1963; Chen Zhongyu 1972; Xia Chaoxiong 1982; K. C. Chang 1986:5–12; Chen Huiling 1988; Cui Wenyin 1993; Harrist 1995; and Chen Fangmei 2000, 2001, 2005.

3. Cf. Clunas 1991 on similar processes in the late Ming period.

4. A. Pan 2000.

5. SS 291.9732, 9735; SWGWJ 51.776–77; MXBT 25.824–26; Pan Meiyue 1980:57–59. For a rich discussion of collating practices in Song times, see Cherniak 1994. Song Shou's standing as a calligrapher is discussed in chapter 7.

6. SWGWJ 51.776; QWJW 4.141. Wang Anshi especially appreciated Song Minqiu's collection of works by Tang poets and made use of them when he compiled a selection of poems by Tang poets (SSWJHL 19.147). The Song family book collection outlasted Minqiu, but only by two decades, as it was consumed in a fire in the Yuanfu period (1098–1100; RZSB xu 15.398).

7. On Ouyang Xiu, see J. Liu 1967; Egan 1984; and Kobayashi 2000.

8. OYXQJ Jigu lu Muxu 1087. See also Egan 2006b:7–59 for a detailed analysis of Ouyang Xiu as a collector of rubbings. His catalogue has been partially reconstructed from the rearranged version prepared by his son. See Egan 2006b:9–10.

9. OYXQJ Jigu lu bawei 4.1135.

10. OYXQJ Jigu lu bawei 7. 1177; trans. Egan 1989:372.

11. OYXQJ 44.305–6; trans. Egan 1984:223.

12. OYXQJ 6.43; trans. Egan 1984:199.

13. OYXQJ Jigu lu bawei Muxu 1087; Egan 2006b:11–13.

14. For Wang Shen's biography, see Weng Tongwen 1968.

15. THJWZ 2.93; Soper 1951:38; ShuS 27–28.

16. ShuS 27–28; BJYGJ 7.58–59 (both translated in Ledderose 1979:98, 99); QBZZ 5.227–28 (trans. in Sturman 1997:222). See also Egan 2006b:204–5.

17. Nakata 1970:229–38; HS 210–11.

18. Maeda 1970:39–40, modified. See also translation in Soper 1951:172.

19. Besides figure 3.2, see the colophon to Wang Qihan's *Examining Books* (reproduced in Jin Weinuo 1984 annotations, p. 32).

20. Barnhart 1997:125–26. Barnhart (1983, 1994) sees this as the beginning of the powerful tradition of the scholar-painters of China, an art not only distinct from the art of the court but in tension with it. For a study of *Misty River,* including the poetry written for it by Su Shi and Wang Shen, see Murck 2000:129–56.

21. Quite a few of his pieces appear in KGT.

22. Nakata 1970:232–34; HS 190.

23. Studies of Li Gonglin include Barnhart 1976, 1993; Harrist 1995, 1998; and Brotherton 2000.

24. HJ 3.287; KGT passim; ZS 11–12 (trans. Harrist 1995:242).

25. Harrist 1998:18.

26. XHHP 7.132–33. On this painting, see Edwards 1993.

27. His father was Zhao Tingzhi, who served from Shenzong's through Huizong's reign.

28. JSL ba 1b; trans. Owen 1986:85.

29. JSL ba 1b; trans. Owen 1986:85, modified.

30. JSL ba 1b, 2a, 2b; trans. Owen 1986:85, 97.

31. SSWJ 11.359.

32. GSJ 36.15a–b; OYXQJ Jigulu bawei 5.1151; KGT preface; ZS 12 (trans. Harrist 1995:242).

33. Egan 1989:383.

34. See Egan 2006b:194–218.

35. KGT 1.19a–b; cf. Harrist 1995:257. See also Rudolph 1963:171 for Zhao Mingcheng's critique of the way Li Gonglin jumped to conclusions in this and other passages.

36. LDMHJ 2.184; cf. Acker 1954:199.

37. MXBT 17.540; trans. Bush and Shih 1985:99–100, modified.

38. Pan Meiyue 1980:95.

39. ShuS 27–28; cf. Ledderose 1979:98.

40. HS 195.

41. QDYY 12.216–17; DJMHLZ 3.91, 3.99; JZDSZ 4C.466; SSJW 10.183. On Song book culture, see also McDermott 2005.

42. HS 217; Sullivan 1982:168.

43. HS 207; ShuS 8–9, 26; cf. H. Liu 1997:40–44; Ledderose 1979:103–4.

44. HS 213–14, 216; ShuS 2 (trans. Ledderose 1979:97–98); MXBT bu 2.955.

45. An example discussed by Ouyang Xiu were the various versions of the inscriptions made by the First Emperor of Qin (OYXQJ Jigulu bawei 1.1100).

46. For a convenient compilation of inscriptions on paintings preserved in Song collected works, see Chen Gaohua 1984.

47. ShuS 42, 55; HS 206; cf. Van Gulik 1958:184, 188, 189, 194.

48. QSB 3.210–11. The collector was Wang Shu (997–1057) and his son was Wang Qinchen (fl. 1050–1100).

49. Brief introductions to the Stone Drums are found in K. Y. Chang 1978 and Y. Tseng 1993:44–45, and a full study in Mattos 1988. The stones are now thought to have been made by the rulers of the state of Qin (and thus to be unrelated to Shi Zhou, who served the Zhou king).

50. Wei was a late-eighth-century Tang poet who wrote a song on the drums. See Owen 1981:303–16.

51. King Wen was the last of the predynastic rulers of Zhou (ca. 1060 BCE). King Xuan reigned from 827 to 782 BCE.

52. Tang official who died in 820. Late in his career, he served as governor of Fengxiang. XTS 165.5059–60; JTS 158.4163–66.

53. Son of Xiang Minzhong (948–1019); SS 282.9557.

54. See SuiS 32.945.

55. Shi Zhou was considered the creator of the great seal script. He served at court under King Xuan of Zhou (9th century BCE).

56. OYXQJ Jigulu bawei 1.1097–98.

57. Discussed later in Ouyang Xiu's book; OYXQJ Jigulu bawei 1.1099–1100.

58. JSL 13.4a–b.

59. For instance, he discussed a rubbing someone had shown him that was supposed to date from the Qin period and to have been from huge metal statues made by the First Emperor. Dong You traced the history of these statues, showing that all of them had either

been melted down or thrown in the river, so that the rubbing in question must have been made from a recarving of the text recorded in the *Annotated Classic of Rivers* (SJZ 4.130–31; GCSB 4.17b–18a).

60. GCSB 1.12a–13a.

61. KGT preface; Ledderose 1976:119 and 1979:49.

62. Pan Meiyue 1980:88; XHSP 6.50; SSWJ 11.354, 11.356–57. For a poem Su Shi wrote to commemorate Sun's hall, see Egan 1989:395–96.

63. Several scholars have examined specific exchanges in detail. See Sargent 1992; Murck 2000:130–51; and Foong 2000.

64. HS 203. Seals themselves were also becoming collectibles in this period. Mi Fu mentioned that Zhao Lingrang had a seal of Li Yu's (HS 208).

65. Pan Meiyue 1980:14–17 lists twenty-four Northern Song book collectors mentioned in Song sources as preparing catalogues of their collections (none of which survive).

66. WXTK 207.1711A.

67. ZS 1.10b–11a; KGT passim; Harrist 1995:44–45; Chen Fangmei 2001:51, 2005:271–72.

68. HS 203.

69. Egan 2006b:17–26, 43–50.

70. See Owen 1986:80–98.

71. SSWJ 11:359–60.

72. SSWJ 11.356–57; trans. Egan 1989:404–5. See also Egan 1994:159. For Su Shi's chiding of Mi Fu, see Sturman 1997:69–73.

73. Egan 2006b:177.

74. A. Pan 2000; Harrist 1998:24; Sturman 1997:122, 215.

CHAPTER 4

TWSCT 4.80.

1. For a list of these works, see appendix 2. Perhaps for this reason, Huizong as a collector has received very little attention from scholars. Takatsu 2004 directly addresses this issue, but the discussion is only two pages long.

2. Bickford 2002–3.

3. In TWSCT 3.53 Cai Tao reports that he was fourteen at the end of the Daguan period (1109 or 1110), when his father went to Hangzhou after being dismissed as grand councilor. This would mean that he was born in 1096 or, more likely, 1097.

4. SS 472.13730–32, 248.8783; SHY Dixi 8.40a–b; TWSCT 2.38–39. The numbers indicate the man's sequence among his brothers, siblings, or cousins (depending on the family's customs).

5. SHY Zhiguan 69.13a, Xuanju 9.16b; SS 472.13727, 472.13731; SZFBNL 12.809–10; BTL 5.62 (trans. Djang and Djang 1989:524–25).

6. SS 472.13728, 472.13732; SSY 40.13b–15a. The history, *Guoshi houbu,* does not survive in full, but lengthy passages were copied into several Southern Song works, such as SCBM, CBBM, and SZFBNL. *Tiewei shan* literally means "mountains surrounded by iron," and is a Buddhist phrase referring to the limits of personal knowledge.

7. SKQSZMTY 141.2913–15; Hervouet 1978:105. On the biases in the historical sources for Cai Jing, see Hartman 2006.

8. TWSCT 1.5–6.

9. Wu's biography in XHHP 19.294 mentions an early appointment in the princely establishment of Huizong's uncle Zhao Hao, but not a similar appointment to Huizong's establishment, suggesting that his role there may have been informal.

10. I have not been able to identify Xu Bijian. Perhaps Bijian is an alternative name for the well-known Five Dynasties flower painter Xu Xi, for whom no alternative names have been recorded.

11. TWSCT 4.78.

12. TWSCT 4.76–77; trans. Djang and Djang 1989:521, modified. It is possible that Huizong had more than one fan with Cai Jing's calligraphy of a Du Fu poem on it. In his account of the banquet in 1119, Cai Jing reported a conversation with Huizong about the time when he was a prince and had approached Cai Jing with a fan and asked him to write on it. Huizong remembered the Du Fu poem he had written on it and was able to recite it. See HZL yuhua 1.279.

13. Song Zifang was the nephew of Song Di, a scholar-painter of the 1060s–1070s (see Murck 2000:42–44, 61–67). Deng Chun said of his appointment, "In that era my late grandfather happened to be in the government, and he recommended Song Di's nephew, Song Zifang, as suitable for selection as the professor. At that time Zifang's brushwork and use of ink were the most outstanding of his generation; hence everyone said that he was the appropriate choice" (HJ 1.269; trans. Bush and Shih 1985:134).

14. This work, by Wang Xizhi, is not listed in the XHSP. Mi Fu described how he acquired it in ShuS 12 (trans. Ledderose 1979:106). Huang Bosi added to the account that Mi Fu acquired it in 1103 and paid 150,000 for it (DGYL 2.3b).

15. By Wang Xianzhi; XHSP 16.124.

16. On Cao, see XHHP 5.99, where his name is given as Fuxing.

17. TWSCT 4.78–79.

18. SCZCZY 6.59.

19. SS 472.13722; SSWJHL 27.214.

20. HJ 10.417; trans. Maeda 1970b:60–61, modified. These paintings by Zhan Ziqian do not survive, but a different painting that Huizong attributed to Zhan is extant. See plates 23 and 24.

21. TWSCT 4.76.

22. Cf. SS 129.3002. See also chapter 6.

23. TWSCT 4.79–80. Wen Weng was a model official in Sichuan (Western Shu) in Han times. See HanS 89.3625–26. Shao Bowen also gave a large number for the antiquities in Harmony Revealed Hall, saying they numbered several thousand (SSWJHL 27.211).

24. BSLH 2.18b–19b.

25. The bronzes that did enter Huizong's collection include eight owned by Li Gonglin, seven owned by Liu Chang, three owned by Wang Qincheng, and two each owned by Zhang Shunmin and Wen Yanbo. In all of these cases, it was likely a descendant who sold or gave the vessel. See the tables in Ye Guoliang 1984:336–92.

26. The catalogue, XQGT, was prepared between 1104 and 1108, according to Ye Guoliang 1982:95–98. The close ties between Huizong and Zhao Zhonghu are evident from his inclusion in the 1119 party discussed later in this chapter.

27. Here it is interesting to note that in the late 1990s, after several decades of active archaeological excavations, the Palace Museum in Beijing had approximately 10,000 pre-Qin bronzes. See Liu Yu and Ding Meng 1999:19.

28. JSL 13.1b; 13.2a; YJZ bu 23.1761.

29. TWSCT 1.9–10, supplemented by CBBM 128.4b–6a and CBSB 31.1040–42, which give a somewhat fuller account. Wang is said to have paid 1,700 in gold, but "gold" here probably just means "money." Perhaps the cost was 1700 strings of cash.

30. GCSB 2.14b–15a; SS 319.10388–89. The object does not appear in the BGT. Two bronze vessels that belonged to another man on the banned list, Zhang Shunmin, did end up in the catalogue. See KGT 4.23a–24a, 4.44a–45a; BGT 8.6a–7a, 9.13a–14b; SS 347.1005–6.

31. HLSZ 20a–b. See also Sturman 1997:183. MZML 2.15 says Huizong gave him eighteen silver tablets. Certainly not every piece in Mi Fu's collection entered Huizong's, but a dozen or more apparently did. Mi Fu does not provide a list of his entire collection, and he was constantly trading things, so exactly what he had in 1105 is impossible to determine. However, by comparing the list of items Mi Fu mentions as being in his collection compiled by Nakata with those in the XHSP, it is clear that only a tiny number of the items in the *Xuanhe* catalogue are listed by Mi Fu as being in his collection. For instance, of the forty pieces by Ouyang Xun in the *Xuanhe shupu*, only two have titles that match ones listed by Mi Fu as his own. See Nakata 1970:229–38.

32. BZZFSZ 20.300; trans. Sturman 1989:386. For other examples of paintings that were given to the palace, or that "returned" there, knowing where they belonged, see GTL 325; MZML 2.63.

33. Nakata 1979:234–36; BSLH 2.31b–32a.

34. See Sturman 1997:182–84 and 245n22 on the likelihood that it was Cai Jing who advanced Mi Fu's career. Wang Shen, however, would be another good candidate. Mi Fu also sought help from two other men who held high posts at the time, Jiang Zhiqi and Deng Xunwu. Letters to both of them survive, the one to Jiang amusing in suggesting language Jiang could use to Huizong, such as "[Mi Fu] relies on his own talents and has nothing to do with party cliques. He is old now and hampered by his qualifications. If it were his misfortune to die one day without having the opportunity to enrich His Majesty's enterprise and thus embellish His Majesty's magnanimity, this official would consider it a pity" (trans. Sturman 1997:218).

35. MZML 6.64; trans. Sturman 1997:219–20, modified. For other anecdotes, see Sturman 1997:215–19.

36. TWSCT 1.9–10.

37. CBBM 128.4b–6a; TWSCT 1.9–10; CBSB 31.1040–42; SSQWXZZTJ 14.899. The connections between collecting antiquities and reforming court ritual are analyzed more fully in chapter 6.

38. TWSCT 4.80.

39. CBSB 32.1061.

40. HZL yuhua 1.277; CBSB 40.1251.

41. SHY Zhiguan 18.17b.

42. LTGS 1.35–36. SHY Zhiguan 18.21b.

43. HMZ 207.

44. QDYY 6.93.

45. In making this list, I tried to err on the side of inclusion rather than exclusion, so this list almost surely includes a few works that have fake Huizong seals on them. However, in order to consider the full range of Huizong's practice with regard to inscriptions and seals, I did not want to limit myself to the more secure set of works with the Xuanhe mount-

ing set, since he could not have used that set of practices before 1119 and is likely to have put some seals on works before that date.

46. The best studied example is the *Admonitions of the Instructress*, attributed to Gu Kaizhi, which seems to have a genuine copy of the Ruisi dongge seal but quite a few forged Huizong seals as well. See Y. Wang 2003.

47. Cf. Xu Bangda 1981a:36–39, 1981b; Barnhart 1983; Niu Kecheng 2005.

48. For citation of good illustrations of all the works with Huizong's seals on them, see appendix 2.

49. It is not visible in the reproductions I have been able to inspect of the Liang Shimin, and I have not seen the painting. However, from the description of the seals in the Qing period *Shiju baoji*, most likely it was on the final seam of the work. See Gugong 1981: fulu, 8. See appendix 2 for citations to illustrations.

50. I have come across no other plausible works with this Daguan seal. There is another Daguan seal, shaped like a gourd, that I have not seen associated with Huizong in existing scholarship. It appears on at least five Song album leaves in the collections of the Beijing and Taipei palace museums. See National Palace Museum 1995b:204, 216; Zheng Zhenduo et al. 1957: plates 12, 33, and 77. (Other Daguan seals are listed in SQBJ as on Song album leaves in Qianlong's collection, but without pictures, it is impossible to tell if they match). One of the published leaves is signed Li Anzhong; the others are anonymous. They are all of the bird/flower/insect genre, in a style generally associated more with the Southern Song than with the Northern Song. It is certainly possible that this seal was placed on these fans falsely, but it is also possible that these were products of Huizong's court, rather than of earlier artists. Since Li Anzhong served in the painting academies of both Huizong and Gaozong, and Huizong's court was clearly a period of transition between the high Northern and high Southern Song styles, it is possible that these were up-to-date works done at Huizong's court that he placed his seal on. Another alternative is that he used this as an artist's seal, and was taking credit for making them himself, perhaps to give away as gifts.

51. On this seal, see Y. Wang 2003:196–98; and Bickford 2006:509–10.

52. On the activities of other buildings in the Sagacious Thoughts compound, see Bickford 2006:503–11.

53. Another complication of the Eastern Pavilion of Sagacious Thoughts seal is that Gaozong also had a hall with that name, and he had several seals with the same term on them, seals that are visually quite distinct (see Shanghai bowuguan 1987 2:1358–61, seal numbers 5, 14, and 18). There are several reasons for considering this particular version of the seal to be Huizong's rather than Gaozong's. The Zhou Fang entered Jin Zhangzong's collection, something much more likely to be true of objects from Huizong's rather than Gaozong's collection. The Ruisi dongge seals on the Han Gan and the Han Huang, *Literary Gathering*, are directly over Huizong's inscription, a very odd place for Gaozong to put his seal. Y. Wang 2003:196–98 also comes to the conclusion that this Ruisi dongge seal is Huizong's, not Gaozong's.

54. Barnhart 1983, 1994, attributes this "Guo Xi" to Wang Shen. For citations of illustrations of these paintings, see appendix 2.

55. The only other painting I have found with this seal is a Zhang Sengyou, which also has some of the seals in the Xuanhe mounting set, but in at least one case placed anomalously, making it more problematic. The linked Xuanhe, normally found in the lower right, is also found in the upper left; other reported seals are not visible in the reproductions available to me.

56. P. Foong 2000 reads the *mi/bi* 秘 character in this seal as referring to what I translate as the Palace Library, and the Xuanhe as referring to the reign period rather than the hall. I am not sure how she reads the *zhong* 中 character.

57. Paintings attributed to Huizong with this small square "imperial writing" seal include most of his best-known works, such as *Auspicious Cranes* (plate 21), *Five-Colored Parakeet* (plate 4), *Auspicious Dragon Rock, Two Birds on a Wax-Plum,* and his cursive-script calligraphy of the *Thousand Character Essay* done in 1122 (plate 19). For illustrations of these works, see Bo Songnian 1998:3, 4, 6, 8, 11, 12, 15, and 29.

58. Y. Wang 2003:198. For his fuller study of this painting, see Wang Yaoting 2007.

59. T. Wu 1997:144.

60. Published in T. Wu 1997:58. For other examples, see appendix 2. "Trace" is a somewhat ambiguous term. Its basic meaning is something close to footprint, a trace of a person's presence. A man's writings and calligraphy are traces of his thoughts and feelings. "True trace" thus would mean something that a person did himself that left a physical sign of his actions. However, a fourteenth-century source (THBJ 1.5a–b) says "true trace" was used in the old Palace Library (probably meaning the Song one) to identify copies.

61. The painting is the landscape hanging scroll in the Osaka City Museum. The two pieces of calligraphy are edicts, the one to Cai Xing, and the one that concerns sacrificial ceremonies, both in the collection of the Liaoning Provincial Museum. For illustrations, see Ōsaka shiritsu bijutsukan 1975:2:34 and Zhu Huiliang and Yang Meili 1985:86–108. The calligraphies are quite likely by Huizong, but the painting is made somewhat dubious by the existence of a related version (reversed left to right) in the National Palace Museum, Taipei (illustrated in National Palace Museum 2000:212).

62. NSGGL xu 3.179–80.

63. When they are present there is always the suspicion that they have been forged. See, for instance, the *Four Birds* (illustrated in Bickford 1996a, plate 2). Since many more paintings circulated that had once been in Huizong's collection than ones that he had done himself, the collector seals were very well known, and forgers may not have recognized the distinction between Huizong's artist and collector seals. Moreover, his collector seals used on calligraphy were widely reproduced in published reproductions of calligraphy, such as the *Sanxitang fatie* (SXTFT) that Qianlong issued.

64. For some of the fans, see Bo Songnian 1998:4, 5, and 14. The seal is also found on two large landscapes, the ones in the National Palace Museum, Taipei, and the Palace Museum, Beijing (see National Palace Museum 2000:212 and Gugong 1981:92).

65. For Zhao, see GCHB 6.9a–b. XHHP 12.204 lists a copy Wang Shen did of a painting titled *Wintry Forest* by Li Cheng.

66. XHHP 1.33; SHY Zhiguan 18.22b. This occasion is discussed in detail below.

67. QJJ 27.12a–b, 95.2b; HJian 423; Weitz 2002:85.

68. GXZZ xu B.212; QRJSJ 45.768.

69. For larger color illustrations, see T. Wu 1997:56–57; and Shanghai shuhua chubanshe 2004:32–40.

70. TWSCT 1.10.

71. TWSCT 4.80.

72. HZL yuhua 1.274.

73. The source for this story is HZL yuhua 1.276–79; supplemented by CB shibu 40.1251–52; and SF han 114.5238–39.

74. HZL does not list him, nor does the CBSB version, though the SF one does.

75. HZL yuhua 1.276–77.

76. Records of such gatherings are very numerous. For other gatherings Huizong held, see HZL yuhua 1.273–76, 1.279–81. Deng Chun reports that at a banquet held in 1116 at an imperial garden outside the palace, Huizong showed a picture of drakes he had recently painted and inscribed. "All those present at the banquet stood around to look at it. Each viewed the painting with awe and praised the work as the most exquisite and spirited one under Heaven" (HJ 1.266–67; trans. Ecke 1972:98).

77. For a large illustration of this painting, see National Palace Museum 1993:127–29. On this painting, see Yi Ruofen 2006.

78. On the protocols of imperial excursions, see Ebrey 1999.

79. TWSCT 1.15–16. The inauspiciousness Cai Tao refers to at the end concerns the fact that Minghuang (Xuanzong) was not visiting Shu as an outing, but fleeing from rebel armies and would soon lose the throne. Perhaps Cai Tao thought this was inauspicious at the time, but it is more likely that it was only after Huizong also lost his throne that Cai Tao, looking back, saw this gift as ill-omened.

80. LTGS 5.207–8; SHY Chongru 6.12a–b, Zhiguan 18.21b–23b; CLJ 1.17b–18a; HJ 1.266–67.

81. SHY Chongru 6.12a–b.

82. LTGS 5.207–8.

83. LTGS 5.208.

84. SHY Chongru 6.12a–b.

85. LTGS 5.207–8; HJ 1.266–67; SHY Zhiguan 18.22b, Chongru 6.12a–b; CLJ 1.17b–18a.

86. LTGS 5.207–8; SHY Zhiguan 18.21b–23b, Chongru 6.12b; HJ 1.266–67.

87. SHY Chongru 6.12a–b.

88. TWSCT 6.107–8.

89. XHSP 1.2–3, 20.162.

90. Acker 1954:231.

91. On Li Yu, see Chen Baozhen 1997, 1998, and 1999; P. Chen 1999; and R. Davis 2004:501–3. On Huizong's view of Li Yu, see also H. Wu 1996:29–48.

92. THJWZ 6.251; trans., Soper 1951:101–2, slightly modified. On Li Yu's practices, see also Chen Baozhen 1999.

CHAPTER 5

SHY Zhiguan 18.24a.

1. WXTK 202.1690B. Peng Mountain refers to Penglai, the home of the immortals. Referring to the Palace Library as the land of the immortals evokes both the stature of the men who worked there and its desirability as a place to work. Luo Ji was not the first to write an account of the Palace Library. Almost twenty years earlier, Song Feigong wrote a fifteen-chapter *Record of the Literary Institutes of the Song Dynasty* (Huang Song guange lu). See Zhang Fuxiang's preface to LTGS, 1. Nor would Luo Ji be the last to write such a book. Cheng Ju (1078–1144), who served in the Palace Library for long stretches beginning in 1117, wrote a similarly conceived book in 1131, titled *Affairs of the Unicorn Terrace* (Lintai gushi; see LTGS). Much lengthier texts survive from it than the earlier two books, and it will be regularly cited here.

2. SCSSLY 2.23, 3.31, 5.47, 16.187, 28.359, 24.301, 31.390–400, 50.655–56. These have recently been assembled in Wang He and Zhen Li 2003:396–405.

3. SCSSLY 31.394–95, 50.655.

4. SCSSLY 24.301, 31.392–93, 31.398–99, 5.23.

5. SCSSLY 31.395–98.

6. See Gong Yanming 1997:237–40.

7. SHY Xuanju 19.21b, 12.4a–b; YH 204.22a. On Luo's career, see also Wang He and Zhen Li 2003:393–96.

8. SHY Li 14.72b, 20.9b, 34.7b, Shihuo 12.3b, Zhiguan 18.14b, Chongru 5.28b.

9. SHY Zhiguan 18.19a, 23a; SS21.398; LTGS 183.

10. FRJ 26.45b.

11. FRJ 26.51a–b.

12. For another biography that makes the point that a Library official did not curry favor with Liang Shicheng, see HQJSJ 34.29b–30a.

13. SS 164.3873–75, with ranks from Hucker. In 1120 the number of appointees was altered, adding three editorial directors, dropping two editors, and adding two proofreaders. See also Gong Yanming 1997:140–42.

14. BSJ 35.4a–8a; RZSB 13.173.

15. JXTZ 80.19a; HQJSJ 34.22a, 25a–b; BSJ 33.6b.

16. The fourth was Ye Mengde. See DQZL 11.1a–b.

17. E.g., Zhai Ruwen, SS 372.11544.

18. BSJ 33.4b–5a. For the listing of Cheng Ju and Mao Sui, see CBBM 123.5b, 7b. In addition, Teng Yu's father and uncle had been on the banned list (WZJ 29.29b).

19. ZHJ fulu 2b.

20. YH 204.22a, 23b; SHY Xuanju 33.23b–24a; WZJ 29.26a–27b; FXJ 26.317; HQJSJ 38.16b–17a.

21. SSHY 6.47a; ZHJ fulu 11.21b–23a; HJ 4.295; HQJSJ 34.31a; GCSB preface.

22. ZHJ fulu 2b–3a; HQJSJ 34.20b; FXJ 26.317.

23. GCSB; GCHB. Dong You's son wrote a preface for GCSB that says he compiled the two books in 1157. He stressed that not much remained of his father's once-extensive collection, much having been lost when he fled south to escape the Jurchen invasion or in the subsequent wars. In all probability, the notes were also incomplete.

24. This is not a direct quote from Xie He's famous text on painting. For a study and translation of it, see Acker 1954:1–32.

25. GCHB 4.41–42; largely translated in Bush and Shih 1985:222, which has been used here with minor modifications. For other passages from Dong You, see Bush and Shih 1985:209–11, 214–17, 221–22, 229–30, 232–33, 236–37.

26. DGYL 1.1a–34a.

27. LXJ 168.4a–b; cf. SS 443.13106. Perhaps because these notes had not been edited for publication, in them Huang Bosi was not as consistent as Dong You in mentioning when the objects he discussed were part of the palace collection.

28. See DGYL passim; Bush and Shih 1985:204–5, 221.

29. SD 1.102. Tang Xuandu was a Tang calligrapher.

30. DGYL 1.52b–53b. For other examples of Huang Bosi's writings on calligraphy, see DGYL 1.53b–54a, 1.55a–59b.

31. SHY Zhiguan 18.14a–b. The standard explanation for the color of the paper is that treating it to deter insects turned it yellow. Shen Gua offered an additional reason: the large yellow volumes were too distinctive for officials to take home and thus cut pilferage (MXBT 1.75).

32. SHY Chongru 4.19a–b. He calculated that the Han dynasty had 33,090 *juan* (chapters/scrolls) of books, the Sui dynasty 370,000 *juan*, the Tang in the early eighth century 89,600 *juan*, but the Song (when its catalogue was prepared in 1041) only 30,669 *juan*. He's figure for the Sui is not plausible. SuiS 35.1099 stated that the catalogue of both secular and religious books, including ones both extant and lost, came to 56,881 *juan* (6520 titles). YH 52.16b gave the larger figure for the Sui, but included duplicates and other extraneous volumes. When they were removed, the total was 37,000 *juan*.

33. SHY Chongru 4.19a–b; SHY Zhiguan 18.14b–15a. The call for collecting was reiterated in 1112.

34. SHY Zhiguan 18.15b–16a; LTGS Canben 2B.275–76, 280.

35. SHY Zhiguan 18.16b–17b.

36. YH 52.42a; WXTK 174.1509C–10A; SHY Zhiguan 8.19a; SS 202.5033.

37. SHY Zhiguan 18.21b, 18.24a; SHY Chongru 4.19b–20a.

38. Two Southern Song authors cite it. See SCTSM 50b; LX 5.1b, 2.5a.

39. SHY Chongru 4.20a–b. To do the checking, the Library officials used the checklists (*zhang mu*) of the various collections in the Palace Library. As late as 1125/4/9 work was being done to add titles to the Palace Library. On that day it was reported that a comparison of the titles in one private collector's library and those in the Palace Library resulted in finding 658 titles in 1,051 volumes or scrolls, totaling 2,417 chapters. After the Palace Library checked the books, they were classed as good editions of rare books and the owner was granted official status.

40. HZL qian 1.10. See also SHY Chongru 4.12a–13a; SHY Zhiguan 18.24b; WXTK 174.1510A; SS 202.5033.

41. DGYL 2.79a–80b.

42. GCSB 5.16a, 3.7a, 4.8b, 6.26a, 30b, 1.2a, 3.8a.

43. XHHP lists thirty-one paintings of dragons by the Five Dynasties monk painter Chuangu. See also GCHB 5.49.

44. These three painters are all well represented in the XHHP (1.37–39, 17.268–70, 17.272–740), with many paintings on themes similar to the ones listed here, even if not these particular ones.

45. GCHB 3.28.

46. GCHB 6.64.

47. See CBBM 130.21b.

48. GCHB 3.30. *The Record of Peng Mountain* also mentioned that this painting had proven, on inspection of its seals, to have been in the palace collection early in the dynasty. No one in the library could account for how it had ended up in private hands (SCSSLY 50.655).

49. GCHB 5.50, 2.20–22.

50. GCHB 5.57.

51. GCHB 5.57.

52. Sirén 1936:33–37; HJ 9.407; trans. Maeda 1970b:55 or Bush and Shih 1985:102.

53. Discussed in Dong You's previous entry. The tests for skills were part of the traditional celebration of the seventh day of the seventh month.

54. Ding Wei was a leading official who was purged in 1037 and his property seized. On the paintings seized, see also THJWZ 6.235–36; trans. Soper 1951:95. Another painting confiscated from Ding Wei is mentioned in GCHB 5.49.

55. This is also the rank he was given by Liu Daochun. See SCMHP 8–9; trans. Lachman 1989:18–21.
56. GCHB 3.29.
57. GCHB 1.3–4.
58. Nothing matching this description is in the extant version of KGT.
59. GCSB 1.14b.
60. GCHB 1.1.
61. GCHB 6.64.
62. GCHB 3.30, 5.57.
63. GCSB 3.8a , 2.14b–15a.
64. GCHB 5.55.
65. GCHB 5.57, 3.30.
66. E.g., DGYL 1.67b–68b, 71a–81a; GCSB 3.10a–b, 3.16a–17a.
67. DGYL 1.69a.
68. GCSB 1.17b–18a, 2.14b; DGYL 1.77b–78b, 1.63b–64b.
69. GCSB 1.4a–b; DGYL 1.65a–b.
70. DGYL 1.65a–b, 1.63b, 1.78b; GCSB 1.16b–17a; GCHB 2.20–22.
71. DGYL 1.39a–b.
72. DGYL 2.20b–21a.
73. It is not clear whether this note was done while Huang Bosi was working in the palace or not. A work with this title is listed in XHSP 13.102, so it is possible that this note was prepared as part of his work at the Library.
74. An official during the late seventh century.
75. DGYL 1.44b–46a.
76. Three of the *dui* he lists had already been published in KGT. See KGT 3.1a–4a, 3.17a–18a, 3.23a–24b. Another is in BGT 16.43a–48b.
77. GCSB 1.2a.
78. LXJ 168.3a.
79. HQJSJ 34.20a–b.

CHAPTER 6

ZHJ 8.3a–b.

1. JXLL 1.11b–13a. On the Stone Drums see Zhu Jia Jin 1986:44–45; Y. Tseng 1993:44; and for the fullest account, Mattos 1988.
2. NGZML 14.402.
3. See Barnard 1973.
4. See appendix 1 on editions of the catalogue.
5. Gao Renjun 1987; Zhang Linsheng 1996:5.
6. OYXQJ Jigulu bawei 1091–93; KGT 1.6a–8b; BGT 2.7a–b, 2.3a–5a, *juan* 22–26, 28–30.
7. Because this is the most widely available edition, it is the one cited here. For other editions, see appendix 1. To show the style of the illustrations in different editions, illustrations in this chapter are drawn from several editions. In this chapter and elsewhere in this book, to avoid cluttering the discussion with Chinese terms, whenever feasible I refer to vessel types by the translations in this table.
8. LJ 37.3b; cf. Legge 1967 2:93.

9. ZL 18.27a.

10. See Legge 1967 2:117. See also DeWoskin 1982:87–95.

11. ZL 19.4b. Cf. Biot 1851 1:445–46. There are also several other passages in the *Zhou li* that mention one or more of these vessels with reference to particular rites.

12. There had also been earlier *Illustrations of the Three Ritual Classics*, the earliest by the Later Han scholar Ruan Kan.

13. SLT 14.1a–2b, 14.4a–5a. Cf. L. Chang 2000.

14. SS 431.12797; YH 56.13b–16a.

15. ZS 1.10b–11b. See also L. Chang 1996:6; and Ye Guoliang 1984:135.

16. KGT 4.27a–28a, 4.59a–b.

17. SS 128.2997. Earlier Song emperors had also initiated reforms of court music. See J. Lam 2006.

18. DeWoskin 1982:59–60, 81–83. On the connections between bells and tuning in China, see Bagley 2004.

19. CBBM 135.1a–b; CBSB 23.787–88.

20. See Barnard 1973:468–79; K. C. Chang 1986:95–101; and H. Wu 1995:4–10 on the Nine Cauldrons; and Falkenhausen 1993:23–39, 51–66, on bells.

21. The local official was Ren Yingshi, and he wrote an essay on the bells that he sent with them, which his biographer claimed had influence on the scholars at court. XYJ 8.6a–b.

22. On the development of *bo* bells, see Falkenhausen 1993:168–89. For his date of these bells, see p. 367. The closest *bo* bell that survives from the period seems to be one in the National Palace Museum called Nengyuan bozhong. For pictures of it, see Chen Fangmei 2001:131 plate 28; 132, plate 29. There is also a very close bell in the Minneapolis Institute of Art. See Jacobsen 2002:24.

23. Already in Southern Song times some scholars read the name of the duke as Xu 戌 rather than Cheng 成. See ZDKS 47b; and Li Youping 2004:25. This may well be the correct reading, but Huizong, his curators, and most later authors referred to the bells as the Duke Cheng bells.

24. The SS 129.3002 does not fully understand the meaning of "the place where the mandate was received," associating it with Huizong's fief as a prince rather than with Taizu.

25. SDZLJ 149.551; CBSB 29.986; SCSS 14.223–24. The CBSB passage has a misprint of *hua* 華 for *jing* 莖.

26. According to Chen Mengjia 1964:51, the Song scholars were misreading the character for "song" (*ge* 謌) as *jing* 謽, so the analysis of the meaning of *jing* is beside the point.

27. Cf. SDZLJ 149.551.

28. The *jing* character here is different from the one on the bells.

29. Song Jun lived during the Later Han. See HHS 41.1411–14. The citation here is to commentaries to the *Record of Ritual*. See LJYS 51.6a.

30. *Lüshi chunqiu* 5, "The Music of the Ancients," discusses the traditions concerning these and other ancient forms of music. See Knoblock and Riegel 2000:146–51.

31. DGYL 1.76a–b.

32. Legge 1961 5:627.

33. DGYL 1.76b–77a.

34. GCSB 3.6b–7a. On the names of the absolute pitches and the movable notes (like do, re, mi), see DeWoskin 1982:43–52; and Falkenhausen 1992. On the failure of officials during Renzong's reign to cast chime bells that worked properly, see Ebrey n.d.

35. SS 129.3001; CBSB 25.834–36, 25.844; TWSCT 1.11–12; SCSS 14.222. On the cranes' response to music and cranes as an auspicious sign, see Sturman 1990:33–68.

36. SS 128.2999. Reportedly the cauldron was turned over to serve as a bell (CBSB 25.836; SS 128.2999), but this seems somewhat difficult to imagine, especially if nine feet tall. But a cauldron standing on its three legs would certainly also give a sound when struck on its rim with a wooden mallet. Perhaps skilled craftsmen could design a large cauldron that would sound the right note when so struck.

37. Chen Mengjia 1964; Chen Fangmei 2001:95–99; Li Youping 2004. See also Zhongguo yinyue wenwu daxi zongbian jibu 1996–2001, especially the volumes on Beijing, Henan, Shanghai, and Shaanxi.

38. Because these bells were seized by the Jurchen as booty in 1127, some of them had their name changed in 1174 because the word *sheng*, here translated as "brilliance," violated the taboo of the Jin emperor. These ones have Dahe instead of Dasheng; see Chen Mengjia 1964 and Rudolph 1948.

39. Li Youping 2004:68, 95.

40. XQGJ 36.5a–8a; XQXJYB 17.17a–19a.

41. SS 129:3001.

42. CBSB 25.851; SCSS 14.222.

43. Li Youping 2004:131.

44. SS 129:3017–18; J. Lam 2006.

45. BGT 22.3b.

46. See Pratt 1976, 1981; and Provine 1996:63–65. A first gift of 167 musical instruments in 1114 had included music and instructions, but not the heavy bells or stone chimes.

47. Huang Tipei 1983:76.

48. CBBM 133.1a.

49. The earliest reference to this proverbial saying is in HanS 30.1746, where it is attributed to Confucius.

50. CBBM 133.1b–2a; CBSB 28.950.

51. CBBM 133.3a–b; ZHWLXY 5.4a–4b. For other ways the ZHWLXY innovated, see Kojima 1992.

52. ZHJ fulu 21b–23a.

53. SS 356.11206; GCSB 1.10b; DGYL 1.73b.

54. ZS 1.1b.

55. CBSB 32.1057, 32.1062.

56. TWSCT 4.80.

57. ZS 1.1b–4b; SHY Li 28.17b, 28.60b; YH 56.15b–16a.

58. The best evidence of this comes from the efforts of the Southern Song government to make vessels on the model of those made during the Zhenghe period. See YH 69.24a–25b.

59. ZHJ 10.1a–4a; CBSB 35.1129.

60. CBSB 35.1130–31; ZHJ fulu 19a–b; SS 119.2810. The other officials granted vessels were Zheng Juzhong, Deng Xunwu, She Shen, Hou Meng, Xue Ang, and Bai Shizhong.

61. SS 119.2810.

62. SHY Li 14.70a–b.

63. Zhou Zheng 1983; Cai Meifen 1991; National Palace Museum 2000:100, 413; Chen Fangmei 2000:302–4; Yan Yiping 1962. See also L. Chang 2000 and Erickson 2001:425–26.

64. ZHJ 8.1b.

65. An exception is Chen Fangmei 2001, especially pp. 82–86. For other studies of Song "metal and stone" studies, see Wang Guowei 1968 5:1924–34; Rudolph 1963; Chen Zhongyu 1972; Chen Huiling 1988; and Chen Wenju 1994. These studies tend to generalize about the state of studies in Song times, not making much effort to distinguish private and government scholarship or detect stages across the three centuries of the Song. On this scholarship, see also Y. Sena n.d.

66. Illustrated in BGT 1.8b.

67. This is not an exact quotation from the *Zhou li*, but there was a tradition of interpreting "sacrificial animal beaker" in this way. See LiS 95.10b.

68. BGT 9.34b–35a. For more sample translations, see K. C. Chang 1986:9–10. In 1851 P. P. Thoms published images from this book with partial translations of the captions. See Thoms 1851.

69. The specific number is omitted in the version of this epitaph included in Li Gang's collected works (LXJ 168.4a), but is found in versions of the epitaph attached as an appendix to some editions of DGYL and in LYZYL 123.26a.

70. This is seen most easily in the tables in Ye Guoliang 1982:336–431.

71. BGT 4.31a–33a; 12.18a–21b.

72. E.g., KGT 4.17a; and BGT 10.29a–30b. See also GCSB 3.3b–4b for Dong You's recognition of the generic meaning of *yi*.

73. BGT 8.5a. These vessels are in BGT 6.35a–36b and 11.3a–9a.

74. On principles used in dating, see also Liu Zhaorui 1992:36.

75. BGT 14.54a, 29a, 1.36a, 9.12a, 10.36a.

76. BGT 9.40b, 3.8a–b, 11.34a. For another example qualified as late Zhou, see BGT 5.7a.

77. BGT 13.7a–9b, 13.12a–14a.

78. See Zheng Xuan's commentary in ZL 20.2b.

79. These two vessels are illustrated in BGT 8.45a, 8.46a. One would have imagined that they were inscribed and named as "wine bowls" (*zhou*), but in fact neither is inscribed, making it unclear why the author is sure that they are wine bowls.

80. BGT 8.4a–5a.

81. BGT 7.6a–b.

82. BGT 7.7b–8a. KGT 4.59a–b identifies a quite different vessel as an "elephant beaker." It is a covered vessel with a sculpted elephant on its lid.

83. KGT 4.67a–b identifies a quite different vessel as a "settled beaker."

84. BGT 7.17a–b. See also the discussion of bottle beakers in BGT 7.19a–b. In some cases, the authors of the BGT accepted the suggestions in KGT for identification with terms used in *The Rites of Zhou*, and in other cases they did not. For instance, BGT 8.18a–19a suggests that a vessel should be identified as a "tiger libation cup," an idea first suggested by KGT 4.27a–28a. However, the BGT 6.36a–37b authors did not repeat the idea that an inscribed beaker was a "mountain beaker," as suggested in KGT 4.57a–58b.

85. Harrist 1995:257.

86. BGT 6.19a–20a.

87. BGT 10.14a–16b, although there the character is read as *gan* 干 instead of *ge* 戈.

88. BGT 1.53a–b.

89. According to a search of the digital version of the SKQS, Wang Anshi is cited twenty-four times in the BGT, and the *Rites of Zhou* fifty-four times (*Zhou guan* forty-eight times and *Zhou li* six times).

90. BGT 14.4b–5a.

91. No extant books include such essays, but there is always the possibility that books that had such essays were available in Song times but have not survived. I have not found any references to specific titles that would be likely candidates, however.

92. BGT 1.3a–b. Modern archaeology confirms the practice of numbered sets of vessels but not the practice of making them of gold or silver.

93. BGT 1.6a–7b and 1.29a–32b.

94. The Gui cauldron is discussed in BGT 1.14a–16a, but the Xin cauldron is not in BGT (perhaps there has been a copyist error here).

95. BGT 1.3b–4a. The last two vessels mentioned are in BGT 1.42a–43b and 1.52a–53b.

96. BGT 1.4a–5b.

97. RZSB 14.181–82, san 13.565–67, discussed in Rudolph 1963:170–71. On the other hand, Hong Mai also appreciated the way BGT had corrected earlier commentators' mistaken understandings of vessels. See RZSB san 13.564–65.

98. BGT 15.23a–b; compare to 15.22a–b; Chen Fangmei 1989:76; L. Chang 1999:7–8; and K. C. Chang 1986:11–12.

99. XQGJ, passim.

100. See in particular *Record of an Ancient Mirror* (Gujing ji; GJJ). On this story, see Koffler 1995; Warner 2002–3; and J. Chen 2004a, 2004b.

101. MXBT 19.630, 19.634–35; discussed in Needham 1962:93–95.

102. Only one dated mirror is included in *Antiquities Illustrated* (BGT 29.16a–b). This mirror is illustrated in appendix 1 (fig. A.7). In a few cases, mirrors are dated in the catalogue as Han that would today be dated to the Tang period. See in particular BGT 29.27b, 29.28a, 29.30a–33b.

103. For similar inscriptions, see also Karlgren 1934:38–39; Loewe 1979:194–95; and J. Chou 2000:56. There are also mirrors that have a similar decoration to this one (that is, with seven bosses or "stars" with creatures between them). See Bulling 1960, plates 46–51.

104. To translate *yi,* Karlgren 1934 prefers "may you have," while Loewe 1979:192–202 consistently uses "fitting."

105. Much has been written about the design of these mirrors. See Yang 1947; Cammann 1948; Loewe 1979:60–85; and Loewe 1982:117–18. For a dissent, see Brashier 1995. There are many surviving mirrors with similar inscriptions to the mirror in figure 6.25. See Karlgren 1934:30–33; Loewe 1979:196–97; and J. Chou 2000:44.

106. For other similar examples, see Bulling 1960: plate 75–79.

107. The three *shang* elements are copper, lead, and tin. *Shang* here just means "metal," on the basis of five phases correlations and the note *shang.* See S. Cahill 1986 or Karlgren 1934:52–55.

108. BGT 28.13b. This inscription is very close to Karlgren 1934's number 177 (pp. 55–57), and I have largely followed his interpretation, thus in a few cases reading the characters differently than the editors of the BGT.

109. See Cammann 1953 and Thompson 1967.

110. See Sturman 1990, Bickford 2002–3, and Egan 2006a.

111. BGT 28.26a–29b.

112. For concerns about the inauspiciousness of objects from graves, see the controversy over the presentation of an ancient bronze to the throne in 1099 by the imperial clansman Zhonghu. CB 516.12283; JSL 11.4a; BGT 2.5a.

113. Eugene Wang described the ornamental design of Han mirrors as having evolved "from a more regulated symbolic order to a rollicking riot of immortals. It became increasingly saturated with an overall Later Han ethos: the collective yearning for immortality and the fantasy about the paradise presided over by the Queen Mother of the West" (1994:512). For accounts of the Daoist side of mirrors as observed in the nineteenth century, see Doolittle 1865 1:150–51, 2:313, 316–17; Hirth 1906:229; and de Groot 1892–1910, vol. 6:1000–1005.

114. Trans. Schipper 1993:171.

115. Schipper and Verellen 2004:618–19; BGT 30.14a. For scholars who stress the Daoist side of mirrors, see Kaltenmark 1974, Schafer 1978–79, and S. Cahill 1986. For a scholar who takes a more cautious approach, see Stephen Little, who wrote, "While mirrors are not Taoist per se, they are significant in a Taoist context because they give visual form to the basic principles underlying the structure of the cosmos in ancient China" (Little 2000:140).

116. On *Cloudy Bookcase,* see Boltz 1987:229–31. Part of the section on mirrors comes from a Tang Daoist text titled "The Scripture of the Essentials of the Clear Mirror," which gives brief instructions on techniques of meditation using mirrors, and the Six Dynasties text "Most High True Scripture of the Clear Mirror." On these texts, see Schipper and Verellen 2004:343, 97–98.

117. Schipper and Verellen 2004:97. On use of mirrors in tantric and other Buddhist practice, see Strickmann 2002:215–17, 277–79; and E. Wang 2005:247–62.

118. BGT 28.27a–b. Cf. BGT 28.29a–b. Similar inscriptions are found in Karlgren 1934:65–67; Swallow 1937:21; Loewe 1979:198–99; and J. Chou 2000:6, 45.

119. BGT 28.14a–b.

120. BGT 28.7 a–b. The translation "fitting for the market" is based on Karlgren's (1934) reading of similar phrases rather than the deciphering offered in the BGT (which has 木 instead of 市). It is not entirely clear where this inscription begins, since it circles the mirror with no break and does not start with a standard phrase. I have adopted the reading in DHWJ 32.38a.

121. This is evident in Karlgren 1934, as he often cites several divergent readings by Chinese and Japanese scholars and proposes yet another alternative. His analysis shows that Huizong's scholars made many mistakes, for instance reading the seal form of 無 as 典, and 其 as 與. These errors continued into modern times, as the Han seal forms of these characters were very close to each other.

122. Huang Bosi does briefly discuss two mirror inscriptions in DGYL 1.50b–51a.

123. Reference to the Yellow Emperor making fifteen mirrors is found in "The Record of a Magic Mirror." See Koffler 1995:178, 193n10; and J. Chen 2004b:34n5.

124. According to the appendix to *The Book of Changes,* the five numbers of heaven are the odd numbers 1, 3, 5, 7, and 9, and the five numbers of earth are the even numbers 2, 4, 6, 8, and 10.

125. ZL 36.23a. Cf. Biot 1851 2:381.

126. Based loosely on TPGJ 231.1771–72.

127. From XJZJ 3.97. This mirror was supposed to be four feet tall and five feet nine inches wide, and could be used to see internal ailments as well as feelings. The First Qin emperor had used it to detect disloyalty among palace ladies. This story is also given in TPGJ 403.3246–47.

128. *Fushui* mirrors were mentioned in *The Rites of Zhou.* They came to be associated with using mirrors to concentrate sunlight to start fires. See Needham 1962:87–89.

129. BGT 28.4a–6b.

CHAPTER 7

XHSP 1.6.

1. ShuS 14–15. See also Y. Tseng 1993:257–59. The text is translated in Chang and Frankel 1995.

2. W. Fong 1999:35–37. For a similar assessment, see National Palace Museum 1981:104. For a less positive assessment of this piece as a work of calligraphy, see Y. Tseng 1993:258. She writes that compared to the great Tang calligraphers, Sun's writing "appears thin and frail" and that he "handles the brush intellectually rather than emotionally." For a formal analysis of Sun's calligraphy in the piece, see also Goepper 1992.

3. See appendix 1 on the history of this text.

4. On the origins of calligraphy as an art in the Later Han period, see Nylan 1999.

5. On the connections between social standing and calligraphy, see Ledderose 1986 and Goldberg 1988–89.

6. On early aesthetic theory and its application to both literature and calligraphy, see Z. Cai 2004a. Although there are only a few translations of texts on calligraphy into English (see especially Chang and Frankel 1995), quite a few scholars have discussed the development of this literature and have quoted many significant passages. An overview of the full tradition is found in W. Fong 1999. Many translations are also interspersed in Driscoll and Toda 1935 and Y. Tseng 1993. For studies of particular aspects or stages of calligraphy theory and criticism, see Barnhart 1964, Chaves 1977, Hay 1983, and Egan 1989, 2004. For brief synopses of some of the key texts, see McNair 1987.

7. They did, however, sometimes doubt rubbings said to come from ancient artifacts, as these could be forged without actually casting a bronze (one could simply carve an inscription into clay and make the rubbing from the clay tablet without ever having to make a bronze vessel). Note also that once *Antiquities Illustrated* circulated widely in Ming and Qing times, forgers used it to make plausible-looking bronze vessels. See L. Chang 1999, 2000.

8. Most studies of calligraphy include a discussion of copies and forgeries. See in particular Zürcher 1955; S. Fu 1977:1–39; Ledderose 1979:33–39; and Harrist 2004.

9. This is also the format used for the painting catalogue, and since both were done at about the same time, it is not clear whether one was modeled on the other or the format was arrived at after considering the needs of both collections.

10. Lothar Ledderose, for instance, analyzed Mi Fu's understanding of Wang Xizhi (Ledderose 1979). Shen Fu examined the reception of Yan Zhenqing's works in later centuries (S. Fu 1987). Ronald Egan examined shifting standards for judging calligraphers from Tang to Northern Song times (Egan 1989). Hui-liang Chu brought attention to the renewed interest in Zhong You in the late Northern Song (H. Chu 1990). Amy McNair looked at the ways Song scholars made the Tang master Yan Zhenqing serve their purposes (McNair 1990, 1998). Peter Sturman examined Song scholars' approaches to the Tang master of the cursive script, Zhang Xu (Sturman 1999). Adele Schlombs analyzed later uses and understandings

of the Tang cursive master and monk Huaisu (Schlombs 1998). Eugene Wang looked at early Tang uses of Wang Xizhi (E. Wang 1999).

11. McNair 1994; McNair 1998:5; C. K. Ho 1996. There are also modern reproductions of Song copies of this work, such as STCHGT.

12. Rong Geng 1980:1–11.

13. Ledderose 1979; Goldberg 1988–89.

14. McNair 1994:213–15.

15. Egan 1989:382–84. On the notion that moral character is expressed through art, see also J. Cahill 1960b:130.

16. McNair 1998:79–82. On Huang Tingjian's attitude toward Wang Xizhi, see S. Fu 1976:202–4.

17. S. Fu 1976:199–217; McNair 1998:90–91; Sturman 1997:121–72; Ledderose 1979:58; H. Chu 1990, especially pp. 57–58 and 95–106.

18. Sturman 1997:157–58, 28; McNair 1995:107; GCSB 10.5a–6a.

19. Rong Geng 1980:67–108; Ma Ziyun 1985; McNair 1995. No complete copy of the original rubbing set has survived, nor even very many incomplete sets. A recent reprint puts together chapters from five incomplete sets. See DGTQLT and its postface.

20. The late Ming *Yuqingzhai tie* has one piece by Wang Xizhi with Huizong's seals that are not in the XHSP. See Onoe et al. 1954–68 4:79. Similarly, the eighteenth-century SXTFT (ce 8) has a piece by Fan Zhongyan with Huizong's seals, but Fan is not in the XHSP. SXTFT also has a Wang Xizhi not in the XHSP but with Huizong's seals (cf. Onoe et al. 1954–68 4:184).

21. Eighty-four of the 419 pieces in the *Chunhua Model Letters* are in the *Xuanhe Calligraphy Catalogue.* Of course, not all 419 pieces would necessarily have been in the imperial collection in 992. Some could have been borrowed from other collectors. One modern scholar has speculated that some could have been based on earlier rubbings rather than originals, though there is nothing in the primary sources to indicate this. See C. H. Ho 1996:60n4.

22. TWSCT 4.78–79.

23. 1220 works are listed by title; however, a different total (1259) is reached by adding together the number of works mentioned at the end of each artist's biography. In other words, sometimes a biography will end with a statement such as "the palace currently has eight of his works," then list only seven. There are also ambiguous entries that complicate counting and could account for some but not all discrepancies.

24. See, for instance, the entry for Yan Zhenqing in XHSP 3.24–25; translated in McNair 1998:136–37.

25. FSYL 1. 5–8, 1.8–11, 1.11–13, 2.26–32.

26. The fifth had fifteen; the sixth, eighteen; the seventh, twenty; the eighth, fifteen; and the ninth, twenty-three.

27. FSYL 3.43–49, 5.77–6.100.

28. On this text, see Escande 1997.

29. The exception is Shen Chuanshi (769–827). The Tang list in the *Model Letters* was much shorter; only fourteen men were included. Still, three of them do not appear in Huizong's catalogue.

30. Egan 1989:385–92.

31. Wang Yuanjun 1995:10–12; HYMY 2; Sturman 1999:207, 215; XHSP 1.3–4, 3.26, 6.48, 18.139, 19.149.

32. SSWJ 69.2192, 2187 (the latter trans. Sturman 1997:33). By contrast, Ouyang Xiu wrote that "Li Jianzhong was pure, scrupulous, gentle, and refined. Those who appreciate his calligraphy do so together with appreciation of his character" (Sturman 1997:26). And Huang Tingjian wrote of him as "standing above the crowd; full, without any excess flesh, like a worldly beauty who is plump but with a fine and elegant manner" (S. Fu 1976:198).

33. Egan 1989:417; S. Fu 1976:210. In the same passage he similarly criticized Xue Ji and Shen Quanshi, who were left out of the XHSP.

34. The term "critics" does not always refer to Su Shi or one of his followers. Often it refers to Zhu Changwen or Zhang Huaiguan. On the other hand, critics other than Su and his followers are mentioned by name from time to time. For instance, the entry on Shi Yannian cites by name both Fan Zhongyan and Ouyang Xiu. Li Bo and Dou Ji are mentioned in the entry for Huaisu, and Han Yu is cited by name in the entry for Gao Xian (XHSP 6.48, 19.147, 19.149).

35. Ledderose 1979:28; based on FSYL 3.38–43.

36. Based on Rong Geng 1980:8–10; and Ledderose 1979:116–18.

37. HMZ 207.

38. DGYL 1.35a–b.

39. For the opinion of those publishing them that these are early copies, see Onoe et al. 1954–68 4:167; Nakata 1979–82 1:206; Nakata 1983:169; Jiang Zhaoshen 1989:16; Gugong et al. 2002:47, and so on.

40. S. Fu 1977:82; Harrist and Fong 1999:92.

41. Harrist 1999:253–56.

42. These three works are among the works by Wang Xizhi illustrated in the recent Chinese book (Wang Jingxian 1986) along with the eight works of ink on paper listed in appendix 3.

43. For instance, Schlombs 1998:143–46 rejects Huaisu's *Lunshu* (however, C. K. Ho 1994:98 sees it as a genuine work of his early period). Similarly McNair 1998:139 labels Yan Zhenqing's *Zhushan* and *Huzhou* "not genuine" (Gugong et al. 2002:127 agrees on *Huzhou*; Yang Renkai 1989:40 agrees on *Zhushan*). Sturman 1999:215 disputes the attribution to Zhang Xu of the Four Poems, an attribution Yang Renkai (1999:58–59) defends.

44. On these works, see Schlombs 1998:50–72 and McNair 1998:44–50.

45. Zhou Mi (1232–1308) thought that Zhangzong probably did; see Weitz 2002:73.

46. Nakata 1977–95, vols. 5 and 6, passim.

47. Based on TGSB 2.9a.

48. The reference to watching the summer clouds comes from Lu Yu's biography of Huaisu. See QTW 433.16. The reference to attaining enlightenment from it is attributed to Sikong Tu in another XHSP entry (see XHSP 19.178).

49. Based on Mi Fu's description of Huaisu. See Nakata 1977–95 4:460n281.

50. On what basis Zhang attributed this to Yan Zhenqing is unclear. Huaisu in his own *Autobiography* attributes it to Li Zhou. See Pan Yungao 1997:232.

51. XSD 82.

52. The authors apparently confused the calligrapher-monk Huaisu with another monk named Huaisu who had a biography in the *Song Gao seng zhuan*. This other monk lived in the seventh century, had the family name Fan, and did in fact study with Xuanzang. See SGSZ 14.334–35; Schlombs 1998:8.

53. See the sources identified for the similar phrases in the quotation above from Huaisu's biography in Zhu Changwen's *Continued Calligraphy Standards* (see note 47 above).

54. These poems survive, and all were recorded in the Southern Song. See SYJH 17.1b–5a, 17.16a–b.

55. Huaisu used this phrase himself in his autobiography (Pan Yungao 1997:232). It was first used in a Tang poem by Zhang Wei to refer to Zhang Xu (QTS 197.6).

56. From Huaisu's *Autobiography.*

57. Nakata 1977–95 6:199n16 identifies Qin Guan as a possible source for this remark.

58. Lu Yu mentioned his drinking. See QTW 433.15a.

59. XHSP 19.146–47.

60. XSD 134–35.

61. Based on Ouyang Xiu's GTL 1.12.

62. Based on Su Shi's comment in SSWJ 69.2187.

63. Based on Huang Tingjian's comments in SGTB 5.50.

64. I have not identified the critics referred to in this sentence.

65. XHSP 6.46–47. Both the XSD and the XHSP, after discussing Song Shou, go on to discuss his son Minqiu.

66. SS 291.9732–36. Nor does it draw from the earlier DDSL 57.1a–3a.

67. Li Jianzhong's own entry (XHSP 12.90) presents him more favorably.

68. Ouyang Xiu did much the same thing in his *Collected Antiquities* when he knew nothing of the creator of a calligraphy. See Egan 1989:373–74.

69. XHSP 11.88. For similar cases in which the main thing the authors knew about a man was that he had followed Zhong You's style, see XHSP 4.32 and 5.38. In each case they compare the man unfavorably to Zhong You.

70. XHSP 8.63–64.

71. XHSP 18.141.

72. XHSP 19.148–49.

73. XHSP 2.11.

74. XHSP 2.11.

75. OYXQJ Jigulu bawei 1.1099. Nakata 1977–95 5:61n9 points out that the editors of the XHSP are misleading when they imply that this Qin inscription shows small seal script was used as early as King Mu, when the text itself dates from a later king who reigned from 338 to 311 BCE.

76. Both have entries in the catalogue; see XHSP 2.15, 2.16. The prince was Huizong's uncle (Shenzong's younger brother).

77. XHSP 2.11–12. On Wu Guang the Immortal and the "bending leek seal script," see Nakata 1977–95 5:61nn18–19.

78. For an example of Mengying's invented forms, see Y. Tseng 1993:59 (fig. 3.71b).

79. The original is in SJZ 16.550. SD 88–89 relates this story and expresses doubts about its probability.

80. XHSP 2.16–17.

81. XHSP 3.19.

82. XHSP 3.19–20.

83. XHSP 7.54–55.

84. On theories of the meaning of *zhang* cursive, see F. Wang 1987.

85. XHSP 13.99–100. "Copyist style" referred to the style used in the Hanlin Academy to write out government documents. See SCSSLY 50.654. Because *yuanti* has been translated "palace style," one might think Huizong's curators would feel obligated to defend it, but the

term referred to the style used by low-ranking functionaries in the palace to copy government documents, and neither Huizong nor his curators saw themselves as assembling a collection of the work of anonymous copyists but rather work by creative artists.

86. Cai's essay, called "Discussions on Calligraphy" (Fashu lun), is still extant. For the passage referred to here, see FSL 155.

87. XHSP 20.158.

88. On the other hand, Huizong's catalogue was not the final word on the meaning of *bafen*, and in the Southern Song, Chen Si still wrote of Cai Yong in the Eastern Han as excelling at *bafen* script (SXS 283).

89. XHSP 2.14.

90. XHSP 11.84–85.

91. SSF 85–86.

92. XHSP 1.7–8.

93. From Zhou Yue's *Gujin fashu yuan*, identified by Nakata 1977–95 5:34n45.

94. SSF 86.

95. XHSP 1.3–4.

96. OYXQJ Jigulu bawei 6.1166; ShuS 27.

97. National Palace Museum 1977 2:4–5.

98. XHSP 2.16–17, 20.161, 20.162.

99. XHSP 10.80–81. For other comparable examples, see XHSP 9.74–75.

100. Egan 1989:374–76, 2006b:35–37; C. H. Ho 1996:72; Sturman 1997:32–33.

101. XHSP 4.31–32. For other examples, see XHSP 9.74–75, 10.81, 11.87.

102. XHSP 9.76. For other examples, see XHSP 3.24–25, 8.66, 19.76.

103. XHSP 9.73. For other examples, see XHSP 5.37, 6.45–46.

104. XHSP 19.153.

105. On this calligraphy, see Li Meiling 2004.

106. See Ledderose 1984.

107. SD and SSF have entries for only Zhiyong and one other monk, Zhiguo. XSD has an entry for Huaisu and the Song monk Mengying.

108. For a translation of this passage, see Hartman 1986:222–23.

109. See Gimello 1992, Grant 1994. Su Shi did argue against Han Yu's point of view, asserting that the artist need not abandon emptiness and quietude, and could use them to gain greater insight into both the world and himself (Egan 1989:407–8). Liu Jing, a collector and friend of Mi Fu, wrote a text that does not survive that at least briefly characterized several monk calligraphers, comparing Huaisu to jade, Chongguang to pearls, Gaoxian to gold, Guanxiu to gems, and Yaqi to crystal (XHSP 19.152).

110. XHSP 19.151.

111. XHSP 6.50–51.

112. XHSP 5.41.

113. XHSP 2.14.

114. XHSP 11.85.

115. He is not in SHY (according to Wang Deyi 1978) and does not appear in any of the Song *wenji* included in the SKQS, according to the electronic index.

116. SS 320.10397–401. On Cai Xiang, see also McNair 1986.

117. XHSP 6.47.

118. The allusions are to SSWJ 69.2182, 69.2187.

119. XHSP 12.96.

120. Mi Fu also studied the calligraphy of Shen Chuanshi. See Sturman 1997:48. For a fuller description of the evolution of Cai Jing's style, see TWSCT 4.76–78.

121. On the occasion when Cai Jing did this calligraphy, with Mi Fu present, see TWSCT 4.78. To some at the time, writing large characters smacked of professional calligraphers. Li Gonglin reportedly refused to write large characters on that ground (HJ 9.410; trans. Maeda 1970b:57).

122. See earlier discussion of Cai Xiang.

123. See XHSP 15.117, which records that Wang Xizhi once took six plantain fans from an old woman and wrote five characters on each, assuring her that if she told people he had done the writing she could ask 100 cash each for them. In fact, she found people competing for them.

124. XHSP 12.92–93.

125. For another example, see National Palace Museum 1981:17.

126. See Ebrey 2006b.

CHAPTER 8

From the entry for Cao Zhongyuan in the *Xuanhe Painting Catalogue*, which borrows language from a poem by Su Shi. XHHP 3.74. For Su Shi's poem, see SSSJ 29.1522; Egan 1994:298.

1. Nearly life-size illustrations are found in Gugong 1978 1:34–35 and Gugong et al. 2002:57–61. Scholars today believe this is a later painting done in an archaic style, possibly a copy of a Tang work. See H. Wu 1997:64; and Thorp and Vinograd 2001:219.

2. XHHP 1.33. Curiously, Zhan's entry does not list this painting.

3. HJ 1.263.

4. It is difficult to distinguish paintings that Huizong inherited from those he acquired. Probably most of the paintings done by court painters who had served under earlier Song emperors, such as Huang Jucai or Cui Bo, were inherited, but many artists who served at court did not do so their entire careers, and paintings by them also circulated in the art market. See P. Foong 2006 for the example of Guo Xi. Evidence that a particular painting was in the palace before Huizong's time is scarce. Wai-kam Ho (1980:15–19) has argued that two paintings with a seal reading "Shangshu sheng yin" must have entered the palace between 1083 and 1126. These are the Li Cheng in Kansas City and the Juran in Cleveland. He does not explain, however, why this seal is never seen on works with Huizong's seals.

5. The literature on Chinese painting theory in English is quite large. Translations of key texts can be found in Sirén 1936; Sakanishi 1939; Soper 1949, 1951, 1958; Acker 1954, 1974; Y. Lin 1967; Maeda 1970b; Bush 1971; Bush and Shih 1985; Munakata 1974; and Lachman 1989. There is also a large scholarly literature analyzing Chinese painting theory. See, for instance, Soper 1976, J. Cahill 1960b and 1961, Ledderose 1973 and 1983, Bush and Murck 1983, Murck and Fong 1991. Some recent studies include Bush 2004, Z. Cai 2004b, Egan 2004 and 2006b, and Mair 2004.

6. Acker 1954, 1974.

7. See Lachman 1989.

8. THJWZ 1.20–22; trans. Soper 1951:10–12. See also Shen Gua's comments on close observation in MXBT 17.541.

9. Bush and Shih 1985:196.

10. Bickford 1996a:101; Harrist 1998:18, 22–25.

11. XHHP 1.21.

12. XHHP 10.164; trans. Bush and Shih 1985:119–20, supplemented. Parts of the introductions to other sections are also translated in Bush and Shih 1985:103–29, passim.

13. See HJ 10.418 (Maeda 1970b:61–62) for Deng Chun's account of Huizong's disinterest in the large number of paintings by Guo Xi that he had inherited but had had moved to a storehouse. He eventually let Deng Chun's grandfather take some of them. The XHHP 11.191–92 does not exclude Guo Xi, but has only thirty paintings by him.

14. THJWZ 1.50–51; Soper 1951:21–22.

15. H. Kohara 1995:14. This is also largely true of Su Shi. See Egan 2006b:170–74.

16. It is true that in both catalogues a handful of men produced a disproportionate share of the works. In the calligraphy catalogue just six men (3 percent) accounted for 45 percent of the collection, more extreme than in the painting catalogue, in which the top 3 percent (seven men) accounted for 29 percent of the collection.

17. Maggie Bickford (2007) suggests that Huizong might well have had court painters produce paintings that could be attributed to famous painters whose works were no longer extant, toward the goal of having a complete collection, one that could be used to narrate the story of Chinese painting. Perhaps he filled some gaps this way, but he does not seem to have done so systematically, since he does not have entries for all of the pre-Tang painters ranked highest by earlier authorities. (Only four of the nine painters that Li Sizhen in the late seventh century put in the upper three ranks are in the *Xuanhe Painting Catalogue*; see XHPL). By contrast, top-rated Tang painters whose works did circulate in the Northern Song (according to Mi Fu's mention of them) are quite well represented in the *Xuanhe Catalogue*.

18. Another interesting observation about temporal distribution is that many of the Tang painters lived during the reign of the Tang emperor Xuanzong, including Zhou Fang, Wu Daoxuan (Wu Daozi), Wang Wei, Han Gan, and Lu Lengqie. In fact, the catalogue includes more than two dozen depictions of Xuanzong and members of his court, such as his consort Yang Guifei, done by twelve painters. The most prolific were Zhang Xuan with seven, Zhou Fang with four, Han Gan with three, and Zhou Wenju and Wang Fei with two each. See XHHP 5.105, 5.106, 5.109, 6.112, 6.114, 6.116, 7.123, 7.127, 8.144, 8.152, 10.166, and 13.222.

19. For an illustration of the full painting, see McCausland 2003:64–84.

20. Several other figure painters, including Yan Liben, were classed under religious paintings, even though a majority of their listed paintings were not religious. An example of Yan Liben's work listed in the *Xuanhe Catalogue* (XHHP 1.38) is *Taizong in the Sedan Chair* (see plate 34, or Gugong et al. 2002:87–95). Another example is Sun Wei, whose *Lofty Scholars* is also listed in XHHP 2.58. For an illustration of it, see Gugong et al. 2002:129–45.

21. See the chapters in McCausland 2003. The evidence that the painting had been in Huizong's collection is not only that it is listed in his catalogue, but also that it has one of his seals (as well as other forged seals). See Y. Wang 2003. Mi Fu was the first to refer to this painting as a work by Gu, and he may have been the one to make the attribution. See Murck 2003.

22. For the full work, with details reproduced full size, see Gugong 1978:58–69. Sirén

1956 1:118–19 thinks this painting is a Song work, and J. Cahill 1980:16 suggests Southern Song.

23. XHHP 2.53.

24. For an example of a Song Buddhist work that seems, on the basis of his seals, to have been in Huizong's collection, see the anonymous Śakyamuni in the National Palace Museum in Taipei, which has been published in several places, the best of which is in National Palace Museum 2000:82–83. Since there is no title attributing this painting to a particular artist, it is possible that it is listed in Huizong's catalogue under an artist who can no longer be identified.

25. XHHP 5.106.

26. For the full painting, see T. Wu 1997:56–57. The other copy of a Zhang Xuan painting, titled *Lady Guoguo on an Outing*, is in the Liaoning Provincial Museum. For an illustration, see plate 16 or Shanghai shuhua chubanshe 2004:32–40.

27. T. Wu 1997:141–43. Other works by painters classed as figure painters likely to have been in Huizong's collection include *Literary Gathering*, attributed to Han Huang, in the Palace Museum, Beijing; *Groom and Horse*, attributed to Hao Cheng, in the Boston Museum of Fine Arts; and *Inspecting a Horse,* attributed to Zhao Yan, in the Shanghai Museum. In all of these cases, the painting may well have been made in Song times (perhaps as a copy of an earlier work), but has Huizong's seals or inscription or was listed in his catalogue. The Hao Cheng was illustrated in chapter 4 (fig. 4.7). For illustrations of the other two, see Gugong 1978:44–45; and Jin Weinuo 1984:113.

28. On this painting see Barnhart 1993.

29. XHHP 8.142–43.

30. On this painting, see J. Cahill 1982 and H. Liu 2002. Huizong's title to this painting is missing, so whether or not he attributed it to Wei Xian is not clear, but Wei Xian is the only artist in the catalogue with a painting titled *Waterwheel*, which led later scholars to attribute the painting to him. The attribution to Wei Xian has recently been questioned because of what seems to be a signature in the margin (see H. Liu 2002).

31. HHS 83.2768. Another artist listed under architecture, Guo Zhongshu (910–977), has a painting attributed to him, *Traveling on the River in Clearing Snow*, that has Huizong seals. For a good illustration, see National Palace Museum 1989:127. For a discussion, see Barnhart 1997:102–4.

32. XHHP 8.147–48.

33. XHHP 8.148. For a reproduction of the full painting, see Gugong 1978:76–79. Another painting attributed to Hu Gui is held in Taipei. See National Palace Museum 1995a:95–100. This painting has been extant since the twelfth century (see Loehr 1961:253 for the 1145 colophon). A painting attributed to the Khitan Li Zanhua, another of the artists listed in this category, is held in the Museum of Fine Arts in Boston. See T. Wu 1997:50–52. All of these are likely to be Song copies and thus could have been done at Huizong's court.

34. XHHP 9.157, 162. See Barnhart 1997:118 for an illustration of the full handscroll and a discussion of it. The painting does not have Huizong's seals.

35. For a full, large reproduction, see National Palace Museum 1993:50–55.

36. XHHP 11.193. On this painting, see Hay 1972. Another extant Five Dynasties landscape listed in the XHHP is Dong Yuan's *Awaiting a Crossing at the Mountain Pass in Summer* in the Liaoning Provincial Museum. See XHHP 11.180–81; and Gugong et al. 2002:217–27.

37. For the full painting, see Gugong et al. 2002:299–305.

38. XHHP 12.203–4. On this painting, see Barnhart 1997:125. Other Song landscape paintings with strong evidence of having been Huizong's collection are another painting by Wang Shen (plate 9) and *Summer Mountains*, in the Metropolitan Museum, attributed to Qu Ding (see W. Fong 1975).

39. XHHP 14.236–37. For the full painting, see Gugong et al. 2002:347–67; for discussions of it, see B. Xu 1964; Edwards 1993; and Barnhart 1997:113. Another Song copy is the painting ascribed to Han Gan in the National Palace Museum, which Wang Yaoting believes was done by Huizong himself. See National Palace Museum 1993:25; and Y. Wang 2003:198.

40. For a full illustration, see Fu Xinian 1988:15–17 or Yu Jianhua and Chen Songlin 1999:74–75. This painting has Zhangzong title and seals, adding to the likelihood that it was in Huizong's collection. For an example of a painting of a cat and monkey by Yi Yuanji, which has Huizong's seal and inscription, see plate 15.

41. A good illustration is in National Palace Museum 1993:68–69 and 2000:112–13. See also the painting attributed to Huang Jucai's father, Huang Quan, illustrated in chapter 9 (plates 35 and 36).

42. XHHP 17.268.

43. See Gugong 1981:52–59 for a full reproduction. On this painting, see P. Lin 1996.

44. XHHP 20.312.

45. XHHP 20.318.

46. On the prevalence of Song copies among the works that stand in for the great names in Chinese painting history, see Bickford 2004.

47. SHY Zhiguan 18.22b; HJ 1.266–67.

48. For the full painting, see National Palace Museum 1993:127. On this painting, see also Yi Ruofen 2006. The National Palace Museum also has two handscrolls (NPM 1995a:351–64) that clearly make use of several elements of this scroll and bear even more calligraphy purporting to be by Huizong and Cai Jing, but this calligraphy is much less likely to be authentic, suggesting that these scrolls are later works with forged inscriptions.

49. XHHP 7.130.

50. HJ 1.270.

51. HJ 1.263. Several paragraphs later Deng Chun mentions another collection of paintings with a similar title (called *Xuanhe ruilance* instead of *Xuanhe ruilanji*). The second set consisted of pictures of auspicious objects, the pictures made during Huizong's reign, and so is clearly a different work than the one mentioned earlier that ended with the early Song painter Huang Jucai. In the Yuan period, Tang Hou, author of *Huajian*, seems to have conflated these two references, referring only to the second, but taking the number of items from the first. Many scholars have discussed the albums of auspicious images (e.g., Sturman 1990:36; T. Wu 1997:140–41; and Bickford 2002 3:85–88), but I have not come across comparable analysis of what the first-mentioned albums must have been like. Ecke 1972:97–101 translates the entire passage but does not provide any analysis.

52. Barnhart 1997:113; T. Wu 1997:143; H. Wu 1997:76.

53. See Ledderose 1973.

54. Murck 2007.

55. Of the more plausible paintings with Huizong's seals listed in appendix 2, only three have signatures: the Liang Shimin handscroll (fig. 8.6), Li Gonglin's copy of Wei Yan's *Pasturing Horses* (plate 11), and Huang Quan's *Studies from Nature* (plates 35 and 36), all of which are Song-period paintings.

56. There are two paintings with Li Yu's attribution on them (Han Gan's *Night Shining White*, fig. 3.1, and Zhao Gan's *Along the River at First Snow*, fig. 8.3). See Chen Baozhen 1997. Of course, inscriptions that attributed a painting to a living artist were an entirely different matter, and presumably were based on direct personal knowledge.

57. TCMHL 111; trans. Soper 1958:222–23, modified.

58. LDMHJ 239–40; trans. Acker 1974:248–49, modified.

59. From a poem by Wang Changling in QTS 143.1445.

60. QTS 219.2306.

61. XHHP 5.106. See also the comparisons of the XHHP entry on Dong Yuan to earlier texts by Guo Ruoxu, Shen Gua, and Mi Fu in Barnhart 1970:23–26.

62. Many other examples of the ways the XHHP went beyond earlier authorities can be seen by skimming through Chen Gaohua 1984 and 1987, which assemble texts by successive authorities on leading painters.

63. XHHP 3.67.

64. XHHP 6.117.

65. XHHP 13.229.

66. XHHP 10.192.

67. See R. Wilhelm 1967:8.

68. See Legge 1961 4:400–401.

69. See Watson 1968:80.

70. From Liu Xiang's *Xinxu*; XX zashi 5.190.

71. The story is recorded in LDMHJ 200–201; Acker 1974:19; and repeated in Cao's entry in XHHP 5.99.

72. XHHP 9.154. I have made use of the partial translation in Bush and Shih 1985:115–16; but with many modifications. Xu Bai appears in THJWZ 4.172; and Soper 1951:70.

73. XHHP 10.164 (trans. Bush and Shih 1985:119), 15.239.

74. For instance, there were twenty-three references to *yizhe* 議者 in the calligraphy catalogue, compared to nine in the painting catalogue; there were twelve references to critics using the term *ping* 評 in the calligraphy catalogue, but only one in the painting catalogue.

75. Discussions of the aesthetic ideas in the *Xuanhe Painting Catalogue* include Bush 1971:74–82; Jin Weinuo 1980; Jie Han 1990; Chen Xiang 1992; Xiao Baifang 1994; and Yi Ruofen 1999.

76. For an example of borrowing from Su Shi, see the quotation at the opening of this chapter; for more, see Yi Ruofen 1999. An example of borrowing from Huang Tingjian is found in the entry for Zhao Lingrang. Compare the text in XHHP 20.306 and SGTB 3.30.

77. H. Kohara 1995:17.

78. HS 193, 205, 202, 192, 203, 198.

79. H. Kohara 1995 suggests that Mi Fu's dismissal of most of the paintings attributed to famous men like Li Cheng may have made him unwelcome, since Huizong's collection, in time at least, had many of them.

80. See XHHP 1.31, 2.46, 2.57–58, 3.69, 5.99.

81. XHHP 13.221–22. A more abbreviated version of the first story is found in LDMHJ 242; Acker 1974:262. Either Huizong's cataloguers embellished the story or, more likely, they had another source no longer extant. The second story is based on YYZZ xu 2.214.

82. XHHP 12.211. For other examples of similar language, see XHHP 10.179, 11.180, 11.182, 11.190, 11.195, 12.204, 12.205, 12.217, 19.300, 20.307–8.

83. XHHP 8.144, 3.74, 2.56.

84. XHHP 15.248.

85. Du Fu's poem is in QTS 221.2334. Stuart Sargent (1992:289) explains these references in this way: "It is [Du Fu]'s 'Trussed Chicken,' in which the poet tells of coming upon a young servant about to take a trussed-up chicken off to market because he dislikes seeing the bird kill insects around the house. Apparently the boy feels sorry for the insects, but he is too young to realize what will happen to the chicken once it is sold at the market; Du Fu rails at him to release the bird, asking which is more important to people, chickens or ants? But then he muses that chickens and insects are locked into an unending chain of 'winning and losing,' and he ends his poem gazing fixedly at a building by a hill over the frigid river, as if to suggest that there is no answer."

86. Tao Qian's poem is in A. Davis 1983 1:191.

87. QTS 219.2309–10.

88. XHHP 7.131. See also the translation in Egan 2005:128.

89. Bush and Shih 1985:203; XHHP 7.131 (trans. Bush and Shih 1985:204).

90. The painting school and painting examinations are discussed many places. See Sirén 1956 2:76–78; and Li Huishu 1984.

91. On "small scenes," see P. Lin 1996.

92. XHHP 20.302 (trans. Bush and Shih 1985:128–29); SCJ Luancheng ji 17.333–34 (trans. Bush and Shih 1985:208–9).

93. SSWJ 11.367; trans. Bush and Shih 1985:220.

94. XHHP 20.310.

95. XHHP 7.130–32. For a translation of his entry, see Meyer 1923:50–55.

96. Soper 1976:38, 31–32.

97. XHHP 18.284; trans. Soper 1976:39.

98. Soper 1976:35 points out that Mi Fu also used the term "lofty and ancient" a couple of times.

99. THJWZ 3.111; Soper 1951:45–46, modified.

100. The passage in *Zhuangzi* reads, "When you're betting for tiles in an archery contest, you shoot with skill. When you're betting for fancy belt buckles, you worry about your aim. And when you're betting for real gold, you're a nervous wreck. Your skill is the same in all three cases—but because one prize means more to you than another, you let outside considerations weigh on your mind. He who looks too hard at the outside gets clumsy on the inside." See Watson 1968:201.

101. An allusion to *Han Feizi*. See HFZ 7.406–7.

102. XHHP 20.317–18.

103. See J. Cahill 1996a:166.

104. SCMHP 8–9; Lachman 1989:18–19.

105. THJWZ 115; Soper 1951:47.

106. SCMHP 51, 61, 101; Lachman 1989:53, 61, 95–96; THJWZ 4.142; Soper 1951:58.

107. On the Osaka painting, see Barnhart 1997:102, 104. On the National Palace Museum painting, see Sickman and Soper 1956:106–7, where the painting is described as "characteristic of the grand manner of early Northern Song."

108. XHHP 8.139.

109. SCMHP 1.30; Lachman 1989:38; THJWZ 3.120–21; Soper 1951:49.

110. XHHP 4.81.

111. SCMHP 75 (trans. Lachman 1989:73); THJWZ 3.129 (trans. Soper 1951:53); XHHP 11.188.

112. XHHP 11.190.

113. XHHP 18.284. It is interesting to note here that Huizong's curator Dong You had a high opinion of Cui Bo. In a colophon Dong You wrote for a painting of sparrows and cicadas by Cui, he discussed the failure of earlier critics to appreciate fully bird-and-flower paintings. He did not see why landscapes and figures should be seen as carrying more spiritual intelligence, since "every creature has its spiritual intelligence. It is just that the ignorant do not know to look for it in paintings like this" (GCHB 6.68).

114. Huang Jucai had 332, Yi Yuanji 245, Cui Bo 241, Cui Que 67, Ge Shouchang 1, and Wu Yuanyu 189. In two of these cases, the label "court painter" is a bit of a stretch. Yi accepted several commissions for Shenzong, but does not seem to have had a regular appointment as a court painter. Wu served under a prince, not in the main palace. On the other hand, two painters listed under the Five Dynasties, Huang Quan and Huang Jubao, finished their careers in Kaifeng, and some of their paintings may have been done there.

115. XHHP 15.242–43; trans. P. Lin 1994:4, slightly modified.

116. XHHP 17.275. Cf. Bickford 1996a:88–89.

117. Sirén 1936:64–66. See also Bush 1971:51–66.

118. Sometimes people mistakenly assume that those labeled *wuchen* were military officers, but many people with military rank never spent time in the army. On this system, see W. Lo 1987:27–28; or Umehara Kaoru 1985:160. On imperial relatives standing in the southern ranks, see Chaffee 1999:43–47.

119. Xiao Baifang 1991. On Song Daoist art, see also S. Huang 2002, which concentrates on the Southern Song period.

120. See the tables in Xiao Baifang 1991:164–85, 233–63. In the relatively small number of cases of painters classified under different specialties, the paintings in their specialty are listed first before their paintings on Daoist or Buddhist subjects.

121. XHHP 8.144, preface 8–9. For the allusion, see Watson 1968:134–36.

122. THJWZ 2.59; Soper 1951:25; XHHP 2.62.

123. For an illustration of the full scroll, see Little and Eichman 2000:132–37.

124. Little and Eichman 2000:132, 137; see also J. Cahill 1960a:15.

125. LDMHJ 230; Acker 1974:200–1; XHHP 1.34. In LDMHJ, this artist is called Dong Boren. In XHHP, Boren is said to be his *zi* and Zhan his *ming*. Yu Jianhua, in his notes to XHHP, argues that the Xuanhe editors were mistaken and the name should be Dong Boren.

126. See Graham 1990:34, 61–63.

127. XHHP 2.62.

128. XHHP 2.64. For a Song period depiction of this deity, see Little and Eichman 2000:240–41.

129. XHHP 4.91.

130. XHHP 4.92.

131. On the cultural accomplishments of Song clansmen, see Chaffee 1999:267–71.

132. XHHP 20.307. See also the translation in Egan 2005:133–34.

133. See J. Cahill 1980 for lists of illustrations of paintings attributed to Zhao Lingrang, Zhao Shilei, Zhao Kexiong, and Zhao Zhonghan, most of which he sees as likely of later date.

134. For the full painting, see T. Wu 1997:53. On this painting and Zhao Lingrang, see Maeda 1970a and Powers 1995:104–7.

135. XHHP 20.306; trans. Sirén 1956 2:71.

136. See Fu Xinian 1988:80–81, 23; and XHHP 16.264–65.

137. The other two were the abdicated ruler of the Southern Tang, Li Yu, and the monk Guanxiu.

138. XHSP 2.15; Nakata 1970. On Jun's interests, see also DDSL 16.5b–6a; and SS 246.8721.

139. XHHP 20.304.

140. XHHP 20:307–8.

141. XHHP 16:261–62. Xiaoying was given a name in 1085 that indicates that he was born that year or late in 1084. See SHY Dixi 3.6b–7a.

142. The *Xuanhe Calligraphy Catalogue* has an entry for only one eunuch, Cen Zongdan (XHSP 12.97–98). See the discussion of him in chapter 7.

143. On eunuchs in the Song period, see Zhang Bangwei 1993:263–303; Wang Mingsun 1981; Umehara 1985:163–65; and Hartwell 1988:21–26. For eunuch involvement in Song court art, see also H. Liu 2003:154–70.

144. XHHP 7.137.

145. XHHP 19.297–98.

146. See appendix 1.

147. See Ebrey 2006a.

148. HZL houlu 2.73. On Liang's role in art under Huizong, see Bickford 2006:505–10.

149. One possible exception: Dong You discussed a painting that had been acquired when Zeng Bu's son Yu had been found guilty of corruption and his property confiscated. But Zeng did not have a reputation as a collector, and there may not have been many paintings involved besides this one. Certainly Huizong did not claim the collections of Su Shi, Huang Tingjian, or anyone else in their circle.

150. W. Ho 1980:xxv. I am not sure how early the habit of seeing literati theory as an act of opposition to court influence can be traced. Susan Bush in 1971 noted that the eleventh-century development of scholar painting "would seem to have begun as a reaction against the more artificial conventions favored at the early Song court" (1971:6). My efforts to trace this idea earlier, however, were not successful. I did not find it in James Cahill's 1958 dissertation or 1960 article on the amateur ideal or 1960 survey on Chinese painting, nor, to go back further, Sirén's 1936 book on painting theory or his 1956 overview of painting. Soper 1957:13 opposed the two, but without clearly saying that literati art started as a reaction to court art. He wrote: "The 'literary man's style' of painting became the implacable enemy of the Academy and all its ways, the enemy of all organization, training, and planning."

151. Powers 1995:103; Bickford 1996a:102.

152. Barnhart 1993:9–10; Murck 2000.

153. Harrist 1998:18, 22–25; J. Cahill 1996b:11–12; Barnhart 1997:125; P. Foong 2000; Bickford 1996b.

154. Egan 2006b:174; S. Jang 1992.

CHAPTER 9

QHSHF 1B:31b–32a.

1. On Northern Song relations with Liao and its alliance with Jin, see G. Wang 1983, J. Tao 1983, and other chapters in Rossabi 1983; J. Tao 1988; Franke and Twitchett 1994; Twitchett and Tietze 1994.

2. SSJSBM 56.569; CBBM 146.4b–5a; SCBM 25.246–50.

3. JKCXL 1.1; CBBM 146.5b–6a.

4. JKCXL 1.1; CBBM 146.7a; SCBM 26.256.

5. SCBM 26.259–60, 27.262–64, 27.267–702, 8.275; JKCXL 1.3–6; SSJSBM 56.571–72.

6. SCBM 28.276–30.294; JKCXL 1.7–8. WZRY 53 differs on some of the figures, giving 10,000 bolts of silk and satin and omitting the camels. See also Franke 1970.

7. SCBM 32.312–13, 36.357–59; JKYL 1.18–19; JKCXL 2.13; WZRY 54–55.

8. JKYL 3.46–50, 3.55, 3.57–59, 3.62, 4.76–77, 4.81–83, 4.87–88, 5.106–7, 6.116–17, 6.123; SHY Zhiguan 69.20a–24b; SCBM 39.389–94, 48.477–79, 48.481–83, 49.491–95; 50.506–7.

9. SSJSBM 55.562–63; SCBM 52.517, 56.557–58; XNYL 1.16.

10. SSJSBM 56.579; JKCXL 2.13–14; trans. Haeger 1971:66.

11. SSJSBM 56.584–85; SCBM 58.4, 60.18; SS 335.10753.

12. SCBM 62.47–49, 63.55–58; XNYL 1.16–17; JKJW 1.

13. SCBM 63.60, 64.67–69, 65.74–75, 65.79–80; JKJW 2–4; SS 353.11137–39.

14. SCBM 65.84, 66.92; JKJW 3–4; JKYL 13.256–63; WZRY 63; SS 23.434.

15. WZRY 64–65; SSJSBM 56.591.

16. JKJW 8–9; SCBM 69.120–22.

17. SSJSBM 56.591; SCBM 69.120–27, 70.130, 70.138; JKYL 14.273–75; JKCYQY 1; JKJW 8–10; WZRY 68–69; Zhou Baozhu 1992:612.

18. JKYL 14.273; JKJW 9–10.

19. CBBM 149.1a–2b; NZLH 127; DJDFL 3.80–81; NZLH 126, 129; SCBM 70.135, 70.137; XNYL 12.244; SSJSBM 59.609; Kaplan 1970:41–56; J. Tao 1989:532–34.

20. JKJW 11–12.

21. SCBM 71.140–43; DJDFL 3.87, 4.120; NZLH 130; JKYL 14.275, 14.277–78; JKJW 12–14.

22. JKYL 14.278. DJGZ 4.65 gives different but still astronomical figures: ten million bars of gold, twenty million bars of silver, and twenty million bolts of silk. Gold was worth about fourteen times as much as silver, since a few weeks later an exchange of cash for silver was announced at 35,000 cash for an ounce of gold, 2,500 for an ounce of silver (JKJW 23).

23. SCBM 71.145–46.

24. SCBM 72.149; JKYL 14.279.

25. SCBM 72.153, 73.160, 73.163, 74.176, 77.20911, 78.211–14, 81.241–42, 81.244; JKYL 15.297, 15.302–4, 15.307.

26. SCBM 73.161–62, 99.408; JKJW 16, 18.

27. SCBM 72.159, 73.165–66; JKJW 17–19.

28. SCBM 74.172. The heir was born in 1117/10, so in 1127/1 he was nine years and two or three months.

29. NZLH 133; SCBM 74.174–75.

30. SCBM 74.175–76, 74.178, 75.197; JKYL 15.302. WZRY 78 says six million ounces of silver.

31. SCBM 96.378. One source said that a third of the students at the National Academy contracted beriberi, half eventually dying of it (SCBM 99.402).

32. SCBM 77.202–3, 77.209, 87.294; JKJW 26.

33. NZLH 136.

34. NZLH 139; SCBM 77.209–210; JKYL 15.303.

35. SCBM 76.198; XNYL 2.40–42.

36. NZLH 141; JKJW 29, 36–38; SCBM 80.232–33, 81.239, 83.258, 99.401.

37. NZLH 155–56.

38. SCBM 79.226; 81.241–42; Mattos 1988:47–48.

39. NZLH 162; JKYL 16.326, 16.331; WZRY 87; SCBM 86.286–88. The document submitted by the Kaifeng prefecture (KFFZ 121–22) gave the breakdown of what Song submitted. Altogether, 247,600 ounces of gold and 7,728,000 ounces of silver were collected, a little less than the year before. At 50 ounces to the bar, this equaled 49,520 bars of gold and 1,545,600 bars of silver. Another 607,700 bars of gold and 2,583,100 bars of silver were credited in exchange for 11,635 women, of whom 129 were princesses and high-ranking consorts, 451 low-ranking consorts or women of the close branches of the imperial clan, 1,241 more-distant clanswomen, 1,083 palace ladies and palace entertainers, 2,091 wives of close clansmen, 2,007 wives of distant clansmen, 1,314 women of the entertainment quarters, and 3,319 women of the families of officials or nobles. The highest-ranking women are listed by name and age (KFFZ 97–118).

40. SFJ 244–45, 49; SCBM 99.401. For a listing as of 1129, see SCBM 99.404–5.

41. Murray 1989:28.

42. HMZ 207.

43. SCBM 208.158–59; Katō 1963:202–30; Franke 1994:297–99; ZDKZ 470–81; JS 5.108.

45. WLJS 9.503–5.

45. Gugong et al. 2002:217–27. Another possibility is Han Huang's *Five Oxen* (plate 35), which has Huizong's version of the Ruisi dian seal in a place that would have been hard to trim off, and Gaozong's seals on the edges. A third possibility is Xu Daoning's *Fishermen* in the Nelson Atkins Museum in Kansas City. The *Xuanhe Catalogue* lists 138 paintings by Xu, several of which could have been this painting, and it does have a seal of Gaozong's that has been judged to be authentic. See W. Ho et al. 1980:21–24.

46. There were also competing versions of some paintings, though usually not nearly so many. See Yang Renkai 1999:129–30 for a discussion of the competing versions of *Night Revels of Han Xizai*, a painting listed in Huizong's catalogue (see plate 1). The extant version (Gugong et al. 2002:237–57) has neither Huizong nor Gaozong seals; the earliest are of Shi Miyuan (1164–1233). One possibility is that it is a copy made at Huizong's court of the original in his collection.

47. See Xu Bangda 1987:34.

48. For instance, the extant version of Huaisu's *Autobiography* (fig. 7.8) has a colophon by Zeng Yu (1073–1135, son of Zeng Bu) dated 1132. It claims that there had been three versions of the *Autobiography* owned in the eleventh century by the Shi, Feng, and Su families. In 1088 the Su version was taken to Kaifeng by Su Ye, where Mi Fu and others added inscriptions. Zeng claimed that the Feng version was the one that entered the palace collection and that the one then owned by Lü Binglao was actually the Su version that had been inscribed by Mi Fu, even though Mi's inscription was no longer attached. See Schlombs 1998:83.

49. On Mi Youren as authenticator, see Sturman 1989:259, 356–58, 503–6.

50. HJ 3.307.

51. For an illustration, see Gugong et al. 2002:147–51.

52. Gugong et al. 2002:53–55. As Peter Sturman (1989:385) noted, this work "bears no credible documentation preceding the late Northern Song, and the fact that it too appears in the *Chunhua fatie* [Model Letters] only encourages suspicion."

53. McNair 1998:45–47. Later this work entered the collection of Xianyu Shu. See M. Fu 1981:392–93. On Empress Wu, see H. Lee 2004:70–76.

54. On its seals, see Y. Wang 2003.

55. NSGGL xu 3.175–88. The Southern Song collection included works of both calligraphy and painting by unknown artists, which Huizong's catalogues did not. Murray 1989:28 accepts Zhou Mi's statement that the Southern Song collection was as large as Huizong's, apparently not considering this quantitative evidence.

56. HZL san 3.264. A Yuan scholar recorded Bo Juyi's poem and explained its reference, suggesting that he had seen it. Although several other versions of this painting survived into modern times, the one with Huizong's inscription of Bo's poem has not. See Chen Gaohua 1984:59; Lawton 1973:34–37; and H. Wu 1996:79–82.

57. DJGZ 14.196; Zhang Linsheng 1996:5–6. Zhang Linsheng also cites a Yuan source to the same effect, ZGZDZY preface 3a.

58. H. Chan 1984:68–69; Franke 1994:243–45.

59. J. Tao 1976:84–89, 99; H. Chan 1984:73–74; Franke 1994:245–50; Mote 1999:242.

60. JS 126.2731; Y. Wang 2003:204.

61. See Jiang Zhaoshen 1989 for illustrations of these two pieces.

62. For a list, see Toyama 1957.

63. For the various seals and colophons on *Taizong*, see Gugong et al. 2002:87–95 or Gugong 1978: back 6–8. For those on *Early Snow*, see National Palace Museum 1995a:153–60. On *Admonitions*, see Y. Wang 2003.

64. XYJZ 2.33; DJGZ 20.275. This, of course, indicates that some antiquities survived Hailing's orders for destruction. Zhangzong seems also to have purchased objects either from the border markets with Song or perhaps from markets in Jin cities, as many items had entered general circulation before Zhangzong acquired them (Toyama 1957).

65. JS 39.882–83.

66. Mote 1999:244–48.

67. Toyama 1955. On Jia Sidao as an official, see Franke 1962.

68. YSSZ 235; Gugong et al. 2002:307–11; Jiang Zhaoshen 1989.

69. Weidner 1982:8–14.

70. Weitz 2002:143. An example of something sold at these markets is a small Lingbi scholar's rock in the shape of a mountain with an eight-character inscription by Huizong. See ibid., 210.

71. Fu Shen 1981: plate 10.

72. Jay-Preston 1983:62; Weitz 2002:11.

73. See Weitz 2002.

74. Weitz 2002: 113–17; XHHP 2.47–48, 2.53, 7.129–30. Note that Wu Daozi has some of the constellations, but none specifically called Mars (Fire Star). Of course, not being listed in the XHHP need not mean that the inscription by Huizong was forged, since, as discussed in chapter 8, not all the paintings in his collection were listed in the catalogue.

75. XHSP 14.108, 5.39–40; Weitz 2002:80, 81.

76. Weidner 1982:32–38; S. Fu 1990; Gugong et al. 2002:57–61; Gugong 1981:54.

77. Weidner 1982:17–32; Weitz 2004; Langlois 1978:106–8.

78. Fu Shen 1981: plate 32A; Weitz 2004:255. On *Waterwheel*, see H. Liu 2002.

79. Fu Shen 1981:56, plate 33; Weidner 1982:25; Gugong et al. 2002:53–55.

80. Weitz 2004:253–55.

81. Mattos 1988:47–49. They remained there until 1933, when they were crated and moved to protect them from the imminent war with Japan. In 1947 they were moved to Nanjing,

but later were moved back to Beijing and finally uncrated at the Palace Museum in 1958, where they remain.

82. MSJZ 6.7b–11a.

83. Yang Renkai 1999:17; L. Chang 1996:8–9.

84. On Xiang, see Zheng Yinshu 1984; on An, Lawton 1969; on Liang, Lee and Ho 1981.

85. See Barnhart 1991 on Dong Qichang's often arbitrary attributions.

86. L. Chang 1996:9, 13; JCSHM 1a–7a. One of those listed as fake was "*Collating Books*, by Wang Qihan of the Northern Song, inscribed by Song Huizong, fake." This would seem to be a version of the painting with that title currently owned by Nanjing University (see Jin Weinuo 1984: plate 60). The Huizong inscription on this painting is not necessarily genuine, but it is probably not the painting Gao refers to, as it has neither Gao's nor Qianlong's seals.

87. Gugong et al. 2002:97–107. The main connection between this painting and Huizong's collection is that it has the Huizong version of the Ruisi dongge seal, as well as Gaozong seals (which would explain why smaller Huizong seals are not extant). There are also plausible matches to paintings listed in Huizong's catalogue (XHHP 6.115).

88. National Palace Museum 1989:147–48. On Qianlong's connoisseurship, see H. Kohara 1988.

89. National Palace Museum 2000:112, 416; National Palace Museum 1965 5.43. L. Chang 1996:5 believes that this painting entered private hands after the fall of Kaifeng, perhaps because it does not have Gaozong or Zhangzong seals, but there is no evidence that every painting in those collections was impressed with seals (nor can one exclude the possibility that seals were later removed). A possible scenario is that this painting was taken by the Jurchen and kept in a Jin palace until the defeat by the Mongols, when it entered the market and ended up being acquired by the late Southern Song court. It is also worth noting that hanging scrolls, especially ones by professional or court painters, are less likely to have inscriptions or colophons added to them, so that other owners could have passed unnoticed.

90. Gugong et al. 2002:347–67.

91. The full list consisted of paintings by Zhao Chang, Xu Xi (two), Wei Yan, Yan Wengui (two), Li Cheng, Liu Yongnian, Li Guizhen, Wu Yuanyu, Zhou Wenju, Wang Qihan, Sun Zhiwei, and Hu Gui (NSGGL xu 3.179–80). The 1199 list also mentions anonymous paintings (perhaps by Huizong's court artists) that Huizong had inscribed, a couple of which do survive (*Two Birds* in the National Palace Museum, Taipei, and *Pheasant* in the Palace Museum, Beijing). These are usually treated as paintings by Huizong.

92. SXZJ 4.9a–b; BGT 3.33a–34a; Weitz 2002:182. For another bronze once in Huizong's collection that he saw, see Weitz 2002:197; and the corresponding BGT 6.35a–36b.

93. Chen Gaohua 1984:130.

94. Weitz 2002:70; XHHP 8.142–43; Gugong et al. 2002:263–69; Gugong 1978 rear 15–16; Yang Renkai 1999:230.

95. J. Kuo 1989:181–82, Harrist 1999:242–43, 253–55; S. Fu 1977:241–42. Note that Dong Qichang gave 143 rather than 243 as the number of Wang Xizhis in Huizong's collection. Over the next several decades, a few connoisseurs recorded seeing the work, which entered the collection of the Korean merchant and collector An Qi (1683–1744), who pressed eleven of his seals on it. After An's death, it entered the collection of the Qianlong emperor, who put nineteen seals on it and added three inscriptions, two on either side of Wang's calligraphy and one elsewhere. This piece of calligraphy left the palace collection like many others

in the twentieth century, and had a couple of owners before it was acquired in 1957 by the artist-collector Zhang Daqian (1899–1983).

96. Gugong et al. 2002:129–43; SQBJ 14.12a–13a. Jin Weinuo 1984: rear 19 identifies the colophon writer as Sima Yin, a man about whom nothing is known.

97. Weitz 2002:72–73; DGL 11.40b; W. Ho et al. 1980:8–10. For other examples of works seen by Zhou Mi but not extant today, see Weitz 2002:281–95 and passim.

98. QHSHF 1B:31b–33b; SHJ 4.109. On the Hans as collectors, see Yang Renkai 1999:17–18.

99. DGL 1.10a–b; Zhang Guangbin 1984:265–67; Xu Bangda 1987:22–27; H. Zhang 2003:277–78, W. Weng and B. Yang 1982:214–15. Another example of a work from Huizong's collection that escaped Qianlong's seals and inscriptions by becoming the property of Yongxing is the Shanghai Museum's *Waterwheel*; see Zheng Wei 1966:18. There are also some works that escaped ownership by any branch of the Qing imperial family, such as Wang Xizhi's *Shangyu tie*. See Xu Bangda 1978; Gugong et al. 2002:50–51.

100. Illustrated in Yang Renkai 1989:206–7.

101. Xu Bangda 1987:102–3.

102. ZDKS 5b; JGZ 1.5a–b; Gao Renjun 1987:106, 110. This article mentions earlier references to the cauldron, but none of them link it to Huizong's collection.

103. On her story, see Owen 1986:80–98.

104. In eighteen other cases she finds the information insufficient to make an identification. Weitz 2002:217–34, 251–55, 260–71.

REFLECTIONS

1. YS 143.3414.

2. R. Huang 1981:12.

3. My description of Qianlong as a collector is based on a series of exhibits and related catalogues and symposia as well as independent monographs. See J. Chou and Brown 1985; J. Chou 1988; Kahn 1985; Guy 1987; H. Kohara 1988; W. Fong and J. Watt 1966; L. Chang 1996; C. Ho and Bronson 2004; National Palace Museum 2002; H. Zhang 2002; Berger 2003; Rawski and Rawson 2005; and Holzwarth 2005.

4. For the Qianlong catalogue totals, see H. Kohara 1988:66. Moreover, Qianlong's catalogues included categories of paintings and calligraphies excluded from Huizong's, such as works believed to be copies, works by current court artists, and works by the dynasty's own emperors.

5. L. Chang 1996:17; Guy 1987:104.

6. Holzwarth 2005:50. Shaughnessy 1991:11 states that a conservative estimate is that at least 50 percent of the antiquities in Qianlong's catalogues were modern reproductions or forgeries. Among them were four of Huizong's Dasheng bells.

7. See H. Kohara 1988:61.

8. In the case of calligraphy, the term "court taste" has been used to refer not to more ornate or embellished styles but to the style of the Two Wangs. These two men were of course not rulers themselves but literati who used only the commonly available materials of brush, ink, and paper. It was only their appreciation by rulers, especially Tang rulers from Taizong on, that associates them with the court.

9. Berger 2003:73–74; Holzwarth 2005:49, 51–52.

10. Cf. Bol 2001.

11. A text on collecting antiquities written in 1388 covers a much wider range of objects than Huizong's *Antiquities Illustrated.* Besides ancient bronzes, it includes ancient paintings and calligraphies, rubbings, ancient zithers, inkstones, jades, pearls, ivory, coral, gold, ancient porcelain, ancient lacquer ware, textiles, and objects made from rare woods or stones. It includes only a few sentences on mirrors: "In ancient times bronze was the only material used for the casting of mirrors. They were beautifully cast. Tang mirrors have particularly high and large knobs, and were therefore nicknamed 'the Big Noses of Tang.'" The next item on the ability of ancient bronzes to repel evil spirits mentions mirrors marked with the twelve "hours" of the day that are a "veritable wonder" (David 1971:12). Craig Clunas, in his study of late Ming collecting, discusses only one book that mentioned mirrors. This book on the sights of the capital mentioned that the temple of the city god had stalls extending three *li* which sold ancient and modern books, Shang and Zhou bronzes, and Qin and Han mirrors (Clunas 1991:137).

12. GZJY chapter 56.

13. GJTSJC Kaogong, *juan* 225–28.

14. XQGJ *juan* 39–40. The Qing catalogue also shares much of the weakness on dating of Huizong's catalogue. It has no mirrors dated to the period between the Han and Tang, and does not correct the date of the "sea creature and grape" mirrors from Han to Tang, maintaining the dating of the BGT.

15. JSS jin 6. Interestingly, despite these signs of interest in mirrors, in the late nineteenth and early twentieth centuries Chinese scholars and collectors did not show as much interest in mirrors as their Japanese counterparts. Zhu Jianxin, in his survey of "metal and stone" written in 1938, devoted only seven out of 300 pages to mirrors and noted that Japanese scholars had done more work on mirrors than Chinese scholars (Zhu Jianxin 1938:160–66). On Japanese interest in early Chinese mirrors, see Tomioka 1920 and S. Umehara 1955.

APPENDIX I

1. ZS 1.1a.

2. ZHWLXY shou, passim.

3. The only scholar I know who argues that Huizong was not involved in any way (at least in the painting and calligraphy catalogues) is Wei Bin (2006), but I do not find his arguments convincing.

4. Chang Bide 1971; Ni Genfa 1985.

5. See Chen Mengjia and Wang Shimin 1998:9–10.

6. TWSCT 4.79–80; ZS 1.1a; JZDSZ 1B.93; TZ 64.765B; SCTSM 68a; ZZSLJT 8.228.

7. DSMQJ 2.164–65; SKQSZMTY 115.2396; PGXLZZ 3.682; Rong Geng 1994:18–27; Cen Zhongmian 1948; Ye Guoliang 1984; Cheng Mengjia and Wang Shimin 1998.

8. Ye Guoliang 1984. Chen Mengjia and Wang Shimin 1998:15–18 instead see a confusion of the two books titled *Bogu tu.*

9. L. Chang 2000:24; Chen Mengjia and Wang Shimin 1998:1.

10. YH 69.25a; SHY Li 14.80a; YLMC 3.38–39; Xu Yahui 2003; LDZD 1.15, 3.3, 10.15, 10.18; TZ 64.765B, 73.841B–C; LuS 24.16a; RZSB 14.181–82, san 13.564–67; LX 14.8a; QBBZ 2.18a.

11. ZZYL 130.3101–2; ZXJ 59.3051; SXZXSDYT 31b. Xu Yahui 2003 thinks it likely that Zhu Xi's access to the pictures was indirect, through the manual Gaozong issued, but since other references show that he had access to the book, it is just as likely that he made his choices from the book itself.

12. LYJ 3.14b–16a; YH 58.126–27; YLMC 6.77; and elsewhere. A search of the electronic *Siku quanshu* found several more citations in Southern Song works, including one in a poem, and others in books on errors in the two Han histories, on ancient vessels, and on children's education.

13. Qu Wanli 1975:272.

14. The 1603 edition could have used the same blocks as the 1588 (as the blocks are more worn, with more breaks), but the 1752 edition seems better in many places, suggesting either entirely new blocks based on careful tracing or selective replacement of damaged blocks.

15. Also see Poor 1965, which compares a page in the 1599, 1603, and 1752 editions.

16. This list is based on Poor 1965; Rong Geng 1994:18–27; Weng Daxi 2005:736, 742–43; and searches of online catalogues, such as WorldCat Online Computer Library Center and comparable sites abroad, especially the rare book page of the National Central Library in Taiwan (http://nclcc.ncl.edu.tw/ttsweb/rbookhiml/nclrbook.htm) and the Web site of the National Library of China (www.nlc.gov.cn/old/english.htm). With one exception, I have not included microfilms.

17. Weng Daxi 2005:742–43.

18. As Nakata 1977–95 5:8–10 shows, the calligraphy catalogue must have been done between 1120 and 1125, as it says that Cai Jing had retired after three terms as grand councilor (he began a fourth term late in 1125). One could go further and note that some of the pieces of calligraphy by Cai Jing that mention Genyue Garden are unlikely to have been written before 1122, when the garden was completed. In the case of the painting catalogue, it mentions Tong Guan as holding a title he had in 1120, not later titles, but that means only that his entry was finished at that date. It could be that other entries were finished later.

19. YTJH 3.2b–3a. See also Wei Bin 2006.

20. YTJH 3.2b–3a; SKQSZMTY 112.2336–38; Yu Shaosong 1968:6.2–7; Yu Jiaxi 1958:781–82; Chang Bide 1971; Ni Genfa 1985; Chen Quanxi 1986; Wang Yuanjun 1995; Xie Wei 1998:161–64; Wei Bin 2006.

21. I consulted Xie Wei 1998:161 as well as online catalogues to make this list.

Bibliography

ABBREVIATIONS USED IN THE BIBLIOGRAPHY

CSJC *Congshu jicheng* 叢書集成. Published by Shanghai, Commercial Press, 1936–39.
SBCK *Sibu congkan* 四部叢刊. Published by Shanghai, Hanfen lou, 1936.
SKQS *Siku quanshu* 四庫全書. Published by Taipei, Commercial Press, 1983.
SKSLXB *Shike shiliao xinbian* 石刻史料新編. Published by Taipei, Xinwenfeng, 1977.
XXSKQS *Xuxiu siku quanshu* 續修四庫全書. Published by Shanghai, Guji chubanshe, 1995–99.

PRIMARY SOURCES

BGT *Chongxiu Xuanhe bogu tu* 重修宣和博古圖, 30 *juan*, attributed to Wang Fu 王黼 (d. 1126). SKQS ed. if not otherwise indicated. Other editions are cited as the Yuan, 1528, 1588, 1596, 1599, and 1752 editions. For more on them, see appendix 1.
BJYGJ *BaoJin yingguang ji* 寶晉英光集, 8 *juan*, by Mi Fu 米芾 (1051–1107). CSJC ed.
BQS *Baqiong shi jinshi buzheng* 八瓊室金石補正, 130 *juan*, by Lu Zengxiang 陸增祥 (1816–1882). SKSLXB ed.
BSJ *Beishan ji* 北山集, 40 *juan*, by Cheng Ju 程俱 (1078–1144). SKQS ed.
BSLH *Bishu luhua* 避暑錄話, 2 *juan*, by Ye Mengde 葉夢得 (1077–1148). SKQS ed.
BTL *Bintui lu* 賓退錄, 10 *juan*, by Zhao Lingshi 趙令時 (1175–1231). Song Yuan biji congshu ed. Shanghai: Shanghai guji chubanshe, 1983.
BZZFSZ *Baozhen zhai fashu zan* 寶真齋法書贊, 28 *juan*, by Yue Ke 岳珂 (1183–1240). Yishu congshu ed. Taipei: Shijie shuju, 1962.
CB *Xu zizhi tongjian changbian* 續資治通鑒長編, 520 *juan*, by Li Tao 李燾 (1115–1184). Beijing: Zhonghua shuju, 1985.
CBBM *Tongjian changbian jishi benmo* 通鑑長編紀事本末, 150 *juan*, by Yang Zhongliang 楊仲良 (fl. ca. 1170–1230). Songshi ziliao cuibian ed. Taipei: Wenhai chubanshe, 1967.
CBSB *Xu zizhi tongjian changbian shibu* 續資治通鑑長編拾補. Beijing: Zhonghua shuju, 2004.
CHGT *Song ta Chunhua ge tie* 宋拓淳化閣帖. Reprint of You Xiang 游相 ed. Shanghai: Commercial Press, 1924.
CLJ *Chuliao ji* 初寮集, 8 *juan*, by Wang Anzhong 王安中 (1076–1134). SKQS ed.

CWZM *Chongwen zongmu* 崇文總目, 5 *juan*, by Wang Yaochen 王堯臣 (1001–1056) et al. CSJC ed.
DDSL *Dongdu shilue* 東都事略, 130 *juan*, by Wang Cheng 王偁 (twelfth century). Songshi ziliao cuibian ed. Taipei: Wenhai chubanshe, 1967.
DGL *Daguan lu* 大觀錄, 20 *juan*, by Wu Sheng 吳升 (eighteenth century). XXSKQS ed.
DGTQLT *Daguan Taiqinglou tie Song ta zhenben* 大觀太清樓帖宋拓真本. Beijing: Wenwu chubanshe, 2001. Each chapter is issued as a separate softcover volume.
DGYL *Dongguan yulun* 東觀餘論, 2 *juan*, by Huang Bosi 黃伯思 (1079–1118). SKQS ed.
DHWJ *Dong Han wen ji* 東漢文紀, 32 *juan*, by Mei Dingzuo 梅鼎祚 (1553–1619). SKQS ed.
DJDFL *DaJin diaofa lu* 大金弔伐錄, 4 *juan*. Anon. CSJC ed.
DJGZ *DaJin guozhi* 大金國志, 40 *juan*, by Yuwen Maozhao 宇文懋昭. Beijing: Zhonghua shuju, 1986.
DJMHL *Dongjing menghua lu* 東京夢華錄, 10 *juan* (1147), attrib. to Meng Yuanlao 孟元老 (fl. 1126–1147). In *Dongjing menghua lu wai si zhong* 東京夢華錄外四種. Shanghai: Zhonghua shuju, 1962.
DJMHLZ *Dongjing menghua lu zhu* 東京夢華錄注, 10 *juan* (1147), attrib. to Meng Yuanlao 孟元老 (fl. 1126–1147), edited by Deng Zhicheng 鄧之誠 (1887–1960). Beijing: Commercial Press, 1959.
DQZL *Danqian zhailu* 丹鉛摘錄, 13 juan, by Yang Shen 楊慎 (1488–1559). SKQS ed.
DSMQJ *Dushu minqiu ji* 讀書敏求記, 4 *juan*, by Qian Zeng 錢曾 (1629–1701). XXSKQS ed.
DYJ *Danyang ji* 丹陽集, 24 *juan*, by Ge Shengzhong 葛勝仲 (1072–1144). SKQS ed.
DZ *Daozang* 道藏, 36 vols. Beijing: Wenwu chubanshe, 1988.
FRJ *Feiran ji* 斐然集, 30 *juan*, by Hu Yin 胡寅 (1098–1156). SKQS ed.
FSL *Fashu lun* 法書論, by Cai Xizong 蔡希綜 (eighth century). In *Zhongwan Tang Wudai shulun* 中晚唐五代書論, edited by Pan Yungao 潘運告. Changsha: Hunan meishu chubanshe, 1997.
FSYL *Fashu yaolu* 法書要錄, 10 *juan*, by Zhang Yanyuan 張彥遠 (ca. 815–ca. 880). CSJC ed.
FXJ *Fuxi ji* 浮溪集, 32 *juan*, by Wang Zao 汪藻 (1079–1154). CSJC ed.
GCHB *Guangchuan huaba* 廣川畫跋, 6 *juan*, by Dong You 董逌 (fl. 1100–1130). In *Huapin congshu* 畫品叢書, edited by Yu Anlan 于安瀾. Shanghai: Shanghai Renmin meishu chubanshe, 1982.
GCSB *Guangchuan shuba*, 廣川書跋, 10 *juan*, by Dong You 董逌 (fl. 1100–1130). SKQS ed.
GJJ *Gujing ji* 古鏡記, 1 *juan*, by Wang Du 王度 (Sui). In *Shuofu sanzhong*, han 114 (vol. 8, pp. 5259–64).
GJTSJC *Gujin tushu jicheng* 古今圖書集成, edited by Chen Menglei 陳夢雷 (1651–1741). Shanghai: Zhonghua shuju, 1934 reprint.
GSJ *Gongshi ji* 公是集, 54 *juan*, by Liu Chang 劉敞 (1019–1068). SKQS. ed.
GTL *Guitian lu* 歸田錄, 2 *juan*, by Ouyang Xiu 歐陽修 (1007–1072). TangSong shiliao biji congkan ed. Beijing: Zhonghua shuju, 1981.
GuoTL *Guoting lu* 過庭錄, 1 *juan*, by Fan Gongcheng 范公偁 (twelfth century). Beijing: Zhonghua shuju, 2002.
GXJ *Guixi ji* 龜谿集, 12 *juan*, by Shen Yuqiu 沈與求 (1086–1137). SKQS ed.
GXZZ *Guixin zazhi* 癸辛雜識, 6 *juan*, by Zhou Mi 周密 (1232–1308). Beijing: Zhonghua shuju, 1988.
GZJY *Gezhi jingyuan* 格致鏡原, 100 *juan*, by Chen Yuanlong 陳元龍 (1652–1736). SKQS ed.
HanS *Han shu* 漢書, 100 *juan*, by Ban Gu 班固 (32–92). Beijing: Zhonghua shuju, 1962.

HBJSZ *Hubei jinshi zhi* 湖北金石志, 14 *juan*, by Zhang Zhongxin 張仲炘 (*jinshi* 1877). SKSLXB ed.

HFZ *Han Fei zi* 韓非子, 20 *juan*. Taipei: Chengwen chubanshe, 1980.

HHS *Hou Han shu* 後漢書, 120 *juan*, by Fan Ye 范曄 (398–445). Beijing: Zhonghua shuju, 1971.

HJ *Huaji* 畫繼, 10 *juan*, by Deng Chun 鄧椿 (fl. 1127–1167). In *Tuhua jianwen zhi, Huaji* 圖畫見聞志, 畫繼, edited by Pan Yungao 潘運告. Changsha: Hunan meishu chubanshe, 2000.

HJian *Hua jian* 畫鑑, 1 *juan*, by Tang Hou 湯垕 (fl. 1322). In *Huapin congshu* 畫品叢書, edited by Yu Anlan 于安瀾. Shanghai: Shanghai Renmin meishu chubanshe, 1982.

HLSZ *Helinsi zhi* 鶴林寺志, 1 *juan*, by Mingxian 明賢 (fl. 1610–1614). Late Ming ed., microfilm of Rare Books in the National Library Peiping, roll 501.

HMZ *Hanmo zhi* 翰墨志, 1 *juan*, by Song Gaozong 宋高宗. In *Songren shulun* 宋人書論, edited by Pan Yungao 潘運告 and Shui Caitian 水采田. Changsha: Hunan meishu chubanshe, 1999.

HQJSJ *Hongqing jushi wenji* 鴻慶居士文集, 42 *juan*, by Sun Di 孫覿 (1081–1169). SKQS ed.

HS *Huashi* 畫史 by Mi Fu 米芾 (1051–1107), 1 *juan*. In *Huapin congshu* 畫品叢書, edited by Yu Anlan 于安瀾. Shanghai: Shanghai Renmin meishu chubanshe, 1982.

HSSL *HuangSong shulu* 皇宋書錄, 3 *juan* (1242), by Dong Shi 董史 (thirteenth century). Zhibuzuzhai congshu ed.

HYMY *Haiyue mingyan* 海岳名言, 1 *juan*, by Mi Fu 米芾 (1051–1107). Taipei: Shijie shuju, 1962.

HYSJ *Hunyuan shengji* 混元聖紀, 9 *juan*, by Xie Shouhao 謝守灝 (1134–1212). In *Daozang* 道藏, vol. 17. Beijing: Wenwu chubanshe, 1988.

HZL *Huizhu lu* 揮麈錄, 20 *juan*, by Wang Mingqing 王明清 (1127–1214+). Beijing: Zhonghua shuju, 1961.

JCSHM *Jiangcun shuhua mu* 江村書畫目, 1 *juan*, by Gao Shiqi 高士奇 (1645–1703). Hong Kong: Longmen shuju reprint, n.d.

JGZ *Jiguzhai zongding yiqi kuanshi* 積古齋鐘鼎彝器款識, 10 *juan*, by Ruan Yuan 阮元 (1764–1849). In *Wenxuanlou congshu* 文選樓叢書, 1842 ed.

JKCXL *Jingkang chuanxin lu* 靖康傳信錄, 3 *juan*, by Li Gang 李綱 (1083–1140). CSJC ed.

JKCYQY *Jingkang chaoye qianyan* 靖康朝野僉言, 1 *juan*, anon. CSJC ed.

JKJW *Jingkang jiwen* 靖康紀聞, 1 *juan*, by Ding Teqi 丁特起 (d. 1135+). CSJC ed.

JKYL *Jingkang yaolu* 靖康要錄, 16 *juan*, anon. CSJC ed.

JS *Jinshi* 金史, 135 *juan*, edited by Tuo Tuo 脫脫 (1313–1355) et al. Beijing: Zhonghua shuju, 1975.

JSCB *Jinshi cuibian* 金石萃編, 160 *juan*, by Wang Chang 王昶 (1725–1806). SKSLXB ed.

JSL *Jinshi lu* 金石錄, 30 *juan*, by Zhao Mingcheng 趙明誠 (1081–1129). SKSLXB ed.

JSS *Jinshi suo* 金石索, 12 *juan*, by Feng Yunpeng 馮雲鵬 (nineteenth century) and Feng Yunyuan 馮雲鵷 (nineteenth century). XXSKQS ed.

JSWZJ *Jinshi wenzi ji* 金石文字記, 12 *juan*, by Gu Yanwu 顧炎武 (1613–1682). SKSLXB ed.

JSXB *Jinshi xubian* 金石續編, 21 *juan*, by Lu Yaoyu 陸耀遹 (1771–1836). SKSLXB ed.

JTS *Jiu Tang shu* 舊唐書, 200 *juan* (945), by Liu Xu 劉煦 (887–946) et al. Beijing: Zhonghua shuju, 1975.

JXLL *Jinxie linlang* 金薤琳琅 , 20 *juan*, by Du Mu 都穆 (1458–1525). SKSLXB ed.

JXTZ *Jiangxi tongzhi* 江西通志, 162 *juan*, edited by Xie Min 謝旻 (eighteenth century) et al. SKQS ed.

JZDSZ *Junzhai dushu zhi* 郡齋讀書志, 4 *juan*, by Chao Gongwu 晁公武 (1105–1180). Taipei: Commercial Press reprint.

KFFZ *Kaifeng fuzhuang* 開封府狀, 1 *juan*, anon. In *Jingkang baishi jianzheng* 靖康稗史箋証, compiled by Cui An 確庵 and Nai An 耐庵, edited by Cui Wenyin 崔文印. Beijing: Zhonghua shuju, 1988.

KGT *Kaogu tu* 考古圖, 10 *juan*, by Lü Dalin 呂大臨 (1044–1093). SKQS ed.

KGT 1752 ed. *Kaogu tu* 考古圖, 10 *juan*, by Lü Dalin 呂大臨 (1044–1093). Part of 1752 reprint of 1603 *Sangu tu* 三古圖.

LDMHJ *Lidai minghua ji* 歷代名畫集, 10 *juan*, by Zhang Yanyuan 張彥遠 (fl. 820–850). In *Tang Wudai hualun* 唐五代畫論, edited by He Zhiming 何志明 and Pan Yungao 潘運告. Changsha: Hunan meishu chubanshe, 1997.

LDZD *Lidai zhongding yiqi kuanshi fatie* 歷代鐘鼎彝器款識法帖, 20 *juan*, by Xue Shanggong 薛尚功 (d. 1144). SKQS ed.

LiS *Li shu* 禮書, 150 *juan*, by Chen Xiangdao 陳祥道 (1053–1093). SKQS ed.

LJ *Li ji* 禮記. In *Shisan jing zhushu* 十三經注疏. Reprint of 1815 ed. Taipei: Yiwen yinshuguan, 1981.

LJYS *Liji yishu* 禮記義疏, 83 *juan*, commissioned by the Qianlong 乾隆 emperor (r. 1735–1796). SKQS ed.

LSZX *Lishi zhenxian tidao tongjian* 歷世真仙體道通鑑, 53 *juan*, by Zhao Daoyi 趙道一 (Yuan). In DZ, Harvard-Yenching 296.

LTGS *Lintai gushi* 麟臺故事, 5 *juan*, by Cheng Ju 程俱 (1078–1144), annotated by Zhang Fuxiang 張富祥. TangSong shiliao biji ed. Beijing: Zhonghua shuju, 2000.

LuS *Lu shi* 路史, 47 *juan*, by Luo Bi 羅泌 (d. 1176+). SKQS ed.

LX *Li xu* 隸續, 21 *juan*, by Hong Gua 洪适 (1117–1184). SKSLXB ed.

LXABJ *Laoxuean biji* 老學庵筆記, 10 *juan*, by Lu You 陸游 (1125–1210). TangSong shiliao biji ed. Beijing: Zhonghua shuju, 1979.

LXJ *Liangxi ji* 梁溪集, 180 *juan*, by Li Gang 李綱 (1083–1140). SKQS ed.

LYJ *Lingyan ji* 靈巖集, 8 *juan*, by Tang Shichi 唐世恥 (ca. 1180–ca. 1240). SKQS ed.

LYZYL *Liu yi zhi yi lu* 六藝之一錄, 406 *juan*, by Ni Tao 倪濤 (*jinshi* 1709). SKQS ed.

LZJSZ *Liangzhe jinshi zhi* 兩浙金石志, 18 *juan* + 1, by Ruan Yuan 阮元 (1764–1849). SKSLXB ed.

MCB *Mochi bian* 墨池編, 6 *juan*, by Zhu Changwen 朱長文 (1039–1098). Reprint of Ming Wanli ed. Taipei: National Central Library, 1978.

MSJZ *Mishujian zhi* 秘書監志, 11 *juan*, by Wang Shidian 王士點 (fourteenth century). SKQS ed.

MSZ *Maoshan zhi* 茅山志, 33 *juan*, edited by Liu Dabin 劉大彬 (fl. 1317–1328). In DZ (HY 304).

MXBT *Mengxi bitan jiaozheng* 夢溪筆談校證, 26 *juan*, by Shen Gua 沈括 (1031–1095), edited by Hu Daojing 胡道静. Shanghai: Shanghai chubangongsi, 1956.

MYHG *Moyuan hui guan* 墨緣彙觀, 4 *juan*, by An Qi 安岐 (b. 1683). XXSKQS ed.

MZML *Mozhuang manlu* 墨莊漫錄, 10 *juan*, by Zhang Bangji 張邦基 (fl. 1140s). TangSong shiliao biji ed. Beijing: Zhonghua shuju, 2002.

NGZML *Nenggai zhai manlu* 能改齋漫錄, 18 *juan* (1157), by Wu Zeng 吳曾 (d. 1170+). Shanghai: Shanghai guji chubanshe, 1979.

NSGGL *NanSong guange lu, xulu* 南宋館閣錄, 續錄, 10 *juan*, by Chen Kui 陳騤 (1128–1205) and anonymous. Beijing: Zhonghua shuju, 1998.

NZLH *Nanzheng luhui* 南征錄彙, by Li Tianmin 李天民 (Jin). In *Jingkang baishi jianzheng* 靖康稗史箋証, compiled by Cui An 確庵 and Nai An 耐庵, edited by Cui Wenyin 崔文印. Beijing: Zhonghua shuju, 1988.

OYXQJ *Ouyang Xiu quanji* 歐陽修全集, 157 *juan*, by Ouyang Xiu 歐陽修 (1007–1072). Taipei: Shijie shuju, 1961.

PGXLZZ *Pangu xiaolu zazhu* 攀古小廬雜著, 12 *juan*, by Xu Han 許瀚 (1797–1866). XXSKQS ed.

QBBZ *Qingbo biezhi* 清波別志, 12 *juan*, by Zhou Hui 周輝 (1127–1198+). SKQS ed.

QBZZ *Qingbo zazhi* 清波雜志, 12 *juan*, by Zhou Hui 周輝 (1127–1198+). Beijing: Zhonghua shuju, 1994.

QDYY *Qidong yeyu* 齊東野語, 20 *juan*, by Zhou Mi 周密 (1232–1308). Beijing: Zhonghua shuju, 1983.

QHSHF *Qinghe shuhua fang* 清河書畫舫, 12 *juan*, by Zhang Chou 張丑 (1577–1643). SKQS ed.

QJJ *Qiujian ji* 秋澗集, 100 *juan*, by Wang Yun 王惲 (1227–1304). SKQS ed.

QRJSJ *Qingrong jushi ji* 清容居士集, 50 *juan*, by Yuan Jue 袁桷 (1266–1327). CSJC ed.

QSB *Quesao bian* 卻掃編, 3 *juan*, by Xu Du 徐度 (d. 1156). CSJC ed.

QSS *Quan Song shi* 全宋詩, edited by Fu Xuancong 傅璇琮 et al. Beijing: Beijing Daxue chubanshe, 1991–1998.

QSW *Quan Song wen* 全宋文, edited by Zeng Zaozhuang 曾枣庄 and Liu Lin 劉琳. Sichuan: Bashu shushe, 1988–1994.

QTS *Quan Tang shi* 全唐詩, 900 *juan*, edited by Peng Dingqiu 彭定求 (1645–1719). Beijing: Zhonghua shuju, 1979.

QTW *Quan Tang wen* 全唐文, 1,000 *juan*, edited by Dong Gao 董誥 (1740–1818) et al. Reprint of 1814 ed. Tainan: Jingwei shuju, 1965.

QWJW *Quwei jiuwen* 曲洧舊聞, 10 *juan*, by Zhu Bian 朱弁 (?–1138). Beijing: Zhonghua shuju, 2002.

QYT *Qianyan tang jinshi wen bawei* 潛研堂金石文跋尾, 20 *juan*, by Qian Daxin 錢大昕 (1728–1804). SKSLXB ed.

QYTMT *Qunyu tang Mi tie* 群玉堂米帖, 3 *juan*, by Mi Fu 米芾 (1051–1107). Shanghai: Shanghai shuhua chubanshe, 1982.

RZSB *Rongzhai suibi* 容齋隨筆, 74 *juan*, by Hung Mai 洪邁 (1123–1202). Shanghai: Shanghai guji chubanshe, 1978.

SCBM *Sanchao beimeng huibian* 三朝北盟會編, 250 *juan*, by Xu Mengxin 徐夢莘 (1126–1207). Reprint of Shixue yanjiushe 1939 punctuated ed. Taipei: Dahua shuju, 1979.

SCJ *Su Che ji* 蘇轍集, 97 *juan*, by Su Che 蘇轍 (1039–1112). Beijing: Zhonghua shuju, 1990.

SCMHP *Songchao minghua ping* 宋朝名畫評, 6 *juan*, by Liu Daochun 劉道醇 (fl. 1050s). In *Songren huaping* 宋人畫評, edited by Pan Yungao 潘運告. Changsha: Hunan meishu chubanshe, 1999.

SCSS *Songchao shishi* 宋朝事實, 20 *juan*, by Li You 李攸 (fl. 1134). CSJC ed.

SCSSLY *Songchao shishi leiyuan* 宋朝事實類苑, 78 *juan* (1145), by Jiang Shaoyu 江少虞 (*jinshi* ca. 1115–d. 1145+). Shanghai: Shanghai guji chubanshe, 1981.

SCTSM *Suichu tang shumu* 遂初堂書目, 1 *juan*, by You Mao 尤袤 (1127–1193). SKQS ed.

SCZCZY *Songchao zhuchen zouyi* 宋朝諸臣奏議, 150 *juan*, edited by Zhao Ruyu 趙汝愚 (1140–1196). Shanghai: Shanghai guji chubanshe, 1999.

SD *Shu duan* 書斷, 4 *juan*, by Zhang Huaiguan 張懷瓘 (fl. 720s). In *Zhang Huaiguan shu lun* 張懷瓘書論, edited by Pan Yungao 潘運告. Changsha: Hunan meishu chubanshe, 1997.

SDJK *Song Dongjing kao* 宋東京考 , 20 *juan*, by Zhou Cheng 周城 (eighteenth century). Beijing: Zhonghua shuju, 1988.

SDPQJ *Su Dongpo quanji* 蘇東坡全集, by Su Shi 蘇軾 (1036–1101). Taipei: Shijie shuju, 1982.

SDSL *Songdai shulun* 宋代書論, edited by Lao Shuifan 老水番. Changsha: Hunan meishu chubanshe, 1999.

SDZLJ *Song dazhaoling ji* 宋大詔令集, 196 *juan*, anon. Beijing: Zhonghua shuju, 1962.

SF *Shuofu* 說郛, 120 *juan*, by Tao Zongyi 陶宗儀 (fl. 1360). In *Shuofu sanzhong* 三種. Shanghai: Shanghai guji chubanshe, 1988.

SFJ *Song fu ji* 宋俘記, by Kegong 可恭 (Jin). In *Jingkang baishi jianzheng* 靖康稗史箋証, compiled by Cui An 確庵 and Nai An 耐庵, edited by Cui Wenyin 崔文印. Beijing: Zhonghua shuju, 1988.

SGSZ *Song gaoseng zhuan* 宋高僧傳, 30 *juan*, by Zanning 贊寧 (919–1001). Beijing: Zhonghua shuju 1987.

SGTB *Shangu tiba* 山谷題跋, by Huang Tingjian 黃庭堅 (1045–1105). CSJC ed.

SHJ *Shuhua ji* 書畫集, 6 *juan*, by Wu Qizhen 吳其貞 (fl. 1630s–1670s). XXSKQS ed.

ShuS *Shushi* 書史, 1 *juan*, by Mi Fu 米芾 (1051–1107). CSJC ed.

SHY *Song huiyao jigao* 宋會要輯稿, 460 *juan*, edited by Xu Song 徐松 (1781–1848) et al. Beijing: Zhonghua shuju, 1957.

SJZ *Shuijing zhu* 水經注, 40 *juan*, by Li Daoyuan 酈道元 (d. 527), edited by Wang Guowei 王國維. Shanghai: Shanghai Renmin chubanshe, 1984.

SKQSZMTY *Siku quanshu zongmu tiyao* 四庫全書總目提要, 200 *juan*, edited by Ji Yun 紀昀 (1724–1805) et al. Shanghai: Commercial Press, 1931.

SKTB *Beijing tushuguan cang Zhongguo lidai shike taben huibian* 北京圖書館藏中國歷代石刻拓本匯编, 100 vols. Zhengzhou: Zhongzhou guji chubanshe, 1989–1991.

SLGJ *Shilin guangji* 事林廣記, 50 *juan*, by Chen Yuanjing 陳元靚 (ca. 1200–1266). XXSKQS ed.

SLT *Sanli tu* 三禮圖, 20 *juan*, by Nie Chongyi 聶崇義 (tenth century). Shanghai: Tongwen shuju, ca. 1910.

SMCYXL *Song mingchen yanxing lu, wai ji* 宋名臣言行錄, 外集, 17 *juan*, by Li Youwu 李幼武 (fl. 1261). N.p., 1638.

SMTJ *Siming tujing (Qiandao)* 四明圖經 (乾道).12 *juan* (1169). By Zhang Jin 張津. Songyuan difang zhi congshu ed. Taibei: Dahua, 1980.

SQBJ *Shiqu baoji* 石渠寶笈, 44 *juan*, edited by Zhang Zhao 張照 (b. 1650) et al. SKQS ed.

SS *Song shi* 宋史, 496 *juan*, edited by Tuo Tuo 脫脫 (1313–1355) et al. Beijing: Zhonghua shuju, 1977.

SSF *Shu shu fu* 述書賦, by Dou Ji 竇泉 (fl. 750s–760s). In *Songren shulun* 宋人書論, edited by Pan Yungao 潘運告. Changsha: Hunan meishu chubanshe, 1999.

SSHY *Shushi huiyao* 書史會要, 9 *juan*, by Tao Zongyi 陶宗儀 (fl. 1360–1368). SKQS ed.

SSJSBM *Songshi jishi benmo* 宋史紀事本末, 40 *juan*, by Chen Bangzhan 陳邦瞻 (d. 1623). Beijing: Zhonghua shuju, 1977.

SSJW *Sushui jiwen* 涑水記聞, 16 *juan*, by Sima Guang 司馬光 (1019–1086). TangSong shiliao biji congkan ed. Beijing: Zhonghua shuju, 1989.

SSQW *Songshi quanwen* 宋史全文, 36 *juan*, anon., (Yuan), edited by Li Zhiliang 李之亮. Harbin: Heilongjiang renmin chubanshe, 2005.

SSQWXZZTJ *Songshi quanwen xu zizhi tongjian* 宋史全文續資治通鑑, 36 *juan*, anon. Songshi ziliao cuibian ed. Taipei: Wenhai chubanshe, 1969.

SSSJ *Su Shi shiji* 蘇軾詩集, 50 *juan*, by Su Shi 蘇軾 (1036–1101). Beijing: Zhonghua shuju, 1982.

SSWJ *Su Shi wenji* 蘇軾文集, 73 *juan*, by Su Shi 蘇軾 (1036–1101). Beijing: Zhonghua shuju, 1986.

SSWJHL *Shaoshi wenjian hou lu* 邵氏聞見後錄, 30 *juan*, by Shao Bowen 邵伯溫 (1056–1134). TangSong shiliao biji cong kan ed. Beijing: Zhonghua shuju, 1983.

SSY *Song shi yi* 宋史翼, 40 *juan*, by Lu Xinyuan 陸心源 (1834–1894). Reprint of Qing Guangxu ed. Songshi ziliao cuibian ed. Taipei: Wenhai, 1967.

SSZ *Sanshan zhi* 三山志, 42 *juan*, by Liang Kejia 梁克家 (1128–1187). In *Song Yuan difangzhi congshu* 宋元地方誌叢書. Taipei: Dahua, 1980.

STCHGT *Song ta Chunhua ge tie* 宋拓淳化閣帖, edited by Wang Zhu 王著. Shanghai: Commercial Press, 1934.

SuiS *Sui shu* 隋書, 85 *juan*, by Wei Zheng 魏徵 (580–643) and Linghu Defen 令狐德棻 (583–666). Beijing: Zhonghua shuju, 1973.

SWGWJ *Su Weigong wenji* 蘇魏公文集, 72 *juan*, by Su Song 蘇頌 (1020–1101). Beijing: Zhonghua shuju, 1988.

SXS *Shu xiao shi* 書小史, 10 *juan*, by Chen Si 陳思 (ca. 1200–1259+). In *Songren shulun* 宋人書論, edited by Pan Yungao 潘運告. Changsha: Hunan meishu chubanshe, 1999.

SXTFT *Sanxi tang fatie* 三希堂法帖, 10 *juan*, issued by Qing Gaozong 清高宗 (r. 1735–1796). N.p.: Wensheng tang shuju, 1935.

SXZJ *Songxuezhai ji* 松雪齋集, 10 *juan*, by Zhao Mengfu 趙孟頫 (1254–1322). SKQS ed.

SXZXSDYT *Shaoxi zhouxian shidian yitu* 紹熙州縣釋典儀圖, 1 *juan*, by Zhu Xi 朱熹 (1130–1200). SKQS ed.

SYJH *Shuyuan jinghua* 書苑菁華, 20 *juan*, by Chen Si 陳思 (fl. 1225–1264). SKQS ed.

SZFBNL *Song zaifu biannian lu jiaobu* 宋宰輔編年錄校補, 20 *juan*, by Xu Ziming 徐自明 (d. 1220+), edited by Wang Ruilai 王瑞來. Beijing, Zhonghua shuju, 1986.

SZJSZ *Shanzuo jinshizhi* 山左金石志, 24 *juan*, by Bi Yuan 畢沅 (1730–1797). SKSLXB ed.

TCMHL *Tangchao minghua lu* 唐朝名畫錄, 1 *juan*, by Zhu Jingxuan 朱景玄 (ninth century). In *Tang Wudai hualun* 唐五代畫論, edited by He Zhiming 何志明 and Pan Yungao 潘運告. Changsha: Hunan meishu chubanshe, 1997.

TGSB *Tang guoshi bu* 唐國史補, 3 *juan*, by Li Zhao 李肇 (fl. 806–820). SKQS ed.

THBJ *Tuhui baojian* 圖繪寶鑑, 5 *juan*, by Xia Wenyan 夏文彥 (fourteenth century). SKQS ed.

THJWZ *Tuhua jianwenzhi* 圖畫見聞誌, by Guo Ruoxu 郭若虛 (fl. 1070–1075). In *Tuhua jianwenzhi, Huaji* 圖畫見聞誌, 畫繼, edited by Pan Yungao 潘運告 and Mi Tianshui 米田水. Changsha: Hunan meishu chubanshe, 2000.

TPGJ *Taiping guangji* 太平廣記, 500 *juan*, by Li Fang 李昉 (925–996) et al. Beijing: Renmin chubanshe, 1959.

TWSCT *Tiewei shan congtan* 鐵圍山叢談, 6 *juan*, by Cai Tao 蔡絛 (?–1147+). TangSong shiliao biji congkan ed. Beijing: Zhonghua shuju, 1983.

TZ *Tongzhi* 通志, 200 *juan*, by Zheng Qiao 鄭樵 (1104–1162). Reprint of Shitong ed. Guoxue jiben congshu ed. Taipei: Xinxing shuju, 1962.

WJTJXJ *Wujun tujing xuji* 吳郡圖經續記, 3 *juan*, by Zhu Changwen 朱長文 (1039–1098). In *SongYuan difang zhi congshu*. Taipei: Dahua, 1980.

WLCQJ *Wang Linchuan quanji* 王臨川全集, 100 *juan*, by Wang Anshi 王安石 (1021–1086). Taipei: Shijie shuju, 1966.

WLJS *Wulin jiushi* 武林舊事, 10 *juan*, by Zhou Mi 周密 (1232–1308). In *Dongjing Menghua lu wai sizhong* 東京夢華錄外四種. Shanghai: Zhonghua shuju, 1962.

WXTK *Wenxian tongkao* 文獻通考, 348 *juan*, by Ma Duanlin 馬端臨 (ca. 1250–1325). Reprint of Shitong ed. Taipei: Xinxing shuju.

WZJ *Wenzhong ji* 文忠集, 200 *juan*, by Zhou Bida 周比大 (1126–1204). SKQS ed.

WZRY *Wengzhong renyu* 甕中人語, 1 *juan*, anon. (Song). In *Jingkang baishi jianzheng* 靖康稗史箋証, compiled by Cui An 確庵 and Nai An 耐庵, edited by Cui Wenyin 崔文印. Beijing: Zhonghua shuju, 1988.

XHHP *Xuanhe huapu* 宣和畫譜, 20 *juan*, anon., edited by Yu Jianhua 俞劍華. Beijing: Renmin meishu, 1964. (For other editions, see appendix 1.)

XHPL *Xu huapin lu* 續畫品錄, 1 *juan*, by Li Sizhen 李嗣真 (d. 696). In *Tang Wudai hualun* 唐五代畫論, edited by He Zhiming 何志明 and Pan Yungao 潘運告. Changsha: Hunan meishu chubanshe, 1997.

XHSP *Xuanhe shupu* 宣和書譜, 20 *juan*, anon. Shanghai: Shanghai shuju, 1984. (For other editions, see appendix 1.)

XJZJ *Xijing zaji* 西京雜記, 6 *juan*, attributed to Liu Xin 劉歆 (d. 23). In *Han Wei liuchao biji xiaoshuo daguan* 漢魏六朝筆記小說大觀. Shanghai: Shanghai guji chubanshe, 1999.

XNYL *Jianyan yilai xinian yaolu* 建炎以來繫年要錄, 200 *juan*, by Li Xinchuan 李心傳 (1166–1243). Beijing: Zhonghua shuju, 1956.

XQGJ *Qin ding Xiqing gujian* 欽定西淸古鑑, 40 *juan*, by Liang Shizheng 梁詩正 (1697–1763). SKQS ed.

XQXJYB *Xiqing xujian, yibian* 西淸續鑑乙編, 20 *juan*, edited by Wang Jie 王杰 (1725–1805). XXSKQS ed.

XSD *Xu shuduan* 續書斷, 2 *juan*, by Zhu Changwen 朱長文 (1041–1098). In *Songren shulun* 宋人書論, edited by Pan Yungao 潘運告. Changsha: Hunan meishu chubanshe, 1999.

XTS *Xin Tang shu* 新唐書, 225 *juan*, by Ouyang Xiu 歐陽修 (1007–1072) and Song Qi 宋祁 (998–1061). Beijing: Zhonghua shuju, 1975.

XX *Xinxu* 新序, 10 *juan*, by Liu Xiang 劉向 (77?–6? BCE). Taipei: Commercial Press, 1984.

XYJ *Xueyi ji* 學易集, 8 *juan*, by Liu Qi 劉跂 (d. 1117). SKQS ed.

XYJZ *Xu yijian zhi* 續夷堅志, 4 *juan*, by Yuan Haowen 元好問 (1190–1257). Beijing: Zhonghua shuju, 1986.

XZZTJ *Xu zizhi tongjian* 續資治通鑑, 220 *juan*, by Bi Yuan 畢沅 (1730–1797) et al. Beijing: Zhonghua shuju, 1957.

YDJSL *Yuedong jinshi lue* 粵東金石略, 9 *juan*, by Weng Fanggang 翁方綱 (1733–1818). SKSLXB ed.

YH *Yuhai* 玉海, 204 *juan*, by Wang Yinglin 王應鱗 (1223–1296). Shanghai: Shanghai shudian, 1987.

YLMC 雲麓漫鈔, 15 *juan*, by Zhao Yanwei 趙彥衛 (1140–1210). Shanghai: Gudian wenxue chubanshe, 1957.

YJZ *Yijian zhi* 夷堅志, 207 *juan*, by Hong Mai 洪邁 (1123–1202). Beijing: Zhonghua shuju, 1981.

YS *Yuan shi* 元史, 210 *juan*, edited by Song Lian 宋濂 (1310–1381) et al. Beijing: Zhonghua shuju, 1976.

YSSZ *Yuesheng suocang shuhua bielu* 悅生所藏書畫別錄. In *Zhongguo gudai meishu congshu* 中國古代美術叢書, edited by Deng Shi 鄧實, vol. 21. Beijing: Guoji wenhua chubanshe.

YTJH *Yutang jiahua* 玉堂嘉話, 4 *juan*, by Wang Yun 王惲 (1227–1304). SKQS ed.

YYZZ *Youyang zazu* 酉陽雜俎, 30 *juan*, by Duan Chengshi 段成式 (d. 863). Beijing: Zhonghua shuju, 1981.

YZTJ *Yanzhou tujing* 嚴州圖經, 3 *juan*, by Chen Gongliang 陳公亮 (twelfth century). In *Song Yuan difangzhi congshu* 宋元地方誌叢書. Taipei: Dahua, 1980.

ZBYL *Zeng Bu yilu* 曾布遺錄, 3 *juan*, by Zeng Bu 曾布 (1035–1107). In *Ouxiang lingshi* 藕香零拾, edited by Miao Quansun 繆荃孫. Beijing: Zhonghua shuju, 1998.

ZDKS *Zhongding kuanshi* 鐘鼎款識, 1 *juan*, by Wang Houzhi 王厚之 (1131–1204). XXSKQS ed.

ZGZDZY *Zeng guang zhongding zhuan yun* 增廣鐘鼎篆韻, by Yang Jun 楊鉤 (13th/14th century). XXSKQS ed.

ZHJ *Zhonghui ji* 忠惠集, 10 *juan*, by Zhai Ruwen 翟汝文 (1076–1141). SKQS ed.

ZHWLXY *Zhenghe wuli xinyi* 政和五禮新儀, 220 *juan*, edited by Zheng Juzhong 鄭居中 (1059–1123) et al. SKQS ed.

ZL *Zhou li* 周禮, 42 *juan*. Shisanjing zhushu ed. Reprint of 1815 ed. Taipei: Yiwen yinshu guan, 1981.

ZS *Zhou shi* 籀史, 1 *juan*, by Zhai Qinian 翟耆年 (twelfth century). Shoushan ge congshu ed.

ZXJ *Zhu Xi ji* 朱熹集, 100 + 26 *juan*, by Zhu Xi 朱熹 (1130–1200). Chengdu: Sichuan jiaoyu chubanshe, 1996.

ZZSLJT *Zhizhai shulu jieti* 直齋書錄解題, 22 *juan*, by Chen Zhensun 陳振孫 (1183–1261). CSJC ed.

ZZYL *Zhu Zi yulei* 朱子語類, 140 *juan* (1270), by Zhu Xi 朱熹 (1130–1200). Beijing: Zhonghua shuju, 1986.

SECONDARY SOURCES

Acker, William, trans. 1954, 1974. *Some T'ang and Pre-T'ang Texts on Painting.* 2 vols. Leiden: E. J. Brill.

Adamson, John, ed. 1999. *The Princely Courts of Europe, 1500–1750*. London: Seven Dials.

Akin, Marjorie. 1996. "Passionate Possession: The Formation of Private Collections." In *Learning from Things: Method and Theory of Material Culture Studies,* edited by W. David Kingery, 102–28. Washington: Smithsonian Institution Press.

Alsop, Joseph. 1982. *The Rare Art Traditions: The History of Art Collecting and Its Linked Phenomena Wherever These Have Appeared.* New York: Harper & Row.

Asch, Ronald G., and Adolf M. Birke, eds. 1991. *Princes, Patronage, and the Nobility: The Court at the Beginning of the Modern Age, c. 1450–1650.* Oxford: Oxford University Press.

Bagley, Robert. 2004. "The Prehistory of Chinese Music Theory." *Proceedings of the British Academy* 131:41–90.

Barnard, Noel. 1973. "Records of Discoveries of Bronze Vessels in Literary Sources—and

Some Pertinent Remarks on Aspects of Chinese Historiography." *Journal of the Institute of Chinese Studies of the Chinese University of Hong Kong* 6.2:455–544.
Barnhart, Richard. 1964. "Wei Fu-jen's *Pi Chen t'u* and the Early Texts on Calligraphy." *Archives of the Chinese Art Society of America* 18:13–25.
———. 1970. *Marriage of the Lord of the River: A Lost Landscape by Tung Yuan.* Ascona, Switzerland: Artibus Asia Publishers.
———. 1976. "Li Kung-lin's Use of Past Styles." In *Artists and Traditions,* edited by Christian Murck, 51–71. Princeton: Princeton University Press.
———. 1983. "Wang Shen and Late Northern Sung Landscape Painting." *International Symposium on Art Historical Studies 2: Ajia ni okeru sansui hyōmen ni tsuite.* Kyoto: Kyoto National Museum and Taniguchi Foundation.
———. 1991. "Tung Ch'i-ch'ang's Connoisseurship of Sung Painting and the Validity of His Historical Theories: A Preliminary Study." In *Proceedings of the Tung Ch'i-ch'ang International Symposium*, edited by Wai-ching Ho, 11.1–11.20. Kansas City: Nelson-Atkins Museum of Art.
———. 1993. *Li Kung-lin's Classic of Filial Piety.* New York: Metropolitan Museum of Art.
———. 1994. "Landscape Painting around 1085." In *The Power of Culture: Studies in Chinese Cultural History*, edited by Willard J. Peterson, Andrew H. Plaks, and Ying-shih Yü, 195–205. Hong Kong: Chinese University of Hong Kong Press.
———. 1997. "The Five Dynasties and the Song Period." In *Three Thousand Years of Chinese Painting,* edited by Yang Xin et al., 87–137. New Haven: Yale University Press.
———. 1998. "Three Song Landscape Paintings." *Orientations* 29.2:54–58.
Berger, Patricia. 2003. *Empires of Emptiness: Buddhist Art and Political Authority in Qing China.* Honolulu: University of Hawaii Press.
Bickford, Maggie. 1996a. *Ink Plum: The Making of a Chinese Scholar-Painting Genre.* New York: Cambridge University Press.
———. 1996b. "The Painting of Flowers and Birds in Sung-Yüan China." In *Arts of the Sung and Yüan,* edited by Maxwell K. Hearn and Judith G. Smith, 293–315. New York: Metropolitan Museum of Art.
———. 2002–3. "Emperor Huizong and the Aesthetic of Agency," *Archives of Asian Art* 53:71–104.
———. 2004. "Relic, Replica and Romance: Possessing the Past at the Courts of Song China." Paper presented at the symposium Song Painting and Its Legacy, Yale University, April 3, 2004.
———. 2006. "Huizong's Paintings: Art and the Art of Emperorship." In *Emperor Huizong and Late Northern Song China: The Politics of Culture and the Culture of Politics,* edited by Patricia Buckley Ebrey and Maggie Bickford, 453–513. Cambridge, MA: Harvard Asia Center, 2006.
———. 2007. "Making the Chinese Cultural Heritage at the Courts of the Northern Sung." In *Conference on Founding Paradigms: The Art and Culture of the Northern Sung Dynasty, Conference Papers.* Taipei: National Palace Museum.
Biot, Édouward, trans. 1851. *Le Tcheou-li, ou Rites des Tcheou.* 2 vols. Paris: l'Imprimerie Nationale.
Bo Songnian 薄松年. 1998. *Zhao Ji* 趙佶. Beijing: Wenwu chubanshe.
Bol, Peter K. 1992. *This Culture of Ours: Intellectual Traditions in T'ang and Sung China.* Stanford: Stanford University Press.

———. 1993. "Government, Society, and State: On the Political Visions of Ssu-ma Kuang and Wang An-shih." In *Ordering the World: Approaches to State and Society in Sung Dynasty China,* edited by Robert P. Hymes and Conrad Schirokauer, 128–92. Berkeley: University of California Press.

———. 2001. "Whither the Emperor? Emperor Huizong, the New Policies, and the Tang-Song Transition." *Journal of Song-Yuan Studies* 31:103–34.

———. 2006. "Emperors Can Claim Antiquity Too—Emperorship and Autocracy under the New Policies." In *Emperor Huizong and Late Northern Song China: The Politics of Culture and the Culture of Politics,* edited by Patricia Buckley Ebrey and Maggie Bickford, 173–205. Cambridge, MA: Harvard Asia Center.

Boltz, Judith M. 1987. *A Survey of Taoist Literature, Tenth through Seventeenth Centuries.* Berkeley: Institute of East Asian Studies.

———. 1993. "Not by the Seal of Office Alone: New Weapons in Battles with the Supernatural." In *Religion and Society in T'ang and Sung China*, edited by Patricia Buckley Ebrey and Peter N. Gregory, 241–305. Honolulu: University of Hawaii Press.

Bossler, Beverly J. 1998. *Powerful Relations: Kinship, Status, and the State in Sung China (960–1279).* Cambridge, MA: Council on East Asian Studies, Harvard University.

Brashier, K. E. 1995. "Longevity Like Metal and Stone: The Role of the Mirror in Han Burials." *T'oung Pao* 81:201–29.

Brotherton, Elizabeth. 2000. "Beyond the Written Word: Li Gonglin's Illustrations to Tao Yuanming's *Returning Home,*" *Artibus Asiae* 59.3–4:225–63.

Brown, Jonathan. 1994. *Kings and Connoisseurs: Collecting Art in Seventeenth-Century Europe.* Princeton: Princeton University Press.

Bulling, A. 1960. *The Decoration of Mirrors of the Han Period: A Chronology.* Ascona, Switzerland: Artibus Asiae Publishers.

Bush, Susan. 1971. *The Chinese Literati on Painting: Su Shih (1037–1101) to Tung Ch'i-ch'ang (1555–1636).* Cambridge, MA: Harvard University Press.

———. 1983. "Tsung Ping's Essay on Painting Landscape and the 'Landscape Buddhism' on Mount Lu." In *Theories of the Arts in China,* edited by Susan Bush and Christian Murck, 132–64. Princeton: Princeton University Press.

———. 2004. "The Essay on Painting by Wang Wei (415–453) in Context." In *Chinese Aesthetics: The Ordering of Literature, the Arts, and the Universe in the Six Dynasties,* edited by Zong-qi Cai, 60–80. Honolulu: University of Hawaii Press.

Bush, Susan, and Christian Murck, eds. 1983. *Theories of the Arts in China*. Princeton: Princeton University Press.

Bush, Susan, and Hsio-yen Shih. 1985. *Early Chinese Texts on Painting.* Cambridge, MA: Hoarvard University Press.

Cahill, James. 1958. "Wu Chen, A Chinese Landscapist and Bamboo Painter of the Fourteenth Century." PhD diss., University of Michigan.

———. 1960a. *Chinese Painting.* Geneva: Skira.

———. 1960b. "Confucian Elements in the Theory of Painting." In *The Confucian Persuasion,* edited by Arthur F. Wright, 115–40. Stanford: Stanford University Press.

———. 1961. "The Six Laws and How to Read Them." *Ars Orientalis* 4:132–63.

———. 1963. "Collecting Painting in China." *Arts Magazine* 37.7:66–72.

———. 1980. *An Index to Early Chinese Paintings*. Berkeley: University of California Press.

———. 1982. "Some Aspects of Tenth Century Painting as Seen in Three Recently-

Published Works." *Proceedings of the International Conference on Sinology: Section on History of Art,* 1–21. Taipei: Academia Sinica.

———. 1996a. "The Imperial Painting Academy." In *Possessing the Past: Treasures from the National Palace Museum, Taipei,* edited by Wen C. Fong and James C. Y. Watt, 159–99. New York: Metropolitan Museum of Art.

———. 1996b. *The Lyric Journey: Poetic Painting in China and Japan.* Cambridge: Harvard University Press.

Cahill, Suzanne. 1980. "Taoism at the Sung Court: The Heavenly Text Affair of 1008." *Bulletin of Sung and Yüan Studies* 16:23–44.

———. 1986. "The World Made Bronze: Inscriptions on Medieval Chinese Bronze Mirrors." *Archives of Asian Art* 39:62–70.

Cai Meifen 蔡玫芬. 1991. "Zhenghe ding" 政和鼎. *Gugong wenwu yuekan* 104:1.

Cai, Zong-qi, ed. 2004a. *Chinese Aesthetics: The Ordering of Literature, the Arts, and the Universe in the Six Dynasties.* Honolulu: University of Hawaii Press.

———. 2004b. "The Conceptual Origins and Aesthetic Significance of 'Shen' in Six Dynasties Texts on Literature and Painting." In *Chinese Aesthetics: The Ordering of Literature, the Arts, and the Universe in the Six Dynasties,* edited by Zong-qi Cai, 310–42. Honolulu: University of Hawaii Press.

Cammann, Schuyler. 1948. "The 'TLV' Pattern on Cosmic Mirrors of the Han Dynasty." *Journal of the American Oriental Society* 68.4:159–67.

———. 1953. "The Lion and Grape Patterns on Chinese Bronze Mirrors." *Artibus Asiae* 16.4:265–91.

Cen Zhongmian 岑仲勉. 1948. "*Xuanhe bogu* tu zhuanren" 宣和博古圖撰人. *Guoli zhongyang yanjiuyuan lishi yuyan yanjiusuo jikan* 12:353–61.

Chaffee, John W. 1985. *The Thorny Gates of Learning in Sung China: A Social History of Examinations.* Cambridge: Cambridge University Press.

———. 1990–92. "Chao Ju-yu, Spurious Learning, and Southern Sung Political Culture." *Journal of Sung-Yüan Studies* 22:23–61.

———. 1999. *Branches of Heaven: A History of the Imperial Clan of Sung China.* Cambridge, MA: Harvard University Asia Center.

———. 2006. "Huizong, Cai Jing, and the Politics of Reform." In *Emperor Huizong and Late Northern Song China: The Politics of Culture and the Culture of Politics,* edited by Patricia Buckley Ebrey and Maggie Bickford, 31–77. Cambridge, MA: Harvard Asia Center, 2006.

Chan, Hok-lam. 1984. *Legitimation in Imperial China: Discussions under the Jurchen-Chin Dynasty (1115–1234).* Seattle: University of Washington Press.

Chang Bide 昌彼得. 1971. "Ba Yuan dade ben *Xuanhe huapu*" 跋元大德本宣和畫譜. *Gugong tushu jikan* 2.2:73–76.

Chang, Ch'ung-ho, and Hans H. Frankel, trans. 1995. *Two Chinese Treatises on Calligraphy.* New Haven: Yale University Press.

Chang, Curtis Chung. 1968. "Inheritance Problems in the First Two Reigns of the Sung Dynasty." *The Hong Kong Baptist College Academic Journal* 3.1:48–74.

Chang Kuang-yuan. 1978. "The Stone Drums and the Glory of Ch'in Culture: The Successor to the Culture of Western Chou, Parts I and II," *National Palace Museum Bulletin* 13.3:1–20; 13.4:1–17.

Chang, Kwang-chih. 1983. *Art, Myth, and Ritual.* Cambridge, MA: Harvard University Press.

———. 1986. *The Archaeology of Ancient China*, 4th ed. New Haven: Yale University Press.

Chang, Lin-sheng (see also Zhang Linsheng). 1996. "The National Palace Museum: A History of the Collection." In *Possessing the Past: Treasures from the National Palace Museum, Taipei*, edited by Wen C. Fong and James C. Y. Watt, 1–25. New York: Metropolitan Museum.

———. 1999. "The Wen-wang *Fang-ting* and Chung-chü-fu *Kuei*: A Study of Archaistic Bronzes in the National Palace Museum." *National Palace Museum Bulletin* 34.5:1–20.

———. 2000. "The Wen-wang *Fang-ting* and Chung-chü-fu *Kuei*: A Study of Archaistic Bronzes in the National Palace Museum (continued)." *National Palace Museum Bulletin* 34.6:21–36.

Chao, Shin-yi. 2003. "Daoist Examinations and Daoist Schools during the Northern Song Dynasty." *Journal of Chinese Religions* 31:1–37.

———. 2006. "Huizong and the Divine Empyrean Palace Temple Network." In *Emperor Huizong and Late Northern Song China: The Politics of Culture and the Culture of Politics*, edited by Patricia Buckley Ebrey and Maggie Bickford, 324–58. Cambridge, MA: Harvard Asia Center.

Chaves, Jonathan. 1977. "The Legacy of Ts'ang Chieh: The Written Word as Magic." *Oriental Art* 23.2:200–15.

Chen Baozhen 陳葆真 (see also Chen Pao-chen). 1993. "Song Huizong huihua de meixue tezhi—Jianlun qi yuanyuan he yingxiang" 宋徽宗繪畫的美學特質—兼論其淵源和影響. *Wenshizhe xuebao* 40 (1993.6):293–344.

———. 1997. "Yishu de wang Li Houzhu, 1" 藝術的王李后主 (一), *Guoli Taiwan daxue meishushi yanjiu jikan* 4:43–58.

———. 1998. "Yishu de wang Li Houzhu, 2" 藝術的王李后主 (二), *Guoli Taiwan daxue meishushi yanjiu jikan* 5:41–76.

———. 1999. "Yishu de wang Li Houzhu, 3" 藝術的王李后主 (三), *Guoli Taiwan daxue meishushi yanjiu jikan* 6:71–130.

———. 2005. "Cong NanTang dao BeiSong—Qijian Jiangnan he Sichuan diqu huihua shili de fazhan" 從南唐到北宋—其間江南和四川地區繪畫勢力的發展. *Guoli Taiwan daxue meishushi yanjiu jikan* 18:155–208.

Chen Chuanxi 陳傳席. 1986. "Xuanhe huapu de zuozhe kao ji qita"《宣和畫譜》的作者考及其他. *Fuyang shiyuan xuebao* 1986.2: 89–91.

Chen Fangmei 陳芳妹. 1989. "Jiaguo zhongqi: chide juzun" 家國重器: 齒德俱尊 *Gugong wenwu yuekan* 81:70–81.

———. 2000. "Zaixian Sandai: Cong Gugong Songdai fanggu tongqi shuoqi" 再現三代—從故宮宋代仿古銅器說起. *Qianxi nian Songdai wenwu dazhan* 千禧年宋代文物大展, edited by Lin Boting 林柏亭, 293–320. Taipei: National Palace Museum.

———. 2001. "Song guqiwu xue de xingqi yu Song fanggu tongqi" 宋古器物學的興起與宋仿古銅器. *Meishu shi yanjiu jikan* 10:37–160.

———. 2005. "Zhui sandai yu dingyi zhi jian—Songdai cong *Kaogu* dao *Wangu* de zhuanbian" 追三代於鼎彝之間—宋代從「考古」到「玩古」的轉變. *Gugong xueshu jikan* 23.1:267–332.

Chen Gaohua 陳高華. 1984. *Song Liao Jin huajia shiliao* 宋遼金畫家史料. Beijing: Wenwu chubanshe.

———. 1987. *Sui Tang huajia shiliao* 隋唐畫家史料. Beijing: Wenwu chubanshe.

Chen Huiling 陳慧玲. 1988. "Lun Songdai jinshixue zhi fada ji qi jiazhi" 論宋代金石學之發達及其價值. *Guoli fanyiguan guankan* 17.2:245–58.

Chen, Jue. 2004a. "History and Fiction in the *Gujing ji* (Record of an Ancient Mirror)," *Monumenta Serica* 52:161–97.

———. 2004b. "The Mystery of an 'Ancient Mirror': An Interpretation of *Gujing ji* in the Context of Medieval Chinese Cultural History." *East Asian History* 24:33–50.

Chen Mengjia 陳夢家. 1964. "Song Dasheng bianzhong kaoshu" 宋大晟編鐘考述. *Wenwu* 1964.2:51–53.

Chen Mengjia and Wang Shimin 王世民. 1998. "*Bogu tu* kaoshu" 《博古圖》考述. *Hunan-sheng bowuguan wenji* 4:8–20.

Chen Pao-chen (see also Chen Baozhen). 1999. "Emperor Li Hou-chu as a Calligrapher, Painter, and Collector." In *Selected Essays on Court Culture in Cross-Cultural Perspective,* 133–69. Taipei: National Taiwan University Press.

Chen Wenju 陳溫菊. 1994. "Songdai jingxue de shengsi—You Songren guqi wuxue yu jinshixue yanjiu tanqi" 宋代經學的省思—由宋人古器物學與金石學研究談起 *Kong-meng yuekan* 32.7:34–42.

Chen Xiang 陳翔. 1992. "*Xuanhe huapu* de huihua meixue sixiang" 《宣和畫譜》的繪畫美學思想. In *Zhongguo huihua yanjiu lunwen ji* 中國繪畫研究論文集, edited by Duoyun 朵雲. Shanghai: Shanghai shudian. Reprinted from *Duoyun* 25.2 (1990):70–77, 23, where the author is listed as Jie Han 頡翰.

Chen Zhongyu 陳仲玉. 1972. "Lun Songdai jinshixue zhi fada ji qi jiazhi" 論宋代金石學之發達及其價值. *Shihuo* n.s. 2:18–30.

Cherniak, Susan. 1994. "Book Culture and Textual Transmission in Sung China." *Harvard Journal of Asiatic Studies* 54:5–125.

Chou, Ju-hsi. 1988. *Chinese Painting under the Qianlong Emperor.* Special issue of *Phøebus* 6.1.

———. 2000. *Circles of Reflection: The Carter Collection of Chinese Bronze Mirrors.* Cleveland: Cleveland Museum of Art.

Chou, Ju-hsi, and Claudia Brown. 1985. *The Elegant Brush: Chinese Painting Under the Qianlong Emperor, 1735–1795.* Phoenix: Phoenix Art Museum.

Chu, Hui-liang. 1990. "The Chung Yu (A.D. 151–220) Tradition: A Pivotal Development in Sung Calligraphy." PhD diss., Princeton University.

Chuang Shang-yen. 1967. "The Slender Gold Calligraphy of Emperor Sung Hui Tsung." *National Palace Museum Bulletin* 2:1–9.

Clunas, Craig. 1991. *Superfluous Things: Material Culture and Social Status in Early Modern China.* Cambridge, MA: Polity.

———. 1996. "Commodities, Collectables, and Trade Goods: Some Modes of Categorizing Material Culture in Sung-Yüan Texts." In *Arts of the Sung and Yüan*, edited by Maxwell K. Hearn and Judith G. Smith, 45–56. New York: Metropolitan Museum Department of Asian Art.

Crossley, Pamela K. 1992. "Review Article: The Rulerships of China." *American Historical Review* 97.5:1468–83.

———. 1999. *A Translucent Mirror: History and Identity in Qing Imperial Ideology.* Berkeley: University of California Press.

Cui Wenyin 崔文印. 1993. "Songdai de jinshi xue" 宋代的金石學. *Shixueshi yanjiu* 2:62–71.

David, Sir Percival, trans. and ed. 1971. *Chinese Connoisseurship: The Ko ku yao lun, The Essential Criteria of Antiquities.* New York: Praeger.

Davis, A. R. 1983. *T'ao Yüan-ming, AD 365–427: His Works and their Meaning.* 2 vols. New York: Cambridge University Press.

Davis, Edward L. 2001. *Society and the Supernatural in Song China.* Honolulu: University of Hawaii Press.

Davis, Richard L., trans. 2004. *Historical Records of the Five Dynasties,* by Ouyang Xiu. New York: Columbia University Press.

de Bary, Wm. Theodore, and Irene Bloom, eds. 1999. *Sources of Chinese Tradition.* 2nd ed. New York: Columbia University Press.

de Groot, J. J. M. 1892–1910. *The Religious System of China: Its Ancient Forms, Evolution, History and Present Aspect, Manners, Customs and Social Institutions Connected Therewith.* Leyden: E.J. Brill.

DeWoskin, Kenneth J. 1982. *A Song for One or Two: Music and the Concept of Art in Early China.* Ann Arbor: University of Michigan Center for Chinese Studies.

Djang, Chu, and Jane C. Djang, trans. 1989. *A Compilation of Anecdotes of Sung Personalities.* Compiled by Ting Ch'uan-ching. N.p.: St. John's University Press.

Doolittle, Justus. 1865. *Social Life of the Chinese.* 2 vols. New York: Harper & Brothers.

Drège, Jean-Pierre. 1991. *Les bibliothèques impériales en Chine au temps des manuscrits (jusqu'au Xe siècle).* Paris: École française d'Extrême-Orient.

Driscoll, Lucy, and Kenji Toda. 1935. *Chinese Calligraphy.* Chicago: University of Chicago Press.

Duindam, Jeroen. 1994. *Myths of Power: Norbert Elias and the Early Modern European Court.* Amsterdam: Amsterdam University Press.

Ebrey, Patricia Buckley. 1999. "Taking Out the Grand Carriage: Imperial Spectacle and the Visual Culture of Northern Song Kaifeng," *Asia Major* 12.1:33–65.

———. 2000. "Taoism and Art at the Court of Song Huizong." In *Taoism and the Arts of China,* edited by Stephen Little and Shawn Eichman, 95–111. Chicago: Art Institute of Chicago.

———. 2002. "The Emperor and the Local Community in the Song Period." In *Chūgoku no rekishi sekai—Tōgō no shisutemu to tagen teki hatten* 中國の歴史世界—統合のシステム—多元的發展, 373–402. Tokyo: Tokyo toritsu daigaku shuppankai.

———. 2006a. "Huizong's Stone Inscriptions." In *Emperor Huizong and Late Northern Song China: The Politics of Culture and the Culture of Politics,* edited by Patricia Buckley Ebrey and Maggie Bickford, 229–74. Cambridge, MA: Harvard Asia Center.

———. 2006b. "Literati Culture and the Relationship between Huizong and Cai Jing," *Journal of Song-Yuan Studies* 36:1–24.

———. 2006c. "Succession to High Office: The Chinese Case." In *Technology, Literacy, and the Evolution of Society: Implications of the Work of Jack Goody,* edited by David R. Olson and Michael Cole, 49–71. Mahwah: Lawrence Erlbaum.

———. 2007. "Rethinking Imperial Art Collecting: The Case of the Northern Sung." In *Conference on Founding Paradigms: The Art and Culture of the Northern Sung Dynasty, Conference Papers.* Taipei: National Palace Museum.

———. N.d. "Replicating Zhou Bells at the Northern Song Court." In *Reinventing the Past: Archaism and Antiquarianism in Chinese Art and Visual Culture,* edited by Wu Hung. Chicago: Paragon Press, forthcoming.

Ebrey, Patricia Buckley and Maggie Bickford, eds. 2006. *Emperor Huizong and Late Northern Song China: The Politics of Culture and the Culture of Politics.* Cambridge, MA: Harvard Asia Center.

Ecke, Betty Tseng Yu-ho (see also Tseng, Yuho). 1972. "Emperor Hui Tsung, the Artist: 1082–1136." PhD diss., New York University.

Edwards, Richard. 1993. "Li Gonglin's Copy of Wei Yan's *Pasturing Horses*." *Artibus Asiae* 53:168–93.

Egan, Ronald C. 1984. *The Literary Works of Ou-yang Hsiu (1007–72).* Cambridge: Cambridge University Press.

———. 1989. "Ou-yang Hsiu and Su Shih on Calligraphy." *Harvard Journal of Asiatic Studies* 49.2:365–419.

———. 1994. *Word, Image, and Deed in the Life of Su Shi.* Cambridge, MA: Council on East Asian Studies, Harvard University.

———. 2004. "Nature and Higher Ideals in Texts on Calligraphy, Music, and Painting." In *Chinese Aesthetics: The Ordering of Literature, the Arts, and the Universe in the Six Dynasties*, edited by Zong-qi Cai, 277–309. Honolulu: University of Hawaii Press.

———. 2005. "The Emperor and the Ink Plum: Tracing a Lost Connection between Literati and Huizong's Court." In *Rhetoric and the Discourses of Power in Court Culture: China, Europe, and Japan,* edited by David R. Knechtges and Eugene Vance, 117–48. Seattle: University of Washington Press.

———. 2006a. "Huizong's Palace Poems." In *Emperor Huizong and Late Northern Song China: The Politics of Culture and the Culture of Politics,* edited by Patricia Buckley Ebrey and Maggie Bickford, 361–94. Cambridge, MA: Harvard Asia Center, 2006.

———. 2006b. *The Problem of Beauty: Aesthetic Thought and Pursuits in Northern Song Dynasty China.* Cambridge, MA: Harvard University Asia Center.

Elias, Norbert. 1983. *The Court Society.* Trans. by Edmund Jephcott. Oxford: B. Blackwell.

Elliott, Jeannette Shambaugh, with David Shambaugh. 2005. *The Odyssey of China's Imperial Treasures.* Seattle: University of Washington Press.

Erickson, Susan N. 2001. "Investing in the Antique: Bronze Vessels of the Song Dynasty (960–1279)." In *Die Gegenward des Altertums: Formen und Funktionen des Altertumsbezugs in den Hochkulturen der Alten Welt,* edited by Dieter Kuhn and Helga Stahl, 423–35. Heidelberg: Edition Forum.

Escande, Yolaine. 1997. "Classements et évaluations à partir du Shuduan (Critères de la calligraphie) de Zhang Huaiguan." *Études chinoises* 16.2:39–113.

Falkenhausen, Lothar von. 1992. "On the Early Development of Chinese Musical Theory: The Rise of Pitch-Standards." *Journal of the American Oriental Society* 112.3:433–39.

———. 1993. *Suspended Music: Chime-Bells in the Culture of Bronze Age China.* Berkeley: University of California Press.

Fisher, Carney T. 1987. "The Ritual Dispute of Sung Ying-Tsung." *Papers on Far Eastern History* 36:109–38.

———. 1990. *The Chosen One: Succession and Adoption in the Court of Ming Shizong.* Sydney: Allen and Unwin.

Fong, Wen C. 1975. *Summer Mountains: The Timeless Landscape.* New York: Metropolitan Museum.

———. 1999. "Chinese Calligraphy: Theory and History." In *The Embodied Image: Chinese Calligraphy from the John B. Elliott Collection*, edited by Robert E. Harrist, Jr. and Wen C. Fong, 28–84. Princeton: Princeton University Art Museum.

Fong, Wen C., and James C. Y. Watt. 1996. *Possessing the Past: Treasures from the National Palace Museum, Taipei.* New York: Metropolitan Museum of Art.

Foong, Ping. 2000. "Guo Xi's Intimate Landscapes and the Case of Old Trees, Level Distance," *Metropolitan Museum Journal* 35:87–115.

———. 2006. "Li Cheng and a Landscape Past for the Northern Song Court." Paper presented at the Conference on "Reinventing the Past: Antiquarianism in East Asian Art and Culture," University of Chicago, November 3-4, 2006.

Franke, Herbert. 1962. "Chia Ssu-tao (1213–1275): A 'Bad Last Minister.'" In *Confucian Personalities*, edited by Arthur F. Wright and Denis Twitchett. Stanford: Stanford University Press.

———. 1970. "Treaties between Sung and Chin." *Études Song in Memoriam Étienne Balazs.* Series 1, part 1. Edited by Francoise Aubin, 55–84. Paris: Mouton.

———. 1994. "The Chin Dynasty." *The Cambridge History of China.* Vol. 6, *Alien Regimes and Border States, 907–1368,* edited by Herbert Franke and Denis Twitchett, 215–320. Cambridge: Cambridge University Press.

Franke, Herbert, and Denis Twitchett. 1994. "Introduction." *The Cambridge History of China.* Vol. 6, *Alien Regimes and Border States, 907–1368,* edited by Herbert Franke and Denis Twitchett, 1–42. Cambridge: Cambridge University Press.

Freeman, Michael Dennis. 1973. "Lo-yang and the Opposition to Wang An-shih: The Rise of Confucian Conservatism, 1068–1086." PhD diss., Yale University.

Fu, Marilyn Wong. 1981. "The Impact of the Reunification: Northern Elements in the Life and Art of Hsien-yü Shu (1257?–1302) and Their Relations to Early Yüan Literati Culture." In *China Under Mongol Rule,* 371–433, edited by John D. Langlois, Jr. Princeton: Princeton University Press.

Fu, Shen C. Y. 1976. "Huang T'ing-chien's Calligraphy and His *Scroll for Chang Ta-t'ung*: A Masterpiece Written in Exile." PhD diss., Princeton University.

———. 1977. *Traces of the Brush: Studies in Chinese Calligraphy.* New Haven: Yale University Art Gallery.

——— 傅申. 1981. *Yuan dai huang shi shu hua shou cang shi lüe* 元代皇室書畫收藏史略. Taipei: National Palace Museum.

———. 1987. "Periodization of Yen Chen-ch'ing's Calligraphic Influence." In *The International Seminar on Chinese Calligraphy in Memory of Yen Chen Ching's 1200th Posthumous Anniversary*, edited by Chen Chi-lu, 103–48. Taipei: Shen's Art Publishing Co.

———. 1990. "Princess Sengge Ragi: Collector of Painting and Calligraphy." In *Flowering in the Shadows: Women in the History of Chinese and Japanese Painting,* edited by Marsha Weidner, 55–80. Honolulu: University of Hawaii Press.

Fu Xinian 傅熹年. 1988. *Zhongguo meishu quanji* 中國美術全集 *Huihua bian* 繪畫編 3. Beijing: Wenwu chubanshe.

Gao Renjun 高仁俊. 1987. "Ding lu, si" 鼎錄, 四. *Gugong wenwu yuekan* 48:105–12.

Gimello, Robert M. 1992. "Mārga and Culture: Learning, Letters, and Liberation in Northern Sung Ch'an." In *Paths to Liberation: The Mārga and Its Transformations in Buddhist Thought*, edited by Robert E. Buswell, Jr., and Robert M. Gimello, 371–437. Honolulu: University of Hawaii Press.

Goepper, Roger. 1992. "Methods of Formal Analysis of Chinese Calligraphy, Taking Sun Guo-t'ing's *Shu-p'u* as an Example." *International Colloquium on Chinese Art History, 1999: Proceedings,* 599–626. Taipei: National Palace Museum.

Goldberg, Stephen J. 1988–89. "Court Calligraphy of the Early T'ang Dynasty." *Artibus Asiae* 49.3–4:189–237.

Gong Yanming 龔延明. 1997. *Songdai guanzhi cidian* 宋代官制辭典. Beijing: Xinhua shudian.

Graham, A. C., trans. 1990. *The Book of Lieh-tzu: A Classic of Tao.* New York: Columbia University Press.
Grant, Beata. 1994. *Mount Lu Revisited: Buddhism in the Life and Writings of Su Shih.* Honolulu: University of Hawaii Press.
Gugong bowuyuan 故宮博物院. 1935. "Song Xuanhe tongzun" 宋宣和銅尊. *Gugong zhoukan* 432:1204.
Gugong bowuyuan 故宮博物院, Liaoningsheng bowuguan 遼寧省博物館, Shanghai bowuguan 上海博物館, ed. 2002. *JinTangSongYuan shuhua guobao teji.* 晉唐宋元書畫國寶特集 Shanghai: Shanghai shuhua chubanshe.
Gugong bowuyuan canghua jibianji weiyuanhui 故宮博物院藏畫集編輯委員會. 1978. *Zhongguo lidai huihua* 中國歷代繪畫. Vol. 1. Beijing: Palace Museum.
———. 1981. *Zhongguo lidai huihua* 中國歷代繪畫. Vol. 2. Beijing: Palace Museum.
Guy, R. Kent. 1987. *The Emperor's Four Treasuries: Scholars and the State in the Late Ch'ien-lung Era.* Cambridge, MA: Harvard East Asian Monographs.
Gyss-Vermande, Caroline. 1995. "Lettres de Song Huizong au maître du Maoshan Liu Hunkang, ou le patronage impérial comme pratique de dévotion." In *Hommage À Kwong Hing Foon: Études d'histoire culturelle de la Chine,* 239–53. Paris: College de France, Institute des Hautes Études Chinoises.
Haeger, John Winthrop. 1968. "The Significance of Confusion: The Origins of the *T'ai-p'ing yü-lan,*" *Journal of the American Oriental Society* 88.3:401–10.
———. 1971. "Sung Government at Midstream: Translation of and Commentary on the *Ching-k'ang ch'uan-hsin lu.*" PhD diss., University of California, Berkeley.
Hargett, James M. 1988–89. "Huizong's Magic Marchmount: The Genyue Pleasure Park of Kaifeng." *Monumenta Serica* 38:1–48.
Harrist, Robert E. Jr. 1995. "The Artist as Antiquarian: Li Gonglin and His Study of Early Chinese Art." *Artibus Asiae* 55:237–80.
———. 1998. *Painting and Private Life in Eleventh-Century China: Mountain Villa by Li Gonglin.* Princeton: Princeton University Press.
———. 1999. "A Letter from Wang Hsi-chih and the Culture of Chinese Calligraphy." In *The Embodied Image: Chinese Calligraphy from the John B. Elliott Collection*, edited by Robert E. Harrist, Jr., and Wen C. Fong, 240–59. Princeton: Princeton University Art Museum.
———. 2004. "Replication and Deception in Calligraphy of the Six Dynasties Period." In *Chinese Aesthetics: The Ordering of Literature, the Arts, and the Universe in the Six Dynasties,* edited by Zong-qi Cai, 31–59. Honolulu: University of Hawaii Press.
Harrist, Robert E. Jr., and Won C. Fong, eds. 1999. *The Embodied Image: Chinese Calligraphy from the John B. Elliott Collection.* Princeton: The Art Museum, Princeton University.
Hartman, Charles. 1986. *Han Yü and the T'ang Search for Unity.* Princeton: Princeton University Press.
———. 1990. "Poetry and Politics in 1079: The Crow Terrace Poetry Case of Su Shih." *Chinese Literature: Essays, Articles, Reviews* 12:15–44.
———. 2001. "Poetry and Painting." In *Columbia History of Chinese Literature*, edited by Victor H. Mair, 466–90. New York: Columbia University Press.
———. 2006. "A Textual History of Cai Jing's Biography in the *Songshi.*" In *Emperor Huizong and Late Northern Song China: The Politics of Culture and the Culture of Poli-*

tics, edited by Patricia Buckley Ebrey and Maggie Bickford, 517–64. Cambridge, MA: Harvard Asia Center, 2006.
Hartwell, Robert M. 1982. "Demographic, Political, and Social Transformations of China, 750–1550." *Harvard Journal of Asiatic Studies* 42.2:365–442.
———. 1988. "The Imperial Treasuries: Finance and Power in Song China." *Bulletin of Sung-Yuan Studies* 20:18–89.
Hay, John. 1972. "'Along the River during Winter's First Snow': A Tenth-Century Handscroll and Early Chinese Narrative." *The Burlington Magazine* 114:294–304.
———. 1983. "The Human Body as a Microcosmic Source of Macrocosmic Values in Calligraphy." In *Theories of the Arts in China,* edited by Susan Bush and Christian Murck, 74–102. Princeton: Princeton University Press.
Hennessey, William O., trans. 1981. *Proclaiming Harmony.* Ann Arbor: Center for Chinese Studies, University of Michigan.
Hervouet, Yves. 1978. *A Sung Bibliography.* Hong Kong: Chinese University Press.
Hirth, Friedrich. 1906. "Chinese Metallic Mirrors, With Notes on Some Ancient Specimens of the Musée Guimet." In *Anthropological Papers Written in Honor of Franz Boas,* 208–56. New York: Stechert.
Ho, Ch'ing-ku. 1994. "The Artistic Achievement and Historical Position of Huai-su's Draft-Script Calligraphy." *T'ang Studies* 12:97–116.
Ho Chuan-hsing. 1996. "The Revival of Calligraphy in the Early Northern Sung." In *Arts of the Sung and Yüan*, edited by Maxwell K. Hearn and Judith G. Smith, 59–85. New York: Metropolitan Museum of Art, Department of Asian Art.
Ho, Chuimei, and Bennet Bronson. 2004. *Splendors of China's Forbidden City: The Glorious Reign of Emperor Qianlong.* Chicago: Field Museum.
Ho, Wai-kam. 1980. "Aspects of Chinese Painting from 1100 to 1350." In *Eight Dynasties of Chinese Painting: The Collections of the Nelson Gallery-Atkins Museum, Kansas City, and the Cleveland Museum of Art*, xxv–xxxiv. Cleveland: Cleveland Museum of Art.
Ho, Wai-kam, Sherman E. Lee, Laurence Sickman, and Marc F. Wilson. 1980. *Eight Dynasties of Chinese Painting: The Collections of the Nelson Gallery-Atkins Museum, Kansas City, and the Cleveland Museum of Art.* Cleveland: Cleveland Museum of Art.
Holzwarth, Gerald. 2005. "The Qianlong Emperor as Art Patron and the Formation of the Collections of the Palace Museum, Beijing." In *China: The Three Emperors 1662–1795,* edited by Evelyn S. Rawski and Jessica Rawson, 41–53. London: Royal Academy of Arts.
Huang Chaozong 黃潮宗. 1973. "Songdai de guoli tushuguan" 宋代的國立圖書館. *Dalu zazhi* 46.2:20–36.
Huang, Chi-chiang. 1994. "Imperial Rulership and Buddhism in the Early Northern Song." In *Imperial Rulership and Cultural Change in Traditional China,* edited by Frederick P. Brandauer and Chun-chieh Huang, 144–87. Seattle: University of Washington Press.
Huang, Ray. 1981. *1587: A Year of No Significance.* New Haven: Yale University Press.
Huang, Shih-shan Susan. 2002. "The Triptych of *Daoist Deities of Heaven, Earth and Water* and the Making of Visual Culture in the Southern Song Period (1127–1279)." PhD diss., Yale University.
Huang Tipei 黃體培. 1983. *Zhonghua yuexue tonglun* 中華樂學通論. Vol. 2. Taipei: Xingzengyuan wenhua jianshe weiyuanhui.
Hucker, Charles O. 1985. *A Dictionary of Official Titles in Imperial China.* Stanford: Stanford University Press.

Hymes, Robert P. 1986. *Statesmen and Gentlemen: The Elite of Fu-chou, Chiang-hsi in Northern and Southern Sung.* Cambridge: Cambridge University Press.

Ihara Hiroshi 伊原弘. 2004. *Kisō to sono jidai* 徽宗とその時代 (Special issue of journal *Ajia yōgaku* 64).

Inglis, Alister D. 2006. *Hong Mai's* Record of the Listener *and Its Song Dynasty Context.* Albany: State University of New York Press.

Jacobsen, Robert D. 2002. *Appreciating China.* Minneapolis: Minneapolis Institute of Arts.

Jang, Scarlett. 1992. "Realm of the Immortals: Paintings Decorating the Jade Hall of the Northern Song." *Ars Orientalis* 22:81–96.

Jay-Preston, Jennifer. 1983. "The Life and Loyalism of Chou Mi (1232–1298) and His Circle of Friends." *Papers on Far Eastern History* 28:49–105.

Ji, Xiao-bin. 2005. *Politics and Conservatism in Northern Song China.* Hong Kong: The Chinese University Press.

Jiang Zhaoshen 江兆申. 1989. "Yuan cang fashu mingji gaiguan" 院藏法書名蹟概觀. *Gugong wenwu yuekan* 80:14–27.

Jie Han 頡翰. 1990. "Qian tan *Xuanhe huapu* de huihua meixue sixiang" 淺談《宣和畫譜》的繪畫美學思想. *Duoyun* 25:70–77, 23.

Jin Weinuo 金維諾. 1980. "Song Yuan huihua shouzang zhulu" 宋元繪畫收藏著錄. *Meishu yanjiu* 1980.3:68–71.

———. 1984. *Zhongguo meishu quanji* 中國美術全集, *huihua bian* 繪畫編. Vol. 2. Beijing: Renmin meishu chubanshe.

Jin Zhongshu 金中樞. 1966, 1967. "Lun BeiSong monian zhi chongshang Daojiao" 論北宋末年之崇尚道教(上,下). *Xinya xuebao* 1966.7.2:323–414; 1967.8.1:187–257.

Kahn, Harold. 1985. "A Matter of Taste: The Monumental and Exotic in the Qianlong Reign." In *The Elegant Brush: Chinese Painting Under the Qianlong Emperor 1735–1795,* 288–302. Phoenix: Phoenix Art Museum.

Kaltenmark, Max. 1974. "Miroirs Magiques." In *Mélanges de Sinologie offerts à Monsieur Paul Demiéville* (Bibliothèque de l'Institut des Hautes Études Chinoises XX), 151–66. Paris: Presses Universitaires de France.

Kaplan, Harold. 1970. "Yueh Fei and the Founding of Southern Sung China." PhD diss., Iowa State University.

Karlgren, Bernhard. 1934. "Early Chinese Mirror Inscriptions." *Bulletin of the Museum of Far Eastern Antiquities* 6:9–79.

———. 1941. "Huai and Han." *Bulletin of the Museum of Far Eastern Antiquities* 13:1–125.

Katō Shigeshi 加籐繁. 1963. *Zhongguo jingjishi kaozheng* 中國經濟史考證. Vol. 2. Beijing: Xinhua shuju.

Kaufmann, Thomas Dacosta. 1994. "From Treasury to Museum: The Collections of the Austrian Habsburgs." In *The Cultures of Collecting,* edited by John Elsner and Roger Cardinal, 137–54. Cambridge, MA: Harvard University Press.

Keene, Donald. 2003. *Yoshimasa and the Silver Pavilion: The Creation of the Soul of Japan.* New York: Columbia University Press.

Knoblock, John, and Jeffrey Riegel, trans. 2000. *The Annals of Lü Buwei.* Stanford: Stanford University Press.

Kobayashi, Yoshihiro 小林義廣. 2000. *Ōyō Shū: Sono shōgai to sōzoku* 欧陽脩: その生涯と宗族. Tokyo: Sōbunsha.

Koffler, Pauline Bentley. 1995. "The Story of the Magic Mirror (*Gujingji*) by Wang Du. Translated with an Introduction and Notes." In *Hommage à Kwong Hing Foon: Études d'Histoire Culturelle de la Chine,* 165–214. Paris: Collège de France Institut des Hautes Études Chinoises.

Kohara, Hironobu. 1988. "The Qianlong Emperor's Skill in the Connoisseurship of Chinese Painting." *Phoebus* 6.1 (*Chinese Painting under the Qianlong Emperor*), 56–73.

———. 1995. "Notes on Reading Mi Fu's *Huashi*." *Ars Orientalis* 25:11–18.

Kojima Tsuyoshi. 小島毅. 1992. "Sōdai no kokka saishi—*Seiwa gorei shingi* no tokuchō" 宋代の國家祭祀「政和五禮新儀」の特徵. In *Chūgoku reihō to Nihon ritsuryōsei* 中國禮法と日本律制, edited by Ikeda On 池田溫, 463–84. Tokyo: Tōhō shuppan.

Kong Xiangxing 孔祥星 and Liu Yiman 劉一曼. 1984. *Zhongguo gudai tongjing* 中國古代銅鏡. Beijing: Wenwu.

Kracke, Edward A. Jr. 1947. "Family versus Merit in Chinese Civil Service Examinations under the Empire." *Harvard Journal of Asiatic Studies* 10:103–23.

———. 1953. *Civil Service in Sung China: 960–1067.* Harvard-Yenching Institute Monographs, 13. Cambridge, MA: Harvard University Press.

———. 1977. "The Expansion of Educational Opportunity in the Reign of Hui-tsung and Its Implications." *Sung Studies Newsletter* 13:6–30.

Kuo, Jason Chi-sheng. 1989. "Huichou Merchants as Art Patrons in the Late Sixteenth and Early Seventeenth Centuries." In *Artists and Patrons: Some Social and Economic Aspects of Chinese Painting,* edited by Chu-tsing Li, 177–88. Seattle: University of Washington Press.

Kurz, Johannes L. 2001. "The Politics of Collecting Knowledge: Song Taizong's Compilations Project." *T'oung Pao* 87:289–315.

Lachman, Charles, trans. 1989. *Evaluations of Sung Dynasty Painters of Renown: Liu Tao-ch'un's* Sung-ch'ao ming-hua p'ing. Leiden: Brill.

Lam, Joseph S. C. 2006. "Huizong's Dashengyue, a Musical Performance of Emperorship and Officialdom." In *Emperor Huizong and Late Northern Song China: The Politics of Culture and the Culture of Politics,* edited by Patricia Buckley Ebrey and Maggie Bickford, 395–452. Cambridge, MA: Harvard Asia Center.

Langlois, John D. Jr. 1978. "Yü Chi and His Mongol Sovereign: The Scholar as Apologist," *Journal of Asian Studies* 38.1:99–116.

Lapina, Zinaida. 1980. "Recherches épigraphiques de Ou-yang Hsiu," *Etudes Song/Sung Studies,* n.s. 2:99–111.

Lawton, Thomas. 1969. "The *Mo-yuan Hui-kuan* by An Ch'i." Special issue, *National Palace Museum Quarterly* 1:13–35.

———. 1973. *Chinese Figure Painting.* Washington, DC: Freer Gallery of Art.

Ledderose, Lothar. 1973. "Subject Matter in Early Chinese Painting Criticism." *Oriental Art* n.s. 19.1:69–83.

———. 1976. "Mi Fu." In *Song Biographies: Painters*, edited by Herbert Franke, 116–27. Wiesbaden: Franz Steiner Verlag.

———. 1978–79. "Some Observations on the Imperial Art Collection in China." *Transactions of the Oriental Ceramic Society* 43: 33–45.

———. 1979. *Mi Fu and the Classical Tradition of Chinese Calligraphy.* Princeton: Princeton University Press.

———. 1983. "The Earthly Paradise: Religious Elements in Chinese Landscape Art."

In *Theories of the Arts in China,* edited by Susan Bush and Christian Murck, 165–83. Princeton: Princeton University Press.

———. 1984. "Some Taoist Elements in the Calligraphy of the Six Dynasties." *T'oung Pao* 70.4–5:246–278.

———. 1986. "Chinese Calligraphy: Its Aesthetic Dimension and Social Function." *Orientations* 17.10:35–50.

Lee, Hui-shu (see also Li Huishu). 1994. "The Domain of Empress Yang (1162–1233): Art, Gender and Politics at the Southern Sung Court." PhD diss., Yale University.

———. 2004. "The Emperor's Lady Ghostwriters in Song-Dynasty China." *Artibus Asiae* 64.1:61–101.

Lee, Sherman E., and Wai-kam Ho. 1981. "The Nature and Significance of the Collection of Liang Ch'ing-piao." *Proceedings of the International Conference on Sinology, Section of History of Arts,* 101–57. Taipei: Academia Sinica.

Lee, Thomas Hong-chi. 1985. *Government Education and Examinations in Sung China.* Hong Kong: The Chinese University of Hong Kong.

———. 1995. "Books and Bookworms in Song China: Book Collection and the Appreciation of Books." *Journal of Sung-Yuan Studies* 25:193–218.

Legge, James, trans. 1961. *The Chinese Classics.* 5 vols. Reprint of 1865–95 Oxford edition. Hong Kong: Hong Kong University Press.

———. 1967. *Li Chi, Book of Rites.* 2 vols. Reprint of 1885 Oxford Sacred Books of the East edition. New York: University Books.

Levine, Ari Daniel. 2002. "A House in Darkness: The Politics of History and the Language of Politics in the Late Northern Song, 1066–1104." PhD diss., Columbia University.

———. 2006. "Terms of Estrangement: Factional Discourse in the Early Huizong Reign, 1100–1104." In *Emperor Huizong and Late Northern Song China: The Politics of Culture and the Culture of Politics,* edited by Patricia Buckley Ebrey and Maggie Bickford, 131–70. Cambridge, MA: Harvard Asia Center.

Li Huarui 李華瑞. 1993. "Songdai huashichang chutan" 宋代畫市場初探. *Meishu shilun* 45 (1993.1):68–76.

Li Huishu 李慧淑 (see also Lee Hui-shu). 1984. "Songdai huafeng zhuanbian zhi qiji—Huizong meishu jiaoyu chenggong zhi shili" 宋代畫風轉變之契機—徽宗美術教育成功之實例（上,下）. *Gugong xueshu jikan* 1.4:71–91; 2.1:9–36.

Li Meiling 李美玲. 2004. "Shishu jie mei—Du Mu 'Zhang Haohao shi' pingxi" 詩書皆美—杜牧「張好好詩」評析." *Zhongguo wenhua yuekan (Donghai daxue)* 284:70–85.

Li Xueqin 李學勤, ed. 1986. *Zhongguo meishu quanji* 中國美術全集, Gongyi 工藝 5: Qingtong qi 青銅器 2. Beijing: Wenwu.

Li Youping 李幼平. 2004. *Dasheng zhong yu Songdai huangzhong biaozhun yingao yanjiu* 大晟鍾與宋代黃鍾標準音高研究. Shanghai: Shanghai yinyue xueyuan chubanshe.

Liaoningsheng bowuguan, 遼寧省博物館 ed. 1998. *Shuhua zhulu: shuhua juan* 書畫著錄:書畫卷. Shenyang: Liaoning meishu chubanshe.

Lin, Yutang. 1967. *The Chinese Theory of Art.* New York: Putnam Sons.

Lin Po-ting 林柏亭. 1994. "Changes in the Meaning of *Hsieh-sheng.*" *National Palace Museum Bulletin* 28.6:1–17.

———. 1996. "The Relationship Between Intimate Scenery and Shoal-and-Waterfowl Paintings in the Sung Dynasty." In *Arts of the Sung and Yuan,* edited by Maxwell K. Hearn and Judith G. Smith, 87–107. New York: Metropolitan Museum of Art.

Little, Stephen, with Shawn Eichman. 2000. *Taoism and the Arts of China*. Berkeley: University of California Press.

Liu, Cary Y. 1999. "Sung Dynasty Painting of the T'ai-ch'ing-lou Library Hall: From Historical Commemoration to Architectural Renewal." In *Arts of the Sung and Yüan: Ritual, Ethnicity, and Style in Painting*, edited by Cary Y. Liu and Dora C. Y. Ching, 95–119. Princeton: The Art Museum, Princeton University.

Liu Cunren 柳存仁 (see also Liu, Ts'un-yan). 1991. "Daozang ben san sheng zhu Daode jing huijian" 道藏本三聖注道德經會箋. In *Hefeng tang wenji* 和風堂文集, 223–495. Shanghai: Shanghai guji chubanshe.

Liu, Heping. 1997. "Painting and Commerce in Northern Song Dynasty China, 960–1126." PhD diss., Yale University.

———. 2002. "*The Water Mill* and Northern Song Imperial Patronage of Art, Commerce, and Science." *Art Bulletin* 84.4:566–95.

———. 2003. "Empress Liu's *Icon of Maitreya*: Portraiture and Privacy at the Early Song Court," *Artibus Asiae* 63.2:129–90.

Liu, James T. C. (see also Liu Zijian). 1957. "An Early Sung Reformer: Fan Chung-yen." In *Chinese Thought and Institutions*, edited by John K. Fairbank, 105–31. Chicago: University of Chicago Press.

———. 1959. *Reform in Sung China: Wang An-shih (1021–1086) and His New Policies*. Cambridge, MA: Harvard University Press.

———. 1962. "An Administrative Cycle in Chinese History." *Journal of Asian Studies* 21.3:137–52.

———. 1967. *Ou-yang Hsiu: An Eleventh-Century Neo-Confucianist*. Stanford: Stanford University Press.

Liu, Ts'un-yan (see also Liu Cunren). 1974. *On the Art of Ruling a Big Country: Views of Three Chinese Emperors*. Canberra: Australian National University Press.

Liu Yu and Ding Meng. 1999. "Inscriptions on Zhou Dynasty Bronze Bells." *China Archaeology and Art Digest* 3.2–3:19–28.

Liu Zhaorui 劉昭瑞. 1992. "Jianlun Songren de gu qiwu xue yanjiu" 簡論宋人的古器物學研究. *Wenbo* 1992.2:34–38, 79.

Liu Zijian 劉子健 (see also Liu, James T. C.). 1987. *Liang Song shi yanjiu huibian* 兩宋史研究彙編. Taipei: Lianjing.

Lo, Winston W. 1987. *An Introduction to the Civil Service of Sung China, with an Emphasis on Its Personnel Administration*. Honolulu: University of Hawaii Press.

Loehr, Max. 1961. "Chinese Paintings with Sung Dated Inscriptions." *Ars Orientalis* 4:219–84.

Loewe, Michael. 1979. *Ways to Paradise: The Chinese Quest for Immortality*. London: George Allen & Unwin.

———. 1982. *Chinese Ideas of Life and Death: Faith, Myth and Reason in the Han Period (202 BC–AD 220)*. London: Allen and Unwin.

———, ed. 1993. *Early Chinese Texts: A Bibliographical Guide*. Berkeley: Institute of East Asian Studies, University of California.

Luoyang Bowuguan 洛陽博物館, ed. 1988. *Luoyang chutu tongjing* 洛陽出土銅鏡. Beijing: Wenwu chubanshe.

Ma Ziyun 馬子云. 1985. "Tan jiao gugong cang Song ta Chunhua, Jiangtie, Daguan santie" 談校故宮藏宋拓《淳化》,《絳帖》,《大觀》三帖. *Gugong bowuyuan yuankan* 1985.3:95–104.

Maeda, Robert J. 1970a. "The Chao Ta-nien Tradition." *Ars Orientalis* 8:243–53.

———. 1970b. *Two Twelfth Century Texts on Chinese Painting.* Ann Arbor: Michigan Papers in Chinese Studies.

Mair, Victor H. 2004. "Xie He's 'Six Laws' of Painting and Their Indian Parallels." In *Chinese Aesthetics: The Ordering of Literature, the Arts, and the Universe in the Six Dynasties,* edited by Zong-qi Cai, 81–122. Honolulu: University of Hawaii Press.

Mattos, Gilbert L. 1988. *The Stone Drums of Ch'in.* Nettetal, West Germany: Steyler.

Mayo, Margaret Ellen. 2005. "Collecting Ancient Art: A Historical Perspective." In *Who Owns the Past? Cultural Policy, Cultural Property, and the Law,* edited by Kate Fitz Gibbon, 133–41. New Brunswick: Rutgers University Press.

McCausland, Shane, ed. 2003. *Gu Kaizhi and the Admonitions Scroll.* London: The British Museum Press.

McDermott, Joseph P. 2005. "The Ascendance of the Imprint in China." In *Printing and Book Culture in Late Imperial China,* edited by Cynthia J. Brokaw and Kai-wing Chow, 55–104. Berkeley: University of California Press.

McMullen, David L. 1988. *State and Scholars in T'ang China.* Cambridge: Cambridge University Press.

McNair, Amy. 1986. "The Sung Calligrapher Ts'ai Hsiang." *Bulletin of Sung-Yuan Studies* 18:61–75.

———. 1987. "*Fa shu yao lu,* a ninth-century compendium of texts on calligraphy." *T'ang Studies* 5:69–86.

———. 1990. "Su Shih's Copy of the *Letter on the Controversy over Seating Protocol.*" *Archives of Asian Art* 43:38–48.

———. 1994. "The Engraved Model-Letters Compendia of the Song Dynasty." *Journal of the American Oriental Society* 114.2:209–25.

———. 1995. "Engraved Calligraphy in China: Recension and Reception." *Art Bulletin* 77.1:106–14.

———. 1998. *The Upright Brush: Yan Zhenqing's Calligraphy and Song Literati Politics.* Honolulu: University of Hawaii Press.

Meyer, Agnes E. 1923. *Chinese Painting as Reflected in the Thought and Art of Li Lung-mien, 1070–1106.* New York: Duffield and Co.

Miyakawa, Hisayuki 宮川尚志. 1975a. "Rin Reiso to Sō no Kisō" 林靈素と宋の徽宗. *Tōkai daigaku kiyō (bunkaku bu)* 2:1–8.

———. 1975b. "Sō no Kisō to dōkyō" 宋の徽宗と道教. *Tōkai daigaku kiyō (bunkaku bu)* 23:1–10.

Mote, Frederick. 1999. *Imperial China 900–1800.* Cambridge, MA: Harvard University Press.

Munakata, Kiyohiko. 1974. *Jing Hao's* Bifaji: *A Note on the Art of Brush.* Ascona, Switzerland: Artibus Asiae Publishers.

———. 1991. *Sacred Mountains in Chinese Art.* Urbana: University of Illinois Press.

Murck, Alfreda. 2000. *Poetry and Painting in Song China: The Subtle Art of Dissent.* Cambridge, MA: Harvard Asia Center.

———. 2003. "The Convergence of Gu Kaizhi and *Admonitions* in the Literary Record." In *Gu Kaizhi and the Admonitions Scroll,* edited by Shane McCausland, 138–45. London: British Museum Press.

———. 2007. "Titles of Paintings: The Northern Sung Paradigm." In *Conference on*

Founding Paradigms: The Art and Culture of the Northern Sung Dynasty, Conference Papers. Taipei: National Palace Museum.

Murck, Alfreda, and Wen C. Fong, eds. 1991. *Words and Images: Chinese Poetry, Calligraphy, and Painting.* New York: Metropolitan Museum of Art.

Murray, Julia K. 1989. "Song Kao-tsung as Artist and Patron: The Theme of Dynastic Revival." *Artists and Patrons: Some Social and Economic Aspects of Chinese Painting,* edited by Chu-tsing Li, 27–36. Seattle: University of Washington Press.

Nakata Yūjirō 中田勇次郎. 1970. *Chūgoku shoron shū* 中國書論集. Tokyo: Nigensha.

———. 1977–95. *Chūgoku shoron taikei* 中國書論大系. 18 vols.; vols. 5 and 6 include annotated translation into Japanese of XHSP. Tokyo: Nigensha.

———. 1979–82. *Shodō geijutsu* 書道藝術. Tokyo: Chūō kōronsha.

———. 1983. *Chinese Calligraphy.* Tokyo: Weatherhill.

National Palace Museum. 1958. *Gugong tongqi tulu* 故宮銅器圖錄. Taipei: National Palace Museum.

———. 1964. *Signatures and Seals on Painting and Calligraphy.* Hong Kong: Cafa Co.

———. 1965. *Gugong shuhua lu, zeng ding ben* 故宮書畫錄, 增訂本. Taipei: National Palace Museum.

———. 1970. *Masterpieces of Chinese Calligraphy.* Taipei: National Palace Museum.

———. 1973. *Masterpieces of Chinese Figure Painting.* Taipei: National Palace Museum.

———. 1977. *Gugong lidai fashu quanji* 故宮歷代法術全集. Vol. 2. Taipei: National Palace Museum.

———. 1981. *Masterpieces of Chinese Calligraphy: Supplement.* Taipei: National Palace Museum.

———. 1985. *Haiwai yizhen huihua* 海外遺珍繪畫. Taipei: National Palace Museum.

———. 1989. *Gugong shuhua tulu* 故宮書畫圖錄. Vol. 1. Taipei: Guoli Gugong bowuyuan.

———. 1993. *Gugong canghua daxi* 故宮藏畫大系. Vol. 1. Taipei: Guoli Gugong bowuyuan.

———. 1995a. *Gugong shuhua tulu* 故宮書畫圖錄. Vol. 15. Taipei: Guoli Gugong bowuyuan.

———. 1995b. *Songdai shuhua ceye mingpin tezhan* 宋代書畫冊頁名品特展. Taipei: Guoli Gugong bowuyuan.

———. 2000. *Qianxi nian Songdai wenwu dazhan* 千禧年宋代文物大展. Taipei: National Palace Museum.

———. 2002. *Qianlong huangdi de wenhua daye* 乾隆皇帝的文化大業. Taipei: National Palace Museum.

Needham, Joseph. 1962. *Science and Civilization in China.* Vol. 4, *Physics and Physical Technology.* Part 1, *Physics.* Cambridge: Cambridge University Press.

Ni Genfa 倪根法. 1985. "*Xuanhe huapu* de chengshu niandai ji yu Mi Fu de guanxi" 《宣和畫譜》的成書年代及與米芾的關係. *Huadong shifan daxue xuebao* (Zhexue shehui dexue ban) 1985.3:81–83.

Niu Kecheng 牛克誠. 2005. "Xuanhe yufu yin geshi yanjiu" 宣和御府印格式研究. *Gugong bowuyuan yuankan* 2005.1:53–76.

Nylan, Michael. 1999. "Calligraphy, the Sacred Text and Test of Culture." In *Character and Context in Chinese Calligraphy,* edited by Cary Y. Liu, Dora C. Y. Ching, and Judith G. Smith, 16–77. Princeton: Princeton University Art Museum.

Onoe Hachirō 尾上八郎 et al., eds. 1954–68. *Shodō zenshū* 書道全書. 28 vols. Tokyo: Heibonsha.

Ōsaka shiritsu bijutsukan. 1975. *Chūgoku kaiga* 中國繪畫. Tokyo: Mainichi shimbunsha.

Owen, Stephen. 1981. *The Great Age of Chinese Poetry: The High T'ang.* New Haven: Yale University Press.

———. 1986. *Remembrances. The Experience of the Past in Classical Chinese Literature.* Cambridge, MA: Harvard University Press.

Pan, An-yi. 2000. "Painting and Friendship, Political and Private Life: The Case of Li Gonglin." *Journal of Sung-Yuan Studies* 30:97–113.

Pan Meiyue 潘美月. 1980. *Songdai cangshujia kao* 宋代藏書家考. Taipei: Xuehai chubanshe.

Pan Mingshen 潘銘燊 (see also Poon Ming-sun). 1971. "Songdai sijia cangshu kao" 宋代私家藏書考. *Huaguo* 6:201–62.

Pan Yungao 潘運告, ed. 1997. *Zhongwan Tang Wudai shulun* 中晚唐五代書論. Changsha: Hunan meishu chubanshe.

———. 1999. "Du *Xuanhe shupu* de ganxiang" 讀《宣和書譜》的感想. In *Xuanhe shupu,* 1–8. Changsha: Hunan meishu chubanshe.

Pearce, Susan M. 1995. *On Collecting: An Investigation into Collecting in the European Tradition.* London: Routledge.

Peng Huiping 彭慧萍. 2005. "Liang Song gongting shuhua chucang zhidu zhi bian: yi bige wei hexin de jiancang jizhi yanjiu" 兩宋宮廷書畫儲藏制度之變: 以秘閣為核心的鑒藏機制研究. *Gugong yuankan* 117:12–40.

Poon Ming-sun (see also Pan Mingshen). 1979. "Books and Printing in Sung China (960–1279)." PhD diss., University of Chicago.

Poor, Robert. 1965. "Notes on the Sung Dynasty Archaeological Catalogues." *Archives of the Chinese Art Society of America* 19:33–44.

Powers, Martin J. 1995. "Discourses on Representation in Tenth- and Eleventh-Century China." In *The Art of Interpreting,* edited by Susan C. Scott, 89–125. University Park: Pennsylvania State University Press.

Pratt, Keith. 1976. "Music as a Factor in Sung-Koryŏ Diplomatic Relations, 1069–1126." *T'oung Pao* 62.4–5:199–218.

———. 1981. "Sung Hui Tsung's Musical Diplomacy and the Korean Response." *Bulletin of the School of Oriental and African Studies* 44.3:509–21.

Provine, Robert C. 1996. "State Sacrificial Music and Korean Identity." In *Harmony and Counterpoint: Ritual Music in Chinese Context,* edited by Bell Yung, Evelyn S. Rawski, and Rubie S. Watson, 54–75. Stanford: Stanford University Press.

Qu Wanli 屈萬里. 1975. *Pulinsidun daxue Geside dongfang tushuguan zhongwen shanben shumu* 普林斯敦大學葛思德東方圖書館中文善本書目. Taipei: Yiwen yinshu guan.

Rawski, Evelyn S. 1998. *The Last Emperors: A Social History of Qing Imperial Institutions.* Berkeley: University of California Press.

Rawski, Evelyn S., and Jessica Rawson, eds. 2005. *China: The Three Emperors 1662–1795.* London: Royal Academy of Arts.

Ren Chongyue 任崇岳. 1998. *Song Huizong, Song Qinzong* 宋徽宗, 宋欽宗. Changchun: Jilin wenshi chubanshe.

Robinet, Isabelle. 1997. *Taoism: Growth of a Religion*, trans. Phyllis Brooks. Stanford: Stanford University Press.

Rong Geng 容庚. 1980. *Cong tie mu* 叢帖目. 3 vols. Hong Kong: Zhonghua shuju.

———. 1994. "Songdai jijin shuji shuping" 宋代吉金書籍述評. In *Rong Geng xuanji* 容庚選集, 3–73. Tianjin: Tianjin renmin chubanshe.

Rossabi, Morris, ed. 1983. *China among Equals: The Middle Kingdom and Its Neighbors, 10th–14th Centuries.* Berkeley: University of California Press.
Rowland, Benjamin. 1951. "The Problem of Hui Tsung." *Archives of the Chinese Art Society of America* 5:5–22.
Rudolph, Richard C. 1948. "Dynastic Booty: An Altered Chinese Bronze." *Harvard Journal of Asiatic Studies* 11:174–83.
———. 1963. "Preliminary Notes on Sung Archaeology." *Journal of Asian Studies* 22.2:169–77.
Rupert, Milan, and O. J. Todd. 1935. *Chinese Bronze Mirrors.* Peiping: San Yu Press.
Sakanishi, Shio. 1939. *The Spirit of the Brush, Being the Outlook of Chinese Painters on Nature from the Eastern Chin to Five Dynasties, A.D. 317–960.* London: J. Murray.
Sargent, Stuart H. 1992. "Colophons in Countermotion: Poems by Su Shih and Huang T'ing-chien on Paintings." *Harvard Journal of Asiatic Studies* 52.1:263–302.
Sariti, Anthony. 1972. "Monarchy, Bureaucracy, and Absolutism in the Political Thought of Ssu-ma Kuang." *Journal of Asian Studies* 32.1:53–76.
Schafer, Edward H. 1978–79. "A T'ang Taoist Mirror." *Early China* 4:56–59.
Schipper, Kristofer. 1993. *The Taoist Body,* trans. Karen C. Duval. Berkeley: University of California Press.
Schipper, Kristofer, and Franciscus Verellen. 2004. *The Taoist Canon: A Historical Companion to the* Daozang. Chicago: University of Chicago Press.
Schlombs, Adele. 1998. *Huai-su and the Beginnings of Wild Cursive Script in Chinese Calligraphy.* Stuttgart: Franz Steiner Verlag.
Schmidt-Glintzer, Helwig. 1988. "Zhang Shangying (1043–1122)—An Embarrassing Policy Adviser under the Northern Song." *Liu Tzu-chien hakushi shoshū kinen Sōshi kenkyū ronshū,* edited by Kinugawa Tsuyoshi. Kyoto: Dohōsha.
Sena, Yun-Chiahn C. n.d. "Cataloguing Antiquity: Song Scholarship on Ancient Objects." In *Reinventing the Past: Archaism and Antiquarianism in Chinese Art and Visual Culture,* edited by Wu Hung. Chicago: Paragon Press, forthcoming.
Shanghai bowuguan 上海博物館. 1987. *Zhongguo shuhuajia yinjian kuanshi* 中國書畫家印鑑款識. 2 vols. Beijing: Wenwu chubanshe.
Shanghai shuhua chubanshe 上海書畫出版社, ed. 2003a. *Linquan gaoshi* 林泉高士. Shanghai: Shanghai shuhua chubanshe.
———, ed. 2003b. *Junma qingji* 駿馬輕騎. Shanghai: Shanghai shuhua chubanshe.
———, ed. 2004. *Yanyou yaji* 宴游雅集. Shanghai: Shanghai shuhua chubanshe.
———, ed. 2005. *SongYuan huaniao* 宋元花鳥. Shanghai: Shanghai shuhua chubanshe.
Shaughnessy, Edward L. 1991. *Sources of Western Zhou History: Inscribed Bronze Vessels.* Berkeley: University of California Press.
She Cheng 佘城. 1988. *Bei Song tuhua yuan zhi xintan* 北宋圖畫院之新探. Taipei: Wenshizhe chubanshe.
Shen Peng 沈鵬. 1986. *Zhongguo meishu quanji* 中國美術全集. *Shufa zhuanke* 書法篆刻 4. Beijing: Wenwu chubanshe.
Shen Zhiyu, ed. 1983. *The Shanghai Museum of Art.* New York: Abrams.
Shui Laiyou 水賚佑. 1995. *Zhao Ji de shufa yishu* 趙佶的書法藝術. Beijing: Renmin meishu.
Sickman, Laurence, and Alexander Soper. 1956. *The Art and Architecture of China.* Baltimore: Penguin.

Sirén, Osvald. 1936. *The Chinese on the Art of Painting: Translations and Comments.* Peiping: Henri Vetch.

———. 1956. *Chinese Painting: Leading Masters and Principles.* 7 vols. London: Lund, Humphries and Co.

Smith, Paul. N.d. "Shen-tsung's Reign (1068–1085)." Draft chapter for the *Cambridge History of China*. Vol. 5: *The Song Dynasty*. Cambridge: Cambridge University Press, forthcoming.

Soper, Alexander C. 1949. "A Northern Sung Descriptive Catalogue of Paintings (The *Hua P'in* of Li Ch'ih)." *Journal of the American Oriental Society* 69.1:18–33.

———. 1951. *Kuo Jo-hsü's Experiences in Painting (T'u-hua chien-wen chih): An Eleventh Century History of Chinese Painting.* Washington, DC: American Council of Learned Societies.

———. 1957. "Standards of Quality in Northern Sung Painting." *Archives of the Chinese Art Society of America* 11:8–15.

———. 1958. "*T'ang ch'ao ming hua lu*: Celebrated Painters of the T'ang Dynasty by Chu Ching-hsüan of T'ang." *Artibus Asiae* 31:204–30.

———. 1976. "The Relationship of Early Chinese Painting to Its Own Past." In *Artists and Traditions: Uses of the Past in Chinese Culture*, edited by Christian F. Murck, 21–47. Princeton: The Art Museum, Princeton University.

Strickmann, Michel. 1978. "The Longest Taoist Scripture." *History of Religions* 17.3–4: 331–54.

———. 2002. *Chinese Magical Medicine,* edited by Bernard Faure. Stanford: Stanford University Press.

Sturman, Peter C. 1989. "Mi Youren and the Inherited Literati Traditions: Dimensions of Ink-play." PhD diss. Yale University.

———. 1990. "Cranes Above Kaifeng: The Auspicious Image at the Court of Huizong." *Ars Orientalis* 20:33–68.

———. 1997. *Mi Fu: Style and the Art of Calligraphy in Northern Song China*. New Haven: Yale University Press.

———. 1999. "Wine and Cursive: The Limits of Individualism in Northern Sung China." In *Character and Context in Chinese Calligraphy,* edited by Cary Y. Liu, Dora C.Y. Ching, and Judith G. Smith, 200–31. Princeton: Princeton University Art Museum.

Sullivan, Michael. 1982. "Some Notes on the Social History of Chinese Art." *Proceedings of the International Conference on Sinology: Section on History of Art,* 159–70. Taipei: Academia Sinica.

Sun Kekuan 孫克寬. 1965. *SongYuan daojiao zhi fazhan* 宋元道教之發展. Taipei: Sili Donghai daxue.

Swallow, R. W. 1937. *Ancient Chinese Bronze Mirrors.* Peiping: Henri Vetch.

Takatsu Takashi 高津孝. 2004. "Korekutaa to shite no Kisō" コレクターとしての 徽宗. *Ajia yōgaku* 64:32–33.

Tang Daijian 唐代劍. 1992. "*Songshi* 'Lin Lingsu zhuan' buzheng" 《宋史, 林靈素傳》補正. *Shijie zongjiao yanjiu* 49 (1992):23–28.

———. 1994. "Bei Song Shenxiaogong jiqi weiyi gouji" 北宋神霄宮及其威儀鉤稽. *Zhongguo daojiao* 1994.3:47–48.

Tao, Jing-shen. 1976. *The Jurchen in Twelfth-Century China: A Study of Sinification*. Seattle: University of Washington Press.

———. 1983. "Barbarians or Northerners: Northern Sung Images of the Khitan." *China among Equals: The Middle Kingdom and Its Neighbors, 10th–14th Centuries,* edited by Morris Rossabi, 66–86. Berkeley: University of California Press.

———. 1988. *Two Sons of Heaven: Studies in Sung-Liao Relations.* Tucson: University of Arizona Press.

———. 1989. "The Personality of Sung Kao-tsung (r. 1127–1162)." *Liu Tzu-chien hakushi shoshū kinen Sōshi kenkyū ronshū,* edited by Kinugawa Tsuyoshi, 531–43. Kyoto: Dohōsha.

Teng, Ssu-yü, and Knight Biggerstaff. 1971. *An Annotated Bibliography of Selected Chinese Reference Works.* 3rd ed. Cambridge, MA: Harvard University Press.

Thompson, Nancy. 1967. "The Evolution of the T'ang Lion and Grapevine Mirror." *Artibus Asiae* 29.1:25–54.

Thoms, Peter Perring. 1851. *A Dissertation on the Ancient Chinese Vases of the Shang Dynasty.* London: James Gilbert.

Thorp, Robert L., and Richard Ellis Vinograd. 2001. *Chinese Art and Culture.* New York: Abrams.

Tomioka Masutarō 富岡謙蔵. 1920. *Kokyō no kenkyū* 古鏡の研究. Kyoto: Maruzen.

Toyama Gunji 外山軍治. 1955. "Ka Shidō ni tuite" 賈似道について. *Shodō zenshū* 16:25–27.

———. 1957. "Kin Shoshu shōsō no shoga ni tsuite" 金章宗收藏の書畫について. In *Kanda Hakushi Kanreki kinen shoshigaku ronshū* 神田博士還曆記念書誌学論集, 531–39. N.p.: Kanda Hakushi Kanreki Kinenkai.

Tseng Yuho (see also Ecke, Betty Tseng Yu-ho). 1993. *A History of Chinese Calligraphy.* Hong Kong: The Chinese University Press.

Tsukamoto Maromitsu. 2005. "On 'Overseas Calligraphy': An Investigation into the Historical Role of Fine Art Diplomacy and the Collection of Artifacts in the Northern Song." *Transactions of the International Conference of Eastern Studies* 50:97–116.

Twitchett, Denis, and Klaus-Peter Tietze. 1994. "The Liao." In *The Cambridge History of China,* Vol. 6, *Alien Regimes and Border States, 907–1368,* edited by Herbert Franke and Denis Twitchett, 43–153. Cambridge: Cambridge University Press.

Umehara Kaoru 梅原郁. 1985. *Sōdai kanryō seido kenkyū* 宋代官僚制度研究. Kyoto: Dōhōsha.

Umehara, Sueji. 1955. "The Late Mr. Moriya's Collection of Ancient Chinese Bronzes." *Artibus Asiae* 18:238–56.

Van der Loon, Piet. 1984. *Taoist Books in the Libraries of the Sung Period: A Critical Study and Index.* London: Ithaca Press.

Van Gulik, R. H. 1958. *Chinese Pictorial Art as Viewed by the Connoisseur.* Rome: Instituto Italiano per il Medio ed Estremo Oriente.

Vandier-Nicholas, Nicole. 1964. *Le Houa-che de Mi Fou, ou le carnet d'un connaisseur à l'époque des Song du Nord.* Paris: Presses Universitaires de France.

Vittinghoff, Helmolt. 1975. *Proskription und Intrige gegen Yüan-yu-Parteigänger: Ein Beitrag zu den zur Kontroversen nach den Reformen des Wang An-shih, dargestellt an den Biographien des Lu Tien (1042–1102) und des Ch'en Kuan (1057–1124).* Frankfurt: Peter Lang.

Wang, Eugene Y. 1994. "Mirror, Death, and Rhetoric: Reading Later Han Chinese Bronze Artifacts." *Art Bulletin* 76.3:511–34.

———. 1999. "The Taming of the Shrew: Wang Hsi-chih (303–361) and Calligraphic Gentrification in the Seventh Century." In *Character and Context in Chinese Calligraphy,* edited by Cary Y. Liu, Dora C. Y. Ching, and Judith G. Smith, 132–73. Princeton: Princeton University Art Museum.

———. 2005. *Shaping the Lotus Sutra: Buddhist Visual Culture in Medieval China.* Seattle: University of Washington Press.

Wang, Fang-yu. 1987. "The Historical Development of Chang-ts'ao (Chang Cursive Script)." In *The International Seminar on Chinese Calligraphy in Memory of Yen Chen Ching's 1200th Posthumous Anniversary*, edited by Chen Chi-lu, 223–48. Taipei: Shen's Art Publishing Co.

Wang, Gungwu. 1983. "The Rhetoric of a Lesser Empire: Early Sung Relations with Its Neighbors." *China among Equals: The Middle Kingdom and Its Neighbors, 10th–14th Centuries,* edited by Morris Rossabi. Berkeley: University of California Press.

Wang Guowei 王國維. 1968. *Wang Guantang xiansheng quanji* 王觀堂先生全集. 10 vols. Taipei: Wenhua.

Wang He 王河 and Zhen Li 真理. 2003. *Songdai yizhu ji kao* 宋代佚著輯考. Nanchang: Jiangxi renmin chubanshe.

Wang Jingxian 王靖憲. 1986. *Zhongguo meishu quanji* 中國美術全集, *Shufa zhuanke* 書法篆刻 2. Beijing: Wenwu chubanshe.

Wang Mingsun 王明蓀. 1981. "Tan Songdai de huanguan" 談宋代的宦官. *Dongfang zazhi* 15.5:57–60.

Wang Shimin 王世民. 2002. "Bei Song shiqi de zhili zuoyue yu guqi yanjiu" 北宋時期的制禮作樂與古器研究. In *Yifen ji* 揖芬集, 135–38 Beijing: Shehui kexue wenxian chubanshe.

Wang Yao-t'ing. 1988. "Images of the Heart: Chinese Painting on a Theme of Love." *National Palace Museum Bulletin* 22.6:1–21.

———. 2003. "Beyond the *Admonitions* Scroll: A Study of its Mounting, Seals and Inscriptions. In *Gu Kaizhi and the Admonitions Scroll*, edited by Shane McCausland, 192–218. London: British Museum Press.

———. 2007. "Tang Han Gan *Muma tu* yu Huizong chao mogu" 唐韓幹《牧馬圖》. In *Conference on Founding Paradigms: The Art and Culture of the Northern Sung Dynasty, Conference Papers.* Taipei: National Palace Museum.

Wang Yuanjun 王元軍. 1995. "Guanyu *Xuanhe shupu* de jige wenti" 關于《 宣和書譜》的幾個問題. *Shumu jikan* 29.2. Also in *Shufa yanjiu* 1997.6:31–45.

Wang Zhenghua 王正華. 1998. "*Ting qin tu* de zhengzhi yihan: Huizong chao yuanhua fengge yu yiyi wangluo" 《聽琴圖》的政治意涵：徽宗朝院畫風格與意義網絡. *Guoli Taiwan daxue meishu shi yanjiu jikan* 5:77–122.

Warner, Ding Xiang. 2002–3. "Rethinking the Authorship and Dating of 'Gujingji' 古鏡記." *T'ang Studies* 20–21:1–38.

Watson, Burton, trans. 1968. *The Complete Works of Chuang Tzu*. New York: Columbia University Press.

Wei Bin 韋賓. 2006. "*Xuanhe huapu* ming chu Jin Yuan shuo" 《宣和畫譜 》名出金元說. *Meishu guancha* 2006.10:103–6.

Weidner, Marsha Smith. 1982. "Painting and Patronage at the Mongol Court of China, 1260–1368." PhD diss., University of California, Berkeley.

Weitz, Ankeney, trans. 2002. *Zhou Mi's* Record of Clouds and Mist Passing Before One's Eyes. Leiden: Brill.

———. 2004. "Art and Politics at the Mongol Court of China: Tugh Temür's Collection of Chinese Paintings." *Artibus Asiae* 64.2:243–80.

Weng Daxi 翁達溪, ed. 2005. *Zhongguo guji shanben zongmu* 中國古籍善本總目. 7 vols. Beijing: Xianzhuang shuju.

Weng Tongwen 翁同文. 1968. "Wang Shen shengping kaolue" 王詵生平考略. *Nanyang daxue xuebao* 2 (1968):172–82. Reprinted in *Song shi yanjiu ji* 5 (1970): 135–168.

Weng, Wan-go, and Yang Boda. 1982. *The Palace Museum: Peking, Treasures of the Forbidden City.* New York: Abrams.

West, Stephen H. 2006. "Crossing Over: Huizong in the Afterglow, Or the Deaths of a Troubling Emperor." In *Emperor Huizong and Late Northern Song China: The Politics of Culture and the Culture of Politics,* edited by Patricia Buckley Ebrey and Maggie Bickford, 565–608. Cambridge, MA: Harvard Asia Center.

Wilhelm, Richard, trans. 1967. *The I Ching or Book of Changes.* Princeton: Princeton University Press.

Williamson, Henry Raymond. 1935. *Wang An-shih: A Chinese Statesman and Educationalist of the Sung Dynasty.* London: Arthur Probsthain.

Worthy, Edmond H. 1976. "The Founding of Sung China, 950–1000: Integrative Changes in Military and Political Institutions." PhD diss., Princeton University.

Wu Hung. 1995. *Monumentality in Early Chinese Art and Architecture.* Stanford: Stanford University Press.

———. 1996. *The Double Screen: Medium and Representation in Chinese Painting.* London: Reaktion Books.

———. 1997. "The Origins of Chinese Painting." In *Three Thousand Years of Chinese Painting,* by Yang Xin et al, 15–85. New Haven: Yale University Press.

———. 2003. "The *Admonitions* Scroll Revisited: Iconology, Narratology, Style, Dating." In *Gu Kaizhi and the Admonitions Scroll*, edited by Shane McCausland, 89–99. London: British Museum Press.

Wu Tung. 1997. *Tales from the Land of Dragons: 1,000 Years of Chinese Painting.* Boston: Museum of Fine Arts.

Xia Chaoxiong 夏超雄. 1982. "Songdai jinshixue de zhuyao gongxian ji qi xingqi de yuanyin" 宋代金石學的主要貢獻及其興起的原因. *Beijing daxue xuebao* 1982.1:66–76.

Xiao Baifang 蕭百芳. 1990a. "Cong *Daozang* ziliao tansuo Song Huizong chong dao de mudi" 從道藏資料探索宋徽宗崇道的目的. *Daojiao xue tansuo* 3:130–83.

———. 1990b. "Song Huizong chong dao shenhua de tantao" 宋徽宗崇道神話的探討. *Daojiao xue tansuo* 3:95–129.

———. 1991. "Cong Song Huizong chong dao, shi yishu de juedu guan *Xuanhe huapu* de daoshi huihua" 從宋徽宗崇道嗜藝術的角度觀《宣和畫譜》的道釋繪畫. *Daojiao xue tansuo* 4:122–328.

———. 1994. "You *Xuanhe huapu* de huihua meixue tantao Song Huizong shidai huayuan shanshui huafeng" 由《宣和畫譜》的繪畫美學探討宋徽宗時代畫院山水畫風. *Guoli chenggong daxue lishi xuebao* 20:138–97.

Xie Wei 謝巍. 1998. *Zhongguo huaxue zhuzuo kaolu* 中國畫學著作考錄. Shanghai: Shanghai shuhua chubanshe.

Xie Zhiliu 謝稚柳. 1989a. *Song Huizong Zhao Ji quanji.* 宋徽宗趙佶全集. Shanghai: Shanghai Renmin chubanshe.

———, ed. 1989b. *Zhongguo lidai fashu moji daguan.* 中國歷代法書墨跡大觀. Shanghai: Shanghai shudian. 1989.

Xu Bangda 徐邦達. 1964. "Li Gonglin and His 'Horses.'" *Chinese Literature* 6:109–16.

———. 1978. "Jin Wang Xizhi *Shangyu tie*" 晉王羲之《上虞帖》. *Yiyuan duoying* 2:44.
———. 1979. "Song Huizong Zhao Ji qinbihua yu daibihua de kaobian" 宋徽宗趙佶親筆畫與代筆畫的考辨. *Gugong bowuyuan yuankan* 1:62–67, 50.
———. 1981a. *Gu shuhua jianding gailun* 古書畫鑑定概論. Beijing: Wenwu chubanshe.
———. 1981b. "Song Jin neifu shuhua de zhuanghuang biaoti cangyin he kao" 宋金內府書畫的裝潢標題藏印合考. *Meishu yanjiu* 1:83–85.
———. 1987. *Gu shuhua guoyan yaolu* 古書畫過眼要錄. Changsha: Hunan meishu chubanshe.
Xu Lingzhi 徐淩志, ed. 2004. *Zhongguo lidai zangshu shi* 中國歷代藏書史. Nanchang: Jiangxi renmin chubanshe.
Xu Yahui 許雅惠. 2003. "*Xuanhe bogu tu* de jianjie liuchuan—yi Yuandai sai yin chi da hu mu chutu de taoqi yu *Shaoxi zhouxian shidian yitu* wei li" 《宣和博古圖》的「間接」流傳—以元代賽因赤答忽墓出土的陶器與《紹熙州縣釋典儀圖》為例. *Meishu shi yanjiu jikan* 14:1–26.
Yan Yiping 嚴一萍. 1962. "Song guwenzi guqiwu xuezhe Zhai Ruwen ji qi suozuo qi" 宋古文字古器物學者翟汝文及其所作器. *Zhongguo wenzi* 8:1a–8b.
Yang Huarong 羊華榮. 1985. "Song Huizong yu daojiao" 宋徽宗與道教. *Shijie zongjiao yanjiu* 3:70–79.
Yang, Lien-sheng. 1947. "A Note on the So-called TLV Mirrors and the Game *Liu-po*." *Harvard Journal of Asiatic Studies* 9:202–6.
Yang Renkai 楊仁愷 . 1988. "Song Huizong Zhao Ji shufa yishu suotan" 宋徽宗趙佶書法藝術瑣談. *Shufa congkan* 14:4–10.
———. 1989. *Zhongguo meishu quanji* 中國美術全集. *Shufa zhuanke* 書法篆刻. Vol. 3. Beijing: Wenwu chubanshe.
———. 1999. *Guobao chenfu lu* 國寶沉浮錄. Shenyang: Liaohai chubanshe.
Yao Yingting 姚瀛艇. 1992. *Songdai wenhua shi* 宋代文化史. Kaifeng: Henan daxue chubanshe.
Ye Guoliang 葉國良. 1982. "Songdai jinshixue yanjiu" 宋代金石學研究. PhD diss., National Taiwan University.
———. 1984. "*Bogu tu* xiuzhuan shimo ji qi xiangguan wenti" 博古圖修撰始末及其相關問題. *Youshi xuezhi* 18.1:130–42.
Yi Ruofen 衣若芬. 1999. "*Xuanhe huapu* yu Su Shi huihua sixiang" 宣和畫譜與蘇軾繪畫思想. In *Zhongguo di shijie Su Shi yanjiu huiyi wenji* 中國第十屆蘇軾研究會議文集, edited by Li Zengpo 李曾坡, 209–38. Jinan: Qilu shushe chubanshe.
———. 2006. "'Hunjun' yu 'jianchen' de duihua—Tan Song Huizong *Wenhuitu* tishi" 「昏君」與「奸臣」的對話—談宋徽宗《文繪圖》題詩. *Wen yu shi* 8:253–78.
Yu Jianhua 俞建華 and Chen Songlin 陳松林. 1999. *Zhongguo huihua quanji: Wudai Song Liao Jin* 中國繪畫全集：五代宋遼金. Vol. 1. Hangzhou: Zhejiang renmin meishu chubanshe.
Yu Jiaxi 余嘉錫. 1958. *Siku tiyao bianzheng* 四庫提要辨證. Beijing: Kexue chubanshe.
Yu Shaosong 余紹宋. 1968. *Shuhua shulu jieti* 書畫書錄解題. Hong Kong: Zhong Mei tushu gongsi.
Yuan Tongli 袁同禮. 1928. "Songdai sijia cangshu gailue" 宋代私家藏書概略. *Tushuguan xue jikan* 2.2:179–87.

Zeng Yifen 曾貽芬 and Cui Wenyin 崔文印. 1991. "Songdai de wenxian shouji yu guanfang cang shumu" 宋代的文獻收集與官方藏書目. *Shixueshi yanjiu* 3:54–60.

Zhang Bangwei 張邦煒. 1993. *Songdai huangqin yu zhengzhi* 宋代皇親與政治. Chengdu: Sichuan renmin chubanshe.

———. 2005. *Songdai zhengzhi wenhua shi lun* 宋代政治文化史論. Beijing: Renmin chubanshe.

Zhang Guangbin 張光賓, ed. 1984. *Zhonghua wuqian nian wenwu jikan* 中華伍仟年文物集刊. *Fashu bian* 法書編. Vol. 1. Taipei: Zhonghua wuqian nian wenwu jikan bianji weiyuanhui.

———. 1992. "Xuanhe shu hua er pu Song ke zhiyi" 宣和書畫二譜宋刻質疑. *Gugong wenwu yuekan* 115:130–35.

Zhang, Hongxing. 2002. *The Qianlong Emperor: Treasures from the Forbidden City.* Edinburgh: National Museum of Scotland.

———. 2003. "The Nineteenth-Century Provenance of the *Admonitions* Scroll: A Hypothesis." In *Gu Kaizhi and the Admonitions Scroll*, edited by Shane McCausland, 277–87. London: British Museum Press.

Zhang Linsheng (see also Chang, Lin-sheng) 張臨生. 1996. "Guoli Gugong Bowuyuan shoucang yuanliu shilue" 國立故宮博物院收藏源流史略. *Gugong xueshu jikan* 13.3:1–82.

Zheng Wei 鄭為. 1966. "Zhakou panche tujuan" 閘口盤車圖卷. *Wenwu* 184:17–25.

———. 1978. "Zhakou panche tujuan" 閘口盤車圖卷. *Yiyuan duoying* 2:18–19.

Zheng Yinshu 鄭銀淑. 1984. *Xiang Yuanbian zhi shuhua shouzang yu yishu* 項元汴之書畫收藏與藝術. Taipei: Wenshizhe chubanshe.

Zheng Zhenduo 鄭振鐸, Zhang Heng 張珩, and Xu Bangda 徐邦達. 1957. *Songren huace* 宋人畫冊. Beijing: Zhongguo gudian yishu chubanshe.

Zheng Zhenman 鄭振滿 and Ding Hesheng 丁荷生 (Kenneth Dean). 1995. *Fujian zongjiao beiming huibian* 福建宗教碑銘彙編. Fuzhou: Fujian renmin chubanshe.

Zhongguo yinyue wenwu daxi zongbian jibu 中國音樂文物大系總編輯部, ed. 1996–2001. *Zhongguo yinyue wenwu daxi* 中國音樂文物大系. 9 vols. Zhengzhou: Daxiang chubanshe.

Zhou Baozhu 周寶珠. 1992. *Songdai dongjing yanjiu* 宋代東京研究. Kaifeng: Henan Daxue chubanshe.

Zhou Zheng 周錚. 1983. "Xuanhe shanzun kao" 宣和山尊考. *Wenwu* 1983.11:74–75, 67.

Zhu Huiliang 朱惠良 and Yang Meili 楊美莉. 1985. *Zhonghua wuqian nian wenwu jikan* 中華伍仟年文物集刊. *Fashu bian* 法書編. Vol. 3. Taipei: Zhonghua wuqian nian wenwu jikan bianji weiyuanhui.

Zhu Jia Jin. 1986. *Treasures of the Forbidden City.* New York: Viking.

Zhu Jianxin 朱劍心. 1938. *Jinshi xue* 金石學. Changsha: Commercial Press.

Zito, Angela. 1997. *Of Body and Brush: Grand Sacrifice as Text/Performance in Eighteenth-Century China*. Chicago: University of Chicago Press.

Zürcher, Erik. 1955. "Imitation and Forgery in Ancient Chinese Painting and Calligraphy." *Oriental Art* n.s. 1.4:141–46.

Glossary-Index

Titles of works of art and books are listed under the author/artist unless anonymous. Page numbers in italics refer to figures.